The
Guinness Sports
Yearbook 1994

GUINNESS PUBLISHING

Published in Great Britain by Guinness Publishing Ltd, 33 London Road, Enfield, Middlesex

Cover design by Ad Vantage Studios, text design and layout by Oddball Publishing, Brighton
using Quark Xpress on Apple Mac computers
Typeset in Helvetica and Palatino by Perfect Setting, Brighton
Printed and bound in Great Britain by The Bath Press, Bath, Avon

'Guinness' is a registered trademark of Guinness Publishing Ltd

A catalogue record for this book is available from the British Library

ISBN 0-85112-745-2

Foreword

The sporting year gets ever more crowded. In this supposedly quiet post-Olympic year we have had Ryder Cup golf, Ashes Tests, a British Lions tour, World Cup qualifying football, the World Athletics Championships and a World Student Games as well as the annual round of major competitions in tennis, golf and motor racing. There was barely time to recover from one major event, before the next came along. For much of the year, though, there was little British success to applaud. Our footballers have struggled, our cricketers will never want another year like it. Their record for 1993 reads, played 10, won 1, drew 1, lost 8. Even the Lions, who looked to capture some glory after a brilliant second test victory, came unstuck at the final hurdle.

It was left to a quartet of largely unsung heroes to show the way. Richard Fox unassuming but brilliant, won his fifth world title in canoe slalom; Richard Phelps achieved what no Briton before him could, and won the world modern pentathlon crown; and two cyclists, Chris Boardman and Graeme Obree astonished the continental world with their record-breaking exploits.

Then, on August 15th, along came Linford Christie to run arguably the greatest 100m of all time to win the World Championship in Stuttgart. Christie was just one hundredth of a second outside Carl Lewis's world record, set on a faster track in Tokyo two years ago. On the same day, Damon Hill won his first grand prix. In the week following, Sally Gunnell and Colin Jackson achieved what Christie hadn't quite when they both broke world records on the way to their respective world titles.

September saw Nigel Mansell win the Indy Car title, Britain's rowers, including the incomparable Steven Redgrave collect four gold medals at the World Championship and Spencer Smith, in that most daunting of events, the Triathlon, carried off another title. And the Ryder Cup, though lost, provided an enduring spectacle.

Between the moments of exhilaration in 1993, there were moments of sadness. Bobby Moore and James Hunt both died too young. In their time they painted vivid colours on the canvas of sport and will be greatly missed.

It was a year of records broken and new champions born. A year of retirements; of Botham bowing out and Clough climbing down. It was a year when money seemed more important than ever and China didn't get the Olympics. It is all here in the next 400 pages. Enjoy it.

David Coleman

Introduction

"It's not a hobby, it's a way of life," says husky racer Martin Bundy. You find a lot of bits of paper with things like that written on when you do a book like this. They go into a file for things you don't know what to file under (no, we don't have a file for husky racing) and the file gets bigger and bigger and when you've finished the book the file sits back and laughs at you because you probably haven't used one of the cuttings.

It's only a sporting year, but it doesn't take long to realise that you could fill one of these books a week with everything that's available. We've trodden a fairly straight path, trying to keep our first priority that the book must be an accurate record, a results book for the year gone. We've generally steered clear of historical records. If you want to know who won the Running Deer Rifle title in 1908, then Guinness already has a book to cater for your needs; Peter Matthews' estimable 'Encyclopedia of Sports Records and Results'. We have, though, included a certain amount of oddball information to lighten the load a little, plus a diary and major events' preview for the year ahead.

Within each sport, we have organised the information so that world championships always take precedence, followed by European events, then national results. Our first thanks must go to all the federations that supplied us with that material. Without their assistance, compiling this would be impossible. Most of them understood that sending us more and early rather than little and late helped enormously. The governing bodies (even the couple that weren't helpful) are listed at the back of the book.

Our credit list must start with **The Daily Telegraph** which we constantly referred to, for both results and stories. **L'Equipe** and **The Guardian** were also vital sources of information and **The Daily Mirror, The Press Association** and **Nottingham Evening Post** gave valuable assistance.

Athletics Weekly, AIMS (the Association of International Marathons), Cycling Weekly, Motorcycle News, Rally Sport, Raceform, Racenews and **Regatta Magazine** tolerated us pestering them, either for back copies or technical help. **John Burton, Michael Butcher** (who also wrote the in-section piece on Chinese athletes), **Mick Cleary, David Hunn, Phil Liggett** and **Frank Keating** contributed the 'Landmarks' articles. **Mike Collett** helped with the preview material and **John Trachim** supplied the 1994 calendar. **Rosie Weekes** and **Jill Faulkner** diligently typed away, **John Mitchell** pointed me in the right technical direction and **Charles Richards**, at Guinness, supplied the eaglest of eyes when an eagle's eye was vital. It only remains to thank **David Luckes**, who assiduously sought out enough material so that we almost could do that one book a week. Without his help, I probably wouldn't have got past this page.

Peter Nichols

Contents

Abbreviations

Where a time is shown, the hours minutes and seconds are separated by a colon. A full point is used only as a decimal point for parts of a second. eg 3 hours 23 minutes and 7.5 seconds is shown as 3:23:7.5

J	Junior
CR	Championship record
NR	National record
ER	European record
WR	World record

Countries

ALB	Albania
ALG	Algeria
ANG	Anguilla
ANO	Angola
ANT	Antigua
ARG	Argentina
ARM	Armenia
AUS	Australia
AUT	Austria
AZE	Azerbaijan
BAH	Bahamas
BAR	Barbados
BEL	Belgium
BER	Bermuda
BHR	Bahrain
BLS	Belarus
BOS	Bosnia-Herzegovina
BRA	Brazil
BUL	Bulgaria
BUR	Burundi
CAN	Canada
CAY	Cayman Islands
CGO	Congo
CHI	Chile
CHN	People's Republic of China
CIV	Ivory Coast
CMR	Cameroon
COL	Colombia
CRC	Costa Rica
CRO	Croatia
CUB	Cuba
CYP	Cyprus
DEN	Denmark
DJI	Djibouti
DMN	Dominica
DOM	Dominican Republic
ECU	Ecuador
EGY	Egypt
ENG	England
ESA	El Salvador
ESP	Spain
EST	Estonia
ETH	Ethiopia
FIJ	Fiji
FIN	Finland

FRA	France
GAB	Gabon
GAM	The Gambia
GBR	Great Britain and N Ireland
GEO	Georgia
GER	Germany
GHA	Ghana
GRE	Greece
GRN	Grenada
GUA	Guatemala
GUY	Guyana
HKG	Hong Kong
HOL	Holland
HON	Honduras
HUN	Hungary
INA	Indonesia
IND	India
IRL	Ireland
IRN	Iran
IRQ	Iraq
ISL	Iceland
ISR	Israel
ISV	US Virgin Islands
ITA	Italy
JAM	Jamaica
JOR	Jordan
JPN	Japan
KEN	Kenya
KGZ	Kyrgyzstan
KOR	Korea
KUW	Kuwait
KZK	Kazakhstan
LAT	Latvia
LES	Lesotho
LIE	Liechtenstein
LTU	Lithuania
LUX	Luxembourg
MAD	Madagascar
MAL	Malaysia
MAR	Morocco
MEX	Mexico
MLD	Moldova
MOZ	Mozambique
MRI	Mauritius
MYA	Myanmar
NAM	Namibia
NCA	Nicaragua
NGR	Nigeria
NGU	Papua New Guinea
NIR	Northern Ireland
NOR	Norway
NZL	New Zealand
OMA	Oman
PAK	Pakistan
PAN	Panama
PAR	Paraguay
PER	Peru
PHI	Philippines
POL	Poland
POR	Portugal
PRK	North Korea
PUR	Puerto Rico

QUT	Qatar
ROM	Romania
RSA	South Africa
RUS	Russia
RWA	Rwanda
SAU	Saudi Arabia
SCO	Scotland
SEN	Senegal
SEY	Seychelles
SIN	Singapore
SLE	Sierra Leone
SLO	Slovenia
SOM	Somalia
SRI	Sri Lanka
STL	St Lucia
SUD	Sudan
SUI	Switzerland
SUR	Surinam
SWE	Sweden
SYR	Syria
TAN	Tanzania
TCH	The Czech Republic
THA	Thailand
TJK	Tadjikistan
TKM	Turkmenistan
TPE	Taiwan (Chinese Taipeh)
TRI	Trinidad & Tobago
TUN	Tunisia
TUR	Turkey
UAE	United Arab Emirates
UGA	Uganda
UKR	Ukraine
URU	Uruguay
USA	United States
UZB	Uzbekistan
VEN	Venezuela
WAL	Wales
YUG	Yugoslavia
ZAM	Zambia
ZIM	Zimbabwe

A Year in Brief   October 1992 - September 1993

October
Stuttgart qualified for the next round of the European Cup by scoring at Leeds in a 4-1 defeat....four days later UEFA rules that Stuttgart fielded one foreigner too many and the game was awarded to Leeds 3-0, with a deciding tie to be played at Barcelona.....Vinnie Jones charged by FA over 'Hard Men' video......Europe's women golfers win historic victory in the Solheim Cup.....Nigel Benn beats Italian Mauro Galvano to claim WBC super-middleweight title.....Subotica wins the Prix de l'Arc de Triomphe.....Australian cricketer Greg Matthews fined by the Australian Cricket Board for scrunching up a Benson & Hedges packet in a magazine anti-smoking advert......Leeds beat Stuttgart 2-1 in the replayed game.....Nick Faldo wins the World Matchplay tournament at Wentworth beating the American Jeff Sluman a massive 8 & 7 in the final....England draw 1-1 with Norway in the World Cup qualifier....Duke McKenzie beats Jesse Benavides to become WBO super-bantamweight champion....Frank Bruno beats South Africa's Pierre Coetzer and Micky Duff talks of a £10m heavyweight title fight against Evander Holyfield in London...England beat Scotland in the final of golf's Dunhill Cup....England's rugby team beat Canada at Wembley 26-13....Glasgow Rangers beat Leeds 2-1 in European Cup second round, 1st leg .....Bruce Grobbelaar sent off in Liverpool's 4-2 away defeat by Spartak Moscow.....Sunday League cricketers show off their new pyjama strips at the Oval.....Racing was halted at Newbury when a plane crashed onto the track.....Toronto Blue Jays beat Atlanta Braves 4-2 to become the first Canadian team to win Baseball's World Series....Australian rugby league team beat England 10-6 in the World Cup final at Wembley.....Graeme Souness suspended for five matches by UEFA for abusing the Swedish referee in Liverpool's match against Spartak Moscow.....Jim Parker, a football referee is suspended following allegations that he swore at a player.....Craig Reedie, former president of the International Badminton Federation, is confirmed as the new chairman of the British Olympic Association.....Lennox Lewis knocks out Donovan 'Razor' Ruddock in 46 seconds of the second round at Earls Court.....

November
Ireland's rugby union team sent to a crashing defeat by the Australian touring team 42-17. Australia's captain Michael Lynagh dislocated his shoulder and put out of the rest of the tour....Lester Piggott suffers fractured clavicle and broken rib in an accident at the Breeders Cup in Gulfstream Park, Miami. The horse, Mr Brooks, broke a leg mid-race.....Andrew Davies and Andrew Saxton, sent home from the Barcelona Olympics following the results of a drug test, are cleared by the British Amateur Weightlifting Association. BAWLA decides that there was uncertainty over the status of the drug involved, Clenbuterol.....Sandy Lyle wins the Volvo Masters at Valderrama in Spain.....Rangers qualify for the next round of the European Cup beating Leeds 2-1 at Leeds....Swansea beat the Australian rugby union tourists 21-6.....Bobby Fischer beat Boris Spassky 10 games to five in Belgrade to win £2.2m.....Richard Dunwoody wins with all five of his mounts at the Chepstow National Hunt meeting on November 7....Nigel Mansell's last Formula One race before he switches codes ends on a sour note when Ayrton Senna

crashes into the back of his car on lap 19 of the Australian Grand Prix.....USA beat Sweden in the final of golf's World Cup.....Australia's rugby team beat the Barbarians 30-20 at Twickenham.....England defeat South Africa 33-16 at Twickenham and, in Nantes, Argentina have a shock win over France 24-20.....Jones fined £20,000 by the FA.....England beat Turkey 4-0 in World Cup qualifier at Wembley.....Barnet fined £50,000 for financial breaches of League regulations.....Chris Eubank makes a successful fifth defence of his WBO super-middleweight title when he defeats Juan Carlos Gimenez at Manchester.....British tennis launches a £63m five year plan to produce British winners.....Desert Orchid in intensive care after an operation for an intestinal blockage.....Rangers draw 2-2 with Marseilles in the opening game of the Champions League.....Carlos Sainz wins Lombard RAC Rally....Roy Inman resigns as women's national judo coach......

December

Allan Border fined 50% of his match fee for dissent in the first Test against the West Indies at Brisbane.....Harry 'Butch' Reynolds, banned from athletics for two years following a drugs test in 1991, awarded $27.3m against the International Amateur Athletic Federation by a court in Columbus, Ohio....British Judo Association withdraws Inman's licence on the grounds of "financial irregularities".....United States win the Davis Cup beating Switzerland.....Dan Maskell dies.....WBC crown Lennox Lewis heavyweight world champion after Riddick Bowe dumps the belt in a dustbin.....Nigel Benn retains his WBC super-middleweight title by beating Nicky Piper.....BBC TV's Match of the Day shows Arsenal's Ian Wright punching Spurs' David Howells during the north London derby.....Michael Stich wins $2m when he takes the Compaq Grand Slam title in Munich.....Liverpool lose 5-1 to Coventry, their heaviest defeat in 16 years.....Nick Faldo beats Greg Norman in a play-off for the Johnnie Walker World Championship in Jamaica.....Norwich lead the Premier Division at Christmas.....The Fellow wins the King George VI Chase at Kempton for the second year running.....Border hits 25th Test hundred, playing against the West Indies at Melbourne.....Baseball star, Mark McGwire signs a five year $28m contract with the Oakland Athletics.....sprinter Jason Livingston fails in his attempt to overturn a four year drugs ban.....US golfer John Daly admitted to an alcohol rehabilitation centre.....

January

Nigel Mansell's opening Indy Car test session at Phoenix.....Test and County Cricket Board discount one of Graham Gooch's centuries, made on the unofficial South African tour of 1982, to reduce his number of first-class centuries from 99 to 98.....Germany defeat England 8-3 in the women's European Indoor Cup for hockey.....Brian Lara scores 277 for the West Indies in the third Test against Australia at Sydney.....North Korea thrown out of the World Gymnastics Championships because of the disputed age of one of their team.....Bolton Wanderers knock Liverpool out of the FA Cup.....England, aiming for their third grand slam, start the Five Nations rugby tournament with a 16-15 victory over France at Twickenham.....Olympic triple gold medallist rower Steve Redgrave threatens to retire unless he can find a sponsor.....Steve Cauthen retires after failing to agree terms with Sheikh Mohammed, Michael Roberts takes over.....English Table Tennis

Association outlaw toxic glues.....The Maleeva sisters (Magdalena, Mañuela & Katerina) make history when all three reached the last 16 of the Australian Open tennis.....Paul Gascoigne belches into an Italian microphone.....Nigel Short becomes the first Briton ever to reach the chess World Championship final when he defeats Jan Timman.....West Indies win the closest Test match in history when they beat Australia, in the fourth Test at Adelaide, by one run.....a motion of no confidence in the MCC, proposed by businessman Dennis Olver, is defeated by 6135-4600 at an extraordinary general meeting at Central Hall, Westminster.....Jim Courier and Monica Seles win the Australian Open titles.....

February
Sunderland dismiss manager Malcolm Crosby nine months after he led the team out in the FA Cup final.....Dallas Cowboys win Super Bowl XXVII in Pasadena, destroying the Buffalo Bills 52-17.....India win the first Test in Calcutta by eight wickets.....Paul Hodkinson retains his WBC featherweight title beating Ricardo Cepeda.....Wales defeat England 10-9 at Cardiff Arms Park to shatter England's dream of an unprecedented three rugby grand slams in a row.....Riddick Bowe defeats Mike Dokes in 2 minutes and 19 seconds of their fight, to retain his WBA/IBF world heavyweight title.....Mighty Mogul, one-time Champion Hurdle favourite, is put down after an operation on his knee went wrong.....Mark Foster breaks the world record for the 50m butterfly, recording a time of 23.72 in the World Cup meeting at Gelsenkirchen in Germany.....Mike Tyson's appeal against his rape conviction begins in an Indiana courtroom.....England lose second Test at Madras by an innings and 22 runs.....Mark Foster breaks the world record for the 50m (21.60) in the World Cup meeting at Sheffield.....Chris Eubank retains his WBO super-middleweight title by beating Lindell Holmes on points.....Kjetil Andre Aamodt of Norway dominates the World Skiing championships in Morioka, Japan, winning the slalom and giant slalom titles.....Scotland comfortably beat Wales 20-0 and Gavin Hastings scores 14 points.....Graeme Hick scores his first Test century for his adopted country, Hick scores 178.....England lose third Test at Bombay by an innings and 15 runs.....Gary Kasparov and Nigel Short establish the Professional Chess Association after falling out with FIDE over the dates and venue of their World Championship match.....On Feb 24, Bobby Moore dies.....Zeta's Lad stretches his unbeaten run to five and establishes his position as favourite for the Grand National.....Richard Corsie wins his third successive World Indoor singles bowls title.....Allan Border passes Sunil Gavaskar's Test aggregate of 10,122 in Australia's first innings against New Zealand at Christchurch.....Paul Gascoigne sent off for violent conduct during Lazio's 3-2 win in Genoa.....

March
Sue Slocombe appointed Great Britain women's hockey coach.....Ben Johnson tests positive again and is banned for life.....England beat Scotland 26-12 in the Five Nations rugby and Scotland stand-off Craig Chalmers breaks his arm.....Yvonne Murray and Tom McKean, in the 3000m and 800m respectively, win gold medals in the World Indoor championships.....Stephen Hendry scores a maximum 147 in the Nescafé Asian at Bangkok.....Alain Prost wins at Kyalami, South Africa, the opening race in the Formula One season.....Granville Again wins the Champion Hurdle.....Sri Lanka defeat England by 5

wickets at Colombo.....Jodami wins the Cheltenham Gold Cup.....Gloucester and England fast bowler David Lawrence re-fractures his left kneecap during a weight training session.....Ireland rugby team beat England 17-3, but France win Five Nations championship.....Nigel Mansell wins his debut Indy Car race at Surfer's Paradise in Queensland.....Scotland's Gavin Hastings chosen as captain of the British Lions touring party to New Zealand.....Brian Clough made an honorary freeman of the city of Nottingham.....Cambridge enjoy only their second victory in 18 years when they defeat Oxford in the Boat Race by 11 seconds.....Kenyan athletes win seven of the eight titles at the World Cross-country championships in Spain.....

April
England win 2-0 in Turkey, while the Turkish crowd pelt the team and its supporters.....Wales has a 2-0 victory over Belgium in another World Cup qualifier at Cardiff, to inflict upon Belgium its first defeat in seven matches.....the Grand National has two false starts, the second time a large number of horses continue on unaware of the recall flag, Esha Ness wins the race that never was.....judo player Elvis Gordon had a set-to with his former trainer Malcolm Abbots at the British Open championships in Birmingham.....Nigel Mansell, in his second Indy Car race, crashes at 185 mph at Phoenix.....jockey Peter Scudamore retires after winning his final race on Sweet Duke.....Zambia loses all but three of its top footballers in a plane crash....Marseilles and Rangers draw 1-1 in Marseilles in the European Champions League.....on April 8th, Manchester United top the Premier League for the first time in the season.....Bernhard Langer wins the US Masters at Augusta, with Ian Woosnam in 17th Britain's highest finisher.....Ayrton Senna wins the European Grand Prix at Donington.....Vinnie Jones banned for four matches and fined £1,000 for reaching 40 points.....Rob de Castella, former world champion from Australia, announces he will retire after running in the NutraSweet London Marathon.....Eamonn Martin wins the London Marathon, but Liz McColgan, on $250,000 appearance money, can finish only third in the women's race to 1992 winner, Germany's Katrin Dörre.....Vitaly Scherbo, winner of six golds at Barcelona Olympics, and America's Shannon Miller are the all-round champions at the World Gymnastic championships at Birmingham, Neil Thomas become Britain's first ever medallist with a silver in the floor exercises.....Rangers draw with CSKA Moscow at Ibrox Park and are eliminated from the European Cup.....Steve Robinson wins the WBO featherweight title to become the first Welshman since Howard Winstone in 1968 to hold a world crown.....Frank Bruno defeats Carl 'The Truth' Williams in the 10th round at Birmingham.....Arsenal beat Sheffield Wednesday 2-1 to win the Coca-Cola Cup.....TCCB decides to use a third umpire in domestic one-day competitions.....England draw with Holland 2-2 at Wembley in World Cup match and Gascoigne fractures a cheekbone.....Scotland eclipsed 5-0 by Portugal in Lisbon to write off their World Cup hopes and Ally McCoist breaks his leg.....Sayyedati wins the 1000 Guineas.....Graham Gooch is reappointed England captain for the forthcoming series against Australia.....Monica Seles stabbed on court in Hamburg.....

May

Manchester United win the Premier League for the first time since 1967 when Oldham, struggling against relegation, surprisingly beat Aston Villa 1-0.....Nottingham Forest are relegated.....Leicester win rugby union's Pilkington Cup....Hounslow hockey team win the HA Cup to complete a cup and league double.....in Athens, judo player Nicola Fairbrother gains her second European lightweight title in a row.....French horse Zafonic justifies his high reputation by storming home in the 2000 Guineas.....Wigan beat Widnes 20-14 in rugby league's Challenge Cup final at Wembley.....Stephen Hendry wins his third world snooker title, defeating Jimmy White in the final at Sheffield.....Ginny Leng, on Houdini, wins her third Badminton three-day victory.....Lennox Lewis outpoints American Tony Tucker in his first defence of the WBC world title.....Halifax relegated from the football league.....Tottenham sack Terry Venables as chief executive and the battle between Venables and Alan Sugar begins.....Arsenal beat Sheffield Wednesday to win the FA Cup 2-1 after a replay at Wembley. The teams drew 1-1 in the first game.....MCC make Geoff Boycott a life member.....Robin Smith hits the highest score by an English batsman in international one-day cricket, 167, against the Australians at Edgbaston and England still lose.....the yacht Nuclear Electric wins the British Steel Challenge round the world race.....Australian clean sweep in the Texaco Trophy, one-day matches.....Ayrton Senna wins a record six Monaco Grands Prix, eclipsing Graham Hill's record. Damon Hill, son of Graham, finishes second.....England draw 1-1 in Poland, with Gascoigne wearing a mask to protect his cheekbone.....in the European Cup final at Munich, Marseilles beat AC Milan 1-0.....

June

Nigel Mansell wins at West Allis, Wisconsin, his first victory on an oval track.....Sergei Bruguera and Steffi Graf win at the French Open.....Norway beat England 2-0 in Oslo.....Commander-in-Chief springs a surprise Derby win as the hot favourite Tenby struggles.....Glenn Hoddle leaves Swindon to become manager of Chelsea.....Intrepidity wins the Oaks.....Gooch becomes the fifth Test batsman in history to be given out handled ball. Gooch made 133 first.....England lose the first Test against Australia.....England beaten 2-0 by the United States, to revive memories of the 1-0 defeat in 1950.....British Lions lose the first Test against the All Blacks by 20-18.....Paul Ince becomes the first black footballer to captain England and, at 25, the youngest for 18 years.....British Horseracing Board takes over from the Jockey Club as rulers of British racing.....Chris Lillywhite makes it a British victory in cycling's Milk Race.....Sampras and Graf top the Wimbledon seedings.....On June 14th, James Hunt dies.....Ossie Ardiles appointed manager of Tottenham Hotspur.....Australia win the second Test by an innings and 62 runs to continue England's disastrous sequence.....Chicago Bulls win the National Basketball Association title.....a sub-committee from the American House of Representatives denounces Peking's Olympic bid on the grounds of human rights.....four British men reach Wimbledon's third round and Andrew Foster, ranked 332 in the world, goes one stage further before losing to world number one Pete Sampras.....Nigel Benn knocks out Lou Gent to retain his WBC super-middleweight title.....the British Lions dominate the second Test winning by 20-7.....in spite of seven individual winners, Britain's men finish second to Russia in athletics World Cup at Rome.....Commander-in Chief completes the Derby double when he wins the Irish Derby .....

July

Sampras beats Courier at Wimbledon and Graf snatches a victory against Jana Novotna who, in defeat, cries on the Duchess of Kent's shoulder.....Tour de France begins.....Marseilles football club are threatened by bribery accusations.....British Lions struggle as All Blacks wrap up the third Test 30-13 to win the series 2-1.....Kenyan Richard Chelimo breaks the world 10,000m record in Stockholm, recording 27:07.91.....Graham Thorpe scores a century on his Test debut.....Alain Prost wins the British Grand Prix, his 50th grand prix victory.....Richard Fox wins his fifth world title when he takes the honours in the K1 slalom at the world championships in Mezzano, Italy.....Derbyshire defeat Lancashire by six runs to win the Benson & Hedges Cup.....Leicester v Surrey cricket match at Grace Road is abandoned because the pitch is too dangerous.....Yobes Ondieki becomes the first man to run under 27 minutes for the 10,000m when he wins in Oslo in 26:58.38.....bribery allegations threaten Polish football title holders Legia Warsaw.....IOC Commission report favours Sydney Olympic bid.....on July 12, Miguel Induráin assumes the yellow jersey in the Tour de France and is never again headed..........Juan Antonio Samaranch, President of the International Olympic Committee visits Manchester.....IAAF loses first appeal against the $27.3 award won by Butch Reynolds.....Sampdoria pay £5.2m to Juventus for David Platt and Rangers agree a fee of £4m for Dundee United's Duncan Ferguson.....FISA, the ruling body of Formula One bans active suspensions.....Roy Keane moves from Nottingham Forest to Manchester United for £3.75m....the Inland Revenue threatens an investigation into league clubs' finances.....Linford Christie fails to gain an automatic place for the world championships 200m when he eases up at the Panasonic AAA Championships and does not qualify for the final.....Greg Norman beats Faldo by two shots to secure his second Open golf title, seven years after the first.....Ian Botham retires.....Liz McColgan, Britain's only reigning world athletics champion withdraws from the team for Stuttgart.....the clubs vote against a Football League recommendation to expel Barnet.....Endsleigh Insurance complete a £3.5m three year deal to become sponsors of the Football League replacing Barclays Bank..... on Jul 18, Graeme Obree breaks the world one hour cycling record in Oslo.....on Jul 23, Chris Boardman breaks Obree's one hour cycling record to complete the most extraordinary five days in the history of British cycling.....Opera House wins the King George VI and Queen Elizabeth Diamond Stakes beating the double Derby winner Commander-in-Chief.....Miguel Induráin wins his third successive Tour de France.....England lose out for the seventh time in eight Tests when they are beaten in the fourth Test by Australia.....Graham Gooch quits as captain, but chairman of the selectors, Ted Dexter, stays on.....2000 Guineas winner and wonderhorse Zafonic finishes seventh in the Sussex Stakes at Goodwood.....Mike Atherton named as the new England cricket captain.....Linford Christie comfortably beats Carl Lewis in a 100m race at Gateshead and they each collect £100,000.....Willie Carson reaches a career total of 3,500 winners when King's Signet wins the Stewards Cup on July 31.....

August

England's women cricketers win the World Cup, which is rather embarrassing for England's men.....spinner John Emburey recalled to the England Test team shortly before his 41st birthday.....fast bowler David Lawrence returns to action in a benefit match at Cheltenham.....horserace trainer Reg Akehurst accuses the Jockey Club of a

Newmarket bias.....Prince Philip, after colliding with a yacht in his first race and a buoy in his second, wins an event at Cowes Week.....Linford Christie loses out to American Leroy Burrell at the Zurich Grand Prix.....Dudley Wood, secretary of the Rugby Football Union refutes newspaper claims that he made racist comments at a press lunch.....Niche, Lord Carnavon's filly who placed second in the 1000 Guineas, is killed when she bolted onto the road near trainer Richard Hannon's stable.....Nick Gillingham wins his third European 200m breaststroke title when he fends off the Hungarian Karoly Guttler in the Sheffield championships.....Zafonic is retired to stud.....Manchester United win the Charity Shield on penalties.....Australian leg-spinner Shane Warne takes his 29th wicket against England to equal the record for a leg-spinner.....Richard Phelps takes the world title in the modern pentathlon after the first one-day competition in its history at Darmstadt in Germany..... on Monday, August 9th, while England are still fighting to save the fifth Test, chairman of the selectors Ted Dexter resigns.....England lose the fifth Test to make it eight defeats in nine outings.....M J K Smith named as manager for the West Indies tour.....Australian Phil Anderson wins the Kellogg's Tour of Britain.....Linford Christie wins the world 100m title in Stuttgart, winning in 9.87 seconds, one hundredth of a second outside Carl Lewis' world record.....Damon Hill, having just missed out in the British and German Grands Prix, finally earns his debut victory in Hungary.....Paul Azinger beats Greg Norman in a play-off to win the US PGA championship, with Nick Faldo a shot away third.....Karen Lunn, from Australia, wins the British Women's Open championship.....Chinese women athletes finish first, second and third in the 3000m at the world championships.....Scot Graeme Obree beats Boardman and the world record twice en route to the world 4000m pursuit title in Hamar, Norway.....on Thursday, August 19, Sally Gunnell wins the world 400m hurdles title and breaks the world record with a time of 52.74 seconds.....on Friday, Colin Jackson wins the 110m hurdles title and he, too, breaks the world record with a time of 12.91 seconds.....USA win the Walker Cup 19-5.....Chris Boardman signs professional terms with GAN, France's leading team.....Gooch passes Gower's total of 8231 in the sixth Test at the Oval to become England's highest scoring batsman of all time.....Spencer Smith wins the world triathlon title in Manchester.....England win the sixth Test for their first victory in 13 months.....floodlit horse racing given the go-ahead.....the enquiry into the Grand National decides that in future there will be two recall men with flags.....Peter Reid dismissed as Manchester City's manager.....Damon Hill wins his second successive grand prix in Belgium.....Middlesex win the Britannic Assurance County Championship when Northants, the only team who could have caught them, only draw with Leicester.....

September
Terry Venables sells his 3,542,937 shares in Tottenham Hotspur for £3.2m.....Sussex and Essex hit 1,808 runs in their match at Hove to break the English record for aggregate runs in a game.....the day after that match finishes Sussex score a record 321 runs in the NatWest final, but are beaten by Warwickshire who immediately break Sussex's record.....Redgrave and Pinsent, the Searle brothers, Peter Haining and the women's lightweight coxless four all win gold at the World Rowing Championships in Roudnice, Czech Republic.....three boats disintegrate and four competitors are hospitalised at the

British Powerboat Grand Prix.....Wayne Rainey crashes in the Italian Motorcycle Grand Prix and is paralysed from the chest down.....Noureddine Morceli runs 3:44.39 in Rieti, Italy to take Steve Cram's world mile record.....Marseilles are banned from the European Cup.....England beat Poland 3-0 in World Cup qualifier, while Scotland and Wales draw.....Wang Junxia of China shatters the world 10,000m record by over 42 seconds, three more records fall in the next five days.....Monaco replace Marseilles in the European Cup.....Bob's Return wins the St Leger.....Damon Hill completes a hattrick of grand prix wins when he takes the Italian race.....Sampras and Graf win the US Open tennis.....Mexican Julio Cesar Chavez, after winning 87 consecutive fights, can only draw with American Pernell Whitaker.....Andy Roxburgh resigns as Scotland manager.....100 Cardiff City supporters are arrested in Liège.....Nigel Mansell signs on for two more years in the USA and two days later he wins at Nazareth and claims the Indy Car championship title in his debut season.....Glamorgan win the AXA Equity & Law Sunday League.....Chris Pyatt retains his WBO middleweight title by beating Hugo Corti.....on 21 September the cricket season closes and Malcolm Marshall, Derek Randall, Viv Richards and Chris Tavaré bow out.....Michael Roberts' riding contract with Sheikh Mohammed is not renewed, Frankie Dettori set to take his place.....Marseilles stripped of their French league title.....Sydney chosen for the Olympics 2000, just pipping Beijing by 45-43. Manchester's best score is 13 votes.....Alain Prost announces his retirement from F1.....the United States win the Ryder Cup at the Belfry by two points, winning five of the last six singles played on the final day.....Prost finishes second in Portugal to claim his fourth title.....

The Olympic Games

Sometimes sport gets on the front page; sometimes it *is* the front page. When the white smoke puffed out of the chimney of the Stade Louis II into the sullen evening air of the Principality of Monaco to signify Sydney had succeeded, it was an end to the biggest, noisiest, most expensive and most political campaign for Olympic selection in history.

It began with eight candidates: Beijing, Berlin, Brasilia, Istanbul, Manchester, Milan, Sydney and Tashkent. Tashkent, overly ambitious in the first flush of independence, bowed out first. Milan redid its calculations and Brasilia was just about forced out after the publication of the Olympic Enquiry Commission's report on the applications. Brasilia's bid was considered one of the weakest for many a day. That left five.

Beijing did everything but win the competition. They leaned heavily on the IOC, enjoying the tacit support of the President who had one eye on History, with a capital H. There were even those willing to suggest that Juan Antonio (aka Marques de) Samaranch harboured a Nobel Peace Prize. The President did not distance himself from the idea of the Games as a force for political change. "In Tokyo 1964, it was the turning point for the economy.....in Seoul there were big changes and now there is full democracy in Korea," he said at a meeting with journalists in London last June.

The International Olympic Committee would be playing for the highest stakes if Beijing was selected. The political gains could be momentous, the losses could threaten the very future of the Olympic movement. Had the Chinese played their cards more astutely, the Games would probably have gone there, but they didn't. Almost every manoeuvre back-fired. When they released a token number of political prisoners, it served only to highlight how many remained. When they reacted to the hostility of the American congress, it turned

THE VOTING

First round: Beijing 32, Sydney 30, Manchester 11, Berlin 9, Istanbul 7

Second round: Beijing 37, Sydney 30, Manchester 13, Berlin 9

Third round: Beijing 40, Sydney 37, Manchester 11

Fourth round: Sydney 45, Beijing 43

into a threat of a boycott of the Atlanta Olympics (though this story has bizarre conspiratorial links with a group of American businessmen who visited China earlier). And when female athletes turned out at the national championships to shatter world records, the rest of the world simply ascribed it to the use of drugs.

That Sydney's was the best sporting bid was almost beyond dispute. The IOC Enquiry Commission rated it so and if the decision was not to be a political one, the Australian city should have been out ahead. Yet, at the Machiavellian pre-voting stage, John Coates, president of the Australian Olympic Committee, was making a last-ditch bid to secure the Games by expanding a previously made offer to the African IOC members. He had already stated that should Sydney get the Games, each country would be entitled to two 12 month scholarships to the Canberra Institute of Sport. Anxious that Beijing had eased ahead in the final hours, Coates increased his offer from 12 months worth of scholarships to seven years worth. Putting a modest value of £15,000 a year on each scholarship, that made Australia's offer worth £210,000 to each country.

The IOC saw nothing wrong with this. Their head of public relations Andrew Napier said there was nothing underhand, it was, "scrupulously clean and fair". The IOC had previously committed itself to tidying up the bidding system when the offer of 'presents' was getting out of hand. It appears that the only change they have made is that now the money is passed over the table and not under it.

Berlin began its Olympic dream in the post-Wall euphoria of 1989 and 1990. Technically, it was a sound bid, but the revival of right-wing extremism in Rostock and the towns of east Germany took its toll. Eventually, even the Germans were not sure that the Games should come their way. The Berlin marathon, traditionally held on the last weekend in September, considered bringing its event forward a week, from September 26, so that it could assist the Berlin bid. It decided against changing its date, for fear its event would become the target of protesters.

Manchester came with a late run and a sense of misplaced optimism. John Major eventually made a full commitment to the idea, but in the infancy of his office, he was far too cautious. The Manchester bid had no clout until all the clout had been apportioned. Even as recently as the spring of 1993, Linford Christie was happily espousing the cause of Sydney. Like Major, he saw the error of his ways, but it was too late to acquire a unity of purpose. Manchester's 2000 bid was the third successive British bid to fall short: Birmingham in 1992 and Manchester in 1996 preceded it.

The future for any British bids is in the balance. The IOC vice-president (and Australian) Kevin Gosper immediately invited the Chinese to rebid for the 2004 Games. Should they respond positively, it will be hard for anyone to prise their grip off the ultimate in sporting prizes. It should not be forgotten that Beijing played the donations game much earlier in this bidding sequence when they made an inaugural present to the IOC museum in Lausanne of a 2,200 year old 'grave soldier' from Xi'an. The figure had an estimated value of around $40m which made it worth

OLYMPIC SHORTS

Has the International Olympic Committee thoughts above its station? Well, probably yes. It has applied for observer status at the United Nations. Now, it runs a very good sports meeting every four years, but......

Primo Nebiolo, much-loved President of the IAAF and member of the IOC (well, much-loved by Primo) was so sure that Beijing had won the Games that an hour before the official announcement, he issued, through his henchman Enrico Jacomini, a press release to the Italian press saying just that.....later it was amended.

The Australian team were nothing, if not honest. "We went to the Brothel des Paris every morning to prostitute ourselves and try and get one more vote for Sydney," said Frank Sarlor, the lord mayor of Sydney, on his daily visits to the Hotel des Paris in Monaco where the IOC members stayed. "The Best Little Whores on the Riviera" said one Australian newspaper's headline.

From the inception of its bid, until the vote was taken on September 23rd, 630 criminal offences were committed in Germany against the Berlin bid and its organisers.

about one and a half times the cost of the entire museum.

As daunting is the queue that is forming behind them. Rio de Janeiro (to compensate for the humiliating late withdrawal of Brasilia?); Johannesburg, Durban or Cape Town (when they have sorted out their political problems, said Samaranch. He didn't use the same line against China); Paris (a very strong potential bid); Buenos Aires (like Rio chasing the fact that South America, like Africa, has never hosted the Games); The Ruhr District (Essen & Dusseldorf); Stockholm (with the most beautiful Olympic stadium in the world and our choice); and Istanbul ('cos it almost got forgotten this time around).

Manchester would be better opting for the next available Commonwealth Games to capitalise on the good publicity it has generated. If there is to be a bid from Britain for the 2004 Games, it may be necessary to look elsewhere. Glasgow would be great, but London may be the only viable option. Then you have to ask whether the money that it would cost is worth it. Manchester may have only spent around £5m on the actual machinery of the bid, but it couldn't have been carried forward without the investment in the sporting infrastructure. The government ploughed in £75m, half of which has gone on the indoor arena above Victoria station, and would have to do at least the same again were London to bid. Manchester may be left with some fine facilities, but it will still have look at the balance sheet some time ahead and wonder if it really was worth it. We hope so.

Landmarks

Botham Bows Out

"At the end of a lovely day, the coltish local tailender, Botham, made the pitch look easy and the bowling even more so." So wrote The Guardian's **Frank Keating** *in a summer of Botham's boyhood. In the 19 years that followed, Botham broke all the records and added a shimmering lustre to English cricket. This summer, without so much as a by-your-leave, he retired. Keating, having watched the boy become a man become a master, bids farewell.*

Not since those two black-edged sepia Septembers of 1914 and 1939 can sheer fluke and a perverse conjunction of the generations have conspired to make a cricket season end with such laments and last-post bugles for the going of cricketers of grandeur.

On the sunlit fields of the shires we will not see again those two mighty monarchs writ large and forever in the annals of an ancient game - Vivian Richards and Allan Border. But their presence here in a way was always only a bonus. And as home is where the heart is, it is hard to believe that next summer we are unlikely to see emerging through the Test match wicket-gate any one of that great triumvirate, Ian Botham, Graham Gooch, or David Gower. As well, no more Dilley, no more Foster; no more dear deadpan, deadbat Tavare; and, alas, no more Randall, the Retford imp...

And the grandest of all was Botham - for his bold and baronial wholeheartedness, his larks, his wolfish grin, his runs, his sixers, his wickets, his catches, his utter <u>hooraymanship</u>. 'A working-class hero is something to be', wrote John Lennon. Ian Botham rampagingly made flesh of the lyric.

Can it be that Botham was so long with us, for so long part of the furniture and fabric, that we took him too much for granted? We shall be poignantly aware of his absence this coming summer - particularly on June 12, 1994, I fancy, which will be to all intents the exact 20th anniversary of his announcing himself to cricket's wider world. On that evening in 1974, the 18-year old laddo from Yeovil came in as a tailender in a crucial cup-tie against Hampshire with Somerset standing forlorn at 113 for eight and needing an impossible 70 to win. Andy Roberts, the cruel West Indian demon, at once knocked out three of the boy's teeth with a fearful bouncer. He put them in his pocket, sipped a glass of water, clouted the next bouncer out of the field and into the carpark - and his half-century secured a famous victory with an over and one wicket to spare.

The callow youngster had, at almost the first time of asking, defined how courage in sport is that glorious contradiction in terms - the strong desire to live, taking the form of a readiness to die. It was to be ever thus with Botham.

Two decades of staggering all-round feats were set in train that day. But even as he filled the Test match record books to the brim, it always remained the fact that it was never so much what he got, but the way that he got them - and every succeeding feat and broken record was logged with swash and buckle and foe-honouring chivalry and the promise of foaming pints or vintage wines shared with friend and opponent at close of play -

'For St. George he was for England

And before he slayed the dragon

He drank a pint of English ale

Out of an English flagon'

The Merrie Englander has laid down his bat, sheathed sword in its scabbard. But methinks his zest for life itself remains unmellowed and one activity from which he has not retired - nor, he says, never will - are his epic tramps in aid of leukaemia, for which he has so far raised over £5 million. Far more steps for that cause than all his resplendent Test match runs or wickets or sixers or blinding catches.

There were, said Chesterton, two distinct types of great men: "One type is so great as to make every man feel small. The other, the true great, makes every man great". Ian Botham was a true great.

BOTHAM BY NUMBERS

BATTING

	Plyd	Inngs	NO	Runs	HS	Ave	100s	50s	Catches
Test Matches	102	161	6	5,200	208	33.54	14	22	120
One-day Ints	116	106	15	2,113	79	23.22	-	9	36
Career	402	617	46	19,399	228	33.97	38		354

BOWLING

	Plyd	Balls	Runs	Wkts	Ave	Best	5wkts	10wkts
Test matches	102	21,815	10,878	383	28.40	8-34	27	4
One-day Ints	116	6,271	4,139	154	28.54	4-31	-	-
Career	402		31,902	1,172	27.22	8-34	59	8

Honours: Two County Championships with Worcester in 1988 & 1989; two NatWest/Gillette wins, 1979 & 1983, with Somerset; two Benson & Hedges wins with Somerset, 1981 & 1982; three John Player/Refuge victories, 1979 with Somerset, 1987 & 1988 with Worcester; BBC Sports Personality of the Year in 1981; OBE in 1992

King of the River

Few competitors in British sport have been more sensationally successful than Richard Fox, and none who has achieved as much has been honoured by so few. In July, Fox became the world champion of slalom canoeing for the fifth time and also won his fifth gold medal as a member of the winning team. **David Hunn**, *of the Sunday Times, charts the path down the river of an astonishing sportsman.*

Try as they do, it is difficult for the British press and public to dismiss slalom canoeing as one of those 'Mickey Mouse' sports on which they can conveniently turn their backs. The sport is vigorously contested by almost every nation in Europe, east and west, as well as by the United States and Canada, and by several in south America and the far east. What is more, Fox competes in a solo kayak (K1), the class in which competition is fiercest and most widespread.

In sleek, Eskimo style craft weighing only a few pounds, the competitors use double-bladed paddles. The so-called 'Canadian' canoes require the paddler to kneel upright and dig a single blade into the water. But this is not straightforward, flatwater racing, this is a turbulent, downhill hell in which they must steer at breakneck speed over boulders, down rapids and through a bewildering array of 'gates'.

The 'gates' are pairs of poles suspended just above the water, usually 25 of them on a course less than 400 metres long. They are placed with evil intent: at the foot of a drop or close to a maelstrom of water. Some demand that the paddler cuts right across the torrent, and some that he passes through the gate against the water, turning to force himself upstream with no more (if he is to win) than a single, mighty stroke of the blade.

Speed is not quite everything. Though the winner will probably have to complete the course in about two minutes, he will be penalised by five seconds for every gate he touches. In world and Olympic contests, the competitor is allowed two runs and the better total counts. Technique, tactics and strength have never been subjected to a more brutal assault.

When Richard Fox was 11 years old, he was given a do-it-yourself canoe kit. His father, Roger Fox, was a devotee of the sport who went on to become chairman of the slalom committee of the British Canoe Union. Richard's younger sister, now Rachel Crosbee, is a physiotherapist who was British national and open champion in 1992 and in the women's team that won bronze in July.

At 12, Richard watched the Olympic slalom on the man-made course outside

---

FOX FACTS

Full Name: Richard Munro Fox
Age: 33
Height: 176cm Weight: 70kg
Lives: Marseilles
Honours: MBE

Individual World Champion

1981, 1983, 1985, 1989 & 1993

Team World Champion

1979, 1981, 1983, 1987 & 1993

World Cup Champion

1988, 1989 & 1991

Munich. At 17, he had qualified for his first world championships, in 1977. Fox was champion in 1981, 1983, 1985 and 1989, adding the World Cup (a seven-race series) in 1988, 1989 and 1991. There has never been a record to equal it nor, in any sport, a British world champion of greater appeal.

The women's K1 champion in 1989 was the French paddler, Myriam Jerusalmi. In fairy-tale style, they married. It was a rare union of two supreme athletes and in 1993 they both won their world championships again, Richard at an age (33) regarded as well beyond the pale for so physically testing a sport. It was some compensation for his desperate disappointment at being placed fourth in the Barcelona Olympics, the only Games of his competitive lifetime to include slalom canoeing.

His first run was at a stunning speed (less than 105 seconds), he hit three gates. His second run was clear, but he took two strokes to get through one of the raging uphill gates. Such a fragment of error can cruelly puncture a dream of glory. Fox finished 33 one-hundredths of a second outside the bronze medal and two seconds slower than the winner.

The flash of time will haunt this perfectionship for ever. The rest of us are content to have known the greatest slalom canoeist the world has ever seen.

Rare Talents

For 100 years the world's best cyclists have chased the one hour target. That blue riband of records has been held by many of the great riders, but never before by a Briton. Suddenly this year, there were two. **Phil Liggett,** *of the Daily Telegraph tells the story.*

Chris Boardman, Olympic 4,000m champion, and Graeme Obree, never before seen in international competition, became the first amateur riders since Italian Ercole Baldini, almost 40 years ago, to break the most coveted track record in the world - the hour - in July.

In a heady six-day period for the British sport, first Obree and then Boardman pushed the figures away from some of the most famous idols of the post-War period, leaving millionaire pedallers like five-times Tour de France winner, Eddy Merckx, and erstwhile hour record holder, Francesco Moser, shaking their heads in disbelief.

Two amateur riders whose characters could not be more different, stepped into the most sacred corner of record-breaking and then returned home to leave continental Europeans incredulous at their achievements.

Obree, a 27-year-old eccentric Scot from Ayr who was persuaded to continue as an amateur rider for one more year by his wife, destroyed the myth of sleek, ultra-light £3000 machines backed by multi-million pounds in research, when he turned up in Norway with his homemade "old faithful" - a machine patched together with washing machine bearings and made from parts salvaged from obsolete bicycles.

Norway had just finished building a new velodrome for the World Championships due in August and after Boardman had objected to Obree going for the record at Bordeaux, where the Olympic champion was planning a later attempt, the Scot decided on Oslo.

A cameraman, five photographers and an inquisitive French journalist were all who were on-hand when Obree, riding in his unique style which resembles a downhill skier on wheels, rewrote the record books. Next day, the French sports paper L'Equipe gave two pages to "Mister O'Bree and old faithful".

Until that moment, Britain had never had a rider - amateur or professional - with the ability to attempt the record. Now, with the dust still swirling around the stadium in Oslo, Boardman was in position in Bordeaux to register his claim.

In Britain, Obree's ride caused hardly a ripple, only the French, Belgian and Italian Press reported the happening at length. They understood what riding 51.596 kilometres in an hour really meant.

But, Britain was catching on, too, and when Boardman launched into his attempt six days later, everyone was suddenly an expert. Riding a monocoque bicycle similar to the one on which he won the Olympic title, Boardman took eight kilometres to catch up with Obree's schedule. From that moment on he was gaining almost a second a kilometre until at the end, in the heat of the velodrome in a humid Bordeaux, Boardman's hour ran out at 52.270 kilometres - the first rider to beat 52 kilometres. Because of the deafening roar from the crowd, Boardman did not even hear the gun fire to end the attempt.

This time, instead of a handful of people, Boardman had drawn a packed stadium and, again, a British amateur destroyed the myth that has surrounded the hour record since Francesco Moser set it at altitude in Mexico in 1984.

"I had no idea what breaking this record meant to Europe", said Boardman afterwards. "If I had, I would have been scared stiff."

In six days, two young British riders had achieved more publicity in Europe than any home rider since the halcyon days of sprinter Reg Harris.

TRACKING THE RECORD

Date	Rider		Kms
29.06.56	Jacques Anquetil	FRA	46.159
19.09.56	Ercole Baldini	ITA	46.393
23.09.58	Roger Riviere	FRA	47.346
30.10.67	Ferdi Bracke	BEL	48.093
10.10.68	Ole Ritter	DEN	48.653
25.10.72	Eddy Merckx	BEL	49.431
23.01.84	Francesco Moser	ITA	51.151
18.07.93	Graeme Obree	GBR	51.596
23.07.93	Chris Boardman	GBR	52.270

Obree, who since breaking the record has beaten Boardman on the way to winning the World pursuit championship in Norway, still uses his white old faithful, and will attack Boardman's new record when he feels the conditions are right in 1994.

Frenchman Henri Desgrange, a 28-year-old amateur, became the first holder of the hour record when he covered 35.325 kms on the Paris (Buffalo) track on the 11th May 1893. Desgrange became the founder of the Tour de France, first held in 1903. Since the Second World War, the record has been attempted by only the greatest names in the sport.

The Clough Years

On April 26, Brian Clough retired from football after a career that spanned nine years as a player and 28 years as a manager, 18 of which were with Nottingham Forest. Clough (and a few others) tell it how it was.

"Age doesn't count. It's what you know about football that matters. I am better than the 500 or so managers who have been sacked since the war. If they had known anything about the game they would not have lost their jobs."

Clough, in 1985, after his appointment to the manager's job at Hartlepool. At 29, he was the youngest manager in the League.

"In this business, you've got to be a dictator or you haven't got a chance."

The same year, confirming that he might be a socialist, but he wasn't a democrat.

"Leaving Derby was the worst clanger of my career, an absolute tragedy. I quit in disgust and learnt one thing: never resign on a point of principle."

Clough won the League title with Derby in 1972, but left 18 months later following a disagreement with the directors.

"I couldn't accept that I'd swapped the England centre-half and six other internationals for a bunch of players who couldn't put their boots on the right feet. It was like asking Lester Piggott to win the Derby with a Skegness donkey."

Clough on his short spell as manager of Brighton & Hove Albion. Clough and Peter Taylor went to Brighton in November 1973 and Clough stayed for less than eight months, leaving in July 1974 for Leeds.

"When all the hurt of being out of work had gone, I wanted to kiss the Leeds board, not strangle them. I was the luckiest man alive because I won the pools without filling in the coupon."

Clough succeeded Don Revie at Elland Road, but player unrest led to a very brief stay. With players like skipper Billy Bremner and Jackie Charlton

refusing to play for the new manager, the chairman of the board Manny Cussins sacked him. Clough's pay-off, for less than a month and a half's work, was £120,000 (a lot of money in those days) and a Mercedes car.

"A Rolls-Royce communist"

Malcolm Allison on Brian Clough

"Football Hooligans? Well, there are the 92 club chairmen for a start...."

Clough on trouble on the terraces.

"If the game was meant to be played in the air, He would have put grass in the sky."

In Clough's golden spell he won two European Cups, a League title and two League Cups in just three seasons and all with a style of football that embellished the English game.

"Me"

When asked who the biggest influence on his career was. Clough, throughout his career, constantly referred to himself as "Old Big 'Ead".

THE LONG
AND THE SHORT

Longest Serving League Managers

24 years	Matt Busby	Man Utd 1945-69
23 years	Jimmy Seed	Charlton 1933-56
23 years	Joe Smith	Blackpool 1935-58
21 years	Billy Walker	Notts F 1939-60
20 years	Eddie Davidson	Sheff Utd 1932-52
18 years	Brian Clough	Notts F 1975-93

Shortest Serving League Managers

3 days	Bill Lambton	Scunthorpe 1959
	(Verbal contract cancelled)	
4 days	Dave Bassett	Crystal Pal 1984
	(Returned to Wimbledon)	
13 days	Johnny Cochrane	Reading 1939
	(Sacked)	
18 days	Jimmy McIlroy	Bolton 1970
	(Resigned)	
25 days	Tim Ward	Exeter 1953
	(Returned to Barnsley)	
44 days	Brian Clough	Leeds 1974
	(Sacked - player unrest)	

"One of the reasons why I never became England manager was because the Football Association thought I'd take over and run the show. They were dead right."

The England managership twice came up when Clough was at the height of his powers, but he was overlooked both times. In 1977, the FA chose Ron Greenwood. In 1982, the post went to Bobby Robson.

"I can't promise to give the team talk in Welsh, but from now on I shall be taking my holidays in Porthcawl and I've got a complete set of Harry Secombe albums."

On being offered the job of manager of Wales in 1988. Clough turned it down.

"I'm the worst judge of centre-forwards since Walter Winterbottom, who only gave me two England caps."

Clough hit 251 League goals in 274 matches and was the fastest ever to 200 goals, but his only games for England were against Sweden and Wales in 1959. His career was ended by injury in 1962.

"I'm going nowhere. Resignations are for Prime Ministers and cabinets and those caught with their trousers down."

In 1988, responding to suggestions that he might walk away from Forest.

"In case you haven't noticed, people like to keep pointing out that I've never won the FA Cup."

Clough, in 1991. While Forest won the League Cup four times, only once in Clough's years did they reach an FA Cup final. That was in 1991 against Spurs when the game went to extra time.

"I have always felt like royalty. You are how you feel. It's not conceit, it just happens to be true."

On receiving the freedom of the city of Nottingham.

"This is a beautiful city with a beautiful river and I know - I've walked on it for 18 years."

Again, on receiving the freedom of the city.

"Don't worry, next year I'll be standing here again having won more cups and leagues..."

To a fan, after receiving the freedom of the city.

"I'm staying here till they shoot me because I am finishing after that."

Clough, on Notts Forest

"Can't avoid the truth. Can't make it look better than it is. Only one thing to be said. We're in the shit."

April, 1993.

Postscripts

"A glorious chapter..."

Graham Taylor

"A brilliant tactician..."

Jack Charlton

'By far the best manager I ever played under and I played under quite a few, including Bill Shankly and Bob Paisley."

Larry Lloyd, former Nottingham Forest defender.

"I remember one morning at training. It was a really cold day and we all had tracksuit bottoms on. Clough comes along and says: 'Right, tracksuit bottoms off, run in and out of there', pointing to a field of nettles next to the training ground. We were stung to high heaven, but we all went - Shilton, Burns, Francis and Lloyd - all experienced internationals. In fact, we all had to go through again. It was the law of the playground, but it worked because nobody argued back. Even now, I'd probably do the same..."

Viv Anderson, Nottingham Forest and England fullback.

With Bells On

Britain might have hoped for some success in the Stuttgart world athletics championship. Sally Gunnell was a clear favourite for the 400m hurdles; Linford Christie and Colin Jackson close favourites for their events. Hope, however, travelled beyond expectation and two world records and three titles later, the British team, with ten medals in all, could revel in its best world championships yet. **Michael Butcher**, *of The European, catalogues the happy days.*

It was not so long ago that Britain was seen as the home of the middle distances. It was a tag that had been with us from the Victorian era of Walter George down to the incomparable Sebastian Coe in the 1980s. Well, this year the world has been turned upside down. All eyes have been on the sprinting Titans from the British Isles instead of our once untameable transatlantic cousins. And that's not the only change in the order of things.

A 33-year-old man winning the World title within 0.01 of the world record? Unreal as it might sound, Linford Christie turned the age to speed ratio on its head to take Britain's first World 100 metre title since the championships started in 1983. Add that to his Olympic crown and you have one of the most extraordinary Tales of the Unexpected in the history of sport. Christie did not win his first decent title, the European Indoor, until he was 26. Since then his progression has been of the juggernaut variety.

Even more, Stuttgart was reckoned to be the greatest 100 metres ever seen, with Christie tantalisingly close to tearing up the record book. Remember all the showboating surrounding Carl Lewis's Tokyo time of 9.86 seconds? Well, he was scooted along with a 1.2 metres per second wind while the 0.3 behind Christie had about as much puff as you need to ruffle an eiderdown feather.

It was not only the win that was important, but the stature of the man. Since his Olympic victory, the haughty American Kings of Speed have been obliged to eat humble pie. This year it was double helpings. The world's greatest, Carl Lewis, was disposed of almost insultingly in the dollar-strewn head-to-head in Gateshead. In Stuttgart, he was an also-ran in fourth place.

The real threat was supposed to come from Andre Cason but he was beaten even before the gun went off. Spotted the night before the final in one of the snack stands outside the Gottlieb-Daimler stadium, he was staring morosely into a corner. His depression was well-founded. He was not really in the race for gold.

One aspect of the Christie aura that he shares with Carl Lewis is that in the minor races he does not feel the need to win. Grands Prix come and go. They do not matter any more when you are the best in the world. Why bother with the Roxy at Rochdale when the West End awaits?

In hurdling as in sprinting the story was the same. The Americans have dominated for more than 100 years. Not this year, though. Colin Jackson smashed through the athletes' equivalent of writers' block to win the World title and lay a troublesome ghost to rest, as well as the best from the US.

Plagued by ill luck and injury since his win in the European Championships in 1990, Jackson finally kissed his bad luck goodbye in Stuttgart. It was quite a send-off. The Welsh wizard thrust his torso through the beam in the world record time of 12.91 seconds to take the major title that had eluded him for so long. He also turned the clock back 128 years to the last time a British hurdler set a world record. He, too, was called Jackson, initial C, which is weird if you care about those things.

There had been a minor fright just before the championships when Jackson took the first flight out of Zurich and missed competing in the most glittering grand prix on the circuit. Just a precaution you understand, said his coach. But we held our breath and whispered "Not again, surely." Bad faith was amply chastised in Stuttgart by a flawless performance that seemed unreal in its perfection.

THE MARCH OF TIME
The progression of world records in the 110m hurdles and the women's 400m hurdles

110m Hurdles
Electronically timed

12.91	Colin Jackson	GBR	Stuttgart	20.8.93
12.92	Roger Kingdom	USA	Zurich	16.8.89
12.91	Renaldo Nehemiah	USA	Zurich	19.8.81
13.00	Renaldo Nehemiah	USA	LA	6.5.79
13.16	Renaldo Nehemiah	USA	San José	14.4.79
13.21	Alejandro Casanas	CUB	Sofia	21.8.77
13.24	Rod Milburn	USA	Munich	7.9.72
13.33	Willie Davenport	USA	Mexico	17.10.68

the first(hand-timed)

16.0	Clement Jackson	GBR	Oxford	14.11.1865

400m Hurdles

52.74	Sally Gunnell	GBR	Stuttgart	19.8.93
52.94	Marina Stepanova	URS	Tashkent	17.9.86
53.32	Marina Stepanova	URS	Stuttgart	30.8.86
53.55	Sabine Busch	GDR	Berlin	22.9.85
53.58	Marga Ponomaryeva	URS	Kiev	22.6.84
54.02	Anna Ambraziené	URS	Moscow	11.6.83
54.28	Karin Rossley	GDR	Jena	17.5.80
54.78	Marina Makeyeva	URS	Moscow	27.7.79
54.89	Tatyana Zelentsova	URS	Prague	2.9.78

the first(hand-timed and unratified)

61.1	Sandra Dyson	GBR	Bonn	15.5.71

The men were not the only ones to whip the Americans into submission. Of the three golds in Stuttgart, one was fully expected by all and sundry, Sally Gunnell's in the 400 metres hurdles. That makes it more difficult to win not easier, but when we saw it happen, we smiled and said "I told you so".

Another world record, too, but it was Sally who warned us about that in the girl-next-door way she has. But don't be fooled, there's a killer instinct under the surface that would do credit to a rattler. When the WR flashed up on the dinky digital display she strode off to take the applause while another defeated Yank, Sandra Farmer-Patrick, lay prostrate on the track, blind with fatigue.

Yes, it's been a good year to be British. Records have fallen and reputations have been carved with pride. In the 1988 Olympics, when I asked an American sprint coach for an interview with his star athlete, he looked pityingly at me and said, "OK, two minutes for the Mother Country". Well, the Mother Country has hit back. I'll see if I can find two minutes next time I see him.

All in a Day's Work

"Where do all the ladders start," said the poet Yeats,"In the foul rag and bone shop of the heart." Richard Phelps would appreciate that. For years, he has worked diligently to a timetable designed to make him the finest modern pentathlete in the world. Yet, he has fallen short. This year, he threw the book away, relied on the heart and, on the busiest sporting day of his life, became Britain's first ever world champion in the event. **Mick Cleary,** *of the Observer, found a relaxed Renaissance man.*

It was a warm August day in Darmstadt, just over half an hour's drive away from Frankfurt. Richard Phelps had a couple of hours to kill. What should he do? Pen a sonnet to his loved one perhaps? The modern pentathlete faces these sort of dilemmas all the time. He is the Renaissance man of Sport. A bit of exercise, a spot of intellectualising. It's all in a day's work.

In fact the modern Renaissance man does not have much time for the fancy stuff.

"It's not romantic," says Phelps. "It's just hard work."

Ah, but we incurables on the sidelines can dream though: of great athletic feats, of battles fought, enemies defeated, pressures resisted, and of a noble spirit pervading all. The modern pentathlon traces its roots back to the oldest of times, based on the exploits of the loyal soldier bearing the news of war through hostile terrain. Distilled into its contemporary essence, the sport requires the athletes to shoot, fence, run, swim and ride. No-one does it better than Phelps.

At long last those words can be writ large. For at the beginning of August Phelps, at the age of 32, won the world title. So many championships, so many near misses. And so to Darmstadt. Phelps had modest expectations.

"It had been a funny old year", said Phelps. "I'd thrown away the rule book and done everything my way. Perhaps I should have done that years ago."

Phelps, married, baby on the way, without sponsorship and obliged to work full-time in the family scrap-iron business in Gloucester, had cut right back on his training schedule. If circumstances pushed him to this end, so too did his own inclinations. He'd had enough of the grind. The Barcelona Olympics had sapped his morale.

Going into the final event he was lying in sixth place. The show jumping is a brute of a discipline. Not because of any mountainous obstacles or excessive time restrictions. No, all those elements Phelps, or any modern pentathlete, can take in their stride. What brings them to their knees however is the draw for which horse they are to ride. It is a complete lottery and can destroy a man. Imagine Lester Piggott in the paddock fingers crossed behind his back hoping to draw Zafonic. Phelps duly pulled the three-legged mule from the hat and that was that. He finished 13th.

"It's such a cruel climax," says Phelps. "We all know it's coming but when it goes against you, it still hurts like hell. I found it very hard to take because I felt I was in with a real chance of a medal."

He returned home and contemplated retirement. After all he'd certainly done his time. Maybe there was still a bit of oxygen left in the tank, but was there any fire in the belly? He wasn't sure himself. He'd started in the sport at the age of 12, his sense of ambition fuelled by the exploits of his uncle, Robert, veteran of three Olympic Games, who had been introduced to the sport by a Hungarian refugee he met while playing water polo.

The sport had been the preserve of the military. The Phelps family introduced a bit of bluff Gloucestershire common sense to the proceedings. In 1979, aged 18, Richard Phelps became British champion for the first of ten times. An individual bronze at the worlds in 1987 was followed by another bronze at Seoul in the team event. The modern pentathlon used to take place over two days but pressure from the Olympic powers-that-be, desperate to make everything televisual, suggested that if the sport weren't telescoped into one day, then maybe it might disappear from the Olympic schedules. Nice lot aren't they? Phelps adapted better than some. But still the Big One eluded him.

"I'd tried so hard but never quite pulled it off", says Phelps. "So this year I thought I'd have some fun. I stopped travelling to London for shooting and fencing practice. And I also cut down on my competitions. I had to pay my way out to Australia for the world qualifiers but, that apart, I did very little. I competed in a triathlon the week before the worlds. Normally we're banned from doing that. Seven days before that I'd been lying on a beach in Majorca on holiday. Our governing body weren't too impressed."

They may not have been. The rest of the world certainly were.

Indy Pink

Last summer, Nigel Mansell became the first Briton in 16 years to win the Fomula One world championship. Then, amid rumour, counter-rumour and a deal of acrimony, Mansell quit the circuit and signed up with the Newman/Haas Indy Car team. America was a new challenge and a daunting one, but Mansell's commitment was whole-hearted. He moved the family to Florida and set about learning the rules of a new game. He learnt them better than anyone could ever have expected.

If Nigel Mansell was searching for a grail, then he could not have arrived at a more appropriate town than Nazareth. Not in Lower Galilee, though; in Pennsylvania, USA. There, on September 19th, the 40-year-old became the first driver in motor racing history to take the Formula One and Indy Car crowns in successive years. Mansell certainly found it a spiritual occasion: "One of the five great moments of my life," he said, ranking it alongside the birth of his three children. If such a comparison appears misplaced, it nevertheless offers an insight into the mind of Mansell. The line of ambition seldom ran straighter. Why else should a middle-aged man with no financial worries put his life repeatedly on the line unless the desire to achieve is all-consuming?

Mansell didn't need a long memory to remind himself of the risks; his debut victory in Australia was followed by a near-calamity in Phoenix when he clunked into one of those great concrete walls. Mansell might have been reminded of that day in Nazareth when another Briton, Steve Robertson in the support race, found that concrete was harder than steel, and like Mansell in Phoenix was airlifted to hospital. "You can't say I have had a rosy baptism," said Mansell. "I have the scars to prove it."

Throughout the summer, though, Mansell was unwavering. He had the best car and the best team when he was at Williams; he has the best car and the best team at Newman/Haas. He has served them both well. That opening win in Surfer's Paradise was followed by victories at Wisconsin (race 5), Michigan (race 10) and New Hampshire (race 11). Two days prior to the Nazareth event, Mansell confirmed where his heart now lies by signing a new two year contract with the American team. The deal is worth a reputed $7.5m + bonuses for two years. At Nazareth, Mansell indicated that it would be money well spent. He drove a perfect race; on the 45th and 46th laps he took Emerson Fittipaldi and Paul Tracy in succession to take a lead. It was a race he didn't need to win to take the title. The necessity was only to finish within eight points of his nearest rival, Fittipaldi. This was one, though, the Briton wanted to complete in style. "It was the most thrilling race I have been in," said a euphoric Mansell afterwards. "I have been teetotal for 14 years, but I'm actually going to get drunk tonight. I'm going to drink like there's no tomorrow."

Mansell's contract will keep him in America till 1996. However, he has not ruled out returning to F1 then. He has been sorely missed. If he does not endear himself to everyone Mansell still draws in the crowds like no-one else. The management at Silverstone reckoned that his absence alone from the 1993 British grand prix cost them £1m in losses because of the drop in the number of spectators. Mansell will be welcomed back with open arms; whenever he comes.

Bruno meets Lewis

It was the only time that two Britons had fought for a heavyweight title in history. Bruno, the popular favourite with 'True Brit' on his pants against Lewis, the Brit-come-lately, who won his Olympic gold medal for Canada. **John Burton** *of the Daily Mail tells the story of a fight that answered one question, but left another unanswered.*

In the very early hours of Saturday morning, October 1, in a chilly Cardiff Arms Park, Lennox Lewis won the heavyweight battle of Britain against Frank Bruno, but failed miserably in his quest to convince detractors that he is the best heavyweight in the world.

There were too many moments when 32-year-old Bruno was able to dominate the champion with a forceful left jab to leave serious questions about Lewis' credentials at the highest level. If Bruno, known throughout the game for being ponderous and mechanical, could find the target so easily, what damage could Riddick Bowe do?

One thumping right third-round cross which, fortunately for Lewis landed on the side of his head and not flush on his chin, could have been the beginning of the end. But Bruno did not have the mobility or speed of thought to capitalise. It was reminiscent of the crashing right cross he exploded on Mike Tyson's jaw in 1989 when, fleetingly, the undisputed heavyweight championship beckoned.

However, it would have been a step back in time if Bruno had managed to sustain his titanic effort and upset the odds-on favourite. And on the credit side, Lewis demonstrated for the second successive fight, that he has a dependable chin and more importantly a desire to survive. When Bruno's bombs were flying he came in close to give himself those vital seconds to clear his head and unscramble the millions of dollar signs that were in danger of scattering in the stratosphere.

Lewis regrouped and restored some sanity to the proceedings in round five, when he began to use his left jab. Bruno was leading on points at this stage, but his world fell apart when Lewis detonated a left hook on his chin. It didn't matter a jot that the punch was thrown in desperation. It had its desired effect and the fight was all over in the seventh round. It showed, too, that the 28-year-old Lewis can be one of the most ruthless finishers in a ruthless business. While he can continue to find that explosive force in either hand, he will remain one of the major players.

For Bruno, it was the best performance of his career, but there is little left to contemplate now except retirement. Not even the negotiating skills of Micky Duff could conjure up a fourth tilt at the richest prize in sport and domestic scraps against European champion Henry Akinwande or British champion Herbie Hide would be a backward step.

Lewis, in holding the WBC version of the divided crown, is giving British boxing a prestige never known in the history of the sport. But only when he meets Riddick Bowe, generally regarded as the world number one, can we gain a true measure of his abilities.

On this evidence, while Bruno goes back into pantomime, Lewis, if he wants to join the all time greats of the sport, must go back to school.

Lists

NEW YEAR HONOURS

DBE	Mary Alison Glen-Haig	IOC member
CBE	Arthur Edward Jones	Badminton
OBE	David Coleman	Commentator
	George Hubert Graham Doggert	Cricket
	David Michael Barclay Sole	Rugby
	Michael James Stewart	Cricket
	Gordon David Strachan	Football
MBE	Christopher Miles Boardman	Cycling
	Elly Maria Ellis	Wembley Stdm.
	Sharron Davies	Swimming
	Nicholas Gillingham	Swimming
	Tanni Carys Davina Grey	Paralympian
	Sally Jane Janet Gunnell	Athletics
	Garry Gerard Paul Herbert	Rowing
	Christopher Holmes	Paralympian
	Sean Robert Kerly	Hockey
	Timothy Marshall	Sport/Disabl.
	Matthew Pinsent	Rowing
	Gregory Mark Pascoe Searle	Rowing
	Denise Jacqueline Smith	Sport/Disabl.
BEM	Hugh Blair	Sport/Scotland
	Robert Joseph Garbutt	St John's
	Robert Ian Graham	Boxing

QUEEN'S BIRTHDAY HONOURS

Knight Bachelor

	Eddie(Elias George) Kulukundis	Benefactor
CBE	Prof. John Allen Patmore	Sports Council
	Susan Elizabeth Anne Devoy	Squash
OBE	Lt.Col. Colin Cheshire	Shooting
	Andrew Robert Mitchell	Sport/Disabl.
	Andrew Roxburgh	Football
	Prof. Margaret Jean Talbot	Sport & PE
	Michelle (Micky) Walker	Golf
MBE	George Leslie Baldwin	Athletics
	George Barraclough	Swimming
	Carole Bradley	Sport/Disabl.
	Majorie May Davies	Football
	Neal Dickinson	Athletics
	Thomas Richard Dunwoody	Horse Racing
	Stephen Gordon Hendry	Snooker
	Harold Larwood	Cricket
	John (Jack) McDiarmid McMillen	Golf
	Sharon Rendle	Judo
	Johnny Wallis	Football
	Raymond Colin Wilkins	Football

BBC SPORTS PERSONALITY OF THE YEAR 1992 AWARDS

Winner: **Nigel Mansell**
International Award: **Andre Agassi**
Team Award: **GB Rowing Squad**

TELEVISION SPORTS RATINGS
From Sept 1 1992-Sept 1 1993

1	Horse Racing (April 3) Grand National	BBC1	15.17m
2	Football (May 20) FA Cup Final Replay	BBC1	13.44m
3	Athletics (Aug 15) Men's 100m Final WC	BBC1	11.49m
4	Boxing (Oct 17) Bruno v Coetzer	BBC1	11.43m
5	Football (May 15) FA Cup Final	BBC1	10.92m
6	Athletics (Jul 30) Christie v Lewis 100m	ITV	10.73m
7	Football (Apr 18) Coca-Cola Cup Final	ITV	10.48m
8	Boxing (Sept 19) Eubank v Thornton	ITV	10.38m
9	Boxing (Feb 20) Eubank v Holmes	ITV	10.06m
10	Football (Apr 7) Rangers v Marseilles	ITV	9.97m
11	Football (June 13) England v Brazil	ITV	9.89m
12	Football (Oct 21) Rangers v Leeds	ITV	9.88m
13	Football (Apr 21) Rangers v CSKA Moscow	ITV	9.64m
14	Football (May 29) England v Poland	ITV	9.64m
15	Athletics (Aug 4) Zurich GP	ITV	9.44m
16	Football (June 2) England v Norway	BBC1	9.18m
17	Football (June 19) England v Germany	ITV	9.16m
18	Boxing (Nov 28) Eubank v Giminez	ITV	8.88m
19	General Sport (Dec 13) Sports Review of 1992	BBC1	8.76m
20	Football (May 26) European Cup Final	ITV	8.68m

BRITISH SPORTS WRITERS 1992 AWARDS
Organised by the Sportswriters' Association
Pat Besford Trophy(Oustanding Achievement): **Chris Boardman**
Sportsman of the Year: **Linford Christie**
(2nd: Nigel Mansell; 3rd: Nick Faldo)
Sportswoman of the Year: **Sally Gunnell**
Sports Team of the Year: **England Rugby Union**
Peter Wilson Trophy: **Simon Terry**
J L Manning Award (Services to Sport): **Bill Slater**
Disabled Sportsperson: **Chris Holmes**
Evian Award (Winter Sports): **Michael Dixon**

BRITAIN'S TOP EARNING SPORTSMEN IN 1993

1 **Lennox Lewis**   **Boxing**   **£10.5m**
With £6m from the Tucker fight and £3m+ from his Bruno clash, Lewis is comfortably clear.

2 **Nigel Mansell**   **Motor Racing**   **£5.0m**
A quiet year for Mansell, whose Indy Car salary does not match up to his F1 earnings. A low basic augmented by substantial bonuses of maybe, £2.5m

3 **Nick Faldo**   **Golf**   **£3.5m**
Again, not as profitable as last year, but Faldo ticks along with a high level of endorsement earnings.

4 **David Platt**   **Football**   **£3.1m**
Platt's £5.5m transfer to Sampdoria has made it a bumper year for the former Crewe player. A signing-on fee, plus a salary of around £800,000 before tax, a new boot deal with Mizuno.

5 **Paul Gascoigne**   **Football**   **£2.6m**
No transfer for Gascoigne, so his figure is below Platt although his basic salary, at around £1.2m before tax, is higher. Bonuses and a boot deal with Lotto are the next big earners.

6 **Frank Bruno**   **Boxing**   **£2.5m**
Approaching £1m for the Lewis fight pushed up Bruno's earnings. Two other fights plus advertising contracts all help. The pantos don't pay a lot.

7 **Linford Christie**   **Athletics**   **£1.75m**
His Olympic win upped the ante. Christie probably earned in excess of £600,000 from racing. His Puma deal is purported to be worth £250,000+ a year, but Lucozade may be the biggest contributor of all.

8 **Nigel Benn**   **Boxing**   **£1.7m**
Most of his income from fighting, has had four fights in 12 months, including £1m for Eubank.

9 **Chris Eubank**   **Boxing**   **£1.5m**
A healthy £850,000 or so from the Benn fight is the biggest contribution, but two other fights also.

9 **Gary Lineker**   **Football**   **£1.5m**
He may not have had the greatest starts in Japanese football, but Lineker still paying in the cheques.

11 **Stephen Hendry**   **Snooker**   **£1.4m**
Hendry is comfortably snooker's biggest earner, the majority of his earnings coming from the table.

12 **Steve Davis**   **Snooker**   **£1m**
These days, more of Davis' earnings come from endorsements than playing major events.

12 **Pat Eddery**   **Horse Racing**   **£1m**
A long-standing and lucrative retainer from Khalid Abdullah gets Eddery in the list.

12 **Nigel Short**   **Chess**   **£1m**
Almost £700,000 comes from the Kasparov match.

12 **Ian Woosnam**   **Golf**   **£1m**
About 40% from playing, 60% from 'services' and endorsements.

Note: Because of our deadlines, these figures are estimated for a year that runs October 1992-October 1993

BEST-SELLING SPORTS BOOKS

Oct 1, 1992 to Sept 30 1993

1	Mansell & Williams Challenge (Orion)	£20.00
2	Playfair Cricket Annual 1993 (Headline)	£3.99
3	WHSmith/Sunday Times Chronicle of Sport (Reed)	£15.99
4	Rothmans Football Yearbook (Headline)	£14.99
5	WHS/Complete Coarse Fisherman (Boxtree)	£10.99
6	David Gower: The Autobiography (Collins)	£14.99
7	Premier League Handbook (Collins)	£3.99
8	WHS/Complete Book of Golf (Colour Library)	£14.99
9	Nigel Mansell World Champion (Simon & Schuster)	£3.99
10	Wisden Cricketers' Almanac '93 (Wisden)	
11	Playfair Football Annual 92/93 (Headline)	£3.99
12	Non-League Club Directory '93 (Football Directories)	
13	From the Wood to The Trees by Tom O'Connor (Robson)	£10.95
14	WWF Official Wrestling Book (Hamlyn)	£9.99
15	Champions - Manchester United's Winning Season (Simon & Schuster)	£9.99
16	Superform Races & Racehorses '92/'93 (Superform)	£17.95
17	Match of the Day (BBC Books)	£12.95
18	Grey Horse - Desert Orchid (Penguin)	£15.99
19	Guinness Soccer Who's Who by Jack Rollin (Guinness Pblg)	£6.99
20	Gary Lineker's Soccer Quiz Book (Collins)	£3.99
20	Muhammed Ali - His Life and Times (Pan/McMillan)	£6.99

List Compiled by WH Smith

COACHES OF THE YEAR

*Awarded by the British
Institute of Sports Coaches*

Valerie Mellor (Swimming), **Pete Keen** (Cycling)
Maggie Souyave (Hockey), **Jack Rowell**(Rugby U)
Dina Murdie (Swimming), **Terry Potter** (V'Ball)
Moira Hinkles (Hockey), **Hugh Mantle** (Sl Canoe)

Aerial Sports

World Gas Balloon Championship

Obertraun, Austria   Oct 4-10, 1992

1.	David Levin/Jim Schiller	USA	7598
2	Thomas Fink/Rain Hassold	GER	5732
3	Josef Strakbaum/Gert Scholz	AUT	5057
4	Alan Fraenckel/Jacky Robertson	ISV	4572
5	Silvia Wagner/Thomas Lewwtz	AUT	4386
6	Helma Sjuts/Hermann Nienhaus	GER	3577

World Gliding Championship

Borlänge, Sweden   June 12-26

15 Metre Class

1=	Gilbert Gerbaud	FRA	8220
1=	Eric Napoleon	FRA	8220
3	Wolfgang Janowitsch	AUT	8216
4	Stasys Skalskis	LIT	8120
5	Martin Theisinger	GER	8062
6	Justin Wills	GBR	8049

Standard Class

1	Andrew Davis	GBR	7285
2	Eric Borgmann	NED	7059
3	Tomasz Rubaj	POL	7002
4	Jiri Stepanek	TCH	6813
5	Joha Sorri	FIN	6802
6	Jean-Claude Lopitaux	FRA	6739

Open Class

1	Janusz Centka	POL	9897
2	Goran Ax	SWE	9525
3	Brian Spreckley	GBR	9391
4	Gerard Lherm	FRA	9292
5	Stanislaw Wujczak	POL	9050
6	Alister Kay	GBR	9040

World Hang Gliding Championships

Men

Owens Valley, USA   Jun 26-Jul 10, 1993

1	Tomas Suchanek	TCH	6982
2	Chris Arai	USA	6971
3	Mark Gibson	USA	6831
4	Steve Moyes	AUS	6724
5	John Pendrey	GBR	6635

Teams

1	USA	20568
2	Australia	19964
3	Great Britain	19653
4	Switzerland	19286
5	Austria	18954

Women

Nanyo City, Japan   Apr 19-May 2, 1993

1	Francoise Dieuzeide-Banet	FRA	3192
2	Kari Castle	USA	3169
3	Isabelle Piaget	SUI	3157
4	Diane Ecoeur	SUI	3094
5	Judy Leden	GBR	2861

Teams

1	Switzerland	8786
2	France	6598
3	Germany	6517
4	Australia	5812
5	Great Britain	5683

British Championships

Men

1. Peter Harvey
2. Darren Arkwright
3. Graham Phipps
4. Gordon Rigg
5. Chris Ashman

Women

1. Kathleen Rigg
2. Paula Bowyer
3. Judy Leden
4. Jenny Auckland
5. Pam Sykes

World Paragliding Championships

Aug 2-12

Final Positions

1	Hans Bollinger	SUI
2	Ernst Stadri	GER
3	John Pendry	GBR
4	Christian Tamegger	AUT
5	Patrick Berod	FRA

Leading Women

6	Camilla Perner	AUT
28	Manou Berger	FRA
41	Miyuki Tanaka	JPN
42	Claire Bernier	FRA
72	Sarah Fenwick	GBR
75	Judy Leden	GBR

American Football
Super Bowl XXVII

It was the kind of hattrick the Buffalo Bills could have done without; hitting your third successive defeat in a Super Bowl is nobody's idea of a good day at the office. Only if you were looking for the smallest of mercies was there anything to be thankful about; that tiny mercy was that the other two defeats were nothing like as humbling.

It began sunnily enough for the Bills with a three yard touchdown to open the scoring. It would be kinder not to catalogue the deluge that followed. Enough to say that, after Jay Novacek (who represented the US at decathlon in the 1984 Olympics) had brought the Cowboys level, the floodgates could no longer be held back. The Cowboys poured it on, whilst in the second and fourth quarters, the poor Bills did not even register a point.

When it was all over, the Cowboys had logged the second highest score in a Super Bowl (behind only the 55 points that San Francisco had put over Denver three years ago) and the game aggregate of 69 points was the highest ever. The record that the Bills will most want to forget was the nine turnovers that were converted into five touchdowns by Dallas. Thank you and goodnight.

So Dallas became the ninth succesive NFC champions to take the Super Bowl and with the youngest team in the Conference threaten to dominate for a while. Quarterback Troy Aikman was labelled the game's most valuable player, having completed 22 of 30 passes for 273 yards with no interceptions (and with passes for four touchdowns in there somewhere). A good day at the office.

Buffalo Bills 17
Dallas Cowboys 52

Pasadena, California   Jan 31
Att: 98,374

INDIVIDUAL STATISTICS

	Buffalo		Dallas	
Rushing	K Davis	15-86	E Smith	22-108-1
	T Thomas	11-19-1	Aikman	3-28
	Gardner	1-3	Gainer	2-1
	Reich	2-0	Johnston	1-0
			Beuerlein	1-0
Passing	Reich		Aikman	
	18-31-194-1-2		22-30-273-4-0	
	Kelly			
	4-7-82-0-2			
Receiving	Reed	8-15-2	Irvin	6-114-2
	Beebe	2-50-1	Novacek	7-72-1
	Tasker	2-30	Harper	1-45-1
	K Davis	3-16	E Smith	6-27
	Metzelaars	2-12	Johnston	2-15
	T Thomas	4-10		
	McKeller	1-6		
Intercept's			Everett	2-22
			Washington	1-13
			Brown	1-0
Sacks	Smith		Everett, Jeffcoat	
			Haley, Lett	

Scoring
Buffalo	T Thomas 2yd run (Christie kick)	5.00(1)
Dallas	Novacek 23yd from Aikman	13.24(1)
Dallas	J Jones 2yd fumble return (Elliott)	13.39(1)
Buffalo	Field Goal by Christie 21yd	11.36(2)
Dallas	Irvin 19yd pass from Aikman (Elliott)	13.06(2)
Dallas	Irvin 18yd pass from Aikman (Elliott)	13.24(2)
Dallas	Field Goal by Elliott 20yd	6.39(3)
Buffalo	Beebe 40yd pass from Reich (Christie)	15.00(3)
Dallas	Harper 45yd pass from Aikman(Elliott)	4.56(4)
Dallas	E Smith 10yd run (Elliott)	6.48(4)
Dallas	Norton 9yd fumble return (Elliott)	7.29(4)

TEAM STATISTICS
	Buffalo	Dallas
Points	17	52
Rushing yards	108	137
Passing yards	254	271
Return yards	90	114
Sacked yards lost	4-22	1-2
Punts	3-45.3	3-43.7
Third downs	5-11	5-11
Fourth downs	0-2	0-1
Time of possession	28.48	31.12

1992 NFL Final Standings

NATIONAL FOOTBALL CONFERENCE

Eastern Division	W	L	T	Pct	PF	PA
Dallas	13	3	0	.813	409	243
Philadelphia	11	5	0	.688	354	245
Washington	9	7	0	.563	300	255
N Y Giants	6	10	0	.375	306	367
Phoenix	4	12	0	.250	243	332

Central Division	W	L	T	Pct	PF	PA
Minnesota	11	5	0	.688	374	249
Green Bay	9	7	0	.563	276	296
Tampa Bay	5	11	0	.313	267	365
Chicago	5	11	0	.313	295	361
Detroit	5	11	0	.313	273	332

Western Division	W	L	T	Pct	PF	PA
San Francisco	14	2	0	.875	431	236
New Orleans	12	4	0	.750	330	202
Atlanta	6	10	0	.375	327	414
L A Rams	6	10	0	.375	313	383

AMERICAN FOOTBALL CONFERENCE

Eastern Division	W	L	T	Pct	PF	PA
Miami	11	5	0	.688	340	281
Buffalo	11	5	0	.688	381	283
Indianapolis	9	7	0	.563	216	302
N Y Jets	4	12	0	.250	220	315
New England	2	14	0	.125	205	363

Central Division	W	L	T	Pct	PF	PA
Pittsburgh	11	5	0	.688	299	225
Houston	10	6	0	.625	352	258
Cleveland	7	9	0	.438	272	275
Cincinnati	5	11	0	.313	274	364

Western Division	W	L	T	Pct	PF	PA
San Diego	11	5	0	.688	335	241
Kansas City	10	6	0	.625	348	282
Denver	8	8	0	.500	262	329
L A Raiders	7	9	0	.438	249	281
Seattle	2	14	0	.125	140	312

PLAY-OFF MATCHES

First round
NFC - **Washington Redskins 24** Minnesota Vikings 7
    Philadelphia Eagles 36 New Orleans Saints 20
AFC - **San Diego Chargers 17** Kansas City Chiefs 0
    Buffalo Bills 41 Houston Oilers 38 (OT)

Second Round
NFC - **San Francisco 49ers 20** Washington Red'ns 13
    Dallas Cowboys 34 Philadelphia Eagles 10
AFC - **Buffalo Bills 24** Pittsburgh Steelers 3
    Miami Dolphins 31 San Diego 0

CONFERENCE CHAMPIONSHIPS

NFC - **Dallas Cowboys 30** San Francisco 49ers 20
AFC - **Buffalo Bills 29** Miami Dolphins 10

NFC STATISTICS

SCORING
Records: Points 176-Paul Hornung, Green Bay 1960
    Touchdowns 24-John Riggins, Washington 1983
    Field Goals 35-Ali Haji-Sheikh, New York 1983
    Extra points 62-Mark Moseley, Washington 1983

Team	Td	Tdr	Tdp	Tdm	Xp	Fg	Saf	Pts
San Francisco	54	22	29	3	53	18	0	431
Dallas	48	20	23	5	47	24	1	409
Minnesota	45	19	18	8	45	19	1	374
Philadelphia	44	19	20	5	40	16	1	354
New Orleans	35	10	19	6	33	29	0	330
Atlanta	39	3	33	3	39	18	0	327
L A Rams	38	12	23	3	38	15	1	313
N Y Giants	36	20	14	2	36	18	0	306
Washington	30	10	15	5	30	30	0	300
Chicago	34	15	17	2	34	19	0	295
Green Bay	30	7	20	3	30	22	0	276
Detroit	30	9	16	5	30	21	0	273
Tampa Bay	33	12	17	4	33	12	0	267
Phoenix	29	11	15	3	28	13	1	243

NICE LITTLE EARNER

In March of this year, players became free agents and without a salary limit imposed by the NFL (though it's sure to happen next year) the world turned upside down. Below are some of the players whose Christmases came all at once.

Reggie White, formerly of Philadelphia Eagles, signed for the Green Bay Packers for $17m over three years. The first $9m coming this year.

Cody Carlson, a modest backup quarterback, re-signed for Houston Oilers for a not too modest $8.85 over three years.

Carlton Bailey, a backup linebacker from the Buffalo Bills, who didn't even get a game in the Super Bowl, took his salary from last season's $275,000, to $5.25m over the next three years when he moved to the New York Giants

Brian Habib, the Minnesota Viking's *fifth* best offensive lineman, transfered his allegiance to the Denver Broncos for the princely sum $4.2 over three years. Well, you would, wouldn't you?

KICKERS

	Xp	Xpa	Fg	Fga	Pts
Morten Andersen (New Orleans)	33	34	29	34	120
Chip Lohmiller (Washington)	30	30	30	40	120
Lin Elliott (Dallas)	47	48	24	35	119
Mike Cofer (San Francisco)	53	54	18	27	107
Fuad Reveiz (Minnesota)	45	45	19	25	102

NON-KICKERS

	Td	Tdr	Tdp	Tdm	Pts
Emmitt Smith (Dallas)	19	18	1	0	114
Terry Allen (Minnesota)	15	13	2	0	90
Rodney Hampton (NY Giants)	14	14	0	0	84
Sterling Sharpe (Green Bay)	13	0	13	0	78
Neal Anderson (Chicago)	11	5	6	0	66
Jerry Rice (San Francisco)	11	1	10	0	66

PASSING

Records Completions: 353-Don Majkowski, Green Bay 1989
Touchdowns: 36-Y A Tittle, New York 1963
Yards: 4,614-Neil Lomax, St Louis 1984
Longest for Td: 99yds-Frank Filchock, Wash'ton '39
George Izo, Washington 1963
Karl Sweetan, Detroit 1966
Sonny Jurgensen, Wash'ton '68
Ron Jaworski, Philadelphia 1985

	Att	Com	Pct	Yds	Ave	Td	Rating
Steve Young (SF)	402	268	66.7	3465	8.62	25	107.0
Chris Miller (Atl)	253	152	60.1	1739	6.87	15	90.7
Troy Aikman (Dall)	473	302	63.8	3445	7.28	23	89.5
R Cunningham (Phil)	384	233	60.7	2775	7.23	19	87.3
Brett Favre (GB)	471	302	64.1	3227	6.85	18	85.3

PUNTING

Records Number: 114-Bob Parsons, Chicago 1981
Average: 51.4yds-Sammy Baugh, Washington 1940
Longest: 94yds-Joe Lintzenich, Chicago 1931

	No	Yds	Lg	Ave	Ret yds	Net ave
Harry Newsome (Mn)	72	3243	84	45.0	339	35.7
Tom Barnhardt (NO)	67	2947	62	44.0	218	37.7
Jim Arnold (Det)	65	2846	71	43.8	356	34.7
Sean Landeta (NY G)	53	2317	71	43.8	356	31.5
Mike Saxon (Dall)	61	2620	58	43.0	397	33.5

RUSHING

Records Carries: 407-James Wilder, Tampa Bay 1984
Yards: 2,105-Eric Dickerson, Los Angeles 1984
TDs: 24-John Riggins, Washington 1983

	Att	Yds	Avg	Long	TD
Emmitt Smith (Dall)	373	1713	4.6	t68	18
Barry Sanders (Det)	312	1352	4.3	t55	9
Terry Allen (Minn)	266	1201	4.5	51	13
Reggie Cobb (TB)	310	1171	3.8	25	9
Rodney Hampton (Gts)	257	1141	4.4	t63	14

PASS RECEIVING

Records Receptions 108-Sterling Sharpe, Green Bay 1992
Yards 1570-Jerry Rice, San Francisco 1986
TDs 22-Jerry Rice, San Francisco 1987

	No	Yds	Avg	Long	TD
Sterling Sharpe (GB)	108	1461	13.5	t76	13
Andre Rison (Atl)	93	1119	12.0	t71	11
Jerry Rice (SF)	84	1201	14.3	t80	10
Michael Irvin (Dall)	78	1396	17.9	t87	7
Mike Pritchard (Atl)	77	827	10.7	t38	5

QUOTES

"Most of my cliches aren't original"

Chuck Knox, veteran coach of the Los Angeles Rams.

"Everywhere I looked, I saw my name and it was spelt right"

Karl Mecklenburg, of the Denver Broncos, after visiting Mecklenburg in Germany.

"We can beat this team. All we have to do is capitalise on our mistakes"

Bill Peterson, Florida coach, famed for his Malapropisms, who died in August.

"It's no fun sitting here on the beaches of Malibu in 85 degree weather"

Footballer Keith Jackson, offering to end his dispute with the Philadelpia Eagles.

"I only want to be in 'Kill' movies, it ain't no fun unless you get to kill somebody. I don't want to be in no love story. I want to be the black Rambo. I want to be Rambro."

Giants linebacker Lawrence Taylor, on being offered a part in Robert de Niro's new film.

"We had to take them down the grainstore to weigh them"

Ellsworth Community College coach Mike Doyle, on the problems of his four offensive players weighing in. Little wonder when they go: 30 stones, 26 stones, 23.5 stones and, the little ol' lightweight of the quartet, who weighs in at just 23 stones.

INTERCEPTIONS

Records Number: 14-Dick Lane, Los Angeles 1952
Yards: 301-Don Droll, Detroit 1949
Longest Return: 102yds - Bob Smith, Detroit 1949
Erich Barnes, New York 1961
TDs: 3-Dick Lynch, New York 1963
Herb Adderley, Green Bay 1965
Monte Jackson, LA 1976
Rod Perry, LA 1976
Ronnie Lott, San Francisco 1981
Wayne Haddix, Tampa Bay 1990
Robert Massey, Phoenix 1992

	No	Yds	Avg	Long	TD
Audray McMillian (Mn)	8	157	19.6	t51	2
Donnell Woolford (Chi)	7	67	9.6	32	0
Brad Edwards (Wash)	6	157	26.2	t53	1
Toi Cook (NO)	6	90	15.0	t48	1
Robert Massey (Phoe)	5	147	29.4	t46	3
Todd Scott (Minn)	5	79	15.8	t35	1

PUNT RETURNS

Records Number: 70-Danny Reece, Tampa Bay 1979
Yards: 646-Eddie Brown, Washington 1976
Longest for TD: 98yds-Gill Lefebvre, Cinn 1933
Charlie West, Minn 1968
Dennis Morgan, Dallas 1974

	No	FC	Yds	Avg	Long	TD
Johnny Bailey (Phoe)	20	8	263	13.2	65	0
Kelvin Martin (Dall)	42	18	532	12.7	t79	2
Vai Sikahema (Phil)	40	10	503	12.7	t87	1
Anthony Parker (Minn)	33	17	336	10.2	42	0
Terrell Buckley (GB)	21	5	211	10.0	t58	1
Brian Mitchell (Wash)	29	9	271	9.3	t84	1

KICK RETURNS

Records Number: 60-Drew Hill, Los Angeles 1981
Yards: 1,345-Buster Rhymes, Minnesota 1985
Longest: 106yds-Al Carmichael, Green Bay 1956
Roy Green, St Louis 1979
TDs: 4-Travis Williams, Green Bay 1967
Cecil Turner, Chicago 1970

	No	Yds	Avg	Long	TD
Jon Vaughn (NE)	20	564	28.2	t100	1
Randy Baldwin (Cle)	30	675	22.5	47	0
Alton Montgomery (D)	21	466	22.2	64	0
Clarence Verdin (Ind)	39	815	20.9	42	0
Eric Ball (Cin)	20	411	20.6	48	0
Harvey Williams (KC)	21	405	19.3	37	0

AFC STATISTICS

SCORING

Records: Points 155-Gino Cappelleti, Boston 1964
Touchdowns 23-O J Simpson, Buffalo 1975
Field Goals 34-Jim Turner, New York 1968
34-Nick Lowery, Kansas City 1990
Extra points 66-Uwe von Schamann, Miami 1984

Team	Td	Tdr	Tdp	Tdm	Xp	Fg	Saf	Pts
Buffalo	44	18	23	3	43	24	1	381
Houston	41	10	27	4	41	21	1	352
Kansas City	40	14	15	11	39	23	0	348
Miami	36	9	24	3	34	30	0	340
San Diego	36	18	16	2	35	26	3	335
Pittsburgh	31	13	15	3	29	28	0	299
Cincinnati	31	11	16	4	31	19	0	274

Cleveland	30	7	18	5	29	21	0	272
Denver	29	11	16	2	28	20	0	262
LA Raiders	29	7	20	2	28	15	1	249
NY Jets	23	8	12	3	23	19	1	220
Indianapolis	24	8	13	3	24	16	0	216
New England	25	6	13	6	22	11	0	205
Seattle	14	4	9	1	14	14	0	140

KICKERS

	Xp	Xpa	Fg	Fga	Pts
Pete Stoyanovich (Miami)	34	36	30	37	124
Steve Christie (Buffalo)	43	44	24	30	115
Gary Anderson (Pittsburgh)	29	31	28	36	113
John Carney (San Diego)	35	35	26	32	113
Nick Lowery (Kansas City)	39	39	22	24	105
Al Del Greco (Houston)	41	41	21	27	104

NON-KICKERS

	Td	Tdr	Tdp	Tdm	Pts
Thurman Thomas (Buffalo)	12	9	3	0	72
Barry Foster (Pittsburgh)	11	11	0	0	66
Earnest Givins (Houston)	10	0	10	0	60
Rodney Culver (Indianapolis)	9	7	2	0	54
Haywood Jeffires (Houston)	9	0	9	0	54
Derrick Fenner (Cincinnati)	8	7	1	0	48

PASSING

Records Completions: 404-Warren Moon, Houston 1991
Touchdowns: 48-Dan Marino, Miami 1984
Yards: 5,084-Dan Marino, Miami 1984
Longest for Td: 99yds-Jim Plunkett, Los Angeles '83

	Att	Com	Pct	Yds	Ave	Td	Rating
Warren Moon (Hou)	346	224	64.7	2521	7.29	18	89.3
Dan Marino (Mia)	554	330	59.6	4116	7.43	24	85.1
Neil O'Donnell (Pit)	313	185	59.1	2283	7.29	13	83.6
Jim Kelly (Buf)	462	269	58.2	3457	7.48	23	81.2
Cody Carlson (Hou)	227	149	65.6	1710	7.53	9	81.2
Dave Kreig (KC)	413	230	55.7	3115	7.54	15	79.9

PUNTING

Records Number: 105-Bob Scarpitto, Denver 1967
Average: 46.9-Greg Montgomery, Houston 1992
Longest: 98yds-Steve O'Neal, New York 1969

	No	Yds	Lg	Ave	Ret yds	Net ave
Greg Montgomery (H)	53	2487	66	46.9	255	37.3
Rohn Stark (Ind)	83	3716	64	44.8	313	39.3
Rick Tuten (Sea)	108	4760	65	44.1	416	38.7
Bryan Barker (KC)	75	3245	65	43.3	300	35.3
Mark Royals (Pit)	73	3119	58	42.7	308	35.6
John Kidd (SD)	68	2899	65	42.6	244	36.4

RUSHING

Records Carries: 390-Barry Foster, Pittsburgh 1992
Yards: 2,003-O J Simpson, Buffalo 1973
TDs: 19-Earl Campbell, Houston 1979
19-Chuck Muncie, San Diego 1981

	Att	Yds	Avg	Long	TD
Barry Foster (Pit)	549	1690	4.3	69	11
Thurman Thomas (Buf)	312	1487	4.8	44	9
Lorenzo White (Hou)	265	1226	4.6	44	7
Harold Green (Cin)	265	1170	4.4	53	2
Chris Warren (Sea)	223	1017	4.6	52	3
Mark Higgs (Mia)	256	915	3.6	23	7

PASS RECEIVING

Records *Receptions 101-Charlie Hennigan, Houston 1964*
Yards 1,746-Charlie Hennigan, Houston 1961
TDs 18-Mark Clayton, Miami 1984

	No	Yds	Avg	Long	TD
Haywood Jeffires (Hou)	90	913	10.1	47	9
Curtis Duncan (Hou)	82	954	11.6	72	1
Ronnie Harmon (SD)	79	914	11.6	72	1
John L Williams (Sea)	74	556	7.5	27	2
Anthony Miller (SD)	72	1060	14.7	t67	7
Earnest Givins (Hou)	67	787	11.7	41	10

INTERCEPTIONS

Records *Number: 13-Lester Hayes, Oakland 1980*
Yards: 349-Charlie McNeil, San Diego 1961
Longest Return: 103yds-Venice Glenn, S Diego 1987
Louis Oliver, Miami 1992
TDs: 4-Ken Houston, Houston 1971
Jim Kearney, Kansas City 1972

	No	Yds	Avg	Long	TD
Henry Jones (Buf)	8	263	32.9	t82	2
Eugene Robinson (Sea)	7	126	18.0	49	0
Dale Carter (KC)	7	65	9.3	t36	1
Mark Kelso (Buf)	7	21	3.0	13	0
Darren Carrington (SD)	6	152	25.3	69	1
Michael Brim (Jets)	6	139	23.2	t77	1

PUNT RETURNS

Records *Number: 62-Fulton Walker, Los Angeles 1985*
Yards: 692-Fulton Walker, Los Angeles 1985
Longest for TD: 98yds-Terance Mathis, NY 1990

	No	FC	Yds	Avg	Long	TD
Rod Woodson (Pit)	32	13	364	11.4	t80	1
Clarence Verdin (Ind)	24	12	268	11.2	t84	2
Arthur Marshall (Den)	33	16	349	10.6	47	0
Dale Carter (KC)	38	6	398	10.5	t86	2
Tim Brown (Raiders)	37	19	383	10.4	40	0
Cliff Hicks (Buf)	29	6	289	10.0	42	0

KICK RETURNS

Records *Number: 55-Bruce Harper, New York 1978-9*
David Turner, Cincinnati 1979
Yards: 1,317-Bobby Jancik, Houston 1963
Longest: 106yds-Nolan Smith, Kansas City 1967
TDs: 3-Ray Clayborn, New England 1977

	No	Yds	Avg	Long	TD
Jon Vaughn (NE)	20	564	28.2	t100	1
Randy Baldwin (Cle)	30	675	22.5	47	0
Alton Montgomery (D)	21	466	22.2	64	0
Clarence Verdin (Ind)	39	815	20.9	42	0
Eric Ball (Cin)	20	411	20.6	48	0
Harvey Williams (KC)	21	405	19.3	37	0

British & European Results

As early as February, discussions about a revival of the World League of American Football were tentative enough to signal the likely outcome. "We are looking for large multi-national firms who see the marketing advantages of being involved with America's most famous sport. But I don't see the NFL owners doing it by themselves," said Neil Austrian, President of the NFL. It was to be expected. When the last sally had cost around £12m in losses, the 28 franchise owners that constitute the vested interests in America were unlikely to fork out again. The NFL did acknowledge that the European Division, which comprised of London Monarchs, Barcelona Dragons and Frankfurt Galaxy, was a success, but the problem was the failure of the League to make an impact on US television. Discussions centred around a new competition with a heavier accent on Europe and teams in Paris, Dusseldorf, Milan or Amsterdam added to the itinerary, but the reduction in trans-atlantic rivalry was not appealing enough and in September came the announcement that the competition had been ruled out for 1994 and 1995.

NDMA Division 1

Final Standings

NORTHERN CONFERENCE

	P	W	L	T	PF	PA	Pct
Glasgow Lions	6	6	0	0	205	35	100
Leeds Cougars	6	2	4	0	112	129	33
Gateshead Senators	6	0	6	0	28	253	0

Only 6 games were played due to a team withdrawing from the competition 2 weeks before the start of the season.

MIDLANDS CONFERENCE

	P	W	L	T	PF	PA	Pct
London Olympians	7	7	0	0	213	114	100
Leicester Panthers	10	7	3	0	303	209	70
Nottingham Hoods	8	5	3	0	207	142	63
Northants Storm	9	4	5	0	165	208	44
Birmingham Bulls	10	4	6	0	180	155	40
Coventry Jaguars	9	0	9	0	26	201	0

Olympians only played 7 matches due to their participation in the Euro-Bowl. Other matches were abandoned due to water-logged pitches.

SOUTHERN CONFERENCE

	P	W	L	T	PF	PA	Pct
Thames Valley Chgrs	8	8	0	0	184	42	100
Brighton B52's	8	5	3	0	163	73	63
Milton Keynes Pioneers	8	4	4	0	197	144	50
West London Aces	8	3	5	0	41	110	38
Cardiff Mets	8	0	8	0	50	175	0

PLAY OFFS
Glasgow Lions (1) **42** Milton Keynes Pioneers (8) **8**
Leicester Panthers (4) **28** Brighton B52's (5) **0**
Thames Valley Chargers (2) **21** Leeds Cougars (7) **18**
London Olympians (3) **48** Nottingham Hoods (6) **14**
( ) *denotes seeding*

Glasgow Lions **27** Leicester Panthers **24**
Thames Valley Chargers **14** London Olympians **41**

FINAL
Maidenhead Rugby Club   Aug 1
Glasgow Lions   14
London Olympians 40

STATISTICS
Tackles (Solo)

	T	A	No
B Veira (Brighton B52's)	**70**	25	95
C Nash (Birmingham Bulls)	57	43	100
J McMullan (Birmingham Bulls)	52	54	106

Sacks (Number)

	No	Yds
K Mills (Northants Storm)	**14.0**	105
M Piper (Glasgow Lions)	**6.5**	43
G Cross (Birmingham Bulls)	**6.5**	33

Interceptions (Number)

	No	Yds	Lg	TD
S Whybrow (Thames Valley Chgrs)	5	63	30	1
P Jones (Thames Valley Chargers)	5	60	18	2
J Wyse (Leicester Panthers)	5	20	20	0

Passing (rating)

	Att	Com	Pct	Yds	Lgt	Td	Rating
W Norton (Leic P)	163	88	54	1391	55	20	**163.71**
L Valentine (Lndn O)	142	78	55	1281	69	14	**157.61**
D Trainor (Glasg L)	122	52	43	876	50	8	**118.02**

Qualification 100 attempts

Rushing (Yardage)

	Att	Yds	Avg	Long	TD
W Sweetman (Leic P)	167	**1091**	6.53	53.0	13
R Dunkley (Lndn O)	156	**966**	6.19	35.0	12
T Bell (Leeds Cgrs)	131	**945**	7.21	70.0	7

Receiving (Yardage)

	Att	Yds	Avg	Long	TD
L Innis (Lndn O)	31	568	18.3	69.0	4
D Sweetman (Leic P)	28	565	20.2	55.0	5
A Okiwe (Nttgham H)	32	459	14.3	32.0	3

Eurobowl 1993

First Round
Cardkey Raiders(Den Haag) **50** St Gallen Raiders **20**
Amsterdam Crusaders **56** Leuven Lions **0**
Leuven Lions **0** SAFIR Argonautes(Aix-en-Prov.) **106**
Dusseldorf Panthers **29** London Olympians **32**
LEVIS Giants Graz **7** Pharaones Milano **35**
St Gallen Raiders **28** Cardkey Raiders **31**
Pharones Milano **35** LEVIS Giants Graz **7**
SAFIR Argonautes **26** Amsterdam Crusaders **54**
East City Giants(Helsinki) **40** Uppsala 86ers **35**

Intermediate Round
Cardkey Raiders **36** Pharaones Milano **34**

Semi-Finals
Cardkey Raiders **7** Amsterdam Crusaders **22**
East City Giants **29** London Olympians **34**
FINAL
Heysel Stadium, Brussels   July 3
London Olympians 42
Amsterdam Crusaders 21

	EUROBOWL WINNERS	
	(Ulrico-Lucarelli Trophy)	
1986	Taft Vantaa, Finald	
1988	Helsinki Roosters, Finland	
1989	Legnano Frogs, Italy	
1990	Manchester Spartans, UK	
1991	Amsterdam Crusaders, Holland	
1992	Amsterdam Crusaders	
1993	London Olympians	

European Championships

Semi-Finals
Italy **9** Sweden **0**
Germany **0** Finland **10**

Third Place
Sweden **3** Germany **21**

FINAL
Italy **7**
Finland **17**

Angling

Fly Fishing
World Championship

Kamloops, British Columbia, Canada   June 9-11

Team

1 England	260 placings	
2 Poland	320	
3 Italy	327	
4 Wales	·337	
5 Czech Republic	340	
6 Finland	348	

Individual

1 **Russell Owen**	WAL	22 placings
2 Franciszek Sjanik	POL	31
3 Jeremy Lucas	ENG	33
7 John Lindsey	ENG	39
11 Chris Ogborne	ENG	53
22 Moc Morgan	WAL	60
28 Paul Miller	ENG	65
37 John Pawson	ENG	70

From anchored boats on clear lakes in the Kamloops region of British Columbia, England's fly fishermen proved themselves the world's best for their third team title in seven years. Sponsored by Drennan, the England team took the lead in the second of the six three hour sessions and were never headed. Russell Owen took ten large trout to become the first Welshman ever to win the individual title.

Spring Home International

Draycote Water   May 22

Team

1 England	
2 Scotland	
3 Ireland	
3 Wales	

Individual

1 Jeremy Herrmann	ENG
2 Chris Timothy	ENG
3 John Pawson	ENG
4 David Wood	SCO
5 Alan Lyness	IRL
6 Bill Latham	ENG

Autumn Home International

Llyn Brenig, Wales   Sept 4

Team

1 England	
2 Ireland	
3 Scotland	
4 Wales	

Individual

1 Jeremy Herrmann	ENG

In practice, Ireland's Eddy Harte caught a rainbow trout of 111lbs 2.5ozs to break the fishery record.

River Home International

River Wharfe, Yorkshire   July 2

Team

1 **Scotland**	1668pts
2 Wales	1334
3 Wales	1283
4 Ireland	812

Individual

1 **Paul Buchanan**	SCO
2 Ian Wilson	SCO
3 Matt Walker	SCO
4 Franz Grimley	SCO

English National River Championship

River Wye, Bakewell   July 14

1 **Ian Warrilow**	Severn-Trent	1580pts
2 Ian Greenwood	Severn-Trent	
3 Jeremy Lucas	South-East	
4 Trevor Colclough	Severn-Trent	
5 Baz Reece	South-East	
6 Chris Howitt	South-East	

English National Boat Championship

Bewl Water   Sept 11

1 **David Grove**	6 fish - 9lb 9oz
2 Richard Hearth	6 fish - 9lb 2oz
3 Michael Dwyer	4 fish - 9lb 2oz

Jeanette Ford, who finished 12th, became the first women ever to qualify for the England team.

Coarse Angling
World Championship

Day 1		Day 2	
Italy	19	France	25
San Marino	31	Italy	30
Scotland	38	Austria	34
Austria	42	Ireland	34
France	43	England	37
Hungary	48	Wales	42
Ireland	52	10th Scot.	69
16 th Wales	80		
17th Eng.	84		

Overall Result

Italy	49
France	69
Austria	76
Ireland	87
8th Scot.	108
9th Eng.	122
10th Wales	123

Individual World Champion
Mario Barros from Portugal

National Championships
Sept 11 1993

Division 1

Pos	Association	Pts	Peg	Pos
1	Liverpool & Dist.	803	12	51
2	Essex County	760	83	52
3	Izaak Walton Preston	733	61	53
4	St Hellens AA	712	47	54
5	Wakefield AC	663	34	55
6	Colchester APS	660	84	56
7	Nottingham & Dist.	652	81	57
8	Doncaster & Dist.	650	2	58
9	Rotherham & Dist.	639	37	59
10	Dorking AS	638	29	60

Division 2

Pos	Association	Pts	Peg	Pos
1	Scunthorpe & Dist.	768	27	51
2	Pro-Rod Bedford M.G.	767	24	52
3	Clay Lane Social	758	20	53
4	Disley & New Mills	750	22	54
5	Erne Anglers	741	38	55
6	Delcac	729	2	56
7	Highfield A.S.	707	25	57
8	Tek Neek Niddmen	690	74	58
9	Remenham A.S.	676	52	59
10	Bourne A.S.	676	81	60

Division 3

Pos	Association	Pts	Peg	Pos
1	Chelmsford A.A.	832	83	51
2	Driffield Hearts	801	85	52
3	Mohmar A.C.	740	6	53
4	Ossett Anglers	737	75	54
5	Cambs & Isle of Ely	706	61	55
6	Swadlincote & Dist.	704	42	56
7	Kings Lynn A.A.	701	74	57
8	Association Phoenix	687	21	58
9	Firth Park WMC	666	7	59
10	Team Bristol Amal.	665	15	60

Division 4

Pos	Association	Pts	Peg	Pos
1	Langroyd AC	767	17	51
2	Image Blackhorse	742	66	52
3	Avon Bait	701	76	53
4	Ashfield Anglers	674	59	54
5	Kingfisher MG	658	68	55
6	Mansfield Pisc.	643	15	56
7	Cutlers Arms AC	642	60	57
8	Papermakers Arms	641	13	58
9	Bridgnorth R.B.L.	621	22	59
10	Beverley & Dist.	607	74	60

NFA Team Challenge
Arrow Valley Lakes, Redditch Oct 26, 1992

Final Standings

1	Lancashire	381
2	Van Den Eynde	333
3	Wolverhampton JTE	288

Individual

1 Kim Milsom(VDE)
2 Billy Reynolds(VDE)
3 Steve O'Rourke(VDE)
4 Gary Powell(Highfield)

Sea Angling
World Shore Championships
Almeria, Spain   Oct 11-19, 1992

MEN
Team
  1 **Spain;** 2 France; 3 Portugal; 4 England.
British Individual Placings:
  6 Peter Owen; 8 Chris Clarke; 14 Ian Golds

WOMEN
Team
  1 **Spain;** 2 France; 3 Germany; 4 England.
British Individual Placings:
  13 Jill Waterhouse; 14 Carole Green; 15 Pat Heath.

Home Nations Shore International
Chesil Beach, Dorset   Nov 21-22

Team

1	Ireland	190 zone pts
2	Wales	160
3	England	150
4	Scotland	135

Individuals

1	Jim Dobie	ENG	141.69 wt + pts
2	Scott McCarthy	SCO	72.75
3	Sam Roche	IRL	71.81

Archery

World Championships

Turkey   Sept

MEN

Britain's Steve Hallard qualified for the final rounds, but was eliminated at the first stage.

Semi-finals

K Park (KOR) 119 S Zabrodskiy (UKR) 107

Park's score was a new world record

K Kim (KOR 109   K Shkolny (UKR) 107

Final

K Park 113 K Kim 109

MEN'S TEAM

1 France
2 Korea
3 Holland

WOMEN

Semi-finals

K Hyo Jung (KOR) 106   L Tuniants (KZK) 105

C Youn Jeong (KOR) 111 F Lai (TPE) 102

Final

K Hyo Jung 104 C Youn Jeong 98

WOMEN'S TEAM

1 Korea
2 Russia
3 China

World Indoor Championships

Perpignan, France   Mar 5-7

The top 16 from the qualifying rounds go forward to a knock-out competition. The final placings are as indicated on the left, the qualifying score and position is shown in brackets. * indicates a British record.

RECURVE

Men	1	Gennady Metrofanov	RUS	(1170/6)
	2	Wu Tsung	TPA	(1170/5)
	3	Stanislas Zabrodski	BLS	(1167/8)
		Richard Priestman	GBR	(1164/14)
Women	1	Jennifer O'Donnell	USA	(1171/1)
	2	Natalia Valeeva	MOL	(1142/7)
	3	Olga Yakoucheva	BLS	(1137/11)
		Alison Williamson	GBR	(1141*/8)

COMPOUND

Men	1	Kirk Ethridge	USA	(1183/2)
	2	Paw Lassew	DEN	(1174/4)
	3	Dee Wilde	USA	(1184/1)
	8	Simon Tarplee	GBR	(1173*/5)
		Chris Sweeney	GBR	(1157/17)
		Edward Parsons	GBR	(1154/20)
Women	1	Inga Low	USA	(1119/6)
	2	Glenda Doran	USA	(1155/1)
	3	Helene Joigner	FRA	(1141/2)
		Jeanette Wright	GBR	(1112/10)
		Nikki Simpson	GBR	(1104/14)
		Wendy Lesinski	GBR	(1081/18)

National Indoor Target Championships

National Indoor Arena, Birmingham   Mar 28

RECURVE

Men	1	Dale Hughes	Dunlop
	2	Dave Winfield	Eccles
	3	Greg Hill	Wales
Women	1	Pauline Edwards	Atkins
	2	Fiona German Lloyd	CCB
	3	Kath Nellis	Scarborough

COMPOUND

Men	1	Simon Tarplee	Evesham
	2	Neil Wakelin	Stortford
	3	Barry Allen	Wrexham
Women	1	Nikki Simpson	Oxford
	2	Wendy Lesinski	Clophill
	3	Kay Bent	Bowmen of the Deans

SEVERN CUP

1 England
2 Wales
3 Nothern Ireland
4 Scotland

MOST GOLDS TROPHY

Rick McKinney   USA

British Championships

Beacon Park, Lichfield, Staffs   Aug 14-15

RECURVE

Men	1	Richard Priestman	Nethermoss	2336
	2	Dave Winfield	Eccles	2326
	3	R Crich	Rolls Royce	2264
Women	1	Pauline Edwards	Atkins	2352
	2	Y Oakshott	B'n of Hatch	2284
	3	S Snowden	Lincoln	2266

County Titles

Men	1	Worcestershire	8716
		(Preece, Nott, Pearson & Nash)	
Women	1	Nottinghamshire	8202
		(Smeeton, Hood, Attwood & Palmer)	

COMPOUND

Men	1	Neil Wakelin	Stortford	2410*
Women	1	M Bell	Stortford	2188

UK Masters Tournament

Lilleshall   June 12-13

RECURVE

Men	1	Steve Hallard	Rugby	1262
	2	Simon Terry		1254
	3	J Shales		1250
Women	1	K Tarplee		1223
	2	C Attwood		1204
	3	J Edens		1200

COMPOUND

Men	1	Simon Tarplee	Evesham	1325
	2	B Dicks		1274
	3	J Lesinski		1263
Women	1	Wendy Lesinski	Clophill	1292
	2	J Wright		1239
	3	A Hartfield		1201

140th Grand National Archery Meeting

Lilleshall   June 30-July 2

RECURVE
Double Hereford

Women	1	J Eley	2250
	2	C Attwood	2218
	3	B Thomas	2207

Double York

Men	1	J Shales	2334
	2	J Pugh	2186
	3	G Hardinges	2177

County Teams

Men	Worcester
Women	Berkshire

COMPOUND

Men	1	T Ward	2021
Women	1	S Jones	2197

Association Football

Has British football lost its way? Well, you'd have to believe it if you took the FIFA rankings at face value. England slumped down to 11th in the rankings that came out in August and even 3-0 wins against Poland (rated a mere 20th) won't do a lot to help that. Scotland would have left the room when they saw where FIFA had placed them: 30th and below Wales. No wonder Andy Roxburgh resigned. Graham Taylor didn't, but that wasn't because nobody asked him to. The tabloid papers hounded him - more vitriolically even than they hounded his predecessor, Bobby Robson. Taylor, though, hung on (however briefly) and even earned something close to a eulogy for the performance against Poland. Most damning, however, are the statistics: up till September 1993, Taylor had used 57 players for England and only once kept the same team. Wales entered the new season with a lingering outside chance of a World Cup place (a bit like England) and Northern Ireland had none at all. All round, not the greatest of years.

Even our exports weren't doing too well: Gascoigne, got himself sent off for Lazio. Lineker started his Japanese career on a very low note (and even got himself booked for careless driving back home - Lineker, careless?); and Des Walker found all that Italian coaching did his game no end of good. So much good, in fact, that he was dropped from the England team for a succession of defensive errors. The only surprise there was that John Barnes wasn't called in to replace him. There was even more distressing news when a questionnaire amongst 8-12 year olds revealed that 11% of them believed that Jacques Delors was a striker for Marseilles. Was he the one, though, who allegedly buried all that money in a garden?

Britain's most successful export could even have been that great fisher of men, Jack Charlton who, with a blend of football that you wouldn't define as exotic, has lifted the Republic of Ireland into the FIFA's top six. Whether they have really reached such an elevated status or not is arguable. What is beyond argument is that Charlton's team is the most successful to come from anywhere near our shores.

FIFA RANKINGS		
As at Aug 8, 1993		
Figures in brackets show placings as at Dec 31, 1992		
1 (1)	Germany	57.50
2 (2)	Italy	56.99
3 (12)	Switzerland	56.81
4 (4)	Sweden	56.35
5 (10)	Argentina	56.20
6 (6)	Republic of Ireland	55.38
7 (8)	Russia	54.67
8 (3)	Brazil	54.49
9 (14)	Norway	54.35
10 (11)	Denmark	53.47
11 (5)	England	52.89
12 (19)	France	51.90
13 (15)	Spain	50.83
14 (25)	Mexico	50.27
15 (18)	RCS (TCH & SVK)	50.03
16 (7)	Holland	49.97
17 (13)	Nigeria	49.53
18 (17)	Belgium	47.77
19 (35)	Columbia	47.67
20 (20)	Poland	47.57
21 (11)	Rumania	47.18
22 (16)	Uruguay	45.97
23 (33)	Portugal	45.91
24 (22)	Cameroon	45.03
25 (32)	Zambia	44.77
26 (21)	Egypt	44.43
27 (28)	Wales	44.40
28 (24)	USA	44.13
29 (27)	Côte d'Ivoire	42.96
30 (23)	Scotland	41.79
40 (43)	Northern Ireland	37.17

Rangers gave Britain its most sustained interest in European competitions, finishing second in their group to the eventual winners Marseilles. Rangers also so dominated the Scottish premiership that everyone else lost interest; they compiled a 44 match unbeaten run that was ended in March by an away defeat at Celtic.

Manchester United won the English Premier Division for the first time since 1967, which wouldn't be a cause for celebration of all those non-United fans out there, except for one thing: the United team included Eric the Great, the best thing to happen to British football since Peter Osgood. Cantona, even if he is slower than a Skegness donkey, is a joy to watch. Why, even before the doors to the 1993/4 season were half open, the Frenchman had illustrated his skills with two magical moments. The first came against Chelsea when, from the halfway line, he hoiked a clearance back over the Chelsea keeper Kharine's head and unluckily hit the crossbar. The second touch of class came a week later when a piercing free-kick against Arsenal left Seaman with no hope. During the close season, Cantona appeared as a model for Paco Rabanne's spring/summer 94 collection, wearing a 'Raj' inspired range of suits. Even Peter Osgood didn't have that much class.

It was the first year of the Premier League, a competition which, if you believe the Second and Third Division clubs, is simply designed so that fewer and fewer clubs could corner more and more of the market. The FA sold the television rights for a mammoth £304m to BSkyB, with the left-overs going to the BBC's Match of the Day.

The wisdom of such a deal was called into question when the FA saw the not-so-mammoth audiences that Sky was pulling in. A figure of between 300-400 thousand being hardly enough to entice the local sweet-shop to take a board on the ground. Fortunately the FA was pulling enough in on the swings not to worry too much about the roundabouts. The Swiss Bank Corporation were initially not too enamoured of the FA; they issued a writ for £2.5m which was the commission on the Sky deal they felt they were owed.

The winners of Divisions 1, 2 and 3 were utterly predictable; well, they were if your name was Jimmy Wright. Jimmy, the brother of Cardiff City chairman Rick, had a small £1,000 each way bet on Newcastle, Stoke and Cardiff to pick up the treble. They did and Jimmy was £500,000 richer. Newcastle, with the new Messiah Kevin Keegan, were so superior they had virtually stopped taking bets by Christmas. Lou Macari's Stoke, too, won in a canter. From November 21, they were not headed at the top of the Division. Cardiff, however, were off the pace in Division 3 and had to put together a second half of note (they won 17 of their last 22 games) to ensure they had a future in Division 2.

A PLAGUE ON ALL YOUR WORKS

It took the skills of clairvoyant Adeline Lee to salvage Derby County's season. In the dark and distant past, a malevolent gypsy had put a curse on the ground and the Rams were suffering as the home defeats piled on. Lee, who works in Skegness, was brought in as a last-ditch attempt to cure the problem. Did it work? Well, see below.

DERBY HOME LEAGUE MATCHES

Before the Curse was lifted
Played: 12 Won: 3 Lost: 9

After the Curse was lifted
Played: 11 Won: 8 Drawn: 2 Lost: 1

Down among the dead men, there was nothing to celebrate. Halifax, despite employing 23 managers since the war, found that the secret of success remained as elusive as ever. With about as many pounds in the bank as they had points in the League, the Shaysiders finally said goodbye to League football. In their place came Wycombe Wanderers with a manager, Martin O'Neill, bold enough to say no to Nottingham Forest.

Others almost went the way of Halifax; the most likely candidates to go down with all hands were Barnet and Brighton, but somehow or other both survived to start the 1993/4 season. Unfortunately the odds are now stacked against the lower reaches; the gap between the top and bottom of the league so vast that it will be a small miracle if at least one or two clubs do not go the the wall this winter.

Glenn Hoddle went to the Bridge and the Wall this year. Hoddle went to Stamford Bridge, which could stretch his Christianity to the limit, while his sports shop in Bishop's Stortford went into liquidation owing £36,500, which probably only amounts to about two months worth of his Chelsea salary. Hoddle's ex-boss Terry Venables was surely wishing that he was dealing in such modest sums - well, maybe not.

There was individual unruliness throughout the year; Vinnie Jones, to no-one's surprise collected 41 points, but he has been superseded by James Major, who put it about a bit in the Huntingdon League. Major was sent off on four occasions to make him almost as unpopular as his dad, the Prime Minister. "I don't care who your father is, son". You can almost here the ref saying it, can't you? Manchester City fans were naughty, too. They flooded onto the pitch before the end of a match against Tottenham and cost the club an FA fine of £50,000. Peter Swales, the subject of much of the fans' abuse that day, deserves some sort of award for remaining as chairman for so long against such hostility.

Brentford's Gary Blissett was taken to court by Torquay's John Uzzell in December, the charge of grevious bodily harm (relating to an incident in a match a year earlier which shattered Uzzell's cheekbone) did not stick after the FA chief executive, Graham Kelly gave evidence in Blissett's favour, which was strange.

HOT SEATS
The Managerial Moves in England summer 1993

Premier League

Chelsea	G'bye:	David Webb
	Hello:	Glenn Hoddle
Swindon	G'bye:	Glenn Hoddle
	Hello:	John Gorman
Spurs	G'bye:	Terry Venables
		Doug Livermore
	Hello:	Ossie Ardiles
Division 1		
Barnsley	G'bye	Mel Machin
	Hello:	Viv Anderson
Brentford	G'bye:	Phil Holder
	Hello:	David Webb
Crystal Palace	G'bye:	Steve Coppell
	Hello:	Alan Smith
Notts Forest	G'bye:	Brian Clough
	Hello:	Frank Clark
West Brom	G'bye:	Ossie Ardiles
	Hello:	Keith Burkinshaw
Watford	G'bye:	Steve Perryman
	Hello:	Glenn Roeder
Division 2		
Barnet	G'bye:	Edwin Stein
	Hello:	Gary Phillips
Cambridge	G'bye:	Ian Atkins
	Hello:	Gary Johnson
Huddersfield	G'bye:	Ian Ross
	Hello:	Neil Warnock
Division 3		
Gillingham	G'bye:	Glenn Roeder
	Hello:	Mike Flanagan
Lincoln	G'bye:	Steve Thompson
	Hello:	Keith Alexander
Scarborough	G'bye:	Ray McHale
	Hello:	Phil Chambers
Torquay	G'bye:	Paul Compton
	Hello:	Don O'Riordan
Wigan	G'bye:	Dave Philpotts
	Hello:	Kenny Swain

World Cup
(Qualifying Rounds)
Includes results of matches played prior to October 1992.

GROUP 1
Table as at Sept 30

	P	W	D	L	F	A	Pts
Switzerland	8	5	3	0	19	5	13
Italy	8	5	2	1	18	6	12
Portugal	7	4	2	1	14	4	10
Scotland	8	3	3	2	11	10	9
Malta	9	1	1	7	3	21	3
Estonia	8	0	1	7	1	20	1

Ibrox Park, Oct 14, 1992
Scotland (0) 0   Portugal (0) 0
Scotland produced a lacklustre display against a skilful Portuguese side for whom Paulo Futre impressed. The Atletico Madrid striker twice came within an inch of giving Portugal the lead, his closest effort when Goram's legs repelled his shot. Scotland could manage only a couple of harmless long range efforts from McCall and McStay and did not have the cause aided when Gallacher limped off with a torn hamstring. Manager Andy Roxburgh accused the visitors of playing negatively, but he could hardly have been inspired by his own team's efforts
Scotland: Goram, Malpas, Boyd, McCall, Whyte, Levein, Gallacher (McClair 33), Mc Stay, McCoist, McAllister, Collins (Durrant 71).
Portugal: Baia, Joao Pinto I, Helder, Veloso, Couto, Oceano, Paneira, Semedo (Figo 53), Domingos, Futre, Andre.

Ibrox Park, Nov 18, 1992
Scotland (0) 0   Italy (0) 0
The Italians were allowed to dictate matters in the first half and, without Goram's determination, the game could have lost by half-time. After the break, it was a different story. McLaren tied up Roberto Baggio, the Scots controlled the game, and a victory looked on the cards. That it did not happen was due to poor Scottish finishing.
Scotland: Goram, McPherson, Malpas, McStay, McLaren, Whyte, Durie (Jess 71), McAllister, McCoist, Durrant (Robertson 88), Boyd.
Italy: Pagliuca, Mannini, Di Chiara (Costacurta 7), Maldini, Baresi, Lentini, Albertini, Eranio, Bianchi, Signori (Donadoni 46), R Baggio.

Ibrox Park, Feb 17, 1993
Scotland (1) 3   Malta (0) 0
Ally McCoist needed only 15 minutes to prise open the massed defence of the Maltese. He scored a second when Eoin Jess, making his international debut, set him up with an easy tap in. McCoist, with 41 club goals under his belt already throughout the season, could have made it a hattrick day but failed to convert another Jess assist. McAllister was also profligate, missing a penalty. It was left to Pat Nevin to add a third to cheer the 17,500 schoolchildren who had been given free tickets for the game. Their screams of delight disguised the reality.

Against this sort of opposition, it should have been more.
Scotland: Goram, McPherson (Robertson 64), Boyd, McStay, McLeich, McLaren, Nevin, McAllister (Ferguson 73), McCoist, Collins, Jess.
Malta: Cluett, S Vella, Buhagiar (E Camilleri 83), Galea, Brincat, Buttigieg, Busuttil, Saliba, J Camilleri, Laferia, Sultana (R Vella 74).

Lisbon, Apr 28, 1993
Portugal (2) 5   Scotland (0) 0
Barros 5, 70
Cadete 45, 72
Futre 67
In the Stadium of Light, Scotland had one of their darkest hours. Rui Barros eluded the offside trap to open the scoring and Jorge Cadete added another in the 44th minute. Roxburgh switched tactics for the second half, in an effort to salvage the match. It simply made matters worse. Three goals came in five minutes, through Futre, Barros and Cadete, and Scotland found themselves with their worst international result for 18 years. It could have been more if the home team had not been so wasteful of their chances. On this occasion, Roxburgh did not accuse the Portuguese of negative tactics.
Portugal: Baia, Xavier, Costa, Costa (Veloso 53), Couto, Oceano, Barros, Sousa, Semedo, Futre, Cadete (Domingos 81).
Scotland: Goram, Gough, McInally, McPherson, McKimmie, Levein (Nevin 60), McStay, McCall, McCoist, Collins (Durrant 75), Gallacher.

Tallinn, May 19, 1993
Estonia (0) 0   Scotland (1) 3
                       Gallacher 43, Collins 59
                       Booth 73
The £1.5m price-tag on his move from Coventry to Blackburn obviously did wonders for Kevin Gallacher's confidence. His rich vein of scoring continued when he struck the first goal just before time. He was instrumental in the second too, which John Collins scored and a neat display was tidily wrapped up by Aberdeen's Scott Booth. After Portugal, this was a desperately needed morale booster.
Estonia: Poom, R Kallaste, Lensalu, Prins, Kaljend, T Kallaste, Borisov, Kristal (Hepner 46), Reim, Veensalu (Pustov 76), Bragin.
Scotland: Gunn, Wright (McLaren 80), Boyd, McStay, Hendry, Irvine, Gallacher, Bowman, Robertson (Booth 61), McClair, Collins.

Aberdeen, June 2, 1993
Scotland (2) 3   Estonia (0) 1
McClair 16   *Bragin 57*
Nevin 27, 72 (pen)
A rare international goal by Brian McClair helped to settle the nerves and create a platform for a second successive win against Estonia. It was only McClair's second goal for his country in 30 appearances. Nevin, who supplied the cross for McClair had a happy time scoring both the second and the third goals; the latter coming from a penalty. That was a timely intervention by Nevin. Sergei Bragin had brought the Estonians back into the game with a searing goal after the interval. Nevin's strike put the game back into Scotland's pocket.

Scotland: Gunn, McLaren (Robertson 72), Boyd, McStay, Hendry, Irvine, Gallacher, Ferguson (Booth 55), McClair, Collins, Nevin.
Estonia: Poom, R Kallaste, Lensalu (Bragin 46), Prins, Kaljend, T Kallaste, Borisov, Kristal, Reim, Olumets (Veensalu 73), Rajala.

Pittodrie, Sept 8 1993
Scotland (0) 1   **Switzerland (0) 1**
Collins 50   *Bregy (pen) 69*
Scotland surrendered any chance of qualifying for America when Switzerland came away from this match with a point. Gordon Durie almost set up an early goal, but the Swiss side showed evidence of the talent that has made them one of the tidiest sides in Europe. Against the run of play, though, Scotland scored first and looked then to have a chance of two points, but twenty minutes later, keeper Gunn upended Ciri Sforza and Bregy scored from the spot to virtually book Switzerland's place in the World Cup finals. Scotland's consolation is that they were probably drawn in the toughest group of all.
Scotland: Gunn, McKimmie, Robertson, Bowman (O'Donnell 75), Irvine, McAllister, Levein, Collins, Booth (Jess 69), Durie, Nevin
Switzerland: Pascolo, Quentin, Rothenbuhler (Grassi 61), Herr, Geiger, Bregy (Rueda 87), Sutter, Ohrel, Sforza, Knup, Chapuiat

Cagliari, Oct 14, 1992
Italy (0) 2   **Switzerland (2) 2**
R Baggio 83   *Ohrel 17, Chapuisat 21*
Eranio 89

Valetta, Oct 25, 1992
Malta (0) 0   **Estonia (0) 0**

Berne, Nov 18, 1992
Switzerland (2) 3   **Malta (0) 0**
Bickel 2, Sforza 42
Chapuisat 89

Valetta, Dec 19, 1992
Malta (0) 1   **Italy (0) 2**
Gregory 85   *Vialli 59, Signori 62*

Valetta, Jan 24, 1993
Malta (0) 0   **Portugal (0) 1**
                       Aguas 56

Oporto, Feb 24, 1993
Portugal (0) 1   **Italy (2) 3**
Couto 57   *R Baggio 2, 75*
                       Casiraghi 24

Palermo, March 24, 1993
Italy (2) 6   **Malta (0) 1**
D Baggio 19   *Busuttil 68 (pen)*
Signori 38
Vierchowod 48
Mancini 59, 89
Maldini 73

Berne, March 31, 1993
Switzerland (1) 1   **Portugal (1) 1**
Chapuisat 39   *Semedo 44*

Trieste, April 14, 1993
Italy (1) 2   **Estonia (0) 0**
R Baggio 21
Signori 86

Valletta, April 17, 1993
Malta (0) 0   **Switzerland (1) 2**
                       Ohrel 31, Turkyilmaz 89

Berne, May 1, 1993
Switzerland (0) 1   **Italy (0) 0**
Hottiger 55

Tallinn, May 12, 1993
Estonia (0) 0   **Malta (1) 1**
                       Laferla 16

Oporto, June 19, 1993
Portugal (3) 4   **Malta (0) 0**
Nogueira 2
Costa 9, Joao Pinto II 23
Cadete 8

Riga, Sept 22, 1993
Estonia (0) 0   **Italy (1) 3**
                       Baggio (pen) 19, 73
                       Mancini 59

GROUP 2

Table as at Sept 30

	P	W	D	L	F	A	Pts
Norway	8	6	2	0	21	3	14
Holland	8	4	3	1	24	8	11
England	8	4	3	1	19	6	11
Poland	7	3	2	2	8	7	8
Turkey	8	1	1	6	7	17	3
San Marino	9	0	1	8	1	39	1

Wembley, Oct 14, 1992
England (0) 1   **Norway (0) 1**
Platt 55   *Rekdal 76*
It was Paul Gascoigne's first match back at Wembley since being stretchered off in the 1991 Cup Final. Gascoigne curbed any inclination to repeat his tackling excesses and for 75 minutes it looked as if everything was hunky-dory. England were a goal ahead - Platt continuing the extraordinary run that saw him score every England goal for seven matches - and set fair for home when a crashing volley from Kjetil Rekdal stunned the Wembley crowd.
England: Woods, Dixon (Palmer 89), Walker, Adams, Pearce, Batty, Ince, Platt, Gascoigne, Wright (Merson 69), Shearer.
Norway: Thorstvedt, Nilsen, Bratseth, Pedersen (Berg 19), Bjornebye, Halle, Jakobsen, Ingebritsen, Mykland (Flo 78), Rekdal, Sorloth.

Wembley, Nov 18, 1992
England (2) 4   **Turkey (0) 0**
Gascoigne 16, 61
Shearer 28, Pearce 60
With Palmer and Ince supplying the midfield graft, Gascoigne was left to indulge his Arts. It was an

impressive performance which rewarded him with the first and last goals. Shearer discovered his scoring touch for England and everything in the English garden looked well on the way to rosy. Taylor, for once, could look relaxed.

England: Woods, Dixon, Pearce, Palmer, Walker, Adams, Platt, Gascoigne, Shearer, Wright, Ince.
Turkey: Hayrettin, Recep, Bulent, Gokhan, Ogun, Orhan, Hami (Riza 69), Unal, Mehmet (Ugur 46), Oguz, Hakan.

Wembley   Feb 17, 1993
England (2) 6   **San Marino (0) 0**
Platt 13, 24, 67, 83
Palmer 76
Ferdinand 86
As debuts go, Platt's as England's captain could hardly have been happier. The Juventus player found the net on four occasions as England thumped San Marino. Platt's tally was the biggest haul since Malcom Macdonald hit five against Cyprus in 1975. John Barnes suffered the disapproval of the crowd and Gascoigne overelaborated, but it didn't remove the smile from Graham Taylor's face. Two games and ten goals; it was almost the days of wine and roses.

England: Woods, Dixon, Walker, Adams, Dorigo, Gascoigne, Batty, Platt, Palmer, Ferdinand, Barnes.
San Marino: Benedettini, Muccioli, Zanotti, M Mazza, Gennari, Canti, Guerra, Manzaroli, Bacciocchi (P Mazza 63), Bonini, Francini (Matteoni 80).

Izmir, March 31, 1993
Turkey (0) 0   **England (2) 2**
        Platt 6, Gascoigne 44
On and off the field Turkey proved an inhospitable place for the English. Missiles came from off the pitch, fierce tackling was the order of the day on it. Platt scored his tenth goal in his last ten internationals and Gascoigne scored with his head to settle the match. Wright and Dixon left the field injured and coins rained on the English players as they left the field. Nevertheless, the record, in the last three games, read; played three, won three, goals for 12, goals against none.

Turkey: Engin (Hayrettin 42), Recep (Hami 69), Ogun, Ali, Tugay, Bulent, Feyyaz, Unal, Mehmet, Oguz, Orhan.
England: Woods, Dixon (Clough 46), Sinton, Palmer, Walker, Adams, Platt, Gascoigne, Barnes, Wright (Sharpe 84), Ince.

Wembley, April 28, 1993
England (2) 2   **Holland (1) 2**
Barnes 2, Platt 23 *Bergkamp 34, Van Vossen 85 (pen)*
Des Walker, once lauded as the fastest defender in the whole damn world, fell rather short of such standards when he was roundly outpaced by Holland's Marc Overmars in the dying minutes of the game. Walker did what any mere mortal would and pulled him back by his shirt. But Walker, a mere mortal? It cost a penalty, duly dispatched by Van Vossen and the scores were brought level. Barnes, for once the hero, had established an early lead; Platt (who else?) doubled it. Bergkamp pulled one back for Holland, Gascoigne took an elbow in the eye from Wouters and left the field, then Holland equalised with that penalty. They are not long the days of wine and roses.

England: Woods, Dixon, Walker, Adams, Keown, Ince, Gascoigne (Merson 46), Palmer, Barnes, Platt, Ferdinand.
Holland: De Goey, Blind, De Boer, Rijkaard, Winter, Wouters, Witschge, Gullit (Van Vossen 69), Bergkamp, Bosman (De Wolf 46), Overmars.

Chorzow, May 29, 1993
Poland (1) 1   **England (0) 1**
Adamczuk 34   *Wright 84*
Ian Wright's first international goal saved this one for England. The Arsenal forward had come on as a substitute for Carlton Palmer. Bardsley, brought into the team late when Dixon pulled out through illness, had looked the best Englishman on the field prior - which was not high praise. Gascoigne wore a mask to protect his damaged cheekbone. It looked theatrical; it may even have protected the cheekbone. It certainly didn't help his football. Woods and Walker (two mistakes in two games) offered Poland the early opportunity for a goal when they misread each others intentions. Adamczuk took it gratefully.

Poland: Bako, Czachowski, Szewczyk, Kozminski, Lesiak, Brzeczek (Jalocha 84), Szierczewski, Adamczuk, Furtok, Kosecki, Lesniak (Wegrzyn 75).
England: Woods, Bardsley, Dorigo, Palmer (Wright 72), Walker, Adams, Platt, Gascoigne (Clough 79), Sharpe

---

Graham Taylor's
Breakfast Reading

After 2-0 defeat by Norway

GAME FOR OLAF - The Star
VIKE OFF TAYLOR - The Sun
NORSE MANURE - The Mirror

After 2-0 defeat by USA (in Boston)

STARS AND TRIPE - The Mirror
YANKS 2 PLANKS 0 - The Sun

A day later

THE BOSTON DANGLER - The Sun

Oslo, June 2, 1993
Norway (1) 2   **England (0) 0**
Leonhardsen 42
Bohinen 48
Walker confirmed his relegation to the ranks of mere mortal, by making his third crucial mistake in three games. His foul on Fjørtoft led to the free-kick which Dixon, in turn, deflected past Woods. It was one of those days. The misery continued for Walker and England as Mykland turned him inside out to set up the second for Bohinen. What was there to say? In defence, it was pointed out that Norway are nobody's fall guys any more. No, but England were moving that way.

Norway: Thorstvedt, Halle, Pedersen, Bratseth (Nilsen 82), Bjornebye, Flo, Mykland, Leonhardsen, Fjortoft (Sorloth 57), Rekdal, Bohinen.
England: Woods, Dixon, Pallister, Palmer, Walker (Clough 63), Adams, Platt, Gascoigne, Ferdinand, Sheringham (Wright 46), Sharpe.

Wembley, Sept 8, 1993
England (1) 3   **Poland (0) 0**
Ferdinand 5
Gascoigne 48
Pearce 53
The reaction to this victory told the whole story; it was
greeted as rousing and emphatic and a sure sign that
England was back on the road. It was rousing, because
England's supporters needed someting to cheer about. It
was emphatic, too, but largely because Poland played no
sort of game and resorted to niggling tactics. England
were good for a while and Ferdinand collected his
opening goal with panache, but it was still alarming how
long it took the England players simply to control the
ball. Should they get to America, they'd be given much
less time there. Gascoigne scored, but that was slight
compensation for a booking which left him out of the
Holland game. Pearce blasted the third for a set-piece
move. It was a relief, but was it any more?

Oslo, Sept 9, 1992
Norway (4) 10   **San Marino (0) 0**
Rekdal 5, 79
Halle 6, 51, 69
Sorloth 15, 21
Nilsen 46, 67
Mykland 74

Oslo, Sept 23, 1992
Norway (1) 2   **Holland (1) 1**
Rekdal 9 (pen)   *Bergkamp 10*
Sorloth 78

Poznan, Sept 23, 1992
Poland (1) 1   **Turkey (0) 0**
Waldoch 33

Serravalle, Oct 7, 1992
San Marino (0) 0   **Norway (2) 2**
                        Jakobsen 7, Flo 19

Rotterdam, Oct 14, 1992
Holland (1) 2   **Poland (2) 2**
Van Vossen 43, 46   *Kosecki 18, Kowalczyk 20*

Ankara, Oct 28, 1992
Turkey (1) 4   **San Marino (0) 0**
Hakan 37, 89
Orhan 87, Hami 90

Istanbul, Dec 16, 1992
Turkey (0) 1   **Holland (0) 3**
Feyyaz 60   *Van Vossen 57, 87*
              Gullit 59

Utrecht, Feb 24, 1993
Holland (2) 3   **Turkey (1) 1**
Overmars 4   *Feyyaz 36 (pen)*
Witschge 37, 57

Serravalle, March 10, 1993
San Marino (0) 0   **Turkey (0) 0**

Utrecht, March 24, 1993
Holland (2) 6   **San Marino (0) 0**
Van den Brom 2
Canti (og) 29
De Wolf 52, 85
R De Boer 68 (pen)
Van Vossen 78

Oslo, April 28, 1993
Norway (2) 3   **Turkey (0) 1**
Rekdal 14   *Feyyaz 57*
Fjortoft 17
Jakobsen 55

Lodz, April 28, 1993
Poland (0) 1   **San Marino (0) 0**
Furtok 68

Serravalle, May 19, 1993
San Marino (0) 0   **Poland (0) 3**
                        Lesniak 52, 80
                        Warzycha 56

Rotterdam, June 9, 1993
Holland (0) 0   **Norway (0) 0**

Bologna, Sept 22, 1993
San Marino (0) 0   **Holland (3) 7**
                        Bosman 1, 66, 76
                        Jonk 21, 43
                        de Boer 51
                        Koeman (pen) 79

Oslo, Sept 22, 1993
Norway (0) 1   **Poland (0) 0**
Flo 54

GROUP 3
Table as at Sept 30

	P	W	D	L	F	A	Pts
Rep of Ireland	10	7	3	0	17	2	17
Denmark	10	6	4	0	14	1	16
Spain	10	6	3	1	23	3	13
N Ireland	10	5	2	3	13	11	12
Lithuania	12	2	3	7	8	21	5
Latvia	12	0	5	7	4	21	5
Albania	12	1	2	9	6	26	4

Windsor Park, April 28, 1992
N Ireland (2) 2   **Lithuania (1) 2**
Wilson 13   *Narberkovas 41*
Taggart 16   *Fridrikas 48*
N Ireland: Fettis, Donaghy (Fleming 46), Taggart,
McDonald, Worthington, Black, Magilton, Wilson,
Hughes, Quinn, Dowie (Rogan 80).
Lithuania: Martinkenas, Buzmakovas, Mika, Janonis,
Mazeikis, Tautkas, Urbonas, Fridrikas (Zhuta 90),
Narbekovas, Baranauskas, Ivanauskas (Danisevicius 89).

Dublin, May 26, 1992
Rep of Ireland (0) 2   Albania (0) 0
Aldridge 60
McGrath 80
Rep of Ireland: Bonner, Irwin, Staunton, O'Leary,
McGrath, Townsend, Keane, Houghton, Quinn, Aldridge

(Coyne 83), Sheedy (McCarthy 52).
Albania: Dani, Zmijani, Qendro (Pali 71), Peqini, Vata, Abazi, Kushta, Vasi, Rraklli, Zola (Sokoll 80), Demollari.

Dublin, Sept 9, 1992
Rep of Ireland (1) 4 Latvia (0) 0
Sheedy 30
Aldridge 59, 82 (pen), 86
Rep of Ireland: Bonner, Irwin, Staunton, Kernaghan, McGrath, Townsend, Keane, Whelan, Quinn (Coyne 61), Aldridge, Sheedy (Phelan 76).
Latvia: Igochine, Astajevs, Alexeyenko, Bulders, Gnedois, Popkovs (Semionovs 63), Sprogis, Abzinovs (Sidorovs 36), Yeliseyevs, Linards, Glazovs.

Windsor Park, Sept 9, 1992
N Ireland (3) 3   Albania (0) 0
Clarke
Wilson
Magilton
N Ireland: Wright, Fleming, Worthington, Taggart, McDonald, Donaghy, Wilson, Magilton, Clarke (O'Neil 77), Dowie, Hughes.
Albania: Strakosha, Zmijani, Peqini, Lekbello, Vata, Abazi, Kushta, Milori (Bilali 69), Millo, Kepa, Rraklli.

Copenhagen, Oct 14, 1992
Denmark (0) 0   Rep of Ireland (0) 0
Moran and Kernaghan locked up the Irish defence as Denmark struggled to live up to their billing as European champions. Laudrup had two chances to put his team ahead, but could not convert either and a point was enough to take Eire to the top of Group 3.
Denmark: Schmeichel, Olsen, Piechnik, Sivebaek, Heintze, Rieper, Jensen, Vilfort, Larsen, Laudrup, Povlsen (Christensen 77).
Rep of Ireland: Bonner, Irwin, Phelan, Moran, Kernaghan, Keane, Townsend, Houghton (Kelly 73), Quinn, Aldridge, McGoldrick.

Windsor Park, Oct 14, 1992
N Ireland (0) 0   Spain (0) 0
Against a technically superior Spanish team, Tommy Wright kept the Irishmen in the game, first denying Hierro then Michel. Michael Hughes almost brought the points to Northern Ireland in the 82nd minute, but was cut down by a lunging tackle from Antonio Munoz. Munoz took a slightly early bath for his trouble, but he was probably relieved to be out of a dreary game played on a rain-lashed night at Windsor Park.
N Ireland: Wright, Fleming, Worthington, Taggart, McDonald, Donaghy, Black (Morrow 61), Wilson, Clarke, Quinn, Hughes.
Spain: Zubizarreta, Ferrer, Toni, Solozabal, Lopez, Hierro, Amor, Michel, Claudio (Guardiola 63), Martin Vazquez, Manolo (Alfonso 60).

Windsor Park, Nov 18, 1992
N Ireland (0) 0   Denmark (0) 1
Larsen 51
Another capacity crowd turned out, but probably more in hope than expectation. The home team were stretched by the hard-running Danish team and in the 51st minute Larson scored the goal that left Billy Bingham's team an uphill struggle to qualify.

N Ireland: Fettis, Fleming, Taggart, McDonald, Worthington, Donaghy, Magilton, Wilson (Black), Hughes, Clarke (Gray), Quinn.
Denmark: Schmeichel, Sivebaek (Rjeldberg 46), Rieper, Olsen, Heintze, Vilfort, Jensen, Larsen (Goldbaek 73), Povlsen, Laudrup, Elstrup.

Seville, Nov 18, 1992
Spain (0) 0   Rep of Ireland (0) 0
Roy Keane produced his best international performance to date and could count himself unlucky not to be on the winning side. Up front, Aldridge caused a mountain of problems for the Spanish, in particular Juan Lopez who decided that Aldridge would be less of a threat if he up-ended him. For his troubles, Lopez was sent off. Aldridge looked to have scored in the 73rd minute, but the goal was disallowed for offside.
Spain: Zubizarreta, Ferrer, Goicoechea, Solozabal, Lopez, Hierro, Salinas (Bakero 52), Michel, Butragueno (Beguiristain 60), Vazquez, Amor.
Rep of Ireland: Bonner, Irwin, Phelan, Moran, Keane, Townsend, McGrath, Houghton, Staunton, Aldridge, Quinn.

Tirana, Feb 17, 1993
Albania (0) 1   N Ireland (0) 2
Rrakli 89   Magilton 14, McDonald 38
The Northern Irish went two goals clear before Tommy Wright earnt his spurs with a penalty save. Albania pulled one back in the dying minutes, but this victory on the dire Quemel Stadium surface at least kept some hope alive for the World Cup finals.
Albania: Kapliani, Zmijani (Peqini 46), Kacaj, Bano, Vata, Bazgo, Lekbello (Shulku 46), Fortuzi, Abazi, Rraklli, Demollari.
N Ireland: Wright, Fleming, Morrow, Taggart, Magilton, McDonald, Donaghy, Gray, Dowie (Quinn 73), O'Neill, Black.

Dublin, March 31, 1993
Rep of Ireland (3) 3 N Ireland (0) 0
Townsend 20
Quinn 22,
Staunton 28
Three goals in eight minutes sealed the fate of this match. Andy Townsend scored his fourth goal in 35 international appearances to set Eire in motion, Niall Quinn knocked in a Houghton cross for the second and Steve Staunton curled one in for the third. After that, Northern Ireland settled down to think about the 1998 World Cup.
Rep of Ireland: Bonner, Irwin, Phelan, McGrath, Moran, Keane, Townsend, Houghton, Quinn (McGoldrick 84), Coyne (Cascarino 78), Staunton.
N Ireland: Wright, Donaghy, Worthington, Taggart, McDonald, Morrow, Magilton (Quinn 51), O'Neil (Black 74), Dowie, Gray, Hughes.

Dublin, April 28, 1993
Rep of Ireland (0) 1 Denmark (1) 1
Quinn 75   Vilfort 27
Denmark used Schmeichel to pump balls upfield and then closed in on any attempts to play football. It irritated the Irish, not so much because they found it hard to play against, but because they thought they had copyrighted

the idea. Jack Charlton considered that Reiper, Olsen and Kjeldberg were outstanding, which gave us one insight. Ireland weren't about to change their tactics.

Rep of Ireland: Bonner, Irwin, McGoldrick, McGrath, Kernaghan, Keane, Towsend, Houghton, Quinn, Aldridge (Cascarino 62), Staunton.
Denmark: Schmeichel, Nielsen, Rieper, Olsen, Kjeldbjerg, Hansen, Jensen, Vilfort, Pingel (Kristensen 60), Elstrup, Laudrup.

Seville, April 28, 1993
Spain (3) 3   **N Ireland (1) 1**
Salinas 22, 27   *Wilson 11*
Hierro 41

Memories, all be them faint, of Northern Ireland's 1-0 victory over Spain in the 1982 World Cup, were awakened when Notts County's Kevin Wilson scored after 12 minutes. The memories didn't linger long. Two goals in five minutes by Salinas tipped the balance in Spain's favour. Flickering Irish hopes were extinguished by a third goal from Hierro and with seven of their 12 games played and only six points under their belt, Northern Ireland, even with two games against Latvia and one against Albania to come, could forget the American dream.

Spain: Zubizarreta, Ferrer, Fernando, Toni, Akorta, Hierro, Guerrero, Adolfo, Beguiristain (Bakero 76), Salinas, Claudio (Kiki 59).
N Ireland: Wright, Fleming, Worthington, Donaghy, Taggart, McDonald, Black (Dennison 73), Wilson, O'Neill (Dowie 73), Gray, Hughes.

Vilnius, May 25, 1993
Lithuania (0) 0   **N Ireland (1) 1**
                         Downie 8

Southampton's Ian Dowie scored the winning goal just nine minutes into the game at the rain-soaked National Stadium. A shot from Michael Hughes rebounded off a defender and Dowie volleyed in from 10 yards. Wright was outstanding in the second half.

Lithuania: Martinkenas, Blatusnikas, Buzmakovas (Vichka 68), Mazeikis, Zhukas, Lushanskis (Shlenskis 46), Baranauskas, Sukristovas, Kirilovas, Fridrikas, Zdanicius.
N Ireland: Wright, Fleming, Taggart, McDonald, Worthington, Donaghy, Magilton, O'Neill, Wilson, Hughes, Dowie.

Tirana, May 26, 1993
Albania (1) 1   **Rep of Ireland (1) 2**
Kushta 7   *Staunton 13, Cascarino 77*

Paul McGrath, who had pulled out of the match two days prior with a knee injury, was sorely missed. Staunton, who scored the Republic's first from a free-kick, and Townsend were the only Irish players to emerge with credit although Tony Cascarino won't be too displeased with his evening's work. On the field for just three minutes, and with only his second touch, he put the game beyond Albania's reach.

Albania: Musta, Zmijani (Fortuzi 58), Shulku, Shala, Vata, Lekbello, Kushta, Peqini, Rraklli (Bozgo 76), Milori, Demollari.
Rep of Ireland: Bonner, Irwin, Phelan, Kernaghan, Moran, Keane, Townsend, Houghton, Quinn, Aldridge (Cascarino 74), Staunton.

Riga, June 2, 1993
Latvia (0) 1   **N Ireland (2) 2**
Linards 55   *Magilton 4, Taggart 15*

Two thousand Latvians, about the same sort of crowd that Darlington get of a Saturday, found little to cheer about. Northern Ireland won their second qualifier in a row, but national pride was the only thing at stake.

Latvia: Karavayev, Erglis, Shevljakovs, Ivanovs, Gnedois, Popkovs, Sarnado (Yeliseyevs 46), Astafjevs, Zelberlins (Babicevs 63), Linards, Gorjacilovs.
N Ireland: Wright, Fleming, McDonald, Taggart, Worthington, O'Neill (Quinn 85), Magilton, Donaghy, Wilson, Hughes, Dowie.

Riga, June 9, 1993
Latvia (0) 0   **Rep of Ireland (2) 2**
                         Aldridge 14, McGrath 42

McGrath returned to bolster an Irish side that needed to secure two points to stay one step ahead of Spain and Denmark in the hunt for World Cup places. Denmark and Spain, it should be noted, had both failed to win here. An early strike by Aldridge, Ireland's 400th goal in world football, and a goal from McGrath just before the interval was enough and Ireland moved on to 13 points in Group 3. The same total as Spain, but a game in hand.

Latvia: Karavayev, Erglis, Shevljakovs, Astafjevs, Ivanovs, Gnedois, Popkovs, Bulders, Babicevs (Yeliseyevs 46), Sharando (Gorjacilovs 54), Linards.
Rep of Ireland: Bonner, Irwin, Kernaghan, McGrath, Phelan, Houghton, Townsend, Keane, Staunton, Aldridge (Sheridan 80), Quinn (Cascarino 74).

Vilnius, June 16, 1993
Lithuania (0) 0   **Rep of Ireland (1) 1**
                         Staunton 38

For the first time in its sporting history, the Republic's team managed three consecutive away victories. However, it was not a pretty game to watch. A greasy surface and tired teams combined to produce a dreadful game of football. Still, for Irish hearts the end justified the means. They leap to the top of Group 3 and now know that, with an easy home fixture against Lithuania next, if they can hold Spain to a draw at home on October 13th, they will be on their way to America. Unless the Northern Irish chose to spoil the story in the final match in November. But they wouldn't do that, surely?

Lithuania: Martinkenas, Zhukas, Baltusnikas, Mazeikis, Buzmakovas, Skarbalius (Zdanicius 46), Baranauskas, Urbonas (Ramelis 67), Stumprys, Kirilovas, Slekys.
Rep of Ireland: Bonner, Irwin, Phelan, McGrath, Kernaghan, Keane, Townsend, Houghton, Quinn, Aldridge (Whelan 76), Staunton.

Dublin, Sept 8, 1993
Rep of Ireland (2) 2   Lithuania (0) 0
Aldridge 4
Kernaghan 25

For half a game it looked a doddle for the Republic, as Aldridge put away his 13th international goal before the game was half awake and man-of-the-match Kernaghan added another before the interval. However, Charlton was wise to counsel caution as the Lithuanians made a game of it in the second half and almost stole a point. It still put the Republic in the driving seat for the US, but they still had a little way to go.

Windsor Park, Sept 8, 1993
N Ireland (1) 2   **Latvia (0) 0**
Quinn 35
Gray 80
Latvia has yet to win a game in this group and another defeat was notched up against Northern Ireland.

Seville, April 22, 1992
Spain (1) 3   **Albania (0) 0**
Michel 2, 66 (pen)
Hierro 87

Tirana, June 3, 1992
Albania (0) 1   **Lithuania (0) 0**
Abazi 77

Riga, Aug 12, 1992
Latvia (0) 1   **Lithuania (0) 2**
Linards 15   *Poderis 65, Tereskinas 86*

Riga, Aug 26, 1992
Latvia (0) 0   **Denmark (0) 0**

Riga, Sept 23, 1992
Latvia (0) 0   **Spain (0) 0**

Vilnius, Sept 23, 1992
Lithuania (0) 0   **Denmark (0) 0**

Vilnius, Oct 28, 1992
Lithuania (0) 1   **Latvia (1) 1**
Fridrikas 85   *Linards 44*

Tirana, Nov 11, 1992
Albania (0) 1   **Latvia (1) 1**
Kepa 67   *Alexeyenko 3*

Seville, Dec 16, 1992
Spain (0) 5   **Latvia (0) 0**
Bakero 49
Guardiola 51
Alfonso 79
Beguiristain 81, 82

Seville, Feb 24, 1993
Spain (3) 5   **Lithuania (0) 0**
Christobal 5
Bakero 13
Beguiristain 18
Christiansen 86
Aldana 89

Copenhagen, March 31, 1993
Denmark (1) 1   **Spain (0) 0**
Povlsen 20

Copenhagen, April 14, 1993
Denmark (1) 2   **Latvia (0) 0**
Vilfort 23, Strudal 76

Vilnius, April 14, 1993
Lithuania (2) 3   **Albania (0) 1**
Baltusnikas 20   *Demollari 86*
Sukristovas 25
Baranauskas 63

Riga, May 15, 1993
Latvia (0) 0   **Albania (0) 0**

Vilnius, June 2, 1993
Lithuania (0) 0   **Spain (0) 2**
     Guerrero 73, 77

Copenhagen, June 2, 1993
Denmark (4) 4   **Albania (0) 0**
Jensen 11
Pingel 20, 40
Moller 28

Tirana, Sept 8, 1993
Albania (0) 0   **Denmark (0) 1**
     Pingle 63

Tirana, Sept 22, 1993
Albania (1) 1   **Spain (3) 5**
Kushta 40   *Salinas 3, 31, 60*
     Toni 19
     Caminero 67

GROUP 4
Table as at Sept 30

	P	W	D	L	F	A	Pts
Belgium	8	7	0	1	15	3	14
Romania	8	5	1	2	25	10	11
RCS	8	3	4	1	18	9	10
Wales	8	4	2	2	16	10	10
Cyprus	8	2	1	5	8	13	5
Faroe islands	10	0	0	10	1	38	0

Bucharest, May 20, 1992
Romania (5) 5   **Wales (0) 1**
Hagi 5, 35   *Rush 50*
Lupescu 7, 24
Balint 31
Romania: Stelea, Petrescu, Mihali, Belodedici, Munteanu, Sabau (Timofte 80), Popescu, Lupescu, Hagi (Gerstenmaier 71), Lacatus, Balint.
Wales: Southall, Phillips, Bowen (Blackmore 71), Aizlewood, Melville, Horne, Speed, Pembridge (Giggs 59), Hughes, Rush, Saunders.

Cardiff, Sept 9, 1992
Wales (3) 6   **Faeroes (0) 0**
Rush 5, 64, 89
Saunders 28
Bowen 37
Blackmore 71
Wales: Southall, Phillips, Bowen (Giggs 66), Symons, Young, Blackmore, Horne, Saunders, Rush, Hughes, Speed.
Faeroes: Knudsen, Jakobsen, T Hansen, Danielsen, O Hansen, Morkore, Simonsen, Dam (Justinussen 56), Jonsson, Reynheim, Muller.

Nicosia, Oct 14, 1992
Cyprus (0) 0   **Wales (0) 1**
     Hughes 51
Mark Hughes' first international goal for two years secured the points for Wales in a difficult tie played on a bumpy pitch in sapping humidity. Hughes, operating in

midfield, met a Phillips cross in the 51st minute to record his tenth goal for Wales. Rush was in search of something grander, the Welsh goalscoring record which he shared with Allchurch and Ford at 23. Only the acrobatics of Michalis Christofi in the Cyprus goal, in fending off a 30 yard strike, denied him. It wouldn't be long coming though.

Cyprus: Christofi, Costa, Pittas (Hadjilukas 71), Constantinou, Nicolau, Yiangudakis, D Ioannou, Charalambous, Sotiriou (Y Ioannou 59), Papavasiliou, Savidis.

Wales: Southall, Phillips, Bowen, Blackmore, Young, Symons, Horne, Saunders, Rush, Hughes, Speed.

Brussels   Nov 18, 1992
Belgium (0) 2   Wales (0) 0
Staelens 53
Degryse 58
Having contained a lively Belgian midfield for the first half, Wales conceded two soft goals in five minutes to surrender the game. Gary Speed, who needed stitches in a facial wound, finally gave a performance that mirrored his contributions for Leeds, but it wasn't enough.

Belgium: Preud'homme, Medved, Grun, Albert, Smidts, Staelens (Wilmots 82), Van der Elst, Boffin, Degryse, Scifo, Szerniatynski (Nilis 46).

Wales: Southall, Phillips, Bowen (Giggs 60), Blackmore, Young, Symons, Horne, Saunders, Rush, Hughes, Speed (Pembridge 80)

Cardiff, March 31, 1993
Wales (2) 2   Belgium (0) 0
Giggs 18, Rush 39
It was Ryan Giggs' international debut and predictably he marked it with a goal. Horne stepped over the ball, Giggs swung a left-footed drive past Preud'homme. Simple as that. Rush scored the second and reached his landmark, the 24 goals needed to top Ford and Allchurch's Welsh record. It was a landmark for Belgium too. They sacrificed their 100% record in Group 4.

Wales: Southall, Horne, Bodin, Aizlewood, Young, Ratcliffe, Saunders, Speed (Phillips 88), Rush, Hughes, Giggs (Bowen 89).

Belgium: Preud'homme, Medved (Oliveira 46), Grun, Albert, Smidts, Staelens, Van der Elst, Boffin, Degryse, Scifo, Czerniatynski (Severeyns 67)

Ostrava, April 28, 1993
RCS (1) 1   Wales (1) 1
Latal 41   Hughes 31
Wales scored on effectively their first attack of the game, but as that was after 31 minutes it gives you some idea which team dominated the first half. It was never going to be an easy game against the combined teams of the Czech Republic and Slovakia. Young and Aizlewood were absent through suspension and Ratcliffe was injured and the point they eventually came away with probably satisfied them.

Representation of Czechs and Slovaks: Kouba, Glonek (Bejbl 66), Kedlec, Novotny, Vrabec, Latal, Nemec (Dubovsky 79), Kubik, Nemecek, Kuka, Luhovy.

Wales: Southall, Phillips, Bodin (Bowen 52), Melville, Symons, Blackmore, Horne, Saunders, Rush, Hughes, Giggs.

Toftir, June 6, 1993
Faeroes (0) 0   Wales (2) 3
                     Saunders 22, Young 31
                     Rush 69
In the dramatic setting of the Svangaskaro Stadium, Wales plotted their path to America with a comfortable 3-0 victory. Giggs was the tormentor, providing the cross for Saunder's goal which sent them on their way, for Young's 32 minute header that made it 2-0, and for Rush's final and spectacular volley.

Faeroes: Knudsen, Jakobsen, T Hansen, Johannesen, Justinussen, Reynatugvu (Ramussen 49), Nielsen, Dam, A Hansen, Reynheim (Mohr 59), Arge.

Wales: Southall, Phillips, Bodin, Aizlewood, Young (Melville 49), Symons, Horne, Saunders, Rush, Hughes (Speed 75), Giggs

Cardiff, Sept 8, 1993
Wales (2) 2   RCS (1) 2
Giggs 21   Kuka 16
Rush 35   Dubrovsky 67
A rare mistake by Mark Hughes let in Kuka to give the RCS team an early lead. Giggs pulled Wales back into the contest and Rush put them ahead, but in the 67th minute, Dubrovsky, the £2.5m forward with Real Madrid scored from a 25 yard free-kick.

Brussels, April 22, 1992
Belgium (1) 1   Cyprus (0) 0
Wilmots 24

Bucharest, May 6, 1992
Romania (5) 7   Faeroes (0) 0
Balint 4, 40, 78
Hagi 14, Lacatus 28 (pen)
Lupescu 44, Pana 55

Toftir, June 3, 1992
Faeroes (0) 0   Belgium (1) 3
                     Albert 30, Wilmots 65, 71

Toftir, June 16, 1992
Faeroes (0) 0   Cyprus (1) 2
                     Sotiriu 30, Papavasiliu 58

Prague, Sept 2, 1992
RCS(0) 1   Belgium (1) 2
Kadlec 77   Chovanec (og) 44
                  Czerniatynski 83

Kosice, Sept 23, 1992
RCS (1) 4   Faeroes (0) 0
Nemecek 24
Kuka 85, 87
Dubovsky 89 (pen)

Brussels, Oct 14, 1992
Belgium (1) 1   Romania (0) 0
Smidts 27

Bucharest, Nov 14, 1992
Romania (0) 1   RCS (0) 1
Dumitrescu 48   Nemecek 79 (pen)

Larnaca, Nov 29, 1992
Cyprus (1) 1   **Romania (2) 4**
Pittas 39 (pen)   *Popescu 4, Raducioiu 36*
                      Hagi 73, Hanganu 86

Nicosia, Feb 13, 1993
Cyprus (0) 0   **Belgium (2) 3**
                      Scifo 2, 4, Albert 87

Limassol, March 24, 1993
Cyprus (0) 1   **RCS (1) 1**
Sotiriou 47   *Moravcik 33*

Bucharest, April 14, 1993
Romania (1) 2   **Cyprus (1) 1**
Dumitrescu 33, 55   *Sotiriou 23*

Limassol, April 25, 1993
Cyprus (2) 3   **Faeroes (0) 1**
Xiuruppas 7   *Arge 82*
Sotiriou 43
Ioannou 75

Brussels, May 22, 1993
Belgium (1) 3   **Faeroes (0) 0**
Wilmots 32, 75
Scifo 50 (pen)

Kosice, June 2, 1993
RCS (2) 5   **Romania (1) 2**
Vrabec 13   *Raducioiu 26, 55*
Latal 37
Dubovsky 58, 83, 89

Toftir, June 16, 1993
Faeroes (0) 0   **RCS (3) 3**
                      Hasek 3, Postulka 38, 44

Toftir, Sept 8,1993
Faeroes (0) 0   **Romania (1) 4**
                      Raducioiu 23, 58, 60, 76

GROUP 5
Table us at Sept 30

	P	W	D	L	F	A	Pts
Russia	7	5	2	0	15	3	12
Greece	6	4	2	0	6	1	10
Iceland	7	2	2	3	6	6	6
Hungary	7	1	1	5	5	11	3
Luxembourg	5	0	1	4	1	12	1

Athens, May 13, 1992
Greece (1) 1   **Iceland (0) 0**
Sofanidis 28

Budapest, June 3, 1992
Hungary (1) 1   **Iceland (0) 2**
Kiprich 3   *Orlygsson 51, Magnusson 73*

Luxembourg, Sept 9, 1992
Luxembourg (0) 0 **Hungary (1) 3**
                      Detari 16, Kovacs 52, 79

Reykjavik, Oct 7, 1992
Iceland (0) 0   **Greece (0) 1**
                      Tsaluhidis 61

Moscow, Oct 14, 1992
Russia (0) 1   **Iceland (0) 0**
Yuran 64

Moscow, Oct 28, 1992
Russia (2) 2   **Luxembourg (0) 0**
Yuran 4
Radchenko 23

Salonika, Nov 11, 1992
Greece (0) 0   **Hungary (0) 0**

Athens, Feb 17, 1993
Greece (1) 4   **Luxembourg (0) 0**
Dimitriadis 30 (pen)
Mitropoulos 65

Budapest, March 31, 1993
Hungary (0) 0   **Greece (0) 1**
                      Apostolakis 70

Luxembourg, April 14, 1993
Luxembourg (0) 0 **Russia (1) 4**
                      Kiriakov 12, 46
                      Shalimov 57, Kulkov 90

Moscow, April 28, 1993
Russia (0) 3   **Hungary (0) 0**
Kanchelskis 55
Kolivanov 60
Yuran 86

Luxembourg, May 20, 1993
Luxembourg (0) 1 **Iceland (1) 1**
Birgisson (og) 70   *Gudjohnsen 40*

Moscow, May 23, 1993
Russia (0) 1   **Greece (1) 1**
Dobrovolski 75 (pen) *Mitropoulos 45*

Reykjavik, June 2, 1993
Iceland (1) 1   **Russia (1) 1**
Sverrisson 26   *Kiriakov 38*

Reykjavik, June 16, 1993
Iceland (1) 2   **Hungary (0) 0**
Sverrisson 13
Gudjohnsen 77

Budapest, Sept 8,1993
Hungary (1) 1   **Russia (1) 3**
Nikiforov 21   *Pyatnitski 15*
                      Kiryakov 53
                      Borodyuk 90

GROUP 6
Table as at Sept 30

	P	W	D	L	F	A	Pts
France	8	6	1	1	14	5	13
Sweden	8	5	2	1	15	5	12
Bulgaria	8	4	2	2	13	8	10
Austria	7	3	0	4	12	10	6
Finland	8	1	1	6	4	14	3
Israel	7	0	2	5	5	21	2

Helsinki, May 14, 1992
Finland (0) 0　　**Bulgaria (2) 3**
　　　　　　　　　　Balakov 16
　　　　　　　　　　Kostadinov 25, 85

Sofia, Sept 9, 1992
Bulgaria (2) 2　　**France (0) 0**
Stoichkov 21 (pen)
Balakov 29

Halsinki, Sept 9, 1992
Finland (0) 0　　**Sweden (0) 1**
　　　　　　　　　　Ingesson 77 (pen)

Stockholm, Oct 7, 1992
Sweden (0) 2　　**Bulgaria (0) 0**
Dahlin 56
Pettersson 76

Paris, Oct 14, 1992
France (1) 2　　**Austria (0) 0**
Papin 3, Cantona 77

Vienna, Oct 28, 1992
Austria (2) 6　　**Israel (0) 2**
Herzog 41, 46　　*Zohar 57, 77*
Polster 49, Stoger 56
Ogris 87

Tel Aviv, Nov 11, 1992
Israel (1) 1　　**Sweden (1) 3**
Banin 42　　　　*Limpar 37, Dahlin 58*
　　　　　　　　　　Ingesson 74

Paris, Nov 14, 1992
France (2) 2　　**Finland (0) 1**
Papin 17　　　　*Jarvinen 54*
Cantona 31

Tel Aviv, Dec 2, 1992
Israel (0) 0　　**Bulgaria (0) 2**
　　　　　　　　　　Sirakov 55, Penev 83

Tel Aviv, Feb 17, 1993
Israel (0) 0　　**France (1) 4**
　　　　　　　　　　Cantona 28, Blanc 62, 84
　　　　　　　　　　Roche 89

Vienna, March 27, 1993
Austria (0) 0　　**France (0) 1**
　　　　　　　　　　Papin 58

Vienna, April 14, 1993
Austria (2) 3　　**Bulgaria (0) 1**

Pfeifenberger 11　　*Ivanov 54*
Kuhbauer 25
Polster 89

Paris, April 28, 1993
France (1) 2　　**Sweden (1) 1**
Cantona 42 (pen), 82　*Dahlin 14*

Sofia, April 28, 1993
Bulgaria (2) 2　　**Finland (0) 0**
Stoichkov 14
Yankov 43

Sofia, May 12, 1993
Bulgaria (1) 2　　**Israel (0) 2**
Stoichkov 35 (pen)　*R Harazi*
Sirakov 60　　　　*Rosenthal 53*

Pori, May 13, 1993
Finland (2) 3　　**Austria (0) 1**
Paatelainen 17　　*Zisser 89*
Rajamaki 20
Hjelm 50

Stockholm, May 19, 1993
Sweden (0) 1　　**Austria (0) 0**
Eriksson 50

Stockholm, June 2, 1993
Sweden (2) 5　　**Israel (0) 0**
Brolin 17, 41, 65
Zetterberg 55
Landberg 89

Lahti, June 16, 1993
Finland (0) 0　　**Israel (0) 0**

Sofia, Sept 8,1993
Bulgaria (1) 1　　**Sweden (1) 1**
Stoichkov 21　　*Dahlin 26*

Helsinki, Sept 8, 1993
Finland (0) 0　　**France (0) 2**
　　　　　　　　　　Blanc 47
　　　　　　　　　　Papin (pen) 55

CONCACAF
Pre-preliminary round
Dominican Republic 1 Puerto Rico 2; Puerto Rico 1
Dominican Republic 1; St Lucia 1 St Vincent 0; St Vincent
3 St Lucia 1.

Preliminary round
Bermuda 1 Haiti 0; Haiti 2 Bermuda 1; Jamaica 2 Puerto
Rico 1; Puerto Rico 0 Jamaica 3; Cuba withdrew St
Vincent w.o; Netherlands Antilles 1 Antigua 1; Antigua 3
Netherlands Antilles 0; Guyana 1 Surinam 2; Surinam 1
Guyana 1; Barbados 1 Trinidad & Tobago 2; Trinidad &
Tobago 3 Barbados 0.

First round
Central Region
Guatemala 0 Honduras 0; Honduras 2 Guatemala 0;
Panama 1 Costa Rica 0; Costa Rica 5 Panama 1;

Nicaragua 0 El Salvador 5; El Salvador 5 Nicaragua 1.

Caribbean Region
Surinam 0 St Vincent 0; St Vincent 2 Surinam 1; Antigua 0
Bermuda 3; Bermuda 2 Antigua 1; Trinidad & Tobago 1
Jamaica 2; Jamaica 1 Trinidad & Tobago 1.

Second Round
Group A: Costa Rica 2 Honduras 3; St Vincent 0 Mexico
4; Mexico 2 Honduras 0; St Vincent 0 Costa Rica 1;
Mexico 4 Costa Rica 0; St Vincent 0 Honduras 4;
Honduras 4 St Vincent 0; Costa Rica 2 Mexico 0;
Honduras 2 Costa Rica 1; Mexico 11 St Vincent 0; Costa
Rica 5 St Vincent 0; Honduras 1 Mexico 1.

Group B: Bermuda 1 El Salvador 0; Jamaica 1 Canada 1;
Bermuda 1 Jamaica 1; El Salvador 1 Canada 1; Canada 1
Jamaica 0; El Salvador 4 Bermuda 1; Canada 2 El
Salvador 3; Jamaica 3 Bermuda 2; Canada 4 Bermuda 2;
Jamaica 0 El Salvador 2; Bermuda 0 Canada 0; El
Salvador 2 Jamaica 1.

Third Round
Honduras 2 Canada 2; El Salvador 2 Mexico 1; Canada 2
El Salvador 0; Mexico 3 Honduras 0; Canada 3 Honduras
1; Mexico 3 El Salvador 1; Honduras 2 El Salvador 0;
Mexico 4 Canada 0; Honduras 1 Mexico 4; El Salvador 1
Canada 2; Canada 1 Mexico 2; El Salvador 2 Honduras 1.
Mexico qualified for finals in USA.

OCEANIA

Group 1: Solomon Islands 1 Tahiti 1; Solomon Islands 1
Australia 2; Tahiti 0 Australia 3; Australia 2 Tahiti 0;
Australia 1 Solomon Islands 1; Tahiti 4 Solomon Islands
2.

Group 2: New Zealand 3 Fiji 0; Vanuatu 1 New Zealand
4; New Zealand 8 Vanuatu 0; Fiji 3 Vanuatu 0; Fiji 0 New
Zealand 0; Vanuatu 0 Fiji 3.

Second round
New Zealand 0 Australia 1; Australia 3 New Zealand 0.

Fourteen members of the Ugbowo Bombers football
team from Nigeria disappeared in Sweden after
competing in the Gothia Cup competition in
Gothenberg.

AFRICA

First round
Group A: Algeria 3 Burundi 1; Burundi 1 Ghana 0;
Ghana 2 Algeria 0; Burundi 0 Algeria 0; Ghana 1 Burundi
0; Algeria 2 Ghana 1.
Uganda withdrew

Group B: Zaire 4 Liberia 2; Cameroon 5 Swaziland 0;
Swaziland 1 Zaire 0; Zaire 1 Cameroon 2; Swaziland 0
Cameroon 0; Zaire v Swaziland not played; Cameroon 0

Zaire 0.
Liberia withdrew

Group C: Zimbabwe 1 Togo 0; Egypt 1 Angola 0; Togo 1
Egypt 4; Zimbabwe 2 Egypt 1; Angola 1 Zimbabwe 1;
Togo 1 Zimbabwe 2; Angola 0 Egypt 0; Egypt 3 Togo 0;
Zimbabwe 2 Angola 1; Angola v Togo not played; Egypt
0 Zimbabwe 0; Togo 0 Angola 1.

Group D: Nigeria 4 South Africa 0; South Africa 1 Congo
0; Congo 0 Nigeria 1; South Africa 0 Nigeria 0; Congo 0
South Africa 1; Nigeria 2 Congo 0.
Libya withdrew

Group E: Ivory Coast 6 Botswana 0; Niger 0 Ivory Coast
0; Botswana 0 Niger 1; Botswana 0 Ivory Coast 0; Ivory
Coast 1 Niger 0; Niger 2 Botswana 1.
Sudan withdrew

Group F: Morocco 5 Ethiopia 0; Tunisia 5 Benin 1; Benin
0 Morocco 1; Ethiopia 0 Tunisia 0; Ethiopia 3 Benin 1;
Tunisia 1 Morocco 1; Benin 0 Tunisia 5; Ethiopia 0
Morocco 1; Morocco 5 Benin 0; Tunisia 3 Ethiopia 0;
Benin 1 Ethiopia 0; Morocco 0 Tunisia 0.

Group G: Gabon 3 Mozambique 1; Mazambique 0
Senegal 1; Gabon 3 Senegal 2; Mozambique 1 Gabon 1;
Senegal 6 Mozambique 1; Senegal 1 Gabon 0.
Mauritania withdrew

Group H: Madagascar 3 Namibia 0; Zambia 2 Tanzania
0; Tanzania 0 Madagascar 0; Namibia 0 Zambia 4;
Tanzania 2 Namibia 0; Madagascar 2 Cambia 0; Tanzania
1 Zambia 3; Namibia 0 Madagascar 1; Zambia 4 Namibia
0; Zambia 3 Madagascar 1
Tanzania withdrew

Group I: Guinea 4 Kenya 0; Kenya 2 Guinea 0
Mali and Gambia withdrew

Second round
Group A: Algeria 1 Ivory Coast 1; Ivory Coast 2
Nigeria 1; Nigeria 4 Ivory Coast 1
Group B: Morocco 1 Senegal 0; Zambia 2 Morocco 1 (*This
was Zambias first international since the Apr 28 air crash that
wiped out their national squad*); Zambia 4 Senegal 0

Group C: Cameroon 3 Guinea 1; Guinea 3 Zimbabwe 0;
Zimbabwe 1 Guinea 0

MORE SERIOUS THAN THAT

After Iraq beat China 1-0 in the World Cup
qualifying match, nine people died during the
celebrations. Another 120 were injured by what
was described as 'rogue' gunfire.

Celebrations in Columbia after its 5-0 win over
Argentina in a World Cup qualifier left 20 dead
and 100 injured

ASIA

First round

Group A: Jordan 1 Yemen 1; Pakistan 0 China 5; Jordan 1 Iraq 1; Yemen 5 Pakistan 1; Iraq 6 Yemen 1; Jordan 0 China 3; Iraq 8 Pakistan 0; Yemen 1 China 0; Iraq 1 China 0; Jordan 3 Pakistan 1; China 3 Pakistan 0; Yemen 1 Jordan 1; Iraq 4 Jordan 0; Yemen 3 Pakistan 0; China 4 Jordan 1; Iraq 3 Yemen 0; Iraq 4 Pakistan 0; China 1 Yemen 0; Pakistan 5 Jordan 0; China 2 Iraq 1.

Group B: Syria 2 Taiwan 0; Iran 0 Oman 0.
Myanmar withdrew

Group C: Korea DPR 3 Vietnam 0; Qatar 3 Indonesia 1; Korea DPR 2 Singapore 1; Qatar 4 Vietnam 0; Korea DPR 4 Indonesia 0; Vietnam 2 Singapore 3; Qatar 4 Singapore 1; Vietnam 1 Indonesia 0; Indonesia 0 Singapore 2; Qatar 1 Korea DPR 2; Indonesia 1 Qatar 4; Vietnam 0 Korea DPR 1; Singapore 1 Korea DPR 3; Vietnam 0 Qatar 4; Indonesia 1 Korea DPR 2; Singapore 1 Vietnam 0; Indonesia 2 Vietnam 1; Singapore 1 Qatar 0; Korea DPR 2 Qatar 2; Singapore 2 Indonesia 1

Group D: Hong Kong 2 Bahrain 1; Lebanon 2 India 2; Bahrain 0 Korea Rep 0; Lebanon 2 Hong Kong 2; India 1 Hong Kong 2; Lebanon 0 Korea Rep 1; India 0 Korea Rep 3; Lebanon 0 Bahrain 0; Bahrain 2 India 1; Hong Kong 0 Korea Rep 3; Bahrain 0 Lebanon 0; Korea Rep 4 Hong Kong 1; Bahrain 3 India 0; Korea Rep 2 Lebanon 0; Korea Rep 7 India 0; Lebanon 2 Hong Kong 1; Lebanon 2 India 1; Bahrain 3 Hong Kong 0; Korea Rep 3 Bahrain 0; India 3 Hong Kong 1

Group E: Macao 0 Saudi Arabia 6; Malaysia 1 Kuwait 1; Macao 1 Kuwait 10; Malaysia 1 Saudi Arabia 1; Kuwait 0 Saudi Arabia 0; Malaysia 9 Macao 0; Kuwait 2 Malaysia 0; Saudi Arabia 8 Macao 0; Kuwait 8 Macao 0; Saudi Arabia 3 Malaysia 0; Macao 0 Malaysia 5; Saudi Arabia 2 Kuwait 0

Group F: Japan 1 Thailand 0; Sri Lanka 0 UAE 4; Japan 8 Bangladesh 0; Thailand 1 Sri Lanka 0; Sri Lanka 0 Bangladesh 1; UAE 1 Thailand 0; Japan 5 Sri Lanka 0; UAE 1 Bangladesh 0; Japan 2 UAE 0; Thailand 4 Bangladesh 1; Thailand 0 Japan 1; UAE 3 Sri Lanka 0; Bangladesh 1 Japan 4; Thailand 1 UAE 2; Bangladesh 0 UAE 7; Sri Lanka 0 Thailand 3; Bangladesh 1 Thailand 4; Sri Lanka 0 Japan 6; Bangladesh 3 Sri Lanka 0; UAE 1 Japan 1

THE 100 CAPS CLUB		
As at Aug 20		
1	Peter Shilton (ENG)	125
2	Pat Jennings (NIR)	119
3	Heinz Hermann (SUI)	117
4	Björn Nordqvist (SWE)	115
5	Dino Zoff (ITA)	112
6	Héctor Chumpitaz (PER)	111
7	Oleg Blochin (RUS)	109
8	Ladislau Bölöni (ROM)	108
	Bobby Moore (ENG)	108
10	Bobby Charlton (ENG)	106
11	Billy Wright (ENG)	106
12	Grzegorz Lato (POL)	104
	Torbjørn Svenssen (NOR)	104
14	Franz Beckenbauer (GER)	103
15	Soon-Ho Choi (KOR)	102
	Kenny Dalglish (SCO)	102
	Kazimierz Deyna (POL)	102
	Morton Olsen (DEN)	102
	Joachim Streich (GDR)	102
20	Lothar Matthäus (GER)	101
	Thomas Ravelli (SWE)	101
22	Joszef Bozsik (HUN)	100
	Djalma Santos (BRA)	100
	Hans-Jürgen Dörner (GDR)	100

The Tottenham Roadshow

In 1991 (was it really that recent?) Terry Venables brought Alan Sugar into Tottenham Hotspur in order to fend off the undesirable attentions of Robert Maxwell who, as we now know, was planning to spend a bit more pension money acquiring the aforesaid club. Venables and Sugar was a marriage made in Heaven (ish), but within two years they were talking like this........

"Alan Sugar has voted to dismiss me and I am talking to my solicitors..." Venables on May 14. The same day, Venables got an injunction against his dismissal until a full court hearing on May 25. That hearing reinstated Venables until June 8th

"My first aim, in a nutshell, is to professionalise the club" Sugar, after the board had sacked Venables.

"I'm overwhelmed by the support I've received from the fans, it makes all the difference" Venables

"I know there is no point in trying to take Terry on in the press, especially in the back pages. I know that if Terry was seen stabbing someone in public his supporters would simply swear the guy fell on the knife" Sugar

"He wants me out. He wants to run the whole show. But I will not let it die because when it comes to shares and money, I will be the loser. My life is on the line, I have invested everything and more in Tottenham" Venables

"I promise you, Terry has picked on the wrong bloke. He's not dealing with a Barmitzvah boy" Sugar

"I'd rather fight my corner and pay for the fight than surrender. If I get done, I'll walk away. At least I'll be able to sleep at night" Venables

"Mr Venables told me Brian Clough likes a bung..." Sugar in court, allegations that Clough denies, threatening to "sue the socks off" Sugar. The court hearing fails to grant an injunction against Venables' sacking. Five days later, Ossie Ardiles is appointed the new manager of Tottenham. His popularity helping to defuse some of the fans unrest. Venables has to put a bond of £300,000 into court if he is to continue his action.

"This does not affect anything. I am determined to go ahead" Venables in July, a month later Sugar applies for a court order to strike out Venables' action on the grounds that he still has not paid the bond. On September 2nd, Venables sells all but a nominal holding in Spurs. His 3,542,937 shares sell for 91p each, realising a total of £3,224,072 which, Venables states, will allow him to repay his total borrowings. He maintains that he will continue with his action for wrongful dismissal.

"I have an open mind about what to do next" Venables, after selling his shares. Two weeks later, a Panorama television programme alleges that Venables acted illegally when he raised the money to buy the Tottenham Hotspur shares in the first place, selling assets from a company in which he no longer owned. *To be continued.............*

United at Last

"There's been a lot of talk about me getting married, but if Manchester United win the championship I definitely will," said a confident George Best in January. At that stage Norwich City had taken their tidy football to the top of the League, although they were nobody's favourites to stay the course. Ron Atkinson's Villa looked likeliest and on February 13, victory at Chelsea took them over Norwich. Villa did themselves no favours by losing to Oldham at the final hurdle, but the title was won by an impressive show of form in the home straight. Where United had faded in 1992, they flourished in 1993.

Seven straight victories, beginning with a crucial 3-1 away win at Carrow Road, made the championship theirs. They did it with some panache, too. But you would expect that in a side that contains Cantona, Giggs and Kanchelskis. It took a time coming and it cost a lot of money, as well, the list below is a formidable account sheet. It only shows one side of the balance sheet, but then they haven't really sold a lot of players during Ferguson's reign. To their eternal shame, though, Manchester United finished bottom of the Meat Pie League. BBC2's Standing Room Only compiled the League, visiting 15 clubs and tasting the fare on offer. The verdict on United's pies was that they "tasted like pre-chewed dog food". Top of the League was Notts County. We have no information on the pies at Villa, but the team hung on to second place, ahead of Norwich. Blackburn have spent almost as much money as United in their quest for success, but Dalglish's team were checked by the absence of Alan Shearer, the costliest of all, for the second half of the season.

Leeds almost followed a League title with relegation and Liverpool and Arsenal both had poor seasons. Liverpool eventually finished sixth, but were a long way off the pace. Arsenal couldn't score goals; their 40 goals for was the lowest in the division. Even Nottingham Forest got more. Arsenal, though, had a couple of cups as compensation, Forest didn't.

Nottingham Forest occupied bottom spot for most of the year, so their demise was greeted with sadness, but not surprise. Their manager and two best players left immediately and the chimes rang for the end of an era. Crystal Palace went down, but only by a hair's breadth and Middlesbrough by a bit more

MONEY LIKE WATER

In just over six years at Manchester United, Alex Ferguson has spent almost £23 million to create a championship winning team. It's a tactic that appears to be working; not only did United win the League title, but the company decared a profit(91/92) of £5.1m. Below are the signings that Ferguson has made.

Brian McClair	Celtic (June 87)	£850,000
Viv Anderson	Arsenal (Jul 87)	£250,000
Steve Bruce	Norwich (Dec 87)	£825,000
Lee Sharpe	Torquay (May 88)	£180,000
Jim Leighton	Aberdeen (May 88)	£750,000
Mark Hughes	Barcelona (Jun 88)	£1,800,000
Mal Donaghy	Luton (Oct 88)	£650,000
Ralph Milne	Bristol C (Nov 88)	£170,000
Guiliano Maiorana	Histon (Nov 88)	£30,000
Mike Phelan	Norwich (Jun 89)	£750,000
Neil Webb	Notts F (Jun 89)	£1,500,000
Brian Carey	Cork (Jul 89)	£100,000
Gary Pallister	M'boro (Aug 89)	£2,300,000
Danny Wallace	Soton (Sept 89)	£1,200,000
Paul Ince	West Ham (Sept 89)	£1,500,000
Dennis Irwin	Oldham (Jun 90)	£625,000
Neil Whitworth	Wigan (Jun 90)	£150,000
Andrei Kanchelskis	Donetsk (Apr 91)	£650,000
Peter Schmeichel	Brondby (Jul 91)	£550,000
Paul Parker	QPR (Aug 91)	£2,000,000
Dion Dublin	Cambridge (Aug 92)	£1,000,000
Pat McGibbon	Portadown (Aug 92)	£100,000
Eric Cantona	Leeds (Nov 92)	£1,200,000
Roy Keane	Notts F (June 93)	£3,750,000
	TOTAL	£22,880,000

English Football

FA Premier League 1992-93

		P	W	D	L	GF	GA	W	D	L	GF	GA	PTS	GD
1	Manchester United	42	14	5	2	39	14	10	7	4	28	17	84	+36
2	Aston Villa	42	13	5	3	36	16	8	6	7	21	24	74	+17
3	Norwich City	42	13	6	2	31	19	8	3	10	30	46	72	-4
4	Blackburn Rovers	42	13	4	4	38	18	7	7	7	30	28	71	+22
5	Queens Park Rangers	42	11	5	5	41	32	6	7	8	22	23	63	+8
6	Liverpool	42	13	4	4	41	18	3	7	11	21	37	59	+7
7	Sheffield Wednesday	42	9	8	4	34	26	6	6	9	21	25	59	+4
8	Tottenham Hotspur	42	11	5	5	40	25	5	6	10	20	41	59	-6
9	Manchester City	42	7	8	6	30	25	8	4	9	26	26	57	+5
10	Arsenal	42	8	6	7	25	20	7	5	9	15	18	56	+2
11	Chelsea	42	9	7	5	29	22	5	7	9	22	32	56	-3
12	Wimbledon	42	9	4	8	32	23	5	8	8	24	32	54	+1
13	Everton	42	7	6	8	26	27	8	2	11	27	28	53	-2
14	Sheffield United	42	10	6	5	33	19	4	4	13	21	34	52	+1
15	Coventry City	42	7	4	10	29	28	6	9	6	23	29	52	-5
16	Ipswich Town	42	8	9	4	29	22	4	7	10	21	33	52	-5
17	Leeds United	42	12	8	1	40	17	0	7	14	17	45	51	-5
18	Southampton	42	10	6	5	30	21	3	5	13	24	40	50	-7
19	Oldham Athletic	42	10	6	5	43	30	3	4	14	20	44	49	-11
20	Crystal Palace	42	6	9	6	27	25	5	7	9	21	36	49	-13
21	Middlesbrough	42	8	5	8	33	27	3	6	12	21	48	44	-21
22	Nottingham Forest	42	6	4	11	17	25	4	6	11	24	37	40	-21

QUOTES

"I don't think we'll go down, but then the captain of the Titanic probably said the same thing"

Neville Southall, as Everton came dangerously close to the relegation zone

"There's more ice down there [in the dressing room] than sank the Bismarck"

Gerry Francis, referring to QPR's injuries and getting his boats in a twist.

"Compared to the chairman I had at my previous club, Ken Bates is Mary Poppins"

David Webb, in February, when he was still manager at Chelsea.

"I've got nine black players at our club. What's racist about calling someone 'big nose' ?"

Wimbledon manager Joe Kinnear accused of making anti-Semitic gestures at Tottenham fans.

"I scored the goal that won the championship, but I'm not happy. I'm a Liverpool supporter"

Oldham's Nick Henry, whose winner against Aston Villa secured the title for Manchester United.

"Alex has had to wait seven years for this, but I've been waiting for 26"

United chairman, Martin Edwards.

"It's not like Vinnie. He certainly knows his way to the FA"

Wimbledon chief executive Dave Barnard when Jones was late for a disciplinary hearing.

PREMIER LEAGUE SCORERS

Leading Scorers		League	Other Comps
Teddy Sheringham	Tottenham (Notts F)	22 (1)	7
Les Ferdinand	QPR	20	4
Mick Quinn	Coventry	19 (2)	3 (3)
Dean Holdsworth	Wimbledon	19	0
Alan Shearer	Blackburn	16	6
David White	Man City	16	3
Ian Wright	Arsenal	15	16
Brian Deane	Sheff Utd	15	5
Matthew Le Tissier	Southampton	15	3
Eric Cantona	Man Utd (Leeds)	15 (6)	2 (2)
Mark Hughes	Man Utd	15	1
Ian Rush	Liverpool	14	4
Lee Chapman	Leeds	14	4
Dean Saunders	Aston Villa (L'pool)	14 (1)	4

Total Premier League attendances 9,759,809

	Arsenal	Aston Villa	Blackburn	Chelsea	Coventry	Crystal Pal	Everton	Ipswich	Leeds U	Liverpool	Man City	Man United	Middlesboro	Norwich C	Notts Forest	Oldham A	QPR	Sheff U	Sheff Weds	Southamptn	Tottenham	Wimbledon
Arsenal	****	0-1	0-1	2-1	3-0	3-0	1-0	2-1	3-0	3-0	1-0	0-1	1-1	2-4	1-1	2-0	1-1	1-1	2-1	4-3	1-3	0-1
Aston Villa	1-0	****	0-0	1-3	3-0	3-0	1-0	1-1	1-1	2-1	1-1	1-0	2-3	1-0	0-1	1-3	2-1	0-2	1-2	2-0	0-0	1-0
Blackburn	1-0	0-0	****	0-1	2-0	1-2	2-3	2-1	1-1	0-0	1-0	0-0	3-2	0-0	1-3	0-1	0-3	1-3	0-0	1-1	1-2	0-0
Chelsea	1-0	0-1	2-0	****	2-1	1-2	2-1	1-1	1-1	2-1	2-4	1-0	0-0	0-0	3-0	1-0	3-1	4-2	3-3	1-0	1-2	4-2
Coventry	0-2	3-0	2-5	2-1	****	2-2	2-0	0-0	2-2	4-1	1-0	0-1	1-1	1-1	1-1	0-1	1-1	1-1	2-2	2-2	0-2	0-2
Crystal Palace	1-2	1-0	3-3	1-2	2-2	****	0-2	3-1	1-0	1-1	0-0	0-1	0-2	4-1	4-2	1-3	1-3	2-0	2-1	1-0	2-2	4-0
Everton	0-0	1-0	2-1	2-1	3-1	0-2	****	3-0	2-0	2-1	3-1	0-2	2-2	1-1	0-2	1-0	4-2	1-0	1-0	2-1	2-1	1-3
Ipswich	1-2	1-1	2-1	1-1	2-1	3-1	3-0	****	1-0	2-2	3-1	1-2	2-2	3-1	2-2	2-2	0-1	0-3	1-1	4-3	1-1	1-0
Leeds	3-0	1-1	5-2	1-1	2-1	0-0	2-0	4-2	****	2-2	4-0	0-2	4-1	2-2	1-4	2-0	2-1	3-1	1-1	0-0	5-0	1-0
Liverpool	0-2	2-1	1-2	2-1	4-0	5-0	1-0	2-2	2-0	****	2-3	2-2	1-2	1-0	1-0	1-0	3-2	0-1	2-2	1-1	6-2	2-3
Man City	0-1	1-1	3-2	0-1	1-0	0-0	2-5	3-1	4-0	1-1	****	2-1	2-0	2-1	0-2	0-1	0-1	3-0	0-1	0-1	0-1	0-1
Man United	0-0	3-1	3-1	3-0	5-0	1-0	0-3	1-2	0-0	2-2	1-1	****	1-1	1-3	1-3	1-0	2-1	1-3	1-3	2-1	4-1	1-2
Middlesboro	1-0	2-3	3-2	0-0	0-2	4-1	2-2	0-1	3-0	1-2	2-0	1-3	****	1-0	1-2	2-3	0-1	2-	2-1	3-2	3-0	2-0
Norwich City	1-1	1-0	0-0	0-0	1-1	4-2	1-1	3-1	4-2	1-0	2-3	1-3	3-0	****	0-3	0-2	2-1	0-2	1-0	1-2	0-0	3-0
Notts Forest	0-1	0-1	1-3	3-0	1-1	1-1	1-0	2-1	1-4	0-0	2-1	1-2	1-2	0-2	****	1-3	1-0	0-3	1-0	1-2	2-1	1-0
Oldham	0-1	1-1	0-1	1-0	0-1	1-1	2-2	0-0	2-0	3-0	0-1	0-1	3-0	2-1	3-3	****	2-0	1-2	2-2	4-3	2-1	5-2
QPR	0-0	2-1	0-3	3-1	2-0	1-3	4-2	0-1	2-1	1-0	3-5	2-1	0-1	1-0	1-0	2-0	****	1-0	1-2	4-3	2-1	0-2
Sheff United	1-1	0-2	1-3	4-2	1-2	2-0	1-0	0-3	3-1	0-1	3-0	1-3	2-	0-2	0-3	1-2	1-0	****	1-1	2-0	2-0	1-1
Sheff Weds	1-0	1-2	0-0	3-3	2-2	1-0	1-0	1-1	1-1	2-2	0-1	1-3	2-1	1-0	1-0	2-2	1-0	1-1	****	5-2	2-0	2-0
Southampton	2-0	2-0	1-1	1-0	1-2	2-2	2-1	4-3	0-0	0-0	0-1	1-0	2-1	1-2	1-2	4-3	1-1	3-2	1-2	****	0-0	1-2
Tottenham	1-0	0-0	1-2	1-2	0-2	2-2	2-1	0-2	0-0	2-0	0-1	1-1	3-0	0-0	2-1	2-1	1-1	0-0	0-2	4-2	****	1-1
Wimbledon	3-2	2-3	1-1	0-0	1-2	4-0	1-3	0-1	1-0	0-1	1-2	1-2	2-0	3-0	1-0	5-2	0-2	1-1	1-2	1-2	1-1	****

Barclays League 1992-93

Division One

		P	W	D	L	GF	GA	W	D	L	GF	GA	PTS	GS
1	Newcastle United	46	16	6	1	58	15	13	3	7	34	23	96	92
2	West Ham United	46	16	5	2	50	17	10	5	8	31	24	88	81
3	Portsmouth	46	19	2	2	48	9	7	8	8	32	37	88	80
4	Tranmere Rovers	46	15	4	4	48	24	8	6	9	24	32	79	72
5	Swindon Town	46	15	5	3	41	23	6	8	9	33	36	76	74
6	Leicester City	46	14	5	4	43	24	8	5	10	28	40	76	71
7	Millwall	46	14	6	3	46	21	4	10	9	19	32	70	65
8	Derby County	46	11	2	10	40	33	8	7	8	28	24	66	68
9	Grimsby Town	46	12	6	5	33	25	7	1	15	25	32	64	58
10	Peterborough United	46	7	11	5	30	26	9	3	11	25	37	62	55
11	Wolverhampton Wndrs	46	11	6	6	37	26	5	7	11	20	30	61	57
12	Charlton Athletic	46	10	8	5	28	19	6	5	12	21	27	61	49
13	Barnsley	46	12	4	7	29	19	5	5	13	27	41	60	56
14	Oxford United	46	8	7	8	27	30	6	6	11	24	35	56	53
15	Bristol City	46	10	7	6	29	25	4	7	12	20	42	56	49
16	Watford	46	8	7	8	27	30	6	6	11	30	41	55	57
17	Notts County	46	10	7	6	33	21	2	9	12	22	49	52	55
18	Southend United	46	9	8	6	33	22	4	5	14	21	42	52	54
19	Birmingham City	46	10	4	9	30	32	3	8	12	20	40	51	50
20	Luton Town	46	6	13	4	26	26	4	8	11	22	36	51	48
21	Sunderland	46	9	6	8	34	28	4	5	14	16	36	50	50
22	Brentford	46	7	6	10	28	30	6	4	13	24	41	49	52
23	Cambridge United	46	8	6	9	28	30	3	10	10	19	37	49	48
24	Bristol Rovers	46	6	6	11	30	42	4	5	14	25	45	41	55

QUOTES

"I would say that football is bent from the top downwards. There is dodgy dealing, a lot of brown paper-bagging"

David Kohler, chairman of Luton Town.

"It may be a dump, but it's our dump"

Millwall fans on the last day of the old Den, before moving round the corner to a swish new ground.

"The only reason I used to go into bars was to see if any of my players were there"

Malcolm Allison, Bristol Rovers manager reflecting on his past playboy image and being ironic (we think).

"When I lose my temper at home I don't take it out on my wife, Kay, and the two kids. I go for a walk so I can beat the dog up instead"

West Ham(now Liverpool) hard man Julian Dicks being ironic (we hope).

"Tell Alex Ferguson, we're on our way. Unless he's too busy celebrating"

Kevin Keegan, manager of Newcastle.

LEADING SCORERS

		League	Other Comps
Guy Whittingham	Portsmouth	42	5
Andy Cole	Newcastle (Br C)	24 (12)	4 (4)
Gary Blissett	Brentford	21	8
John Aldridge	Tranmere Rovers	21	5
David Kelly	Newcastle	21	4
Trevor Morley	West Ham	20	2
Craig Maskell	Swindon Town	19	5
Paul Furlong	Watford	19	3
Paul Gray	Luton Town	19	1
Paul Kitson	Derby County	17	6
Tony Adcock	Peterborough	16	3
Steve Bull	Wolverhampton	16	3
Stan Collymore	Southend	15	3

Division One attendances 5,874,017

Barclays League 1992-93

Division Two

		P	W	D	L	GF	GA	W	D	L	GF	GA	PTS	GS
1	Stoke City	46	17	4	2	41	13	10	8	5	32	21	93	73
2	Bolton Wanderers	46	18	2	3	48	14	9	7	7	32	27	90	80
3	Port Vale	46	14	7	2	44	17	12	4	7	35	27	89	79
4	West Bromwich Albion	46	17	3	3	56	22	8	7	8	32	32	85	88
5	Swansea City	46	12	7	4	38	17	8	6	9	27	30	73	65
6	Stockport County	46	11	11	1	47	18	8	4	11	34	39	72	81
7	Leyton Orient	46	16	4	3	49	20	5	5	13	20	33	72	69
8	Reading	46	14	4	5	44	20	4	11	8	22	31	69	66
9	Brighton & Hove Albion	46	13	4	6	36	24	7	5	11	27	35	69	63
10	Bradford City	46	12	5	6	36	24	6	9	8	33	43	68	69
11	Rotherham United	46	9	7	7	30	27	8	7	8	30	33	65	60
12	Fulham	46	9	9	5	28	22	7	8	8	29	33	65	57
13	Burnley	46	11	8	4	38	21	4	8	11	19	38	61	57
14	Plymouth Argyle	46	11	6	6	38	28	5	6	12	21	36	60	59
15	Huddersfield Town	46	10	6	7	30	22	7	3	13	24	39	60	54
16	Hartlepool United	46	8	6	9	19	23	6	6	11	23	37	54	42
17	AFC Bournemouth	46	7	10	6	28	24	5	7	11	17	28	53	45
18	Blackpool	46	9	9	5	40	30	3	6	14	23	45	51	63
19	Exeter City	46	5	8	10	26	30	6	9	8	28	39	50	54
20	Hull City	46	9	5	9	28	26	4	6	13	18	43	50	46
21	Preston North End	46	8	5	10	41	47	5	3	15	24	47	47	65
22	Mansfield Town	46	7	8	8	34	34	4	3	16	18	46	44	52
23	Wigan Athletic	46	6	6	11	26	34	4	5	14	17	38	41	43
24	Chester City	46	6	2	15	30	47	2	3	18	19	55	29	49

QUOTES

"Don't you know there's a recession on in the Midlands? We've always paid over the top for players....but we've won nothing"

West Brom chairman Trevor Summers to team manager Ossie Ardiles.

"Rotherham reminds me of Bermuda. It's small, so you bump into the same people two or three times a day"

Rotherham striker Shaun Goater, a Bermudan international

"The listening bank refused to listen and the bank that likes to say yes, said no"

Garry Gibson, chairman of Hartlepool, on his club's efforts to finance a new stand.

LEADING SCORERS

		League	Other Comps
Bob Taylor	WBA	30	7
Kevin Francis	Stockport	28	10
Mark Stein	Stoke	26	7
Andy Walker	Bolton	26	7
Tony Ellis	Preston	22	3
Kurt Nogan	Brighton	20	2
Stuart Rimmer	Chester	20	0
Adrian Heath	Burnley	19	3
Robert Taylor	Leyton Orient	18	0
Sean McCarthy	Bradford City	17	8
Jimmy Quinn	Reading	17	6
John McGinlay	Bolton	16	6
David Eyres	Blackpool	16	3
Paul Jewell	Bradford City	16	3

Division Two attendances   3,483,073

Barclays League 1992-93

Division Three

		P	W	D	L	GF	GA	W	D	L	GF	GA	PTS	GS
1	Cardiff City	42	13	7	1	42	20	12	1	8	35	27	83	77
2	Wrexham	42	14	3	4	48	26	9	8	4	27	26	80	75
3	Barnet	42	16	4	1	45	19	7	6	8	21	29	79	66
4	York City	42	13	6	2	41	15	8	6	7	31	30	75	66
5	Walsall	42	11	6	4	42	31	11	1	9	34	30	73	76
6	Crewe Alexandra	42	13	3	5	47	23	8	4	9	28	33	70	75
7	Bury	42	10	7	4	36	19	8	2	11	27	36	63	63
8	Lincoln City	42	10	6	5	31	20	8	3	10	26	33	63	57
9	Shrewsbury Town	42	11	3	7	36	30	6	8	7	21	22	62	57
10	Colchester United	42	13	3	5	38	26	5	2	14	29	50	59	67
11	Rochdale	42	10	3	8	38	29	6	7	8	23	41	58	70
12	Chesterfield	42	11	3	7	32	28	4	8	9	27	35	56	59
13	Scarborough	42	7	7	7	32	30	8	2	11	34	41	54	66
14	Scunthorpe United	42	8	7	6	38	25	6	5	10	19	29	54	57
15	Darlington	42	5	6	10	23	31	7	8	6	25	22	50	48
16	Doncaster Rovers	42	6	5	10	22	28	5	9	7	20	29	47	42
17	Hereford United	42	7	9	5	31	27	3	6	12	16	33	45	47
18	Carlisle United	42	7	5	9	29	27	4	6	11	22	38	44	51
19	Torquay United	42	6	4	11	18	26	6	3	12	27	41	43	45
20	Northampton Town	42	6	5	10	19	28	5	3	13	29	46	41	48
21	Gillingham	42	9	4	8	32	28	0	9	12	16	36	40	48
22	Halifax Town	42	3	5	13	20	35	6	4	11	25	33	36	45

QUOTES

"If you didn't know him, you would think he was an absolute ignorant pig. He is, in many ways, but he does care for the club"

Barnet manager, Barry Fry, about his club chairman, Stan Flashman.

If you take that picture, I'll smash that camera over your head"

Barnet chairman, Stan Flashman, to a photographer outside a Football League enquiry into allegations of financial irregularities at the club.

"Barnet has been a big part of my life. I took a second mortgage out to save them. I gave my testimonial money. I got arrested driving the tractor on Christmas Day to flatten the pitch and when I said I was the manager, the policeman said he was George Best"

Barnet manager Barry Fry.

"Watching it go in, I felt like Monica Seles. It was like somebody sticking a big knife in my back"

John Bond, manager of Shrewsbury, on the Northampton goal that cost his club a place in the play-offs.

"When I'm managing Maidenhead in two years time, I'm quite sure I'll know I made the wrong decision"

Martin O'Neill, on choosing to stay with newly promoted Wycome Wanderers, than join Notts Forest.

LEADING SCORERS

		League	Other Comps
Darren Foreman	Scarborough	27	4
Carl Griffiths	Shrewsbury	27	4
Wayne Clark	Walsall	21	3
Andy Barnes	York City	21	0
Steve Watkin	Wrexham	18	2
Gary Bull	Barnet	17	2
Phil Stant	Cardiff (Mansf'd)	17 (6)	2 (1)
Tony Naylor	Crewe	16	9
Gary Bennett	Wrexham	16	5
Michele Cecere	Walsall	16	2
Ian Blackstone	York City	16	0
George Oghani	Carlisle	15	1
Phil Clarkson	Crewe	13	4
Ian Helliwell	Scunthorpe	13	4

Division Three Attendances 1,540,428

English Non-League Football 1992-93

GM Vauxhall Conference

FINAL TABLE

	P	W	D	L	GF	GA	Pts
Wycombe Wanderers	42	24	11	7	84	37	83
Bromsgrove Rovers	42	18	14	10	67	49	68
Dagenham & Redbridge	42	19	11	12	75	47	67
Yeovil Town	42	18	12	12	59	49	66
Slough Town	42	18	11	13	60	55	65
Stafford Rangers	42	18	10	14	55	47	64
Bath City	42	15	14	13	53	46	59
Woking	42	17	8	17	58	62	59
Kidderminster Harriers	42	14	16	12	60	60	58
Altrincham	42	15	13	14	49	52	58
Northwich Victoria	42	16	8	18	68	55	56
Stalybridge Celtic	42	13	17	12	48	55	56
Kettering Town	42	14	13	15	51	63	55
Gateshead	42	14	10	18	53	56	52
Telford United	42	14	10	18	55	60	52
Merthyr Tydfil	42	14	10	18	51	79	52
Witton Albion	42	11	17	14	62	65	50
Macclesfield Town	42	12	13	17	40	50	49
Runcorn	42	13	10	19	58	76	49
Welling United	42	12	12	18	57	72	48
Farnborough Town	42	12	11	19	68	87	47
Boston United	42	9	13	20	50	69	40

Total Attendance 567,609

Leading Scorers

	League	Other
David Leworthy (Farnborough)	32	7
Mark Whitehouse (Bromsgrove)	23	3
Malcolm O'Connor (Northwich)	21	6
Keith Scott (Wycombe)	20	8
Paul Cavell (Dagenham)	19	10
Terry Robbins (Welling)	19	4
Karl Thomas (Witton)	19	3
Andy Sayer (Slough)	19	2
Gary Abbott (Welling)	17	2
Phil Brown (Kettering)	16	2

HFS Loans League

PREMIER DIVISION - FINAL TABLE

	P	W	D	L	GF	GA	Pts
Southport	42	29	9	4	103	31	96
Winsford United	42	27	9	6	91	43	90
Morecambe	42	25	11	693	51	86	
Marine	42	26	8	8	83	47	86
Leek Town	42	21	11	10	86	51	74
Accrington Stanley	42	20	13	9	79	45	73
Frickley Athletic	42	21	6	15	62	52	69
Barrow	42	18	11	13	71	55	65
Hyde United	42	17	13	12	87	71	64
Bishop Auckland	42	17	11	14	63	52	62
Gainsborough Trinity	42	17	8	17	63	66	59
Colwyn Bay	42	16	6	20	80	79	54
Horwich	42	14	10	18	72	79	52
Buxton	42	13	10	19	60	75	49
Matlock Town	42	13	11	18	56	79	47
Elmey	42	13	6	23	62	91	45
Whitley Bay	42	11	8	23	57	96	41
Chorley	42	10	10	22	52	93	40
Fleetwood Town	42	10	7	25	50	77	37
Droylsden	42	10	7	25	47	84	37
Mossley	42	7	8	27	53	95	29
Goole Town	42	6	9	27	47	105	27

Leading Scorers

	League	Other
John Coleman (Morecambe)	33	12
Steve Haw (Southport)	32	12
Paul Beck (Accrington)	26	15
Chris Camden	26	8
Andy Graham (Hyde)	26	0
Bevan Blackwood (Winsford)	24	13

FIRST DIVISION - FINAL TABLE

	P	W	D	L	GF	GA	Pts
Bridlington Town	40	25	11	4	84	35	86
Knowsley Town	40	23	7	10	86	48	76
Ashton United	40	22	8	10	81	54	74
Guiseley	40	20	10	10	90	64	70
Warrington Town	40	19	10	11	85	57	67
Gretna	40	17	12	11	64	47	63
Curzon Ashton	40	16	15	9	69	63	63
Great Harwood Town	40	17	9	14	66	57	60
Alfreton Town	40	15	9	16	80	80	54
Harrogate Town	40	14	12	14	77	81	54
Worksop Town	40	15	9	16	66	70	54
Radcliffe Borough	40	13	14	13	66	69	53
Workington	40	13	13	14	51	61	52
Eastwood Town	40	13	11	16	49	52	50
Netherfield	40	11	14	15	68	63	47
Caernarvon Town	40	13	8	19	66	74	47
Farsley Athletic	40	12	8	20	64	77	44
Lancaster City	40	10	12	18	49	76	42
Shepshed Albion	40	9	12	19	46	66	39
Congleton Town	40	10	7	23	59	95	37
Rossendale United	40	5	5	30	50	126	20

Leading Scorers

	League	Other
Andy Whittaker (Netherfield)	27	6
Peter Coyne (Radcliffe)	26	4
Chris Shaw (Ahston)	23	10
Steve French (Harrogate)	22	4
Graeme Jones (Bridlington)	21	7
Gary Waller (Worksop)	21	7

Diadora League

PREMIER DIVISION - FINAL TABLE

	P	W	D	L	GF	GA	Pts
Chesham United	42	30	8	4	104	34	98
St Albans City	42	28	9	5	103	50	93
Enfield	42	25	6	11	94	48	81
Carshalton Athletic	42	22	10	10	96	56	76
Sutton United	42	18	14	10	74	57	68
Grays Athletic	42	18	11	13	61	64	65
Stevenage Borough	42	18	8	16	62	60	62
Harrow Borough	42	16	14	12	59	60	62
Hayes	42	16	13	13	64	59	61
Aylesbury United	42	18	6	18	70	77	60
Hendon	42	12	18	12	52	54	54
Basingstoke Town	42	12	17	13	49	45	53
Kingstonian	42	14	10	18	59	58	52
Dulwich Hamlet	42	12	14	16	52	66	50
Marlow	42	12	11	19	72	73	47
Wokingham Town	42	11	13	18	62	81	46
Bromley	42	11	13	18	51	72	46
Wivenhoe Town	42	13	7	22	41	75	46
Yeading	42	11	12	19	58	66	45
Staines Town	42	10	13	19	59	77	43
Windsor & Eton	42	8	7	27	40	90	31
Bognor Regis	42	5	10	27	46	106	25

Leading Scorers	League	Other
Jimmy Bolton (Carshalton)	37	3
Steve Clark (St Albans)	36	0
Dave Pearce (Kingstonian)	27	4
Chris Townsend (Chesham)	24	0
Graham Westley (Aylesbury)	23	4
Darren Collins (Enfield)	23	3
Tommy Langley (Wokingham)	21	0
Martin Gittings (Stevenage)	20	0

DIVISION ONE - FINAL TABLE

	P	W	D	L	GF	GA	Pts
Hitchin Town	40	25	7	8	67	29	82
Molesey	40	23	11	6	81	38	80
Dorking	40	23	9	8	73	40	78
Purfleet	40	19	12	9	67	42	69
Bishop's Stortford	40	19	10	11	63	42	67
Abingdon Town	40	17	13	10	65	47	64
Tooting & Mitcham Utd	40	17	12	11	68	46	63
Billericay Town	40	18	6	16	67	61	60
Wembley	40	14	15	11	44	34	57
Walton & Hersham	40	14	12	14	58	54	54
Boreham Wood	40	14	12	14	44	43	50
Maidenhead United	40	10	18	12	45	50	48
Leyton Wingate	40	11	14	15	56	61	47
Whyteleafe	40	12	10	18	63	71	46
Uxbridge	40	11	13	16	50	59	46
Heybridge Swifts	40	11	9	20	47	65	42
Croydon	40	11	9	20	54	82	42
Chalfont St Peter	40	7	17	16	48	70	38
Barking	40	10	8	22	42	80	38
Lewes	40	9	10	21	34	80	37
Aveley	40	9	7	24	45	87	34

Leading Scorers	League	Other
Mark Hynes (Whyteleafe)	30	0
Steve Lunn (Dorking)	22	6

Neil Pearson (Molesey)	22	4
John Collins (Tooting)	21	2
Michael Rose (Molesey)	18	3
Steve Jones (Billericay)	18	2

DIVISION TWO - FINAL TABLE

	P	W	D	L	GF	GA	Pts
Worthing	42	28	11	7	105	50	91
Ruislip Manor	42	25	12	5	78	33	87
Berkhampstead Town	42	24	8	10	77	55	80
Hemel Hempstead	42	22	12	8	84	52	78
Metropolitan Police	42	22	6	14	84	51	72
Malden Vale	42	20	9	13	78	54	69
Chertsey Town	42	20	7	15	84	60	67
Saffron Walden	42	19	10	13	63	49	67
Newbury Town	42	14	18	10	53	51	60
Hampton	42	16	11	15	59	59	59
Edgware Town	42	16	10	16	84	75	58
Egham Town	42	16	9	17	60	71	57
Banstead Athletic	42	14	13	15	67	52	55
Leatherhead	42	14	11	17	66	61	53
Ware	42	12	11	19	68	76	47
Witham Town	42	10	16	16	54	65	46
Tilbury	42	12	8	22	55	101	44
Barton Rovers	42	9	14	19	40	66	41
Hungerford Town	42	11	8	23	37	93	41
Rainham Town	42	9	10	23	56	80	37
Harefield United	42	10	7	25	37	72	37
Southall	42	7	7	28	43	106	28

Leading Scorers	League	Other
Steve Newing (Hemel)	27	2
Peter Skerritt (Egham)	23	0
Andy Linsell (Hemel)	20	0
Daniel Freeman (Worthing)	19	2
Richard Tiltman (Worthing)	18	2

DIVISION THREE - FINAL TABLE

	P	W	D	L	GF	GA	Pts
Aldershot Town	38	28	8	2	90	35	92
Thame United	38	21	11	6	84	38	74
Collier Row	38	21	11	6	68	30	74
Leighton Town	38	21	10	7	89	47	73
Cove	38	21	8	9	69	42	71
Northwood	38	19	11	8	84	68	68
Royston Town	38	17	8	13	59	42	59
East Thurrock Utd	38	17	7	14	69	58	58
Kingsbury Town	38	15	9	14	62	59	54
Hertford Town	38	14	10	14	61	64	52
Flackwell Heath	38	15	6	17	82	76	51
Tring Town	38	12	11	15	59	63	47
Hornchurch	38	11	13	14	53	52	46
Horsham	38	12	7	19	63	72	43
Epsom & Ewell	38	10	11	17	52	67	41
Bracknell Town	38	7	13	18	52	94	34
Clapton	38	8	7	23	46	74	31
Camberley Town	38	8	7	23	37	72	31
Petersfield United	38	6	12	20	36	90	30
Feltham & Hounslow B	38	5	4	29	47	119	19

Leading Scorers	League	Other
Steve Drew (Leighton)	30	3
Dave Whitehead (Hertford)	29	1
Tony Read (Collier Row)	28	0
Stephen Stairs (Aldershot)	27	4
Nigel Mott (Thame)	26	4

Beazer Homes League

PREMIER DIVISION - FINAL TABLE

	P	W	D	L	GF	GA	Pts
Dover Athletic	40	25	11	4	65	23	86
Cheltenham Town	40	21	10	9	76	40	73
Corby Town	40	20	12	8	68	43	72
Hednesford Town	40	21	7	12	72	52	70
Trowbridge Town	40	18	8	14	70	66	62
Crawley Town	40	16	12	12	68	59	60
Solihull Borough	40	17	9	14	68	59	60
Burton Albion	40	16	11	13	53	50	59
Bashley*	40	18	8	14	60	60	59
Halesowen Town	40	15	11	14	67	54	56
Waterlooville	40	15	9	16	59	62	54
Chelmsford City	40	15	9	16	59	69	54
Gloucester City	40	14	11	15	66	68	53
Cambridge City	40	14	10	16	62	73	52
Atherstone United*	40	13	14	13	56	60	50
Hastings Town	40	13	11	16	50	55	50
Worcester City	40	12	9	19	45	62	45
Dorchester Town	40	12	6	22	52	74	42
Moor Green	40	10	6	24	58	79	36
V S Rugby	40	10	6	24	40	63	36
Weymouth**	40	5	10	25	39	82	23

Bashley & Atherstone had 3 points deducted
Weymouth had 2 points deducted
Dartford results were discounted

Leading Scorers

J Smith (Cheltenham) 29, R Carter (Solihull) 25, K Bayliss (Gloucester) 22, C Burton (Solihull) 22, P Fishendon (Crawley) 22, G Manson (Dorchester) 21, L O'Connor (Hednesford) 21.

MIDLAND DIVISION - FINAL TABLE

	P	W	D	L	GF	GA	Pts
Nuneaton Borough	42	29	5	8	102	45	92
Gresley Rovers	42	27	6	9	94	55	87
Rushden & Diamonds	42	25	10	7	85	41	85
Barri	42	26	5	11	82	49	83
Newport AFC	42	23	8	11	73	58	77
Bedworth United	42	22	8	12	72	55	74
Stourbridge	42	17	9	16	93	79	60
Sutton Coldfield TN	42	17	9	16	82	78	60
Redditch United	42	18	6	18	75	79	60
Tamworth	42	16	11	15	65	51	59
Weston Super Mare	42	17	7	18	79	86	58
Leicester United	42	16	9	17	67	67	57
Grantham Town	42	16	9	17	60	73	57
Bilston Town	42	15	10	17	74	69	55
Evesham United	42	15	8	19	67	83	53
Bridgnorth Town	42	15	7	20	61	68	52
Dudley Town	42	14	8	20	60	75	50
Yate Town	42	15	5	22	63	81	50
Forest Green Rovers	42	12	6	24	61	97	42
Hinckley Town*	42	9	11	22	56	89	37
King's Lynn	42	10	6	26	45	90	36
Racing Club Warwick	42	3	7	32	40	88	16

Hinckley had one point deducted

Leading Scorers

E Wright (Stour) 46, P Culpin (Nuneaton) 39, D Draper (Bedworth) 25, D Withers (Barri) 24, J Baker (Bilston) 23, T Hall (Stourbridge) 23, D Watkins (Rushden) 23.

SOUTHERN DIVISION - FINAL TABLE

	P	W	D	L	GF	GA	Pts
Sittingbourne	42	26	12	4	102	43	90
Salisbury	42	27	7	8	87	50	88
Witney Town	42	25	9	8	77	37	84
Gravesend & Northfleet	42	25	4	13	99	63	79
Havant Town	42	23	6	13	78	55	75
Sudbury Town	42	20	11	11	89	54	71
Erith & Belvedere	42	22	5	15	73	66	71
Ashford Town	42	20	8	14	91	66	68
Braintree Town	42	20	6	16	95	65	66
Margate	42	19	7	16	65	58	64
Wealdstone	42	18	7	17	75	69	61
Buckingham Town	42	16	11	15	61	58	59
Baldock Town	42	15	9	18	59	63	54
Poole Town	42	15	7	20	61	69	52
Fareham Town	42	14	8	20	67	65	50
Burnham	42	14	8	20	53	77	50
Canterbury City	42	12	10	20	54	76	46
Newport IOW	42	9	16	17	44	56	43
Fisher Athletic	42	8	9	25	38	98	33
Andover	42	7	9	26	42	99	29
Bury Town	42	8	5	29	46	119	29

Leading Scorers

S Portway (Gravesend) 58, P Smith (Sudbury) 34, M Buglione (Margate) 31, S Parnell (Sudbury) 27, L McRobert (Ashford) 26, K Clarke (Witney) 25, D Arter (Sittingbourne) 23.

The Neville Ovenden Football Combination

DIVISION ONE - FINAL TABLE

	P	W	D	L	GF	GA	Pts
Millwall	38	21	10	7	71	42	73
Chelsea	38	20	11	7	78	49	71
Crystal Palace	38	18	12	8	66	44	66
Southampton	38	18	10	10	56	39	64
Tottenham Hotspur	38	16	15	7	75	38	63
Oxford United	38	16	12	10	58	57	60
Watford	38	15	12	11	62	61	57
Wimbledon	38	15	10	13	60	43	55
Ipswich Town	38	16	7	15	58	62	55
Arsenal	38	12	15	11	57	46	51
Charlton Athletic	38	14	6	18	48	57	48
Luton Town	38	13	9	16	53	64	48
West Ham Utd	38	13	6	19	56	59	45
Norwich City	38	11	12	15	66	78	45
Swindon Town	38	10	12	16	53	60	42
Bristol City	38	8	12	18	39	60	36
Portsmouth	38	8	10	20	43	73	34
Brighton & Hove Albion	38	9	7	22	38	81	34
Fulham	38	5	7	26	28	76	22

DIVISION TWO - FINAL TABLE

	P	W	D	L	GF	GA	Pts
Bristol Rovers	27	18	5	4	61	36	59
Swansea City	27	17	6	4	78	33	57
Birmingham City	27	14	9	4	61	42	51
AFC Bournemouth	27	10	6	11	52	44	36
Yeovil Town	27	9	6	12	49	67	33
Cheltenham Town	27	7	9	11	43	56	30
Cardiff City	27	7	8	12	48	51	29

The Pontins League

DIVISION ONE - FINAL TABLE

	P	W	D	L	GF	GA	Pts
Aston Villa	34	21	8	5	64	32	71
Notingham Forest	34	20	8	6	77	46	68
Blackburn Rovers	34	18	10	6	60	37	64
Leeds United	34	15	8	11	59	44	53
Bolton Wanderers	34	15	8	11	48	49	53
Manchester United	34	13	13	8	58	50	52
Liverpool	34	13	10	11	47	43	49
Sheffield Wednesday	34	13	10	11	51	48	49
Leicester City	34	12	12	10	42	38	48
Wolverhampton Wndrs	34	13	6	15	46	55	45
Notts County	34	12	8	14	56	52	44
Newcastle United	34	12	7	15	36	43	43
Sheffield United	34	10	10	14	54	59	40
Sunderland	34	11	6	17	57	57	39
Barnsley	34	9	11	14	48	58	38
Stoke City	34	8	8	18	38	56	32
Manchester City A	34	7	9	18	34	68	30
Rotherham United	34	5	6	23	29	69	21

DIVISION TWO - FINAL TABLE

	P	W	D	L	GF	GA	Pts
Derby County	34	26	5	3	103	28	83
Everton	34	21	10	3	78	44	73
Coventry City	34	19	5	10	53	31	62
York City	34	17	8	9	48	31	59
West Bromwich Albion	34	18	5	11	54	50	59
Oldham Athletic	34	17	6	11	70	52	57
Port Vale	34	14	8	12	51	49	50
Bradford City	34	14	7	13	60	58	49
Huddersfield Town	34	15	4	15	61	56	49
Grimsby Town	34	13	7	14	51	45	46
Middlesbrough	34	14	4	16	47	53	46
Blackpool	34	13	6	15	40	55	45
Burnley	34	11	8	15	46	56	41
Mansfield Town	34	11	6	17	41	49	39
Scunthorpe United	34	10	4	20	46	64	34
Hull City	34	7	6	21	33	76	27
Wigan Athletic	34	6	5	23	25	68	23
Preston North End	34	5	6	23	43	85	21

ANOTHER HAND OF GOD?

What is it with retired footballers? First of all Franz Beckenbauer says he's coming back as a woman, now Pele says reckons he's got the gift of healing. "Boys and girls confined to wheelchairs start walking again after I visit them in hospitals. Parents call me saying their kid has cancer, has one month to live and wants to see me while still conscious. I go to the hospital and the kid recovers". Pele had never spoken of this before because he was afraid of being misunderstood. Well, in short Pele mate, you will be. More interesting, perhaps, is that the Beckenbauer scoop (I want to come back as a woman) appeared in Penthouse. Pele's scoop appeared in Playboy. Looks like they are winding each other up......

FA Cup

All we wanted was a song and dance from Waddle and everything would have been right with the world. He was out there somewhere, his tap shoes on and ready to roll, but did we see him? Did we heck! We saw instead sheer drudgery. It's amazing that clubs can work so hard to get to the final and then make it such a dour occasion. Arsenal must bear the brunt; they offered nothing much in the way of constructive football, content only to pin Wednesday down. That took surprisingly little effort. The fact that Travor Francis decided to play Warhurst at the back was indicative: they didn't want to do too much attacking.

"I've had letters from psychologists telling me that Arsenal now have the upper hand," said Trevor Francis, before the Thursday replay. Psychologists should have been more concerned with why over two and a half million more people watched the replay on television than watched the first game. Quite probably they couldn't believe their eyes the first time.

Again it went to extra time and again what went first wasn't up to much. Ian Wright, playing despite a toe broken in the first match, gave Arsenal the lead in the 35th minute. Nothing much else happened until a spark of imagination was lit in the Sheffield Wednesday ranks with about 20 minutes of the game remaining. John Harkes, who had made some impression on the game, combined with Waddle and the latter's shot was deflected past Seaman. At that point, Wednesday's star looked in the ascendancy and if you had to bet who would last extra time better, you would have bucked the psychologist and gone for Francis' team.

But no, there was, at least, some real drama to come. Andy Linighan, only playing in the final because Martin Keown was cup-tied, came thundering into attack, at the bell, to secure it for Arsenal. There were cheers from north London (as Arsenal became the first club to do the League Cup and the FA Cup double) and there were tears from Wednesday, who were bracing themselves for penalties.

The rest of us breathed a sigh of relief. Too often, these days, the showpiece of the game is a poor shadow of its old self. The excuses were made about football saturation by George Graham (and both clubs played seven games in the first three weeks of May), but this dirgeful final was as much about not wanting to play imaginatively as being too tired to.

While that 13 million plus watched it on television, only 62,267 turned out in person for the replay, the smallest crowd ever for an FA Cup Final in Wembley Stadium.

Of conquering minnows in the earlier rounds, Bolton stood out. They drew at home to Liverpool in the third round and then whopped them at the Kop. They went to the once-great acres of Molineux in the fourth round and served a similar dish to Wolves. In the fifth round, when it was just getting exciting and people had started arguing again about whether Nat Lofthouse had really fouled Harry Gregg in the 1958 final, they got turned over by Derby at the Baseball Ground.

English Cup Competitions

FA Cup

COMPETITION PROPER
First Round
Accrington Stanley 3 *(Beck 3)*
Gateshead 2 *(Lamb, Bell)*

Blackpool 1 *(Mitchell)*
Rochdale 1 *(Whitehall)*

Blyth Spartans 1 *(Howie)*
Southport 2 *(Haw, Withers)*

Bolton Wandrs 2 *(Reeves, Walker)*
Sutton Coldfield 1 *(Dale)*

Bournemouth 0
Barnet 0

Bradford City 1 *(Jewell)*
Preston NE 1 *(Fowler)*

Brighton 2 *(Kennedy, Codner)*
Hayes 0

Burnley 2 *(Conroy, Curran og)*
Scarborough 1 *(Mockler)*

Bury 2 *(Knill-pen, Robinson-pen)*
Witton Albion 0

Cardiff 2 *(Millar, Blake)*
Bath City 3 *(Withey, Gill, Vernon)*

Chester City 1 *(Ryan)*
Altrincham 1 *(Comstive og)*

Colchester 4 *(Sorrell, Bennett 2, Ball)*
Slough Town 0

Crewe A 6 *(Hignett 4, McKearney 2)*
Wrexham 1 *(Bennett)*

Dagenham 4 *(Broom, Connor, Cavell,*
Butterworth)
Leyton O 5 *(Howard, Whitbread,*
Cooper 2, Jones)

Darlington 1 *(Dobie)*
Hull City 2 *(Atkinson, Norton)*

Doncaster Rovers 1 *(Quinlan)*
Hartlepool 2 *(Johnrose, Saville-pen)*

Exeter City 1 *(Moran)*
Kidderminster 0

Gillingham 3 *(Clark, Crown, Forster)*
Kettering Town 2 *(Brown, Hill-pen)*

Kingstonian 1 *(Russell)*
Peterborough 1 *(Adcock)*

Lincoln City 0
Stafford Rangers 0

Macclesfield 0
Chesterfield 0

Marine 4 *(Ward, Gautrey, Rowland,*
Camden)
Halifax Town 1 *(German)*

Marlow 3 *(Lay, Watkins, Glasgow)*
Salisbury 3 *(Loveridge, Saunders,*
Fletcher)

Northampton 3 *(Wilkin, Brown,*
Terry)
Fulham 1 *(Farrell)*

Rotherham 4 *(Goodwin 2, Howard,*
Cunningham)
Walsall 0

Scunthorpe United 0
Huddersfield Town 0

Shrewsbury Town 3 *(Summerfield,*
Lyne, L Williams)
Mansfield Town 1

Solihull 2 *(Canning, Carter)*
VS Rugby 2 *(Bufton, Green)*

St Albans City 1 *(Duffield)*
Cheltenham 2 *(Willetts-pen, Purdie)*

Sutton United 1 *(Quail)*
Hereford United 2 *(Pickard,*
Barton og)

Torquay United 2 *(Foster, Herd)*
Yeovil Town 5 *(Wilson, Kepple,*
Betty 3)

WBA 8 *(Donovan 3, McNally, Taylor,*
Robson, Raven, Hamilton)
Aylesbury 0

Wigan Athletic 3 *(Williams og,*
Dalziel og, Powell)
Carlisle United 1 *(Arnold)*

Woking 3 *(Clement, Biggins, Carroll)*
Nuneaton 2 *(Bullock, Culpin)*

Wycombe W 3 *(Scott, Carroll,*
Stapleton)
Merthyr T 1 *(Rogers)*

York City 1 *(Canham)*
Stockport County 3 *(Todd, Francis 2)*

Dorking 2 *(Grainger, Lunn)*
Plymouth A 3 *(Dalton 2, Marshall)*

Reading 1 *(Quinn)*
Birmingham 0

Stoke City 0
Port Vale 0

- -
First Round Replays
Port Vale 3 *(Foyle 2, Porter)*
Stoke City 1 *(Sandford)*

Altrincham 2 *(Harris, Freeman)*
Chester City 0

Barnet 1 *(Carter)*
Bournemouth 2 *(Lovell, Mundee)*

' Chesterfield 2 *(Turnbull, Williams)*
Macclesfield Town 2 *(Mitchell 2)*

Huddersfield Town 2 *(Barnett 2)*
Scunthorpe United 1 *(Buckley)*

Peterborough 9 *(Philliskirk 5, Cooper*
Adcock 2, Harlow og)
Kingstonian 1 *(Finch)*
Match ordered to be replayed after a
missile thrown from the crowd.

Preston NE 4 *(Graham, Davidson,*
Ellis, Callaghan)
Bradford City 5 *(McCarthy 2, Blake,*
Tinnion pen, Jewell)

Rochdale 1 *(Reid)*
Blackpool 0

VS Rugby 2 *(Green, Smith)*
Solihull 1 *(Canning pen)*

Stafford R 2 *(Boughly, Bradshaw)*
Lincoln City 1 *(Costello)*

Peterborough United 1 *(Sterling)*
Kingstonian 0

Salisbury 2 *(Chalk, Sanders)*
Marlow 2 *(Hannigan, Glasgow)*

Second Round
Accrington Stanley 1 *(Cooper)*
Crewe Alex 6 *(Carr, Naylor 2,*
Whalley 2, Clarkson)

Altrincham 1 *(Dyson)*
Port Vale 4 *(Swan, Foyle, Taylor,*
Van der Lann)

Bolton Wdrs 4 *(McAteer, Walker,*
McGinley 2,
Rochdale 0

Brighton & Hove A 1 *(Kennedy)*
Woking 1 *(S Wye)*

Burnley 1 *(Conroy)*
Shrewsbury Town 1 *(Griffiths)*

Cheltenham Town 1 *(Warren)*
Bournemouth 1 *(Shearer)*

Exeter City 1 *(Dolan)*
Swansea 2 *(Cornforth, Jenkins)*

Gillingham 1 *(Crown)*
Colchester United 1 *(McGavin)*

Macclesfield Town 0
Stockport Co 2 *(Preece, B Williams)*

Marine 3 *(Murray 2, Gautrey)*
Stafford R 2 *(Berry pen, Palgrave)*

Reading 3 *(Parkinson,*
Quinn 2 - 1 pen)
Leyton Orient 0

Rotherham United 1 *(Cunningham)*
Hull City 0

Yeovil Town 0
Hereford 0

Bath City 2 *(Smart, Randall)*
Northampton T 2 *(Brown, Chard)*

Bradford City 0
Huddersfield T 2 *(Dunn,*
O'Regan-pen)

Hartlepool 4 *(Peverell, Saville 3)*
Southport 0

Wycombe W 2 *(Creaser,Thompson)*
WBA 2 *(Bradley, Taylor)*

Plymouth A 3 *(Marshall 2, Castle)*
Peterborough U 2 *(Philliskirk,*
Sterling)

VS Rugby 0
Marlow 0

Exeter City 2 *(Moran, Cook)*
Swansea City 5 *(West, Wimbleton,*
Legg, Cullen, Bowen)

Wigan Athletic 1 *(Griffiths - pen)*
Bury 1 *(Hulme)*
- - - - - - - - - - - - - - - - - -
Second Round Replays
Northampton Town 3 *(McParland,*
Wilkin, Bell)
Bath City 0

Shrewsbury Town 1 *(Griffiths)*
Burnley 2 *(Pender, Conroy)*

WBA 1 *(Taylor)*
Wycombe Wanderers 0

Bournemouth 3 *(Mundee, Morgan,*
McGorry)
Cheltenham Town 0

Colchester United 2 *(Ball 2)*
Gillingham 3 *(Forster, Arnott,*
Henry-pen)

Hereford 1 *(Pickard)*
Yeovil Town 2 *(Sanderson, Coates)*

Marlow 2 *(Watkins, Bushay)*
VS Rugby 0

Woking 1 *(Senior)*
Brighton 2 *(Codner, Crumplin)*

Bury 1 *(Mauge)*
Wigan Athletic 0

Third Round
Aston Villa 1 *(Cox)*
Bristol Rovers 1 *(Browning)*

Blackburn Rvrs 3 *(Ripley 2, Newell)*
Bournemouth 1 *(Ekoku)*

Brentford 0
Grimsby Town 2 *(Mendonça, Dobbin)*

Brighton & Hove A 1 *(Edwards)*
Portsmouth 0

Derby County 2 *(Short, Miller og)*
Stockport County 1 *(McCord)*

Gillingham 0
Huddersfield Town 0

Hartlepool United 1 *(Saville-pen)*
Crystal Palace 0

Leeds United 1 *(Speed)*
Charlton Athletic 1 *(Nelson)*

Manchester City 1 *(Sheron)*
Reading 1 *(Taylor)*

Marlow 1 *(Lay)*
Tottenham 5 *(Sheringham, Barmby 2,*
Samways 2)

Newcastle United 4 *(Peacock 2, Lee,*
Sheedy)
Port Vale 0

Oldham Athletic 2 *(Olney, Bernard)*
Tranmere Rovers 2 *(Aldridge-pen,*
Nevin)

Sheffield United 2 *(Hodges, Beesley)*
Burnley 2 *(Heath 2)*

Swansea City 1 *(West)*
Oxford United 1 *(Cusack)*

Watford 1 *(Nogan)*
Wolverhampton 4 *(Downing, Mutch,*
Holdsworth og, Bull)

WBA 0
West Ham 2 *(C Allen, Robson)*

Wimbledon 0
Everton 0

Yeovil Town 1 *(Batty-pen)*
Arsenal 3 *(Wright 3)*

Bolton Wanderers 2 *(McGinlay,*
Seagraves)
Liverpool 2 *(Winstanley og, Rush)*

Nottingham F 2 *(Keane, Webb)*
Southampton 1 *(Le Tissier)*

QPR 3 *(Ferdinand 2, Penrice)*
Swindon Town 0

Manchester Utd 2 *(Phelan, Gillespie)*
Bury 0

Crewe Alex 3 *(McKearney-pen,*
Edwards, Clarkson)
Marine 0

Ipswich 3 *(Thompson, Dozell,*
Whitton)
Plymouth Argyle 1 *(Castle)*

Northampton Town 0
Rotherham United 1 *(Howard)*

Notts County 0
Sunderland 2 *(Cunningham,*
Goodman)

Cambridge Utd 1 *(Heathcote)*
Sheffield Weds 2 *(Bright, Harkes)*

Leicester C 2 *(Thompson-pen,*
Oldfield)
Barnsley 2 *(Whitlow og, Redfearn)*

Middlesbrough 2 *(Wright, Falconer)*
Chelsea 1 *(Mohan)*

Norwich City 1 *(Beckford)*
Coventry City 0

Southend 1 *(Collymore)*
Millwall 0

Luton Town 2 *(Gray, Hughes)*
Bristol City 0
- - - - - - - - - - - - - - - - - -
Third Round Replays
Burnley 2 *(Heath, Monington)*
Sheffield Utd 4 *(Deane 3, Littlejohn)*

Everton 1 *(Watson)*
Wimbledon 2 *(Fashanu, Earle)*

Oxford Utd 2 *(Magilton-pen,*
Beauchamp)
Swansea City 2 *(Cornforth, Legg)*

Tranmere R 3 *(Vickers, Morrissey)*
Oldham Athletic 0

Charlton Athletic 1 *(Pitcher-pen)*
Leeds Utd 3 *(Speed, Garland og*
McAllister)

Huddersfield T 2 *(Robinson, Dunn)*
Gillingham 1 *(Green-pen)*

Liverpool 0
Bolton Wdrs 2 *(McGinlay, Walker)*

Reading 0
Manchester City 4 *(Sheron, Holden,*
Flitcroft, Quinn)

Barnsley 1 *(Archdeacon)*
Leicester City 1 *(Joachim)*
Barnsley win 5-4 on penalties

Bristol Rovers 0
Aston Villa 3 *(Saunders 2, Houghton)*

Fourth Round
Aston Villa 1 *(Yorke)*
Wimbledon 1 *(Elkins)*

Crewe Alex 0
Blackburn Rovers 3 *(Wegerle, Newell*
Moran)

Huddersfield T 1 *(Mitchell)*
Southend Utd 2 *(Collymore 2)*

Luton Town 1 *(Telfer)*
Derby County 5 *(Short, Pembridge 3,*
Gabbiadini)

Manchester Utd 1 *(Giggs)*
Brighton & Hove A 0

Nottingham F 1 *(Webb)*
Middlesbrough 1 *(Falconer)*

QPR 1 *(Holloway)*
Manchester City 2 *(White, Vonk)*

Rotherham Utd 1 *(Johnson)*

Newcastle Utd 1 *(Lee)*

Sheffield Utd 1 *(Cork)*
Hartlepool Utd 0

Tranmere Rovers 1 *(Nevin)*
Ipswich Town 2 *(Dozzell,
                    Guentchev)*

Barnsley 4 *(Rammell 3, Redfearn)*
West Ham Utd 1 *(Morley-pen)*

Norwich City 0
Tottenham H 2 *(Sheringham 2)*

Sheffield Wed 1 *(Bright)*
Sunderland 0

Wolverhampton Wdrs 0
Bolton Wdrs 2 *(Green, McGinlay)*

Arsenal 2 *(Parlour, Merson)*
Leeds Utd 2 *(Speed, Chapman)*

Swansea City 0
Grimsby Town 0
- - - - - - - - - - - - - - - - -
Fourth Round Replays
Leeds Utd 2 *(Shutt, McAllister)*
Arsenal 3 *(Smith, Wright 2)*

Middlesbrough 0
Nottingham F 3 *(Bannister, Clough,
                    Woan)*

Newcastle Utd 2 *(Kelly, Clark)*
Rotherham Utd 0

Wimbledon 0
Aston Villa 0
Wimbledon win 6-5 on penalties

Grimsby Town 2 *(Mendonca,
                    Gilbert)*
Swansea City 0

Fifth Round
Arsenal 2 *(Wright 2)*
Nottingham F 0

Blackburn Rovers 1 *(Wegerle)*
Newcastle Utd 0

Derby County 3 *(Short 2, Williams)*
Bolton Wdrs 1 *(Walker)*

Ipswich Town 4 *(Guentchev 3, Wark)*
Grimsby Town 0

Manchester City 2 *(White 2)*
Barnsley 0

Sheffield Weds 2 *(Warhurst 2)*
Southend United 0

Sheffield Utd 2 *(Hoyland, Hodges)*
Manchester Utd 1 *(Giggs)*

Tottenham 3 *(Anderton, Sheringham,
                    Barmby)*
Wimbledon 2 *(Dobbs, Cotterill)*

Sixth Round
Blackburn Rovers 0
Sheffield Utd 0
Ipswich Town 2 *(Kiwomya,*

Guentchev)
Arsenal 4 *(Adams, Wright pen,
                    Whelan og, Campbell)*

Manchester City 2 *(Sheron, Phelan)*
Tottenham 4 *(Nayim 3, Sedgley)*

Derby County 3 *(Nicholson, Kitson,
                    Gabbiadini)*
Sheffield Weds 3 *(Sheridan pen,
                    Warhurst 2)*
- - - - - - - - - - - - - - - - -
Sixth Round Replays
Sheffield Utd 2 *(Ward 2)*
Blackburn Rovers 2 *(Livingstone,
                    Newell)*
Sheffield win 5-3 on penalties.

Sheffield Weds 1 *(Warhurst)*
Derby County 0

Semi-finals
Sheffield Utd 1 *(Cork)*
Sheffield Weds 2 *(Waddle, Bright)*

Arsenal 1 *(Adams)*
Tottenham 0

FA CUP FINAL
Wembley   May 15   79,347
Arsenal 1 *(Wright)*
Sheffield Weds 1 *(Hirst)*

Arsenal: Seaman, Dixon,
Winterburn, Davis, Linigham,
Adams, Jensen, Wright (O'Leary),
Campbell, Merson, Parlour (Smith).
Sheffield Weds: Woods, Nilsson,
Worthington, Palmer, Anderson
(Hyde), Warhurst, Harkes, Waddle
(Bart-Williams), Hirst, Bright,
Sheridan.

FA CUP FINAL REPLAY
Wembley   May 20   62,267
Arsenal 2 *(Wright, Linighan)*
Sheffield Weds 1 *(Waddle)*

Arsenal: Seaman, Dixon,
Winterburn, Davis, Linighan,
Adams, Jensen, Wright (O'Leary),
Smith, Merson, Campbell.
Sheffield Weds: Woods, Nilsson
(Bart-Williams), Worthington,
Harkes, Palmer, Warhurst, Wilson
(Hyde), Waddle , Hirst, Bright,
Sheridan.

Coca Cola Cup

(Originally the Football League Cup, but also the Milk, Littlewoods & Rumbelows Cup)

First Round (over 2 legs)

Bolton Wdrs 2 *(Stubbs, Green)*
Port Vale 1 *(Foyle)*

Port Vale 1 *(Taylor)*
Bolton Wdrs 1 *(Walker)*
Bolton Wdrs win 3-2 on aggregate
- - - - - - - - - - - - - - - - - - - -
Cardiff City 1 *(Dale)*
Bristol City 0

Bristol City 5 *(Cole 3, Rosenoir,*
Allison)
Cardiff City 1 *(Dale)*
Bristol City win 5-2 on aggregate
- - - - - - - - - - - - - - - - - - - -
Carlisle Utd 4 *(Gabbiadini 2, Watson*
Barnsley-pen)
Burnley 1 *(Sonner)*

Burnley 1 *(Pender)*
Carlisle Utd 1 *(Oghani)*
Carlisle Utd win 5-2 on aggregate
- - - - - - - - - - - - - - - - - - - -
Chesterfield 2 *(Morris, Norris)*
York City 0

York City 0
Chesterfield 0
Chesterfield win 2-0 on aggregate
- - - - - - - - - - - - - - - - - - - -
Colchester Utd 1 *(English)*
Brighton & Hove A 1 *(Wilkins)*

Brighton & Hove A 1 *(Wilkins)*
Colchester Utd 0
Brighton & Hove win 2-1 on aggregate
- - - - - - - - - - - - - - - - - - - -
Crewe Alex 4 *(Hignett, Harvey,*
Clarkson, Naylor)
Rochdale 1 *(Reeves)*

Rochdale 1 *(Ryan)*
Crewe Alex 2 *(Garvey, Hignett)*
Crewe Alex win 6-2 on aggregate
- - - - - - - - - - - - - - - - - - - -
Darlington 1 *(Mardenborough)*
Scunthorpe Utd 1 *(Helliwell)*

Scunthorpe Utd 2 *(Daws, Alexander)*
Darlington 0
Scunthorpe Utd win 3-1 on aggregate
- - - - - - - - - - - - - - - - - - - -
Doncaster Rovers 0
Lincoln City 3 *(Finney, Bressington,*
Carmichael)

Lincoln City 1 *(Dunphy)*
Doncaster Rovers 1 *(Hewitt)*
Lincoln City win 4-1 on aggregate
- - - - - - - - - - - - - - - - - - - -
Exeter City 0
Birmingham City 0

Birmingham City 1 *(Sale)*
Exeter City 4 *(Dolan 2, Kelly, Hodge)*
Exeter City win 4-1 on aggregate
- - - - - - - - - - - - - - - - - - - -
Fulham 0

Brentford 2 *(Booker, Blissett)*

Brentford 2 *(Bates, Blissett)*
Fulham 0
Brentford win 4-0 on aggregate
- - - - - - - - - - - - - - - - - - - -
Gillingham 2 *(Crown, Lovell)*
Northampton T 1 *(Terry)*

Northampton T 0
Gillingham 2 *(Crown, Aylott)*
Gillingham win 4-1 on aggregate
- - - - - - - - - - - - - - - - - - - -
Halifax Town 1 *(Megson)*
Hartlepool Utd 2 *(MacPhail, Johnrose)*

Hartlepool Utd 3 *(Johnrose 2,*
Southall)
Halifax Town 2 *(Thomas, Lucketti)*
Hartlepool win 5-3 on aggregate
- - - - - - - - - - - - - - - - - - - -
Hereford Utd 2 *(Pickard 2)*
Torquay Utd 2 *(Fashanu, Darby)*

Torquay Utd 5 *(Fashanu, Foster,*
Saunders 3 (1 pen))
Hereford Utd 0
Torquay Utd win 7-2 on aggregate
- - - - - - - - - - - - - - - - - - - -
Hull City 2 *(Atkinson, Hockaday)*
Rotherham Utd 0

Rotherham Utd 1 *(Todd (pen))*
Hull City 0
Rotherham Utd win 3-2 on aggregate
- - - - - - - - - - - - - - - - - - - -
Leyton Orient 2 *(Tomlinson, Cooper)*
Millwall 2 *(Roberts, Stevens)*

Millwall 3 *(Armstrong, Allen 2)*
Leyton Orient 0
Millwall win 5-2 on aggregate
- - - - - - - - - - - - - - - - - - - -
Oxford Utd 3 *(Cusack, Allen 2)*
Swansea City 0

Swansea City 1 *(McFarlane)*
Oxford Utd 0
Oxford Utd win 3-1 on aggregate
- - - - - - - - - - - - - - - - - - - -
Peterborough Utd 4 *(Adcock 2,*
Charlery, Costello)
Barnet 0

Barnet 2 *(Bull 2 (2 pens))*
Peterborough Utd 2 *(Cooper (pen)*
Charlery)
Peterborough Utd win 6-2 on aggregate
- - - - - - - - - - - - - - - - - - - -
Preston NE 2 *(Tinkler, Ellis)*
Stoke City 1 *(Stein)*

Stoke City 4 *(Stein, Overson,*
Biggins 2)
Preston NE 0
Stoke City won 5-2 on aggregate
- - - - - - - - - - - - - - - - - - - -
Shrewsbury T 1 *(Griffiths)*
Wigan Athletic 2 *(Daley, Tankard)*

Wigan Athletic 0
Shrewsbury T 1 *(Smith)*
Wigan Athletic win on away goals
- - - - - - - - - - - - - - - - - - - -
Stockport Co 1 *(Gannon)*
Chester City 1 *(Comstive)*

Chester City 1 *(Bishop)*
Stockport Co 2 *(Beaumont, Carstairs)*
Stockport County win 3-2 on aggregate
- - - - - - - - - - - - - - - - - - - -
Sunderland 2 *(Butcher, Ball)*
Huddersfield T 3 *(Starbuck, Parsley,*
Roberts)

Huddersfield T 0
Sunderland 1 *(Davenport)*
Huddersfield T win on away goals
- - - - - - - - - - - - - - - - - - - -
Wrexham 1 *(Pejic)*
Bury 1 *(Hulme)*

Bury 4 *(Valentine 2, Kearney,*
Robinson)
Wrexham 3 *(Reid (og), Bennett 2)*
Bury win 5-4 on aggregate
- - - - - - - - - - - - - - - - - - - -
Grimsby Town 1 *(Mendonca)*
Barnsley 1 *(Redfearn)*

Barnsley 1 *(Liddell)*
Grimsby Town 1 *(Mendonca)*
Grimsby Town win 5-3 on penalties
- - - - - - - - - - - - - - - - - - - -
Newcastle Utd 2 *(Peacock 2)*
Mansfield Town 1 *(Stant)*

Mansfield Town 0
Newcastle Utd 0
Newcastle Utd win 2-1 on aggregate
- - - - - - - - - - - - - - - - - - - -
Scarborough 3 *(Mooney, Lee,*
Oliver (og))
Bradford City 0

Bradford City 3 *(Reid, Jewell,*
McCarthy)
Scarborough 5 *(Hirst, Lee, Foreman*
Mooney 2)
Scarborough win 8-3 on aggregate
- - - - - - - - - - - - - - - - - - - -
Tranmere Rvrs 3 *(Aldridge 2, Garnett)*
Blackpool 0

Blackpool 4 *(Garnett (og), Murphy,*
Robinson, Eyres)
Tranmere Rvrs 0
Blackpool win 4-3 on aggregate
- - - - - - - - - - - - - - - - - - - -
Walsall 1 *(Clarke)*
Bournemouth 1 *(Morris)*

Bournemouth 0
Walsall 1 *(McDonald)*
Walsall win 2-1 on aggregate
- - - - - - - - - - - - - - - - - - - -
WBA 1 *(Taylor)*
Plymouth Arg 0

Plymouth Arg 2 *(Marker, Poole
(pen))*
WBA 0
Plymouth Arg win 2-1 on penalties

Second Round (over 2 legs)

Tottenham H 3 *(Sheringham,
Watson, Durie)*
Brentford 1 *(Blissett)*

Brentford 2 *(Blissett, Millen)*
Tottenham H 4 *(Anderton,
Sheringham 2 (1 pen),
Turner)*
Tottenham H win 4-2 on aggregate

Arsenal 1 *(Campbell)*
Millwall 1 *(Roberts)*

Millwall 1 *(Dixon (og))*
Arsenal 1 *(Campbell)*
Arsenal won 3-1 on penalties

Bolton Wdrs 1 *(Stubbs)*
Wimbledon 3 *(Fashanu, Ardley,
Jones)*

Wimbledon 0
Bolton Wdrs 1 *(Philliskirk)*
Wimbledon won 3-2 on aggregate

Bristol City 2 *(Edwards, Scott (pen))*
Sheffield Utd 1 *(Rogers)*

Sheffield Utd 4 *(Whitehouse,
Bradshaw, Deane 2)*
Bristol City 1 *(Cole)*
Sheffield Utd won 5-3 on aggregate

Bury 0
Charlton Athletic 0

Charlton Athletic 0
Bury 1 *(Hulme)*
Bury won 1-0 on aggregate

Cambridge Utd 2 *(Philpott, Chapple)*
Stoke City 2 *(Stein 2)*

Stoke City 1 *(Shaw)*
Cambridge Utd 2 *(Fowler, Francis)*
Cambridge Utd win 4-3 on aggregate

Carlisle Utd 2 *(Barnsley (pen),
Edmondson)*
Norwich City 2 *(Robins, Goss)*

Norwich City 2 *(Sutton 2)*
Carlisle Utd 0
Norwich win 4-2 on penalties

Crystal Palace 3 *(Southgate, Salako
McGoldrick)*
Lincoln City 1 *(Bressington)*

Lincoln City 1 *(Puttnam)*
Crystal Palace 1 *(Southgate)*
Crystal Palace win 4-2 on penalties

Exeter City 0
Oldham Athletic 1 *(Henry)*

Oldham Athletic 0

Exeter City 0
Oldham Athletic win 1-0 on aggregate

Leeds Utd 4 *(Strachan, Chapman
Speed, Shutt)*
Scunthorpe 1 *(Helliwell)*

Scunthorpe 2 *(Helliwell 2)*
Leeds Utd 2 *(Wallace, Chapman)*
Leeds Utd win 6-3 on aggregate

Liverpool 4 *(Rosenthal, Hutchison
Walters, Wright)*
Chesterfield 4 *(Norris 2, Lancaster 2)*

Chesterfield 1 *(Hebberd)*
Liverpool 4 *(Hutchison, Redknapp
Walters, Rush)*
Liverpool win 8-5 on aggregate

Notts County 3 *(Lund 2, Robinson)*

Wolverhampton W 2 *(Bull,
Cook (pen))*

Wolverhampton W 0
Notts County 1 *(O'Riordan)*
Notts County win 4-2 on aggregate

Watford 2 *(Furlong 2)*
Reading 2 *(Quinn, Williams)*

Reading 0
Watford 2 *(Drysdale, Lavin)*
Watford win 4-2 on aggregate

Wigan Athletic 2 *(Johnson,
Worthington)*
Ipswich Town 2 *(Johnson,
Robertson (og))*

Ipswich Town 4 *(Johnson,
Kiwomya 3)*
Wigan Athletic 0
Ipswich Town win 6-2 on aggregate

Blackpool 0
Portsmouth 4 *(Clarke, McLoughlin 2,
Murray)*

Portsmouth 2 *(Whittingham 2)*
Blackpool 0
Portsmouth win 6-0 on aggregate

Brighton & Hove A 1 *(Edwards)*
Manchester Utd 1 *(Wallace)*

Manchester Utd 1 *(Hughes)*
Brighton & Hove A 0
Manchester Utd win 2-1 on aggregate

Coventry City 2 *(Borrows (pen)
Ndlovu)*
Scarborough 0

Scarborough 3 *(Mooney, Foreman,
Hirst)*
Coventry City 0
Scarborough win 3-2 on aggregate

Gillingham 0
Southampton 0

Southampton 3 *(Dowie,

Le Tissier 2 (1 pen))*
Gillingham 0
Southampton win 3-0 on aggregate

Huddersfield T 1 *(Omara)*
Blackburn Rvrs 1 *(Shearer)*

Blackburn Rvrs 4 *(Shearer 2,
Wegerle, Newell)*
Huddersfield T 3 *(Barnett, Roberts,
Ireland)*
Blackburn Rvrs win 5-4 on aggregate

Leicester City 2 *(Lowe, Thompson)*
Peterborough Utd 0

Peterborough Utd 2 *(Halsall,
Charlery)*
Leicester City 1 *(Joachim)*
Leicester City win 3-2 on aggregate

Luton Town 2 *(Claridge 2)*
Plymouth Arg 2 *(Regis 2)*

Plymouth Arg 3 *(Nugent, Poole,
Regis)*
Luton Town 2 *(Claridge, Preece)*
Plymouth Arg win 5-4 on aggregate

Manchester City 0
Bristol Rovers 0

Bristol Rovers 1 *(Reece)*
Manchester City 2 *(Maddison (og)
Holden)*
Manchester City win 2-1 on aggregate

Newcastle Utd 0
Middlesbrough 0

Middlesbrough 1 *(Wilkinson)*
Newcastle Utd 3 *(Kelly 2, O'Brien)*
Newcastle Utd win 3-1 on aggregate

Oxford Utd 1 *(Beauchamp)*
Aston Villa 2 *(McGrath, Teale)*

Aston Villa 2 *(Atkinson, Richardson)*
Oxford Utd 1 *(Cusack)*
Aston Villa win 4-2 on aggregate

QPR 2 *(Ferdinand 2)*
Grimsby Town 1 *(Watson)*

Grimsby Town 2 *(Watson, Woods)*
QPR 1 *(Bailey)*
QPR won 6-5 on penalties

Rotherham Utd 1 *(Goater)*
Everton 0

Everton 3 *(Rideout 2, Cottee)*
Rotherham Utd 0
Everton win 3-1 on aggregate

Sheffield Wed 3 *(Watson, Bright,
Wilson)*
Hartlepool Utd 0

Hartlepool Utd 2 *(Saville (pen)
Johnrose)*
Sheffield Wed 2 *(Bright, Warhurst)*
Sheffield Wed win 5-2 on aggregate

Southend Utd 1 *(Benjamin)*
Derby County 0

Derby County 7 *(Kitson, Martin (og),*
Gabbiadini 2, Simpson 2,
Johnson)
Southend Utd 0
Derby County win 7-1 on aggregate
- - - - - - - - - - - - - - - - - -
Stockport Co 2 *(Francis 2)*
Nottingham F 3 *(Bannister, Clough*
Orlygsson)

Nottingham F 2 *(Black, Gannon (og))*
Stockport Co 1 *(Beaumont)*
Nottingham F win 5-3 on aggregate
- - - - - - - - - - - - - - - - - -
Torquay Utd 0
Swindon Town 6 *(Maskell, Ling*
Mitchell 2, Taylor,
White)

Swindon Town 3 *(Hoddle, White,*
Mitchell)
Torquay Utd 2 *(Myers, Foster)*
Swindon Town win 9-2 on aggregate
- - - - - - - - - - - - - - - - - -
Walsall 0
Chelsea 3 *(Wise, Newton, Townsend)*

Chelsea 1 *(Fleck (pen))*
Walsall 0
Chelsea win 4-0 on aggregate
- - - - - - - - - - - - - - - - - -
West Ham Utd 0
Crewe Alex 0

Crewe Alex 2 *(Naylor, Hignett)*
West Ham Utd 0
Crewe Alex win 2-0 on aggregate

Third Round

Bury 0
QPR 2 *(Peacock, Allen)*

Notts County 2 *(Draper, Agana)*
Cambridge Utd 3 *(Clayton, Danzey,*
White)

Plymouth Arg 3 *(Dalton, Joyce,*
Nugent)
Scarborough 3 *(Curran, Jules,*
Ashdjian)

Portsmouth 0
Ipswich Town 1 *(Thompson)*

Sheffield Wed 7 *(Hirst, Worthington,*
Bright 2, Watson 2,
Bart-Williams)
Leicester City 1 *(Davidson)*

Swindon Town 0
Oldham Athletic 1 *(Bernard)*

Aston Villa 1 *(Saunders)*
Manchester Utd 0

Blackburn Rvrs 2 *(Shearer, May)*
Norwich City 0

Chelsea 2 *(Sinclair, Hartford)*
Newcastle Utd 1 *(Lee)*

Crewe Alex 0
Nottingham F 1 *(Orlygsson)*

Derby County 1 *(Simpson (pen))*
Arsenal 1 *(Campbell)*

Everton 0
Wimbledon 0

Manchester City 0
Tottenham H 1 *(Samways)*

Sheffield Utd 0
Liverpool 0

Southampton 0
Crystal Palace 2 *(McGoldrick, Salako)*

Watford 2 *(Holdsworth,*
Drysdale (pen))
Leeds Utd 1 *(McAllister)*

Third Round Replays

Wimbledon 0
Everton 1 *(Beardsley)*

Liverpool 3 *(McManaman 2,*
Marsh (pen))
Sheffield Utd 0

Scarborough 2 *(Mooney, Mockler)*
Plymouth Arg 1 *(Dalton)*

Arsenal 2 *(Wright, Campbell)*
Derby County 1 *(Pembridge (pen))*

Fourth Round

Cambridge Utd 1 *(Rowett)*
Oldham Athletic 0

Liverpool 1 *(Marsh (pen))*
Crystal Palace 1 *(Coleman)*

Aston Villa 2 *(Atkinson, Saunders)*
Ipswich Town 2 *(Kiwomya 2)*

Everton 2 *(Beardsley, Barlow)*
Chelsea 2 *(Harford, Stuart)*

Nottingham F 2 *(Woan, Keane)*
Tottenham H 0

Scarborough 0
Arsenal 1 *(Winterburn)*

Sheffield Wed 4 *(Bright, Hirst,*
Palmer, Nilsson)
QPR 0

Blackburn Rvrs 6 *(Atkins, Shearer 2,*
Newell 2, Wegerle)
Watford 1 *(Furlong)*

Fourth Round Replays

Ipswich Town 1 *(Kiwomya)*
Aston Villa 0

Chelsea 1 *(Townsend)*
Everton 0

Crystal Palace 2 *(Watts, Thorn)*
Liverpool 1 *(Marsh (pen))*

Fifth Round

Blackburn Rvrs 3 *(Newell 2, Wegerle)*
Cambridge Utd 2 *(Clayton,*
Heathcote)

Crystal Palace 3 *(Coleman, Ndah,*
Watts)
Chelsea 1 *(Townsend)*

Arsenal 2 *(Wright 2)*
Nottingham F 0

Ipswich Town 1 *(Whitton (pen))*
Sheffield Wed 1 *(Sheridan)*

Second Replay

Sheffield Wed 1 *(Warhurst)*
Ipswich Town 0

Semi-Finals (over 2 legs)

Crystal Palace 1 *(Osborn (pen))*
Arsenal 3 *(Wright (pen), Smith 2)*

Arsenal 2 *(Linighan, Wright)*
Crystal Palace 0
Arsenal win 5-1 on aggregate
- - - - - - - - - - - - - - - - - -
Blackburn Rvrs 2 *(Wegerle,*
Palmer (og))
Sheffield Wed 4 *(Harkes, Sheridan*
Warhurst 2)

Sheffield Wed 2 *(Hirst, Bright)*
Blackburn Rvrs 1 *(Andersson)*

COCA COLA CUP FINAL

Wembley   Apr 18   74,007
Arsenal 2 (Merson, Morrow)
Sheffield Wed 1 (Harkes)

Arsenal: Seaman, O'Leary,
Winterburn, Parlour, Adams,
Linighan, Morrow, Merson, Wright,
Campbell, Davis
Sheffield Wed: Woods, Nilsson, King
(Hyde), Palmer, Anderson, Harkes,
Wilson (Hirst), Waddle, Warhurst,
Bright, Sheridan

Autoglass Trophy (for clubs from Divs II and III)

North Area Quarter-Finals
Bradford City 3 *(Williams 3 (1 pen))*
Stockport Co 4 *(Ward 2, Francis 2)*

Chesterfield 3 *(Lancaster 3 (1 pen))*
Burnley 0

Huddersfield T 3 *(Roberts, Stubbs (og), Stuart)*
Bolton Wdrs 0

Wigan Ath 2 *(Langley, Sharratt)*
Scunthorpe Utd 1 *(Humphries (pen))*

South Area Quarter-Finals
Port Vale 4 *(Swan,Smith,Kerr,Walker)*
Northampton T 2 *(Scott, Chard)*

Swansea City 1 *(West (pen))*
Leyton Orient 0

Stoke City 2 *(Stein 2)*
WBA 1 *(Taylor)*

Brighton & Hove A 0
Exeter City 1 *(Daniels)*

North Area Semi-Finals
Stockport 2 *(PA Williams, Francis)*
Chesterfield 1 *(Morris)*

Wigan 5 *(Woods 3, Griffiths, Daley)*
Huddersfield T 2 *(Roberts, Starbuck)*

South Area Semi-Finals
Swansea City 2 *(Daniels (og), Legg)*
Exeter 3 *(Dolan, McIntyre, Jepson)*

Stoke City 0
Port Vale 1 *(Van der Laan)*

North Area Final
Wigan Ath 2 *(Daley, Griffiths)*
Stockport Co 1 *(Gannon)*

South Area Final
Port Vale 2 *(Kerr (pen), Taylor)*
Exeter City 1 *(Bailey)*

AUTOGLASS FINAL
Wembley   May 22   35,885
Port Vale 2 *(Kerr, Slaven)*
Stockport Co 1 *(Francis)*
Port Vale: Musselwhite, Aspin, Kent, Porter, Swan, Glover, Slaven, Van der Laan (Billing), Foyle, Kerr, Taylor. *Stockport Co:* Edwards, Todd, Wallace, Finley, Miller, Williams B, Gannon, Ward, Francis, Beaumont (Preece), Duffield

Anglo-Italian Cup

INTERNATIONAL STAGE
Group A
Ascoli 1 *(Bierhoff)*
Brentford 3 *(Bates, Gayle, Blissett)*

Birmingham City 1 *(Cooper)*
Bari 0

Lucchese 1 *(Venison (og))*
Newcastle Utd 1 *(Kristensen)*

Portsmouth 2 *(Walsh, Symons)*
Cesena 0

Bari 3 *(Caggianelli, Alessio Capocchiano)*
Portsmouth 0

Brentford 1 *(Allon)*
Lucchese 0

Newcastle Utd 0
Ascoli 1 *(Bierhoff)*

Cesena 1 *(Hubner (pen))*
Birmingham 2 *(Frain (pen),Sturridge)*

Bari 3 *(Capocchiano 2, Tovalieri)*
Newcastle Utd 0

Bimingham City 1 *(Sturridge)*
Ascoli 1 *(D'Ainzara)*

Cesena 0
Brentford 1 *(Allon)*

Portsmouth 2 *(Powell 2)*
Lucchese 1 *(Paci)*

Ascoli 1 *(Bierhoff)*
Portsmouth 2 *(Whittingham, Aspinall)*

Brentford 2 *(Godfrey, Luscombe)*
Bari 1 *(Capocchiano)*

Lucchese 3 *(Bettari, Paci, Rastelli)*

Birmingham City 0
Newcastle Utd 2 *(Peacock 2)*
Cesena 2 *(Hubner, Pazzaglia)*

Group B
Bristol City 0
Cosenza 2 *(Negri, Signorelli)*

Cremonese 2 *(Florjancic 2)*
West Ham Utd 0

Derby 3 *(Johnson, Forsyth,Pembridge)*
Pisa 0

Reggiana 0
Tranmere Rvrs 0

Cosenza 0
Derby County 3 *(Comyn, Kitson, Gabbiadini)*

Pisa 4 *(Rocco, Scarafoni, Bosco, Vieri)*
Bristol City 3 *(Edwards, Shelton, Scott (pen))*

Tranmere Rvrs 1 *(Malkin)*
Cremonese 2 *(Florjancic, Verdelli)*

West Ham Utd 2 *(C Allen 2)*
Reggiana 0

Bristol City 1 *(Allison)*
Reggiana 2 *(Pacione, Accardi)*

Cosenza 0
West Ham Utd 1 *(C Allen 2)*

Derby County 1 *(Kitson)*
Cremonese 3 *(Florjancic 2,Wassall og)*

Pisa 0
Tranmere Rvrs 1 *(Irons)*

Cremonese 2 *(Florjancic 2)*
Bristol City 2 *(Cole, Rosenoir)*

Reggiana 0
Derby County 3 *(Kitson, Pembridge, Gabbiadini)*

Tranmere 2 *(Irons, Morrissey)*
Cosenza 1 *(Signorelli)*

West Ham Utd 0
Pisa 0

Semi-finals (over 2 legs)
Brentford 3 *(Allon 3)*
Derby County 4 *(Patterson 2, Gabbiadini, Kitson)*

Derby County 1 *(Gabbiadini)*
Brentford 2 *(Blissett 2)*
Derby County win 5-3 on aggregate

Cremonese 4 *(Nicolini, Florjancic Tentoni, Lombardini)*
Bari 1 *(Verdelli (og))*

Bari 2 *(Jarni, Cucchi)*
Cremonese 2 *(Dezotti 2)*
Cremonese win 6-3 on aggregate

ANGLO-ITALIAN CUP FINAL

Wembley   Mar 27   37,024
Cremonese 3 *(Verdelli, Maspero (pen), Tentoni)*
Derby County 1 *(Gabbiadini)*
Cremonese: Turci, Gualco, Pedroni, Cristiani, Colonnese, Verdelli, Giandebiaggi, Nicolini, Tentoni (Montorfano), Maspero (Lombardini), Florjancic
Derby County: Taylor, Patterson, Forsyth, Nicholson, Coleman, Pembridge, Micklehite, Goulooze (Hayward), Kitson, Gabbiadini, Johnson, Simpson

Scottish Football

It was all Rangers, who remained unbeaten at Ibrox on the way to the club's fifth successive title. Celtic beat them at Parkhead and Aberdeen, Dundee and Partick all had their glory day, but that was that in domestic competition. If the day to day Premier matches became almost mundane for the Rangers supporters, there was nevertheless a very rich icing with the European Cup fixtures. The defeat of Leeds made it unarguable that Rangers were the best team in Britain. The comeback from two goals down against Marseilles was stirring. In all, Rangers played 10 matches in Europe and did not lose one of them. It also generated a considerable sum of money for a club which has been more used to spending it (the £4m on Duncan Ferguson being the biggest investment yet). Five million was the estimate of the income, which made the premature exit from the 1993/4 competition all the more galling. The leading Rangers scorer was again Ally McCoist, who managed 34 before he broke his leg and missed the last month of the season. He was still comfortably the League's top scorer. On a slightly different scale of things, Raith Rovers could also claim to have swept the domestic opposition before them. They took the First Division without a home defeat and it was almost Christmas before they lost any game.

Premier Division Full Results

	Aberdeen	Airdrie	Celtic	Dundee	Dundee Utd	Falkirk	Hearts	Hibernian	Motherwell	Partick T	Rangers	St Johnstone
Aberdeen		0-0	1-1	2-1	0-1	3-1	6-2	3-0	2-0	2-0	0-1	3-0
		7-0	1-1	0-0	0-0	2-2	3-2	2-0	1-0	1-0	1-0	1-1
Airdrie	1-2		1-1	0-0	1-2	2-0	1-0	2-0	0-2	2-2	1-1	0-2
	1-1		0-1	2-2	1-3	0-1	0-0	3-1	1-2	2-2	0-1	1-1
Celtic	2-2	2-0		1-0	2-0	3-2	1-1	2-3	1-1	1-2	0-1	3-1
	1-0	4-0		2-0	0-1	1-0	1-0	2-1	1-1	0-0	2-1	5-1
Dundee	1-2	2-0	0-1		1-3	1-2	1-3	1-1	2-1	0-2	4-3	1-1
	1-2	1-1	0-1		0-4	2-1	1-0	3-1	1-1	0-1	1-3	1-0
Dundee Utd	2-2	0-0	1-1	0-1		2-0	1-1	1-0	1-1	2-1	0-4	2-1
	1-4	3-0	2-3	1-0		2-1	0-1	0-3	-0-	3-1	0-0	1-2
Falkirk	0-1	5-1	4-5	2-2	1-1		2-1	2-1	1-0	0-1	1-2	2-2
	1-4	0-1	0-3-	1-0	1-2		6-0	3-3	1-3	4-2	2-1	2-2
Hearts	1-0	1-3	0-1	1-0	1-0	3-0		1-0	1-0	2-1	1-1	1-1
	1-2	1-1	1-0	0-0	1-0	3-1		1-0	0-0	1-1	2-3	2-0
Hibernian	1-3	2-2	1-2	0-0	2-1	3-1	0-0		2-2	1-0	0-0	3-1
	1-2	3-1	3-1	1-3	2-1	1-1	0-0		1-0	0-1	3-4	2-2
Motherwell	2-1	2-0	1-3	1-3	0-1	3-1	1-3	1-2		0-2	1-4	3-3
	0-2	0-0	2-0	1-2	2-0	2-1	2-1	0-0		2-3	0-4	1-1
Partick T	0-7	1-0	2-3	6-3	0-1	1-2	1-1	2-2	2-2		1-4	1-0
	1-3	1-1	0-1	2-0	0-4	0-1	1-1	0-33	0-1		3-0	1-1
Rangers	3-1	2-0	1-1	3-1	3-2	4-0	2-0	1-0	4-2	3-0		1-0
	2-0	2-2	1-0	3-0	1-0	5-0	2-1	3-0	1-0	3-1		2-0
St Johnstone	0-3	3-0	0-0	4-4	2-0	3-2	1-1	1-1	2-0	1-1	1-5	
	0-2	1-0	1-1	1-1	1-4	1-0	3-1	2-0	0-0	0-0	1-1	

PREMIER DIVISION - FINAL TABLE

		P	W	D	L	GF	GA	W	D	L	GF	GA	PTS	GD
1	Rangers	44	20	2	0	52	11	13	5	4	45	24	73	+62
2	Aberdeen	44	13	7	2	41	13	14	3	5	46	23	64	+51
3	Celtic	44	13	5	4	37	18	11	7	4	31	23	60	+27
4	Dundee United	44	8	7	7	25	27	11	2	9	31	22	47	+7
5	Hearts	44	12	6	4	26	15	3	8	11	11	20	44	-5
6	St Johnstone	44	8	10	4	29	27	2	10	10	23	39	40	-14
7	Hibernian	44	8	8	6	32	28	4	5	13	22	36	37	-10
8	Partick Thistle	44	5	6	11	26	41	7	6	9	24	30	36	-21
9	Motherwell	44	7	4	11	27	37	4	9	9	19	25	35	-16
10	Dundee	44	7	4	11	25	34	4	8	10	23	34	34	-20
11	Falkirk	44	7	5	10	40	39	4	2	16	20	47	29	-26
12	Airdrieonians	44	4	9	9	22	27	2	8	12	13	43	29	-35

DIVISION ONE - FINAL TABLE

		P	W	D	L	GF	GA	W	D	L	GF	GA	PTS	GD
1	Raith Rovers	44	17	5	0	54	14	8	10	4	31	27	65	+44
2	Kilmarnock	44	13	6	3	43	14	8	6	8	24	26	54	+27
3	Dunfermline Athletic	44	10	5	7	33	27	12	3	7	31	20	52	+17
4	St Mirren	44	11	5	6	33	20	10	4	8	29	32	51	+10
5	Hamilton Academicals	44	11	7	4	36	23	8	5	9	29	22	50	+20
6	Morton	44	11	3	8	36	27	8	7	7	29	29	48	+9
7	Ayr United	44	9	9	4	27	19	5	9	8	22	25	46	+5
8	Clydebank	44	10	8	4	42	22	6	5	11	29	44	45	+5
9	Dumbarton	44	10	3	9	30	30	5	4	13	26	41	37	-15
10	Stirling Albion	44	7	5	10	23	31	4	8	10	21	30	35	-17
11	Meadowbank Thistle	44	6	6	10	23	32	5	4	13	28	48	32	-17
12	Cowdenbeath	44	0	5	17	18	55	3	2	17	15	54	13	-76

DIVISION TWO - FINAL TABLE

		P	W	D	L	GF	GA	W	D	L	GF	GA	PTS	GD
1	Clyde	39	11	5	4	37	18	11	5	3	40	24	54	+35
2	Brechin City	39	13	3	3	37	13	10	4	6	25	19	53	+30
3	Stranraer	39	8	9	2	33	21	11	6	3	36	23	53	+25
4	Forfar Athletic	39	10	5	4	47	30	8	5	7	27	24	46	+20
5	Alloa	39	8	4	7	25	28	8	8	4	38	26	44	+9
6	Arbroath	39	8	6	6	34	26	10	2	7	25	24	44	+9
7	Stenhousemuir	39	9	3	8	30	25	6	7	6	29	23	40	+11
8	Berwick Rangers	39	8	5	6	30	25	8	2	10	26	39	39	-8
9	East Fife	39	6	6	8	32	33	8	4	7	38	31	38	+6
10	Queen of the South	39	5	4	11	27	37	7	5	7	30	35	33	-15
11	Queen's Park	39	6	6	7	29	32	2	6	12	22	41	28	-22
12	Montrose	39	5	3	12	24	35	5	4	10	22	36	27	-25
13	East Stirling	39	4	4	12	24	39	4	5	10	26	46	25	-35
14	Albion Rovers	39	4	5	10	22	36	2	5	13	14	40	22	-40

Scottish Cup Competitions

Scottish Cup

First Round

Huntly 4 *(Thompson 3, Copland)*
Stranraer 2 *(Duncan, Cody)*

Inverness T 3 *(MacDonald T 2, Bell)*
Civil Service Strollers 1 *(Givven)*

Queen Of the Sth 3 *(Rowe 2,*
 Henderson)
Spartans 0

Queen's Park 0
Clyde 1 *(McCarron)*

Cove R 2 *(Stephen 2)*
Peterhead 0

Forfar 5 *(Mearns, McKenna, Petrie,*
 Cadden (og), Heddle)
Albion Rvrs 0

Second Round

Clyde 3 *(Thomson, McCarron*
 Dickson)
Brechin City 1 *(Lees)*

Cove R 2 *(Stephen, Cormack)*
Montrose 0

East Fife 1 *(Hope)*
Alloa 1 *(Moffat)*

Gala Fairydean 1 *(Lothian)*
Arbroath 1 *(McNaughton)*

Vale of Leithen 2 *(Hogarth, Ross)*
East Stirling 2 *(McKinnon, Walker)*

Inverness T 0
Berwick Rgrs 1 *(Anderson)*

Stenhousemuir 2 *(Lytwyn,*
 Hallford (pen))
Forfar Ath 3 *(McIntyre, Heddle 2)*

Huntly 2 *(Copland, Rougvie)*
Queen of the Sth 1 *(Henderson)*

Second Round Replays

Alloa 1 *(McAvoy)*
East Fife 1 *(Brown)*

Arbroath 2 *(Macdonald)*
Gala Fairydean 0

East Stirling 3 *(Roberts 2, Geraghty)*
Vale of Leithen 2 *(Hogarth, Selkirk)*

Third Round

Aberdeen 4 *(Booth 3, Irvine)*
Hamilton Acad 1 *(Reid)*

Aidrieonians 0
Clydebank 0

Arbroath 3 *(Sorbie 3)*
Morton 0

Clyde 0
Celtic 0

Cove R 2 *(Megginson, Lavelle)*
East Stirling 2 *(Thomson, Barclay)*

Dundee Utd 3 *(McKinlay, Welsh,*
 Ferguson)
Meadowbank Th 1 *(Rutherford)*

Dunfermline A 1 *(Chalmers)*
Ayr Utd 2 *(Mair (pen), Walker)*

Hearts 6 *(Baird, Ferguson D, Snodin,*
 Robertson, Boothroyd 2)
Huntly 0

Hibernian 5 *(Jackson, McGinlay,*
 Weir 2, Wright)
St Mirren 2 *(Lavety, Gallagher)*

Kilmarnock 5 *(Williamson 3,*
 McCluskey, MacPherson)
Raith Rvrs 0

Motherwell 0
Rangers 2 *(McCoist 2)*

Partick Th 0
Cowdenbeath 1 *(Henderson (pen))*

St Johnstone 6 *(Wright 2, Cherry,*
 Atkins 2, Maskrey)
Forfar 0

Stirling Albion 1 *(McInnes)*
East Fife 2 *(Skelligan 2)*

Dundee 2 *(Wieghorst, Dodds (pen))*
Dumbarton 0

Falkirk 5 *(Sloan 2, McCall, May*
 Cadette)
Berwick Rgrs 2 *(Richardson, Hall)*

Third Round Replays

Clydebank 2 *(Eadie 2)*
Aidrieonians 0

Celtic 1 *(Coyne)*
Clyde 0

East Stirling 2 *(McKinnon,*
 Morland (og))
Cove R 1 *(Stephen (pen))*

Fourth Round

Arbroath 0
East Fife 0

Ayr Utd 0
Rangers 2 *(McCoist, Gordon)*

Cowdenbeath 0
Hibernian 0

Falkirk 2 *(Duffy, May)*

Celtic 0

Hearts 2 *(Baird, Robertson)*
Dundee 0

Kilmarnock 0
St Johnstone 0

Aberdeen 2 *(Jess)*
Dundee Utd 0

East Stirling 1 *(Geraghty)*
Clydebank 2 *(Eadie, Flannigan C)*

Fourth Round Replays

Hibernian 1 *(McGinlay)*
Cowdenbeath 0

St Johnstone 1 *(Davies)*
Kilmarnock 0

East Fife 1 *(Sludden)*
Arbroath 4 *(Tosh 2, Martin 2)*

Quarter-Finals

Aberdeen 1 *(Shearer (pen))*
Clydebank 1 *(McIntosh)*

Arbroath 0
Rangers 3 *(Hateley, Murray,*
 McCoist (pen))

Hearts 2 *(Preston, Robertson (pen))*
Falkirk 0

Hibernian 2 *(Tweed, Wright)*
St Johnstone 0

Quarter-Final Replay

Clydebank 3 *(Eadie, Maher, Henry)*
Aberdeen 4 *(Irvine, Paatelainen,*
 Booth 2)

Semi-Finals

Hibernian 0
Aberdeen 1 *(Booth)*

Rangers 2 *(McPherson, McCoist)*
Hearts 1 *(Preston)*

SCOTTISH CUP FINAL

Celtic Park May 29   50,715

Rangers 2 *(Murray, Hateley)*
Aberdeen 1 *(Richardson)*
Rangers: Goram, McCall, Robertson
D, Brown, Murray, Ferguson,
Durrant, Hateley, Huistra (Pressley)
Aberdeen: Snelders, McKimmie,
Wright (Smith), Grant, Irvine,
McLeish, Richardson, Mason,
Booth, Shearer (Jess), Paatelainen

Skol Cup
(for Scottish League teams)

First Round

East Stirling 0
Alloa 1 *(Moffat)*

Stenhousemuir 2 *(Irvine, Steel)*
Arbroath 3 *(Adam, Tindal,
MacDonald)*

Stranraer 0
East Fife 0
East Fife win 5-4 on penalties

Brechin City 2 *(Brown, Miller)*
Albion Rvrs 1 *(Ferguson)*

Queen's Park 1 *(McCormick)*
Clyde 3 *(D Thompson, Clarke 2)*

Queen of the Sth 3 *(Templeton 3)*
Berwick Rangers 0

Second Round

Aidrieonians 2 *(Conn, Kirkwood)*
Stranraer 3 *(Cody, Sloan, Grant)*

Alloa 1 *(McAvoy)*
St Johnstone 3 *(Curran, Wright 2)*

Brechin City 4 *(Hutt, Ross, Miller
Lees)*
Hamilton Acd 2 *(Clark, Smith)*

Dumbarton 0
Rangers 5 *(Durrant, Gordon, Hateley,
McCoist, Mikhailichenko)*

Dundee Utd 6 *(Johnson 2,Connolly 2,
Mckinlay, Ferreyra)*
Queen of the Sth 0

Meadowbank Th 0
Dundee 3 *(Dodds, McGowan,
D Campbell)*

Morton 2 *(Mathie, Alexander)*
Kilmarnock 3 *(Jack, T Burns 2)*

Motherwell 4 *(Angus, Ferguson 3)*
Clyde 2 *(D Thompson, Speirs)*

Partick Th 2 *(Farningham, Kinnaird)*
Ayr Utd 0

Arbroath 0
Aberdeen 4 *(Paatelainen 2, Shearer
Jess)*

Falkirk 4 *(Drinkell, Smith, May
McAllister)*
Forfar 1 *(Heddle)*

Hearts 1 *(McLaren)*
Clydebank 0

Hibernian 4 *(Evans 2, Hamilton,
McGinlay)*
Raith Rovers 1 *(McStay)*

Montrose 0
Dunfermline A 6 *(O'Boyle 2, Leitch,
Grant, McWilliams,
Davies)*

St Mirren 1 *(Lavety)*
Cowdenbeath 0

Stirling Albion 0
Celtic 3 *(Coyne, Creaney 2)*

Third Round

Dundee Utd 3 *(Ferguson 2, J O'Neill)*
St Mirren 0

Kilmarnock 3 *(McSkimming,
McCluskey, Skilling)*
Hibernian 1 *(Wright)*

Aberdeen 1 *(Paatelainen)*
Dunfermline A 0

Brechin City 1 *(Brown)*
Hearts 2 *(McGinlay, Robertson)*

Celtic 1 *(Payton)*
Dundee 0

Motherwell 0
Falkirk 1 *(Drinkell)*

St Johnstone 2 *(Wright, McAuley)*
Partick Th 2 *(Britton, Shaw)*

Stranraer 0
Rangers 5 *(Hateley 2, McCoist 3)*

Quarter-Finals

Kilmarnock 1 *(Campbell)*
St Johnstone 3 *(Torfason, Maskrey
Wright)*

Dundee Utd 2 *(Ferreyra, Connolly)*
Rangers 3 *(McCoist, Gough, Huistra)*

Falkirk 1 *(McQueen)*
Aberdeen 4 *(Shearer 3, Irvine)*

Hearts 1 *(MacKay)*
Celtic 2 *(Payton, Creaney)*

Semi-Finals

St Johnstone 1 *(Wright (pen))*
Rangers 3 *(McCoist 3)*

Celtic 0
Aberdeen 1 *(Jess)*

SKOL CUP FINAL

Hampden Park Oct 25   45,298

**Rangers 2 *(McCall, Smith (og))*
Aberdeen 1 *(Shearer)***

Rangers: Goram, McCall, Robertson
D, Gough (Mikhailichenko),
McPherson, Brown, Steven
(Gordon), Ferguson, McCoist,
Hateley, Durrant
Aberdeen: Snelders, Wright, Winnie,
Grant, McLeish, Smith, Aitken
(Richardson), Bett (Booth), Jess,
Shearer, Paatelainen

B & Q Cup

Quarter-Finals

Stirling Albion 0
Montrose 1 *(Grant)*

Hamilton Acd 5 *(Clark 2, Weir, Ward,
Smith)*
Berwick Rgrs 2 *(Irvine, Davidson)*

Kilmarnock 1 *(Burns T)*
Morton 2 *(Mathie, Lilley)*

Meadowbank T 3 *(Wilson, Roseburgh,
Kane)*

Queen of the Sth 2 *(Thomson, Rowe)*
Semi-Finals

Morton 3 *(Mathie 2, Alexander)*
Montrose 1 *(Forsyth)*

Hamilton Acd 1 *(McDonald)*
Meadowbank Th 1 *(Wilson)*
Hamilton Acd win 2-1 on aggregate

B & Q FINAL

Love St., Paisley Dec 13   7,391

**Hamilton Acd 3 *(Clark 2, Hillcoat)*
Morton 2 *(Alexander 2)***

Hamilton Acd: Ferguson, Hillcoat,
Miller, Millen, Weir, Reid, Ward,
Clark, Harris, Smith, McDonald
Morton: Wylie, Collins, Pickering,
Rafferty, Doak, Johnston, Mathie,
Mahood (Gahagan), Alexander,
McInnes, Tolmie

Welsh Football

Konica League of Wales

FINAL TABLE

	P	W	D	L	GF	GA	Pts
Cwmbran	38	26	9	3	69	22	87
Inter Cardiff	38	26	5	7	79	36	83
Aberystwyth Town	38	25	3	10	85	49	78
Ebbw Vale	38	19	9	10	76	61	66
Bangor City	38	19	7	12	77	58	64
Holywell Town	38	17	8	13	65	48	59
Conway United	38	16	9	13	51	51	57
Connah's Quay Nomads	38	17	4	17	66	67	55
Porthmadog	38	14	11	13	61	49	53
Haverfordwest County	38	16	5	17	66	66	53
Caersws	38	14	10	14	64	60	52
Afan Lido	38	14	10	14	64	64	52
Mold Alexandra	38	16	4	18	63	69	48*
Llanelli	38	11	8	19	49	64	41
Maesteg Park Athletic	38	9	13	16	52	59	40
Flint Town United	38	11	6	21	47	67	39
Briton Ferry Athletic	38	10	9	19	61	87	39
Newtown	38	9	9	20	55	87	36
Llanidloes Town	38	7	9	22	48	93	30
Abergavenney Thurs	38	7	7	24	36	76	28

* 3 points deducted

Allbright Bitter Welsh Cup

Semi-Finals

Cardiff City 2 Wrexham 0
Wrexham 1 Cardiff 0
Cardiff City win 2-1 on aggregate

Rhyl 2 Connah's Quay Nomads 0
Connah's Quay Nomads 1 Rhyl 0
Rhyl win 2-1 on aggregate

FINAL

National Stadium, Cardiff   May 16   16,443

Cardiff City 5
Rhyl 0
Cardiff City: Ward, James, Searle, Brazil (Pike), Perry,
Millar (Dale), Ramsey, Richardson, Stant, Blake, Griffith
Rhyl: Lichfield, Lee, Jones R, Espley, Lacey, Jones S, Cross
(Norman), Congerton, McMullen, Taylor (Marriott),
Jones A

Welsh Intermediate Cup Final

Brecon Corinthians 0
Llansantffraid 3

Northern Irish Football

Smirnoff Irish League

FINAL TABLE

	P	W	D	L	GF	GA	Pts
Linfield	30	20	6	4	49	15	66
Crusaders	30	21	3	6	53	27	66
Bangor	30	20	4	6	61	32	64
Portadown	30	18	9	3	70	26	63
Distillery	30	20	2	8	61	36	62
Glenavon	30	14	6	10	48	36	48
Glentoran	30	13	8	9	70	40	47
Ards	30	12	9	9	45	45	45
Carrick	30	12	2	16	50	73	38
Ballymena	30	10	6	14	41	51	36
Cliftonville	30	10	3	17	42	48	33
Omagh	30	9	5	16	38	57	32
Larne	30	9	3	18	41	59	30
Newry	30	5	5	20	30	72	20
Coleraine	30	5	3	22	28	63	18
Ballyclare	30	2	6	22	28	75	12

Bass Irish Cup

Quarter-finals   **(Replays)**

Linfield 1 Bangor 2
Ards 0 Distillery 0   Ards 1 Distillery 4
Dundela 1 Glentoran 2
Larne 1 Cliftonville 2   Larne 0 Cliftonville 2

Semi-Finals

Ards 3 Cliftonville 2
Bangor 3 Glentoran 1

FINAL	(First Replay)	(Second Replay)
Windsor Park	May 11	5,000
Ards 1	Ards 1	Ards 0
Bangor 1	Bangor 1	Bangor 1

Budweiser Cup

Semi-Finals

Ards 2 Portadown 4
Ballymena Utd 0 Distillery 0
Ballymena won 4-2 on penalties

FINAL

Windsor Park   Dec 15   2,700

Portadown 3
Ballymena 1

TNT Gold Cup

Semi-Finals

Cliftonville 2 Ballymena 1
Portadown 4 Bangor 0

FINAL

Windsor Park   Nov 11   5,100

Portadown 1
Cliftonville 0

European Football

Alfred Hitchcock could have written this one. The money was buried at the bottom of the garden in Christophe Robert's aunt's home - 250,000 French francs (a little less than £30,000), presumably in used notes. The fraud officers were there when Robert dug it up. A winger with Valenciennes, a French First Division club, Robert had accepted the money to throw a match against the best team in Europe, Marseilles, just six days before the European Cup final in May. The same offer, he claimed, was also made to his teammates, Jacques Glassmann and Jorge Burruchaga. According to Robert, it was made by a Marseilles player, Jean-Jacques Eydelie on the telephone and then the phone was passed to Jean-Pierre Bernes, the Marseilles general secretary, who confirmed the offer.

Robert later collected the money which had been left in an envelope at a Marseilles hotel. It was Glassmann who first confessed to his part in the bribery and Burruchaga and Robert later followed suit. At the end of June, Robert was prosecuted for accepting a bribe and the Marseilles officials began wriggling on the hook. Bernard Tapie, the club president, suggested that Robert had been given the money by Eydelie as a loan to open a restaurant. Eydelie, after denying the story, changed his tune after two weeks solitary confinement in a police cell and admitted it. Bernes was in hospital when the police came round to interview him suffering, according to one report, from a "diplomatic illness".

In July, FIFA, through its general secretary Sepp Blatter, said that Marseilles would be banned from next year's competition if it proved that Bernes, the secretary, had been involved. Not until September 6th did the governing bodies take any futher action. On that day, following the executive committee meeting of UEFA, that governing body decided there was sufficient evidence to ban Marseilles from defending the European Cup.

That decision was made before any ruling in the French courts and was sufficient to spur the never reticent Tapie into action. The club president immediately sought an injuction in court at Berne (the UEFA offices are in Switzerland) to overturn the UEFA decision. On September 9th, the court agreed, but Tapie reckoned without the muscle of FIFA coming into play. Joao Havelange, president of FIFA, went straight to the jugular. He stated that if Marseilles insisted on adherence to the court judgment, then all French clubs and the French national team would be banned from international competition. It was like one of those concrete balls they use for demolition come swinging down from the jib crane. It was lights out time for Tapie.

Monaco were brought in to replace them in the European Cup and, sure as day follows night, FIFA put further pressure on the French governing body and Marseilles had their French championship title taken away from them as well. Will it stop there? No, it won't. The case has still to come to court and the Valenciennes prosecutor M Eric de Montgolfier is known as a zealous man.

By comparison, the Legia Warsaw incident was small beer. Lest we forget, that team and LKS Lodz, were also found guilty of match-fixing and banned from European competition. Of course, you'd never hear of anything like this in Britain.........

FOOTBALL SHORTS

Viitorul Chirnogeni had only six players left on the field with 20 minutes still to go of their Third Division playoff in the Romanian League. The five hadn't been sent off, they fell off. They were all so drunk from a teammate's wedding the night before that the match had to be abandoned. Chirnogeni were losing 21-0.

"You don't have to be a genius to know that something's wrong when your team is booed off in August"
Manchester City's general manager explaining that he is not a genius, but he's still sacking Peter Reid.

What's history worth? Well, about £35,000 if your name's Bill Foulkes. Foulkes, a mainstay of the Manchester United team that won the championship more than once every 26 years, found himself on his uppers and put his trophies up for sale. It included four league championship medals, but the most money came from the sale of his 1968 European Cup winning medal. That one fetched £11,000. It's not a lot is it really....unless you're broke.

"The boy has big feet and big hands. The feet are for playing football and the hands are for picking up the wages"
Johan Cruyff, on his new grandson.

"It's a bloody horrible job and I don't want it to turn me into a horrible person"
Graham Taylor before the Poland match, Afterwards, he wasn't horrible at all.

Jack Belche, 12, scored a hattrick for Goonhavern U13 (wherever Goonhavern is) in just 87 seconds. How big was that pitch then?

BEST ON GASCOIGNE

"It's very difficult to say, but yes"
George Best, when asked if, in his heyday, he was better than Gascoigne.
"I once said Gazza's IQ was less than his shirt number and he asked me 'What's an IQ?'"
Best again

European Leagues 1992-93

BELGIUM - FINAL TABLE

	P	W	D	L	GF	GA	Pts
Anderlecht	34	26	6	2	80	24	58
Standard Liege	34	18	9	7	69	43	45
Mechelen	34	18	6	10	53	33	42
Waregem	34	17	8	9	78	45	42
Antwerp	34	17	7	10	61	42	41
FC Brugge	34	16	8	10	49	32	40
Charleroi	34	16	8	10	58	46	40
Beveren	34	15	7	12	47	42	37
Gent	34	12	10	12	51	51	34
Lierse	34	12	7	15	41	51	31
RWD Molenbeek	34	10	11	13	39	45	31
CS Brugge	34	9	10	15	65	73	28
Liege	34	10	8	16	48	71	28
Ekeren	34	10	7	17	57	67	27
Genk	34	8	11	15	37	50	27
Lommel	34	9	4	21	42	79	22
Lokeren	34	4	12	18	32	58	20
Boom	34	6	7	21	40	95	19

Cup Final: Standard Liege 2 Charleroi 0

RCS (Formerly Czechoslovakia) - FINAL TABLE

	P	W	D	L	GF	GA	Pts
Sparta Prague	30	23	2	5	66	24	48
Slavia Prague	30	18	7	5	70	28	43
Slovan Bratislava	30	17	4	7	61	30	42
Dunaskja	30	16	5	9	46	36	37
Sigma Olomouc	30	14	7	9	44	38	35
Inter Bratislava	30	14	3	13	46	42	31
Brno	30	13	5	12	40	51	31
Banik Ostrava	30	10	11	9	47	38	31
Tatran Presov	30	9	8	13	42	40	28
Hradec Kralove	30	10	7	13	32	36	27
Vitkovice	30	9	9	12	30	44	27
Nitra	30	6	13	10	27	38	25
Budejovice	30	9	5	16	36	39	23
Bohemians	30	5	9	16	23	53	19
Dukla Prague	30	7	5	18	38	74	19
Spartak Travna	30	3	10	17	24	60	16

6 Slovak clubs will play in the Slovak First Division next season. The championship of the Czech Republic will have 16 teams, nine from the Czechoslovakian First Division and 7 promoted teams. Bohemians will be relegated.

Czech Cup Final: Sparta Prague 2 Brno 0
Slovak Cup Final: Kosice 0 Dunaskja 0
Czechoslovakian Cup Final: Kosice 5 Sparta Prague 1

DENMARK - FINAL TABLE

	P	W	D	L	GF	GA	Pts
FC Copenhagen	14	8	3	3	31	23	32
Odense	14	8	3	3	19	15	31
Brondby	14	8	3	3	29	16	30
Aalborg	14	5	5	4	24	22	26
Silkeborg	14	4	5	5	17	17	23
Aarhus	14	4	3	7	24	29	21
Lyngby	14	4	2	8	22	22	18
Naestved	14	1	4	9	16	36	14

Cup Final: Odense 2 Aalborg 0

FRANCE - FINAL TABLE

	P	W	D	L	GF	GA	Pts
Marseille	38	23	9	6	72	36	55
Paris St Germain	38	20	11	7	61	29	51
Monaco	38	21	9	8	56	29	51
Bordeaux	38	18	12	8	42	25	48
Nantes	38	17	11	10	54	39	45
Auxerre	38	18	7	13	57	44	43
St Etienne	38	13	17	8	34	26	43
Strasbourg	38	12	16	10	58	57	40
Lens	38	12	16	10	36	41	40
Montpellier	38	12	12	14	36	41	36
Caen	38	13	9	16	55	54	35
Metz	38	11	13	14	44	45	35
Toulose	38	9	16	13	36	45	34
Lyon	38	9	15	14	40	45	33
Le Havre	38	11	11	16	42	53	33
Sochaux	38	11	10	17	33	50	32
Lille	38	7	16	15	26	48	30
Valenciennes	38	9	11	18	42	57	29
Toulon	38	6	13	19	31	57	25
Nimes	38	3	16	19	32	66	22

Cup Final: Paris St Germain 3 Nantes 0

GERMANY - FINAL TABLE

	P	W	D	L	GF	GA	Pts
Werder Bremen	34	19	10	5	63	30	48
Bayern Munich	34	18	11	5	74	45	47
Eintracht Frankfurt	34	15	12	7	56	39	42
Borussia Dortmund	34	18	5	11	61	43	41
Leverkusen	34	14	12	8	64	45	40
Karlsruhe	34	14	11	9	60	54	39
Stuttgart	34	12	12	10	56	50	36
Kaiserslautern	34	13	9	12	50	40	35
Moenchengladbach	34	13	9	12	59	59	35
Schalke	34	11	12	11	42	43	35
Hamburg	34	8	15	11	42	44	31
Cologne	34	12	4	18	41	51	28
Nuremburg	34	10	8	16	30	47	28
Wattenscheid	34	10	8	16	46	67	28
Dynamo Dresden	34	7	13	14	32	49	27
Bochum	34	8	10	16	45	52	26
Uerdingen	34	7	10	17	35	64	24
Saarbrucken	34	5	13	16	37	71	23

Cup Final: Leverkusen 1 Hertha Berlin 0

GREECE - FINAL TABLE

	P	W	D	L	GF	GA	Pts
AEK Athens	34	24	6	4	78	27	78
Panathinaikos	34	24	5	5	85	21	77
Olympiakos	34	20	8	6	68	31	68
Ofi Crete	34	19	9	6	64	32	66
PAOK Salonika	34	17	6	11	52	38	57
Iraklis	34	16	8	10	51	41	56
Larissa	34	11	10	13	36	42	43
Xanthi	34	11	9	14	56	66	42
Aris Salonika	34	12	6	16	40	50	42

Panachaiki	34	10	9	15	41	50	39
Athinaikos	34	9	12	13	27	37	39
Apollon	34	10	7	17	27	49	37
Doxa Drama	34	9	9	16	34	57	36
Kalamaria	34	7	14	13	28	44	35
Edessaikos	34	9	8	17	38	60	35
Pierikos	34	9	7	18	35	62	34
Ionikos	34	9	6	19	33	49	33
Korinthos	34	6	9	19	28	65	27

Cup Final: Panathinaikos 1 Olympiakos 0

HOLLAND - FINAL TABLE

	P	W	D	L	GF	GA	Pts
Feyenoord	34	22	9	3	82	32	53
PSV Eindhoven	34	22	7	5	81	34	51
Ajax	34	20	9	5	87	30	49
Vitesse	34	16	14	4	58	29	46
Twente	34	17	8	9	64	39	42
Volendam	34	12	13	9	51	34	37
Maastricht	34	15	7	12	49	47	37
Utrecht	34	12	11	11	44	40	35
RKC Waalwijk	34	12	9	13	49	57	33
Willem II	34	12	8	14	41	38	32
Roda	34	11	7	16	51	59	29
Groningen	34	9	11	14	31	49	29
Sparta	34	8	11	15	36	65	27
Cambuur	34	6	13	15	39	58	25
Go Ahead	34	8	9	17	36	64	25
Fortuna Sittard	34	7	7	20	34	76	21
Den Bosch	34	6	9	19	35	79	21
Dordrecht	34	5	10	19	30	66	20

Cup Final: Ajax 6 Heerenveen 2

ITALY - FINAL TABLE

	P	W	D	L	GF	GA	Pts
AC Milan	34	18	14	2	65	32	50
Internazionale	34	17	12	5	59	36	46
Parma	34	16	9	9	47	34	41
Juventus	34	15	9	10	59	47	39
Lazio	34	13	12	9	65	51	38
Cagliari	34	14	9	11	45	33	37
Sampdoria	34	12	12	10	50	48	36
Atalanta	34	14	8	12	42	44	36
Torino	34	9	17	8	38	39	35
Roma	34	8	17	9	42	39	33
Napoli	34	10	12	12	49	50	32
Foggia	34	10	12	12	38	53	32
Genoa	34	7	17	10	41	55	31
Fiorentina	34	8	14	12	53	56	30
Udinese	34	10	10	14	42	48	30
Brescia	34	9	12	13	36	44	30
Ancona	34	6	7	21	40	73	19
Pescara	34	6	5	23	45	74	17

Cup Final: Torino 3,2 Roma 0,5

PORTUGAL - FINAL TABLE

	P	W	D	L	GF	GA	Pts
Porto	34	24	6	4	59	17	54
Benfica	34	22	8	4	60	18	52
Sporting	34	17	11	6	59	30	45
Boavista	34	14	11	9	46	34	39
Maritimo	34	15	7	12	56	48	37

Farense	34	11	13	10	41	36	35
Belenenses	34	11	12	11	42	40	34
Beira Mar	34	10	12	12	24	33	32
Gil Vicente	34	12	7	15	34	42	31
Pacos Ferreira	34	10	11	13	35	44	31
Guimaraes	34	14	3	17	41	53	31
Braga	34	14	3	17	41	53	31
Estoril	34	9	12	13	29	41	30
Famalicao	34	10	10	14	29	48	30
Salgueiros	34	10	9	15	28	44	29
Tirsense	34	10	8	16	27	37	28
Espinho	34	9	10	15	38	55	28
Chaves	34	4	8	22	34	61	16

Cup Final: Benfica 5 Boavista 2

RUSSIA - FINAL TABLE

	P	W	D	L	GF	GA	Pts
Spartak Moscow	14	10	4	0	36	12	24
Vladikavkaz	14	7	3	4	26	20	17
Dynamo Moscow	14	6	4	4	26	21	16
Lokomotiv Moscow	14	5	5	4	14	15	15
CSKA Moscow	14	5	4	5	25	19	14
Novgorod	14	2	7	5	10	18	11
Asmaral Moscow	14	3	3	8	17	36	9
Rostov	14	1	4	9	3	16	6

Cup Final: Torpedo Moscow 1 CSKA Moscow 1
Torpedo Moscow won 5-4 on penalties

SPAIN - FINAL TABLE

	P	W	D	L	GF	GA	Pts
Barcelona	38	25	8	5	87	34	58
Real Madrid	38	24	9	5	75	28	57
La Coruna	38	22	10	6	67	33	54
Valencia	38	19	10	9	60	33	48
Tenerife	38	15	14	9	59	47	44
Atletico Madrid	38	16	11	11	52	42	43
Seville	38	17	9	12	46	44	43
Athletic Bilbao	38	17	6	15	53	49	40
Zaragoza	38	11	13	14	37	52	35
Osasuna	38	12	10	16	42	41	34
Celta	38	9	16	13	25	32	34
Real Sociedad	38	13	8	17	46	59	34
Sporting Gijon	38	11	12	15	38	57	34
Rayo Vallecano	38	8	17	13	40	49	33
Logrones	38	11	11	16	32	48	33
Oviedo	38	11	10	17	42	52	32
Albacete	38	11	9	18	54	59	31
Espanol	38	9	11	18	40	56	29
Cadiz	38	5	12	21	30	70	22
Burgos	38	4	14	20	29	69	22

Cup Final: Real Madrid 2 Zaragoza 0

European Cup Competitions
European Cup

First Round (over 2 legs)

AEK Athens 1 *(Alexandris)*
Apoel 1 *(Hadjilukas)*

Apoel 2 *(Gogic, Sasulitis)*
AEK Athens 2 *(Sabanadzovic,
Alexandris)*
AEK Athens win on away goals
- - - - - - - - - - - - - - - - - - -
FK Austria 3 *(Hasenhuttl, Fridrikas,
Kogler)*
CSKA Sofia 1 *(Shiskov)*

CSKA Sofia 3 *(Metkov, Andonov 2)*
FK Austria 2 *(Flogel, Ivanauskas)*
FK Austria win 5-4 on aggregate
- - - - - - - - - - - - - - - - - - -
Barcelona 1 *(Amor)*
Viking Stavanger 0

Viking Stavanger 0
Barcelona 0
Barcelona win 1-0 on aggregate
- - - - - - - - - - - - - - - - - - -
Glentoran 0
Marseille 5 *(Voller,Martin Vasquez 2,
Sauzee, Ferreri)*

Marseille 3 *(Omam-Biyik, Pele, Boli)*
Glentoran 0
Marseille win 8-0 on aggregate
- - - - - - - - - - - - - - - - - - -
IFK Gothenburg 2 *(Eskeleinen,
Ekstrom)*
Besiktas 0

Besiktas 2 *(Metin, Feyyaz)*
IFK Gothenburg 1 *(Eskeleinen)*
Gothenburg win 3-2 on aggregate
- - - - - - - - - - - - - - - - - - -
Kuuysysi 1 *(Rinne)*
Dinamo Bucharest 0

Dinamo Bucharest 2 *(Gerstenmajer,
Demollari)*
Kuuysysi 0
Dinamo Bucharest win 2-1 on agg.
- - - - - - - - - - - - - - - - - - -
Lech Poznan 2 *(Trzeciak, Podbrozny)*
Skonto Riga 0

Skonto Riga 0
Lech Poznan 0
Lech Poznan win 2-0 on aggregate
- - - - - - - - - - - - - - - - - - -
Maccabi Tel Aviv 0
FC Brugge 1 *(Staelens)*

FC Brugge 3 *(Staelens, Verheyen 2)*
Maccabi Tel Aviv 0
FC Brugge win 4-0 on aggregate
- - - - - - - - - - - - - - - - - - -
AC Milan 4 *(Van Basten 2, Albertini,
Papin)*
Olimpija Ljubljana 0

Olimpija Ljubljana 0

AC Milan 3 *(Massaro, Rijkaard,
Tassotti)*
AC Milan win 7-0 on aggregate
- - - - - - - - - - - - - - - - - - -
PSV Eindhoven 6 *(Koeman,
Ellerman 3, Kieft,
Numan)*
Zalgiris Vilnius 0

Zalgiris Vilnius 0
PSV Eindhoven 2 *(Numan, Romario)*
PSV Eindhoven win 8-0 on aggregate
- - - - - - - - - - - - - - - - - - -
Rangers 2 *(Hateley, Huistra)*
Lyngby 0

Lyngby 0
Rangers 1 *(Durrant)*
Rangers win 3-0 on aggregate
- - - - - - - - - - - - - - - - - - -
Sion 4 *(Hottiger, Tulio, Assis)*
Tavria Simferopol 1
(Shevchenko (pen))

Tavria Simferopol 1 *(Shevchenko)*
Sion 3 *(Tulio, Carlos Luis, Domingos)*
Sion win 7-2 on aggregate
- - - - - - - - - - - - - - - - - - -
Slovan Bratislava 4 *(Gostic,
Dubovsky 2, Morvec)*
Ferencvaros 1 *(Lipcsei)*

Ferencvaros 0
Slovan Bratislava 0
Slovan Bratislava win 4-1 on aggregate
- - - - - - - - - - - - - - - - - - -
Stuttgart 3 *(Walter 2, Buck)*
Leeds Utd 0

Leeds Utd 4 *(Speed, McAllister,
Cantona, Chapman)*
Stuttgart 1 *(Buck)*
*Leeds Utd awarded match 3-0 after
Stuttgart fielded fourth foreign player*
- - - - - - - - - - - - - - - - - - -
Union Luxembourg 1 *(Deville)*
FC Porto 4 *(Semedo, Fernando Couto,
Toni, Domingos)*

FC Porto 5 *(Kostadinov 2, Toni 2,
Jose Carlos)*
Union Luxembourg 0
FC Porto win 9-1 on aggregate
- - - - - - - - - - - - - - - - - - -
Vikingur 0
CSKA Moscow 1 *(Korsakov)*

CSKA Moscow 4 *(Sergeyev,
Korsakov, Grishin,
Kolesnikov)*
Vikingur 0
CSKA Moscow win 5-0 on aggregate
- - - - - - - - - - - - - - - - - - -

First Round Replay

Leeds Utd 2 *(Strachan, Shutt)*
Stuttgart 1 *(Golke)*
_____

Second Round (over 2 legs)

AEK Athens 1 *(Dimitriudis)*
PSV Eindhoven 0

PSV Eindhoven 3 *(Romario 3)*
AEK Athens 0
PSV Eindhoven win 3-1 on aggregate
- - - - - - - - - - - - - - - - - - -
FC Brugge 2 *(Verheyen, Booy)*
FK Austria 0

FK Austria 3 *(Zsak, Fridrikas,
Ivanauskas)*
FC Brugge 1 *(Van der Heyden)*
FC Brugge win on away goals
- - - - - - - - - - - - - - - - - - -
CSKA Moscow 1 *(Grishin)*
Barcelona 1 *(Beguiristain)*

Barcelona 2 *(Nadal, Beguiristain)*
CSKA Moscow 3 *(Buchmanov
Mashkarin, Korsakov)*
CSKA Moscow win 4-3 on aggregate
- - - - - - - - - - - - - - - - - - -
Dinamo Bucharest 0
Marseille 0

Marseille 2 *(Boksic)*
Dinamo Bucharest 0
Marseille win 2-0 on aggregate
- - - - - - - - - - - - - - - - - - -
IFK Gothenburg 1 *(Bengtsson)*
Lech Poznan 0

Lech Poznan 0
IFK Gothenburg 3 *(Ekstrom, Nilsson,
Mild)*
IFK Gothenburg win 4-0 on aggregate
- - - - - - - - - - - - - - - - - - -
Rangers 2 *(Lukic (og), McCoist)*
Leeds Utd 1 *(McAllister)*

Leeds Utd 1 *(Cantona)*
Rangers 2 *(Hateley, McCoist)*
Rangers win 4-2 on aggregate
- - - - - - - - - - - - - - - - - - -
Sion 2 *(Orlando, Assis)*
FC Porto 2 *(Semedo, Fernando Couto)*

FC Porto 4 *(Jorge Costa, Domingos,
Kostadinov, J Malgalhaes)*
Sion 0
FC Porto win 6-2 on aggregate
- - - - - - - - - - - - - - - - - - -
Slovan Bratislava 0
AC Milan 1 *(Maldini)*

AC Milan 4 *(Boban, Rijkaard,
Simone, Papin)*
Slovan Bratislava 0
AC Milan win 5-0 on aggregate

CHAMPION'S LEAGUE

Group A

FC Brugge 1 *(Amokachi)*
CSKA Moscow 0

Rangers 2 *(McSwegan, Hateley)*
Marseille 2 *(Boksic, Voller)*

CSKA Moscow 0
Rangers 1 *(Ferguson)*

Marseille 3 *(Sauzee (pen), Boksic 2)*
FC Brugge 0

FC Brugge 1 *(Dziubinski)*
Rangers 1 *(Huistra)*

CSKA Moscow 1 *(Faizulin)*
Marseille 1 *(Pele)*

Marseille 6 *(Sauzee 3 (2 pen), Pele,*
       Ferreri, Desailly)
CSKA Moscow 0

Rangers 2 *(Durrant, Nisbet)*
FC Brugge 1 *(Staelens)*

CSKA Moscow 1 *(Sergeyev)*
FC Brugge 2 *(Schaessens, Verheyen)*

Marseille 1 *(Sauzee)*
Rangers 1 *(Durrant)*

FC Brugge 0
Marseille 1 *(Boksic)*

Rangers 0
CSKA Moscow 0

FINAL TABLE

	P	W	D	L	F	A	Pt
Marseille	6	3	3	0	14	4	9
Rangers	6	2	4	0	7	5	8
FC Brugge	6	2	1	3	5	8	5
CSKA Moscow	6	0	2	4	2	11	2

Group B

AC Milan 4 *(Van Basten 4 (1 pen))*
IFK Gothenburg 0

FC Porto 2 *(Magalhaes, Jose Carlos)*
PSV Eindhoven 2 *(Romario 2)*

IFK Gothenburg 1 *(Eriksson)*
FC Porto 0

PSV Eindhoven 1 *(Romario)*
AC Milan 2 *(Rijkaard, Simone)*

PSV Eindhoven 1 *(Numan)*
IFK Gothenburg 3 *(Nilsson,*
       Ekstrom 2)

FC Porto 0
AC Milan 1 *(Papin)*

IFK Gothenburg 3 *(Nilsson, Ekstrom,*
       Martinsson)
PSV Eindhoven 0

AC Milan 1 *(Eranio)*
FC Porto 0

IFK Gothenburg 0
AC Milan 1 *(Massaro)*

PSV Eindhoven 0
FC Porto 1 *(Ze Carlos)*

AC Milan 2 *(Simone 2)*
PSV Eindhoven 0

FC Porto 2 *(Ze Carlos, Timofte)*
IFK Gothenburg 0

FINAL TABLE

	P	W	D	L	F	A	Pt
AC Milan	6	6	0	0	11	1	12
IFK Gothenb'rg	6	3	0	3	7	8	6
FC Porto	6	2	1	3	5	5	5
PSV Eindhoven	6	0	1	5	4	13	1

EUROPEAN CUP FINAL

Munich   May 26   64,400

Marseille 1 *(Boli)*
AC Milan 0

Marseille: Barthez, Angloma
(Durand), Boli, Desailly, Pele,
Eydelie, Sauzee, Deschamps, Di
Meco, Boksic, Voller (Thomas)
AC Milan: Rossi, Tassotti,
Costacurta, Baresi, Maldini,
Donadoni (Papin), Albertini,
Rijkaard, Lentini, Van Basten
(Eranio), Massaro

European Cup-Winners Cup

Preliminary Round

Avenir Beggen 1 *(Krings)*
Torshavn 0

Torshavn 1 *(Reynheim)*
Avenir Beggen 1 *(Krahen)*

Branik Maribor 4 *(Simundja 2,*
Tarana, Bonkovski)
Hamrun Spartans 0

Hamrun Spartans 2 *(Brincat 2)*
Branik Maribor 1 *(Parana)*

Stromsgodset 0
Hapoel Petah Tikva 2 *(Bason 2)*

Hapoel Petah Tikva 2 *(Levin, Bason)*
Stromsgodset 0

Vaduz 0
Chernomoretz Odessa 5 *(Tsimbalar,*
Lebed, Sak, Gousev 2)

Chernomoretz Odessa 7 *(Nikiforov 4*
Yablonski, Tsymbalar, Lebed)

First Round

AIK Stockholm 3 *(Simpson,*
Hallstrom, Yevtushenko)
Aarhus 3 *(Tofting, Christensen 2)*

Aarhus 1 *(Harder)*
AIK Stockholm 1 *(Simpson)*

Airdrieonians 0
Sparta Prague 1 *(Sopko)*

Sparta Prague 2 *(Vrabec, Vonasek)*
Airdrieonians 1 *(Black)*

Bohemians 0
Steaua Bucharest 0

Steaua Bucharest 4 *(Andrasi 2,*
Vladoiu, Viorel)
Bohemians 0

Branik Maribor 0
Atletico Madrid 3 *(Alfredo, Garcia 2)*

Atletico Madrid 6 *(Alfaro, Juanito,*
Sabas, Pizo Gomez, Aguilera, Taraba)
Branik Maribor 1 *(Bicarcik)*

Cardiff 1 *(Pike)*
Admira Wacker 1 *(Abfalterer)*

Admira Wacker 2 *(Marschall,*
Abfalterer)
Cardiff 0

Feyenoord 1 *(Kiprich)*
Hapoel Petah Tikva 0

Hapoel Petah Tikva 2 *(Levin,*
Kakkon)
Feyenoord 1 *(Fraser)*

Glenavon 1 *(Smith)*
Antwerp 1 *(Lehnhoff)*

Antwerp 1 *(Kiekens)*
Glenavon 1 *(Farris)*

Levski Sofia 2 *(Borimirov, Getov)*
Lucerne 1 *(Camenzind)*

Lucerne 1 *(Camenzind)*
Levski Sofia 0

Liverpool 6 *(Stewart 2, Rush 4)*
Apollon Limassol 1 *(Spoljaric)*

Apollon Limassol 1 *(Spoljaric)*
Liverpool 2 *(Rush, Hutchison)*

Miedz Legnica 0
Monaco 1 *(Djorkaeff)*

Monaco 0
Miedz Legnica 0

Moscow Spartak 0
Avenir Beggen 0

Avenir Beggen 1 *(Novak)*
Moscow Spartak 5 *(Onopko,*
Piatnitski 2, Radchenko, Povov)

Olympiakos 0
Chernomoretz Odessa 1 *(Sak)*

Chernomoretz Odessa 0
Olympiakos 3 *(Mitsidonas,*
Litovchenko, Protasov)

Parma 1 *(Asprilla)*
Ujpest 0

Ujpest 1 *(Hetesi)*
Parma 1 *(Grun)*

Trabzonspor 2 *(Hami 2)*
TPS Turku 0

TPS Turku 2 *(Kajdu, Lehtonen)*
Trabzonspor 2 *(Hami, Orhan)*

Valur 0
Boavista 0

Boavista 3 *(Marlon 2, Ricky)*
Valur 0

Werden Bremen 3 *(Rufer 2, Bratseth)*

Hannover 1 *(Wojcicki)*

Hannover 2 *(Daschner 2)*
Werder Bremen 1 *(Rufer)*

Second Round

Aarhus 3 *(Andersen, Christensen,*
Nielsen)
Steaua Bucharest 2*(Vladoiu,*
Dumitrescu)

Steaua Bucharest 2 *(Cristescu,*
Vladoiu)
Aarhus 1 *(Christensen)*

Admira Wacker 2 *(Marschall, Bacher)*
Antwerp 4 *(Czerniatynski 2, Segers,*
Severeyens)

Antwerp 3 *(Czerniatynski, Severeyns,*
Van Rethy)
Admira Wacker 4 *(Bacher, Abfalterer,*
Ljung 2)

Lucerne 1 *(Ruda)*
Feyenoord 0

Feyenoord 4 *(Taument, Blinker,*
Kiprich 2)
Lucerne 1 *(Nadig)*

Monaco 0
Olympiakos 1 *(Valtsis)*

Olympiakos 0
Monaco 0

Parma 0
Boavista 0

Boavista 0
Parma 2 *(Di Chiara, Melli)*

Spartak Moscow 4 *(Pisarev, Karpin 2,*
Lediakhov)
Liverpool 2 *(Wright, McManaman)*

Liverpool 0
Spartak Moscow 2 *(Radchenko,*
Piatnitski)

Trabzonspor 0
Atletico Madrid 2 *(Futre, Moya)*

Atletico Madrid 0
Trabzonspor 0

Werder Bremen 2 *(Neubarth, Fufer)*
Sparta Prague 3 *(Sopko, Dvirnik,*
Vonasek)

Sparta Prague 1 *(Siegl)*
Werder Bremen 0

Quarter Finals
Antwerp 0
Steaua Bucharest 0

Steaua Bucharest 1 *(Dumitrescu)*
Antwerp 0

Feyenoord 0
Moscow Spartak 1 *(Piatnitski)*

Moscow Spartak 3 *(Karpin 2, Radchenko)*
Feyenoord 1 *(Kiprich)*

Olympiakos 1 *(Valtsis)*
Atletico Madrid 1 *(Moya)*

Atletico Madrid 3 *(Manolo 2, Alfaro)*
Olympiakos 1 *(Tsaluhidis)*

Sparta Prague 0
Parma 0

Parma 2 *(Melli, Asprilla)*
Sparta Prague 0

Semi Finals
Atletico Madrid 1 *(Luis Garcia)*
Parma 2 *(Asprilla 2)*

Parma 0
Atletico Madrid 1 *(Sabas)*

Moscow Spartak 1 *(Piatnitski)*
Antwerp 0

Antwerp 3 *(Czerniatynski, Jakovljevic, Lehnhoff)*
Moscow Spartak 1 *(Radchenko)*

Final
Wembley   May 12
Parma 3 (Minotti, Melli, Cuoghi)
Antwerp 1 (Seveneyns)

UEFA Cup

Selected matches only from 1st and 2nd rounds
First Round
Cologne 2 *(Jensen, Ordenewitz)*
Celtic 0

Celtic 3 *(McStay, Creaney, Collins)*
Cologne 0
- -
Hibernian 2 *(Beaumont, McGinley)*
Anderlecht 2 *(Degryse pen, Van Vossen)*

Anderlecht 1 *(Nilis)*
Hibernian 1 *(Jackson)*
- -
Manchester United 0
Torpedo Moscow 0

Torpedo Moscow 0
Manchester United 0
Torpedo won 4-3 on penalties

Sheffield Wednesday 8 *(Waddle, Anderson 2, Warhurst 2,*
Bart-Williams 2, Worthington)
Spora Luxembourg 1 *(Cruz)*

Spora Luxembourg 1 *(Cruz)*
Sheffield Wednesday 2 *(Watson, Warhurst)*
- -
Slavia Prague 1 *(Tatarchuk)*
Hearts 0

Hearts 4 *(Mackay, Baird, Levein, Snodin)*
Slavia Prague 2 *(Silhavy, Kuka)*
- -
Standard Liège 5 *(Asselman 2, Goossens 2, Leonard)*
Portadown 0

Portadown 0
Standard Liège 0
- -
Vitesse 3 *(Van der Brom 2, Latuheru)*
Derry City 0

Derry City 1 *(Mooney)*
Vitesse 2 *(Straal, Laamers)*

Second Round
Borussia Dortmund 1 *(Chapuisat)*
Celtic 0

Celtic 1
Borussia Dortmund 2 *(Chapuisat, Zorc)*
- -
Kaiserslautern 3 *(Funkel pen, Marin, Witeczek)*
Sheffield Wednesday 1 *(Hirst)*

Sheffield Wednesday 2 *(Wilson, Sheridan)*
Kaiserslautern 2 *(Witeczek, Zeyer)*
- -
Hearts 0
Standard Liège 1 *(Bettagno)*

Standard Liège 1 *(Wilmots)*
Hearts 0

Third Round
Ajax 2 *(Davids, Jonk)*
Kaiserslautern 0

Kaiserslautern 0
Ajax 1 *(Alften)*
- -
Borussia Dortmund 3 *(Chapuisat, Zorc pen, Povlsen)*
Zaragoza 1 *(Franco)*

Zaragoza 2 *(Poyet, Brehme)*
Borussia Dortmund 1 *(Chapuisat)*
- -
Moscow Dynamo 2 *(Kalitvintsev, Dertkatch)*
Benfica 2 *(Isaias 2)*

Benfica 2 *(Isaias, Yuran)*
Moscow Dynamo 0
- -

Paris St Germain 0
Anderlecht 0

Anderlecht 1 *(Bosman)*
Paris St Germain 1 *(Kombouare)*
- -
Roma 3 *(Aldair 2, Muzzi)*
Galatasaray 1 *(Hakan)*

Galatasaray 3 *(Mustafa 2, Arif)*
Roma 2 *(Caniggia, Hassler)*
- -
Sigma Olomouc 1 *(Marosi)*
Juventus 2 *(Moller, Dino Baggio)*

Juventus 5 *(Vialli 2, Casiraghi, Moller, Ravanelli)*
Sigma Olomouc 0
- -
Standard Liège 2 *(Goossens 2)*
Auxerre 2 *(Verlaat, Baticle)*

Auxerre 2 *(Baticle, Dutuel)*
Standard Liège 1 *(Wilmots)*
- -
Vitesse 0
Real Madrid 1 *(Hierro)*

Real Madrid 1 *Zamorano)*
Vitesse 0

Quarter-finals
Auxerre 4 *(Verlaat, Martins, Vahirua, Dutuel)*
Ajax 2 *(Pettersson, Vink)*

Ajax 1 *(De Boer)*
Auxerre 0
- -
Benfica 2 *Vitor Paneira 2)*
Juventus 1 *(Vialli)*

Juventus 3 *(Kohler, Dino Baggio, Ravanelli)*
Benfica 0
- -
Real Madrid 3 *(Butragueno, Zamorano, Michel)*
Paris St Germain 1 *(Ginola)*

Paris St Germain 4 *(Weah, Ginola, Valdo, Kombouare)*
Real Madrid 1 *(Zamorano)*
- -
Roma 1 *(Mihailovic)*
Borussia Dortmund 0

Borussia Dortmund 2 *(Schulz, Sippel)*
Roma 0

Semi-finals
Borussia Dortmund 2 *(Karl, Zorc)*
Auxerre 0

Auxerre 2 *(Martins, Verlaat)*
Borussia Dortmund 0
Borussia Dortmund win 6-5 on penalties
- -

Juventus 2 *(Roberto Baggio 2)*
Paris St Germain 1 *(Weah)*

Paris St Germain 0
Juventus 1 *(Roberto Baggio)*

Final
Borussia Dortmund 1 *(Rummenigge)*
Juventus 3 *(Dino Baggio, Roberto Baggio 2)*

Juventus 3 *(Dino Baggio 2, Moller)*
Borussia Dortmund 0

Women's Football

NATIONAL LEAGUE
Premier Division

	P	W	D	L	GF	GA	Pts
Arsenal	18	17	0	1	66	8	34
Doncaster Belles	18	16	0	2	80	10	32
Knowsley	18	11	1	6	37	33	23
Wimbledon	18	9	3	6	36	37	21
Red Star Southampton	18	7	3	8	37	41	17
Ipswich Town	18	7	3	8	31	49	17
Stanton Rangers	18	6	1	11	24	45	13
Millwall Lionesses	18	3	2	13	16	41	8
Maidstone Tigresses	18	2	4	12	8	43	8
Bronte	18	2	3	13	16	44	7

Division One South

	P	W	D	L	GF	GA	Pts
District Line	18	15	1	2	93	31	31
Hassocks	18	12	2	4	53	38	26
Town & County	18	9	2	7	51	39	20
Hemel Hempstead	18	8	4	6	38	37	20
Brighton & Hove Albion	18	8	2	8	41	42	18
Horsham	18	6	5	7	34	42	17
Oxford	18	5	5	8	20	34	15
Epsom & Ewell	18	6	2	10	44	52	14
Bristol Backwell	18	4	3	11	31	50	11
Saltdean	18	3	2	13	30	70	8

Division One North

	P	W	D	L	GF	GA	Pts
Leasowe Pacific	18	16	1	1	100	21	33
Nottingham Argyle	18	14	1	3	73	23	29
Abbeydale	18	11	3	4	62	20	25
Sheffield Wednesday	18	9	2	7	68	29	20
St Helens	18	9	1	8	67	49	19
Wolverhampton	18	7	3	8	52	37	17
Villa Aztecs	18	8	1	9	47	45	17
Cowgate Kestrels	18	6	3	9	32	51	15
Sunderland	18	2	0	16	19	103	4
Milton Keynes	18	0	1	17	8	150	1

NATIONAL LEAGUE CUP
Semi Finals
Wimbledon 2 Arsenal 4
Knowsley 5 Leasowe Pacific 4
Final
Arsenal 3 Knowsley 0

WFA CUP
Sixth Round
Arsenal 5 Red Star Southampton 1
Wimbledon 1 Bromley Borough 2
Maidstone Tigresses 1 Bronte 2
Ipswich Town 2 Doncaster Belles 5
Semi Finals
Arsenal 2 Bromely Borough 0
Bronte 1 Doncaster Belles 2
Final
Arsenal 3 Doncaster Belles 0

6TH EUROPEAN CHAMPIONSHIP
Quarter Finals
Norway 3 Holland 0
CIS 0 Germany 7
Sweden 1 Denmark 2
Italy 3 England 2
Denmark 1 Sweden 1
England 0 Italy 3
Holland 0 Norway 3
Germany 0 CIS 0
Semi-Finals
Norway 1 Denmark 0
Italy 1 Germany 1
(Italy won 4-3 on penalties)
Match for 3rd Place
Denmark 3 Germany 1
Final
Norway 1 Italy 0

FOOTBALL POSTSCRIPT

It's been a funny old year for Roy of the Rovers. In March, he was off the park and out of the game when he hit the deck in the wreckage of a helicopter. But Roy wouldn't be Roy if he couldn't turn that one around. Not dead, just sleeping for a few months while the publishers suss out the response to his departing this mortal coil. "Inundated," they said and Roy sprung out of the chopper crash with all his parts together, except his left foot gone walkabout. Well, it's not very clever playing for Melchester without a left foot, is it? So our Roy hops off to Italy to manage a top club and his playing days are over. Well, you can put that in your lunchbox and eat it. Fifty-four years old, one good foot and sidelined for ever. No chance. There'll be a cholera scare, six of the team ruled out and Roy (on your head, stumpy) will be up off the bench to score the winner. You read it here first.

Athletics

These are surely the days of miracles and wonders with two world records and three gold medals from the world championships (*See Landmarks*) and the profile of the sport as high as it has ever been. Sally Gunnell and Colin Jackson may have been the world record breakers, but Linford Christie is what it's about. Over 11 million saw him take the world title in Stuttgart. Why he's even done what everybody does when they get really famous, he's made a record. And to be fair, it's about as good as one of those old Terry Venables songs....mind look what's happened to him.

Credit where credit's due; Christie has reshaped the sport in Britain. Gunnell might carp about her pay scale not equating with Christie's, but nor should it. It is not a matter of being sexist, but simply applying a modicum of market forces to the argument. If he has not yet eclipsed the status of Coe and Ovett a decade ago, he has surely reached it. He's not been Mr Perfect though. Favouring Sydney for the Olympics was silly and the Gateshead clash with Lewis was a bit tacky. It pleased ITV (as 10 million viewers would) but Lewis' manager, Joe Douglas was, according to American sources, fuming the day he did the deal with Andy Norman. It's easy to understand why. Palpably, this was not a race Lewis was interested (or competitive) in. It remains surprising he was tempted over even for £100,000.

Gateshead was also ill-timed. After Barcelona, when the idea was fresh, sackfulls of yen were on offer for an immediate match-race of the world champion against the Olympic champion. But, by the time it reached Gateshead, it was old news. It was run in Britain in August because it was the only place in the world where the interest had been sustained.

That said, there was generally a lot of money about in 1993; more than you'd expect in a world recession. Christie and Lewis collected their £100,000 from Gateshead and Lewis was paid $100,000 by the Lausanne promoter to appear in his grand prix and reportedly double that to make sure he was at the world championships. Noureddine Morceli said he wouldn't go to Stuttgart unless he was paid. He changed his mind at the last minute, but allegedly wasn't paid to do so. Addis Abebe won $500,000 for winning a road race in Djarkarta and Liz McColgan collected three-quarters of a million dollars to run three London marathons.

The British Athletic Federation, still in its infancy, had a few weaning problems. It parted company with its chief executive, Malcolm Jones, with a year of his contract to run. Jones' only fault was in being Malcolm Jones. Given that he had worked for British Athletics for some years before being given the appointment, they knew exactly what they were getting. His dismissal reflected more on those who chose him in the first place. BAF did not replace Jones; instead a triumvirate assumed power. Dave Bedford, John Lister and Peter Radford, after receiving a mandate for change from the clubs, took precedence on the management committee. They have yet to decide on a new executive, or whether they'll have one at all. If the history of the sport is anything to go by, the management committee will make all the major policy changes that it wants and then appoint a chief executive who makes none.

Primo Nebiolo (I wonder what he would have been like if his mother had called him Secundo?), president of the International Amateur Athletic Federation swept all before him. Athletes who threatened to boycott the world championships were brought or bought to heel with the promise of Mercedes cars (with the singular exception of the Ondiekis) and the championships was a considerable success despite many misgivings. Nebiolo even managed to persuade congress to move its head office from London to Monaco. The manner in which the move happened was extraordinary; Nebiolo scheduling the move for February, then scurrying away, four months early, as if the Bailiffs were waiting outside.

There were loads of world records (18 in all) to keep Il Presidente happy, but the most newsworthy came from China, on the eve of its Olympic bid (*See over*). Two other world records were in the landmark category; Yobes Ondieki's sub-27 minute run at the Bislett Games in Oslo and Noureddine Morceli's astonishing mile record in Rieti. Morceli knocked over two seconds off Steve Cram's record, which is record-breaking of Chinese proportions.

The Golden Four was inaugurated; the Grands Prix of Oslo, Zurich, Berlin and Brussels combining to market their products jointly and offer gold bars (worth about $240,000 in total) to athletes who won their events at all four of their meetings. One outcome of their association is that they are set to become an alternative to the hegemony of the IAAF.

British success was considerable; all the more considerable given the number of athletes who missed the summer through injury. Liz McColgan, Roger Black, John Ridgeon missed virtually all of it; Steve Backley, Eamonn Martin, Curtis Robb a good chunk of it; and David Grindley, the bit that really mattered.

Kriss Akabusi said goodbye to international athletics. He said it in Gateshead, in Sheffield, at Crystal Palace. He said it everywhere. Only Akabusi could have got away with

WORLD OUTDOOR RECORDS 1993
Men

Mile	3:44.39	Noureddine Morceli	ALG	Rieti, Italy	Sep 5
10,000m	27:07.91	Richard Chelimo	KEN	Stockholm	Jul 5
10,000m	26:58:38	Yobes Ondieki	KEN	Oslo	Jul 10
110mh	12.91	Colin Jackson	GBR	Stuttgart	Aug 20
High Jump	2.45m	Javier Sotomayor	CUB	Salamanca, Spain	Jul 27
Javelin	95.54	Jan Zelezny	TCH	Peitersburg, SA	Apr 6
Javelin	95.66	Jan Zelezny	TCH	Sheffield	Aug 29
4 x 100m	37.40*	United States		Stuttgart	Aug 21
		(Jon Drummond/Andre Cason/Dennis Mitchell/Leroy Burrell)			
4 x 400m	2:54.29	United States		Stuttgart	Aug 22
		(Andrew Valmon/Quincy Watts/Butch Reynolds/Michael Johnson)			

Women

1500m	3:50.46	Qu Yunxia	CHN	Beijing	Sept 11
3000m	8:22.06	Zhang Linli	CHN	Beijing	Sept 12
3000m	8:12.19	Wang Junxia	CHN	Beijing	Sept 12
3000m	8:06.11	Wang Junxia	CHN	Beijing	Sept 13
10,000m	29:31.78	Wang Junxia	CHN	Beijing	Sept 8
20,000m	1:06:48.8	Izumi Maki	JPN	Amagasaki, Japan	Sept 20
400m Hurdles	52.74	Sally Gunnell	GBR	Stuttgart	Aug 19
Triple Jump	14.97	Yolanda Chen	RUS	Moscow	Jun18
Triple Jump	15.09	Ana Biryukova	RUS	Stuttgart	Aug 21

so many farewells. He remains just about the most popular man in the sport, and rightly so. One story tells it all. Lesley Smith, a bank clerk, stole £3,000 from Akabusi's account and was jailed for six months for the offence. Akabusi, instead of showing any displeasure, offered Smith a job when she came out of jail.

Drugs stayed with us. The usual amount of rumour and innuendo was augmented by an unprecedented spate of positives as well. Ben Johnson's was the most sublime - begging the question of why any person (especially one called Ben Johnson) would take drugs then turn up to a meeting where he knew he would be tested. Conspiracy theories are always seductive, but it's difficult not to read something else into Johnson's positive. The sport was desperate to be rid of him.

On the other hand, nobody wanted Tatyana Dorovshikh to be sidelined, nor Lyudmila Narozhilenko. But they went the way of so many of the female athletes from the old Soviet Union, at least a dozen of whom have been banned this year. It gives credence to the belief that the Soviet sporting machine was doing exactly the same as the East German one, before it was dismantled.

Katrin Krabbe, Jason Livingston and Butch Reynolds all fought their corners against drug bans with varying degrees of success. Livingston failed to change anything; Krabbe got her sentence reduced for a briefish moment; Reynolds got $27m damages from an Ohio court. The Reynolds saga, as Linford might say, will keep on running.

QUOTES

"With Liz the accent is on intimidation. To say she has a high opinion of herself is a gross understatement"

Lisa Ondieki, warming up the war of words with Liz McColgan before this year's NutraSweet London Marathon. Ondieki refused to appear at press conferences with McColgan.

"I'm going to shock the world again, one more time"

Ben Johnson, shortly before the World Indoor Championships in Toronto and very shortly before he was found positive again and banned for life.

"Because of his stutter, Johnson may have a higher level of testosterone than normal people"

Jean-Jacques Kapp, president of the French Stutterers Association.

"Seventy-five percent of our work has to do with drug abuse. I used to count medals and now I count urine samples"

Helmut Meyer, announcing he will not run again as president of the German Athletics Federation.

"My leotard got twisted and stuck right up my bottom just as I was getting to the hurdle. Bit of an unwanted distraction really"

Sally Gunnell, on what caused her to lose her stride pattern in the Stuttgart semi-finals.

"We are good, that's the difference between us and Gazza"

Linford Christie giving the press a good line.

The China Syndrome

In eight September days, China's women runners shook the world with a rapid succession of extraordinary world records at their national championships. In the forefront of this Great Leap Forward was 20-year-old Wang Junxia who also ran one of the world's fastest marathons of 2:24.07 in the seaboard town of Tianjin, south east of Beijing, in April. During the Chinese championships in the Beijing Workers' Stadium, Wang set three new world marks and had a hand in a fourth. Her 10,000 metre record of 29:31.78 and the 1500 metre time of 3:51.92 were equal to that of a male B-string international, her final time in the 3000 metres, after smashing the old record in the semis, quite simply beggared belief. The time of 8:06.13 was just over two seconds slower than Ireland's Frank O'Mara took to win the world indoor championships in 1987. This was record breaking on the grand scale. It was Paavo Nurmi crossed with Flo Jo, mixed with a dash of Bob Beamon for good measure.

The prosaic facts are these. Wang Junxia comes from the northern industrial city of Shenyang - the Birmingham of China - in the province of Liaoning. In common with the 1500 metre record breaker, Qu Yunxia, Wang is advised by Junren Ma, the 48-year-old coach employed by Lioaning region.

There is nothing here to help explain the inexplicable. So, what is Ma's secret? While most in the west suspect illicit chemistry, Ma's response is that hard work is the answer, lots of it. And there is no doubt his athletes work. During the winter months they average a marathon a day and their sessions on the track, witnessed by numerous western athletes in Stuttgart, quickly became the stuff of legend.

In common with many athletes his Army, as his group are popularly known, train at altitude during 'he winter months. This is when they lay down the stamina base for the summer on the track. But there are only so many hours to the day and so many miles the body can absorb. Many athletes have trained as hard and got nowhere.

Ma is a celebrity in China. A self-taught coach who practised karate in the army, he set out to make himself famous and chose athletics as his domain. Ma has talked of the beneficial effects of stewed turtle, caterpillar fungus and jujube berry. Eccentric it may sound, but Herb Elliott's coach, Percy Cerruty, was dismissed in the fifties for this theories on diet. Now, every corner shop stocks the basics of the Cerruty fibre diet. The Austrailian, like Ma, also taught the importance of posture.

So what Ma is doing has been done before in one way or another. There are no training secrets in athletics. Even if Ma's Army are stacking enough steroids to build a Great Wall of China, it hardly explains what they have done. Steroids have been used before but not to this effect. Not only did Ma's Army bridge the gap which stood between the old marks and the new, but took them on another generation in the course of a week.

Before the world championships in Stuttgart, Ireland's Sonia O'Sullivan led the 1993 rankings. Now she is clinging on to a place in the top ten. "I don't know what to say. Everyone keeps asking me about the Chinese and I don't know what to say," she said. Neither does anyone else, Sonia.

World Championships
Stuttgart   August 13-22

MEN				
100m	1	Linford Christie	GBR	**9.87** ER
(w+0.3)	2	André Cason	USA	9.92
	3	Dennis Mitchell	USA	9.99
200m	1	Frankie Fredericks	NAM	**19.85**
(+0.3)	2	John Regis	GBR	19.94
	3	Carl Lewis	USA	19.99
400m	1	Michael Johnson	USA	**43.65**
	2	Butch Reynolds	USA	44.13
	3	Samson Kitur	KEN	44.54
800m	1	Paul Ruto	KEN	**1:44.71**
	2	Guiseppe D'Urso	ITA	1:44.88
	3	Billy Konchellah	KEN	1:44.89
	4	Curtis Robb	GBR	1:45.54
	8	Tom McKean	GBR	1:46.17
1500m	1	Noureddine Morceli	ALG	**3:34.24**
	2	Fermin Cacho	ESP	3:35.56
	3	Abdi Bile	SOM	3:35.96
	6	Matthew Yates	GBR	3:37.61
5000m	1	Ismael Kirui	KEN	**13:02.75**
	2	Haile Gebresilassie	ETH	13:03.17
	3	Fita Bayessa	ETH	13:05.40
10,000m	1	Haile Gebresilassie	ETH	**27:46.02**
	2	Moses Tanui	KEN	27:46.54
	3	Richard Chelimo	KEN	28:06.02
Mrthn	1	Mark Plaatjes	USA	**2:13:57**
	2	Lucketz Swartbooi	NAM	2:14:11
	3	Bert van Vlaanderen	HOL	2:15:12
	13	Steve Jones	GBR	2:20:04
		Paul Evans GBR dnf		
3000msc	1	Moses Kiptanui	KEN	**8:06.36**
	2	Patrick Sang	KEN	8:07.53
	3	Alessandro Lambruschini	ITA	8:08.78
110mh	1	Colin Jackson	GBR	**12.91** WR
(+0.5)	2	Tony Jarrett	GBR	13.00
	3	Jack Pierce	USA	13.06
400mh	1	Kevin Young	USA	**47.18**
	2	Samuel Matete	ZAM	47.60
	3	Winthrop Graham	JAM	47.62
PV	1	Sergey Bubka	UKR	**6.00m**
	2	Grigoriy Yegorov	KZK	5.90m
	3	Maksim Tarasov	RUS	5.80m
HJ	1	Javier Sotomayor	CUB	**2.40m**
	2	Artur Partyka	POL	2.37m
	3	Steve Smith	GBR	2.37
LJ	1	Mike Powell	USA	**8.59m**
	2	Stanislav Tarasenko	RUS	8.16m
	3	Vitaliy Kirilenko	UKR	8.15m
TJ	1	Mike Conley	USA	**17.86m**
	2	Leonid Voloshin	RUS	17.65m
	3	Jonathan Edwards	GBR	17.44m
Shot	1	Werner Günthör	SUI	**21.97m**
	2	Randy Barnes	USA	21.80m
	3	Mike Stulce	USA	20.94m
DT	1	Lars Riedel	GER	**67.72m**
	2	Dmitriy Shevchenko	RUS	66.90m
	3	Jürgen Schult	GER	66.12m
HT	1	Andrey Abduvaleyiv	TJK	**81.64m**
	2	Igor Astapkovich	BLS	79.88m

	3	Tabor Gecsek	HUN	79.54m
Javelin	1	Jan Zelezny	TCH	**85.98m**
	2	Kimmo Kinnunen	FIN	84.78m
	3	Mick Hill	GBR	82.96m
	4	Steve Backley	GBR	81.80m
Decthln	1	Dan O'Brien	USA	**8817**
	2	Eduard Hämäläinen	BLS	8724
	3	Paul Meier	GER	8548
20kmW	1	Valentin Massana	ESP	**1:22:31**
	2	G'vanni de Benedictus	ITA	1:23:06
	3	Daniel Plaza	ESP	1:23:18
50kmW	1	Jesús Angel Garcia	ESP	**3:41:41**
	2	Valentin Kononen	FIN	3:42:02
	3	Valeriy Spitsyn	RUS	3:42:50
4x100m	1	USA		**37.48**
		(Drummond, Cason, Mitchell, Burrell)		
		The same quartet equalled the world record		
		with a 37.40 timing in the heats.		
	2	Great Britain		37.77 ER
		(Jackson, Jarrett, Regis Christie)		
	3	Canada		37.83
4x400m	1	USA		**2:54.29** WR
		(Valmon, Watts, Reynolds, Johnson)		
	2	Kenya		2:29.82
	3	Germany		2:59.99

WOMEN				
100m	1	Gail Devers	USA	**10.82**
	2	Merlene Ottey	JAM	10.82
	3	Gwen Torrance	USA	10.89
200m	1	Merlene Ottey	JAM	**21.98**
(0.0)	2	Gwen Torrance	USA	22.00
	3	Irina Privalova	RUS	22.13
400m	1	Jearl Miles	USA	**49.82**
	2	Natasha Kaiser-Brown	USA	50.17
	3	Sandie Richards	JAM	50.44
800m	1	Maria Mutola	MOZ	**1:55.43**
	2	Lyubov Gurina	RUS	1:57.10
	3	Ella Kovacs	ROM	1:57.92
	4	Diane Modahl	GBR	1:59.42
1500m	1	Liu Dong	CHN	**4:00.50**
	2	Sonia O'Sullivan	IRI.	4:03.48
	3	Hassiba Boulmerka	ALG	4:04.29
3000m	1	Qu Yunxia	CHN	**8:28.71**
	2	Zhang Linli	CHN	8:29.25
	3	Zhang Lirong	CHN	8:31.95
	7	Paula Radcliffe	GBR	8:40.40
10,000m	1	Wang Junxia	CHN	**30:39.30**
	2	Zhong Huandi	CHN	31:12.55
	3	Selina Barsosio	KEN	31:15.38
Marthn	1	Junko Asari	JPN	**2:30:03**
	2	Mañuela Machado	POR	2:30:54
	3	Tomoe Abe	JPN	2:31:01
100mh	1	Gail Devers	USA	**12.46**
(+0.2)	2	Marina Azyabina	RUS	12.60
	3	Lynda Tolbert	USA	12.67
400mh	1	Sally Gunnell	GBR	**52.74** WR
	2	Sandra Farmer-Patrick	USA	52.79
	3	Margarita Ponomaryova	RUS	53.48
HJ	1	Ioamnet Quintero	CUB	**1.99m**
	2	Silvia Costa	CUB	1.97m

	3	Sigrid Kirchmann	AUT	1.97m
LJ	1	**Heike Drechsler**	**GER**	**7.11m**
	2	Larissa Berezhnaya	UKR	6.98m
	3	Renata Nielsen	DEN	6.76m
TJ	1	**Ana Biryukova**	**RUS**	**15.09mWR**
	2	Yolande Chen	RUS	14.70m
	3	Iva Prendzheva	BUL	14.23m
Shot	1	**Zhihong Huang**	**CHN**	**20.57m**
	2	Svetlana Krivelyova	RUS	19.97m
	3	Kathrine Niemke	GER	19.71m
DT	1	**Olga Burova**	**RUS**	**67.40m**
	2	Daniela Costian	AUS	65.36m
	3	Min Chunfeng	CHN	65.26m
JT	1	**Trine Hattestad**	**NOR**	**69.18m**
	2	Karen Forkel	GER	65.80m
	3	Natalya Shikolenko	BLS	65.64m

Hept	1	**Jackie Joyner-Kersee**	**USA**	**6837**
	2	Sabine Braun	GER	6787
	3	Svetlana Buraga	BLS	6635
10kmw	1	**Sari Essayah**	**FIN**	**42.59**
	2	Ileana Salvador	ITA	43.08
	3	Encarnación Granados	ESP	43.21
4x100m	1	**Russia**		**41.49**

(Bogoslovskaya, Malchugina, Voronova, Privalova)

	2	USA		41.49
	3	Jamaica		41.94
4x400m	1	USA		3:16.71

(Torrance, Malone, Kaiser-Brown, Miles)

	2	Russia		3:18.38
	3	GBR		3:23.41

(Keough, Smith, Goddard, Gunnell)

European Cup (Bruno Zauli)

Super League   Rome   June 26-27

MEN

100m	1.Linford Christie	GBR	10.22
(w+1.3)	2.Aleksandr Porkhomovskiy	RUS	10.28
	3.Daniel Sangouma	FRA	10.42
200m	1.John Regis	GBR	20.38
(w-0.9)	2.Andrey Fedoriv	RUS	20.54
	3.Robert Kurnicki	GER	20.59
400m	1.David Grindley	GBR	44.75
	2.Dmitri Golovastov	RUS	45.65
	3.Jean-Louis Rapnouil	FRA	45.91
800m	1.Andrey Bulkovskiy	UKR	1:47.32
	2.Andrea Benvenuti	ITA	1:47.63
	3.Tom McKean	GBR	1:47.67
1500m	1.Andrey Bulkovskiy	UKR	3:37.51
	2.Fermin Cacho	ESP	3:38.09
	3.Pascal Thiebaut	FRA	3:38.12
	5.Curtis Robb	GBR	3:38.56
5000m	1.Rob Denmark	GBR	13:30.02
	2.Alessandro Lambruschini	ITA	13:30.96
	3.Abel Anton	ESP	13:31.35
10,000m	1.Thierry Pantel	FRA	28:02.71
	2.Francesco Panetta	ITA	28:13.99
	3.Carlos Adan	ESP	28:16.19
	dnf Eamonn Martin	GBR	
3000msc	1.Steffen Brand	GER	8:17.77
	2.Francesco Panetta	ITA	8:22.95
	3.Thierry Brusseau	FRA	8:24.60
	6.Tom Buckner	GBR	8:33.39
110m H	1.Colin Jackson	GBR	13.10
(w-0.2)	2.Florian Schwarthoff	GER	13.50
	3.Dan Philibert	FRA	13.62
400m H	1.Stephane Diagana	FRA	48.08 NR
	2.Olaf Hense	GER	48.48
	3.Oleg Tverdokhleb	UKR	48.70
	4.Kriss Akabusi	GBR	48.73
PV	1.Rodion Gataullin	RUS	6.00m
	2.Sergey Bubka	UKR	5.80m
	3.Javier Garcia	ESP	5.70m
	7.Neil Winter	GBR	5.30m

HJ	1.Artur Partyka	POL	2.30m
	2.Jean-Charles Gicquel	FRA	2.30m
	3.Roberto Ferrari	ITA	2.30m
	6.Steve Smith	GBR	2.28m
LJ	1.Giovanni Evangelisti	ITA	8.04m (w)
	2.Angel Hernandez	ESP	8.04m (w)
	3.Stanislav Tarasenko	RUS	7.93m
	6.Fred Salle	GBR	7.63m
TJ	1.Pierre Camara	FRA	17.46m (w)
	2.Jonathan Edwards	GBR	17.27m
	3.Ralf Jaros	GER	17.18m
Shot	1.Aleksandr Bagach	UKR	20.15m
	2.Paolo Dal Soglio	ITA	19.79m
	3.Evgeniy Palchikov	RUS	19.64m
	6.Paul Edwards	GBR	18.33m
Discus	1.Lars Riedel	GER	66.30m
	2.Dmitriy Shevchenko	RUS	63.96m
	3.Vladimir Zinchenko	UKR	62.42m
	6.Robert Weir	GBR	57.42m
HT	1.Sergey Litvinov	RUS	80.78m
	2.Christophe Epallé	FRA	76.08m
	3.Andrey Skvaryuk	UKR	76.00m
	5.Paul Head	GBR	71.90m
JT	1.Jan Zelezny	TCH	89.94m
	2.Mick Hill	GBR	80.76m
	3.Andrey Shevchuk	RUS	79.16m
4 x 100m	1.Great Britain		38.53

(Jason John, Tony Jarrett, Regis, Christie)

	2.France		38.72
	3.Russia		38.89 NR
4 x 400m	1.Great Britain		3:00.25

(Du'aine Ladejo, Akabusi, Regis, Grindley)

	2.Russia		3:00.75 NR
	3.France		3:00.94

MEN'S FINAL TABLE

1 Russia 128; 2 Great Britain 124; 3 France 123;
4 Germany 119; 5 Italy 112; 6 Ukraine 97; 7 Spain 76;
8 Poland 65; 9 Czech Republic 54

Poland and the Czech Republic are relegated to the European Cup B League.

WOMEN

100m	1.Irina Privalova	RUS	11.08
(w-0.3)	2.Marie-José Pérec	FRA	11.27
	3.Dzhanna Tarnopolskaya	UKR	11.29
	5.Bev Kinch	GBR	11.50
200m	1.Irina Privalova	RUS	22.30
(w+0.8)	2.Marie-José Pérec	FRA	22.30
	3.Silke Knoll	GER	22.89
	6.Katharine Merry	GBR	23.27
400m	1.Elena Ruzina	RUS	51.54
	2.Else Devassoigne	FRA	51.92
	3.Linda Keough	GBR	52.14
800m	1.Ella Kovacs	RUM	1:57.5 *
	2.Lyubov Kremlyova	RUS	
	3.Elena Stocchevaya	UKR	
	5.Diane Modahl	GBR	
1500m	1.Vera Chuvasova	RUS	4:16.03
	2.Violeta Beclea	ROM	4:16.36
	3.Yvonne Murray	GBR	4:17.51
3000m	1.Margareta Keszeg	ROM	8:51.88
	2.Yelena Kopytova	RUS	8:52.27
	3.Alison Wyeth	GBR	8:52.98
10,000m	1.Viktoria Nenasheva	RUS	32:33.46
	2.Iulia Negura	ROM	32:36.05
	3.Tamara Koba	UKR	32:39.50
	4.Suzanne Rigg	GBR	32:44.06
100m H	1.Marina Azyabina	RUS	12.63
	2.Jackie Agyepong	GBR	13.17
	3.Liliana Nastase	ROM	13.22
400m H	1.Sally Gunnell	GBR	53.73 CR
	2.Anna Chuprina	RUS	54.42
	3.Nicoleta Carutasu	ROM	54.94
HJ	1.Galina Astefei	ROM	2.00m NR
	2.Heike Henkel	GER	1.96m
	3.Katarzyna Majchrzak	POL	1.92m
	6.Jo Jennings	GBR	1.90m

LJ	1.Heike Drechsler	GER	7.02m
	2.Yelena Sinchukova	RUS	6.94m
	3.Fiona May	GBR	6.73m
TJ	1.Yolande Chen	RUS	14.34m
	2.Helga Radtke	GER	14.04m
	3.Innessa Kravets	UKR	13.99m
	4.Michelle Griffith	GBR	13.54m
Shot	1.Anna Romanova	RUS	19.43m
	2.Valentina Fedyushina	UKR	18.91m
	3.Stephanie Storp	GER	18.85m
Discus	1.Larisa Korotkevich	RUS	64.58m
	2.Larissa Mikhalchenko	UKR	63.04m
	3.Renata Katewicz	POL	61.68m
	8.Jacqueline McKernan	GBR	53.88m
Javelin	1.Felicia Tirlea	ROM	62.68m
	2.Karen Forkel	GER	61.92m
	3.Yekaterina Ivakina	RUS	61.74m
	7.Sharon Gibson	GBR	55.24m
4 x 100m	1.Russia		42.79
	2.France		43.01
	3.Germany		43.46
	6.Great Britain		44.53

(Paula Thomas, Kinch, Merry, Marcia Richardson)

4 x 400m	1.Russia		3:24.23 NR
	2.Ukraine		3:27.37
	3.Germany		3:27.80
	4.Great Britain		3:28.55

(Keough, Modahl, Jennifer Stoute, Gunnell)

WOMEN'S FINAL TABLE
1 Russia 141; 2 Romania 102; 3 Ukraine 97.5;
4 Germany 96; 5 Great Britain 91; 6 France 75;
7 Poland 62; 8 Italy 55.5; 9 Finland 44
*Italy and Finland are relegated. *In the 800m, the electronic timing failed. The timing given is therefore unofficial.*

European Cup First League

Brussels   12-13 June

Men

100m	Patrick Stevens	BEL	10.52(+0.3)
200m	Patrick Stevens	BEL	20.72(+1.5)
400m	Ivanov	BUL	46.32
800m	Atle Douglas	NOR	1:49.78
1500m	Olteanu	ROM	3:51.70
5000m	Olteanu	ROM	13:50.08
10,000m	Jonny Danielson	SWE	28:45.57
3000m St	William van Dijck	BEL	8:37.17
110m H	Georg Boroi	ROM	13.49
400mH	Marc Dolendorf	BEL	49.82
PV	Istvan Bagyula	HUN	5.50m
HJ	Patrick Sjöberg	SWE	2.29m
LJ	Bogdan Tudor	ROM	7.78m
TJ	Tord Henriksson	SWE	17.16m
Shot	Werner Günthör	SUI	21.63m
Discus	Costel Grasu	ROM	63.24m
Hammer	Tibor Gécsek	HUN	74.78m
Javelin	Seppo Räty	FIN	84.22m
4 x 100m	Sweden		39.85
4 x 400m	Sweden		3:08.31

FINAL STANDINGS
1.**Sweden 112**, 2.Rumania 99.5, 3.Hungary 97, 4.Bulgaria 94.5, 5.Switzerland 87.5, 6.Finland 86, 7.Norway 72, 8.Belgium 71.5 *Sweden and Rumania are promoted*

Women

100m	Petya Pendareva	BUL	11.46(+0.3)
200m	Sandra Myers	ESP	23.28(+0.4)
400m	Sandra Myers	ESP	52.23
800m	Natalya Dukhnova	BLS	2:01.94
1500m	Sandra Gasser	SUI	4:16.02
3000m	Daria Nauer	SUI	9:13.81
10,000m	Helena Barócsi	HUN	33:33.92
100mh	Sylvie Dethier	BEL	13.34(+0.3)
400mh	Ann Maenhout	BEL	56.51
HJ	Tatyana Shevchik	BLS	1.90m
LJ	Rita Ináncsi	HUN	6.62m
TJ	Sarka Kaspárková	TCH	13.69m
Shot	Svetla Mitkova	BUL	18.36m
Discus	Ellina Zveryova	BLS	66.32m
Javelin	Tatyana Shikolenko	BLS	61.06m
4 x 100m	Bulgaria		44.83
4 x 400m	Czech Republic		3:32.79

FINAL STANDINGS
1 Belarus 91.5; 2 Spain 81; 3 Switzerland 79; 4 Czech Republic 78; 5 Bulgaria 77.5; 6 Norway 70; 7 Hungary 67; 8 Belgium 67
Belarus and Spain are promoted to the Super League

Second League

GROUP C1
Villach, Austria   June 12-13
Men:1.Greece 125, 2.Austria 107.5, 3.Israel 78, 4.Croatia 69.5, 5.Slovenia 69.5, 6.Cyprus 57.5, 7.Turkey 52
Women:1.Austria 82, 2.Slovenia 78.5, 3.Greece 75, 4.Turkey 49.5, 5.Cyprus 37, 6.Croatia 34, 7.Israel dns

GROUP C2
Copenhagen   June 12-13
Men:1.Denmark 72, 2.Latvia 65, 3.Estonia 62, 4.Lithuania 58, 5.Iceland 41
Women:1.Lithuania 70, 2.Denmark 64, 3.Latvia 53, 4.Iceland 36, 5.Estonia 30

GROUP C3
Rotterdam   June 12-13
Men:1.Belarus 98, 2.Portugal 84, 3.Holland 78, 4.Slovakia 75, 5.Ireland 48, 6.Moldova 38
Women:1.Portugal 75, 2.Sweden 70.5, 3.Holland 69, 4.Ireland 52, 5.Slovakia 51.5, 6.Moldova 38
The top team in each group is promoted to the First League

European Cup
Combined Events

Oulu, Finland   July 10-11
Men's Teams
1. France   22,098 (Plaziat 8277, Blondel 8204, Motti 7682, Mandrou 7370)

2. Germany   22,014
3. Finland   21,299

Men's Individual
1. Meier   GER   8366 (10.96/7.95m/15.52m/2.10m/ 47.42/14.67/47.04/4.40m/54.82m/4:36.37)
2. Plaziat   FRA
3. Blondel   FRA
Women's Teams
1. Russia   18,595 (Zhuravleva 6330, Nikitina 6256, Mikhaylova 6009)

2. Germany   17,708
3. Poland   17,287
Women's Individual
1. Zhuravleva   RUS   6330 (14.38/1.81m/14.30m/24.35/ 6.53m/42.56m/2:13.11)
2. Nikitina   RUS   6256
3. Wlodarczyk   POL   6121

European Junior Championships

San Sebastian   July 29-Aug 1

Men

100m	Danny Joyce	GBR	10.63
200m	Andrea Columbo	ITA	21.14(+2.2)
400m	Guy Bullock	GBR	46.13
800m	Andrzej Zahorski	POL	1:53.49
1500m	Reyes Estevez	ESP	3:45.00
5000m	Kashaev Vener	RUS	13:54.32
10,000m	Ricardo Fernandez	ESP	29:37.75
3000msc	Adam Dobrzynski	POL	8:44.71 CR

110mh	Robin Korving	HOL	13.85(+0.9)
400mh	Carlos Silva	POR	50.27
PV	Khalid Lachheb	FRA	5.40m
HJ	Alexander Juraviev	UKR	2.21m
LJ	Carl Howard	GBR	7.76m
TJ	Paolo Camossi	ITA	16.41m
Shot	Manuel Martinez	ESP	19.02m
Discus	Leonid Crerevko	BEL	54.90m
HT	Vadim Burakov	BEL	67.16m
Javelin	Dimitris Polymedou	GRE	72.80m
Decathlon	Christer Holgar	SWE	7,534
4x100m	GBR(Allyn Condon, Joyce, Paul Bolton, Ejike Wodu)		40.01
10,000mw	Michele Didoni	ITA	40:05.62

Women

100m	Hana Benesova	TCH	11.56
200m	Katharine Merry	GBR	23.35(+0.8)
400m	Mariana Florea	ROM	52.14
800m	Ludmila Formanova	TCH	2:06.88
1500m	Marta Dominguez	ESP	4:17.26
3000m	Gabriela Szabo	ROM	8:50.97 CR
100mh	Diane Allahgreen	GBR	13.42
400mh	Ionela Tirlea	ROM	56.43
HJ	Sabrina DeLeeuw	BEL	1.89m
LJ	Erica Johansson	SWE	6.56m
TJ	Elena Lysak	RUS	13.86 WRJ
Shot	Marika Tuliniemi	FIN	17.93
Discus	Corrie De Bruin	HOL	55.30m
Javelin	Mikaela Ingberg	FIN	56.64
Heptath	Kathleen Gutjahr	GER	5650
4x100m	GBR(Allahgreen, Merry Sophie Smith, Debbie Mant)		44.31
4x400m	Rumania		3:31.13
5000mW	Susana Feitor	POR	21:21.80

European Clubs' Cup

MEN
Budapest   May 29-30

1	Fiamme D'Oro	ITA	127.5
2	Club Larios	ESP	110
3	CSKA Sofia	BUL	99
4	Racing Club de France	FRA	97.5
5	Belgrave Harriers	GBR	93
6	U Saab Badapest	HUN	87
7	PSK Olympia Praha	TCH	69
8	Sport Lisbos	POR	67.5

WOMEN
Limassol, Cyprus   June 5

1	Sisport Fiat	ITA	257.5
2	Levski Sofia	BUL	247
3	IBL Olympja	SLO	239
4	Stade de Français	FRA	239
5	Sport Lisboa	POR	223.5
6	PSK Olympia Praha	TCH	220
7	Birchfield Harriers	GBR	211.5
8	Zalaegerszgi	HUN	162.5

IAAF/Mobil
Grand Prix meetings

SAO PAULO INTERNATIONAL

Ibirapeura Stadium May 16

Men

100m	Robson Da Silva	BRA	10.29(0)
200m	Robson Da Silva	BRA	20.38(-0.8)
400m	Butch Reynolds	USA	44.68
800m	Gilmar Santos	BRA	1:45.88
1500m	Abdi Bile	SOM	3:41.03
3000m	Joe Falcon	USA	7:56.31
110mh	Tong Li	CHN	13.48(-1.5)
PV	Sergey Bubka	UKR	5.80m
LJ	Obinna Eregbu	NGR	7.96m
Discus	Adewale Olukoju	NGR	63.52m

Women

100m	Mary Onyali	NGR	11.46(-3.4)
800m	Maria Mutola	MOZ	1:57.38
100mh	LaVonna Martin	USA	12.94(-0.8)
400mh	Kathy Batten	USA	56.32
HJ	Stefka Kostadinova	BUL	1.98m

NEW YORK GAMES

Wein Stadium May 22

Men

100m	Jon Drummond	USA	10.16(0.0)
200m	Robson Da Silva	BRA	20.43(0.0)
400m	Quincy Watts	USA	45.02
800m	Réda Abdenouz	ALG	1:47.34
Mile	Abdi Bile	SOM	3:58.62
5000m	Philemon Hanneck	ZIM	13:23.52
110mh	Mark Crear	USA	13.31(+0.7)
400mh	Kevin Young	USA	48.71
PV	Denis Petuschinsky	RUS	5.77m
LJ	Mike Conley	USA	7.98m

Women

100m	Michelle Finn	USA	11.28(+0.3)
400m	Sandie Richards	JAM	51.35
800m	Maria Mutola	MOZ	1:56.56
400mh	Sandra Farmer-Patrick	USA	54.69
HJ	Tisha Waller	USA	1.94m
Shot	Valentina Fedyushina	UKR	20.16

BRUCE JENNER CLASSIC SAN JOSE, USA

San Jose City College Stadium May 29

Men

100m	Andre Cason	USA	10.11(+0.3)
200m	Daniel Effiong	NGR	20.37(-0.5)
400m	Andrew Valmon	USA	45.72
1500m	Abdi Bile	SOM	3:39.01
3000m	Marc Davis	USA	7:43.62
110mh	Mark Crear	USA	13.35(+0.3)
400mh	Kevin Young	USA	48.17
PV	Sergey Bubka	UKR	6.00m
Shot	Randy Barnes	USA	20.91m
Discus	Anthony Washington	USA	64.72m

Women

100m	Mary Onyali	NGR	11.25(-0.8)
800m	Maria Mutola	MOZ	2:01.35
1500m	Alisa Hill	USA	4:13.23
400mh	Sandra Farmer-Patrick	USA	55.25

HJ	Angie Bradburn	USA	1.94m
LJ	Jackie Joyner-Kersee	USA	7.09w
Shot	Svetlana Krivelyova	RUS	19.53m

GRAN PREMIO

Estadio de la Cartuja, Seville Jun 5

Men

100m	Dennis Mitchell	USA	10.50(-5.3)
200m	Frankie Fredericks	NAM	20.82(-4.3)
800m	Piotr Pietkarski	POL	1:47.16
1500m	Fermin Cacho	ESP	3:36.30
5000m	Rob Denmark	GBR	13:16.48
3000ms	William Van Dijck	BEL	8:27.19
110mh	Mark McKoy	CAN	13.55(-2.3) TJ
TJ	Leonid Voloshin	RUS	17.55w
HT	Igor Astapkovich	BLS	82.28 Javelin
JT	Patrik Boden	SWE	81.68

Women

100m	Natalya Voronova	RUS	11.51(-5.1)
200m	Natalya Voronova	RUS	23.02(-2.0)
1500m	Carla Sacramento	POR	4:15.81
3000m	Yelena Romanova	RUS	8:54.70
100mh	LaVonna Martin	USA	13.18(-8.1?)
400mh	Vera Ordina	RUS	55.33
HJ	Stefka Kostadinova	BUL	1.97
LJ	Heike Drechsler	GER	7.08m
Shot	Valentina Fedyushina	UKR	19.83m

GOLDEN GALA

Stadio Olimpico, Rome Jun 9

Men

200m	Frankie Fredericks	NAM	20.18(-0.4)
400m	Samson Kitur	KEN	45.03
1500m	Mohamed Suleiman	QAT	3:35.22
5000m	Ezekiel Bitok	KEN	13:10.66
3000msc	Allesandro Lambruschini	ITA	8:17.54
110mh	Colin Jackson	GBR	13.11
PV	Sergey Bubka	UKR	5.90m
LJ	Ivan Pedrosa	CUB	8.16m
Discus	Lars Riedel	GER	67.80m
Javelin	Mick Hill	GBR	82.82m

Women

100m	Merlene Ottey	JAM	11.13(-0.9)
800m	Ella Kovacs	ROM	1:57.48
Mile	Violeta Beclea	ROM	4:21.69
3000m	Yelena Romanova	RUS	8:50.55
400mh	Sally Gunnell	GBR	54.64
HJ	Stefka Kostadinova	BUL	1.98m
TJ	Inna Lasovskaya	RUS	14.64m
Shot	Valentina Fedyushina	UKR	19.15m

BNP D'ATHLETISME

Stadium Nord, Lille, France Jul 2

Men

100m	Andre Cason	USA	10.03(+1.5)
200m	Frankie Fredericks	NAM	20.28(+1.3)
400m	Andrew Valmon	USA	45.00
1000m	Noureddine Morceli	ALG	2:13.73
1500m	Rachid Bashir	MAR	3:36.31
5000m	Khalid Skah	MAR	13:06.82
3000msc	Abdelaziz Sahere	MAR	8:15.25
110mh	Mark McKoy	CAN	13.08(+1.2)
400mh	Kevin Young	USA	47.73
PV	Grigoriy Yegorov	KZK	5.83
LJ	Mike Powell	USA	8.50(+0.9)

Javelin	Jan Zelezny	TCH	91.40m
5000mw	Frants Kostyukevich	BLS	18:31.76
Women			
100m	Gail Devers	USA	10.96(+1.4)
200m	Marie-José Pérec	FRA	21.99(+1.1)
1000m	Ella Kovacs	ROM	2:32.40
400mh	Sandra Farmer-Patrick	USA	54.76
HJ	Stefka Kostadinova	BUL	2.00m
TJ	Yolande Chen	RUS	14.71(+1.6)
Shot	Astrid Kumbernuss	GER	19.03

DN GALAN
Olympic Stadium, Stockholm — *Jul 5*

200m	Frankie Fredericks	NAM	20.21(+2.0)
800m	Mark Everett	USA	1:45.33
1500m	Noureddine Morceli	ALG	3:31.83
Mile	Robert Kiplagat	KEN	3:59.48
10,000m	Richard Chelimo	KEN	27:07.91WR
3000msc	Moses Kiptanui	KEN	8:12.52
110mh	Colin Jackson	GBR	13.45(-0.8)
400mh	Kevin Young	USA	49.61
PV	Rodion Gataullin	RUS	5.70m
HJ	Hollis Conway	USA	2.31m
LJ	Mike Powell	USA	8.38m(+0.3)
Javelin	Jan Zelezny	TCH	84.26m
Women			
100m	Gail Devers	USA	11.04(+0.5)
800m	Kelly Holmes	GBR	2:00.45
1500m	Lyubov Kremlyova	RUS	4:08.57
5000m	Elana Meyer	RSA	14:50.29
400mh	Kim Batten	USA	54.63
TJ	Irina Mushailova	RUS	14.79(+1.7)

ATHLETISSIMA '93
Stade Olympique de la Pontaise, Lausanne — *Jul 7*

Men

100m	Andre Cason	USA	10.04(+0.8)
	2nd Carl Lewis	USA	10.07
200m	Carl Lewis	USA	19.99(+1.1)
400m	David Grindley	GBR	44.53
800m	Johnny Gray	USA	1:44.27
1500m	Mohamed Suleiman	QAT	3:35.54
5000m	Ismael Kirui	KEN	13:06.71
400mh	Kevin Young	USA	47.37
PV	Rodion Gataullin	RUS	5.70m
LJ	Mike Powell	USA	8.51m(+0.4)
Shot	Werner Günthör	SUI	21.72m
Javelin	Jan Zelezny	TCH	88.36m
Women			
100m	Gail Devers	USA	10.82
200m	Irina Privalova	RUS	22.17
800m	Lyubov Gurina	RUS	1:57.56
3000m	Yelena Romanova	RUS	8:51.06
100mh	Aliuska López	CUB	12.85
400mh	Sally Gunnell	GBR	53.86
HJ	Stefka Kostadinova	BUL	2.01m
LJ	Heike Drechsler	GER	7.08m
TJ	Inessa Kravets	UKR	14.61m

MOBIL BISLETT GAMES
Bislett Stadium, Oslo — *Jul 10*

100m	Linford Christie	GBR	10.90(+2.3)
400m	Michael Johnson	USA	44.89
800m	Martin Steele	GBR	1:43.84

Mile	Noureddine Morceli	ALG	3:47.78
	Steve Cram (3rd)	GBR	3:52.17
5000m	Paul Bitok	KEN	13:08.68
10,000m	Yobes Ondieki	KEN	26:58.38WR
3000msc	Richard Kosgei	KEN	8:12.68
110mh	Colin Jackson	GBR	13.21(0.0)
PV	Maksim Tarasov	RUS	5.90m
TJ	Jonathan Edwards	GBR	17.14(+3.3)
Shot	Werner Günthör	SUI	21.42
Women			
100m	Merlene Ottey	JAM	10.94(+1.2)
800m	Maria Mutola	MOZ	1:56.51
3000m	Sonia O'Sullivan	IRL	8:28.74
400mh	Kim Batten	USA	54.18
LJ	Heike Drechsler	GER	7.10m(-0.3)
Javelin	Trina Hattestad	NOR	72.12m

NIKAIA MOBIL MEETIING
Parc des Sports Charles Ehrmann, Nice — *Jul 21*

200m	Frankie Fredericks	NAM	20.41(+0.6)
400m	Samson Kitur	KEN	44.98
800m	William Tanui	KEN	1:46.12
1500m	Simon Doyle	AUS	3:34.39
3000m	Mohamed Issanger	MAR	7:41.06
3000msc	Joseph Keter	KEN	8:21.04
110mh	Colin Jackson	GBR	13.12(+0.8)
PV	Sergey Bubka	UKR	5.93m
Javelin	Jan Zelezny	TCH	90.68m
Women			
100m	Marie-José Pérec	FRA	11.12(+1.7)
200m	Pauline Davis	BAH	23.04(-0.7)
400m	Sandie Richards	JAM	51.39
800m	Argentina Paulino	MOZ	1:57.48
1500m	Sonia O'Sullivan	IRL	4:04.36
3000m	Margareta Keszeg	ROM	8:53.00
100mh	Marina Azyabina	RUS	12.78
400mh	Sally Gunnell	GBR	54.29
HJ	Galina Astefei	ROM	1.97m
TJ	Inessa Kravets	UKR	14.70m

TSB GAMES
Crystal Palace, London — *Jul 23*

Men

100m	Linford Christie	GBR	10.27(-1.9)
200m	John Regis	GBR	20.59(-2)
400m	Quincy Watts	USA	44.78
800m	José Luis Barbosa	BRA	1:45.78
1500m	Matthew Yates	GBR	3:35.83
5000m	William Sigei	KEN	13:14.32
110mh	Colin Jackson	GBR	13.33(-0.8)
400mh	Samuel Matete	ZAM	48.85
HJ	Javier Sotomayor	CUB	2.40m
TJ	Maris Bruziks	LAT	17.21m
PV	Maksim Tarasov	RUS	5.70m
Javelin	Jan Zelezny	TCH	86.78m
Women			
100m	Inger Miller	USA	11.54(-1.4)
400m	Natasha Kaiser-Brown	USA	51.16
200m	Melinda Gainsford	AUS	22.91(-0.5)
800m	Kelly Holmes	GBR	2:00.73
3000m	Yvonne Murray	GBR	8:32.61
100mh	Michelle Freeman	USA	13.07(-0.8)
400mh	Sally Gunnell	GBR	53.85
TJ	Yolande Chen	RUS	14.54m
Shot	Stefanie Storp	GER	19.71m

WELTKLASSE

Müngersdorf Stadium, Cologne Aug 1

Men

100m	Andre Cason	USA	10.11(+0.2)
200m	Linford Christie	GBR	20.39 (-0.1)
400m	Simon Kitur	KEN	44.54
800m	José Luiz Barbosa	BRA	1:45.30
1500m	Mohamed Suleiman	QAT	3:34.13
3000m	Paul Bitok	KEN	7:34.98
110mh	Jack Pierce	USA	13.24(0.0)
400mh	Kevin Young	USA	47.75
4x100m	Cuba		38.87
PV	Rodion Gataullin	RUS	5.88m
LJ	Mike Powell	USA	8.38m
Discus	Tony Washington	USA	66.86m

Women

100m	Gwen Torrance	USA	11.04(-0.1)
800m	Svetlana Masterkova	RUS	1:58.63
3000m	Annette Peters	USA	8:43.67
100mh	Michelle Freeman	JAM	12.86(-0.9)
400mh	Margarita Ponomaryova	RUS	54.45
4x100m	Germany		42.92
HJ	Ioamnet Quintero	CUB	1.97m
Javelin	Natalya Shikolenko	BLS	66.35m

WELTKLASSE

Letzigrund Stadium, Zurich Aug 4

Men

100m	Leroy Burrell	USA	10.02
	Linford Christie (2nd)	GBR	10.03
200m	Daniel Effiong	NGR	20.15
400m	Michael Johnson	USA	44.22
800m	Johnny Gray	GBR	1:44.03
800m B	Billy Konchellah	KEN	1:44.93
1500m	Noureddine Morceli	ALG	3:30.06
5000m	Khalid Skah	MAR	13:04.67
3000msc	Moses Kiptanui	KEN	8:10.29
110mh	Tony Dees	USA	13.19
400mh	Winthrop Graham	JAM	47.60
4x100m	USA(Drummond, Cason C Smith, Dees)		37.99
PV	Sergey Bubka	UKR	5.90m
HJ	Troy Kemp	BAH	2.34m
LJ	Mike Powell	USA	8.43m
Shot	Werner Günthör	SUI	21.49m
Discus	Lars Riedel	GER	66.00m

Women

100m	Merlene Ottey	JAM	10.93
800m	Maria Mutola	MOZ	1:55.62
3000m	Sonia O'Sullivan	IRL	8:30.12
100mh	Gail Devers		12.57
400mh	Sally Gunnell	GBR	53.52
HJ	Stefka Kostadinova	BUL	2.00m
LJ	Heike Drechsler	GER	7.21m
Javelin	Trina Hattestad	NOR	67.96m

GATORADE HERCULIS

Stade Louis II, Monaco Aug 7

100m	Jon Drummond	USA	10.05
200m	Daniel Effiong	NGR	20.16
400m	Quincey Watts	USA	44.67
800m	Nixon Kiprotich	KEN	1:44.09
1500m	Jonah Birir	KEN	3:35.81
3000m	Noureddine Morceli	ALG	7:29.24
3000msc	Richard Kosgei	KEN	8:14.98

110mh	Tony Dees	USA	13.12
400mh	Samuel Matete	ZAM	47.94
PV	Sergey Bubka	UKR	5.94m
TJ	Ralf Jaros	GER	17.18m
Javelin	Tom Pukstys	USA	82.86m

Women

100m	Merlene Ottey	JAM	10.90
200m	Merlene Ottey	JAM	21.77
400m	Gwen Torrance	USA	49.83
1500m	Violeta Beclea	ROM	3:59.35
100mh	Gail Devers	USA	12.77
400mh	Kim Batten	USA	54.24
HJ	Ioamnet Quintero	CUB	2.00m
LJ	Heike Drechsler	GER	6.96m

ISTAF '93

Olympic Stadium, Berlin Aug 27

Men

100m	Leroy Burrell	USA	10.12(+1.0)
	Linford Christie (3rd)	GBR	10.13
400m	Michael Johnson	USA	43.94
800m	Billy Konchellah	KEN	1:44.22
Mile	Noureddine Morceli	ALG	3:46.78
3000m	Mohamed Suleiman	QAT	7:38.21
110mh	Jack Pierce	USA	13.29(0.0)
	Colin Jackson (3rd)	GBR	13.35
3000msc	Patrick Sang	KEN	8:11.08
PV	Sergey Bubka	UKR	5.85m
LJ	Mike Powell	USA	8.13m
Shot	Randy Barnes	USA	21.47m
DT	Lars Reidel	GER	67.02m

Women

100m	Merlene Ottey	JAM	11.01(-0.5)
800m	Maria Mutola	MOZ	1:57.99
5000m	Sonia O'Sullivan	IRL	14:45.92
400mh	Sandra Farmer-Patrick	USA	54.37
HJ	Stefka Kostadinova	BUL	2.00m
LJ	Jackie Joyner-Kersee	USA	7.08m
DT	Olga Burova	RUS	65.64m
JT	Trina Hattestad	NOR	70.44m

IVO VAN DAMME

Heysel Stadium, Brussels Sep 3

Men

100m	Linford Christie	GBR	10.06
200m	Frankie Fredericks	NAM	20.21
400m	Michael Johnson	USA	44.45
Mile	Noureddine Morceli	ALG	3:47.30
110mh	Colin Jackson	GBR	12.99
PV	Maksim Tarasov	RUS	5.90m
Shot	Randy Barnes	USA	21.38m

Women

100m	Gwen Torrance	USA	10.86
200m	Gwen Torrance	USA	21.92
800m	Maria Mutola	MOZ	1:57.90
3000m	Sonia O'Sullivan	IRL	8:30.86
400mh	Sandra Farmer-Patrick	GBR	53.70
HJ	Stefka Kostadinova	BUL	1.92m
	Ioamnet Quintero	CUB	1.92m
LJ	Heike Drechsler	GER	7.07m
Shot	Zhihong Huang	CHN	19.71m

GRAND PRIX FINAL
Crystal Palace, London   *Sep 10*
Men

Event	Athlete	Country	Mark
100m	Leroy Burrell	USA	10.28(-0.5)
200m	Frankie Fredericks	NAM	20.34(0.0)
400m	David Grindley	GBR	44.81
1500m	Noureddine Morceli	ALG	3:31.60
5000m	Ismael Kirui	KEN	13:23.26
110mh	Colin Jackson	GBR	13.14(-0.1)
3000msc	Patrick Sang	KEN	8:15.53
PV	Sergey Bubka	UKR	6.05m
LJ	Mike Powell	USA	8.54m
DT	Lars Reidel	GER	64.90m
JT	Jan Zelezny	TCH	88.28m

Women

Event	Athlete	Country	Mark
100m	Gwen Torrance	USA	11.03(-0.4)
800m	Maria Mutola	MOZ	1:57.35
Mile	Lyubov Kremlyova	RUS	4:24.40
3000m	Sonia O'Sullivan	IRL	8:38.12
400mh	Sandra Farmer-Patrick	USA	53.69
HJ	Stefka Kostadinova	BUL	1.98m
TJ	Yolande Chen	RUS	14.39m
Shot	Svetlana Krivelyova	RUS	19.61m

Final Grand Prix Standings
For the 1st time since its inception, the Grand Prix overall title was decided by comparing performances in different events. The first figure below is the points won for race placings in the GP series; the second figure the points awarded for the performance in the GP final. Where the points are equal, the performance table decides.

Men	**Sergey Bubka**	72	1253
	Jan Zeleny	72	1250
	Colin Jackson	72	1232
	Mike Powell	72	1227
	Noureddine Morceli	72	1221
	Frankie Fredericks	72	1176
Women	**Sandra Farmer-Patrick**	72	1217
	Sonia O'Sullivan	72	1206
	Stefka Kostadinova	72	1195
	Maria Mutola	72	1190
	Sally Gunnell	66	1214
	Gwen Torrance	66	1192

IAAF Invitational Meetings

L'HUMANITÉ
St Denis, France   *June 11*
Men

Event	Athlete	Country	Mark
100m	Jean-Charles Trouabal	FRA	10.34(+0.4)
200m	Waota	CIV	21.40(+2.1)
400m	Hilaire	FRA	46.48
800m	Andrey Sudnik	BLS	1:47.29
1500m	Benfares	FRA	FRA 3:39.36
3000msc	Thierry Brusseau	FRA	8:41.32
110mh	Igor Kazanov	LAT	13.58(+0.3)
PV	Igor Tradenkov	RUS	5.62m
HJ	Roubillard/Gicquel	FRA	2.18m
TJ	Pierre Camara	FRA	17.02m(+0.4)
Javelin	Dmitri Polyunin	RUS	77.56m

Women

Event	Athlete	Country	Mark
100m	Anelia Nuneva	BUL	11.53
200m	Marie-José Pérec	FRA	22.56
400m	Anna Knoroz	RUS	52.78

Event	Athlete	Country	Mark
800m	Lyubov Gurina	RUS	2:00.34
1500m	Tatiana Dorovskikh	UKR	4:10.94
100mh	Yordanka Donkova	BUL	12.88
HJ	Stefka Kostadinova	BUL	1.90m
Javelin	Nadine Auzeil	FRA	60.00m

ADRIAN PAULEN MEMORIAL
Hengelo, Holland   *June 20*
Men

Event	Athlete	Country	Mark
100m	Frankie Fredericks	NAM	10.16
800m	Vebjörn Rodahl	NOR	1:45.83
1500m	Said Aouita	MAR	3:37.60
10,000m	Antonio Serrano	ESP	27:47.33
PV	Jani Lehtonen	FIN	5.65m
LJ	Frans Maas	HOL	7.94m
Discus	Eric De Bruin	HOL	67.06m

Women

Event	Athlete	Country	Mark
800m	Ella Kovacs	ROM	1:56.61
10,000m	Ute Pippig	GER	31:29.70
100mh	Julie Baumann	SUI	13.12
400mh	Ann Maenhout	BEL	55.61
HJ	Galina Astafei	ROM	1.99m
LJ	Heike Drechsler	GER	6.84m
Discus	Daniela Costian	AUS	64.58

XI CUIDAD DE BARCELONA
Barcelona   *Jul 19*
Men

Event	Athlete	Country	Mark
100m	Ray Stewart	JAM	10.43(-0.8)
400m	Samson Kitur	KEN	45.35
800m	Antonio Prieto	ESP	1:48.37
1500m	Fermin Cacho	ESP	3:33.36
110mh	Courtney Hawkins	USA	13.61(-2.3m)
PV	Sergey Bubka	UKR	5.61m
HJ	Javier Sotomayor	CUB	2.30m
Shot	Antonio Peñalver	ESP	16.10m
HT	Sergey Kirmasov	RUS	76.20m
5000mw	Daniel Plaza	ESP	20:44.10
Triathln	Antonio Peñalver	ESP	2471pts

Women

Event	Athlete	Country	Mark
100m	Pauline Davis	BAH	11.51(-2.7)
400m	Claudine Williams	JAM	51.69
1500m	Gwen Griffiths	RSA	4:10.64
100mh	Marie José Mardomingo	ESP	13.53(-0.4)
400mh	Miriam Alonso	ESP	58.02
LJ	Susan Tiedtke	GER	6.69m(+1.3)
Discus	Maritza Martén	CUB	63.46m

SESTRIERE
Italy   *Jul 28*
Men

Event	Athlete	Country	Mark
100m	Frankie Fredericks	NAM	10.16(-2.0)
200m	Frankie Fredericks	NAM	20.08(-1.7)
400m	Quincy Watts	USA	44.13
110mh	Colin Jackson	GBR	12.97(-1.6)ER
400mh	Kevin Young	USA	48.20
PV	Sergey Bubka	UKR	5.80m
LJ	Larry Myricks	USA	8.37(+3.8)
Shot	Luciano Zerbini	ITA	20.27m

Women

Event	Athlete	Country	Mark
100m	Pauline Davis	BAH	11.51(-2.9)
100mh	Yordanko Donkova	BUL	12.93(-3.5)
400mh	Kim Batten	USA	54.74
LJ	Susan Tiedtke	GER	7.19m(+3.7)

VAUXHALL INVITATION

Gateshead   *Jul 30*

Men

100m	Linford Christie	GBR	10.08(+0.4)
	Jon Drummond (2nd)	USA	10.12
	Carl Lewis (3rd)	USA	10.22
200m	Leroy Burrell	USA	20.55(+0.3)
300m	Michael Johnson	USA	31.72
400m	Steve Lewis	USA	45.05
800m	Curtis Robb	GBR	1:45.56
1500m	Mark Davis	USA	3:37.12
3000m	Jon Nuttall	GBR	7:51.58
110mh	Colin Jackson	GBR	13.13(+0.4)
400mh	Kriss Akabusi	GBR	49.45
PV	Rodion Gataullin	RUS	5.60m
TJ	Jon Edwards	GBR	17.22m
Shot	Paul Edwards	GBR	18.71m
Javelin	Phillip Spies	RSA	78.84m

Women

100m	Wendy Vereen	USA	11.36(-0.6)
200m	Melinda Gainsford	AUS	23.02(0.0)
300m	Sally Gunnell	GBR	36.44
400m	Terri Dendy	USA	51.86
800m	Claudette Groenendaal	USA	2:02.20
1500m	Sonia McGeorge	GBR	4:11.89
100mh	Michelle Freeman	USA	13.05(-0.6)
400mh	Kim Batten	USA	55.49
HJ	Tanya Hughes	USA	1.90m
LJ	Terri Horgan	IRL	6.08m
Shot	Grit Hammer	GER	18.31m
Javelin	Sharon Gibson	GBR	55.70m

McDONALDS GAMES

Sheffield   *Aug 29*

Men

100m	Linford Christie	GBR	9.99(+2.5)
200m	Jeff Williams	USA	20.74(+1.1)
400m	Michael Johnson	USA	45.51
800m	Sammy Langat	KEN	1:46.22
1500m	Matthew Yates	GBR	3:38.07
110mh	Colin Jackson	GBR	13.09(+2.1)
400mh	Torrance Zeliner	USA	49.20
PV	Scott Huffman	USA	5.85m
HJ	Javier Sotomayor	CUB	2.36m
LJ	Mike Powell	USA	8.31m
TJ	Jonathan Edwards	GBR	17.27m
JT	Jan Zelezny	TCH	95.66m WR

Women

400m	Jearl Miles	USA	51.46
1000m	Elly van Langen	HOL	2:35.21
2000m	Yvonne Murray	GBR	5:36.03
100mh	Gail Devers	USA	12.62
400mh	Sally Gunnell	GBR	54.25
HJ	Sabrine de Leeuw	BEL	1.93m

RIETI '93

Rieti, Italy   *Sept 5*

100m	Jon Drummond	USA	10.03(+1.7)
	Linford Christie(2nd)	GBR	10.03
200m	Frankie Fredericks	NAM	19.96
	John Regis(3rd)	GBR	20.23
400m	Samson Kitur	KEN	44.59
800m	Nixon Kiprotich	KEN	1:43.54
1500m	Jens-Peter Herold	GER	3:34.82
Mile	Noureddine Morceli	ALG	3:44.39 WR

5000m	Mike Chesire	KEN	13:19.28
400mh	Samuel Matete	ZAM	48.15
PV	Sergey Bubka	UKR	5.80m
Shot	Mike Stulce	USA	20.90m

Women

100m	Irina Privalova	RUS	10.81(+3.8)
200m	Irina Privalova	RUS	21.88
1500m	Sonia O'Sullivan	IRL	4:01.72
400mh	Kim Batten	USA	54.41
HJ	N Topchina	RUS	1.99m
LJ	Keike Drechsler	GER	7.00m

WORLD MILE RECORDS
Since 1954

6.5.54(Oxford)	Roger Bannister	GBR	3:59.40
21.6.54(Turku)	John Landy	AUS	3:57.90
19.7.57(London)	Doug Ibbotson	GBR	3:57.20
6.8.58(Dublin)	Herb Elliott	AUS	3:54.50
27.1.62(Wanganui)	Peter Snell	NZL	3:54.40
17.11.64(Auckland)	Peter Snell	NZL	3:54.10
9.6.65(Rennes)	Michel Jazy	FRA	3:53.60
17.7.66(Berkeley)	Jim Ryun	USA	3:51.30
23.6.67(Bakersfield)	Jim Ryun	USA	3:51.10
17.5.75(Kingston)	Filbert Bayi	TAN	3:51.00
12.8.75(Gothenberg)	John Walker	NZL	3:49.40
17.7.79(Oslo)	Sebastian Coe	GBR	3:48.95
1.7.80(Oslo)	Steve Ovett	GBR	3:48.80
19.8.81(Zurich)	Sebastian Coe	GBR	3:48.53
26.8.81(Koblenz)	Steve Ovett	GBR	3:48.40
28.8.81(Brussels)	Sebastian Coe	GBR	3:47.33
27.7.85(Oslo)	Steve Cram	GBR	3:46.32
5.9.93(Rieti)	**Noureddine Morceli**	**ALG**	**3:44.39**

Other Meetings

REIMS, FRANCE

June 30

Men

100m	James Trapp	USA	10.30(0.0)
400m	Anthuan Maybank	USA	45.49
1500m	Mohamed Taki	MAR	3:36.85
3000m	Jacky Carlier	FRA	7:47.21
110mh	Rod Jett	USA	13.57(0.0)
400mh	Vadim Zadoinov	RUS	50.27
PV	Jean Galfione	FRA	5.92m NR
HJ	Troy Kemp	BAH	2.33m
HT	Sergey Litvinov	RUS	81.14m

Women

100m	Marie-José Pérec	FRA	11.23
800m	Lyubov Gurina	RUS	1:58.80
3000m	Elana Meyer	RSA	8:38.76
100mh	Marina Azyabina	RUS	12.54(0.0)
400mh	Anna Knoroz	RUS	54.75
LJ	Ludmila Ninova	AUT	6.93m(-0.1)

COPENHAGEN
Jul 25
Men

100m	Calvin Smith	USA	10.22
400m	Andrew Valmon	USA	46.06
800m	Nixon Kiprotich	KEN	1:46.12
1500m	William Tanui	KEN	3:38.03
5000m	Richard Chelimo	KEN	13:13.85
HJ	Patrick Sjoberg	SWE	2.30m
Javelin	Tom Pukstys	USA	84.74m

Women

400m	Natasha Kaiser-Brown	USA	51.02
1500m	Sonia O'Sullivan	IRL	4:06.19
3000m	L Zaituc	ROM	8:56.17
TJ	Renata Nielsen	DEN	13.71m

SALAMANCA, SPAIN
Jul 27
Men

100m	Davidson Ezinwa	NGR	10.14(+0.4)
200m	Jason Hendrix	USA	20.47(+1.0)
400m	Sunday Bada	NGR	45.26
800m	José Luiz Barbosa	BRA	1:44.18
1500m	Venuste Nyongabo	BUR	3:39.91
110mh	Emilio Valle	CUB	13.41(-0.3)
HJ	Javier Sotomayor	CUB	2.45m WR
LJ	Mike Powell	USA	8.70m(+0.7)
TJ	Tosi Fasinro	GBR	17.21m(+1.5)
Discus	Roberto Moya	CUB	64.08m

Women

100m	Beverly McDonald	JAM	11.26(+0.1)
400m	Ximena Restrepo	COL	50.37
800m	Meredith Rainey	USA	2:01.96
100mh	Aliuska Lopez	CUB	12.92(+0.4)
Discus	Maritza Martén	CUB	65.96m

US CHAMPIONSHIPS   June 17-20
Men 100m:Andre Cason 9.85(+4.8), 200m:Mike Marsh 19.97(+2.5)(2nd Carl Lewis 20.07), 400m:Michael Johnson 43.74 (2nd Butch Reynolds 44.12), 800m:Mar Everett 1:44.43, 1500m:Bill Burke 3:42.74, 5000m:Matt Giusto 13:32.60, 10,000m:Todd Williams 28:02.05, 3000msc:Mark Davis 8:20.93, 110mh:Jack Pierce 13.19, 400mh:Kevin Young 47.69, PV:Scott Huffman 5.70m, HJ:Hollis Conway 2.31m, LJ:Mike Powell 8.53m(+2.2), TJ:Mike Conley 17.69(+4.2), Shot:Randy Barnes 21.28m, Tony Washington 63.24m, Javelin:Tom Pukstys 83.06, 20kW:James 1:29.09 **Women** 100m:Gail Devers 10.82(+2.2), 200m:Gwen Torrence 22.57(+2.4), 400m:Jearl Miles 50.43, 800m:Joetta Clark 2:01.47, 1500m:Annette Peters 4:11.53, 3000m:Annette Peters 8:48.59, 5000m:Chris McNamara 16:11.85, Lynda Tolbert 12.72(+2.6), 400mh:Sandra Farmer-Patrick 53.96, Tanya Hughes 1.90m, LJ:Jackie Joyner-Kersee 7.02(+2.0), TJ:Claudia Haywood 13.86(+2.9), Shot:Connie Price-Smith 19.02m, Discus:Price-Smith 63.52, Javelin:Donna Mayhew, 10kW:Lawrence 45.55

AFRICAN CHAMPIONSHIPS
Durban   June 23-27
Men
100m:Effiong NGR 10.39(-0.3), 200m:Rossouw RSA 20.65(+1.7), 400m:Ochieng KEN 45.29, 800m:S Kibet KEN 1:45.43, 1500:D Kibet KEN 3:45.67, 5000m:Chemoiywo KEN 13:09.68, 10,000m:Sigei KEN 27:25.23, 3000msc:J Keter KEN 8:22.34, 100mh:Schoerman RSA 13.93(-0.4), 400mh:E Keter

KEN 49.38, PV:Brits RSA 5.40m, HJ:Van Vuuren RSA 2.22m, LJ:Eregbu NGR 8.32(+2.1)TJ:Rabenala MAD 16.72(+0.4), Shot:LeRoux RSA 18.29m, DT:Conjungo 59.92m, HT:Toumi ALG 69.82m, Javelin:Petranoff RSA 82.40m, 20kW:Demissie ETH 1:28.56, 4x100m:Nigeria 39.97, 4x400m:Kenya 3:03.10
Women
100m:Utondu NGR 11.39(-1.2), 200m:Onyali NGR 22.71(+1.9), 400m:Paulino MOZ 51.82, 800m:Mutola MOZ 1:56.36, 1500m:Meyer RSA 4:12.56, 3000m:Griffiths RSA 9:13.92, 10,000m:Adere ETH 32:48.52, 100mh:Ramalalanirina MAD 33.11(+0.3), 400mh:Akinremi NGR 57.59, HJ:Weavers RSA 1.90m, LJ:Opara NGR 6.57(-0.1), TJ:Swart RSA 12.95m, Shot:Meintjies RSA 14.66m, Discus:Etsebeth RSA 54.16m, Javelin:Roux RSA 48.24m, 4x400m:Nigeria 3:33.21

NATIONAL GAMES, CHINA
Peking   Sept 8-13
Men
100:Li Tao 10.24, 200m Huang Tanwei 20.92, 400m: Zhao Cunlin 45.85, 800m: Mu Waiguo 1:49.27, 1500m: Liu Fuxiang 3:48.68, 5000m: Hong Buo 13:32.46, 10,000m: Jin Shangxuan 28:40.81, 3000msc: Sun Ripeng 8:24.97, 110mh: Chen Yanhao 13.59, 400mh: Yang Xianjun 49.59, PV: Liang Xueren 5.30m, HJ: Xu Jang 2.31m, LJ: Huang Gang 8.30m, Shot: Lai Hao 19.72m, DT: Li Shao 60.86m, HT: Bi Zhong 72.52m, JT: Zhang Lianbiao 78.52m
Women
100m: Liu Xiaomei 11.02(0.0), 200m: Chen Zhaojing 22.56(+0.6), 400m: Ma Zuqing 49.81, 800m: Dong Liu 1:55.54 *(Asian Record)*, 1500m: Qu Yunxia 3:50.46 *(World Record)*, 3000m: Zhang Linli 8:22.06 *(Heats - World Record),* Wang Junxia 8:12.19 *(Heats - World Record),* Wang Junxia 8:06.11 *(Final - World Record)* 10,000m: Wang Junxia 29:31.78 *(World Record)*, 100mh: Zhang Yu 12.64, 400mh: Man Qing 53.96, HJ: Jin Ling 1.94m, LJ: Mia Miaolan 7.06m, TJ: Wu Ruiping 14.29m, Shot: Zhou Tianhui 20.00m, DT: Cao Qi 66.08m, JT: Ha Xiayan 65.44m Hept: Ma Miaolan 6,750pts

---

THE RISE AND RISE
OF
JAVIER SOTOMAYOR

2.45m	27.7.93	Salamanca
2.44m	29.7.89	San Juan de Porta Rico
2.43m	8.9.88	Salamanca
2.43m	4.3.89	Budapest (indoors)
2.41m	14.3.93	Toronto(indoors)
2.40m	12.3.89	Havana
2.40m	13.8.89	Bogota
2.40m	19.7.91	St Denis
2.40m	25.5.93	Havana
2.40m	23.7.93	Crystal Palace

Panasonic AAA Championships

(World championships Trials)

Jul 16-17   Alexander Stadium, Birmingham

Each winner automatically earns a world championship team place, provided they have achieved the qualifying standard.

Men

100m	1.Linford Christie	TVH	10.13(+1)
	2.Dean Capobianco	AUS	10.25
	3.John Regis	Belgrave	10.32
200m	1.Jeff Williams	USA	20.47(+2.9)
	2.Toby Box	W & B	20.85
	3.Darren Campbell	Sale	20.89
400m	1.Ochien Kennedy	KEN	45.32
	2.Ade Mafe	TVH	45.64
	3.David McKenzie	Shaftesbury/B	45.75
800m	1.Martin Steele	Longwood	1:47.83
	2.Hezekiel Sepeng	SAF	1:47.84
	3.Tom McKean	Motherwell	1:48.06
1500m	1.Matthew Yates	Newham	3:38.75
	2.Rob Denmark	Basildon	3:39.62
	3.Matthew Barnes	Enfield	3:40.06
5000m	1.Jonathan Brown	Sheffield	13:35.67
	2.Gary Staines	Shaftesbury/B	13:37.08
	3.John Nuttall	Preston	13:38.17
3000msc	1.Colin Walker	Gateshead	8:33.45
	2.Saad Cheddad	SAU	8:34.50
	3.Justin Chaston	Belgrave	8:34.64
110mh	1.Colin Jackson	Brecon	13.15(+1.1)
	2.Tony Jarrett	Haringey	13.37
	3.Kyle Van Der Kuyp	AUS	13.60
400mh	1.Gary Cadogan	Haringey	50.60
	2.Peter Crampton	Spenborough	50.75
	3.Ferrins Pieterse	SAF	50.80
PV	1.Simon Arkell	AUS	5.60m
	2.Tim Bright	USA	5.50m
	3.Pat Manson	USA	5.40m
HJ	1.Tim Forsyth	AUS	2.32m
	2.Steve Smith	Liverpool	2.30m
	3.Dalton Grant	Haringey	2.20m
LJ	1.Fred Salle	Belgrave	7.72m
	2.Barrington Williams	Cannock	7.71m
	3.Ian Simpson	Leeds	7.53m
TJ	1.Francis Agyepong	Shaftesbury/B	16.05m
	2.Dered Browne	Belgrave	15.66m
	3.John McKenzie	Belgrave	15.64m
Shot	1.Mathew Simson	Thurrock	18.79m
	2.Paul Edwards	Belgrave	18.56m
	3.John Minns	AUS	17.93m
Discus	1.Robert Weir	Birchfield	57.44m
	2.Fritz Potgieter	SAF	56.48
	3.Kjell Ove Hauge	Norway	54.58m
HT	1.Paul Head	Newham	72.32m
	2.Jason Byrne	Windsor	68.14m
	3.David Smith	Hull	68.06m
Javelin	1.Colin McKenzie	Newham	81.44m
	2.Mark Roberson	Haringey	78.96m
	3.Andrew Curry	AUS	74.68m
10,000w	1.Martin Bell	Splott RWC	42:29.63
	2.Mark Easton	Surrey WC	42:38.47
	3.Andrew Penn	Coventry RWC	42:51.86

Women

100m	1.Bev Kinch	Hounslow	11.44(+1.1)
	2.Melinda Gainsford	AUS	11.47
	3.Simmone Jacobs	Shaftesbury/B	11.52
200m	1.Cathy Freeman	AUS	22.71(+1.9)
	2.Melinda Gainsford	AUS	23.02
	3.Simmone Jacobs	Shaftesbury/B	23.49
400m	1.Phylis Smith	Wigan	52.15
	2.Kyle Hanigan	AUS	52.68
	3.Solvi Meinseth	NOR	53.45
800m	1.Kelly Holmes	Middx ladies	2:02.69
	2.Linda Keough	Basingstoke	2:03.93
	3.Lynn Gibson	Oxford	2:04.92
1500m	1.Alison Wyeth	Parkside	4:11.03
	2.Kathy Franey	USA	4:13.87
	3.Sonia McGeorge	Brighton	4:14.13
100mh	1.Sally Gunnell	EssexLadies	13.08(+1.8)
	2.Jackie Agyepong	Shaftesbury/B	13.15
	3.Monica Grefstad	NOR	13.33
400mh	1.Jacqui Parker	Essex Ladies	58.14
	2.Jennie Pearson	Ashford	59.09
	3.Jayne Puckeridge	Medway	59.35
PV	1.Katy Staples	Essex Ladies	3.20m
	2.Claire Morrison	Bristol	2.90m
	3.Louise Schramm	Epsom	2.90m
HJ	1.Debbie Marti	Bromley	1,86m
	2.Sharon Foley	IRE	1.83m
	3.Gwen Wentlund	USA	1.83m
LJ	1.Nicole Boegman	AUS	6.50m
	2.Joanne Wise	Coventry	6.26m
	3.Denise Lewis	Birchfield	6.19m
TJ	1.Lene Espegren	NOR	13.43m
	2.Rachel Kirby	Hounslow	13.41m
	3.Ashia Hansen	Essex Ladies	13.16m
Shot	1.Myrtel Augee	Bromley	17.24m
	2.Linda Martensson	SWE	15.67m
	3.Maggie Lynes	Croydon	15.48m
Discus	1.Daniela Costian	AUS	61.58m
	2.Tracy Axten	Hounslow	54.40m
	3.Debbie Calloway	Aldershot	53.28m
HT	1.Debbie Sosimenko	AUS	56.86m
	2.Esther Augee	Essex Ladies	52.22m
	3.Lorraine Shaw	Gloucester	51.76m
Javelin	1.Shelley Holroyd	Sale	60.10m
	2.Sharon Gibson	Notts	59.58m
	3.Amanda Liverton	Exeter	53.22m
5000mw	1.Victoria Lupton	Sheffield	22:34.50
	2.Julie Drake	Brighton	22:37.47
	3.Jane Saville	AUS	23:17.06

Pearl British Championships

June 12-13   Crystal Palace, London

Men. 100m:Linford Christie 10.26(+0.7). 200m:John Regis 20.21(+2.5). 400m:Du'aine Ladejo 46.14. 800m:Martin Steele 1:46.34. 1500m:Curtis Robb 3:39.58. 3000m:Spencer Barden 8:01.86. 5000m:Jon Brown 13:39.68. 10,000m:Paul Evans 28:17.49 *(world championship trial)*. 3000msc:Spencer Duval 8:32.77. 110mh:Andy Tulloch 13.70(+1.2). 400mh:Gary Cadogan 49.80. PV:Neil Winter 5.35m. HJ:Dalton Grant 2.25m. LJ:Ian Simpson 7.55m. TJ:Tosi

Fasinro 17.30w. Shot:Paul Edwards 19.06m.
Discus:Darrin Morris 57.70m. HT:Paul Head 71.48m.
Javelin:Mick Hill 86.94. **Women** 100m:Bev Kinch
11.37(+2). 200m:Katherine Merry 23.20. 400m:Phylis
Smith 51.70. 800m:Kelly Holmes 2:00.86. 1500m:Jayne
Spark 4:14.66. 3000m:Yvonne Murray 8:52.28 *(world
championship trial)*. 100mh:Jackie Agyepong 13.38(+2).
400mh:Gowry Retchakan 56.62. PV:Kate Staples 3.40m.
HJ:Debbie Marti 1.90m. LJ:Fiona May 6.67w. TJ:Michelle
Griffith 13.72m*(Commonwealth record)*.Shot:Myrtle Augee
17.12m. Discus:Jacqui McKernan 56.72m. HT:Lorraine
Shaw 55.14.

Pearl European Relays

Portsmouth   June 5
Relay Events Men 4 x 100m:Ukraine 38.35.
4x200m:Ukraine 1:21.32. 4x400m:Russia 3:01.87.
4x800m:Belarus 7:11.42. Medley:Russia 1:49.68 .4x110mh:
Great Britain (Jarret, Tulloch, Nelson, Jackson) 54.67.
Women. 4x100m: Ukraine 43.55. 4x200m: Russia 1:31.49.
4x400m: Great Britain (Smith, Goddard, Stoute, Gunnell)
3:24.36. 4x800m:Russia 7:57.08 Medley:Russia2:01.10.
4x100mh:Russia 52.00. **Field Events International Men.**
HJ: Dalton Grant GBR 2.26. PV: Andrea Pegorro ITA 5.40.
TJ: Tamas Czingler HUN 17.25. DT: Attila Horvarth
HUN 62.82. HT: Enrico Sgrulletti ITA 77.74. JT: Mick Hill
GBR 81.48. Final Result:1,Great Britain 49; 2,Hungary 42.
3, Italy 41. **Women** LJ:Yinka Idowu GBR 6.42. SP: Myrtle
Augee GBR 16.47. Final Result:1, Great Britain 24. 2. Italy
12. 3, Hungary 8. **Invitation Events Men.** Emsley Carr
Mile: Philemon Hanneck ZIM 3:57.06. 3000m:Steve Cram
GBR 7:54.22. **Women.** 1500m: Yvonne Murray GBR
4:12.37. AAA 10,000m:Vikki McPherson Glas Uni
33:49.29*(World Chamionship Trial)*.

Solent Games

PortsmouthJune 6
Men 100m:Aleksandr Porkhomovsky RUS 10.16(+1.6).
200m:Jiri Valik TCH 21.20(-2.3).300m:Solomon Wariso
GBR 33.46. 400m:Paul Sanders GBR 47.09. 1000m:Sergey
Melnikov RUS 2:22.34. 110mh:Evgeny Pechenkin RUS
13.87(-0.3). LJ:Milko Campus ITA 7.70. SP: Paolo Dal
Sogloi ITA 19.94. 4 x 100 Great Britain 39.95. **Women.**
100m: Zhanna Tarnopolskaya UKR 11.47 (+1.3). 200m:
Yulia Sotnikova RUS 23.51 (-1.3). 300m: Marianna Florea
ROM 36.87. 400m: Tamara Kuprizovich BYL 53.21.
1000m: Oksana Mernikova BYL 2:36.47. 100mh:Marina
Aziubina RUS 12.76 (-1.0). HJ: Jo Jennings GBR I.89. PV
Kate Staples GBR 3.55*(UK Record)*. TJ:Ildikó Fekete HUN
13.49. DT:Sharon Andrews GBR 55.14. HT:Lorraine Shaw
GBR 54.10. JT: Kinga Zsigmond HUN 58.22. 4 x 100:
Czechoslovakia 45.26.

TSB Challenge, GBR v USA

Edinburgh   July 2
Men 100m:Linford Christie GBR 10.06(+1.7). 200m:
John Regis GBR 20.08 (+2.1) 400m:David Grindley GBR
45.43. 800m:Tom McKean GBR 1:48.19. 1500m:David
Strang GBR 3:55.57. 3000m:Rob Denmark GBR 8:08.55.
3000ms/c:Tom Hanlon GBR 8:36.24. 110mh:Colin
Jackson GBR 13.01(+3.6). 400mh:Kriss Akabusi GBR
50.45. HJ:Monterrio Holder USA 2.26. PV:Mike Holloway
USA 5.70. LJ:Dion Bentley USA 7.97 (+2.0). TJ:Jonathan
Edwards GBR 17.70 (+2.9). SP:Mike Stulce USA 20.75.

DT:Steven Muse USA 61.44. HT:Paul Head GBR 69.82.
JT:Mick Hill GBR 85.10. 4x100m:GBR (John, Jarret, Regis,
Christie) 39.45. 4x400m:USA 3:04.49. **Final Results:** 1,
Great Britain 199. 2, United States 190.
Women.100m:Wenda Vereen USA 11.16 (+4.6).
200m:Danette Young USA 22.32 (+4.7). 400m:Sally
Gunnel GBR 51.29. 800m:Meredith Rainey USA 2:05.88.
1500m:Yvonne Murray GBR 4:08.63. 3000m:Sonia
McGeorge GBR 9:20.22. 100mh:Lynda Tolbert USA 12.73
(+4.0). 400mh:Trevaia Williams USA 57.20. HJ:Tanya
Hughes USA 1.91. LJ: Joanne Wise GBR 6.59 (+3.2).
TJ:Michelle Griffith GBR 13.93 (+5.3). SP:Myrtle Augee
GBR 17.68. DT:Carla Garret USA 58.46. JT:Donna
Mayhew USA 61.46. 4x100:USA 44.69. 4x400:USA
3:30.22. **Final Results:** 1,United States 181. 2, Great
Britain 143.

Eastern Electricity AAA U20 Championships

Bedford   July 3-4
Men 100m:D.Joyce Bed 10.46 (+3.1). 200m: D.Joyce Bed
21.60 (+2.1). 400m:G.Bullock LivP 46.96. 800m: E.Sepeng
RSA 1:47.69. 1500m: N.Caddy N&P 3:51.21. 5000:
E.Skosana RSA 14.24.69. 3000ms/c:D.Furmidge
Ryde 9:20.81. 110mh:K.Lumsdon Morp 14.32 (+3.1).
400mh:E.Van der Westhue RSA 53.11. HJ:J.Hames AUS
2.18. PV:N.Winter SB 5.40. LJ:C.Howard Ox C 7.52.
TJ:O.Achike Craw 16.28w. SP:M.Edwards Charn 15.17.
DT:F.Potgeister RSA 59.12. HT:M.Dwight AUS 62.18.
JT:D.MacDonald Cry 65.16. U17-3000m:E.Hankins WS&E
9:33.9. Senior BAF Walking Championships .
10,000m:D.Stone Steyn 42:22.50. **Women.** 100m:K.Merry
Bir 11.40 (+5.1). 200m:Merry 23.43 (+2.5).
400m:D.Adamson AUS 56.00. 800m:V.Kirk Wells 2:13.57.
1500m:J.Mitchell Croy 4:25.47. 3000m:H.Moulder West
9:27.07. 100mh:D.Allahgreen Liv 13.58 (+1.6).
400mh:A.Curbishley M&C 59.16. HJ:C.May G&G 1.76.
LJ:J.Dear WS&E 6.31w (+3.54). TJ:S.Anderson Brom 12.35
(+1.6). SP:D.Passmore AUS 13.88. DT:E.Merry Cov 50.84.
HT:D.Holden Houn 49.44. JT:K.Morrison Med 54.74..
Senior 5000m Walk (Brit. Champs.):J.Drake B&H
23:07.61. U17-3000m:J.Heath Warr 10:20.88.

SHARPE PRACTICE

Since his brilliant success in the 1992 World
Cup, David Sharpe hasn't enjoyed the best of
success. He did win one race though, when an
optimistic policeman tried to catch him after
Sharpe was involved in a fracas outside a
nightclub. Sharpe had no trouble outpacing
the copper, but a Panda car they called up just
had the edge. Sharpe was fined £100.

World Indoor Championships

Toronto, Canada   12-14 March

Ben Johnson got most of the early publicity in Toronto with his second-time-around positive. Briefly, it diverted attention from the fact that these championships are in danger of being one event too many. Indoor athletics is superb theatre, but the quality of competition in many of the events was extremely weak. Butch Reynolds returned to international competition after serving a two year ban and it was no surprise to anyone that it was one medal Primo Nebiolo did not present. Gail Devers added a touch of class; Bruiny Surin assured Canada of the sprint medal that Johnson was chasing; and the men's high jump was comfortably the best event of the meeting. Yvonne Murray and Tom McKean secured a Scottish double, but in truth they've had harder races.

Men

60m	1.Bruny Surin	CAN	6.50	CR
	2.Frankie Fredericks	NAM	6.51	
	3.Talal Mansoor	QAT	6.57	
200m	1.James Trapp	USA	20.63	
	2.Damien Marsh	AUS	20.71	
	3.Kevin Little	USA	20.72	
400m	1.Harry 'Butch' Reynolds	USA	45.26	CR
	2.Sunday Baba	NGR	45.75	
	3.Darren Clark	AUS	46.45	
800m	1.Tom McKean	GBR	1:47.29	
	2.Charles Nkazamyampi	BUR	1:47.62	
	3.Nico Motchebon	GER	1:48.15	
1500m	1.Marcus O'Sullivan	IRE	3:45.00	
	2.David Strang	GBR	3:45.30	
	3Branko Zorko	CRO	3:45.39	
3000m	1.Gennaro Di Napoli	ITA	7:50.26	
	2.Eric Dubus	FRA	7:50.57	
	3.Enrique Molina	ESP	7:51.10	
60m H	1.Mark McKoy	CAN	7.41	CR
	2.Colin Jackson	GBR	7.43	
	3.Tony Dees	USA	7.43	
HJ	1.Javier Sotomayor	CUB	2.14m	
	2.Patrik Sjöberg	SWE	2.39m	
	3.Steve Smith	GBR	2.37m	
LJ	1.Ivan Pedrosa	CUB	8.23m	
	2.Joe Greene	USA	8.13	
	3.Daniel Ivanov	BUL	7.98	
TJ	1.Pierre Camara	FRA	17.59m	
	2.Maris Bruziks	LAT	17.36m	
	3.Nikolay Raev	BUL	17.27m	
PV	1.Rodion Gataullin	RUS	5.90m	
	2.Grigoriy Yegorov	KZK	5.80m	
	3.Jean Galfione	FRA	5.80m	
Shot	1.Mike Stulce	USA	21.27m	
	2.Jim Doehring	USA	21.08m	
	3.Aleksandr Bagach	UKR	20.63m	
Hept*	1.Dan O'Brien	USA	6476	WR
	2.Mike Smith	CAN	6279	
	3.Eduard Hämäläinen	FIN	6075	
5000m W	1.Mikhail Schennikov	RUS	18:32.10	
	2.Robert Korzeniowski	POL	18:35.91	
	3.Mikhail Orlov	RUS	18:43.48	
4 x 400m	1.USA		3:15.10	
	2.Brazil		3:16.11	
	3.Canada		3:16.93	
Medley*	1.USA		3:15.10	
Relay	2.Brazil		3:16.11	
	3.Canada		3:16.93	

Women

60m	1.Gail Devers	USA	6.95	CR
	2.Irina Privalova	RUS	6.97	
	3.Zhanna Tarnapolskaya	UKR	7.21	
200m	1.Irina Privalova	RUS	22.15	CR
	2.Melinda Gainsford	AUS	22.73	
	3.Nataly Voronova	RUS	22.90	
400m	1.Sandie Richards	JAM	50.93	
	2.Tatyana Alekseyeva	RUS	51.03	
	3.Jearl Miles	USA	51.37	
800m	1.Maria Lurdes Mutola	MOZ	1:57.55	CR
	2.Svetlana Masterkova	RUS	1:59.18	
	3.Joetta Clark	USA	1:59.86	
1500m	1.Yekaterina Podkopayeva	RUS	4:09.29	
	2.Violeta Beclea	ROM	4:09.41	
	3.Sandra Gasser	SUI	4:10.99	
3000m	1.Yvonne Murray	GBR	8:50.55	
	2.Margareta Keszeg	ROM	9:02.89	
	3.Lynn Jennings	USA	9:03.78	
60m H	1.Julie Baumann	SUI	7.96	
	2.LaVonna Martin-Floreal	USA	7.99	
	3.Patricia Girard	FRA	8.01	
HJ	1.Stefka Kostadinova	BUL	2.02m	
	2.Heike Henkel	GER	2.02m	
	3.Inga Babakova	UKR	2.00m	
LJ	1.Marieta Ilcu	ROM	6.84m	
	2.Susen Tiedtke	GER	6.84m	
	3.Inessa Kravets	UKR	6.77m	
TJ	1.Inessa Kravets	UKR	14.47m	WR
	2.Yolande Chen	RUS	14.36m	
	3.Inna Lasovskaya	RUS	14.35m	
Shot	1.Svetlana Krivelyova	RUS	19.57m	
	2.Stephanie Storp	GER	19.37m	
	3.Zhang Liuhong	CHN	19.32m	
Pent*	1.Irina Belova	RUS	4787	
	2.Liliana Nastase	ROM	4686	
	3.Urszula Woldarczyk	POL	4667	
3000m W	1.Yelena Nikolayeva	RUS	11:49.73	CR
	2Kerry Junna-Saxby	AUS	11:53.82	
	3.Ileana Salvador	ITA	11:55.35	
4 x 400m	1.Russia		3:28.90	
	2.Jamaica		3:32.32	
	3.USA		3:32.50	
Medley*	1.USA		3:45.90	
Relay	2.Canada		3:56.34	
	No 3rd.			

The heptathlon, pentathlon and the 2 medley relays (800m/200m/200m/400m) were non-championship events.

IAAF International Indoor Meetings

HAMILTON SPECTATOR GAMES — *Jan 15*
Men
50m	Bruny Surin	CAN	5.67
500m	Darnell Hall	USA	1:04.14
Mile	Marcus O'Sullivan	IRL	3:59.30
3000m	Ruben Reina	USA	8:05.15
PV	Bill Payne	USA	5.60mHJ
HJ	Tony Barton	USA	2.29m
LJ	Erick Walder	USA	8.11m

Women
50m	Theresa Neighbours	USA	6.26
500m	Jearl Miles	USA	1:11.54
800m	Maria Mutola	MOZ	2:03.87
1500m	Paula Schnurr	CAN	4:16.20

MONTREAL GRAND PRIX — *Jan 17*
Men
60m	Bruny Surin	CAN	6.60
400m	Darnell Hall	USA	47.44
800m	Freddie Williams	CAN	1:50.37
Mile	Joseph Chesire	KEN	4:01.58
PV	Bill Payne	USA	5.60m
HJ	Kenny Banks	USA	2.21m
LJ	Erick Walder	USA	8.20m

Women
60m	Michelle Freeman	JAM	7.22
400m	Jillian Richardson	CAN	53.17
800m	Alisa Hill	USA	2:05.65
60mh	Michelle Freeman	JAM	8.05
1500mw	Debbie Lawrence	USA	5:53.94
LJ	Beatrice Utondu	NGR	6.54m

USAIR JOHNSON CITY, USA — *Jan 30*
Men
55m	Obinna Eregbu	NGR	6.13
400m	Bryan Irvin	USA	46.84
Mile	Marcus O'Sullivan	IRL	3:59.61
PV	Bill Payne	USA	5.55m
HJ	Tony Barton	USA	2.23m
LJ	Joe Greene	USA	7.90m
Weight	Lance Deal	USA	23.68m

Women
55m	Michelle Freeman	JAM	6.66
400m	Gwen Torrance	USA	52.83
Mile	Shelly Steely	USA	4:38.65
55mh	Michelle Freeman	JAM	7.36

TRICOTEX CUP, BUDAPEST — *Feb 5*
Men
200m	Nicolay Antonov	BUL	21.06
400m	Péter Nyilasi	HUN	48.66
800m	Charles Nkazamyampi	BUR	1:47.21
3000m	Ovidiu Olteanu	ROM	7:55.08
60mh	George Boroi	ROM	7.63
PV	Maksim Tarasov	RUS	5.80m
LJ	Mike Powell	USA	8.44m
TJ	Oleg Gzokhovski	RUS	17.14m
5000mw	Sándor Urbanik	HUN	19:03.02

Women
60m	Olga Bogoslovskaja	RUS	7.30
400m	Marina Shmonina	RUS	53.28

1500m	Violeta Beclea	ROM	4:13.56
60mh	Yordanka Donkova	BUL	7.99
HJ	Siglinde Cadusch	SWE	1.90m
LJ	Yelena Sinchoukova	RUS	6.53m
3000mw	Yekaterina Samolenko	UKR	12:26.37

MILLROSE GAMES, NEW YORK
Feb 5
Men
60m	Michael Green	USA	6.79
400m	Butch Reynolds	USA	47.16
500m	Andrew Valmon	USA	1:03.34
Mile	Noureddine Morceli	ALG	3:55.06
3000m	Joe Falcon	USA	7:55.94
60mh	Greg Foster	USA	7.81

Women
60m	Gail Devers	USA	7.31
800m	Maria Mutola	MOZ	2:02.83
60mh	LaVonna Martin Floreal	USA	8.15
HJ	Yolande Henry	USA	1.85m

SPARKASSEN CUP, STUTTGART — *Feb 7*
Men
60m	Bruny Surin	CAN	6.54
200m	James Trapp	USA	20.83
400m	Michael Johnson	USA	45.75
800m	Johnny Gray	USA	1:45.91
1500m	Moses Miptanui	KEN	3:36.95
3000m	Dieter Baumann	GER	7:43.60
PV	Peter Widen	SWE	5.66m
LJ	Frans Maas	HOL	7.95m
TJ	Oleg Protsenko	RUS	17.00m

Women
60m	Carlette Guidry	USA	7.18
1500m	Sandra Gasser	SUI	4:08.76
60mh	Eva Sokolova	RUS	8.01
HJ	Heike Henkel	GER	2.00m
LJ	Fiona May	GBR	6.57m

MOBIL 1 INVITATIONAL, FAIRFAX — *Feb 7*
Men
60m	Michael Green	USA	6.62	
400m	Butch Reynolds	USA	47.16	
500m	Andrew Valmon	USA	1:03.34	
600 yds	Mark Everett	USA	1:08.90	
800m	Freddie Williams	CAN	1:50.31	
Mile	Noureddine Morceli	ALG	3:55.06	
Mile (+40)	Eamonn Coghlan	IRL	4:05.95	
3000m	Joe Falcon	USA	7:55.94	
60mh	Greg Foster	USA	7.65	
PV	Bill Deering	USA	5.50m	
Shot	Lance Deal	USA	24.82m	WR
Mile w	Allen James	USA	5:50.44	

Women
60m	Gail Devers	USA	7.15
400m	Jearl Miles	USA	53.03
800m	Maria Mutola	MOZ	2:02.83
Mile	Shelly Steely	USA	4:32.27
60mh	LaVonna Martin	USA	7.98
HJ	Yolande Henry	USA	1.85m
Shot	Connie Price	USA	17.37m

DN GAMES, STOCKHOLM *Feb 9*
Men

200m	James Trapp	USA	21.29
400m	David Grindley	GBR	46.91
800m	Johnnie Gray	USA	1:48.21
1500m	Fermin Cacho	ESP	3:42.45
3000m	Moses Kiptanui	KEN	7:38.46
60mh	Gerg Foster	USA	7.58
PV	Igor Trandenkov	RUS	5.72m
HJ	Patrik Sjöberg	SWE	2.31m
LJ	Mike Powell	USA	8.41m
Shot	Jim Doehring	USA	20.56m

Women

60m	Gail Devers	USA	7.14
400m	Sandra Myers	ESP	54.39
1500m	Maria Akraka	SWE	4:11.81
LJ	Larissa Berezhnaya	UKR	6.88m

PAS DE CALAIS, LIEVIN, FRANCE *Feb 13*
Men

60m	Bruny Surin	CAN	6.45	
200m	Frankie Fredericks	NAM	20.37	
1000m	Charles Nkazamyampi	BUR	2:19.37	
60mh	Igor Kazanov	LIT	7.58	
PV	Sergey Bubka	UKR	6.14m	WR
HJ	Gustova Becker	ESP	2.18m	
LJ	Ivan Pedrosa	CUB	8.06m	
5kw	Frantz Kostoukevich	BLS	18:28.50	

Women

60m	Merlene Ottey	JAM	7.01	
200m	Merlene Ottey	JAM	21.87	WR
400m	Yelena Ruzina	RUS	52.06	
1000m	Lyubov Kremlyova	RUS	2:34.84	
60mh	Lyudmile Narozhilenko	RUS	7.69	=WR
LJ	Marieta Ilcu	ROM	6.94m	

TSB INTERNATIONAL, BIRMINGHAM
Feb 20
Men

60m	André Cason	USA	6.65
200m	Nikolay Antonov	BUL	20.84
400m	Michael Johnson	USA	45.14
800m	David Sharpe	GBR	1:48.63
Mile	Noureddine Morceli	ALG	3:50.70
PV	Maksim Tarasov	RUS	5.81m
HJ	Hollis Conway	USA	2.33m
TJ	Jonathan Edwards	GBR	17.16m

Women

60m	Merlene Ottey	JAM	7.12	
200m	Gwen Torrance	USA	23.03	
400m	Sally Gunnell	GBR	52.61	
800m	Diane Modahl	GBR	2:03.08	
2000m	Yvonne Murray	GBR	5:40.90	ER
TJ	Mary Agyepong	GBR	13.42m	

CIUDAD DE SAN SEBASTIAN, SPAIN *Mar 2*
Men

60m	Bruny Surin	CAN	6.52
200m	Christoph Postinger	AUT	20.87
400m	Michael Johnson	USA	45.68
800m	William Tanui	KEN	1:48.84
1500m	Mañual Pancorbo	ESP	3:41.89
3000m	Isaac Viciosa	ESP	7:57.65
60mh	Mark McKoy	CAN	7.55

PV	Sergey Bubka	UKR	5.91m
HJ	Arturo Ortiz	ESP	2.22m

Women

60m	Zhanna Tarnapolskaya	UKR	7.14
200m	Gwen Torrance	USA	22.85
800m	Yelena Storchevaya	UKR	2:02.97
60mh	Lyudmila Narozhilenko	RUS	7.68
LJ	Heike Drechsler	GER	6.95m

A VAULTER TOO MANY

Raymond N'Kounou, a Congolese Olympic pole vaulter, had his application for political asylum in France rejected. This despite the fact that during his brief stay the vaulter had bounded into the Rhone river to rescue a drowning woman. He is likely to receive a medal for his bravery, but no asylum. The real problem is France already has lots of pole vaulters.Now, if he could do a 3:35 1500m, that would be different.......

IAAF World Cross Country Championships

Amorebieta, Spain   28 March

Small wonder that the Europeans are in despair; this time around the Kenyans won seven of the eight prizes on offer with only the women's individual event still an open argument. William Sigei, who finished eighth in last year's championship, loped easily to victory in the absence of John Ngugi. A five-time winner of this event, Ngugi had refused a drugs test in Kenya and been ruled out of the championship. Daunting for the European athletes was that only two of last year's scoring six for Kenya (Sigei and Dominic Kirui) counted for this team. Albertina Dias found the flat, fast course to her liking and won the women's event. Dias, a fine track runner, did a neat role reversal from last year's race when she was third, McKiernan second and Jennings first. Zola Pieterse was fourth, although she did not look in shape to run that fast, and finished ahead of her more favoured compatriot, Elana Meyer. McColgan, in fifth, was comfortably the best of British.

The Courses Grass, and flat bar a few man-made hillocks.
Weather Bright, 14C, 68% hmdty.
Senior Men 11,750m

1.	**William Sigei**	KEN	32:15
2.	Dominic Kirui	KEN	32:56
3.	Ismael Kirui	KEN	32:59
4.	Moses Tanui	KEN	33:14
5.	Ezekiel Bitok	KEN	33:21
6.	Khalid Skah	MAR	33:22
7.	Haile Gebresilasie	ETH	33:23
8.	Addis Abebe	ETH	33:29
9.	Worku Bikila	ETH	33:31
10.	Paul Tergat	KEN	33:35
11.	Brahim Lahlafi	MAR	33:36
12.	Domingos Castro	POR	33:43
13.	Ondoro Osoro	KEN	33:45
14.	Martin Fiz	ESP	33:46
15	James Kariuki	KEN	33:50
16.	Fita Bayessa	ETH	33:53
17.	Thierry Pantel	FRA	33:55
18.	Tenedai Chimusasa	ZIM	33:58
19.	Abrehm Assefa	ETH	33:59
20.	Todd Williams	USA	34:00

Others include:

32.	Andrew Pearson	GBR	34:18
34.	Eamonn Martin	GBR	34:19
45.	Steve Tunstall	GBR	34:34
69.	Andy Bristow	GBR	34:54
71.	Jon Brown	GBR	34:55
102.	Paul Roden	GBR	35:20
111.	David Clarke	GBR	35:28
133.	Darren Mead	GBR	35:49
170.	Paul Dugdale	GBR	36:29

217 Runners Finished

Teams

1.	**Kenya**	25 points
2.	Ethiopia	82
3.	Portugal	167
4.	Spain	187
5.	France	238
6.	Morocco	260
7.	Great Britain	353
8.	USA	376

24 teams finished

Junior Men   7150m

1.	**Phillip Mosima**	KEN	20:18
2.	Christopher Kosgei	KEN	20:20
3.	Josphat Machuka	KEN	20:23
4.	Lazarus Nyakeraka	KEN	20:23
5.	Tegenu Abebe	ETH	20:28
6.	Habte Jifar	ETH	20:50
7.	Tibebu Reta	ETH	20:50
8.	Stanley Kimutai	KEN	21:03
9.	Geta Tsega	ETH	21:04
10.	Toloa Gebre	ETH	21:05

Others Include:

28.	Chris Stephenson	GBR	21:42
34.	Darius Burrows	GBR	21.45
63.	Mark Steinle	GBR	22:07
81.	Mike Griffiths	GBR	22:26
94.	Robert Lynham	GBR	22:35
101.	Ben Sutton	GBR	22:40

150 Runners Finished

Teams

1.	**Kenya**	10 points
2.	Ethiopia	27
3.	Morocco	76
4.	Spain	114
5.	Russia	120
11.	Great Britain	206

26 teams finished

Senior Women   6350m

1.	**Albertina Dias**	POR	20:00
2.	Catherina McKiernan	IRE	20:09
3.	Lynn Jennings	USA	20:09
4.	Zola Pieterse	SAF	20:10
5.	Liz McColgan	GBR	20:17
6	Elana Meyer	SAF	20:18
7.	Pauline Konga	KEN	20:19
8.	Farida Fates	FRA	20:20
9.	Iulia Negura	ROM	20:20
10.	Kazumi Kanbayashi	JPN	20:23
11.	Olga Churbanova	RUS	20:23
12.	Helen Kimayo	KEN	20:24
13.	Olga Bondarenko	RUS	20:24
14.	Odile Ohier	FRA	20:24
15.	Julia Vanquero	ESP	20:28
16.	Esther Kiplagat	KEN	20:30
17.	Jane Ngotho	KEN	20:33
18.	Paula Radcliffe	GBR	20:34
19.	Merina Denboba	ETH	20:36
20.	Tsugumi Fukuyama	JPN	20:37

Others Include:

34.	Annette Sergent	FRA	20:59
38.	Vicky McPherson	GBR	21:01
63.	Suzanne Rigg	GBR	21:21
92.	Alison Wyeth	GBR	21:44
110.	Andrea Whitcombe	GBR	22:05

144 Runners Finished

Teams

1.	**Kenya**	52 points
2.	Japan	93
3.	France	100
4.	South Africa	105
5.	Russia	106
6.	Ethiopia	122
7.	Great Britain	124
8.	Portugal	137

26 teams finished

Junior Women   4450m

1.	**Gladys Ondeyo**	KEN	14:04
2.	Pamela Chepchumba	KEN	14:09
3.	Sally Barsosio	KEN	14:11
4.	Hellen Mutai	KEN	14:14
5.	Susan Power	AUS	14:18
6.	Cathrine Kirui	KEN	14:29
7.	Elena Cosoveanu	ROM	14:32
8.	Akiko Kato	JPN	14:34
9.	Azumi Miyazaki	JPN	14:36
10.	Sachiko Nakahito	JPN	14:40

Others Include:

29.	Sharon Murphy	GBR	15:18
33.	Nicola Slater	GBR	15:22
50.	Julia Mackay	GBR	15:39
52.	Claire O'Connor	GBR	15:41
53.	Michelle Matthews	GBR	15:42
76.	Jeina Mitchell	GBR	16:03

119 Runners Finished

Teams

1.	**Kenya**	10 points
2.	Japan	41
3.	Ethiopia	61
4.	Romania	95
5.	Spain	123
9.	Great Britain	164

IAAF World Cross Challenge

Date	Venue	Men's Winner		Women's Winner	
Nov 29	Bolbec, France	Ezekiel Canario	POR	Lydia Cheromei	KEN
Dec 20	Mol, Belgium	Khalid Skah	MAR	Catherina McKiernan	IRL
Dec 27	São Paulo, Brazil	Simon Chemwoyo	KEN	Albertina Dias	POR
Jan 2	Durham, England	Fita Bayesa	ETH	Derartu Tulu	ETH
Jan 9	Belfast, N.Ireland	Simon Chemwoyo	KEN	Catherina McKiernan	IRL
Jan 17	Seville, Spain	Fita Bayesa	ETH	Catherina McKiernan	IRL
Jan 24	Tourcoing, France	Vincent Rousseau	BEL	Albertina Dias	POR
Jan 31	San Sebastián, Spain	Fita Bayesa	ETH	Luchia Yisak	ETH
Feb 7	Açoteias, Portugal	Ondoro Osoro	KEN	Tecla Lorupe	KEN
Feb 14	Diekirch, Luxemburg	James Kariuki	KEN	Suzanne Rigg	GBR
Feb 21	Chiba, Japan	Mathias Ntawulikura	RWA	Victoriya Nenasheva	RUS
Feb 27	Nairobi, Kenya	William Sigei	KEN	Helen Kimaiyo	KEN
Mar 6	San Vittore, Italy	Fita Bayesa	ETH	Esther Kiplagat	KEN
Mar 28	Amorebieta, Spain	William Sigei	KEN	Albertina Dias	POR

Final Standings - Men

1.	Ismael Kirui	KEN	116pts	$10,000
2.	Fita Bayesa	ETH	110	$ 8000
3.	Dominic Kirui	KEN	103	$ 6000
4.	Ondoro Osoro	KEN	93	$ 5000
5.	James Kariuki	KEN	92	$ 4000
6.	Haile Gebresilasie	ETH	91	$ 3500
7.	Vincent Rousseau	BEL	77	$ 3000
8.	William Sigei	KEN	75	$ 2500
9.	Moses Tanui	KEN	73	$ 2000
10.	Ezequiel Bitok	KEN	71	$ 1500
11.	Steve Tunstall	GBR	71	$ 1000
12.	Jon Brown	GBR	58	$ 500

Final Standings - Women

1.	Catherina McKiernan	IRE	141pts	$10,000
2.	Albertina Dias	POR	138	$8000
3.	Esther Kiplagat	KEN	98	$6000
4.	Tecla Lorupe	KEN	78	$5000
5.	Lydia Cheromei	KEN	78	$4000
6.	Suzanne Rigg	GBR	78	$3500
7.	Pauline Konga	KEN	73	$3000
8.	Colleen De Reuck	SAF	71	$2500
9.	Natalya Sorokivskaya	KZK	67	$2000
10.	Olga Bondarenko	RUS	66	$1500
11.	Anita Håkenstad	NOR	63	$1000
12.	Helen Kimayo	KEN	60	$500

UK World Trials

Corby   Feb 6

Men (12.5k)

1	Steve Tunstall	Lancs	36:33
2	Dave Clarke	Sy	36:44
3	Eamonn Martin	Essex	36:55

Women (5.5k)

1	Suzanne Rigg	Cheshire	18:39
2	Alison Wyeth	Mx	18:51
3	Vikki McPherson	Sco	18:54

English Cross-country Championships

Parliament Hill, London   Feb 27

Senior Men (15km)

1	Richard Nerurkar	Bingley	42:52
2	David Payne	Tipton	43:02
3	Paul Rodens	Horwich	43:08

Senior Men's Team

1	Bingley	162 pts
2	Tipton	308
3	Blackheath	354

Junior Men (10km)

1	S White	Coventry	29:42
2	Kaese Tadesse	Belgrave	29:49
3	S Barden	GEC Av	30:14

Junior Men's Team

1	Coventry	44
2	Oxford University	121
3	Blackheath	193

Reebok Welsh Championships

Singleton Park, Swansea   Feb 28

Senior Men (11.8km)

1	J Hobbs	Cardiff	37:06
2	Ian Hamer	Swansea	38:20
3	A Davies	Brecon	38:26

Senior Mens Team

1	Swansea	64
2	Newport	106
3	Cardiff	132

Senior Women (5.1km)

1	Wendy Ore	Cardiff	14:43
2	H Nash	Cardiff	18:05
3	S Lynch	Newport	18:31

Senior Women's Team

1	Newport	28
2	Cardiff	45
3	Les Croupiers	93

British Fell Running Championships

Whittle Pike   Jul 3

Men

1	I Holmes	Bingley	33:50
2	M Croasdale	Lancaster	33:57
3	A Peace	Bingley	34:02

Men's Team

1	Bingley	33pts

Women

1	C Greenwood	Calder V	39:10
2	J Kenyon	Horwich	40:15
3	L Fairfax	Unatt	40:56

Road-Running

Marathons

BEIJING MARATHON
Oct 11,1992

Men	1	Izumi Takahiro	JPN	2:11:29
	2	Hu Gangjun	CHN	2:12:45
	3	Sato Toshinobu	JPN	2:13:12
	9	Peter Fleming	GBR	2:17:02
Women	1	Xie Lihua	CHN	2:28:53
	2	Li Yemei	CHN	2:30:39
	3	Zheng Guixia	CHN	2:32:49
	9	Marian Sutton	GBR	2:39:46

GATORADE VENICE MARATHON
Oct 11,1992

Men	1	Joaquim Pinheiro	POR	2:13:33
	2	Gabriel Kamau	KEN	2:14:30
	3	Alcidio Costa	POR	2:14:48
Women	1	Emma Scaunich	ITA	2:35:06
	2	Sylvie Laville	FRA	2:42:14

DISCOVERIES MARATHON, LISBON
Oct 18,1992

Men	1	Jacon Ngungu	KEN	2:13:34
Women	1	Ekaterina Kramenkova	RUS	2:38:17

CITIBANK AUCKLAND MARATHON
Oct 25,1992

Men	1	Mark Hutchinson	NZL	2:16:32
	2	Andy Symonds	GBR	2:19:17
Women	1	Anne Roden	GBR	2:39:41

CARPI MARATHON
Oct 25, 1992

Men	1	G Gaduss	POL	2:12:36
	2	Carl Thackery	GBR	2:12:37
	3	Artur Castro	BRA	2:12:52

DB-MARATHON FRANKFURT
Oct 25,1992

Men	1	Steffen Dittmann	GER	2:12:59
Women	1	Bente Moe	NOR	2:23:36

JERUSALEM MARATHON
Oct 27,1992

Men	1	Shaoyan Cai	CHN	2:30.34
Women	1	Mei Wu	CHN	2:50.23

NEW YORK CITY MARATHON
Nov 1,1992

Men	1	Willie Mtolo	RSA	2:09:29
	2	Andres Espinoza	MEX	2:10.53
	3	Kim Woan-Ki	KOR	2:10:54
	4	Osmiro Silva	BRA	2:12:50
	9	David Lewis	GBR	2:13.49
	10	Steve Brace	GBR	2:14:10
Women	1	Lisa Ondieki	AUS	2:24:40
	2	Olga Markova	RUS	2:26:38
	3	Yoshiko Yamamoto	JPN	2:29:58
	4	Kamila Gradus	POL	2:30:09
	8	Sally Easthall	GBR	2:34:05

TOKYO WOMEN'S MARATHON
Nov 15, 1992

	1	Liz McColgan	GBR	2:27:38
	2	Katrin Dörre	GER	2:30:05
	3	Ramilia Burungulova	RUS	2:30:34
	4	Valentina Yegorova	RUS	2:31:27

BANGKOK MARATHON
Nov 29, 1992

Women	1	Lucy Ramwell	GBR	2:48:28

PALERMO MARATHON
Dec 6

Men	1	D Karel	RCS	2:11:47
	2	J Montero	ESP	2:13:31
	3	S Okemwa	KEN	2:14:12

FUKUOKA MARATHON
Dec

Men	1	Tene Negere	ETH	2:09:04
	2	L Peu	RSA	2:10:29
	3	Diego Garcia	ESP	2:10:30
	4	Dionicio Ceron	MEX	2:10:42

COSTA DE CAVLIA MARATHON
Dec 13, 1992 — Spain

Men	1	Ian Bloonfield	GBR	2:18:36
Women	1	Lyubov Klochko	RUS	2:39:48

HONOLULU MARATHON
Dec 13, 1992

Men	1	Benson Masya	KEN	2:14:19
	2	Cosmas N'deti	KEN	2:14:28
	3	David Tsebe	RSA	2:16:45
Women	1	Carla Buerskens	HOL	2:32:13
	2	Lisa Wiedenbach	USA	2:38:51
	3	Ritva Lemettinen	FIN	2:39:21

SAN MIGUEL VIETNAM MARATHON
Jan 3

Men	1	Doug Kurtis	USA	2:39:14
	2	Tim Souter	GBR	2:50:04
Women	1	Thi Teo Dang	VIE	3:25:51

MARRAKECH GRAND ATLAS MARATHON
Jan 10

Men	1	M Chaham	MAR	2:11:55
	2	Viktor Mozgovoy	RUS	2:12:41
	3	M Salim	ALG	2:13:40
Women	1	T Slusser	USA	2:38:01
	2	A Dudaera	RUS	2:42:51
	3	F Rueda-Oppligar	SUI	2:44:42

KATHMANDU MARATHON
Jan 30

Men	1	Ieuan Ellis	GBR	2:24:10

NUTRASWEET LONDON MARATHON
Apr 18

Men

1	Eamonn Martin	GBR	2:10:50
2	Isidro Rico	MEX	2:10:53
3	Grzegorz Gajdus	POL	2:11:07
4	Salvatore Bettiol	ITA	2:11:55
5	Frank Bjørkli	NOR	2:12:23
6	Dave Buzza	GBR	2:12:24
7	Seung-Do Bak	KOR	2:12:34
8	Ahmed Salah	DJI	2:12:40
9	Juan Torres	ESP	2:13:44
10	Steve Brace	GBR	2:14:00

Women

1	Katrin Dörre	GER	2:27:09
2	Lisa Ondieki	AUS	2:27:27
3	Liz McColgan	GBR	2:29:37
4	Renata Kokowska	POL	2:32:30
5	Lorraine Moller	NZL	2:32:56
6	Anna Rybicka	POL	2:34:21
7	Ritva Lemettinen	FIN	2:34:44
8	Alina Ivanova	RUS	2:37:21
9	Galina Zhelyeva	UKR	2:41:50
10	Gillian Horovitz	GBR	2:42:14

W/Chair Men

1	Geroges Vandammo	BEL	1:44:10
2	Ivan Newman	GBR	1:46:15
3	David Holding	GBR	1:51:22

Women

1	Rose Hill	GBR	2:03:05
2	Lily Anggreny	GER	2:09:16
3	Tanni Grey	GBR	2:12:25

With a new sponsor on board, the London Marathon went for the big sell with the grudge match. The sell was Liz McColgan paid a reputed $250,000 to start this event, with the same sum promised for the 1994 and 1995 race (although the event has yet to find a sponsor for that year). The grudge match was the Scot against the Australian Lisa Ondieki. They had raced against each other in the New York Marathon 18 months earlier and the Australian had found the Scot all too arrogant. McColgan was confident then, and won that, her first, marathon. London, was to be a more humbling experience.

The conditions were difficult, but Ondieki and McColgan went out as if it was a two-horse race. Katrin Dörre, winner of last year's event, ran much more cagily. Ondieki broke the Scot, but for Dörre's benefit. Along the Embankment, as a year past, she upped the tempo and was away.

In contrast, the men's event had been almost overlooked. On the day, Eamonn Martin made sure that it wasn't. Martin never looks comfortable until he gets on his toes. For 26 miles he ran on his heels and left us in doubt. Three hundred yards from the finish he was on his toes and away and Mexican Isidro Rico had no chance to stay with him.

OSAKA LADIES MARATHON
Jan 31

1	Junko Asari	JPN	2:26:26
2	Tome Abe	JPN	2:26:27
3	Yoshiko Yamamoto	JPN	2:29:41

BEPPU-OITA MAINICHI MEN'S MARATHON
Feb 7

1	Maurilio Castillo	MEX	2:13:04
2	Leszek Beblo	POL	2:13:42
3	Toru Mimura	JPN	2:14:02

VALENCIA MARATHON
Feb 7

Men	1	Leonid Shvesto	RUS	2;15:04
Women	1	Monica Pont	ESP	2:35:30

TOKYO MARATHON
Feb 14

Men	1	Abebe Mekonnen	ETH	2:12:00
	2	Steve Moneghetti	AUS	2:12:36
	3	Brian Sheriff	ZIM	2:12:55

CITY OF SEVILLE MARATHON
Feb 21

Men	1	Vicente Anton	ESP	2:14:37
Women	1	Karen McLeod	GBR	2:34:30

NAGOYA WOMEN'S MARATHON
Mar 7   Japan

1	Kamila Gradus	POL	2:27:38
2	Akemi Matsuno	JPN	2:27:53
3	Ramilia Burangulova	RUS	2:28:03

LOS ANGELES MARATHON
March 7

Men	1	Joseildo Rocha	BRA	2;14:29
Women	1	Lyubov Klochko	RUS	2:39:49

LAKE BIWA MAINICHI MARATHON, JAPAN
Mar 14

Men	1	Mike O'Reilly	GBR	2:11:01
	2	Weislaw Perszke	POL	2:11:15
	3	Gert Thys	RSA	2:11:40

HAUTS-DE-SEINE
Mar 14   France

Men	1	Chouki Achour	ALG	2:13:43
Women	1	A Andrescu-Barbu	ROM	2:34:38

NIKE ROTTERDAM MARATHON
Apr 18

Men	1	Dionicio Ceron	MEX	2:11:06
	2	Simon Robert Naali	TAN	2:11:44

	3	Harrie Hänninen	FEI	2:11:58
Women	1	Anne Van Schuuppen	HOL	2:34:15
	2	Wima Van Onna	HOL	2:34:28
	3	Ciska Maton	BEL	2:39:24
	4	Brenda Walker	GBR	2:39:36

BAA BOSTON MARATHON
Apr 19

Men	1	Cosmas N'deti	KEN	2:09:33
	2	Kim Jae-Wong	KOR	2:09:43
	3	Lucketz Swartbooi	NAM	2:09:57
	4	Hiromi Taniguchi	JPN	2:11:02
	5	Sammy Lelei	KEN	2:12:12
	6	Mark Plaatjes	USA	2:12:29
Women	1	Olga Markova	RUS	2:25:27
	2	Kim Jones	USA	2:20:00
	3	Carmen De Oliveira	BRA	2:31:18
	4	Mañuela Machado	POR	2:32:20
	5	Albina Galliamova	RUS	2:35:12
	6	Joan Benoit Samuelson	USA	2:35:43

CLEVELAND MARATHON
Apr 25

Men	1	Don Janicki	USA	2:11:39
	2	Mohamed Nazipov	RUS	2:12:15
	3	Peter Maher	CAN	2:12:50
Women	1	Lyubov Klochko	UKR	2:34:47

PARIS MARATHON
Apr 25

Men	1	Leszek Beblo	POL	2:10:46
	2	Belay Wolashe	ETH	2:10:57
	3	S Ah Sakhri	ALG	2:11:09
	10	Andy Green	GBR	2:12:12
Women	1	Mitsuyo Yoshida	JPN	2:29:16
	2	Maria Lelut Rebello	FRA	2:30:36
	3	Ilyina Nadejda	RUS	2:30:44

TURIN MARATHON
Apr 25

Men	1	Walter Durbano	ITA	2:11:13
	2	Raffaele Aliegro	ITA	2:12:11
	3	Abdrew Masai	KEN	2:13:05
Women	1	Emma Scaunich	ITA	2:34:17
	2	Maria Curatolo	ITA	2:36:47

MADRID MARATHON
April 26

Men	1	Martin Vrabel	ESP	2:16:13
Women	1	Alzira Lario	POR	2:43:28

TIANJIN MARATHON
Apr?

Women	1	Wang Junxia	CHN	2:24.07
	2	Qu Yunxia	CHN	2:24:32
	3	Zhang Linli	CHN	2:24:42
	4	Zhang Lihong	CHN	2:24:52
	5	Zhong Huandi	CHN	2:25:36
	6	Ma Liyan	CHN	2:24:42

MUNICH MARATHON
May 9

Men	1	Gidamis Shahanga	TAN	2:14:28
Women	1	Fatima Neves	POR	2:39:34

SHELL HANSE-MARATHON HAMBURG
May 23

Men	1	Richard Nerurkar	GBR	2:10:57
	2	Thomas Robert Naali	TAN	2:11:38
	3	Karel David	TCH	2:11:57
Women	1	Gabi Wolf	GER	2:34:36
	2	Vera Suchova	RUS	2:34:59
	3	Alevtina Naumova	RUS	2:35:19

STOCKHOLM MARATHON
June 5

Men	1	Daniel Mbuli	RSA	2:16:30
	2	Hugh Jones	GBR	2:17:29
Women	1	Grete Kirkeberg	NOR	2:37:58

MELBOURNE MARATHON
June 6

Men	1	Jerry Modiga	RSA	2:15:07
Women	1	Dominique Rembert	FRA	2:44:22

TWENTE MARATHON
June 21   Enschede, Holland

Men	1	Jan Tau	RSA	2:12:19
Women	1	Weronika Troxler	SUI	2:44:33

HELSINKI MARATHON
Aug 7

Men	1	Martin Fiz	ESP	2:12:47
Women	1	Anne Jaaskelainen	FIN	2:43:32

AMSTERDAM MARATHON
Sept 26

Men	1	K Suzuki	JPN	2:11:56
	2	T Dirks	HOL	2:12:27
	3	M Ten Kate	HOL	2:12:39
Women	1	C Beurskens	HOL	2:31:48

BERLIN MARATHON
Sept 26

Men	1	Xolie Yawa	RSA	2:10:57
	2	Driss Dacha	MAR	2:11:43
	3	David Tsebe	RSA	2:12:07
Women	1	Renata Kokowska	POL	2:26:20
	2	Albertina Dias	POR	2:26:48
	3	M Sobranska	POL	2:28:21

TOKYO HALF-MARATHON
Jan 25

Men	1	Steve Moneghetti	AUS	1:00:06
	2	Todd Williams	USA	1:00:11
	3	Dionicio Ceron	MEX	1:00:17
Women	1	Elana Meyer	RSA	1:07:22
	2	Olga Appell	MEX	1:08:34
	3	C D Heining	GER	1:10:04

MIAMI STREET MILE
Jan 25

Men	1	Steve Cram	GBR	3:58:09
Women	1	Alison Hill	USA	4:34:09

JAKARTA 10KM ROAD RACE
Jan 25

Men				
	1	Addis Abebe	ETH	27:40 *WB*
	2	Arturo Barrios	MEX	28:01
	3	Sam Chemoiymo	KEN	28:11
	9	Paul Evans	GBR	30:41

LISBON HALF-MARATHON
Mar 14

Men				
	1	Sammy Lelei	KEN	59:24
	2	Tendai Chimusasa	ZIM	1:00:35
	3	Stephen Freigang	GER	1:00:36
Women	1	Nadezdha Iliyna	RUS	1:09:47

This course was remeasured and found to be 97m short, which disqualifies Lelei's time as a world record

---

EXCUSE ME, COMRADE

The Comrades' Marathon, run over 90km of undulating road from Pietermaritzburg to Durban in South Africa is one of the great distance-running tests in the world and Herman Matthee had every reason to be pleased with his seventh placing in this year's event. It was an even more remarkable run when you consider that he was spotted having breakfast in Durban at the time of the start. Matthee continues to protest his innocence, but so did Rose Ruiz in Boston and we *know* she used the subway.......

BERLIN HALF-MARATHON
Apr 4

Men				
	1	Carsten Eich	GER	1:00:34
	2	Sammy Lelei	KEN	1:00:42
	3	Julius Ondieki	KEN	1:01:23
	7	Billy Dee	GBR	1:02:33
Women	1	Päivi Tikkanen	FIN	1:12:30
	2	Ludmila Matweena	RUS	1:13:03
	3	Izabela Zatorska	POL	1:13:07

PARIS HALF-MARATHON
Apr 4

Men				
	1	Robert Stefko	TCH	1:02:42
	8	Carl Thackery	GBR	1:03:01
Women	1	Maria Lelut Rebello	FRA	1:13:02

BERLIN 25K
May 2

Men				
	1	Tendai Chimusasi	ZIM	1:14:25
	2	Thomas Robert Naali	TAN	1:14:37
	3	Ikaji Salum	TAN	1:14:48
Women	1	Lyudmila Matweena	RUS	1:29:04
	2	Elena Wjasowa	UKR	1:29:04
	3	Gabi Wolf	GER	1:30:22
	4	Karen McLeod	GBR	1:30:52

LYON HALF-MARATHON
May 16

Men				
	1	Andrew Masai	KEN	1:01:35

SCHWEIZER FRAUENLAUF 5KM
(Women's Race)
June 13   Berne, Switzerland

	1	Yelena Romanova	RUS	15:14.5
	2	Uta Pippig	GER	15:19.3
	3	Esther Kiplagat	KEN	15:22.4

UK Road Running

DIET COKE GREAT SOUTH RUN
Portsmouth   Oct 11

Men				
	1	Boay Akonay	TAN	47:04
	2	Paul Davies-Hale	C&S)	47:08
	3	Jack Buckner	Charnw	47:10

DIET COKE GREAT LONDON RUN
Oct 18

Men				
	1	Carl Thackery	Hallam	29:16
	2	Gary Arthy	Blackhth	29:31
	3	Gary Staines	Belgrave	29:58

AAA 10K CHAMPIONSHIP
Nov 29

Men				
	1	Rob Denmark	Basildon	28:36
	2	Keith Cullen	Chelms	28:38
	3	Billy Dee	Luton	28:41

GREAT WEST RUN
Exeter   May 2

Men	1	Richard Nerurkar	Bingley	62:39
Women	1	B Cardy-Wise	Broms	76:43

BUPA INTERNATIONAL ROAD RACES

Aberdeen   May 22

Men				
(5k)	1	Khalid Skah	MAR	13:39
	2	Paul Evans	GBR	13:58
	3	Paul Dugdale	GBR	14:02
Men	1	Curtis Robb	GBR	4:04
(1 mile)	2	John Mayock	GBR	4:05
	3	Rob Denmark	GBR	4:07
Women	1	Yvonne Murray	GBR	15:20
(5k)	2	Liz McColgan	GBR	15:31
	3	Catherina McKiernan	IRL	15:57

BUPA GREAT LONDON RUN (10K)
Sept 12

Women	1	Esther Kiplagat	KEN	32:35
	2	I Negura	ROM	32:48
	3	Zola Pieterse	RSA	33:11

GREAT NORTH RUN
Newcastle–South Shields   Sept 19

Men				
	1	Moses Tanui	KEN	1:00:15
	2	Paul Evans	GBR	1:01:45
	3	Richard Nerurkar	GBR	1:03:04
Women	1	Tecla Lorupe	KEN	1:12:55
	2	Olga Bondarenko	RUS	1:13:13
	3	Zola Pieterse	RSA	1:13:30

BUPA GREAT MIDLAND RUN

Men				
	1	Paul Davies-Hale	GBR	28:37
	2	J Kibor	KEN	28:37
	3	Gary Staines	GBR	28:42
Women	1	Tecla Laroupe	KEN	32:38
	2	Suzanna Rigg	GBR	32:35
	3	Marian Sutton	GBR	33:35

IAAF/Reebok World Race Walking Cup

April 24-25   Monterrey, Mexico

MEN'S 20KM

1. Daniel García		**MEX**	**1:24:26**
2. Valentí Massana		ESP	1:24:32
3. Alberto Cruz		MEX	1:24:37
4. Robert Korzeniowski		POL	1:24:47
5. Mikhail Schennikov		RUS	1:24:49
6. Daniel Plaza		ESP	1:24:52

TEAMS

1. Mexico	**265**	4. Poland	229
2. Italy	244	5. Colombia	225
3. Spain	240	6. Russia	221
13.Great Britain	166		

MEN'S 50KM

1. Carlos Mercenário		**MEX**	**3:50:28**
2. Jesús García		ESP	3:52:44
3. German Sanchez		MEX	3:54:15
4. Miguel Rodríguez		MEX	3:54:22
5. Tim Berrett		CAN	3:55:12
6. Valentin Kononen		FIN	3:57:28

TEAMS

1. Mexico	**275**	4. Italy	243
2. Spain	251	5. Finland	225
3. France	245	6. Poland	223
19.Great Britain	120		

THE LUGANO TROPHY (overall team)

1. Mexico	**265+275=540**
2. Spain	240+251=491
3. Italy	244+243=487

WOMEN'S 10KM

1. Wang Yan		**CHN**	**45:10**
2. Sari Essayah		FIN	45:18
3. Yelena Nikolayeva		RUS	45:22
4. Madelein Svensson		SWE	45:43
5. Kerry Junna-Saxby		AUS	45:55
6. Ileana Salvador		ITA	46:02

TEAMS

1. Italy	**196**	4. Australia	170
2. China	193	5. Hungary	160
3. Russia	193	6. Spain	144

LONDON INTERNATIONAL 200K

Battersea Park	Aug 23	
1. A Radionov	**RUS**	**22:04:39**
2. R Brown	Surrey WC	22:55:30
3. J Cecillon	FRA	23:52:13

AAA WOMEN'S 10K CHAMPIONSHIP

Horsham June 20		
1. V Larby	**A F & D**	**47:10.07**
2. V Lupton	Sheffield	47:37.32
3. E Callinan	Solihull	51:58.80

Australian Rules Football

AFL

Prelim Finals
Sept
Essendon 111 (17.9) bt Adelaide 100 (14.16)
Carlton 86 (13.8) bt Adelaide Crows (8.20)
Final
Melbourne Cricket Ground   Sept 25
Essendon 133 (20.13) bt Carlton 89 (13.11)
Goals
Essendon: Slmon 5, Mercuri 3, Hird 2, Long 2, Harvey,
Wanganeen, C Daniher, Berwick, Wallis, Misiti, Denham,
Calthorpe
Carlton: Kernahan 7, Welsh 2, Williams, Heaver, Bradley,
Alvin

Foster's Cup

Waverley Park, Melbourne   Mar 22
Final
Essendon 102 Richmond 79

British Summer League

ARFL LEAGUE TABLE

		P	W	L	For	Ag	%	Pts
1	London Hawks	12	12	0	1488	371	401.1	48
2	Wandsworth	12	10	2	1445	412	350.7	40
3	Lea Valley	12	8	4	1517	637	238.1	32
4	North London	12	8	4	1293	587	220.3	32
5	West London	12	8	4	1243	659	188.7	32
6	Sussex	12	6	6	746	1058	70.5	24
7	Birmingham	12	4	8	602	1089	55.3	16
8	Liverpool	12	3	9	433	874	49.5	12
9	Bristol	12	3	9	536	1355	39.6	12
10	Earls Court	12	2	10	406	1520	26.7	8
11	East Midland	12	2	10	315	1462	21.5	8

FINALS SERIES

Elimination Final:
North London 76 (10/16) bt West London 31 (4/7)

Qualifying Final:
Lea Valley 63 (9/9) bt Wandsworth 49 (6/13)

First Semi-Final:
Wandsworth 78 (11/12) bt North London 35 (5/5)

Second Semi-Final:
London Hawks 66 (9.12) bt Lea Valley 51 (7/9)

Preliminary Final:
Lea Valley 82 (12/10) bt Wandsworth 47 (6/11)

Grand Final:
London Hawks 85 (12/13) bt Lea Valley 41 (6/5)

Badminton

The world rankings tell most of the story; the world of badminton is dominated by the Koreans, Malaysians, Chinese and Indonesians. In Europe, the Danes have flesh on the bone, but no-one else. It was ironic that when the world championships came to Birmingham, the best chance of a home-based player winning was the typhoid scare that might have ruled out the Indonesian players. Now, if the Chinese had chicken pox, the Malaysians rubella, the Danes hiccups...but no, the championships went as expected. As sure as the tide rolling on the sand, an Indonesian Joko Suprianto, won the men's title, and another Indonesian, Susi Susanti, won the women's. They added, for very good measure, the men's doubles.

Well, what else do they do, you might argue. There were 161 million Indonesians at the last count (1984) and this is their national sport. In a sense that's right. Britain is a catholic (with a small c) nation and we, in sporting terms, spread ourselves thinly. But that argument doesn't please everyone. Lee Jae Bok was the Olympic coach for the British team. In October, Bok, a Korean, rounded on the unprofessional attitude of some of our players. He believed that too many players thought the goal was just to reach the championships, not what you achieved when you were there.

Darren Hall, despite injury problems, added some gloss to the picture when he became the first Briton in a long time to take the Danish Open. But in the major team competition of the season, the Sudirman Cup, the Danes struck back and made a dreadful mess of England, winning 5-0. Indonesia also beat England 5-0 to emphasise the gap.

IBF WORLD RANKINGS
As at July 28, 1993

Men

1	Joko Suprianto	INA
2	Allan Budi Kusuma	INA
3	Heryanto Arbi	INA
4	Ardy B Wiranata	INA
5	Thomas Stuer-Lauridsen	DEN
6	Poul-Erik Hoyer-Larsen	DEN
7	Rashid Sidek	MAL
8	Wenkai Wu	CHN
9	Harmawen Susanto	INA
10	Zhao Jianhua	CHN
18	Stephen Butler	ENG
31	Darren Hall	ENG
39	Anders Nielsen	ENG

Men's Pairs

1	Subagja/Mainaky	INA
2	Holst-Christensen/Lund	DEN
3	C Kang/C Hongyong	CHN
4	Cheah/Soo	MAL
5	Z Yumin/H Zhanzhong	CHN
16	Ponting/Archer	ENG

Women

1	Susi Susanti	INA
2	Ye Zhaoying	CHN
3	Soo Hyun Bang	KOR
4	Huang Hua	CHN
5	Tang Jiuhong	CHN
6	Yao Yan	CHN
7	S Kusumawardhani	INA
8	Lim Xiaoqing	CHN
9	Heung Soon Lee	KOR
10	Shen Lianfeng	CHN
30	Fiona Smith	ENG
36	Alison Humby	ENG
40	Suzanne Louis-Lane	ENG

Women's Pairs

1	Chung/Gil	KOR
2	Lin Yanfen/Yao Fen	CHN
3	Finarsih/Tampi	INA
4	Nong Qunhua/Zhou Lei	CHN
5	Chen Ying/Wu Yuhong	CHN
9	Gowers/Clark	ENG
16	Groves/Davies	ENG

Mixed Pairs

1	Bengtsson/Lund	SWE/DEN
2	Lund/Dupont	DEN
3	Gunawan/Tendean	INA
4	Mirawat/Eliza	INA
5	Clark/Ponting	ENG
12	Sankey/Wright	ENG

World Championships

Birmingham   May 24-June 26, 1993

Men's Singles
From 5th Round

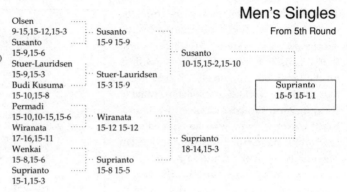

Heryanto Arbi (INA)
Jens Olsen (SWE) — Olsen 9-15,15-12,15-3 — Susanto 15-9 15-9
Hermawen Susanto (INA) — Susanto 15-9,15-6
Sompol Kookasemkit (THA)
Thomas Stuer-Lauridsen (DEN) — Stuer-Lauridsen 15-9,15-3 — Stuer-Lauridsen 15-3 15-9 — Susanto 10-15,15-2,15-10
Lui Jun (CHN)
Allan Budi Kusuma (INA) — Budi Kusuma 15-10,15-8
Foo Kok Keong (MAL)
Fung Permadi (INA) — Permadi 15-10,10-15,15-6 — Wiranata 15-12 15-12
Rashid Sidek (MAL)
Park Sung-Woo (KOR) — Wiranata 17-16,15-11
Ardy B Wiranata (INA)
Wu Wenkai (CHN) — Wenkai 15-8,15-6 — Suprianto 15-8 15-5 — Suprianto 18-14,15-3
Poul-Erik Hoyer-Larsen (DEN)
Erik Lia (NOR) — Suprianto 15-1,15-3
Joko Suprianto (INA)

Suprianto
15-5 15-11

British players results. **1st Rd**: Kevin Scott (SCO) bt Stephen Butler (ENG) 15-6,15-10; Peter Knowles (ENG) bt David Humble (CAN) 12-15,15-7,17-15; Joko Suprianto bt Geraint Lewis (WAL) 15-6,15-2
2nd Rd: Ong Ewe Hock(MAL) bt Peter Bush(ENG) 12-15,15-5,15-8; Bryan Blanshard (CAN) bt Steven Yates (WAL) 15-6,15-4; Darren Hall (ENG) bt Serpa Pinto Horacio MEX) 15-1,15-1; Stephen Butler bt Jeroen van Dijk (HOL) 15-5,15-5; Peter Smith (ENG) bt Hamid Nassimi (IRN) 15-1,15-2; Peter Knowles bt Juraj

Brestovsky (SVK) 15-0,15-2
3rd Rd: Darren Hall bt Arni Hallgrimsson (ISL) 15-5, 15-5; Stephen Butler bt Lee Yong Sun 15-7,15-4; Pan Teng (CHN) bt Pater Smith 15-12,15-3; Peter Knowles bt George Thomas (IND) 15-7,15-9
4th Rd: Sompol Kookasemkit(THA) bt Darren Hall 8-15,18-15,15-4; Allan B Kusuma(INA) bt Stephen Butler 15-18,15-9,15-0; P Hoyer-Larsen (DEN) bt Peter Knowles 15-10,15-3

Women's Singles
From 5th Round

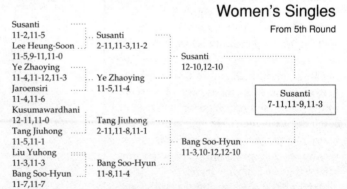

Susi Susanti (INA) — Susanti 11-2,11-5 — Susanti 2-11,11-3,11-2
Hu Ning (CHN)
Lee Heung-Soon (KOR) — Lee Heung-Soon 11-5,9-11,11-0
Juni Kartika (INA)
Ye Zhaoying (CHN) — Ye Zhaoying 11-4,11-12,11-3 — Ye Zhaoying 11-5,11-4 — Susanti 12-10,12-10
Yuliani Santoso (INA)
Chung Eun-Hwa (KOR) — Jaroensiri 11-4,11-6
Somharuehai Jaroensiri (THA)
Guo Jing (CHN) — Kusumawardhani 12-11,11-0 — Tang Jiuhong 2-11,11-8,11-1
S Kusumawardhani (INA)
Lee Wai Leng (MAL) — Tang Jiuhong 11-5,11-1
Tang Jiuhong (CHN)
Liu Yuhong (CHN) — Liu Yuhong 11-3,11-3 — Bang Soo-Hyun 11-8,11-4 — Bang Soo-Hyun 11-3,10-12,12-10
Minarti Timur (INA)
Christine Magnussen (SWE) — Bang Soo-Hyun 11-7,11-7
Bang Soo-Hyun (KOR)

Susanti
7-11,11-9,11-3

British players results. **1st Rd**: Jennifer Allen (SCO) w/o Ana Laura de la Torre (MEX)
2nd Rd: Fiona Smith w/o Gabriel (Melgosa (MEX)
S Louis-Lane (ENG) bt Tan Lee Wai (MAL) 11-4,11-2
Juni Kartika (INA) bt Kelly Morgan (WAL) 11-0,11-1
Hisako Mizui (JPN) bt Gillian Martin (SCO) 11-3,11-4
Tanya Groves (ENG) bt Katy Howell (WAL) 11-3,11-7
A Travers (SCO) bt Brigitte Langthaler (AUT) 11-4,11-1
Jo Muggeridge (ENG) bt Gail Davies (WAL) 11-2,11-0
Kusumawardhani bt Anne Gibson (SCO) 11-3,11-8
Jennifer Allen w/o Liao Yue Jin (NZL); Rhonda Cator w/o Rachael Phipps (WAL)

Sarah Hore bt Erika vanHeiland (USA) 11-3,12-9
Alison Humby bt Pawangadkar (IND) 4-11,11-4,11-5
3rd Rd: Fiona Smith bt Liz Aronsohn (USA) 11-6,12-10
Suzanne Louis Lane bt P V V Lakshmi (IND) 11-6,11-3
Chung Eun-Hwa (KOR) bt Tanya Groves 8-11,11-6,11-4
Guo Jing (CHN) bt Jo Muggeridge 11-4,3-11,12-9
Marina Yakusheva (RUS) bt Jennifer Allen 11-3,11-0
Alison Humby bt Zamaliah Sidek (MAL) 11-1,11-7
4th Rd: Hu Ning (CHN) bt Louis Lane 11-0,11-4
Ye Zhaoying (CHN) bt Fiona Smith 11-1,11-6
Bang Soo-Hyun ((KOR) bt Alison Humby 11-1,11-4

Men's Doubles

*Early round results include only matches involving British
contestants. *Signifies 1st round bye.*
FIRST ROUND
Geraint Lewis/Dayle Blencowe (WAL) w/o
Jerzy Dolhan/Grzegorz Olchowik (POL)

David Gilmour/Craig Robertson (SCO) bt
Svetoslav Stojanov/Michail Popov (BUL) 15-6,15-9

Alistair Gatt/Gordon Haldane (SCO) bt
Jyri Aalto/Jyri Eriksson (FIN) 15-9,15-6

Chris Hunt/Mike Adams (ENG) bt
V Druzhtchenko/V Streltsov (UKR) 18-15,9-15,15-9

Kenny Middlemiss/Russell Hogg (SCO) w/o
Sergey Repka/Leonid Pugach (UKR)

Chris Rees/David Tonks (WAL) bt
Jiang Xin/Yu Qi (CHN) 4-15,15-7,15-7

SECOND ROUND
Nick Ponting/Simon Archer (ENG)* bt
Mikhail Korshuk/Vitaly Shmakov (BLS) 15-9,15-5

Dean Galt/Kerrin Harrison (NZL) bt
Lewis/Blencowe 15-4,15-2

Stephan Kuhl/Kai Mitteldorf (GER) bt
Gilmour/Robertson 15-6,15-9

Gatt/Haldane bt
Richard Banhidi/Tamas Labodi (HUN) 15-9,15-6

Hunt/Adams bt
EtienneThobois/Manuel Dubrulle (FRA) 11-15,15-12,15-3

Jiang Xin/Yu Qi bt
Middlemiss/Hogg 15-6,15-4

Deny Kantano/Antonius (INA) bt
Steven Yates (WAL)/Graham Henderson (IRL)* 15-0,15-3

Dave Wright/Julian Robertson (ENG)* bt
Quinten Van Dalm (HOL)/Boris Kesov (BUL) 15-5,15-4

THIRD ROUND
Ponting/Archer bt
Galt/Harrison 15-4,15-2

Peter Axelsson/Par Gunnar Jonsson (SWE) bt
Gatt/Haldane 15-3,15-8

Hunt/Adams bt
Yap Yee Hup/Yap Yee Guan (MAL) 15-5,15-11

Jan Paulsen/Michael Sogaard (DEN) bt
Wright/Robertson 9-15,15-10,15-13

FOURTH ROUND
Ricky Subagja/Rudy Gunawan (INA) bt
Ponting/Archer 15-9,15-3

Axelsson/Jonsson bt
Hunt/Adams 15-2,15-11

QUARTER-FINALS
Subagja/Gunawan (INA) bt
Razif Sidek/Jalani Sidek (MAL) 15-5,5-15,17-14

Holst Christensen/Lund (DEN) bt
Axelsson/Gunnar Jonsson (SWE) 15-9,9-15,15-4

Yoo Yong-Sung/Ha Tae Kwon (KOR) bt
Cheah Soon Kit/Soo Beng Kiang (MAL) 15-8,15-8

Deny Kantono/Antonius (INA) bt
Chen Kang/Hongyong (CHN) 17-15,16-18,18-16

SEMI-FINALS
Subagja/Gunawan bt
Axelsson/Jonsson 15-9,9-15,15-4

Cheah Soon Kit/Soo Beng Kiang bt
Chen Kang/Chen Hongyong 15-6,15-5

FINAL
Subagja/Gunawan bt
Cheah Soon Kit/Soo Beng Kiang 15-11,15-3

Women's Doubles

SECOND ROUND
Gillian Clark/Gillian Gowers (ENG)* bt
Sheree Jefferson (NZL)/Sonya McGinn (IRL)* 15-6,15-8

Gillian Martin/Jennifer Allen (SCO)* bt
Nely Nedjalkova/Victoria Hristova (BUL)* 15-10,15-10

Joannne Wright/Alison Humby (ENG)* bt
Tove Hol/Camilla Silwer (NOR)* 18-17,15-4

Gail Davies/Katy Howell (WAL)* w/o
Norma Hernandez/Veronica Estrada (MEX)*

Sara Sankey/Julie Bradbury (ENG)* bt
Nicole Baldewein/Karen Stechmann (GER) 15-12,15-10

Natalja Ivanov/Julia Martynenko (RUS)* bt
Jillian Haldane/Aileen Travers (SCO)* 15-6,15-5

THIRD ROUND
Clark/Gowers bt
Eline Coene/Erica van den Heuvel (HOL) 15-9,15-7

Lim Xiao Qing/Christine Magnusson (SWE) bt
Martin/Allen 15-1,15-8

Chen Ying/Wu Yuhong (CHN) bt
Wright/Humby 15-7,15-2

Sankey/Bradbury bt
Davies/Howell 15-,15-1

FOURTH ROUND
Clark/Gowers bt
Irina Serova/Sabine Ploner (AUT) 15-5,15-1

Lotte Olsen/Lisbet Stuer Lauridsen (DEN) bt
Sankey/Bradbury 15-10,18-17

QUARTER-FINALS
Chung So Hung/Gil Young Ah (KOR) bt
Clark/Gowers 12-15,15-2,15-2

Chen Ying/Wu Yihong bt
Marlene Thomsen/A Mette Bille (DEN) 15-4,14-18,15-11

Nong Qunhua/Zhou Lei bt
Maria and Catrine Bengtsson (SWE) 13-15,18-5,15-12

Olsen/Stuer Lauridsen bt
Yao Fen/Lin Yan Fen (CHN) 15-12,13-15,17-16

SEMI-FINALS
Chen Ying/Wu Yuhong bt
Chung So Young/Gil Young Ah 15-7,6-15,15-11

Nong Qunha/Zou Lei bt
Olsen/Stuer Lauridsen 15-12,13-15,17-16

FINAL
Nong Qunha/Zhou Lei bt
Chen Ying/Wu Yihong 15-5,15-10

Mixed Doubles

FIRST ROUND
Julian Robertson/Julie Bradbury (ENG) w/o
Lius Antonio Timm/Indira Bhikha (MOZ)

Akihiro Imai/Haruko Matsuda (JPN) bt
David Tonks/Rachael Phipps (WAL) 15-7,15-3

Simon Archer/Joanne Davies (ENG) bt
Mark Nichols/Rhonda Cator (AUS) 15-12,15-9

Alistair Gatt/Aileen Travers (SCO) w/o
Pawel Wasilewski/Elzbieta Gryzbek

Oleg Morozevich/Tatyana Gerasimovich bt
Kenny Middlemiss/Elinor Allen (SCO) 15-11,5-15,15-6

Yoo Yong-Sung/Jang Hye Ock (KOR) bt
Bruce Flockhart/Anne Gibson (SCO) 15-0,15-1

Trond Waland/Camilla Silwer (NOR) bt
Dayle Blencowe/Katy Howell (WAL) 15-1,15-8

Svetoslav Stojanov/Diana Koleva (BUL) bt
Russell Hogg/Jennifer Allen (SCO) 7-15,15-11,15-11

Dave Wright/Sara Sankey (ENG) bt
Jerzy Dolhan/Bozena Haracz (POL) 15-8,15-2

Gordon and Jillian Haldane (SCO) bt
Ales Babnik/Mateja Slatner (SLO) 15-5,15-4

SECOND ROUND
Robertson/Bradbury bt
Imai/Matsuda 15-7,15-3

Peter Alexsson (SWE)/Gillian Gowers (ENG)* w/o
Enrique Parrales/Norma Hernadez (MEX)*

Bryan Blanchard/Denyse Julien (CAN) bt
Archer/Davies 17-15,15-13

Gatt/Travers bt
Shon Jin-Hwan/Gil Young Ah (KOR) 15-3,15-12

Nick Ponting/Gillian Clark (ENG)* bt
Thorsteinn P Haengsson/Birna Petersen (ISL) 15-1,15-10

Wright/Sankey w/o
Kerrin Harrison/Liao Yue Jin (NZL)

Pat-Gunnar Jonsson/Maria Bengtsson (SWE)* bt
David Gimour/Gillian Martin (SCO)* 15-10,15-2

Chris Hunt/Joanne Wright (ENG)* bt
Jyri Eriksson/Susanna Kauhanen (FIN) 15-3,15-2

Ron Michels/Erica van den Heuvel (HOL) bt
Haldane/Haldane 15-7,15-8

THIRD ROUND
Thomas Lund/Catrine Bengtsson bt
Robertson/Bradbury 15-4,15-4

Axelsson/Gowers bt
Blanshard/Julien 15-7,15-7

Michael Keck/Karen Stechmann bt
Gatt/Travers 15-10,15-10

Ponting/Clark bt
David Humble/Caroline Thorn (CAN) 15-3,15-4

Tim He/Amanda Hardy (AUS) bt
Wright/Sankey 15-7,15-12

Ha Tae-Kwon/Kim Shin Young bt
Hunt/Wright 18-13,6-15,15-12

FOURTH ROUND
Axelsson/Gowers bt
Keck/Stechmann 15-3,15-7

Ponting/Clark bt
Jan Paulsen/Lotte Olsen (DEN) 15-12,11-15,15-13

QUARTER-FINALS
Lund/Bengtsson bt
Axelsson/Gowers 15-6,15-6

Ponting/Clark bt
R Mainaky/E Sulitianingsih (INA) 18-17,12-15,15-11

Aryano Miranat/Elisa (INA) bt
Par Gunnar Jonsson/Maria Bengtsson 8-15,15-7,15-6

Chen Xingdong/Sun Man (CHN) bt
Jon Holst-Christensen/Grete Mogensen 15-10,15-6

SEMI-FINALS
Lund/Bengtsson bt
Ponting/Clark 18-17,12-15,15-11

Holst-Christensen/Mogensen bt
Miranat/Elisa 15-5,15-4

FINAL
Lund/Bengtsson bt
Holst-Christensen/Mogensen 10-15,15-6,15-12

Sudirman Cup

National teams play in nine groups arranged according to ranking. Each team plays every other in its group. The top two groups (1A & 1B) have three teams each and those teams compete for the top six places. The other group matches decide the future rankings with the top team in each group changing places with the bottom team in the group above.

GROUP MATCHES

Group 1A

Korea 4	China 1
China 5	Sweden 0
Korea 3	Sweden 2

	P	W	L	Pts
Korea	2	2	0	2
China	2	1	1	1
Sweden	2	0	2	0

Group 1B

Denmark 5	England 0
Indonesia 5	England 0
Indonesia 3	Denmark 0

	P	W	L	Pts
Indonesia	2	2	0	2
Denmark	2	1	1	1
England	2	0	2	0

Group 2
Japan 3 Malaysia 2
Holland 3 Japan 2
Thailand 3 Japan 2
Holland 4 Malaysia 1
Thailand 3 Malaysia 2
Thailand 3 Holland 2

	P	W	L	Pts
Thailand	3	3	0	3
Holland	3	2	1	2
Japan	3	1	2	1
Malaysia	3	0	3	0

Group 4
Germany 4 Hong Kong 1
Germany 3 India 2
Germany 3 N Zealand 2
Hong Kong 4 India 1
N Zealand 3 Hong Kong 2
N Zealand 3 India 2

	P	W	L	Pts
Germany	3	3	0	3
N Zealand	3	2	1	2
Hong Kong	3	1	2	1
India	3	0	3	0

Group 6
Czech Rep 4 Ireland 1
Czech Rep 5 Iceland 0
Czech Rep 3 USA 2
Iceland 3 Ireland 2
Iceland 4 USA 1
USA 3 Ireland 2

	P	W	L	Pts
Czech Rep	3	3	0	3
Iceland	3	2	1	2
USA	3	1	2	1
Ireland	3	0	3	0

Group 8
Ukraine 5 Belgium 0
Ukraine 4 Hungary 1
Ukraine 3 Kazakhstan 2
Ukraine 5 Pakistan 0
Kazakhstan 5 Belgium 0
Kazakhstan 5 Hungary 0
Kazakhstan 4 Pakistan 1
Hungary 3 Belgium 2
Hungary 4 Pakistan 1
Belgium 4 Pakistan 1

	P	W	L	Pts
Ukraine	4	4	0	4
Kazakhstan	4	3	1	3
Hungary	4	2	2	2
Belgium	4	1	3	1
Pakistan	4	0	4	0

Semi-finals
Korea 3 Denmark 1
Indonesia 3 China 2

Final
Korea 3 Indonesia 2

Group 3
Canada 3 Australia 2
Russia 4 Australia 1
Scotland 3 Australia 2
Russia 3 Canada 2
Canada 5 Scotland 0
Russia 5 Scotland 0

	P	W	L	Pts
Russia	3	3	0	3
Canada	3	2	1	2
Scotland	3	1	2	1
Australia	3	0	3	0

Group 5
Austria 4 Finland 1
Austria 3 Norway 2
Austria 3 Poland 2
Norway 3 Finland 2
Norway 4 Poland 1
Finland 3 Poland 2

	P	W	L	Pts
Austria	3	3	0	3
Norway	3	2	1	2
Finland	3	1	2	1
Poland	3	0	3	0

Group 7
Switzerland 4 Bulgaria 1
Switzerland 4 France 1
Switzerland 3 Wales 2
Bulgaria 3 France 2
Bulgaria 3 Wales 2
Wales 4 France 1

	P	W	L	Pts
Switzerland	3	3	0	3
Bulgaria	3	2	1	2
Wales	3	1	2	1
France	3	0	3	0

Group 9
Peru 5 Cyprus 0
Peru 3 Israel 2
Peru 5 Malta 0
Peru 5 Slovenia 0
Slovenia 5 Cyprus 0
Slovenia 3 Israel 2
Slovenia 4 Malta 1
Cyprus 3 Israel 2
Cyprus 3 Malta 2
Israel 3 Malta 2

	P	W	L	Pts
Peru	4	4	0	4
Slovenia	4	3	1	3
Cyprus	4	2	2	2
Israel	4	1	3	1
Malta	4	0	4	0

5th/6th Play-off
England 3 Sweden 2

World Junior Championships

Jakarta, Indonesia   Nov 8-14, 1992

MEN'S SINGLES
Semi-finals
J Sun (CHN) bt M Tedjakusuma (INA) 15-11 15-5
G Rimarodi (INA) bt S Hartono (INA) 17-15 17-18 15-6
Final
J Sun bt G Rimarodi 15-9 15-11

WOMEN'S SINGLES
Semi-finals
K Yunita (INA) bt M Audina (INA) 11-9 11-5
Yao (CHN) bt Fan (CHN) 11-6 12-9
Final
K Yunita bt Yao 12-11 11-1

MEN'S DOUBLES
Semi-finals
Namrih/Sigit (INA) bt Hwang/Kim (CHN) 8-15 18-17 15-2
Santoso/Kusno (INA) bt Liu/Yu (CHN) 15-3 12-15 15-11
Final
Santoso/Kusno bt Namrih/Sigit 15-11 12-15 15-12

WOMEN'S DOUBLES
Semi-finals
Gu/Han (CHN) bt Anastasia/Indarwati (INA) 15-7 15-3
Tang/Yuan (CHN) bt Audina/Issoliana (INA) 15-6 15-9
Final
Gu/Han bt Tang/Yuan 15-9 15-5

MIXED DOUBLES
Semi-finals
Laugeson/Olsen (DEN) bt Wijaya /Chusnul (INA) 15-13 17-15
Kim/Kim (KOR) bt Liang/Go (CHN) 18-14 15-5
Final
Laugeson/Olsen bt Kim/Kim 15-11 18-17

European Junior Championships

Sofia, Bulgaria   April 11-17

TEAM CHAMPIONSHIP
Final Standings
 1 Denmark
 2 Sweden
 3 Russia
 4 Holland
 5 England
 9 Wales
11 Scotland

INDIVIDUAL CHAMPIONSHIPS
MEN'S SINGLES
Semi-finals
Jim Laugesen (DEN) bt Daniel Eriksson (SWE) 15-3, 15-8
Rasmus Wengberg (SWE) bt Steve Isaac (ENG) 15-3, 15-3
Final
Jim Laugesen bt Rasmus Wengberg 15-9, 15-10

WOMEN'S SINGLES
Kelly Morgan of Wales was Britain's best player and was

eliminated in the quarter-finals.
Semi-finals
Marina Andriavskaja (RUS) bt Lone Sorensen (DEN) 2-11, 11-4, 11-5
Rjkke Olsen (DEN) bt Mette Sorensen (DEN) 11-0, 11-4
Final
Mette Sorensen bt Marina Andriavskaja

MEN'S DOUBLES
Semi-finals
Laugesen/Roos (DEN) bt Richard Doling/Roger Mistri (ENG) 15-8, 15-12
Sogaard/Stavnsgaard (DEN) bt Erikssen/Wengberg (SWE) 15-8, 10-15, 15-11
Final
Laugesen/Roos bt Sogaard/Stavnsgaard 15-8, 10-15, 15-11

WOMEN'S DOUBLES
Chaffin/Hardaker (ENG) and McEwan/Whiteford (SCO) were eliminated in the quarter-finals.
Semi-finals
Sorensen/Olsen (DEN) bt Grether/Beissel (GER) 15-3, 15-7
Runesten/Sorensen (DEN) bt Kurochkina/Karhushina (RUS) 15-6, 15-5
Final
Sorensen/Olsen bt Runesten/Sorensen 15-10, 15-5

MIXED DOUBLES
Semi-finals
Albinus/Monteiro (HOL) bt Carlsson/Tholinsson 18-15, 4-15, 17-16
Runesten/Stavnsgaard bt Hardaker/Boosey (ENG) 15-11, 15-6
Final
Runesten/Stavnsgaard bt Carlsson/Tholinsson 15-8, 15-8

Rothmans World Grand Prix Finals

Kuala Lumpur   Dec 16-20, 1992
MEN'S SINGLES
Semi-finals
Rashid Sidek (MAL) bt Thomas Stuer-Lauridsen (DEN) 15-12 15-8
Allan Budi Kusuma (INA) bt Joko Suprianto (INA) 15-6 15-7
Final
Rashid Sidek bt Allan Budi Kusuma 15-9 5-15 15-7

WOMEN'S SINGLES
Semi-finals
S Kusumawardhani (INA) bt Tang Jiuhong (CHN) 11-7 3-11 11-1
Susi Susanti (INA) bt Y Santoso (INA) 11-9 11-1
Final
Susi Susanti bt S Kumusawardhani 9-11 11-3 11-4

MEN'S DOUBLES
Final
Subagja/Mainaky (INA) bt Cheah/Soo (MAL) 15-11 15-6

WOMEN'S DOUBLES
Final

Lin/Yao (CHN) bt Clark/Gowers (GBR) 15-7 17-16

MIXED DOUBLES
Final
Lund/Dupont (DEN) bt Holst-Christensen/Mogensen (DEN) 15-5 15-2

World Cup

New Delhi   Sept 1-5
MEN'S SINGLES
Semi-finals
Joko Suprianto (INA) bt Rashid Sidek (INA) 15-9, 15-3
Allan Budi Kusuma (INA) bt Harmawen Susanto (INA) 15-11, 15-5
Final
Allan Budi Kusuma bt Joko Suprianto 15-8, 17-16

MEN'S DOUBLES
Semi-finals
Mainaky/Subagja (INA) bt Cheah Soon Kit/Soo Beng Kiang (MAL) 15-9, 15-11
Chen Hongyong/Chen Kang (CHN) bt Jonsson/Axelsson (SWE) 15-9, 15-5
Final
Mainaky/Subagja bt Chen Kang/Chen Hongyong 15-9, 12-15, 15-9

WOMEN'S SINGLES
Semi-finals
Susi Susanti (INA) bt Somharuthai Jaroensiri (THA) 11-0, 11-9
Lim Xiaoqing (SWE) bt Ye Zhaoying (CHN) 11-2, 2-11, 11-6
Final
Susi Susanti bt Lim Xiaoqing 11-7, 11-5

WOMEN'S DOUBLES
Semi-finals
Ching So Young/Gil Young Ah (KOR) bt Yao Fen/Lin Yanfen (CHN) 15-9, 15-10
Lim Xiaoqing/Christine Magnusson (SWE) bt Finarsih/Lili Tampi (INA) 15-10, 15-4
Final
Lim Xiaoqing/Christine Magnusson bt Ching So Young/Gil Young Ah 15-12, 15-7

MIXED DOUBLES
Semi-finals
Peter Axelsson/Gillian Gowers (SWE/GBR) bt Nick Ponting/Gill Clark (GBR) 15-12, 15-11
Aryono Miranat/Eliza (INA) bt Par-Gunnar Jonsson/Maria Bengtsson (SWE) 17-14, 7-15, 15-9
Final
Peter Axelsson/Gillian Gowers bt Aryono Miranat/Eliza 10-15, 15-7, 15-5

Open Events
Dutch Open

Den Bosch   Oct 1-4
Finals only
Men's Singles
Harmawen Susanto (INA) bt Jeroen van Dijk (HOL) 15-6 15-6

Women's Singles
S Kusumawardhani (INA) bt Lim Xiaoqing (SWE)
11-4 11-8
Men's Doubles
Yap/Tan (MAL) bt Michels/Bruil (HOL) 15-9 15-10
Women's Doubles
Bille/Rasmussen (DEN) bt Bradbury/Wright (ENG)
Mixed Doubles
Wright/Sankey (ENG) bt Jakobsen/Rasmussen
(DEN) 5-15 15-8 15-12

German Open

Leverkusen   Oct 8-11
Finals only
Men's Singles
Allan Budi Kusuma (INA) bt Joko Suprianto (INA)
15-11 15-2
Women's Singles
Susi Susanti (INA) bt S Kusumawardhani (INA) 11-7
10-12 11-8
Men's Doubles
Holst-Christense/Lund (DEN) bt
Gunawan/Suprianto (INA) 15-6 2-15 15-9
Women's Doubles
Magnussen/Lim (SWE) bt Bengtssen/Bengtssen
(SWE) 15-9 15-0
Mixed Doubles
Lund/Dupont (DEN) bt Jönsson/Bengtssen (SWE)
15-9 15-12

Danish Open

Aalborg   Oct 15-18
Finals only
Men's Singles
Darren Hall (ENG) bt Poul-Erik Hoyer-Larsen (DEN)
15-11 18-13
Women's Singles
Susi Susanti (INA) bt Lim Xiaoqing (SWE) 11-3 11-3
Men's Doubles
Holst-Christensen-Lund (DEN) bt Svarrer/Paulsen
(DEN) 18-16 15-8
Women's Doubles
Magnussen/Lim (SWE) bt Bengtsson/Bengtsson
(SWE) 15-7 15-3
Mixed Doubles
Lund/Dupont (DEN) bt Holst-Christensen/Bille
(DEN) 15-10 15-9

China Open

Shanghai   Oct 28-Nov 1
Finals only
Men's Singles
Harmawen Susanto (INA) bt Wenkai Wu (CHN)
18-13 15-9
Women's Singles
Yao Yan (CHN) bt Shen Lianfeng (CHN) 11-7 11-8
Men's Doubles
Subagja/Mainaky (INA) bt Sidek/Sidek (INA) 17-15
15-11
Women's Doubles

Lin/Yao (CHN) bt Pan/Wu(CHN) 17-14 15-4
Mixed Doubles
Miranat/Eliza (INA) bt Chen/Sun (CHN) 15-8 9-15
17-16

Hong Kong Open

Hong Kong Nov 2-8
Finals only
Men's Singles
Wenkai Wu (CHN) bt Heryanto Arbi (INA) 15-4
15-13
Women's Singles
Soo Hyun Bang (KOR) bt Susi susanti (INA) 5-11 11-6
11-7
Men's Doubles
Subagja/Mainaky (INA) bt Zheng/Huang (CHN) 15-
13 15-10
Women's Doubles
Nong/Zhou (CHN) bt Sulistianingsih/Tendean
(INA) 15-8 15-6
Mixed Doubles
Lee/Gil (KOR) bt Miranat/Eliza (INA) 15-4 15-11

Thailand Open

Bangkok   Nov 10-15
Finals only
Men's Singles
Joko Suprianto (INA) bt Allan Budi Kusuma (INA)
15-10 10-15 15-10
Women's Singles
Susi Susanti(INA) bt Soo Hyun Bang (KOR) 11-7 11-4
Men's Doubles
Subagja/Mainaky (INA) bt Zheng/Hunag (CHN)
15-9 12-15 15-11
Women's Doubles
Nong/Zhou (CHN) bt Sulistianingsih/Tendean
(INA) 15-4 12-15 15-8
Mixed Doubles
Miranat/Eliza (INA) bt Resiana/Kantono (INA) 15-2
2-15 15-1

Scottish Open

Glasgow   Nov 18-22
Finals only
Men's Singles
Pontus Jantti (FIN) bt Peter Esperen (DEN) 15-9 15-6
Women's Singles
Lim Xiaoqing (SWE) bt Christine Magnussen (SWE)
11-9 11-2
Men's Doubles
Axelsson/Jönsson (SWE) bt Holst-
Christensen/Jacobsen (DEN) 15-10 15-11
Women's Doubles
Lim/Magnussen (SWE) bt Bengtsson/Bengtsson 15-6
15-6
Mixed Doubles
Anonsson/Crabo (SWE) bt Holst-Christensen/Bille
(DEN) 15-11 11-15 15-10

Chinese-Taipei

Taipei   Jan 6-10
Finals only
Men's Singles
Haryanto Arbi (INA) bt Thomas Stuer-Lauridsen 15-18 15-6 15-5
Women's Singles
Lim Xiaoqing (SWE) bt Yuliani Santoso 11-6 9-12 11-5
Men's Doubles
Cheah/Soo (MAL) bt Setiadi/Hendra (INA) 15-3 15-12
Women's Doubles
Magnusson/Lim (SWE) bt Sasge/Matsuo (JPN) 18-15 18-13
Mixed Doubles
Kantono/Zelin (INA) walked over Ponting/Clark (GBR)

Japan Open

Tokyo   Jan 12-17
Finals only
Men's Singles
Heryanto Arbi (INA) bt Joko Suprianto (INA) 15-8 15-12
Women's Singles
Ye Zhaoying (CHN) bt Soo Hyun Bang (KOR) 11-6 11-5
Men's Doubles
Chen/Chen (CHN) bt Thongsari/Teerawiwatana (THA) 15-10 15-10
Women's Doubles
Chung/Gil (KOR) bt Finarsih/Tampi (INA) 15-12 15-5
Mixed Doubles
Lund/Bengtsson (DEN) bt Jakobsen/Thomsen (DEN)

Korean Open

Seoul   Jan 20-24
Finals only
Men's Singles
Joko Suprianto (INA) bt Thomas Stuer-Lauridsen 15-3 18-13
Women's Singles
Soo Hyun Bang (KOR) bt Susi Susanti (INA) 12-9 11-5
Men's Doubles
Zheng/Huang (CHN) bt Holst-Christensen/Lund (DEN) 5-15 15-10 15-4
Women's Doubles
Chung/Gil (KOR) bt Yao/Lin 15-8 15-5
Mixed Doubles
Lund/Bengtssen (DEN) bt Holst-Christensen/Bille 15-9 12-15 15-4

Swiss Open

Basel   Feb 10-14
Finals only
Men's Singles

Fung Permadi (INA) bt Peter Knowles (GBR) 15-11 15-9
Women's Singles
Yuliana Santoso (INA) bt Li Xiaoqing (SWE) 11-6 11-7
Men's Doubles
Axelsson/Jönsson (SWE) bt Osterberg/Gandrup 15-4 15-4
Women's Doubles
Clark/Wright (GBR) bt Andrievskaja/Jakusheva (RUS) 15-8 15-7
Mixed doubles
Jönsson/Bengtsson (SWE) bt Antonsson/Crabo (SWE) 11-15 17-14 15-7

Swedish Open

Taby   Mar 10-14
Finals only
Men's Singles
Thomas Stuer-Lauridsen (DEN) bt Poul-Erik Hoyer-Larsen (DEN) 15-7 14-17 15-13
Women's Singles
Soo Hyun Bang bt Heung Soon Lee (KOR) 11-2 11-6
Men's Doubles
Subagja/Mainaky (INA) bt Axelsson/Jönsson (SWE) 15-12 15-10
Women's Doubles
Chung/Gil (CHN) bt Magnussen/Lim (SWE) 15-9 15-11
Mixed doubles
Lund/Bengtsson (SWE) bt Axelsson/Gowers (SWE/ENG) 15-4 15-10

Yonex All-England Open Championships

Wembley   Mar 17-20
Finals only
Men's Singles
Heryanto Arbi (INA) bt Joko Suprianto (INA) 15-7, 4-15, 15-11

Women's Singles
Susi Susanti (INA) bt Bang Soo-Hyun (KOR) 4-11, 11-4, 11-1

Men's Doubles
Jon Holst-Christensen/Thomas Lund (DEN) bt Chen Hongyong/Chen Kang (CHN) 10-15, 15-4, 15-7

Women's Singles
Chung So Young/Gil Young Ak (KOR) bt Lin Yanfen/Yao Fen (CHN) 5-15, 15-4, 15-7

Mixed Doubles
Jon Holst-Christensen/Grete Mogensen (DEN) bt Thomas Lund (DEN)/Catrine Bengtsson (SWE) 8-1 retd

French Open

Paris   Mar 24-28
Finals only
Men's Singles

G Hendrawan (INA) bt Anders Nielsen (ENG) 15-10
14-18 15-11
Women's Singles
Yao Yan (CHN) bt Ye Zhaoying (CHN) 11-7 5-11 11-5
Men's Doubles
Kantono/Antonius (INA) bt
Haditono/Purwotsugiono (INA) 15-11 18-16
Women's Doubles
Lin/Yao (CHN) bt Nong/Zhou (CHN) 15-10 17-15
Mixed doubles
Miranat/Eliza (INA) bt Gunawan/Tendean (INA)
15-7 15-12

Canadian Open

Calgary   Sept 17-19
Finals only
Men's Singles
Thomas Steur-Lauridsen bt P Espersen (DEN) 15-12, 15-9
Men's Doubles
Lund/Holst-Christensen (DEN) bt Cheng Dand/Chen
Kang (CHN) 15-7, 7-15, 15-5
Women's Singles
C Martin (DEN) bt P Nedergaard (DEN) 11-5, 11-5
Women's Doubles
Lim Xioaqing/Christine Magnusson (SWE) bt L Olsen/ L
Stuer-Lauridsen (DEN) 15-11, 15-5
Mixed Doubles
T Lund/C Benson (DEN/SWE) bt C Jacobsen/L Olsen
(DEN) 15-2, 15-9

US Open

Los Angeles   Sept 20-26
Finals only
Men's Singles
M Mainaky (INA) bt F Permadi (INA) 15-8, 15-8
Women's Singles
Lim Xiaoqing (SWE) bt C Magnusson (SWE) 11-5, 11-0
Men's Doubles
Lund/Holst-Christensen (DEN) bt Kartono/Antonius
(INA) 15-7, 15-7
Women's Doubles
Gil Young Ah/Chung So Young (KOR) bt Lim
Xiaoqing/Magnussen (SWE) 15-5, 15-4

Bulgarian Vintners English National Championships

Norwich   Feb 5-7

MEN'S SINGLES
Semi-finals
Darren Hall (Essex) bt Peter Smith (Surrey) 15-10, 15-5
Anders Nielsen (Surrey) bt Peter Knowles (Kent) 5-15,
15-13, 15-11
Final
Darren Hall bt Anders Nielsen 15-6, 10-15, 8-2 retd

WOMEN'S SINGLES
Semi-finals
Suzanne Louis Lane (Devon) bt Julia Mann (Worcs) 11-6,
11-2

Fiona Smith (Surrey) bt Tracy Dineen (Essex) 11-2, 11-4
Final
Suzanne Louis Lane bt Fiona Smith 11-4, 11-1

MEN'S DOUBLES
Semi-finals
Simon Archer/Nick Ponting (Worcs/Herts) bt James
Anderson/Ian Pearson (Essex) 15-5, 15-5
Julian Robertson/Dave Wright (Notts/Yorks) bt Andrew
Fairhurst/Chris Hunt (Lancs) 11-15, 15-12, 15-7
Final
Robertson/Wright bt Archer/Ponting 15-7, 15-6

WOMEN'S DOUBLES
Semi-finals
Gill Clark/Gillian Gowers (Surrey/Herts) bt Joanne
Davies/Tanya Groves (Lincs/Sussex) 15-7, 15-6
Julie Bradbury/Sara Sankey (Oxon/Lancs) bt Karen
Chapman/Joanne Wright (Sussex) 15-2, 15-9
Final
Clark/Gowers bt Bradbury/Snakey 15-4, 17-14

MIXED DOUBLES
Semi-finals
Nick Ponting/Gill Clark (Herts/Surrey) bt Simon
Archer/Joanne Davies (Worcs/Lincs) 15-8, 15-10
Chris Hunt/Joanne Wright (Lancs/Sussex) bt Dave
Wright/Sara Sankey (Yorks/Lancs) 15-1, 15-10
Final
Ponting/Clark bt Hunt Wright 15-11, 15-7

Baseball

World Series 1992
American League
Championship Series

OAKLAND ATHLETICS v TORONTO BLUE JAYS

Game 1
SkyDome,
Toronto   Oct 7
Toronto 3   Oakland 4
51,039

Game 2
SkyDome,
Toronto   Oct 8
Toronto 3   Oakland 1
51,114

Game 3
Oakland-Alameda
County Coliseum   Oct 10
Oakland 5   Toronto 7
46,911

Game 4
Oakland-Alameda
County Coliseum   Oct 11
Oakland 6   Toronto 7
47,732

Game 5
Oakland-Alameda
County Coliseum   Oct 12
Oakland 6   Toronto 2
44,955

Game 6
SkyDome,
Toronto   Oct 14
Toronto 9   Oakland 2
51,335

TORONTO BLUE JAYS WIN 4-2

National League
Championship Series

ATLANTA BRAVES v PITTSBURGH PIRATES

Game 1
Atlanta-Fulton
County Stadium   Oct 6
Atlanta 5   Pittsburgh 1
51,971

Game 2
Atlanta-Fulton
County Stadium   Oct 7
Atlanta 13   Pittsburgh 5
51,975

Game 3

Three Rivers Stadium
Pittsburgh   Oct 9
Pittsburgh 3   Atlanta 2
56,610

Game 4
Three Rivers Stadium
Pittsburgh   Oct 10
Pittsburgh 4   Atlanta 6
57,164

Game 5
Three Rivers Stadium
Pittsburgh   Oct 11
Pittsburgh 7   Atlanta 1
52,929

Game 6
Atlanta-Fulton
County Stadium   Oct 13
Atlanta 4   Pittsburgh 13
51,975

Game 7
Atlanta-Fulton
County Stadium   Oct 14
Atlanta 3   Pittsburgh 2
51,975

ATLANTA BRAVES WIN 4-3

World Series

ATLANTA BRAVES v TORONTO BLUE JAYS

Game 1
Atlanta-Fulton
County Stadium   Oct 17
Atlanta 3   Toronto 1
51,763

Game 2
Atlanta-Fulton
County Stadium   Oct 18
Atlanta 4   Toronto 5
51,763

Game 3
SkyDome,
Toronto   Oct 20
Toronto 3   Atlanta 2
51,813

Game 4
SkyDome,
Toronto   Oct 21
Toronto 2   Atlanta 1
52,090

Game 5
SkyDome,
Toronto   Oct 22
Toronto 2   Atlanta 7
52,268

Game 6
Atlanta-Fulton
County Stadium   Oct 24
Atlanta 3   Toronto 4
51,763

TORONTO BLUE JAYS WIN 4-2

This was heresy, the first time that a Canadian team had won the World Series. The Americans were so perplexed they even flew the Canadian flag upside down. It didn't matter that most of the Blue Jays team was American, this was still a revolution. It was Dave Winfield's double in the 11th inning that proved to be the winning hit. Winfield, 41, had played baseball for 20 years, serving 15 managers and based in 31 different stadia, but never before been on a World Series winning team. The Blue Jays also looked like never getting there. In 1985, they collapsed in the play-off when leading Kansas 3-1. In 1987, they lost six in a row to lose out in the Division race. In 1989 & 1991, they had the best players, but failed to deliver.

Final League Standings 1993

AMERICAN LEAGUE

East Division

		W	L	Pct	GB
1	Toronto	95	67	.586	-
2	New York	88	74	.543	7
3	Baltimore	85	77	.525	10
4	Detroit	85	77	.525	10
5	Boston	80	82	.494	15
6	Cleveland	76	86	.469	19
7	Milwaukee	69	93	.426	26

West Division

		W	L	Pct	GB
1	Chicago	94	68	.580	-
2	Texas	86	76	.531	8
3	Kansas City	84	78	.519	10
4	Seattle	82	80	.506	12
5	California	71	91	.438	23
6	Minnesota	71	91	.438	23
7	Oakland	68	94	.420	26

NATIONAL LEAGUE

East Division

		W	L	Pct	GB
1	Philadelphia	97	65	.599	-
2	Montreal	94	68	.580	3
3	St Louis	87	75	.537	10
4	Chicago	84	78	.519	13
5	Pittsburgh	75	87	.463	22
6	Florida	64	98	.395	33
7	New York	59	103	.364	38

West Division

		W	L	Pct	GB
1	Atlanta	104	58	.642	-
2	San Francisco	103	59	.636	1
3	Houston	85	77	.525	19
4	Los Angeles	81	81	.500	23
5	Cincinnati	73	89	.451	31
6	Colorado	67	95	.414	37
7	San Diego	61	101	.377	43

QUOTES

"It was a stupid, dumb, foolish, childlike act….." Vince Coleman's lawyer leaving everyone in no doubt what he thought of his client after the New York Mets outfielder had thrown an explosive device into a group of fans. The device estimated to be the equivalent of quarter of a stick of dynamite (yup, dynamite) injured three people, two were kids.

"If the reporters can't take it, forget them. There are always a ton of reporters in here when something bad happens. I don't like a lot of them" Coleman's teammate Bret Saberhagen justifying throwing a firecracker under a table of journalists. Saberhagen, who proved that Coleman doesn't have a patent on stupidity, later admitted spraying reporters with bleach. OK lads, so you had a bad season……..

"We are forced to acknowledge that Canada exists….baseball, Canada and apple pie. Blasphemy" Chicago journalist Jay Marriotti after Toronto Blue Jays reached the World Series in 1992

"When we lose, I can't sleep. When we win, I can't sleep. But when we win, I wake up feeling better" Joe Torre, manager of the St Louis Cardinals

Basketball

England almost hit the big time this year, but according to coach Kevin Cadle just didn't want it enough. A victory against Russia in the qualifying rounds for the European championship in November, 1992 was the highpoint. They looked set fair for Germany until Bulgaria beat them a few days later by just too many points. A lifeline was thrown in June, when a second qualifying competition in Wroclaw, Poland to accommodate all the new nations of Europe, incorporated those countries that had missed earlier qualifying by a single place. It gave England a second chance and Cadle still felt optimistic even with a weakened team. They didn't come close and coach Cadle, recognising a no-win situation when he saw it, took the early train out. "Injuries were a big part of the reason," said Cadle. but his parting shot was more succinct. "It's just that you can't get the players and the administration to come together for England's benefit."

Within three weeks of Cadle's resignation, England's future was even more on the line. The 1995 European Championship qualifying was held in Zalaegerszeg, Hungary and England, following a two point defeat by Finland achieved the dubious distinction of being eliminated from two European championships in four weeks.

Basketball, a distant poor cousin in the UK (although a European championships place might have added a little impetus to the game here) is head of the family in America. Amongst schoolkids, nobody argues about its status. It's the most popular game, easy.

Michael Jordan, the biggest name in the sport, continues the roll of success, driving the Chicago Bulls to their third successive success (isn't that a mouthful) in the NBA. Jordan, whose earnings reputedly amount to around $40 million each and every year, found that, as far as advantages of fame go, the bitter far outweighed the sweet this year when his father, James, was killed.

Jordan, as the famous are wont to, had taken the usual amount of trivial rubbish thrown in his direction when the *New York Times*, and others, cited Jordan's enjoyment of gambling and added fuel to the story that he was a gambling addict. It may be true, but the evidence on offer was that Jordan lost $5,000 one night while gambling in Atlantic City. Given that Jordan earns 22 times that amount **every** day, it's a bit like you or I being pilloried for having a couple of pints on a Friday night (well, I don't know how much you earn, but it's about right for me). Anyway, whatever, Jordan announced his retirement in October.

Jordan, though, couldn't compare with the women of the Santa Rosa basketball club when it comes to big-hit gambling. While Jordan was frittering away $5,000, the slam-dunkers of Santa Rosa in Spain won £17 million in the national Christmas lottery. Apparently (and I don't believe this bit), they could have doubled the prize, but they returned half of their lottery tickets because players and supporters wouldn't buy them.

Still on money, Larry Bird, once of Boston Celtics, may have retired, but is still being paid $30 for each signature on basketballs, photos, jerseys......now, how long does it take to write your name?

European Championships

SELECTED QUALIFYING MATCHES
Group C
Moscow   Nov 13, 1991
CIS (Russia) 77   England 74
Sheffield   Nov 15, 1991
England 84   Denmark 65
Leicester   Nov 20, 1991
England 62   Bulgaria 63
Manchester   Nov 11,1992
England 75   Russia 71
Aarhus   Nov 14, 1992
England 80   Denmark 63
Jambol, Bul   Nov 18
Bulgaria 94   England 69
England finished level on points (8) with Russia and Bulgaria, but lost out on scores difference. Due to the new nations coming into being, a further qualifying competition was held and the third place teams in the original qualifying groups were invited.
Additional Qualifying Competition
Wroclaw, Poland   May/June 1993
England 76   Ukraine 82
England 81   Bosnia-Herzegovina 112
England 91   Slovakia 100
England did not qualify

Finals

Karlsruhe, Berlin & Munich   June 23-July 4

Group A
Russia 99   Bosnia-Herzegovina 77
Sweden 49   Spain 72
Spain 96   Bosnia 89
Sweden 100   Russia 92
Bosnia 89   Sweden 69

Prelim Table	P	W	L	For	Ag	Pts	Av
1 Spain	3	3	0	254	213	6	
2 Russia	3	1	2	266	263	4	(1.12)
3 Bosnia	3	1	2	255	264	4	(0.99)
4 Sweden	3	1	2	218	253	4	(0.93)

Group B
France 69   Turkey 55
Bulgaria 83   Croatia 104
Turkey 78   Bulgaria 70
France 95   Croatia 100
Croatia 113   Turkey 63
France 91   Bulgaria 74

Prelim Table	P	W	L	For	Ag	Pts
1 Croatia	3	3	0	317	241	6
2 France	3	2	1	255	299	5
3 Turkey	3	1	2	196	252	4
4 Bulgaria	3	0	3	227	273	3

Group C
Israel 83   Italy 92
Greece 81   Latvia 62

Italy 79   Latvia 80
Israel 79   Greece 79
Italy 73   Greece 88
Latvia 101   Israel 84

Prelim Table	P	W	L	For	Ag	Pts
1 Greece	3	2	1	243	214	5
2 Latvia	3	2	1	243	243	5
3 Italy	3	1	2	244	251	4
4 Israel	3	1	2	245	267	4

Group D
Germany 103   Estonia 113
Slovenia 61   Belgium 82
Belgium 64   Germany 93
Estonia 63   Slovenia 80
Germany 79   Slovenia 57
Istonia 79   Belgium 78

Prelim Table	P	W	L	For	Ag	Pts
1 Estonia	3	2	1	255	261	5
2 Germany	3	2	1	275	234	5
3 Belgium	3	1	2	224	233	4
1 Slovenia	3	1	2	198	224	4

Group E
Italy 60   Spain 78
Latvia 72   Russia 91
Greece 102   Bosnia 84
Spain 94   Latvia 87
Bosnia 72   Italy 74
Greece 67   Russia 84
Spain 75   Greece 76
Russia 95   Italy 69
Bosnia 102   Latvia 97

Prelim Table	P	W	L	For	Ag	Pts	Av
1 Spain	5	4	1	430	387	9	(1.07)
2 Russia	5	4	1	444	371	9	(0.98)
3 Greece	5	4	1	414	378	9	(0.90)
4 Bosnia	5	1	4	424	468	6	(1.02)
5 Italy	5	1	4	398	448	6	(1.01)
6 Latvia	5	1	4	398	448	6	(0.98)

Group F
France 64   Germany 56
Estonia 77   Turkey 74
Croatia 106   Belgium 74
Estonia 62   France 73
Croatia 70   Germany 63
Turkey 69   Belgium 59
Estonia 80   Croatia 98
Turkey 64   Germany 77
France 83   Belgium 65

Prelim Table	P	W	L	For	Ag	Pts
1 Croatia	5	5	0	487	375	10
2 France	5	4	1	384	338	9
3 Estonia	5	3	2	411	426	8
4 Germany	5	2	3	392	375	6
5 Turkey	5	1	4	325	395	6
6 Belgium	5	0	5	340	398	5

Quarter-finals
Greece 61   France 59
Russia 82   Estonia 61

| Germany 79 | Spain 77 |
| Croatia 98 | Bosnia 78 |

Play offs 5-8th places

Estonia 99	Bosnia 91
Spain 95	France 83
Spain 119	Estonia 80
France 83	Bosnia 75

Semi-finals

| Russia 84 | Croatia 76 |
| Germany 76 | Greece 73 |

Play off for 3rd place

| Croatia 99 | Greece 59 |

Finals

| Germany 71 | Russia 70 |

Final Placings

1 Germany	5 Spain
2 Russia	6 Estonia
3 Croatia	7 France
4 Greece	8 Bosnia

1995 European Championships

QUALIFYING ROUNDS

June: Group A in Vienna, Group B in Zalaegerszeg, Hungary & Group C in Prievidza, Slovakia

Group A

Ukraine 80	Lithuania 75
Austria 91	Scotland 68
Holland 85	Lithuania 93
Ukraine 104	Scotland 64
Holland 113	Scotland 69
Austria 73	Iceland 95
Lithuania 117	Scotland 69
Iceland 70	Ukraine 99
Iceland 78	Holland 87
Austria 71	Ukraine 100
Austria 72	Holland 93
Lithuania 106	Iceland 100
Austria 94	Lithuania 116
Scotland 78	Iceland 81
Ukraine 92	Holland 66

Prelim Table	P	W	L	For	Ag	Pts
1 Ukraine	5	5	0	472	346	10
2 Lithuania	5	4	1	507	428	9
3 Holland	5	3	2	444	404	8
4 Iceland	5	2	3	424	443	7
5 Austria	5	1	4	401	472	6
6 Scotland	5	0	5	348	503	5

Group B

Albania 77	England 96
Romania 84	Finland 92
Hungary 100	Luxembourg 51
England 67	Romania 70
Finland 81	Belarus 78
Hungary 110	Albania 53
England 96	Belarus 80
Hungary 88	Finland 82
Romania 108	Luxembourg 93
England 66	Hungary 64

Albania 87	Romania 104
Belarus 90	Luxembourg 65
Finland 89	Albania 81
England 97	Luxembourg 76
Romania 106	Belarus 75
Luxemb'rg 81	Finland 116
Albania 72	Belarus 99
Hungary 67	Romania 65
England 67	Finland 69
Albania 93	Luxembourg 80
Hungary 95	Belarus 82

Prelim Table	P	W	L	For	Ag	Pts
1 Hungary	6	5	1	524	399	11
2 Finland	6	5	1	529	479	11
3 Romania	6	4	2	537	491	10
4 England	6	4	2	489	436	10
5 Belarus	6	2	4	504	515	8
6 Albania	6	1	5	463	578	7
7 Luxemb'rg	6	0	6	446	604	6

Group C

Poland 86	Portugal 65
Czech Rep 135	Cyprus 60
Switzerland 60	Slovakia 95
Cyprus 63	Poland 123
Switzerland 71	Portugal 94
Slovakia 80	Czech Rep 74
Poland 90	Switzerland 54
Cyprus 64	Slovakia 78
Portugal 74	Czech Rep 91
Portugal 117	Cyprus 77
Czech Rep 85	Switzerland 68
Slovakia 74	Poland 70
Switzerland 78	Cyprus 73
Poland 78	Czech Rep 80
Slovakia 102	Portugal 71

Prelim Table	P	W	L	For	Ag	Pts
1 Slovakia	5	5	0	429	339	10
2 Czech Rep	5	4	1	465	360	9
3 Poland	5	3	2	447	336	8
4 Portugal	5	2	3	421	427	7
5 Switzerl'd	5	1	4	331	437	6
6 Cyprus	5	0	5	337	531	5

Footnote: If the tables confuse you, that's either because we've put a wrong score in, or you didn't realise that Basketball scores 2 pts for a win and 1 for a defeat

---

BIG SHOT

Don Calhoun, an office supplies salesman, chosen randomly from the crowd at a Chicago Bulls game, won a million dollars for one throw when he made a basket from 76 feet. The money was put up by a local restaurant as a regular promotion at the games. I mean, how big was this restaurant?

Carlsberg League

MEN
Division One

1	Worthing Bears	33	31	2	3070	2518	62
2	Thames Valley Tigers	33	28	5	3028	2409	56
3	London Towers	33	25	8	2899	2705	50
4	Guildford Kings	33	25	8	3251	2727	50
5	Birmingham Bullets	33	17	16	2989	2939	34
6	Derby Bucks	33	14	19	2867	2961	28
7	Oldham Celtics	33	14	19	2817	2933	28
8	Leicester Riders	33	12	21	2714	2872	24
9	Manchester Giants	33	12	21	2782	2822	24
10	Cheshire Jets	33	10	23	2548	2935	20
11	Sunderland Saints	33	6	27	2506	2911	12
12	Hemel Royals	33	4	29	2593	3332	8

Division Two

1	Doncaster Panthers	22	20	2	2036	1548	40
2	M'brough Mohawks	22	17	5	1950	1919	34
3	Crystal Palace	22	16	6	1920	1795	32
4	Ware Rebels	22	14	8	1844	1764	28
5	Cardiff Heat	22	13	9	1811	1596	26
6	Coventry Crusaders	22	11	11	1696	1623	22
7	Brixton Topcats	22	11	11	1843	1830	22
8	Bury Lobos	22	10	12	1836	1820	20
9	Plymouth Raiders	22	9	13	1945	1989	18
10	Solent Stars	22	5	17	1653	1873	10
11	Barnsley Generals	22	3	19	1476	1820	6
12	Lewisham Lightning	22	3	19	1650	2083	6

Division Three

1	Sheffield Forgers	20	15	5	1489	1278	30
2	Sedgefield Racers	20	14	6	1538	1428	28
3	Liverpool ATAC	20	13	7	1454	1342	26
4	Guildford Storm	20	13	7	1613	1528	26
5	Swindon Sonics	20	13	7	1530	1392	26
6	S. London Elephants	20	12	8	1418	1431	24
7	Leicester Falcons	20	11	9	1407	1332	22
8	Stevenage Phoenix	20	8	12	1356	1420	16
9	Chiltern Fastbreak	20	6	14	1284	1416	12
10	Camberley Eagles	20	3	17	1416	1662	6
11	Mid Sussex Magic	20	2	18	1137	1413	4

NatWest Trophy
(for Division one men's clubs)
Group Games
South 1

Thames Valley	111	London	104
Birmingham	90	Thames Valley	110
London	94	Birmingham	98

South 2

Hemel Hempstead	61	Guildford	141
Guildford	113	Worthing	106
Worthing	117	Hemel Hempstead	96

North 1

Oldham	80	Derby	95
Sunderland	94	Oldham	79
Derby	92	Sunderland	80

North 2

Manchester	121	Cheshire	70
Leicester	93	Manchester	92
Cheshire	89	Leicester	109

Semi-finals

Leicester	112	Thames Valley	106
Thames Valley	114	Leicester	98
Derby	92	Guildford	114
Guildford	85	Derby	84

Final

Guildford	84	Thames Valley	91

Men's National Trophy

Doncaster
(for all men's clubs except those in Division One)
Final

Guildford	84	Thames Valley	91

League Cup

Birmingham
(for Division One Men's Clubs)
Final

Thames Valley	91	Guildford	84

Founders Cup
(for all men's clubs except those in membership of Nat. Two and Three
Final

Warley	176	Oxford	136

European Women's Championship

Perugia, Italy   June 8-13

Group A

Poland 68	Spain 92
Bulgaria 69	Italy 79
Spain 76	Bulgaria 70
Italy 67	Poland 64
Poland 73	Bulgaria 81
Italy 66	Spain 56

Group B

Russia 53	France 71
Hungary 82	Slovak Rep. 88
Slovak Rep. 75	Russia 80
France 77	Hungary 64
Russia 76	Hungary 89
Slovak Rep. 70	France 51

Semi-finals

Bulgaria 76	Russia 74
Poland 95	Hungary 64
Italy 54	France 56
Spain 73	Slovak Rep. 55

Play-offs

Russia 103	Hungary 83
Bulgaria 72	Poland 77
Italy 67	Slovak Rep. 68

Final

Spain 63	France 53

Final Placings

1 Spain
2 France
3 Slovak Republic
4 Italy
5 Poland
6 Bulgaria
7 Russia
8 Hungary

World Women's Junior Championships

Seoul   Aug 8
Final
Australia 72 Russia 54
3rd/4th Play-off
Poland 74 Korea 53

Carlsberg League Women

Division One

1	Sheffield Hatters	22	21	1	1480	1104	42
2	Northampton 76'ers	22	19	3	1493	1184	38
3	Thames Valley Ladies	22	15	7	1450	1159	30
4	Nottingham Wildcats	22	14	8	1312	1169	28
5	Ipswich	22	14	8	1334	1221	28
6	Rhondda	22	11	11	1381	1352	22
7	Cheshire Cats	22	9	13	1262	1390	18
8	Milton Keynes Q. Cats	22	9	13	1262	1390	18
9	London Centr. YMCA	22	7	15	1271	1600	14
10	London Jets	22	5	17	1227	1422	10
11	Chesham Ladies	22	5	17	1260	1477	10
12	Leicester Ladies	22	3	19	1044	1567	6

Division Two

1	Brixton Lady Topcats	14	13	1	886	634	26
2	South Tyneside	14	10	4	917	760	20
3	Sunderland Strollers	14	10	4	778	684	20
4	Doncaster Free Press	14	9	5	878	696	18
5	Cardiff Flyers	14	6	8	695	782	12
6	Stonebridge Amazons	14	5	9	778	843	10
7	Camberley G. Eagles	14	2	12	687	925	4
8	Houghton R. Raiders	14	1	13	709	1004	2

Women's National Trophy

Doncaster
(for all women's clubs except those in Division One)
Final

Doncaster	66	Sunderland	53

NBA
(Final Standings 1992-3)

ATLANTIC DIVISION

	W	L	%	GB
New York	60	22	.732	-
Boston	48	34	.585	12
New Jersey	43	39	.524	17
Orlando	41	41	.500	19
Miami	36	46	.439	24
Philadelphia	26	56	.317	34
Washington	22	60	.268	38

CENTRAL DIVISION

Chicago	57	25	.695	-
Cleveland	54	28	.659	3
Charlotte	44	38	.537	13
Atlanta	43	39	.524	14
Indiana	41	41	.500	16
Detroit	40	42	.488	17
Milwaukee	28	54	.341	29

MIDWEST DIVISION

Houston	55	27	.671	-
San Antonio	49	33	.598	6
Utah	47	35	.573	8
Denver	36	46	.439	19
Minnesota	19	63	.232	36
Dallas	11	71	.134	44

PACIFIC DIVISION

Phoenix	62	20	.756	-
Seattle	55	27	.671	7
Portland	51	31	.622	11
LA Clippers	41	41	.500	21
LA Lakers	39	43	.476	23
Golden State	34	48	.415	28
Sacramento	25	57	.305	37

Scoring Average

Jordan (Chi)	78	992	476	2541	32.6
Wilkins (Atl)	71	741	519	2121	29.9
K Malone (Utah)	82	797	619	2217	27.0
Olajuwon (Hou)	82	848	444	2140	26.1
Barkley (Pho)	76	716	445	1944	25.6
Ewing (NY)	81	779	400	1959	24.2
Dumars (Det)	77	677	343	1809	23.5
O'Neal (Orl)	81	733	427	1893	23.4
Robinson (SA)	82	676	561	1916	23.4
Manning (LAC)	79	702	388	1800	22.8
Petrovic (NJ)	70	587	315	1564	22.3
Johnson (Cha)	82	728	336	1810	22.1

Stats Leaders

Best Overall record	Phoenix 62-20	.756
Top Offensive	Phoenix	113.4
Top Defensive	New York	95.4
Individual Scoring	Michael Jordan (Chi)	32.6
Indiv Rebounding	Dennis Rodman (Det)	18.3
Assists	John Stockman (Ut)	12.0
Steals	Michael Jordan	2.83
Blocks	Hakeem Olajuwon (Ho)	4.17
Field Goal %	Cedric Ceballos (Ph)	.576
Free Throw %	Mark Price (Cle)	.948
3pt Field Goal %	B J Armstrong (Chi)	.453

NBA play-offs

EASTERN CONFERENCE

New York Knicks v Indiana Pacers
NY 107 Indiana 104
NY 101 Indiana 91
Indiana 116 NY 93
Indiana 100 NY 109
NY win series 3-1

Chicago Bulls v Atlanta Hawks
Chicago 114 Atlanta 90
Chicago 117 Atlanta 102
Atlanta 88 Chicago 98
Chicago win series 3-0

Cleveland Cavaliers v New Jersey Nets
Cleveland 114 New Jersey 98
Cleveland 99 New Jersey 101
New Jersey 84 Cleveland 93
New Jersey 96 Cleveland 79
Cleveland 99 New Jersey 89
Cleveland win series 3-2

Boston Celtics v Charlotte Hornets
Boston 112 Charlotte 101
Boston 98 Charlotte 99
Charlotte 119 Boston 89
Charlotte 104 Boston 103
Charlotte win series 3-1

WESTERN CONFERENCE

Phoenix Suns v LA Lakers
Phoenix 103 LAL 107
Phoenix 81 LAL 86
LAL 102 Phoenix 107
LAL 86 Phoenix 101
Phoenix 112 LAL 104
Phoenix win series 3-2

Houston Rockets v LA Clippers
Houston 117 LAC 94
Houston 83 LAC 95
LAC 99 Houston 111
LAC 93 Houston 90
Houston 84 LAC 80
Houston win series 3-2

Seattle Supersonics v Utah Jazz
Seattle 99 Utah 85
Seattle 85 Utah 89
Utah 90 Seattle 80
Utah 80 Seattle 93
Seattle 100 Utah 92
Seattle win series 3-2

Portland Trail Blazers v San Antonio Spurs
Portland 86 San Antonio 87
Portland 105 San Antonio 96
San Antonio 107 Portland 101
San Antonio 100 Portland 97
San Antonio win series 3-1

THE NUMBERS GAME

A record number of 17,778,295 spectators paid to see the NBA Leagues in 1992/3 season. An average of 16,060 a game at 91.5% capacity......

EASTERN CONFERENCE
SEMI-FINALS
New York Knicks v Charlotte Hornets
New York 111 Charlotte 95
New York 105 Charlotte 101
Charlotte 110 New York 106
Charlotte 92 New York 94
New York 105 Charlotte 101
NY win series 4-1
Chicago Bulls v Cleveland Cavaliers
Chicago 91 Cleveland 84
Chicago 104 Cleveland 85
Cleveland 90 Chicago 96
Cleveland 101 Chicago 103
Chicago win series 4-0

WESTERN CONFERENCE
SEMI-FINALS
Phoenix Suns v San Antonio Spurs
Phoenix 98 San Antonio 89
Phoenix 109 San Antonio 103
San Antonio 111 Phoenix 96
San Antonio 117 Phoenix 103
Phoenix 109 San Antonio 97
San Antonio 100 Phoenix 102
Phoenix win series 4-2
Seattle Supersonics v Houston Rockets
Seattle 99 Houston 90
Seattle 111 Houston 100
Houston 97 Settle 79
Houston 103 Seattle 92
Seattle 120 Houston 95
Houston 103 Seattle 90
Seattle 103 Houston 100
Seattle win series 4-3

EASTERN CONFERENCE
FINAL
New York Knicks v Chicago Bulls
New York 98 Chicago 90
New York 96 Chicago 91
Chicago 103 New York 83
Chicago 105 New York 95
New York 94 Chicago 97
Chicago 96 New York 88
Chicago win series 4-2

WESTERN CONFERENCE
FINAL
Seattle Supersonics v Phoenix Suns
Phoenix 105 Seattle 91
Phoenix 99 Seattle 103
Seattle 97 Phoenix 104
Seattle 120 Phoenix 101
Phoenix 120 Seattle 114
Seattle 118 Phoenix 102
Phoenix 123 Seattle 110
Phoenix win series 4-3

NBA Finals
Chicago Bulls v Phoenix Suns
June 9
Phoenix 92 Chicago 100
June 11
Phoenix 108 Chicago 111

June 13
Chicago 121 Phoenix 129
June 16
Chicago 111 Phoenix 105
June 18
Chicago 98 Phoenix 108
June 20
Phoenix 98 Chicago 99
Chicago win series 4-2

QUOTES
"I kind of put my foot in my mouth when I said that repeating would be easy. It was a lot harder than anything I've done in basketball"
Michael Jordan, on winning the NBA...times three.
"Isiah, Magic and Bird never did this"
Michael Jordan again.
"When Tark goes to the bench, he has two choices - leaded or unleaded"
The *Portland Oregonian* newspaper on the options available to coach Jerry Tarkanian following reports that two reserve players with San Antonio Spurs have bullets lodged in their bodies.
"You could see the fear on their faces, Is it all bandaged up? It's not leaking? Is it all right?"
Magic Johnson, who is HIV positive, on the reasons for his second retirement in a year.

A QUIET NIGHT OUT

Following the Chicago Bulls' third successive NBA victory, Chicago police reported that two people had been killed, several injured and 645 arrested during the celebrations. However, the police said, this year's party was "nice and quiet" compared to last year's.

Billiards

World Professional Championships

Holiday Inn, Bombay   Sept 28-Oct 3, 1992

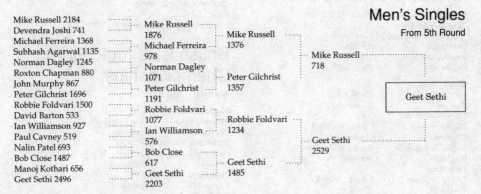

Men's Singles

From 5th Round

Mike Russell 2184
Devendra Joshi 741
Michael Ferreira 1368
Subhash Agarwal 1135
Norman Dagley 1245
Roxton Chapman 880
John Murphy 867
Peter Gilchrist 1696
Robbie Foldvari 1500
David Barton 533
Ian Williamson 927
Paul Cavney 519
Nalin Patel 693
Bob Close 1487
Manoj Kothari 656
Geet Sethi 2496

Mike Russell
1876
Michael Ferreira
978
Norman Dagley
1071
Peter Gilchrist
1191
Robbie Foldvari
1077
Ian Williamson
576
Bob Close
617
Geet Sethi
2203

Mike Russell
1376

Peter Gilchrist
1357

Robbie Foldvari
1234

Geet Sethi
1485

Mike Russell
718

Geet Sethi
2529

Geet Sethi

Final
Robbie Foldvari 4 Geet Sethi 0

Strachan UK Pro

Sheffield   Jan 26-30
First Round
Robbie Foldvari bye
Nalin Patel 4 David Snedden 2
Mark Wildman w-o B Bennett -
Norman Dagley 4 Manoj Kothari 3
Bob Close 4 David Barton 2
Subhash Agarwal 3 Devendra Joshi 4
D Edwards 1 R Williams 4
Peter Gilchrist bye
Mike Russell Bye
Clive Everton 4 David Rees 3
Hugh Nimmo 4 John Caven 0
Ian Williamson w-o Fred Davis OBE -
Michael Ferreira 0 Roxton Chapman 4
John Murphy 4 Paul Cavney 3
Howard Griffiths 4 Des Heald 1
Geet Sethi bye
Second Round
Robbie Foldvari 4 Nalin Patel 0
Mark Wildman 1 Norman Dagley 4
Bob Close 1 Devendra Joshi 4
R Williams 0 Peter Gilchrist 4
Mike Russell 4 Clive Everton 1
Hugh Nimmo 3 Ian Wiliamson 4
Roxton Chapman 2 John Murphy 4
Howard Griffiths 1 Geet Sethi 4
Quarter-finals
Robbie Foldvari 4 Norman Dagley 2
Devendra Joshi 1 Peter Gilchrist 4
Mike Russell 4 Ian Williamson 0
John Murphy 1 Geet Sethi 4
Semi-finals
Robbie Foldvari 4 Peter Gilchrist 2
Mike Russell 1 Geet Sethi 4

Final
Robbie Foldvari 4 Geet Sethi 0

First Radiant Grand Slam Championship

Madras   Apr 3-5
First Round
Clive Everton 4 Howard Griffiths 1
Ray Edmonds - Manoj Kothari w-o
Subhash Agarwal 4 William Turner 0
John Murphy 1 David Sneddon 4
Roxton Chapman w-o Fred Davis OBE -
David Barton 4 David Rees 1
Michael Ferreira PB 1 Devendra Joshi 4
Mark Wildman 4 Alex Higgins 1
Bob Close 4 Des Heald 1
High Nimmo 2 Nalin Patel 4
Second Round
Geet Sethi PS 4 Clive Everton 1
Ian Williamson 4 Manoj Kothari 2
Norman Dagley 2 Subhash Agarwal 4
Peter Gilchrist 4 David Sneddon 2
Robbi Foldvari 4 Roxton Chapman 1
David Barton 0 Devendra Joshi 4
Mark Wildman 4 Bob Close 3
Mike Russell 4 Nalin Patel 0
Quarter-finals
Geet Sethi PS 4 Ian Williamson 0
Subhash Agarwal 1 Peter Gilchrist 4
Robbie Foldvari 4 Devendra Joshi 2
Mark Wildman 3 Mike Russell 4
Semi-finals
Geet Sethi 5 Peter Gilchrist 1
Robbie Roldvari 3 Mike Russell 5
Final
Geet Sethi PS 1 Mike Russell 7

Bowls

World Indoor Championships

Preston   March 15-28
Singles Semi-Final

Richard Corsie 3 sets	Gary Smith 0
(Scotland)	(England)
Jim McCann 3	Tony Allcock 0
(Scotland)	(England)

Singles Final

Richard Corsie 3	Jim McCann 1
(Scotland)	(Scotland)

Pairs Semi-Final

Allcock/Bryant 3	Curtis/Schuback 2
(England)	(Australia)
Smith/Thomson 3	Adamson/McClure 0
(England)	(Ireland)

Pairs Final

Smith/Thomson 3	Bryant/Allcock 0
(England)	(England)

British Isles Indoor Championships

Swansea   March 15-19

Singles Final

J Price 21	N Booth 14
(Wales)	(Ireland)

Pairs Final

Rees/Price 23	Boyle/Boyle 8
(Wales)	(England)

Triples Final

Battersby/Corkill/	Gaskins/Harrington/
McMillan 19	Hanger 8
(Ireland)	(England)

Fours Final

Carruthers/Farish/	Powell/Downey/
Baxter/Bell 22	Jenkins/Lewis 12
(England)	(Wales)

Manchester Unity English Indoor

March 27 - April 4
Singles Final

R Morgan 21	D Bryant 14

Pairs Final

Preston 23	Wymondham Dell 10

Triples Final

Nottingham 20	Teignbridge 13

Fours Final

Cambridge Park 18	Plymouth C.S. 17

Under 25's

Nick Skidmore 21	Jason Norris 20

CIS Insurance Scottish Indoor

Coatbridge, Strathclyde   Dec 1
Final
David Hendry bt Alan Milne 7-6 3-7 7-5 7-5

British Isles (outdoor) Championships

Worthing   Aug 8-20

Singles Final

Robert Proven 13	Alec Lightbody 21
(Scotland)	(Ireland)

Junior Singles Final

Gareth Williams 15	Ian Brown 21
(Wales)	(Scotland)

Pairs Final

England 18	Scotland 17

Triples Final

Ireland 21	Wales 10

Fours Final

Wales 21	England 11

International Series

	W	D	L	Pts	F	A
England	3	-	-	6	391	307
Wales	2	-	1	4	321	336
Ireland	1	-	2	2	326	360
Scotland	-	-	3	0	338	373

EBA National Championships

Singles Final

John Wickham 21	Gordon Charlton 17

Pairs Final

Warwickshire 25	Kent 24
Robinson/Brittan	Smith/Thomson

Triples Final

Suffolk 20	Sussex 21
Sale/Barrell/Cutts	Lewis/Ireland/Williams

HOW LONG?

David Bryant achieved a unique distinction this year when he was dropped by the England selectors for the Home International Series. It was the first time in **33 years** that Bryant had not been selected. During that time he has won the following: 5 Commonwealth Games gold medals, 5 world outdoor titles (& 5 silvers), 6 world indoor titles (& 2 silvers), 23 national outdoor titles, 10 indoor titles and any number of other international competitions.

Champion of Champions
Final
Barney Fernandes 15   Gary Harrington 21

NatWest Bank County Championship (Middleton Cup)
Final
Cumbria 73   Kent 145

NatWest U18 Singles
Final
Neil McKee 20   Graham Shadwell 21

NatWest Club Two Fours
Final
Blackheath & 44   Bournemouth 36
Greenwich

National Championships
Singles Final
Ron Rowlands 21 sets   John Price 5
(Llandrindod Wells)   (Aberavon)
Under 25 Final
Nick Jones 21   Jason Davis 5
(Dinas Powis)   (Pontrhydyfen)
Under 18 Final
Nick Jones 21   Wayne Griffiths 12
(Dinas Powis)   (Welshpool)
Pairs Final
P Howells/G Jones 22   D Weale/R Weale 19
(Haverfordwest)   (Presteigne)
Triples Final
McCarley/Killa/ 20   Shortman/Burgess/ 15
Kingdon   Relland
(Brynhyfryd)   (Cwmbran Park)
Fours Final
Britton/Rosser/ 28   Carey/Rigby/   10
Britton/Mizen   George/Price
(Pontrhydyfen)   (Brynmawr)

Women
World Indoor Championships
Guernsey   May
Singles Semi-Final
Jane Roylance 3sets   Mary Price 2
(England)   (England)
Kate Adams 3   Wilmer LeFeuvre 0
(Scotland)   (Guernsey)
Singles Final
Kate Adams 3   Jane Roylance 1
(Scotland)   (England)

Scottish B.A. Championships
Ayr   August 5-7
Singles Final
George Whitelaw   Stonehouse
Pairs Final
A Grant/R Grant   Overtown & Waterloo
Triples Final
A Frater/R Wilson/   Newmilns
P McCormack (skip)
Fours Final
W Wells/S Wilson/   Hawick
G Lyall/N Amos (skip)
Junior Singles Final
James Meikle   Lesmahagow
Seniors Fours
H Atkin/W Savage/   Blackwood Victoria
GLennox/A Smith (skip)

Irish Championships
Dublin   September 4
Senior Singles Final
Colin Best 21   Noel Weir 13
(Willowfield)   (Rathfriland)
Junior Singles Final
John Nolan 21   Paul Daly 11
(Blackrock)   (Belmont)
Pairs Final
R Oliver/I McClure 26   J Talbot/M Nutt 8
(Portrush)
Triples Final
B Moffett/J Henry 23   W McCandless/J Robinson/ 14
I McClure (skip)   R McCune (skip)
(Portrush)   (Ballymena)
Fours Final
Brian Daly (skip) 27   M McMullan 6
(Belmont)   (Dunluce)

Scottish Championships
Arbroath   Jan 9-10
Singles Final
David Henry 3sets   Alan Milne 1
Pairs Final
Prestwick 22   Turritt 11
Triples Final
Prestwick 16   Buchan 14
Fours Final
Cowal 24   Edinburgh 7
Junior Singles
Joey Strickland 21   Paul Foster 19

HOW MANY?
There are, according to the best possible estimates, **19** governing bodies in British bowls. What do they all govern? Well, there's women, men, indoor, outdoor, crown green, flat green, upstairs, downstairs, living room, back garden and crazy bowls just to start.......

Crown Green Championships

Winners Only

Yorkshire Bank Crown King
Stan Frith (Cheshire)
Henselite All England Merit
John Taylor (Lancs)
Greenmaster Junior Merit
Craig Newton (Yorks)
Martell Cognac Inter County Championship
Yorkshire
Martell Cognac Inter County Supplementary
Greater Manchester

Boxing

To be honest, it's hard enough to feel secure in the knowledge that Lennox Lewis is actually British, without Riddick Bowe throwing the belt in a trash-can. It's ironic, to say the least, that the first and only previous British heavyweight champion of the world never fought for the title in his native Britain and the second (who unlike Fitzsimmons had four titles to tilt for) just doesn't sound British. However, credit where credit's due. Lewis impressively blunted the attacks of Razor Ruddock to earn the chance of the WBC belt, which is more than can be said for the title defences of Bowe who barely had to twitch a muscle to send Michael Dokes back to one rehabilitation centre or another.

Heavyweight boxing is a curious sport. Well, sport is probably not the right word. It's mostly to do with marketing a theatrical event. Only when the rare fighter, who is genuinely skillful and violent, comes along does the theatre transform into the arena. Muhammed Ali, more with skill than violence, and Mike Tyson with the converse qualities, generated genuine awe. Lewis or Bowe has yet to prove they are good enough to lace their gloves.

Frank Bruno stepped off the pantomime boards to fight Pierre Coetzer. There weren't too many calls of 'behind you' as only 3000 turned out to watch Bruno in his day job. Still, his follow-up defeat of the curiously named Carl 'The Truth' Williams set him up for the fight that he wanted, a third shot at the world title against a man that (hype aside) he wasn't kissing cousins with. (*See Landmarks*)

The middleweights (super, in this case), who come a clear second in the pecking order, had a busy year. Nigel Benn survived a missile pelting to overcome the Italian Mauro Galvano, who was forced to retire with a head injury. Next up was the new chairman of the Professional Boxers' Association, Nicky Piper, who faltered in round 11. He was followed by Lou Gent, who lasted only four rounds. Eubank was equally busy, dispensing with three opponents in six months to set himself up with an October bout with Benn. Eubank, who fought a draw with Benn in Manchester, even reckons he took a pay cut to £850,000 because he was so eager to take the fight. Benn collected a full million for that fight and might feel aggrieved he didn't get the decision as well.

As ever, Eubank's problems have tended to be outside the ring, rather than in it. A trip to Manchester's Moss Side was widely criticised earlier this year and he escaped prosecution for driving his Harley Davidson down a pedestrian precinct in Hove. No great crime, but for Eubank it again generated the wrong headlines.

Chris Pyatt, with much less trumpeting, earned and then successfully defended the WBO middleweight title. Paul Hodkinson defeated the Puerta Rican Capeda to hang on to his WBC featherweight title in February, but lost out against Gergoria Vargas in April. Britain's only other current world champions are Steve Robinson, who benefitted in a unique fashion when Columbia's Ruben Palacio was stripped of his title after failing an HIV test and Robinson fought John Davidson for the vacant WBO title, and Scot Paul Weir, who quickly dispensed with Fernando Martinez to take the WBO strawweight crown.

Professional Boxing

World Title Fights

There are currently four governing bodies that dispense world titles. They are: the World Boxing Association (WBA), the World Boxing Organisation (WBO), the World Boxing Council (WBC) and the International Boxing Federation (IBF). If that confuses you, don't worry, you are not the only one.

HEAVYWEIGHT
WBA/IBF
Feb 6   New York
Riddick Bowe (USA) bt Michael Dokes (USA)
Referee stopped fight, round 1.

WBA
May 22   Washington DC
Riddick Bowe bt Jesse Ferguson (USA)
Referee stopped fight, round 2.

WBC
May 8   Las Vegas
Lennox Lewis (ENG) bt Tony Tucker (USA)
Points, 12 rounds.

Oct 1   Cardiff
Lennox Lewis (ENG) bt Frank Bruno (ENG)
Referee stopped fight, round 7.

WBO
February
Michael Moorer (USA) relinquished title.

June 7   Las Vegas
Tommy Morrison (USA) bt George Foreman (USA)
Points, 12 rounds. Morrison wins the vacant title.

CRUISERWEIGHT
IBF
Feb 28   Atlantic City
Alfred Cole (USA) bt Uriah Grant (USA)
Points, 12 rounds.

July 16   Moscow
Alfred Cole bt Glenn McCrory (ENG)
Points, 12 rounds.

WBC
Oct 16, 1992   Paris
Anaclet Wamba (FRA) bt Andrew Maynard (USA)
Points, 12 rounds.

Mar 6   Levallois Perret, France
Anaclet Wamba bt David Vedder (USA)
Points, 12 rounds.

WBO
Oct 2, 1992   Berlin
Tyrone Booze (USA) bt Ralf Rocchigiani (GER)
Points, 12 rounds.

Feb 13   Hamburg
Markus Bott (GER) bt Tyrone Booze
Points, 12 rounds.
June 26   Hamburg
Nestor Giovannini (ARG) bt Markus Bott
Points, 12 rounds.

LIGHT-HEAVYWEIGHT
WBA
Feb 20   Fargo, USA
Virgil Hill (USA) bt Adolpho Washington (USA)
Technical knock-out, round 11.

Apr 3   Levallois Perret, France
Virgil Hill bt Fabrice Tiozzo (FRA)
Points, 12 rounds.

IBF
Mar 20   Dusseldorf
Henry Maske (GER) bt Prince Charles Williams (USA)
Points, 12 rounds.

WBC
Dec 3, 1992   St Jean de Luz, France
Jeff Harding (AUS) bt David Vedder (USA)
Points, 12 rounds.

WBO
Feb 27   Beijing
Leonzer Barber (USA) bt Mike Sedillo (USA)
Points, 12 rounds.

SUPER-MIDDLEWEIGHT
WBA
Jan 30   Memphis, Tennessee
Michael Nunn (USA) bt Victor Cordoba (PAN)
Points, 12 rounds.

Feb 20   Mexico City
Michael Nunn bt Dan Morgan (USA)
Referee stopped fight, round 1.

Apr 23   Memphis
Michael Nunn bt Crawford Ashley (ENG)
Referee stopped fight, round 9.

IBF
Feb 13   Las Vegas
James Toney (USA) bt Iran Barkley (USA)
Referee stopped fight, round 9.

WBC
Oct 3, 1992   Marino, Italy
Nigel Benn (ENG) bt Mauro Galvano (ITA)
Retired, round 3.

Dec 12, 1992   London
Nigel Benn bt Nicky Piper (WAL)
Referee stopped fight, round 11.

Mar 6   Glasgow
Nigel Benn bt Lou Gent (ENG)
Referee stopped fight, round 4.
WBO
Nov 28, 1992   Manchester
Chris Eubank (ENG) bt Juan Carlos Gimenez (PAR)
Points, 12 rounds.

Feb 20   London
Chris Eubank bt Lindell Holmes (USA)
Points, 12 rounds.

May 15   Glasgow
Chris Eubank drew with Ray Close (IRL)
12 rounds.

MIDDLEWEIGHT
WBA
Oct 27, 1992   Houston, Texas
Reggie Johnson (USA) bt Lamar Parks (USA)
Points, 12 rounds.

Jan 19   Boise, Idaho
Reggie Johnson bt Kiyun Song (KOR)
Referee stopped fight, round 8.

May 4   Denver, Colorado
Reggie Johnson bt Wayne Morris (GUY)
Points, 12 rounds.

IBF
May 22   Washington DC
Roy Jones (USA) bt Bernard Hopkins (USA)
Points, 12 rounds. Jones wins the vacant title.

WBC
May 8   Las Vegas
Gerald McClellan (USA) bt Julian Jackson (ISV)
Referee stopped fight, round 5.

Aug 6   Bayamon, Puerto Rico
Gerald McClellan bt Jay Bell (USA)
Knock-out, round 1.

WBO
May 19   Leicester
Chris Pyatt (ENG) bt Sumbu Kalambay (ITA)
Points, 12 rounds. Pyatt wins vacant title.

Sept 18   Leicester
Chris Pyatt bt Hugo Corti (ARG)
Knock-out, round 6.

LIGHT-MIDDLEWEIGHT
WBA
Oct, 1992
Vinny Pazienza (USA) relinquished title because of his inability, through injury, to meet a defence deadline.

QUOTES

"We have options for fights against all the best heavyweights at the moment, with the exception of Mike Tyson. There's nothing we can do about him. The state of Indiana holds a six-year option"

Lou Duva, manager of Evander Holyfield (in October, 1992).

"I am the man who beat the man (Evander Holyfield) who beat the man (James 'Buster' Douglas) who beat the man (Mike Tyson).....

Riddick Bowe

"He is very durable and has a nice moustache"

Frank Bruno's assessment of his opponent, Pierre Coetzer.

"My husband is much funnier than the Spitting Image scriptwriters who produce their childish material. They should get him to write the scripts, I'm sure he could do a better job"

Laura Bruno

"What about hunting? Touché, old bean. Jumping over the fence and chasing all them rabbits"

Bruno defending charges that boxing is out of touch with civilised society

"Herbie Hide is going to be the greatest heavyweight the world has ever seen"

Barry Hearn, his manager.

"Colin McMillan is the best boxer. Nigel Benn has the hardest punch and Paul Hodkinson is the best fighter. I'm the most successful because I can box a little, strut a little and talk a little"

Chris Eubank

Dec 21, 1992   Buenos Aires
Julio Cesar Vasquez (ARG) bt Hitoshi Kamiyama (JPN)
Referee stopped fight, round 1. Vasquez wins vacant title.

Feb 22   Mar Del Plata, Argentina
Julio Cesar Vasquez bt Aquilino Asprilla (PAN)
Knock-out, round 1.

Apr 25   Madrid
J Cesar Vasquez bt Francisco Javier Castillejos (ESP)
Points, 12 rounds.

July 11   Tucumán, Argentina
Julio Cesar Vasquez bt Alejandro Ugueto (VEN)
Points, 12 rounds

Aug 14   Monte Carlo
Julio Cesar Vasquez bt Aaron Davis (USA)
Points, 12 rounds.

IBF
Jan 20   Avoriaz, Italy
Gianfranco Rosi (ITA) bt Gilbert Dele (FRA)
Points, 12 rounds.

WBC
Feb 20   Mexico City
Terry Norris (USA) bt Maurice Blocker (USA)
Referee stopped fight, round 2.

June 19   San Diego, California
Terry Norris bt Troy Waters (USA)
Retired, round 3.

WBO
Dec 19, 1992   San Severo, Italy
John D Jackson (USA) bt Michele Mastrodonato (ITA)
Referee stopped fight, round 10.
July
John David Jackson vacated title.

WELTERWEIGHT
WBA
Oct 31, 1992   London
Crisanto Espana (VEN) bt Meldrick Taylor (USA)
Referee stopped fight, round 8.

May 5   Belfast
Crisanto Espana bt Rodolfo Aquilar (PAN)
Points, 12 rounds.

IBF
June 19   San Diego, Cal.
Felix Trinidad (PUR) bt Maurice Blocker (USA)
Referee stopped fight, round 2.

Aug 6   Bayamon, Puerto Rico
Felix Trinidad bt Luis Garcia (VEN)
Knock-out, round 1.

WBC
Jan 12   New York
Buddy McGirt (USA) bt Genaro Leon (MEX)
Points, 12 rounds.

Mar 6   New York
Pernell Whitaker (USA) bt Buddy McGirt
Points, 12 rounds.
Sept 10   San Antonio, Texas
**Julio Cesar Chavez(MEX) drew with
Pernell Whitaker (USA)**
Over 12 rounds

WBO
Nov 27, 1992   Randers, Denmark
Manning Galloway (USA) bt Gert Bo Jacobsen (DEN)
Points, 12 rounds.

LIGHT-WELTERWEIGHT
WBA
Jan 12   Mar del Plata, Argentina
Juan Martin Coggi (ARG) bt Morris East (PHI)
Knock-out, round 8.

Apr 10   Mar del Plata
Juan Martin Coggi bt Joe Rivera (PUR)
Referee stiopped fight, round 7.

June 23   Tokyo
Juan Martin Coggi bt Hiroyuki Yoshino (JPN)
Referee stopped fight, round 5.

Aug 14   Buenos Aires
Juan Martin Coggi bt José Barboza (VEN)
Points, 12 rounds.

IBF
March
Pernell Whitaker (USA) relinquished title.

May 15   Atlantic City
Charles Murray (USA) bt Rodney Moore (USA)
Points, 12 rounds. Murray wins vacant title.

July 24   Atlantic City
Charles Murray bt Juan Laporte (PUR)
Points, 12 rounds.

THE NUMBERS GAME (2)

Around 136,000 Mexicans watched the world title defence of Julio Cesar Chavez against the American Greg Hausen. That figure broke the record for fight-watchers set by the Gene Tunney/Jack Dempsey bout in 1926, when 120,757 turned out. Chavez' fight was stopped, in his favour in the second minute of the fifth round. Hausen had been subject to a steady barrage of punches since being knocked down in round one. The victory took Chavez' record to 85 wins in as many fights.

WBC
Feb 20   Mexico City
Julio Cesar Chavez (MEX) bt Greg Haugen (USA)
Referee stopped fight, round 5.

May 8   Las Vegas
Julio Cesar Chavez bt Terrence Alli (USA)
Referee stopped fight, round 6.

WBO
Nov 9, 1992   Inglewood
Carlos Gonzalez (MEX) bt Lorenzo Smith (USA)
Retired, round 6.

Mar 22   Inglewood
Carlos Gonzalez bt Tony Baltazar (USA)
Referee stopped fight, round 1.

June 7   Las Vegas
Zack Padilla (USA) bt Carlos Gonzalez
Points, 12 rounds.

LIGHTWEIGHT
WBA
Oct 24, 1992   Portland, USA
Tony Lopez (USA) bt Joey Gamache (USA)
Referee stopped fight, round 11.

Feb 12   Sacramento, USA
Tony Lopez bt Dingaan Thobela (RSA)
Points, 12 rounds.

June 26   Sun City, South Africa
Dingaan Thobela bt Tony Lopez
Points, 12 rounds.

IBF
Jan 10   Atlantic City
Freddie Pendleton (USA) bt Tracy Spann (USA)
Points, 12 rounds.

July 17   Las Vegas
Freddie Pendleton bt Jorge Paez (MEX)
Points, 12 rounds.

WBC
Dec 5, 1992   Mexico City
Miguel Angel Gonzalez (MEX) bt Darryl Tyson (USA)
Points, 12 rounds.

Apr 26   Aguascalientas, Mexico
Miguel Angel Gonzalez bt Hector Lopez (MEX)
Points, 12 rounds.

Aug 13   Guadalajara, Mexico
Miguel Angel Gonzalez bt David Sample (USA)
Points, 12 rounds.

WBO
Apr 16   Rome
Giovanni Parisi (ITA) bt Michael Ayers (ENG)
Points, 12 rounds.

SUPER-FEATHERWEIGHT
WBA
Nov 20, 1992   Tokyo

Genaro Hernandez (USA) bt Yuji Watanabe (JPN)
Referee stopped fight, round 6.

Apr 26   Inglewood
Genaro Hernandez drew with Raul Perez (MEX)
Technical decision, round 1.

June 28   Inglewood
Genaro Hernandez bt Raul Perez
Knock-out, round 8.

IBF
Feb 13   San Juan, Puerto Rico
John Molina (PUR) bt Francisco Segura (MEX)
Referee stopped fight, round 8.

June 26   Atlantic City
John Molina bt Mañuel Medina (MEX)
Points, round 12.

WBC
Nov 7, 1992   Lake Tahoe, Cal
Azumah Nelson (GHA) bt Calvin Grove (USA)
Points, 12 rounds.

Feb 20   Mexico City
Azumah Nelson bt Gabriel Ruelas (USA)
Points, 12 rounds.

FEATHERWEIGHT
WBA
Dec 19, 1992   Changwon, Korea
Yung-Kyun Park (KOR) bt Ever Beleno (VEN)
Points, 12 rounds.

Mar 20   Seoul
Yung-Kyun Park bt Thanomjit Kiatkriengkrai (THA)
Referee stopped fight, round 4.

IBF
Oct 23, 1992   Gravelines, France
Mañuel Medina (MEX) bt Moussa Sangaree (FRA)
Points, 12 rounds.

Feb 26   Melun, France
Tom Johnson (USA) bt Mañuel Medina
Points, 12 rounds.

WBC
Feb 3   London
Paul Hodkinson (ENG) bt Ricardo Capeda (PUR)
Referee stopped fight, round 4.

Apr 28   Dublin
Gregorio Vargas bt Paul Hodkinson
Referee stopped fight, round 7.

WBO
Apr 16
Ruben Palacio (COL) stripped of title after failing an HIV test.

Apr 17   Washington, Tyne and Wear
Steve Robinson (WAL) bt John Davidson (ENG)

Points, 12 rounds. Robinson wins vacant title.

July 10   Cardiff
Steve Robinson bt Sean Murphy (ENG)
Referee stopped fight, round 9.

SUPER-BANTAMWEIGHT
WBA
Dec 5, 1992   Berck-sur-Mer, France
Wilfredo Vasquez (PUR) bt Thierry Jacob (FRA)
Referee stopped fight, round 8.

Mar 6   Levallois Perrat, France
Wilfredo Vasquez bt Luis Mendoza (COL)
Points, 12 rounds.

June 24   Bordeaux, France
Wilfredo Vasquez bt Thierry Jacob
Knock-out, round 10.

IBF
Dec 2, 1992   Tortoli
Kennedy McKinney (USA) bt Welcome Ncita (RSA)
Knock-out, round 11.

Apr 17   Sacramento
Kennedy McKinney bt Richard Duran (USA)
Points, 12 rounds.

July 17   Memphis, USA
Kennedy McKinney bt Rudy Zavala (USA)
Referee stopped fight, round 3.

WBC
Dec 5, 1992   Berck-sur-Mer
**Tracy Harris Patterson (USA) drew with
Daniel Zaragoza (MEX)**
12 rounds.

Mar 13   Poughkeepsie, New York
Tracy Harris Patterson bt Jesse Benavides (USA)
Points, 12 rounds.

WBO
Oct 15, 1992   London
Duke McKenzie (ENG) bt Jesse Benavides
Points, 12 rounds.

June 9   Catford, London
Daniel Jimenez (PUR) bt Duke McKenzie
Points, 12 rounds.

BANTAMWEIGHT
WBA
Oct 10, 1992   Cartagena, Columbia
Jorge Eliecer Julio (COL) bt Eddie Cook (USA)
Points, 12 rounds.

Apr 3   Cartagena
Jorge Eliecer Julio bt Francisco Alvarez (COL)
Retired, round 8.

July 8   Tijuana, Mexico
Jorge Eliecer Julio bt Ricardo Vargas (MEX)
Points, 12 rounds.

IBF
Mar 27   Evian, France
Orlando Canizales (USA) bt Clarence Adams (USA)
Referee stopped fight, round 11.

June 20   Houston
Orlando Canizales bt Derrick Whiteboy (RSA)
No contest, round 3.

WBC
Jan 25   Inglewood
Victor Rabanales (MEX) bt Dio Andujar (PHI)
Points, 12 rounds.

Mar 27   Kyungju, Korea
Jong-Il Byun (KOR) bt Victor Rabanales
Points, 12 rounds.

May 28   Seoul
Jong-Il Byun (KOR) bt Josefino Suarez (MEX)
Points, 12 rounds.

WBO
Mar 24   Conado, Puerto Rico
Rafael Del Valle (PUR) bt Wilfredo Vargas (PUR)
Referee stopped fight, round 5.
June 19   San Juan, Puerto Rico
Rafael Del Valle bt Miguel Lora (COL)
Points, 12 rounds.

SUPER-FLYWEIGHT
WBA
Dec 11, 1992   Tokyo
Katsuya Onizuka (JPN) bt Armando Castro (MEX)
Points, 12 rounds.

May 21   Tokyo
Katsuya Onizuka bt Jae-Shin Lim (KOR)
Points, 12 rounds.

IBF
Jan 16   San Antonio, Texas
Julio Cesar Borboa (MEX) bt Robert Quiroga (USA)
Referee stopped fight, round 12.

May 22   Mexico City
Julio Cesar Borboa bt Joel Luna Zarate (MEX)
Points, 12 rounds.

Aug 21   Kalispel, Montana
Julio Cesar Borboa bt Carlos Mercardo (COL)
Knock-out, round 3.

WBC
Oct 31, 1992   Seoul
Sung-Kil Moon (KOR) bt Greg Richardson (USA)
Points, 12 rounds.

Feb 27   Seoul
Sung-Kil Moon bt Hilario Zapata (PAN)
Referee stopped fight, round 1.

July 3   Seoul
Sung-kil Moon bt Carlos Salazar (ARG)
Points, 12 rounds.

WBO
Mar 26   Copenhagen
Johnny Bredahl (DEN) bt Rafael Caban (PUR)
Points, 12 rounds.

FLYWEIGHT
WBA
June 21   Osaka
David Griman (VEN) bt Hiroki Ioka (JPN)
Referee stopped fight, round 8.

IBF
Nov 29, 1992   Bangkok
Pichit Sitbangprachen (THA) bt Rodolfo Blanco (COL)
Knock-out, round 3.

Mar 6   Uttaradit, Thailand
Pichit Sitbangprachen bt Antonio Perez (MEX)
Referee stopped fight, round 4.

July 11   Bangkok
Pichit Sitbangprachen bt Kyung-Yun Lee (KOR)
Referee stopped fight, round 1.
WBC
Oct 20, 1992   Tokyo
Yuri Arbachakov (RUS) bt Yun-Un Chin (KOR)
Points, round 12.

Mar 20   Bangkok
Yuri Arbachakov bt Muangchai Kittikasem (THA)
Referee stopped fight, round 9.

July 16   Kobe, Japan
Yuri Arbachakov bt Ysaias Zamudio (MEX)
Points, 12 rounds.

WBO
May 15   Glasgow
Jake Matlala (RSA) bt Pat Clinton (SCO)
Knock-out, round 8.

LIGHT-FLYWEIGHT
WBA
Nov 18, 1992   Osaka
Myung Woo Yuh (KOR) bt Hiroki Iota (JPN)
Points, 12 rounds.

July 25   Seoul
Myung Woo Yuh bt Yuichi Hosono (JPN)
Points, 12 rounds.

IBF
Dec 12, 1992   Phoenix, Arizona
Michael Carbajal (USA) bt Robinson Questa (PAN)
Referee stopped fight, round 8.

WBC
Dec 7, 1992   Inglewood

Humberto Gonzalez (MEX) bt Melchor C Castro (MEX)
Points, 12 rounds.

IBF/WBC
Mar 13   Las Vegas
Michael Carbajal bt Humberto Gonzalez
Knock-out, round 7.

July 17   Las Vegas
Michael Carbajal bt Kwang-Sun Kim (KOR)
Knock-out, round 7.

STRAWWEIGHT
WBA
Oct 14, 1992   Tokyo
Hideyuki Ohashi (JPN) bt Hi-Yong Choi (KOR)
Points, 12 rounds.

Feb 10   Tokyo
Chana Porpaoin (THA) bt Hideyuki Ohashi
Points, 12 rounds.

May 9   Ang Thong, Thailand
Chana Porpaoin bt Carlos Murillo (PAN)
Points, 12 rounds.

Aug 22   Bangkok
Chana Porpaoin bt Ronnie Magramo (PHI)
Points, 12 rounds.

IBF
Dec 10, 1992   Bangkok
Ratanapol Sorvorapin (THA) bt Manny Melchor (PHI)
Points, 12 rounds.

June 27   Bangkok
Ratanapol Sorvorapin bt Ala Villamor (PHI)
Referee stopped fight, round 7.

WBC
Oct 11, 1992   Tokyo
Ricardo Lopez (MEX) bt Rocky Lim (THA)
Knock-out, round 2.

Jan 31   Seoul
Ricardo Lopez bt Kwang-Soo Oh (KOR)
Referee stoped fight, round 9.

July 3   Nuevo Laredo, Mexico
Ricardo Lopez bt Saman Sorjaturong (THA)
Referee stopped fight, round 2.

WBO
May 15   Glasgow
Paul Weir (SCO) bt Fernando Martinez (MEX)
Referee stopped fight, round 2.

Commonwealth Title Fights

HEAVYWEIGHT
Oct 31, 1992   London
Lennox Lewis (ENG) bt Razor Rudduck (CAN)
Referee stopped fight, round 2.

January
Lennox Lewis vacated title when awarded the WBC crown.

Mar 18   Catford, London
Hanry Akinwande (ENG) bt Jimmy Thunder (AUS)
Points, 12 rounds.

LIGHT-HEAVYWEIGHT
Apr 7   Leeds
Brent Kosolofski (CAN) bt Michael Gale (ENG)
Referee stopped fight, round 9.

MIDDLEWEIGHT
Oct 1, 1992   Telford, Staffs
Richie Woodall (ENG) bt John Ashton (ENG)
Points, 12 rounds.

LIGHT-MIDDLEWEIGHT
Jan 30   Brentwood, Essex
Lloyd Honeghan (ENG) bt Mickey Hughes (ENG)
Referee stopped fight, round 5.

WELTERWEIGHT
Nov 24, 1992   Doncaster
Eamonn Loughran (NIR) bt Donovan Boucher (CAN)
Referee stopped fight, round 3.

Feb 6   Cardiff
Eamonn Loughran (NIR) bt Mike Benjamin (GUY)
Referee stopped fight, round 6.

LIGHTWEIGHT
Oct 28, 1992   London
Billy Schwer (ENG) bt Carl Crook (ENG)
Retired, round 9.

Feb 24   Wembley
Paul Burke (ENG) bt Billy Schwer
Referee stopped fight, round 7.

FEATHERWEIGHT
Oct 7, 1992   Sunderland
Billy Hardy (ENG) bt Ricky Rayner (AUS)
Referee stopped fight, round 10.

May 19   Sunderland
Billy Hardy bt Barrington Francis (CAN)
Points, 12 rounds.

BANTAMWEIGHT
Dec 3, 1992   Catford
Johnny Armour (ENG bt Albert Musankabele (ZAM)
Referee stopped fight, round 5.

Feb 10   Catford
Johnny Armour bt Morgan Mpande (ZAM)
Points, 12 rounds.

FLYWEIGHT
Francis Ampofo (ENG) bt Albert Musankabele
Referee stopped fight, round 3.

British Title Fights

HEAVYWEIGHT
Feb 27   Dagenham, Essex
Herbie Hide bt Michael Murray
Referee stopped fight, round 5.

SUPER-MIDDLEWEIGHT
April
Henry Wharton vacated title.

MIDDLEWEIGHT
Feb 25   Bradford
Frank Grant bt John Ashton
Retired, round 7.

LIGHT-MIDDLEWEIGHT
Dec 10, 1992   Bethnal Green
Andy Till bt Tony Collins
Referee stopped fight, round 3.

Apr 14   Kensington
Andy Till bt Wally Swift
Referee stopped fight, round 4.

LIGHTWEIGHT
Oct 28, 1992   London
Billy Schwer bt Carl Crook
Retired, round 9.

Feb 24   Wembley
Paul Burke bt Billy Schwer
Referee stopped fight, round 7.

SUPER-FEATHERWEIGHT
Oct 13, 1992   Bury
Neil Haddock bt Michael Armstrong
Referee stopped fight, round 6.

July 25   Oldham
Neil Haddock bt Steve Walker
Referee stopped fight, round 7.

FEATHERWEIGHT
Feb 27 Dagenham
Sean Murphy bt Alan McKay
Referee stopped fight, round 9.

July
British title declared vacant after Murphy lost in nine rounds in a WBO title bid against Steve Robinson.

BANTAMWEIGHT
Jan 25 Glasgow
Drew Docherty bt Donnie Hood
Points, 12 rounds.

FLYWEIGHT
November, 1992
Robbie Regan vacated title after winning European crown.

Dec 22 London
Francis Ampofo bt James Drummond
Points, 12 rounds.

Amateur Boxing
World Championships
Tampere, Finland   May 5-16

SUPER-HEAVYWEIGHT
1	**Roberto Balado**	CUB
2	Svilen Rusinov	BUL
3	Evgeny Belousov	RUS
	Joel Scott	USA

HEAVYWEIGHT
1	**Felix Savon**	CUB
2	Georgi Kandelaki	GEO
3	Stephane Allouane	FRA
	Arshak Avartakian	ARM

LIGHT-HEAVYWEIGHT
1	**Ramon Garbey**	CUB
2	Jacklord Jacobs	NGR
3	Rostislav Zaoulitchny	UKR

MIDDLEWEIGHT
1	**Ariel Hernandez**	CUB
2	Akin Kologlu	TUR
3	Raymond Joval	HOL
	Vasily Zhirov	KZK

LIGHT-WELTERWEIGHT
1	**Francisc Wastag**	ROM
2	Alfredo Duvergel	CUB
3	Geir Hitland	NOR
	Sergey Karavaev	RUS

WELTERWEIGHT
1	**Juan Hernandez**	CUB
2	Vitalis Karpaciauskas	LTU
3	Andreas Otto	GER
	Sergey Gorodnitshev	UKR

LIGHT-WELTERWEIGHT
1	**Hector Vinent**	CUB
2	Jyri Kjäll	FIN
3	Oleg Saitev	RUS
	Oktay Urkal	GER

LIGHTWEIGHT
1	**Damian Austin**	CUB
2	Larry Nicholson	USA
3	Tibor Rafael	SVK
	Vasile Nistor	ROM

FEATHERWEIGHT
1	**Serafim Todorov**	BUL
2	Enrique Carrion	CUB
3	Ramazi Paliani	GEO
	Marcelica Tudoriu	ROM

BANTAMWEIGHT
1	**Alexander Christov**	BUL
2	Joel Casamayor	CUB
3	Ilhan Güler	TUR
	Valdislav Antonov	RUS

FLYWEIGHT
1	**Waldemar Font**	CUB
2	Khikmatulla Akhamadov	UZB
3	Mustafa Hassan	EGY
	Damaen Kelly	IRL

LIGHT-FLYWEIGHT
1	**Nshan Munchian**	ARM
2	Daniel Petrov	BUL
3	Albert Guardado	USA
	Ernednet Tsogtjargal	MON

World Junior Championships
Montreal   Sept 24-Oct 5, 1992

Super-Heavyweight	Mihail Porshnev (RUS)
Heavyweight	Georgi Kandelaki (GEO)
Light-Heavyweight	Samilsan Sinan (TUR)
Middleweight	Islam Arsangaliev (RUS)
Light-Middleweight	Julio Acosta (CUB)
Welterweight	Luyz Brors (GER)
Light-Welterweight	Oleg Saitov (RUS)
Lightweight	Damian Austin (CUB)
Featherweight	Michael Stewart (CAN)
Bantamweight	Neslan Machado (CUB)
Flyweight	Jorenzo O Armenteros (CUB)
Light-Flyweight	Waldemar Font Quintero (CUB)

GBR Representatives: Jamie Branch lost to Arsangaliev in the m-weight quarter-final; Michael Hall bt Moralcs (PUR) in the prelis, but lost to Fleming (CAN) in the quarter-final.

World Rankings
AIBA rankings as at June 30, 1993

SUPER-HEAVYWEIGHT
1 Roberto Balado   CUB
2 Evgeni Belousov   RUS
3 Svilen Rusinov   BUL

HEAVYWEIGHT
1 Felix Savon   CUB
2 Georgios Stefanopoulos GRE
3 Tuakipa Tasefa   NZL

LIGHT-HEAVYWEIGHT
1 Ramon Garbey   CUB
2 Justin Crawford   AUS
3 Sinan Samilsan   TUR

MIDDLEWEIGHT
1 Ariel Hernandez   CUB
2 Akin Kuloglu   TUR
3 Mark Bargero   AUS

LIGHT-MIDDLEWEIGHT
1 Alfredo Duvergel   CUB
2 Francisc Vastag   ROM
3 Sergey Karavaev   RUS

WELTERWEIGHT
1 Juan Hernandez   CUB
2 Andreas Otto   GER
3 Ioannis Ioannidis   GRE

LIGHT-WELTERWEIGHT
1 Hector Vinent   CUB
2 Oktay Urkal   GER
3 Jyri Kjäll   FIN

LIGHTWEIGHT
1 Damian Austin   CUB
2 Marco Rudolph   GER
3 Vasile Nistor   ROM

FEATHERWEIGHT
1 Enrique Carrion   CUB
2 Marcelica Tudoriu   ROM
3 Heiko Hinz   GER

BANTAMWEIGHT
1 Joel Casamayor   CUB
2 Alexander Christov   BUL
3 Timofei Scriabin   MLD

FLYWEIGHT
1 Waldemar Font   CUB
2 Vichai Khadpo   THA
3 Richard Sunee   MRI

LIGHT-FLYWEIGHT
1 Daniel Petrov   BUL
2 Rogelio Marcelo   CUB
3 Nshan Munchian   ARM

BROTHER'S KEEPER?

Two brothers, Kusuo and Katsuaki Eguchi fought for the Japanese straw-weight title in Tokyo in June. Kusuo knocked Katsuaki down in the 1st round, but Katsuaki knocked his brother down in the 2nd round to even the score. The fight was stopped in the 6th round in favour of Katsuaki, who had caught his brother with a couple of whoppers. Kusuo, through the bruises, knew who would get into trouble though when they got home. "Win or lose," he had said before the fight, "I'm the one to be blamed."

Canoeing

Slalom
World Championships

Mezzana, Italy   July 1-11
K1 Men

1	Richard Fox	GBR	1:59.95	0
2	Richard Weiss	USA	2:00.52	0
3	Melvyn Jones	GBR	2:02.37	0
4	Shaun Pearce	GBR	2:03.14	0

C1 Men

1	Martin Lang	GER	2:20.44	0
2	Herve Delamarre	FRA	2:20.92	0
3	Soeren Kaufmann	GER	2:22.98	0
10	Gareth Marriott	GBR	2:22.89	5

C2 Men

1	Czech Rep.		2:24.63	0
2	France		2:28.53	0
3	France		2:25.57	5

K1 Team Men

1	Great Britain	2:33.91	0
	(Pearce/Jones/Fox)		
2	France	2:37.61	0
3	Czech Rep.	2:37.61	0

C1 Team Men

1	Slovak Rep.	2:53.88	0
2	Great Britain	2:54.39	0
	(Horsmann/Delaney/Marriott)		
3	Italy	2:55.85	0

C2 Team Men

1	Czech Rep.	2:52.85	0
2	France	2:53.76	0
3	Slovak Rep.	3:01.08	0
7	Great Britain	3:12.47	35
	(Green/Green + Clough/Clough		
	+ Pitt/Millar)		

K1 Women

1	Myriam Jerusalmi	FRA	2:24.89	0
2	Anne Boixel	FRA	2:29.41	0
3	Marianne Agulhon	FRA	2:30.04	0
5	Lynn Simpson	GBR	2:32.94	0

K1 Team Women

1	France		2:55.78	5
2	USA		3:04.25	5
3	Great Britain		3:04.55	10
	(Lund/Crosbee/Simpson)			

	G	S	B
France	6	6	4
Germany	3	3	2
Great Britain	2	1	4
Czech Rep.	2	-	1
Italy	1	2	3
Slovenia	1	1	1
Austria	1	-	-
USA	-	2	-
Slovak Rep.	-	1	1

British Championships

Holme Pierrepont, Notts   Mar 22
MEN

K1	I Raspin	Tees	2:11.42
C1	G Marriott	Notts	2:34.01
C2	Arrowsmith/Brain		2:51.28

WOMEN

K1	H Corrie	Manc	2:42.09

Women's World Cup

K1 FINAL STANDINGS

1	K Striepecke	GER
2	M Jerusalmi-Fox	FRA
3	L Simpson	GBR

Wildwater
World Championships

Mezzana, Italy   July 1-11
K1 Men

1	Markus Gickler	GER	12:58.61
2	Robert Pontarollo	ITA	13:02.66
3	Cesare Mulazzi	ITA	13:06.39
9	Neil Stamps	GBR	13:14.62
15	Alan Tordoff	GBR	13:20.41
20	Ian Tordoff	GBR	13:21.97
42	Neil Blackmann	GBR	13:53.43

C2 Men

1	France		13:31.91
2	Slovak Rep.		13:41.53
3	Germany		13:45.30
17	Great Britain		14:26.39
	(Clough/Clough)		
18	Great Britain		14:27.79
	(Belbin/Caunt)		
23	Great Britain		14:53.50
	(Simpson/Twigger)		

C1 Men

1	Vladi Panato	ITA	14:12.63
2	Andrej Jelenc	SLO	14:21.89
3	Jean Luc Christin	FRA	14:22.46
18	Mackon Singh	GBR	14:54.05
22	Ros Pumphrey	GBR	15:15.65
24	John Willacy	GBR	15:29.99
26	Mark De Freitas	GBR	15:36.83

K1 Team Men

1	France	13:26.00
2	Italy	13:34.27
3	Great Britain	13:35.27
	(Stamps/Tordoff/Tordoff)	

C1 Team Men

1	France	14:46.05
2	Germany	14:58.12
3	Slovenia	14:58.80
6	Great Britain	15:45.77

(Singh/Pumphrey/Willacy)

C2 Team Men

1	Germany	14:11.23
2	France	14:14.26
3	Italy	14:30.59
6	Great Britain	14:56.79

(Clough/Clough+Belbin/Caunt+Simpson/Twigger)

K1 Women

1	Uschi Profanter	AUT	13:33.76
2	Karin Wirz	GER	13:48.04
3	Sabine Goetschy	FRA	13:48.66
8	Andrea Clayton	GBR	14:33.70
12	Cynthia Berry	GBR	14:44.02
14	Julie Ashton	GBR	14:52.40
18	Karen Porter	GBR	15:03.48

K1 Women Team

1	France	14:29.05
2	Germany	14:55.68
3	Great Britain	15:22.36

(Clayton/Berry/Ashton)

	G	S	B
France	4	1	2
Germany	2	3	1
Italy	1	2	2
Austria	1	-	-
Slovenia	-	1	1
Slovak Rep.	-	1	-
Great Britain	-	-	2

Marathon

World Championships

Brisbane, Australia   October 1992

Distance 45km

K1 Men

1	Ivan Lawler	GBR	3:20:23
2	Stefan Gustarsson	SWE	3:20:30
3	Rug Canilo	POR	3:20:55
7	Gregory Slater	GBR	

K2 Men

1	Australia	3:06:19.0
2	Belgium	3:06:19.9
3	Sweden	3:06:20
16	Great Britain	3:16:05

(Timbrell/Gibbins)

K1 Women

1	Susanne Gunnarsson	SWE	3:34:36
2	Ursula Profanter	AUT	3:34:53
3	Jane Hall	AUS	3:44:11
8	Alison Thorogood	GBR	3:49:15

K2 Women

1	Germany	3:31:00
2	Great Britain	3:31:00

(Troop/Blumenthal)

3	Denmark	3:31:02
8	Great Britain	

(Pagon/Bland)

C1 Canadian

1	Gabor Kulozsvari	HUN	3:49:32
2	Paul Petervari	HUN	3:49:33
3	Paul Bednar	TCH	3:49:43

C2 Canadian

1	Denmark	3:21:22
2	Hungary	3:30:38

TRAINING PARTNER

One canoeist at the World Marathon event was out training at Brisbane when he noticed he was being shadowed by a shark...Don't ever let them tell you that the waters are safe

---

Sprint Racing

World Championships

Copenhagen   Aug 25-29

MEN

K1 500m

1	Mikko Kolehmainen	FIN	1:41.96
2	Renn Crichlow	CAN	1:42.37
3	Danny Collins	AUS	1:42.67

K1 1000m

1	Knut Holmann	NOR	3:42.49
2	Thor Nielsen	DEN	3:44.13
3	Marin Popescu	ROM	3:44.70

K2 10,000

1	Thor Nielsen	DEN	42:12.07
2	Knut Holmann	NOR	42:12.81
3	Atila Szabo	SVK	42:14.41
4	Ivan Lawler	GBR	42:15.92

K2 500m

1	Bluhm/Gutsche	GER	1:32.77
2	Kurpiewski/Freimut	POL	1:33.27
3	S. De Castro/Mangas	ESP	1:34.53

K2 1000m

1	Bluhm/Gutsche	GER	3:21.80
2	Rossi/Scarpa	ITA	3:23.00
3	Sundqvist/Olsson	SWE	3:23.24

K2 10,000m

1	Borhi/Ábrahám	HUN	38:43.34
2	Sundqvist/Olsson	SWE	38:43.98
3	Toppe/Ribe	NOR	38:49.70
24	Bourne/Burns	GBR	Not end.

K4 500m

1	Denisov/Tishyenko/ Ivannik/Gorobyi	RUS	1:24.80
2	Reineck/Kegel/ Wohllebe/Von Appen	GER	1:24.83
3	Gyulay/Rehérváry/ Horváth/Ábrahám	HUN	1:25.49

K4 1000m

1	Reineck/Kegel/ Wohllebe/Von Appen	GER	3:04.80
2	Gyulay/Borhi/ Horváth/Ábrahám	HUN	3:05.11
3	Denisov/Tishyenko/ Ivannik/Gorobyi	RUS	3:07.14

K4 10,000m
1	Reineck/Kegel/ Wohllebe/Von Appen	GER	35:23.38
2	Gryczko/Markiewicz/ Freimut/Kaleta	POL	35:28.50
3	Verlin/Bobreshow/ Tsibuinikov/Galkov	RUS	35:33.75
13	Slater/Block/ Tordoff/Stuart	GBR	37:14.48

C1 500m
1	Nikolay Buhalov	BUL	1:54.02
2	György Kolonics	HUN	1:55.33
3	Steve Giles	CAN	1:56.16
9	Eric Jamieson	GBR	2:00.55

C1 1000m
1	Ivan Klementjev	LAT	4:11.20
2	Victor Partnoi	ROM	4:13.04
3	Matthias Röder	GER	4:13.25
8	Andrew Train	GBR	4:22.37

C1 10,000m
1	Zsolt Bohacs	HUN	47:11.29
2	Pavel Bednar	CZE	47:18.94
3	Andreas Dittmer	GER	47:25.99
4	Andrew Train	GBR	47:52.49

C2 500m
1	Kolonics/Horváth	HUN	1:46.40
2	Nielsson/Frederiksen	DEN	1:46.92
3	Dittmer/Kirchbach	GER	1:47.65

C2 1000m
1	Nielsson/Frederiksen	DEN	3:49.52
2	Boivin/Hoyer	FRA	3:51.22
3	Papke/Spelly	GER	3:51.64
8	Train/Train	GBR	3:56.56

C2 10,000m
1	Nielsson/Frederiksen	DEN	42:18.58
2	Train/Train	GBR	42:26.33
3	Dobrotvorskii/Balabanov	RUS	42:28.77

C4 500m
1	Boldizsár/Novak/ Hoffmann/Szabó	HUN	1:33.95
2	Kabanov/Chemerov/ Konovalov/Kostoglod	RUS	1:35.53
3	Prochazka/Dittrich/ Fibigr/Krivanek	CZE	1:35.86

C4 1000m
1	Pulai/Takács/ Bohacs/Kolonics	HUN	3:30.67
2	Konovalov/Chemerov/ Kabanov/Kostoglod	RUS	3:33.40
3	Dobrotvorskii/Osadtchii/ Kalinitchenko/Balabanov	UKR	3:33.62

WOMEN

K1 500m
1	Birgit Schmidt	GER	1:53.00
2	Anna Olsson	SWE	1:54.08
3	Caroline Brunet	CAN	1:54.72

K1 5000m
1	Susanne Gunnarsson	SWE	22:39.76
2	Rita Köbán	HUN	22:40.63
3	Birgit Schmidt	GER	22:42.91
8	Andrea Dallaway	GBR	23:43.48

K2 500m
1	Olsson/Andersson	SWE	1:48.56
2	Czigány/Mednyánszky	HUN	1:48.59
3	Portwich/Schuck	GER	1:49.56

K2 5000m
1	Portwich/Schuck	GER	21:33.51
2	Dónusz/Mészáros	HUN	21:33.73
3	Simion/Toma	ROM	21:40.32
16	Gilby/Thorogood	GBR	23:26.66

K4 500m
1	Germany	1:37.99
2	Sweden	1:38.16
3	Hungary	1:39.84

National Championships

Pierrepont   June 5-6 1993
Men

K1 500m
1	G Bourne	Elmbridge	1:52.15

K1 1000m
1	G Burns	Elmbridge	3:38.70

K1 10Km
1	G Bourne	Elmbridge	42:46

K2 500m
1	Bourne/Burns	Olympic Sq	1:45.47

K2 1000m
1	Block/Tordoff	Olympic Sq	3:25.49

K4 500m
1	Slater/Block/ Tordoff/Saunt	Wey	1:37.53

K4 1000m
1	Slater/Saunt/ Block/Tordoff	Olympic Sq	3:08.62

C1 500m
1	E Jamieson	Wey	2:06.66

C1 1000m
1	A Train	Fladbury	4:09.40

C1 10Km
1	A Train	Fladbury	47:56

C2 500m
1	Love/Crowther	Olympic Sq	2:06.10

C2 1000m
1	Train/Train	Olympic Sq	3:51.74

Women

K1 500m
1	A Dallaway	Elmbridge	1:57.87

K1 1000m
1	A Dallaway	Elmbridge	4:14.47

K1 6Km
1	A Dallaway	Elmbridge	29:19

K2 500m
1	Dallaway/Dresser	Olympic Sq	1:53.59

K2 1000m
1	Dallaway/Dresser	Olympic Sq	4:04.33

K4 500m
1	Dresser/Gilby/ Dallaway/Bennett	Olympic Sq	1:53.09

Canoe Polo
European Championships
Ponds Forge, Sheffield   July 3-5
Men
Semi-Finals
Germany 7   Holland 6
Great Britain 3   France 2

3rd/4th Play-off
France 2   Holland 1

Final
Germany 4   Great Britain 3

Women
Semi-Finals
Great Britain 5   Ireland 0
Germany 2   France 1

3rd/4th Play-off
France 3   Ireland 1

Final
Germany 10   Great Britain 9

Chess

It was the year in which chess emulated boxing; suddenly there was not just one world title, but two. The cause of the dispute, the selection by FIDE, Chess' governing body, of Manchester as venue for the world title contest between Gary Kasparov and Nigel Short. Well, it hasn't been a good year for Manchester and it missed out on this one too. Kasparov and Short claimed they weren't consulted, established their own governing body (the Professional Chess Association), which then accepted new offers for their version of the Chess World Championship. There was extra spice in the bidding when Noel Alms from Whitley, near Wigan, decided to make a bid of 10 million German marks. This excited everyone until it was pointed out the marks in question were reichmarks and 10 million of them were worth around 0.02 pence. They eventually settled on a bid from *The Times* newspaper worth £1.7m with the Savoy Hotel as the venue. In June FIDE stripped Kasparov and Short of their international ratings and decided to go ahead with a second world championship between the beaten semi-finalists from the original competition Anatoly Karpov and Jan Timman.

When Short finally got to the chess board, he probably wished he hadn't, for he began playing as if he was all too aware of our deadlines. His anxiety was compounded when his advisor Lubosh Kavalek returned to the United States, leaving Short aidless in his most needy hour. Kasparov's now-famous quote must have been ringing in his ear. When asked last year who he would face in the final, Kasparov said: "Short, and it will be short"

PCA World Championship

Savoy Hotel, London Sept
As at Oct 10
Kasparov $10^1/_2$
Short $4^1/_2$

FIDE World Championship

San Lorenzo de el Escorial, Spain   Jan
Semi-final
Best of 14 games
Nigel Short GBR $7^1/_2$
Jan Timman HOL $5^1/_2$

Spassky/Fischer

Belgrade   Oct-Nov 1992
Bobby Fischer bt Boris Spassky 10-5
Fischer collects £2.2m prize money

European Championships

Debrecen, Hungary   Nov 20-30, 1992
Men's team: Nigel Short, Jonathan Speelman, Michael Adams, John Nunn & Anthony Miles (reserve).
Women's team: Susan Arkell, Jana Bellin, Sheila Jackson (reserve)

Final Placings - Men

1	Russia	26
2	Ukraine	$22^1/_2$
3	England	$21^1/_2$
4	Israel	21
5	Lithuania	$20^1/_2$
	Sweden	$20^1/_2$
	Croatia	$20^1/_2$
	Germany	$20^1/_2$

Final Placings - Women

1	Ukraine	$13^1/_2$
2	Georgia	13
3	Azerbaijan	$12^1/_2$
4	Poland	11
	Czechoslovakia	11
6	France	$10^1/_2$
	Spain	$10^1/_2$
	Romania	$10^1/_2$
13	England	$9^1/_2$

World Junior Championship

Buenos Aires   Oct 15-30

Final Placings - Men

1 Zarnicki	ARG	10
2 Milov	ISR	10
3 Michelakis	RSA	$8^1/_2$
Danielian	ARM	$8^1/_2$
Reinderman	HOL	$8^1/_2$
Markovic	YUG	$8^1/_2$
Egger	CHI	$8^1/_2$
Rasik	TCH	$8^1/_2$

Final Placings - Women

1 Dabrowska	POL	$10^1/_2$
2 Radu	ROM	10
Ratna Sulistya	INA	10
Kadimova	AZE	10

World U14 Championship

Bratislava, Slovakia July

Final Placing

1 Ruth Sheldon	GBR	$8^1/_2$ from 11

Goodricke International

Calcutta   Feb

1 Tiviakov	RUS	9
2 Hodgson	GBR	8
3 Murshed	BAN	7
Hickl	GER	
Thipsay	IND	

Interpolis Grand Master Knock-out

Tilburg, Holland   Oct 21-28

Michael Adams GBR bt Boris Gelfand BLS

Adams wins £37,000 prize money

BCF County Championship

Birmingham   June 26

Championship

Kent 8 Essex 8

Kent win on board count

Minor

Oxfordshire 10 Bedfordshire 6

Under 150

Middlesex $12^1/_2$ **Cambridge** $7^1/_2$

Under 125

Hertfordshire 10 Lancashire 6

Leigh Interests National Club Championships

Birmingham   June 27

Open

Wood Green $3^1/_2$ Bristol & Clifton $2^1/_2$

Open Plate

Slough 3 Ilford 3

Slough win on board count

Major

Southend-on-sea 4 Southbourne 1

Major Plate

Guildford $3^1/_2$ Royal Air Force $1^1/_2$

Intermediate

Oxford University $3^1/_2$ Ipswich $1^1/_2$

Intermediate Plate

Great Lever 3 Kings Head 2

Minor

Sun Life (Bristol) 3 Great Lever 2

Minor Plate

Calderdale 3 Waltham Forest 2

Cricket

England, poor England. It wasn't just a bad year, it was no sort of year at all. Thrashed in India, walloped in Sri Lanka and roundly whopped by an Australian team that fell some way short of greatness. It was a year when a chairman of selectors was lost, a captain discarded, 24 players were used in Tests against Australia and all 16 of the tour party used in three Tests against India. Against Sri Lanka only 11 players were used, but in a single Test it's difficult to use more. To cap it all, the only Englishman who has ever seemed likely to win a Test series on his own (he almost did in 1981) I T Botham retired. *See Landmarks.*

It was also the year when a ten year old Simon Penny turned out for the Stogumber village first team and took eight wickets in eleven overs against his elders and wisers. "I'd like to play for Somerset when I grow up," said the talented youngster. An ambition that seemed modest enough. A phone call to Headingley that week could probably have earned him a greater reward.

It was at Headingley, venue for the fourth Australian Test, that England had its first real chance of a victory. Not because the wicket has renown as being difficult (only the Kensington Oval at Bridgetown, Barbados has a higher percentage of results per game), but because the electronic scoreboard bust. By the time we'd reached the fourth Test it was apparent that only a patriot in the scorebox misplacing a few hundred runs gave us any chance at all. Victory came England's way, in the final Test at The Oval, but it was hardly redemption. The Australians accepted their defeat in that sixth and final Test with good grace, which is a sure sign that they weren't bothered.

In The Year of Losing Everything, blame was everywhere, flying like sawdust off the fan. There were stomach problems in India - and not just Fat Gatt's; there was a suspected thrower in Sri Lanka (a tiny Tamil called Muralitharan) who turned the Test; and our Australian defeat was roundly ascribed by the cerebral chairman of the selectors as being a consequence of Venus being in the wrong juxtaposition with the other planets. Was Dexter being ironic? We will probably never know.

There were genuine moments of worry in the year, as when the England team arrived at Bombay for the third and final Test against India. Just two weeks earlier, the city had been riven by religious rioting and 23 people had died. New Zealand had a more frightening time in their tour of Sri Lanka in December - it preceded England's brief sojourn there by two months. During their stay in Colombo for the second Test, a bomb exploded near the team's hotel killing five people. Four of the tour party returned to New Zealand and a fifth, the captain Martin Crowe, would have joined them, but he was instructed to remain by his employers, the New Zealand Cricket Board.

At home, there were more inconsequential moments; even a near-revolution at the MCC, heaven help us, and England lost out in the bidding to host the 1996 World Cup. With a likely deadlock in the offing, England withdrew in what the MCC secretary Lt Colonel John Stephenson described as a "most magnanimous, decent and wonderful gesture". Good as that, ay?

In the Durham Senior League, England's year of misfortune was put into perspective by the even crueller blows that befell the young Seaham Harbour eleven. On a day in May and in response to a not too fearsome target of 132 set by the Gateshead Fells side, Seaham were dismissed for one run. The run came in the final over of eight and was a leg bye. Thus eleven batsmen scored nought. Ray Matthew, secretary of the League proclaimed that he had "scoured the record books and never seen anything like it."

By way of an explanation, the Seaham team, which included players as young as twelve, faced fast bowlers in the opposition team that were on the books of the County side. "Some of the lads were too terrified to bat," said the Seaham secretary Jim Dyson. "They were practically standing at square leg when the bowler came in." Just behind Graham Hick probably.

If English cricket has problems, part of the blame could be laid at the wage structure of the sport. John Emburey might have had cause to complain that after England's solitary one-day success in India his bonus for the match was just £6, but at least Embers was not surviving on the sort of payments that many of his county colleagues were. The game's minimum wage scale shows that a capped county player earns slightly more in a year than Manchester United footballer Roy Keane earns in a week. Let your son go on the stage, by all means, but don't let him take up cricket.

THAT MINIMUM WAGE SCALE	
Age	Minimum Pay(£)
19	5450
20	6005
21	6335
22	7210
23	7540
Capped Players	
1st year	11,195
2nd year	12,405

Middlesex, with the ageing Emburey very much in evidence, ran away with the Britannic Assurance County Championship. Derbyshire enjoyed a rare success in the Benson & Hedges and that followed the rarer still success in the semi-final when they beat Somerset in a bowl-off; only the third time such an expedient has been used. Derbyshire's five bowlers hit the unguarded stumps six times, Somerset's four bowlers (they didn't get as far as using the fifth) three times. It didn't need to happen like that. It was only because Somerset's captain Chris Tavare wanted a 20 over match (20 overs were completed on the first day), while Derbyshire's Kim Barnett insisted on a ten over game, that it went to a bowl off. Something wrong with the rules on that one. The AXA Equity & Law Sunday League had the happiest of all possible endings, unless you were from Kent. That county lost out on the final Sunday of the season to Glamorgan, allowing Viv Richards to depart the stage on a winning note.

Even on the domestic front, one couldn't escape the reality. At the top of the averages stood four Australians and one of those could not even find a place in the Test side. Two Englishmen followed who didn't either, Kim Barnett and Bill Athey, and then came Gooch. For all his failings as a captain, Gooch was the one player to compete on an equal footing with the world's best. In the final Test against Australia, he became England's highest run-getter of all time overtaking Gower's 8231 runs to move up to fifth on the world list. Gower, not having been selected, was obliged to watch from the sidelines.

Allan Border, so old now that he is beginning to resemble the weather vane at Lords, is the man they are all chasing. The Australian had moved to first position on the world list - ahead of new MCC member Sunil Gavaskar - when he reached 50 in an innings of 88 against the New Zealanders at Christchurch in February. Border, who will probably not return as a Test cricketer to these isles (if we are lucky) may however have a few more Tests in the tank. He could, like Bob Beamon's long jump, put the record out of reach for an awful long time.

LEADING TEST RUN SCORERS
As at 1st September 1993

	T	I	NO	Rns	HS	Av	50	100
A R Border	147	252	43	10,695	205	51.17	26	61
S M Gavaskar	125	214	16	10,122	236*	51.12	34	45
Javed Miandad	121	184	21	8689	280*	53.30	23	42
I V A Richards	121	182	12	8540	291	50.23	24	45
G A Gooch	107	194	6	8293	333	44.11	19	45
D I Gower	117	204	18	8231	215	44.25	18	39
G Boycott	108	193	23	8114	246*	47.72	22	42
G St A Sobers	93	160	21	8032	365*	57.78	26	30

GOOCH'S RECORD AGAINST EACH COUNTRY

	T	I	NO	Rns	HS	Av	50	100
Australia	37	66	0	2387	196	35.10	4	15
West Indies	26	51	2	2197	154*	44.83	5	13
New Zealand	12	20	2	925	183	51.38	3	3
India	19	33	2	1725	333	55.64	5	8
Pakistan	10	16	0	683	135	42.68	1	5
Sri Lanka	3	6	0	376	174	62.66	1	1

For Gooch, there was also the hundredth hundred. He couldn't quite contrive, like Boycott to do it at a Test match in front of his home crowd. If only because there are no Tests at Chelmsford. In fact, nobody was quite sure when he did it; the issue being in dispute because of the status of a game for the South African Breweries XI in the Republic in 1982, when Gooch was in his anti-establishment days. If that score is to be counted, then Gooch joined the elite (only 22 others have done it) in January, when he scored a century for England against the Indian U-25 team. If not, he did it in May, at Fenners, against Cambridge.

Glen Chapple's record, for the fastest ever hundred, created less controversy. Absolutely no-one took it seriously. It was one of those silly days when the bowlers spoon-feed the batsmen in order to get a target to make a game of it. Lancashire's Chapple hit his runs in 19 minutes and 27 balls and the only people to get excited were the Old Trafford scorers, Bill Davies and Byron Denning, who couldn't keep up with it. Even Lancashire couldn't get worked up as they still didn't get enough runs to fend off Glamorgan who did as much damage to their serious bowling as Chapple had done to the Mickey Mouse stuff.

In was the year in which England caught up with Australia in one sense; 15 years after Packer set the standard, English umpires also looked like milkmen. The third umpire was introduced to English cricket at The Oval in May for the Benson and Hedges match between Surrey and Lancashire. It wasn't an auspicious opening. When Allan Jones was called upon to adjudicate for the first time (Wasim Akram's possible run out) the replay that was to reveal all, showed little more than a snowy blur. Jones, presented with no evidence, was obliged to find in the batsman's favour. It was one of the few occasions of the summer when umpires did. So eager were most of them (particularly in the Tests) to raise a finger, that one was obliged to wonder if they were receiving a results bonus.

Ian Morris, a farm worker from Cornwall, had his own beef against umpiring standards. Harris, who plays for Veryan, was banned by the umpires from having a runner when playing in the County League. You are only allowed a runner, say the rules, if you are injured during the match. The ban was overturned when Morris, through The Sun newspaper, appealed to the MCC. Harris has one leg.

There were high spots in The Year of Losing Everything. Russell Quentin Cake, a Cambridge student, struck 108 for the Combined Universities against the Australians, to show it was possible. England's women gave a similar object lesson when they won the World Cup, exhibiting a relish for the game too often absent from the men's team. Jo Chamberlain won the 'Woman of the Match' award for a performance that had her likened, in the nicest possible sense, to the lately retired I T Botham.

INTERNATIONAL RESULTS
October 1992 - September 1993
West Indies v Australia 2-1
South Africa v India 1-0
Sri Lanka v New Zealand 1-0
India v England 3-0
Sri Lanka v England 1-0
New Zealand v Australia 1-1
New Zealand v Pakistan 0-1
West Indies v Pakistan 2-0
England v Australia 1-4
Sri Lanka v South Africa 0-1

OUR RANKING LIST

1 **West Indies**
2 **Australia**
3 **Pakistan**
4 **South Africa**
5 **India**
6 **New Zealand**
  Sri Lanka
8 **Anyone you care to mention**
9 **England**

In the men's game, England's ranking in world cricket can seldom have been lower. Taking the 12 months past, the major international results tell the whole story or at least enough to make us miserable. We were patriotic enough to exclude the match at Haarlem against Holland.

In a desperate search for success, scientists at the University of Hertfordshire (the old Hatfield Poly) set out to uncover at least one of the opposition's secrets. This July, they reported back that reverse swing (as used by Pakistan in 1992 against England) was explained by the following formula: $C_y \times 1/4 \times p \times p^2 \times s \div m$ where C_y is the side force coefficient, p is the air density, p is the distance the ball travels, s is the ball's surface area and m is the ball's mass. Equipped with such knowledge, England's bowlers will be able to travel to the West Indies with renewed confidence. There was only one slight drawback. To achieve the reverse swing the ball must be travelling at over 85 miles per hour. Oh dear.

The Cricketer Magazine, which organises the national village knock-out competition, took a less scientific, but still very rational approach to the problem of some people playing cricket better than others. You ban the good ones. In the village competition that meant excluding holders Hursley Park and Hambledon (*yes*, Hambledon for Heaven's sakes, where cricket itself was born).

To cheer us a little, David (Syd) Lawrence returned to the fray, if only at this stage for a cheery knockabout at Cheltenham. Syd only trundled in, but he did manage a bouncer. Dennis Compton was 75 and Gower got married and didn't invite Gooch and the England touring team for the West Indies didn't include Gooch, because he didn't want to go, and Gower, though he did.

The team is: M A Atherton (captain), A R Caddick, A R C Fraser, G A Hick, N Hussain, A P Igglesden, C C Lewis, D E Malcom, M P Maynard, M R Ramprakash, R C Russell, I D K Salisbury, R A Smith, A J Stewart, G P Thorpe, P C R Tufnell and S L Wadkin.

THE MCC EXTRAORDINARY MEETING

It was all rather soppy, yet strangely endearing that, 25 years after the Marylebone Cricket Club ceded control of the England selection policy its members convened in the Central Hall, Westminster on the 27th January to consider the motion of a hitherto unknown 60 year old businessman Dennis Olver that the members had no confidence in the England selectors. The omission of David Gower from the Indian touring side precipitated the insurrection. It was seen as symptomatic of an England hierarchy intent on spurning creative players for a "machine-like efficiency". Although emotions were raised, the debate was largely conducted in the best possible taste; the loudest cheer of the evening reserved for Olver when he announced that "we are all English....". Those in the hall supported the motion 715-412, but postal votes swayed the decision in favour of the establishment 6135-4000. There was no doubt that the divergencies of opinion over Dexter's selection policy were sincerely held, however what united the members was that for a brief while they could relive history and delude themselves that they still played a powerful and central role in English cricket. In fact, the meeting changed nothing (except perhaps the morale of the players in India). Within 24 hours, England had kicked off the Indian Test series. It was the beginning of a run of eight defeats in nine Tests.

QUOTES

"I rate our chances highly. I don't see much to worry about "
> Keith Fletcher's thoughts on India, prior to the winter tour.

"England brownwashed and spin-dried"
> *Guardian* headline after the third Test against India.

"Chris Lewis is becoming a magnificent all-rounder"
> Scyld Berry, in the *Sunday Telegraph* , reviewing the Indian tour.

"Posing with no clothes on doesn't do the game any good and there is far too much of that sort of thing going on"
> Lt Col John Stephenson, MCC secretary, after Chris Lewis posed naked in *For Women* Magazine.

"Two pints of semi-skimmed, please"
> A spectator at Lords to the umpires wearing their new blue polyester coats for the first AXA Equity & Law Sunday League match

"Spin bowling is the one area in which Graham Gooch's side should have a distinct advantage....."
> Alan Lee in *The Times* Sports Calendar, previewing the Australian tour.

"Perhaps Venus is in the wrong juxtaposition with the other planets or something"
> Ted Dexter, chairman of the selectors on England's second Test defeat.

"You 'old it like a bloody chopper and get yer arse over the crease like this"
> Arthur Wood, Yorkshire coach, as quoted by Peter O'Toole.

"Sorry mate, but you don't go on the front foot against 'Big Bird' "
> Joel Garner, playing for Glastonbury, after he hit the Watchet captain on his finger.

England v Australia (The Ashes)

1st Test

Old Trafford, Manchester   **June 3-7**

AUSTRALIA - First Innings

			Min	Bls
M A Taylor	c & b Such		124	322 234
M J Slater	c Stewart	b DeFreitas	58	165 130
D C Boon	c Lewis	b Such	21	108 90
M E Waugh	c & b Tufnell		6	40 37
A R Border*	st Stewart	b Such	17	68 54
S R Waugh		b Such	3	19 19
I A Healy†	c Such	b Tufnell	12	63 48
B P Julian	c Gatting	b Such	0	6 6
M G Hughes	c DeFreitas	b Such	2	9 12
S K Warne	not out		15	33 44
C J McDermott	run out (Lewis)		8	31 17
Extras (B8, LB8, NB7)			23	
Total (112.3 overs, 439 mins)			289	

Fall of wickets: 1-128(Slater), 2-183(Boon), 3-221(M E Waugh), 4-225(Gooch), 5-232(S R Waugh), 6-260(Border), 7-264(Julian), 8-266(Hughes), 9-267(Healy)
Bowling: Caddick 15-4-38-0, DeFreitas 23-8-46-1, Lewis 13-2-44-0, Such 33.3-9-67-6, Tufnell 28-5-78-2

ENGLAND - First Innings

			Min	Bls
G A Gooch*	c Julian	b Warne	65	184 137
M A Atherton	c Healy	b Hughes	19	100 74
M W Gatting		b Warne	4	17 12
R A Smith	c Taylor	b Warne	4	7 6
G A Hick	c Border	b Hughes	34	86 71
A J Stewart†		b Julian	27	73 49
C C Lewis	c Boon	b Hughes	9	16 12
P A J DeFreitas	lbw	b Julian	5	16 17
A R Caddick	c Healy	b Warne	7	32 23
P M Such	not out		14	45 33
P C R Tufnell	c Healy	b Hughes	1	18 22
Extras (B6, LB10, NB5)			21	
Total (74.5 overs, 306 mins)			210	

Fall of wickets: 1-71(Atherton), 2-80(Gatting), 3-84(Smith), 4-123(Gooch), 5-148(Hick), 6-168(Lewis), 7-178(DeFreitas), 8-183(Stewart), 9-203(Caddick)
Bowling: McDermott 18-2-50-0, Hughes 20.5-5-59-4, Julian 11-2-30-2, Warne 24-10-51-4, Border 1-0-4-0

AUSTRALIA - Second Innings

			Min	Bls
M J Slater	c Caddick	b Such	27	64 48
M A Taylor	lbw	b Such	9	37 26
D C Boon	c Gatting	b DeFreitas	93	323 255
M E Waugh		b Tufnell	64	136 107
A R Border*		c & b Caddick	31	131 87
S R Waugh	not out		78	192 134
I A Healy	not out		102	165 133
B P Julian				
M G Hughes				
S K Warne				
C J McDermott				
Extras (B6, LB14, W8)			28	
Total (5 wkts dec, 130 overs, 528 mins)			432	

Fall of wickets: 1-23(Taylor), 2-46(Slater), 3-155(M E Waugh), 4-234(Border), 5-252(Boon)
Bowling: Caddick 20-3-79-1, DeFreitas 24-1-80-1, Such 31-6-78-2, Tufnell 37-4-112-1, Hick 9-1-20-0, Lewis 9-0-43-0

ENGLAND - Second Innings

			Min	Bls
G A Gooch*	handled ball		133	314 217
M A Atherton	c Taylor	b Warne	25	101 72
M W Gatting		b Hughes	23	52 34
R A Smith		b Warne	18	82 65
G A Hick	c Healy	b Hughes	22	93 71
A J Stewart†	c Healy	b Warne	11	33 25
C C Lewis	c Taylor	b Warne	43	93 77
P A J DeFreitas	lbw	b Julian	7	38 26
A R Caddick	c Warne	b Hughes	25	83 74
P M Such	c Border	b Hughes	9	52 36
P C R Tufnell	not out		0	5 0
Extras (LB11, W1, NB4)			16	
Total (120.2 overs, 481 mins)			332	

Fall of wickets: 1-73(Atherton), 2-133(Gatting), 3-171(Smith), 4-223(Gooch), 5-230(Hick), 6-238(Stewart), 7-260(DeFreitas), 8-299(Lewis), 9-331(Caddick)
Bowling: McDermott 30-9-76-0, Hughes 27.2-4-92-4, Warne 49-26-86-4, Julian 14-1-67-1

Umpires: H D Bird & K E Palmer **Toss: England**
Man of the Match: **S K Warne** (Adj J P Agnew)

AUSTRALIA WON BY 179 RUNS

With nine overs remaining in the final hour, Shane Warne dived to his right and held onto a juggling catch to give Australia a deserved win. That Warne was involved was unsurprising considering that he had been the instigator of eight England wickets in a match where spinners reaped large dividends. Mike Gatting will long remember Warne's first ball of the series. Gatting groped outside leg stump. The ball struck the off stump. Australia's bowling was supplemented by Hughes who bristled in all senses. Hughes fired down short pitched balls and verbals in equal measure. Gooch alone handled Warne's guile and Hughes' gusto with equanimity. The England captain struck his 18th Test century before being given out handled ball (only the fifth man ever in Test cricket) after he instinctively knocked it away from the stumps to deny Hughes a five wicket haul. Peter Such, though, was not to be denied that landmark. In his first test he bowled with control and accuracy, to record match figures of 8 - 145. Australia's debutant opener, Michael Slater, also revelled in the occasion striking a half-century to support the phlegmatic Taylor whose hundred showed his liking for both English conditions and bowlers. Ian Healy proved what a valuable wicket-keeper/batsmen he is, rattling off a maiden unbeaten century that set up the basis for Australia's victory.

2nd Test

Lord's   **June 17-21**
AUSTRALIA - First Innings

				Mins	Bls
M A Taylor	st Stewart	b Tufnell	111	325	245
M J Slater	c sub*	b Lewis	152	297	263
D C Boon	not out		138	430	349
M E Waugh		b Tufnell	99	224	162
A R Border*		b Lewis	77	165	121
S R Waugh	not out		0	7	4
I A Healy†					
M G Hughes					
S K Warne					
C J McDermott					
T B A May					
Extras (LB1, W1, NB13)			15		
Total (4 wkts dec, 187 overs, 727 mins)			**592**		

Fall of wickets: 1-260(Slater), 2-277(Taylor), 3-452(M E Waugh), 4-591(Border).
Bowling: Caddick 34-5-109-0, **Foster** 30-4-94-0, **Such** 36-6-90-0, **Tufnell** 39-3-129-2, **Lewis** 31-4-122-2, **Gooch** 9-1-26-0, **Hick** 8-3-21-0 *sub:B F Smith (Leics)

ENGLAND - First Innings

			Min	Bls
G A Gooch*	c May	b Hughes	12	51	32
M A Atherton		b Warne	80	251	210
M W Gatting		b May	5	44	35
R A Smith	st Healy	b May	22	42	43
G A Hick	c Healy	b Hughes	20	52	39
A J Stewart†	lbw	b Hughes	3	14	14
C C Lewis	lbw	b Warne	0	4	5
N R Foster	c Border	b Warne	16	47	50
A R Caddick	c Healy	b Hughes	21	93	97
P M Such	c Taylor	b Warne	7	42	37
P C R Tufnell	not out		2	33	32
Extras (LB8, NB9)			17		
Total (99 overs, 330 mins)			**205**		

Fall of wickets: 1-33(Gooch), 2-50(Gatting), 3-84(Smith), 4-123(Hick), 5-131(Stewart), 6-132(Lewis), 7-167(Foster), 8-174(Atherton), 9-189(Such)
Bowling: Hughes 20-5-52-4, **M E Waugh** 6-1-16-0, **S R Waugh** 4-1-5-0, **May** 31-12-64-2, **Warne** 35-12-57-4, **Border** 3-1-3-0

ENGLAND - Second Innings (Following On)

			Min	Bls
G A Gooch*	c Healy	b Warne	29	91	93
M A Atherton	run out		99	240	215
M W Gatting	lbw	b Warne	59	258	223
R A Smith	c sub*	b May	5	10	14
G A Hick	c Taylor	b May	64	175	158
A J Stewart†	lbw	b May	62	172	166
C C Lewis	st Healy	b May	0	13	7
N R Foster	c M Waugh	b Border	20	89	81
A R Caddick	not out		0	22	19
P M Such		b Warne	4	16	18
P C R Tufnell		b Warne	0	1	1
Extras (B10, LB13)			23		
Total (165.5 overs, 550 mins)			**365**		

Fall of wickets: 1-71(Gooch), 2-175(Atherton), 3-180(Smith), 4-244(Gatting), 5-304(Hick), 6-312(Lewis), 7-361(Stewart), 8-361(Foster), 9-365(Such)
Bowling: Hughes 31-9-75-0, **M E Waugh** 17-0-55-0, **May** 51-23-81-4, **S R Waugh** 2-0-13-0, **Warne** 48.5-17-102-4, **Border** 16-9-16-1

Umpires:**M J Kitchen & D R Shepherd** Toss: **Australia**
Man of the Match: **M J Slater**

AUSTRALIA WON BY AN INNINGS AND 22 RUNS

Like the drowning, the England team must have seen their lives flash past them as Slater and Taylor established the tenor of the series. Their stand, of 260, was a marriage of opposites, and established the perfect platform for Boon and Mark Waugh to carry the attack to England's beleaguered bowlers. That England selected a man who dislikes bowling at Lord's (Foster) was indicative of the English approach. The net result was that Australia lost only four wickets in the course of an oh-so comfortable victory. Boon, on his third tour, recorded his first Test century in England ; that he had scored 14 Test centuries elsewhere beforehand is a measure of how long it took. Border's 77, the least significant of the completed Australian innings, nevertheless took his Test total at Lord's to 503, at an average of 100. Thereafter, the Victorian partnership of Warne and Hughes set about the English batting. McDermott being rushed off to hospital for stomach surgery proved almost incidental to the course of the match (though I'm sure not to McDermott). He was flown home to recuperate and later threatened to come back again. It was a rare act of kindness (to England) that the Australian officials didn't take up his offer. Only Atherton showed any fight, falling one short of a deserved hundred; run out as he lost his footing. The defeat was England's tenth in 14 Tests against Australia and the seventh Test defeat in succession. Only Ted Dexter could follow this with the assertion that England would win the series 4-2.

3rd Test

Trent Bridge, Nottingham **July 1-6**

ENGLAND - First Innings

				Min	Bls
M N Lathwell	c Healy	b Hughes	20	32	29
M A Atherton	c Boon	b Warne	11	76	49
R A Smith		c & b Julian	86	135	113
A J Stewart	c M Waugh	b Warne	25	78	64
G A Gooch*	c Border	b Hughes	38	100	82
G P Thorpe	c S Waugh	b Hughes	6	19	13
N Hussain	c Boon	b Warne	71	254	197
A R Caddick	lbw	b Hughes	15	122	95
M J McCague	c M Waugh	b Hughes	9	24	28
M C Ilott	c Taylor	b May	6	40	44
P M Such	not out		0	2	1
Extras (B5, LB23, W4, NB2)			34		
Total (118.4 overs, 441 mins)			321		

Fall of wickets: 1-28(Lathwell), 2-63(Atherton), 3-153(Stewart), 4-159(Smith), 5-174(Thorpe), 6-220(Gooch), 7-290(Caddick), 8-304(McCague), 9-321(Hussain)

Bowling: Hughes 31-7-95-2, Julian 24-3-84-1, Warne 40-17-74-3, May 14.4-7-31-1, S R Waugh 8-4-12-0, M E Waugh 1-1-0-0

AUSTRALIA - First Innings

				Min	Bls
M J Slater	lbw	b Caddick	40	101	76
M A Taylor	c Stewart	b McCague	28	70	49
D C Boon		b McCague	101	257	177
M E Waugh	c McCague	b Such	70	96	68
S R Waugh	c Stewart	b McCague	13	38	26
I A Healy†	c Thorpe	b Ilott	9	21	17
B P Julian	c Stewart	b Ilott	5	16	14
A R Border	c Smith	b Such	38	176	129
M G Hughes		b Ilott	17	33	19
S K Warne	not out		35	105	70
T B A May	lbw	b McCague	1	11	7
Extras (B4, LB8, W4)			16		
Total (108.3 overs, 471 mins)			373		

Fall of wickets:1-55(Taylor), 2-74(Slater), 3-197(M Waugh), 4-239(S Waugh), 5-250(Healy), 6-262(Julian), 7-284(Boon), 8-311(Hughes), 9-356(Border)

Bowling: McCague 32.3-5-121-4, Ilott 34-8-108-3, Such 20-7-51-2, Caddick 22-5-81-1

ENGLAND - Second Innings

				Min	Bls
M N Lathwell		b Warne	33	121	90
M A Atherton	c Healy	b Hughes	9	27	26
R A Smith	c Healy	b Warne	50	80	71
A J Stewart	lbw	b Hughes	6	29	30
G A Gooch*	c Taylor	b Warne	120	324	265
A R Caddick	c Boon	b Julian	12	84	76
G P Thorpe	not out		114	334	280
N Hussain	not out		47	113	102
M J McCague					
M C Ilott					
P M Such					
Extras (B11, LB11, NB9)			31		
Total (6 wkts dec, 155 overs, 562 mins)			422		

Fall of wickets:1-11(Atherton), 2-100(Smith), 3-109(Lathwell), 4-117(Stewart), 5-159(Caddick), 6-309(Gooch)

Bowling: Hughes 22-8-41-2, Julian 33-10-110-1, May 38-6-112-0, Warne 50-21-108-3, S R Waugh 1-0-3-0, Border 5-0-11-0, M E Waugh 6-3-15-0

AUSTRALIA - Second Innings

				Min	Bls
M A Taylor	c Atherton	b Such	28	94	80
M J Slater		b Such	26	58	36
D C Boon	c Stewart	b Caddick	18	92	62
M E Waugh		b Caddick	1		
A R Border	c Thorpe	b Caddick	2	13	10
S R Waugh	not out		47	196	145
I A Healy†	lbw	b Ilott	5	35	16
B P Julian	not out		56	125	104
M G Hughes					
S K Warne					
T B A May					
Extras (B5, LB5, W4, NB5)			19		
Total (6 wkts, 76 overs, 314 mins)			202		

Fall of wickets:1-46(Slater), 2-74(Taylor), 3-75(M Waugh), 4-81(Border), 5-93(Boon), 6-115(Healy)

Bowling: McCague 19-6-58-0, Ilott 18-5-44-1, Such 23-6-58-2, Caddick 16-6-32-3

Umpires: R Palmer & B J Meyer Toss: England
Man of the Match:G P Thorpe

MATCH DRAWN

Heavens above, a draw and sufficient of an uplift for the England captain to spray champagne into the crowd to celebrate. A re-vamped side even came close to snatching victory. There were English landmarks at Trent Bridge: Gooch recorded his fourth century against Australia and his first at number five; Graham Thorpe became only the third player to score a Test century on his debut in England against Australia. His illustrious forebears were Ranjitsinji in 1896 and WG Grace in 1880. There is a less illustrious comparison. Frank Hayes was England's last debut centurion and, for all his fine county batting, Hayes' England career quickly went on the slide. Hussain's 71 was equally as impressive given that he had to bat with the tail-enders and that every Somerset supporter in the crowd was wishing his demise on account that he had been favoured above Morris and Maynard by the England selectors. Hughes, glorifying in the nickname of 'Sumo', tip-toed in to great effect whilst Warne proved that he can turn a ball on any surface. They weren't the only successful Australian bowlers. Martin McCague, born in Northern Ireland but bred in Australia where, we were repeatedly assured by Australians, "he learnt all his cricket and this is how he repays us" took a useful 4-121 in the first innings. The legitimacy, or otherwise, of McCague's claim to his English heritage generated some interesting arguments, including the one that would have excluded Ted Dexter (born in India) for playing for England. It was also suggested that it might disqualify him from his present incumbency. With Australian reeling at 115-6 on the final day and England scenting victory, Julian blazed his way to a maiden first class half century whilst Waugh kept him patient company. It was enough to deny England.

4th Test

Headingley, Leeds   July 22-26
AUSTRALIA - First Innings

			Min	Bls
M J Slater		b Ilott	67	136 103
M A Taylor	lbw	b Bicknell	27	98 62
D C Boon	lbw	b Ilott	107	310 225
M E Waugh		b Ilott	52	112 75
A R Border*	not out		200	565 399
S R Waugh	not out		157	405 305
I A Healy†				
P R Reiffel				
M G Hughes				
S K Warne				
T B A May				

Extras (B8, LB22, W4, NB9)   43
Total (4 wkts dec, 193 overs, 817 mins)   653
Fall of wickets : 1-86(Taylor), 2-110(Slater), 3-216(M Waugh), 4-321(Boon)
Bowling: McCague 28-2-115-0, Ilott 51-11-161-3, Caddick 42-5-138-0, Bicknell 50-8-155-1, Gooch 16-5-40-0, Thorpe 6-1-14-0

ENGLAND - First Innings

			Min	Bls
M N Lathwell		b May	0	2 3
M A Atherton		b Reiffel	55	225 180
R A Smith	c &	b May	23	59 58
A J Stewart	c Slater	b Reiffel	5	23 22
G A Gooch*	lbw	b Reiffel	59	156 129
G P Thorpe	c Healy	b Reiffel	0	2 3
N Hussain		b Reiffel	15	31 31
A R Caddick	c M Waugh	b Hughes	9	47 44
M P Bicknell	c Border	b Hughes	12	45 32
M J McCague	c Taylor	b Warne	0	6 6
M C Ilott	not out		0	5 5

Extras (B2, LB3, NB17)   22
Total (82.5 overs, 308 mins)   200
Fall of wickets: 1-0(Lathwell), 2-43(Smith), 3-50(Stewart), 4-158(Atherton), 5-158(Thorpe), 6-169(Gooch), 7-184(Hussain), 8-195(Caddick), 9-200(McCague)
Bowling: Hughes 15.5-3-47-3, Reiffel 26-6-65-5, May 15-3-33-1, Warne 23-9-43-1, M E Waugh 3-0-7-0

ENGLAND - Second Innings (Following on)

			Min	Bls
M N Lathwell		b May	25	98 78
M A Atherton	st Healy	b May	63	204 171
R A Smith	lbw	b Reiffel	35	126 120
A J Stewart†	c M Waugh	b Reiffel	78	155 125
G A Gooch*	st Healy	b May	26	63 40
G P Thorpe	c Taylor	b Reiffel	13	62 47
N Hussain	not out		18	113 96
A R Caddick	lbw	b Hughes	12	58 48
M P Bicknell	lbw	b Hughes	0	1 1
M J McCague		b Hughes	11	22 24
M C Ilott	c Border	b May	4	20 23

Extras (B5, LB3, W1, NB11)   20
Total (127 overs, 468 mins)   305
Fall of wickets: 1-60(Lathwell), 2-131(Atherton), 3-149(Smith), 4-202(Gooch), 5-256(Thorpe), 6-263(Stewart), 7-279(Caddick), 8-279(Bicknell), 9-295(McCague)
Bowling: Hughes 30-10-79-3 Reiffel 28-8-87-3 Warne 40-16-63-0 May 27-6-65-4 M E Waugh 2-1-3-0

Umpires: H D Bird & N T Plews Toss: Australia
Man of the Match: A R Border

AUSTRALIA WON BY AN INNINGS AND 148 RUNS

Headingley, scene of some of England's most memorable triumphs, hosted a calamity. If the ghost of 1981 was watching, it was with tears in his eyes. On an easy paced pitch and for the second time in the series, six Australian batsmen compiled a score that England couldn't match with 22. Boon, having scored one Test century in England, found his second simple pie. Waugh and Border it was, though, who put the match beyond England with an unbroken stand of 332, the Australian captain reaching only the second double-century of his career. When England batted, the pitch that had been docile and domesticated became savage and unruly. Reiffel, replacing the injured Julian, looked for the first time on the tour a bowler of menace. He took the heart out of the English batting when he removed Atherton, Thorpe, Gooch and Hussain, in that order, with just 26 runs added to the score. Atherton and Gooch, alone, showed any resistance, but neither could convert a useful innings into a good one. The second innings was marginally better. Stewart finally played an innings of substance and can count himself unfortunate to lose his wicket to an extraordinary catch by Mark Waugh at second slip. It was certainly the catch of the series, quite probably the catch of the season, and maybe the catch of the decade. England could be excused for thinking, at this point, that the Gods too were against them. However, it was not the Gods who decided to select four medium pacers (a fifth, if you count Gooch) as England's only attacking option. It was tactical suicide and, as an honourable captain should, Gooch fell upon his sword shortly after Hughes had wiped up the tail of England's second innings. Gooch's spell as captain, which had begun so well, ended disastrously with this defeat making it eight losses and one draw in the last nine Tests.

5th Test

Edgbaston, Birmingham   **Aug 5-9**

ENGLAND - First Innings

			Min	Bls
G A Gooch	c Taylor	b Reiffel	8	24	20
M A Atherton*		b Reiffel	72	193	157
R A Smith		b M E Waugh	21	66	59
M P Maynard	c S R Waugh	b May	0	11	9
A J Stewart†		c & b Warne	45	83	82
G P Thorpe	c Healy	b May	37	77	53
N Hussain		b Reiffel	3	7	10
J E Emburey	not out		55	160	152
M P Bicknell	c M Waugh	b Reiffel	14	66	59
P M Such		b Reiffel	1	2	3
M C Ilott	c Healy	b Reiffel	3	22	16
Extras (B4, LB6, NB7)			17		
Total (101.5 overs, 364 mins)			321		

Fall of wickets: 1-17(Gooch), 2-71(Smith), 3-76(Maynard), 4-156(Stewart), 5-156(Atherton), 6-160(Hussein), 7-215(Thorpe), 8-262(Bicknell), 9-264(Such)

Bowling: Hughes 19-4-53-0, **Reiffel** 22.5-3-71-6, **M E Waugh** 15-5-43-1, **S R Waugh** 5-2-4-0, **May** 19-9-32-2, **Warne** 21-7-63-1

AUSTRALIA - First Innings

			Min	Bls
M A Taylor	run out(Maynard/Stewart)		19	122	80
M J Slater	c Smith	b Such	22	73	60
D C Boon	lbw	b Emburey	0	10	13
M E Waugh	c Thorpe	b Ilott	137	239	219
A R Border*	c Hussein	b Such	3	9	9
S R Waugh	c Stewart	b Bicknell	59	230	175
I A Healy†	c Stewart	b Bicknell	80	141	107
M G Hughes		b Bicknell	38	142	102
P R Reiffel		b Such	20	108	89
S K Warne	c Stewart	b Emburey	10	43	30
T B A May	not out		3	23	17
Extras (B7, LB8, NB2)			17		
Total (149.5 overs, 579 mins)			408		

Fall of wickets: 1-34(Slater), 2-39(Boon), 3-69(Taylor), 4-80(Border), 5-233(M E Waugh), 6-263(S R Waugh), 7-370(Healy), 8-379(Hughes), 9-389(Warne)

Bowling: Bicknell 34-9-99-3, **Ilott** 24-4-85-1, **Such** 52.5-18-90-3, **Emburey** 39-9-119-2

Umpires: J H Hampshire & D R Shepherd   Toss: England
Man of the Match: **M E Waugh**

ENGLAND - Second Innings

			Min	Bls
G A Gooch		b Warne	48	178	150
M A Atherton*	c Border	b Warne	28	89	66
R A Smith	lbw	b Warne	19	69	70
M P Maynard	c Healy	b May	10	13	15
A J Stewart†		c & b Warne	5	21	26
G P Thorpe	st Healy	b Warne	60	235	192
N Hussain	c S R Waugh	b May	0	4	7
J E Emburey	c Healy	b May	37	200	191
M P Bicknell	c S R Waugh	b May	0	1	2
P M Such	not out		7	50	42
M C Ilott		b May	15	44	41
Extras (B11, LB9, NB2)			22		
Total (6 wkts dec, 155 overs, 562 mins)			251		

Fall of wickets: 1-60(Atherton), 2-104(Smith), 3-115 (Maynard), 4-115(Gooch), 5-124(Stewart), 6-125(Hussain), 7-229(Emburey), 8-229(Bicknell), 9-229(Thorpe)

Bowling: Hughes 18-7-24-0, **Reiffel** 11-2-30-0, **May** 48.2-15-89-5, **Warne** 49-23-82-5, **Border** 2-1-1-0, **M E Waugh** 5-2-5-0

AUSTRALIA - Second Innings

			Min	Bls
M J Slater	c Thorpe	b Emburey	8	43	41
M A Taylor	c Thorpe	b Such	4	35	24
D C Boon	not out		38	112	109
M E Waugh	not out		62	104	87
A R Border*					
S R Waugh					
I A Healy†					
B P Julian					
M G Hughes					
S K Warne					
T B A May					
Extras (B3, LB5)			8		
Total (2 wkts, 43.3 overs, 149 mins)			120		

Fall of wickets: 1-12(Taylor), 2-12(Slater)

Bowling: Bicknell 3-0-9-0, **Such** 20.3-4-58-1, **Emburey** 18-4-31-1, **Ilott** 2-0-14-0

AUSTRALIA WON BY EIGHT WICKETS

To lose one leader is unfortunate, to lose two.... Well, no sooner had Gooch's head rolled than Dexter's toppled after. It wasn't so much a resignation as the promise of a resignation. It came at a curious moment, when England were fighting a backs-to-the-wall attempt to salvage something from the match in Australia's second innings. It couldn't have done much for the team's morale and they quickly wilted as Australia punched off the remaining runs, but it did cheer up the Edgbaston crowd, which spontaneously applauded when the resignation was announced on Radio 3 by Jonathan Agnew. The match could not have greatly heartened the new English captain, Michael Atherton, who appeared to have inherited not only the mantle of captaincy, but the mood of despondency. In England's first innings, Reiffel repeated the message from Headingley, moving the ball sufficiently off the seam to collect a fine 6-71. In England's second innings, it was the spinners who regained control. Turning the ball prodigiously in the bowlers' footmarks, Warne even achieved the not inconsiderable feat of bowling Gooch from a ball that pitched behind his legs. Emburey alone countered the leg-spinner effectively. The 41 year old off-spinner became the mainstay of the batting by the simple expedient of turning face-on to every ball that pitched outside of leg and double-padding-up. It was not a pretty sight, but it did protect his wicket. The net result was that Emburey became England's third highest run-getter in the match. Even so, the Australia victory was comfortable enough. Mark Waugh was the man of the match and it wasn't a difficult decision. Waugh hit 137 in the first innings and 62 not out in the second. The latter performance quelling any remaining optimism (most of it emanating from the England team manager Keith Fletcher) that England were still in with a shout on the final day.

6th Test

The Oval, London   **Aug 19-23**

ENGLAND - First Innings

			Min	Bls
G A Gooch	c Border	b S R Waugh	56	90	66
M A Atherton*		b Reiffel	72	193	157
G A Hick	c Warne	b May	80	141	107
M P Maynard		b Warne	20	36	34
N Hussain	c Taylor	b Warne	30	61	54
A J Stewart†	c Healy	b Hughes	76	117	94
M Ramprakash	c Healy	b Hughes	6	22	22
A R C Fraser		b Reiffel	28	140	92
S L Watkin	c S R Waugh	b Reiffel	13	38	32
P M Such	c M Waugh	b Hughes	4	22	27
D E Malcolm	not out		0	2	0
Extras (LB7, W1, NB9)			17		
Total (101.5 overs, 420 mins)			380		

Fall of wickets: 1-88(Gooch), 2-143(Atherton), 3-177 (Maynard), 4-231(Hick), 5-253(Hussain), 6-272(Ramprakash), 7-339(Stewart), 8-363(Watkin), 9-374(Such)

Bowling: Hughes 30-7-121-2, Reiffel 28.5-4-88-2, **S R Waugh** 12-2-45-2, **Warne** 20-5-70-2, M E Waugh 1-0-17-0, **May** 10-3-32-1

ENGLAND - Second Innings

			Min	Bls
G A Gooch	c Healy	b Warne	79	226	183
M A Atherton*	c Warne	b Reiffel	42	81	62
G A Hick	c Boon	b May	36	95	74
M P Maynard	c Reffeil	b Hughes	9	28	21
N Hussain	c M Waugh	b Hughes	0	1	1
A J Stewart†		c & b Warne	5	21	26
M Ramprakash	c Slater	b Hughes	64	243	184
A R C Fraser	c Healy	b Reiffel	13	52	42
S L Watkin	lbw	b Warne	4	5	4
P M Such	lbw	b Warne	10	54	41
D E Malcolm	not out		0	4	4
Extras (B5, LB12, W1, NB3)			21		
Total (119.2 overs, 470 mins)			313		

Fall of wickets: 1-77(Atherton), 2-157(Hick), 3-180(Maynard). 4-180(Hussain), 5-186(Gooch), 6-254(Stewart), 7-276(Fraser), 8-283(Watkin), 9-313(Such)

Bowling: Hughes 31.2-9-110-3, **Reiffel** 24-8-55-3, **Warne** 40-15-78-3, May 24-6-53-1

AUSTRALIA - First Innings

			Min	Bls
M A Taylor	c Hussain	b Malcolm	70	180	134
M J Slater	c Gooch	b Malcolm	4	11	7
D C Boon	c Gooch	b Malcolm	13	32	23
M E Waugh	c Stewart	b Fraser	10	38	26
A R Border*	c Stewart	b Fraser	48	162	107
S R Waugh		b Fraser	20	37	36
I A Healy†	not out		83	187	117
M G Hughes	c Rampra'sh	b Watkin	7	25	25
P R Reiffel	c Maynard	b Watkin	0	2	3
S K Warne	c Stewart	b Fraser	16	58	45
T B A May	c Stewart	b Fraser	15	66	50
Extras (B5, LB6, W2, NB4)			17		
Total (94.4 overs, 408 mins)			408		

Fall of wickets: 1-9(Slater), 2-30(Boon), 3-53(MWaugh), 4-132(Taylor), 5-164(S R Waugh), 6-181(Border), 7-196(Hughes), 8-196(Reiffel), 9-248(Warne)

Bowling: Malcolm 26.5-86-3, **Watkin** 28-4-87-2, Fraser 26.4-4-87-5, Such 14-4-32-0

AUSTRALIA - Second Innings

			Min	Bls
M J Slater	c Stewart	b Watkin	12	32	25
M A Taylor		b Watkin	8	47	29
D C Boon	lbw	b Watkin	0	1	1
M E Waugh	c Rampra'sh	b Malcolm	49	118	75
A R Border*	c Stewart	b Malcolm	17	90	73
S R Waugh	lbw	b Malcolm	26	100	81
I A Healy†	c Maynard	b Watkin	5	7	10
M G Hughes	c Watkin	b Fraser	12	86	68
P R Reiffel		c & b Fraser	42	74	59
S K Warne	lbw	b Fraser	37	82	63
T B A May	not out		4	15	14
Extras (B2, LB6, W2, NB7)			17		
Total (81.1 overs, 334 mins)			229		

Fall of wickets: 1-23(Slater), 2-23(Boon), 3-30(Taylor), 4-92(Border), 5-95(M Waugh), 6-106(Healy), 7-142(S R Waugh) 8-143(Hughes), 9-217(Reiffel)

Bowling: Malcolm 20-3-84-3, **Watkin** 25-9-65-4, Fraser 19.1-5-44-3, Such 9-4-17-0, Hick 8-3-11-0

Umpires: **M J Kitchen & B J Meyer** Toss: **England**
Man of the Match: **M E Waugh**

ENGLAND WON BY 161 RUNS
Men of the Series: **S K Warne & G A Gooch**

Due to fly home the following day, the Australians gave a good impression of a team putting their seats in the upright position. Boon, whose decline in form was sudden and alarming, was probably even contemplating another record attempt on the drinks trolley. If they didn't look like the team that had cakewalked four of the last five Tests, we should nevertheless give credit to a rejigged England team which did not resemble the one that had been cakewalked over. Malcolm showed that when his radar is in good working order he is to be feared; Fraser, back after his hip injury, was as difficult to play as he ever was; and Watkin took the three wickets in six balls that precipitated the Australian second innings fall. Only a spirited resistance from Healy, Reiffel and Warne stopped the English victory looking like so many Australian ones. The English batsmen, while not exactly clutching the mantle of greatness, could count up a few successes. Mark Ramprakash, due to play for Middlesex against Northants at Lords this weekend, moved across the river to the Oval when Graham Thorpe broke his thumb. Ramprakash, whose England career till then had been rather more straw than substance, made a brick of some significance with his innings of 64. Stewart compiled a useful 76 before being dubiously caught (see also Fraser, Border and Slater who had good arguments on this score). Hick played the innings of the match, didn't look at all uncomfortable against Hughes and reawakened thoughts of the days when he looked about to have greatness thrust upon him. What it will all mean in the months to come on the bony pitches of the West Indies is another matter. For the time being it was enough to enjoy the first victory over Australia since 1986.

England v Australia (Texaco Trophy)

1st One-Day International　　　Old Trafford　　　May 19, 1993

AUSTRALIA				min	ball
M L Hayden	c Stewart	b Lewis	29	61	55
M A Taylor	c Fairbrother	b Illingworth	79	162	126
M E Waugh	c Fairbrother	b Jarvis	56	80	63
D C Boon	c Fairbrother	b Illingworth	2	4	6
A R Border *	c Lewis	b Illingworth	4	20	14
S R Waugh		c &b Lewis	27	42	30
I A Healy†	c Thorpe	b Caddick	20	20	21
M G Hughes	b Lewis		20	24	13
P R Reiffel	run out (Stewart)		2	7	3
C J McDermott	not out		3	3	2
T B A May	not out		1	1	1
Extras (B1, LB8, W2, NB4)			15		
Total (9wkts, 55 overs, 220 minutes)			258		

Fall of wickets: 1-60(Hayden), 2-168(M Waugh), 3-171 (Boon), 4-178(Taylor), 5-186(Border), 6-219(Healy), 7-237 (S Waugh), 8-255(Reiffel), 9-255(Hughes)

Bowling: **Caddick** 11-1-50-1, **Pringle** 10-3-36-0, **Lewis** 11-1-54-3, **Jarvis** 11-0-55-1, **Illingworth** 11-0-48-3, 1-0-6-0

Umpires: **B J Meyer, D R Shepherd** Toss: **England**

Match Award:**C J McDermott** (Adj:A V Bedser)

ENGLAND				min	ball
G A Gooch *	c M Waugh	b McDermott	4	12	14
A J Stewart †	b Hughes		22	37	20
R A Smith		c & b McDermott	9	38	26
G A Hick	b Reiffel		85	143	102
N H Fairbrother	c Reiffel	b S Waugh	59	102	89
G P Thorpe	c Taylor	b McDermott	31	65	38
C C Lewis	run out (S Waugh)		4	14	12
D R Pringle	c Taylor	b S Waugh	6	11	10
R K Illingworth	run out (Healy/Hughes)		12	25	14
P W Jarvis	c Reiffel	b S Waugh	2	7	4
A R Caddick	not out		1	5	4
Extras (LB8, W9, NB2)			19		
Total (54.5 overs, 238 minutes)			254		

Fall of wickets:1-11(Gooch), 2-38(Stewart), 3-44(Smith), 4-171(Fairbrother), 5-194(Hick), 6-211(Lewis), 7-227(Pringle), 8-240(Thorpe), 9-247(Jarvis)

Bowling: **McDermott** 11-2-38-3, **Hughes** 9.5-1-40-1, **May** 11-2-40-0, **Reiffel** 11-0-63-1, **M Waugh** 2-0-12-0, **S Waugh** 10-0-53-3

AUSTRALIA WON BY 4 RUNS

Australia ultimately had to wait until the final over to clinch a victory that had looked likely from the beginning of the England innings, when McDermott was both run-restrictive and penetrative. Hick and Fairbrother gave England the brief odour of victory, if not the full scent, but they finally faltered in the run chase when Illingworth and Caddick found themselves at the same end and the ball in Healy's gloves at the other. The Australians had earlier enjoyed themselves at the expense of the English seamers. The exception was Pringle whose ungainly style (and eccentric fielding) made him something of a crowd favourite. He alone stemmed the flow of runs. After lunch, the Australians faltered when Illingworth was added to the attack and took three key wickets, but they had already done enough.

2nd One-Day International　　　Edgbaston　　　May 21, 1993

ENGLAND					
G A Gooch *	c Healy	b McDermott	17	57	49
A J Stewart †	b McDermott		0	11	5
R A Smith	not out		167	207	163
N H Fairbrother	c Taylor	b S Waugh	23	50	45
G P Thorpe	c Border	b McDermott	36	76	63
C C Lewis	not out		13	11	9
Extras (B2, LB4, W2, NB11)			19		
Total (5 wickets, 55 overs, 220 minutes)			277		

Did not bat: D R Pringle, D G Cork, P W Jarvis, A R Caddick

Fall of wickets: 1-3(Stewart), 2-40(Gooch), 3-55(Hick), 4-105(Fairbrother), 5-247(Thorpe)

Bowling: **McDermott** 11-1-29-3, **Hughes** 11-2-51-0, **Reiffel** 11-1-70-1, **May** 11-0-45-0, **S Waugh** 8-0-55-1, **M Waugh** 3-0-21-0

Umpires: **M J Kitchen, K E Palmer** Toss: **Australia**

Match award:**R A Smith** (Adj:Sir Richard Hadlee)

AUSTRALIA					
M A Taylor	b Lewis		26	68	47
M L Hayden	b Jarvis		14	38	30
M E Waugh	c Fairbrother	b Lewis	113	167	122
D C Boon	c Stewart	b Pringle	21	29	29
A R Border *	not out		86	116	97
S R Waugh	not out		6	7	3
Extras (LB5, W3, NB6)			14		
Total (4 wickets, 53.5 overs, 215 minutes)			280		

Did not bat: I A Healy †, M G Hughes, C J McDermott, P R Reiffel, T B A May.

Fall of wickets: 1-28(Hayden), 2-55(Taylor), 3-95(Boon), 4-263(M Waugh)

Bowling: **Caddick** 11-1-43-0, **Jarvis** 10-1-51-1, **Lewis** 10.3-0-61-2, **Pringle** 11-0-63-1, **Cork** 11-1-57-0

AUSTRALIA WON BY 6 WICKETS

Mark Waugh's classy century and the punchy 86 contributed by his captain Border (off of just 97 balls) were enough to ensure that Australia took the second match of the series to take their first one-day series win in this country in eight attempts. But the Australian success could not dull the shine of the innings which dominated the match. Robin Smith brutalised the Australian bowling, aggregating 167 runs off just 163 balls. For sheer ferocity it ranks alongside Viv Richards' virtuoso performance at Old Trafford in 1984. The fact that McDermott could return figures of 3-29 while those around him were laid waste by the Hampshire batsmen was the highest compliment to the West Australian. Smith's Herculean efforts, however, were to no avail. Even Border was moved enough to offer praise. "If it is not the best one-day innings ever, it is certainly in the grand final," he acknowledged.

3rd One-Day International   Lord's   May 23, 1993

AUSTRALIA				min	ball
M L Hayden	c Stewart	b Caddick	4	22	19
M A Taylor	c Stewart	b Reeve	57	154	104
M E Waugh	c Stewart	b Caddick	14	24	23
D C Boon	b Illingworth		73	145	125
D R Martyn	not out		51	62	43
S R Waugh	c Gooch	b Caddick	8	10	9
I A Healy	not out		12	9	10
Extras (LB3, W6, NB2)			11		
Total (5 wickets, 55 overs, 218 minutes)			230		

Fall of wickets: 1-12(Hayden), 2-31(M Waugh), 3-139(Taylor), 4-193(Boon), 5-208(S Waugh)

Bowling: **Jarvis** 11-1-51-0, **Caddick** 11-3-39-3, **Cork** 9-2-24-0, **Illingworth** 10-0-46-1, **Reeve** 11-1-50-1, **Hick** 3-0-17-0

Umpires: H D Bird, R Palmer   Toss: England

Match Award: B P Julian (Adj:Sir Colin Cowdrey)

AUSTRALIA WON BY 19 RUNS

ENGLAND				min	ball
G A Gooch	c Hughes	b May	42	95	77
A J Stewart	c M Waugh	b Julian	74	172	119
R A Smith	st Healy	b May	6	23	22
G A Hick	b Julian		7	17	13
N H Fairbrother	c Boon	b Julian	18	28	25
G P Thorpe	c Healy	b S Waugh	22	40	24
D A Reeve	run out(S Waugh/Julian)		2	8	8
D G Cork	b Hughes		9	17	10
R K Illingworth	c Healy	b Hughes	9	17	10
P W Jarvis	c Hayden	b McDermott	3	7	5
A R Caddick	not out		2	2	1
Extras (LB6, W8, NB1)			15		
Total (53.1 overs, 223 minutes)			211		

Fall of wickets: 1-96(Gooch), 2-115(Smith), 3-129(Hick), 4-159(Fairbrother), 5-160(Stewart), 6-169(Reeve), 7-195(Cork), 8-201(Thorpe), 9-208(Jarvis)

Bowling: **McDermott** 10-1-35-1, **Hughes** 10.1-0-41-2, **Julian** 11-1-50-3, **May** 11-1-36-2, **S Waugh** 11-0-43-1

England all but handed the Australians the clean sweep on a platter. At tea, needing 127 runs at just four an over and with nine wickets remaining, William Hill would have offered respectable odds against an Australian win. But someone somewhere waved a wand. Julian, who had looked dreadful in his first spell, returned to take three key wickets and claim (perhaps a mite fortuitously) the man-of-the-match award. The England tail, which began at number three on this occasion, offered scant resistance and that was that. Caddick could feel a touch aggrieved. The Somerset bowler had contributed a tidy early spell removing both Hayden and Waugh for nominal sums. The England players, though, learnt one critical lesson. In this Australian team, failure is not contagious. Quite the opposite.

One Day Internationals - Career Records

ENGLAND

Batting	M	In	NO	HS	Runs	Avge	100	50
R A Smith	58	57	8	167*	2068	42.20	4	12
N H Fairbrother	40	38	8	113	1204	40.13	1	9
G A Hick	32	31	5	105*	1038	39.92	1	9
G A Gooch	120	117	6	142	4206	37.89	8	23
D A Reeve	24	16	9	33*	225	32.14	-	-
A J Stewart	51	46	4	103	1278	30.43	1	8
G P Thorpe	3	3	-	36	89	29.67	-	-
D R Pringle	44	30	12	49*	425	23.61	-	-
R K Illingworth	18	7	2	14	61	12.20	-	-
C C Lewis	4	29	8	33	251	11.95	-	-
D G Cork	3	1	-	9	9	9.00	-	-
P W Jarvis	16	8	2	16*	31	5.17	-	-
A R Caddick	3	2	2	2*	3	-	-	-

Bowling	O	R	W	Avge	Best	4w	R/Over
P W Jarvis	146.3	672	24	28.00	5-35	2	4.59
R K Illingworth	182.1	760	24	31.67	3-33	-	4.18
C C Lewis	319.1	1412	45	31.37	4-30	2	4.42
A R Caddick	33	132	4	33.00	1-50	-	4.00
D A Reeve	157.3	671	18	37.28	3-20	-	4.26
D R Pringle	396.3	1677	44	38.11	4-42	1	4.22
G A Gooch	326.2	1436	36	39.88	3-19	-	4.40
G A Hick	37	191	4	47.75	2- 7	-	5.16
D G Cork	31	118	1	118.00	1-37	-	3.81

AUSTRALIA

Batting	M	In	NO	HS	Runs	Avge	100	50
D C Boon	142	138	10	122	4524	35.34	5	26
M A Taylor	43	42	-	94	1380	32.86	-	13
M E Waugh	54	50	3	113	1485	31.60	2	11
A R Border	255	237	36	127*	6171	30.70	3	38
S R Waugh	147	130	33	83*	2916	30.06	2	11
P R Reiffel	18	12	9	23*	79	26.33	-	-
M L M Hayden	3	3	-	29	47	15.67	-	-
I A Healy	91	58	18	50*	786	19.65	-	1
D R Martyn	8	7	1	51*	136	22.67	-	1
M G Hughes	33	17	8	20	100	11.11	-	-
C J McDermott	104	65	15	37	373	7.46	-	-
T B A May	25	7	4	15	22	7.33	-	-
B P Julian	1	-	-	-	-	-	-	-

Bowling	O	R	W	Avge	Best	4w	R/Over
B P Julian	11	50	3	16.67	3-50	-	4.55
M E Waugh	137	655	30	21.83	5-24	2	4.78
C J McDermott	941.1	3862	155	24.92	5-44	5	4.10
P R Reiffel	165	641	25	25.64	4-38	1	3.88
M G Hughes	273.1	1115	38	29.34	4-44	1	4.08
A R Border	407.4	1935	65	29.76	3-20	-	4.74
S R Waugh	997.3	4448	141	31.55	4-33	2	4.46
T B A May	214.2	940	19	49.47	3-51	-	4.39
D C Boon	4.4	41	0	-	0-41	-	8.77

Tetley Bitter Challenge

AUSTRALIA V WORCESTER
Worcester   May 5-7
Australia   262 (Boon 108)
                   287-5 (Boon 105)
Worcester   90
                   458-4 dec (Hick 187)
Australia won by 5 wickets

AUSTRALIA V SOMERSET
Taunton   May 8-10
Australia   431 (Slater 122)
                   40-0 dec
Somerset   151-4 dec
                   285
Australia won by 35 runs

AUSTRALIA V SUSSEX
Hove   May 13-15
Sussex   353
                   92-4
Australia   490-5 dec (Martyn 135, S Waugh 124)
Match Drawn

AUSTRALIA V SURREY
Oval   May 25-27
Australia   378-9 dec (M Waugh 178)
                   171-4 dec
Surrey   231
                   144
Australia won by 174 runs

AUSTRALIA V LEICESTERSHIRE
Leicester   May 29-31
Australia   323-3 dec (Boon 123)
                   88-4 dec
Leicester   158-7 dec
                   146
Australia won by 57 runs

AUSTRALIA V WARWICKSHIRE
Edgbaston   June 9-11
Australia   317-7 (Martyn 116)
Warwicks   184-8
Match Abandoned

AUSTRALIA V GLOUCESTER
Bristol   June 12-14
Gloucester   211
Australia   400
Match Abandoned

AUSTRALIA V HAMPSHIRE
Southampton   June 26-28
Australia   393-7 (Boon 146)
                   271-7 dec (Hayden 115)
Hampshire   374-5 dec (Smith 191)
                   220-5
Match Drawn

AUSTRALIA V DERBYSHIRE
Derby   July 13-15
Derbyshire   305 (Barnett 114)
Australia   258-1 (Slater 133*)
Match Drawn

AUSTRALIA V DURHAM
Durham University July 17-19
Durham   385-8 dec (Larkins 151)
Australia   221 (Brown 7-70)
                   295-3 dec (Hayden 151, Boon 112)
Match Drawn

AUSTRALIA V LANCASHIRE
Old Trafford   July 28-30
Australia   282-3 dec (Taylor 122)
                   194-8 dec
Lancashire   250-7 dec
                   228-5
Lancashire won by 5 wickets

AUSTRALIA V GLAMORGAN
Neath   July 31-Aug 2
Australia   414-4 dec (Bonn 120, M Waugh 152*)
                   235-7 dec
Glamorgan   353-8 dec (Maynard 132)
                   169-5
Match Drawn

AUSTRALIA V KENT
Canterbury   Aug 11-13
Australia   391-4 dec (S Waugh 123, Martyn 105*)
                   34-0 dec
Kent   114-2 dec
                   222
Australia won by 89 runs

AUSTRALIA V ESSEX
Chelmsford   Aug 14-16
Australia   357-5 dec (Hayden 111, M Waugh 108)
                   218
Essex   268
                   277-9 (Knight 87)
Match Drawn

Other Matches (One-day)

AUSTRALIA V ENGLAND AMATEUR XI
Australia won by 94 runs

AUSTRALIA V DUCHESS OF NORFOLK'S XI
Australia won by 7 runs

AUSTRALIA V MIDDLESEX
Australia won by 69 runs

AUSTRALIA V NORTHAMPTONSHIRE
Northant won on faster scoring rate

AUSTRALIA V COMBINED UNIVERSITIES
Australia won by 58 runs

AUSTRALIA V IRELAND
Australia won by 272 runs

Ashes Test Averages

AUSTRALIA

Batting	M	In	NO	HS	Runs	Avge	100	50
S R Waugh	6	9	4	157*	416	83.20	1	2
D C Boon	6	10	2	164*	555	69.37	3	1
M E Waugh	6	10	1	137	550	61.11	1	5
I A Healy	6	7	2	102*	296	59.20	1	2
A R Border	6	9	1	200*	433	54.12	1	1
M A Taylor	6	10	0	124	428	42.80	2	1
M J Slater	6	10	0	152	416	41.60	1	2
S K Warne	6	5	2	37	113	37.66	-	-
B P Julian	2	3	1	56*	61	30.50	-	1
P R Reiffel	3	3	0	42	62	20.66	-	-
M G Hughes	6	5	0	38	76	15.20	-	-
T B A May	5	4	2	15	23	11.50	-	-
C J McDermott	2	1	0	8	8	8.00	-	-

Catches: Healy 21 (5 st); Taylor 11; M Waugh 9; Border 8; S Waugh & Boon 5; Warne 4; Slater, Julian & May 2; Reiffel 1.

Bowling	O	M	R	W	Avge	Best	R/Over
P R Reiffel	140.4	31	396	19	20.84	6-71	2.81
S K Warne	439.5	178	877	34	25.79	5-82	1.99
M G Hughes	296.2	78	845	31	27.25	5-92	2.85
T B A May	278	90	592	21	28.19	5-89	2.12
A R Border	27	11	35	1	35.00	1-16	1.29
S R Waugh	32	9	82	2	41.00	2-45	2.56
B P Julian	82	16	291	5	58.20	2-30	3.54
M E Waugh	56	17	161	1	161.00	1-43	2.87
C J McDermott	48	11	126	0	-	-	2.62

ENGLAND

Batting	M	In	NO	HS	Runs	Avge	100	50
J E Emburey	1	2	1	55*	92	92.00	-	1
G A Gooch	6	12	0	133	673	56.08	2	4
M A Atherton	6	12	0	99	553	46.08	-	6
G P Thorpe	3	6	1	114	230	46.00	1	1
G A Hick	3	6	0	80	256	42.66	-	2
M R Ramprakash	1	2	0	64	70	35.00	-	1
A J Stewart	6	12	0	78	378	31.50	-	3
N Hussain	4	8	2	71	184	30.66	-	1
R A Smith	5	10	0	86	283	28.30	-	2
M W Gatting	2	4	0	59	91	22.75	-	1
A R C Fraser	1	2	0	28	41	20.50	-	-
M N Lathwell	2	4	0	33	78	19.50	-	-
N A Foster	1	2	0	20	36	18.00	-	-
A R Caddick	4	8	1	25	101	14.42	-	-
C C Lewis	2	4	0	43	52	13.00	-	-
M P Maynard	2	4	0	20	39	9.75	-	-
P M Such	5	9	3	14*	56	9.33	-	-
S L Watkin	1	2	0	13	17	8.50	-	-
M C Ilott	3	5	1	15	28	7.00	-	-
M J McCague	2	3	0	11	20	6.66	-	-
M P Bicknell	2	4	0	14	26	6.50	-	-
P A J DeFreitas	1	2	0	7	12	6.00	-	-
P C R Tufnell	2	4	2	2*	3	1.50	-	-
D E Malcolm	1	2	2	0*	0	-	-	-

Catches: Stewart 14 (2 st); Thorpe 5; Caddick, Gatting, Gooch, Hussain, Maynard, Ramprakash, Smith & Such 2; Atherton, DeFreitas, Fraser, Lewis, McCague, Tufnell & Watkin 1.

Bowling	O	M	R	W	Avge	Best	R/Over
A R C Fraser	45.5	9	131	8	16.37	5-87	2.85
S L Watkin	53	13	152	6	25.33	4-65	2.86
D E Malcolm	46	8	170	6	28.33	3-84	3.69
P M Such	239.5	64	541	16	33.81	6-67	2.25
J E Emburey	57	13	150	3	50.00	2-119	2.63
M C Ilott	129	28	412	8	51.50	3-108	3.19
P A J DeFreitas	47	9	126	2	63.00	1-46	2.68
P C R Tufnell	104	12	319	5	63.80	2-78	3.06
M P Bicknell	87	17	263	4	65.75	3-99	3.02
M J McCague	79.3	13	294	4	73.50	4-121	3.69
A R Caddick	153	28	488	5	97.60	3-32	3.19
C C Lewis	58	7	238	2	119.00	2-151	4.10
G P Thorpe	6	1	14	0	-	-	2.33
G A Hick	25	7	52	0	-	-	2.08
G A Gooch	25	6	66	0	-	-	2.64
N A Foster	30	4	94	0	-	-	3.13

Australian Tour Averages

Batting	M	In	NO	HS	Runs	Avge	100	50
D C Boon	14	23	4	164*	1437	75.63	9	2
M E Waugh	16	25	6	178	1361	71.63	4	9
D R Martyn	12	15	3	138*	838	69.83	4	3
S R Waugh	16	21	8	157*	875	67.30	3	2
M L Hayden	13	21	1	151*	1150	57.50	3	7
M J Slater	17	28	4	152	1275	53.12	4	8
A R Border	16	21	3	200*	823	45.72	1	4
M A Taylor	15	25	2	124	972	42.26	3	4
I A Healy	16	20	7	102*	499	38.38	1	3
M G Hughes	14	12	3	71	299	33.22	-	2
B P Julian	13	17	6	66	284	25.81	-	2
P R Reiffel	13	9	1	52	181	22.62	-	1
S K Warne	16	15	4	47	246	22.36	-	-
T J Zoehrer	8	9	1	38	115	14.37	-	-
C J McDermott	6	3	0	23	42	14.00	-	-
T B A May	17	9	5	15	31	7.75	-	-
W J Holdsworth	9	3	0	12	17	5.66	-	-

Catches: Healy 42 (11 st); Taylor 25; M Waugh 18; Zoehrer 17 (4 st); Border 15; Boon 10; Hayden & Martyn 9; Warne 8; Julian & S Waugh 7; Slater 6; Hughes, McDermott & Reiffel 3; Holdsworth 2.

Bowling	O	M	R	W	Avge	Best	R/Over
T J Zoehrer	87.2	21	250	12	20.83	3-16	2.86
S K Warne	765.4	281	1698	75	22.64	5-61	2.21
T B A May	562.5	156	1429	53	26.96	5-89	2.53
M G Hughes	470.2	113	1420	48	29.58	5-92	3.01
P R Reiffel	375.4	85	1113	37	30.08	6-71	2.96
M L Hayden	8.4	1	31	1	31.00	1-24	3.57
M A Taylor	9	0	31	1	31.00	1-4	3.44
S R Waugh	73.1	19	229	7	32.71	2-9	3.13
W J Holdsworth	204.5	32	833	23	36.21	5-117	4.06
B P Julian	318.5	58	1158	29	39.93	5-63	3.63
A R Border	65	17	177	3	59.00	1-12	2.72
M E Waugh	121.1	28	403	6	67.16	3-26	3.33
C J McDermott	143	26	449	6	74.83	2-36	3.14
D R Martyn	8	2	21	0	-	-	2.62

MATCHES PLAYED 30: WON 18, DREW 9, LOST 3.

England in India

1st Test

Eden Gardens, Calcutta   Jan 29- Feb 2
Umpires:P D Reporter, S Venkataraghavan
Toss:India

INDIA	1st Innings		
M Prabhakar	c Lewis	b Salisbury	46
N S Sidhu	c Hick	b Taylor	13
V G Kambli	c Hick	b Jarvis	16
S R Tendulkar	c Hick	b Malcolm	50
M Azharuddin*	c Gooch	b Hick	182
P K Amre	c Hick	b Jarvis	12
Kapil Dev	c Lewis	b Hick	13
K S More†	not out		4
A R Kumble		b Malcolm	0
R K Chauhan		b Malcolm	2
Venkatapathy Raju	c Salisbury	b Hick	1
Extras (B6, LB6, W10, NB10)			32
Total			371

Fall of wickets:1-49, 2-78, 3-93, 4-216, 5-278, 6-346, 7-362, 8-368, 9-370
Bowling:Malcolm 24-3-67-3, Jarvis 27-5-72-2, Lewis 23-5-64-0, Taylor 19-2-65-1, Salisbury 17-2-72-1, Hick 12.5-5-19-3

ENGLAND	1st Innings		
G A Gooch*	c Azharuddin	b Venkatapathy	17
A J Stewart†		b Prabhakar	0
M W Gatting		b Chauhan	33
R A Smith	c Amre	b Kumble	1
G A Hick		b Kumble	1
N H Fairbrother	c More	b Kumble	17
I D K Salisbury	c More	b Chauhan	28
C C Lewis		b Venkatapathy	21
P W Jarvis	c Prabhakar	b Venkatapathy	4
J P Taylor	st More	b Chauhan	17
D E Malcolm	not out		4
Extras (B8, LB8, W4)			20
Total			163

Fall of wickets:1-8, 2-37, 3-38, 4-40, 5-87, 6-89, 7-111, 8-119, 9-149
Bowling:Kapil Dev 6-1-18-0, Prabhakar 9-3-10-1, Kumble 29-8-50-3, Venkatapathy 27-14-39-3, Chauhan 29.1-15-30-3

ENGLAND	2nd Innings		
G A Gooch*	st More	b Kumble	18
A J Stewart†	c Tendulkar	b Kumble	49
M W Gatting		b Chauhan	81
R A Smith	c More	b Chauhan	8
G A Hick	lbw	b Venkatapathy	25
N H Fairbrother	c sub	b Kumble	25
I D K Salisbury	c More	b Kapil Dev	26
C C Lewis	c Amre	b Venkatapathy	16
P W Jarvis	lbw	b Venkatapathy	6
J P Taylor	not out		17
D E Malcolm	lbw	b Kapil Dev	0
Extras (LB13, NB2)			15
Total			286

Fall of wickets:1-48, 2-111, 3-145, 4-192, 5-192, 6-216, 7-234, 8-254, 9-286
Bowling:Kapil Dev 8.2-5-12-2, Prabhakar 9-4-26-0, Kumble 40-16-76-3, Venkatapathy 35-9-80-3, Chauhan 45-17-79-2

INDIA	2nd Innings		
M Prabhakar		b Hick	13
N S Sidhu	st Stewart	b Hick	37
V G Kambli	not out		18
S R Tendulkar	not out		9
Extras (LB4, NB1)			5
Total (2 wickets)			82

Fall of wickets:1-51, 2-62
Bowling:Malcolm 6-1-16-0, Jarvis 5.2-1-23-0, Lewis 3-1-5-0, Taylor 3-1-9-0, Salisbury 6-3-16-0, Hick 6-1-9-2

INDIA WON BY 8 WICKETS
Azharuddin's century was his highest score against England, and his sixth test century against the same country. However, it was only Azharuddin's second success, in 18 attempts, as captain of his country. The previous occasion was almost two years ago, against Sri Lanka

2nd Test

Chidambaram Stadium, Madras   Feb 11-15
Umpires:V K Ramaswamy, R S Rathore
Toss:India

INDIA	1st Innings		
M Prabhakar	c Blakey	b Lewis	27
N S Sidhu	c Hick	b Jarvis	106
V G Kambli	lbw	b Hick	59
S R Tendulkar	c & b Salisbury		165
M Azharuddin*	c Smith	b Jarvis	6
P K Amre	c Jarvis	b Salisbury	78
Kapil Dev	not out		66
K S More†	not out		26
Extras (LB10, W2, NB15)			27
Total (6 wickets)			560

Did not bat:A R Kumble, R K Chauhan, Venkatapathy
Fall of wickets:1-41, 2-149, 3-296, 4-324, 5-442
Bowling:Malcolm 27-7-87-0, Jarvis 28-7-72-2, Lewis 11-1-40-1, Tufnell 41-3-132-0, Hick 29-2-77-1, Salisbury 29-1-142-2

ENGLAND	1st Innings		
R A Smith	lbw	b Kumble	17
A J Stewart*	c sub	b Venkatapathy	74
G A Hick	lbw	b Chauhan	64
M W Gatting	run out		2
N H Fairbrother	c Kapil Dev	b Chauhan	83
R J Blakey†		b Venkatapathy	0
C C Lewis	c Azharuddin	b Venkatapathy	0
I D K Salisbury	lbw	b Kumble	4
P W Jarvis	c sub	b Venkataphy	8
P C R Tufnell	c Azharuddin	b Chauhan	2
D E Malcolm	not out		0
Extras (B14, LB16, NB2)			32
Total			286

Fall of wickets:1-46, 2-157, 3-166, 4-175, 5-179, 6-179, 7-220, 8-277, 9-279
Bowling:Prabhakar 3-2-7-0, Kumble 25-9-61-2, Chauhan 39.3-16-69-3, Venkataphy 54-21-103-4, Kapil Dev 4-0-11-0, Tendulkar 2-1-5-0

ENGLAND — 2nd Innings

R A Smith	c Amre	b Kumble	56
A J Stewart*	lbw	b Kapil Dev	0
G A Hick	c Tendulkar	b Kapil Dev	0
M W Gatting	lbw	b Venkatapathy	19
N H Fairbrother	c Prabhakar	b Kumble	9
R J Blakey†		b Kumble	6
C C Lewis	c & b Kumble		117
I D K Salisbury		b Kumble	12
P W Jarvis	c Tendulkar	b Kumble	2
P C R Tufnell	not out		22
D E Malcolm	c sub	b Venkatapathy	0
Extras (B4, LB5)			9
Total			**252**

Fall of wickets:1-10, 2-12, 3-71, 4-82, 5-88, 6-99, 7-172, 8-186, 9-241

Bowling:Prabhakar 3-2-4-0, Kumble 21-7-64-6, Chauhan 21-4-59-0, Venkatapathy 23.1-3-76-2, Kapil Dev 11-5-36-2, Tendulkar 2-1-4-0

INDIA WON BY AN INNINGS AND 22 RUNS

Kapil Dev,when he reached 35 runs, became the first player in Test history to score 5000 runs and take 400 wickets. Both Tendulkar and Lewis made their highest Test scores.

3rd Test

Wankhede Stadium, Bombay   Feb 19-23
Umpires:P D Reporter, S Venkataraghavan
Toss:England

ENGLAND — 1st Innings

G A Gooch*	c More	b Kapil Dev	4
A J Stewart	run out		13
M A Atherton	c Prabhakar	b Kumble	37
R A Smith	c More	b Venkatapathy	2
M W Gatting	c Kapil Dev	b Venkatapathy	23
G A Hick	c Kapil Dev	b Prabhakar	178
R J Blakey†	lbw	b Kumble	1
C C Lewis	lbw	b Kumble	49
J E Emburey	c More	b Kapil Dev	12
P A J DeFreitas	lbw	b Kapil Dev	11
P C R Tufnell	not out		15
Extras (B4, LB5, W2, NB4)			15
Total			**347**

Fall of wickets:1-11, 2-25, 3-30, 4-58, 5-116, 6-118, 7-211, 8-262, 9-279

Bowling:Kapil Dev 15-3-35-3, Prabhakar 13-2-52-1, Venkatapathy 44-8-102-2, Kumble 40-4-95-3, Chauhan 23-7-54-0

INDIA — 1st Innings

N S Sidhu	c Smith	b Tufnell	79
M Prabhakar	c Blakey	b Hick	44
V G Kambli	c Gatting	b Lewis	224
S R Tendulkar	lw	b Tufnell	78
M Azharuddin*	lbw	b Lewis	26
P K Amre	c DeFreitas	b Hick	57
Kapil Dev	c DeFreitas	b Emburey	22
K S More†	c lewis	b Emburey	0
A R Kumble	c Atherton	b Tufnell	16
Venkatapathy Raju	not out		0
Extras (B5, LB14, W5, NB6)			30
Total			**591**

Fall of wickets:1-109, 2-174, 3-368, 4-418, 5-519, 6-560, 7-560, 8-563, 9-591

Bowling:DeFreitas 20-4-75-0, Lewis 42-9-114-2, Emburey 59-14-144-2, Tufnell 39.3-6-142-4, Hick 29-3-97-2

ENGLAND — 2nd Innings

G A Gooch*		b Prabhakar	8
A J Stewart	lbw	b Prabhakar	10
M A Atherton	c More	b Prabhakar	11
R A Smith		b Kumble	62
M W Gatting	st More	b Chauhan	61
G A Hick	c Amre	b Kumble	47
R J Blakey†		b Kumble	0
C C Lewis	c More	b Venkatapathy	3
J E Emburey	c Tendulkar	b Kumble	1
P A J DeFreitas	st More	b Venkatapathy	12
P C R Tufnell	not out		2
Extras (B4, LB6, W1, NB1)			12
Total			**229**

Fall of wickets:1-17, 2-26, 3-34, 4-155, 5-181, 6-181, 7-206, 8-214, 9-215

Bowling:Kapil Dev 7-1-21-0, Prabhakar 11-4-28-3, Venkatapathy 26.5-7-68-2, Kumble 26-9-70-4, Chauhan 12-5-32-1

INDIA WON BY AN INNINGS AND 15 RUNS

The annihilation continued. Kambli, playing in his third Test, scored the third highest Test score ever by an Indian, and the best ever against England. The Indian innings, for the second Test in succession, was the highest ever against England on Indian soil. There was slight compensation for England with Hick's maiden Test century.

BATTING AVERAGES

India	M	I	NO	Runs	HS	Ave
V G Kambli	3	4	1	317	224	105.66
S R Tendulkar	3	4	1	302	165	100.66
M Azharuddin	3	3	0	214	182	71.33
N S Sidhu	3	4	0	235	106	58.75
Kapil Dev	3	3	1	101	66*	50.50
P K Amre	3	3	0	147	78	49.00
M Prabhakar	3	4	0	130	46	32.50
K S More	3	3	2	30	26*	30.00
R K Chauhan	3	2	0	17	15	8.50
A R Kumble	3	2	0	16	16	8.00
Venkatapathy Raju	3	2	1	1	1	1.00

England	M	I	NO	Runs	HS	Ave
G A Hick	3	6	0	315	178	52.50
M W Gatting	3	6	0	219	81	36.50
C C Lewis	3	6	0	206	117	34.33
J P Taylor	1	2	1	34	17*	34.00
N H Fairbrother	2	4	0	134	83	33.50
P C R Tufnell	2	4	3	28	22*	28.00
A J Stewart	3	6	0	146	74	24.33
R A Smith	3	6	0	146	62	24.33
M A Atherton	1	2	0	48	37	24.00
I D K Salisbury	2	4	0	70	28	17.50
G A Gooch	2	4	0	47	18	11.75
P A J DeFreitas	1	2	0	23	12	11.50
J E Emburey	1	2	0	13	12	6.50
P W Jarvis	2	4	0	20	8	5.00
D E Malcolm	2	4	2	4	4*	2.00
R J Blakey	2	4	0	7	6	1.75

BOWLING AVERAGES

India	O	M	Runs	W	Ave
Kapil Dev	51.2	15	133	7	19.00
A R Kumble	181	53	416	21	19.81
M Prabhakar	48	17	127	5	25.40
Venkatapathy Raju	210	62	468	16	29.25
R K Chauhan	169.4	64	323	9	35.88
S R Tendulkar	4	2	9	0	-

England	O	M	Runs	W	Ave
G A Hick	76.5	11	202	8	25.25
P W Jarvis	60.2	13	167	4	41.75
D E Malcolm	57	11	170	3	56.66
P C R Tufnell	80.3	9	274	4	68.50
J E Emburey	59	14	144	2	72.00
J P Taylor	22	3	74	1	74.00
C C Lewis	79	16	223	3	74.33
I D K Salisbury	52	6	230	3	76.66
P A J DeFreitas	20	4	75	0	-

1st One-Day International

Jaipur   Jan18
Umpires:S K Bansal, S Venkataraghavan
Toss:England

INDIA

M Prabhakar		b Jarvis	25
N S Sidhu		b Jarvis	0
V G Kambli	not out		100
M Azharuddin*	lbw	b Lewis	6
S R Tendulkar	not out		82
Extras (B2, LB7, W1)			10
Total (3 wickets, 48 overs)			**223**

Did not bat:P K Amre, Kapil Dev, V Yadav†, A R
Kumble, Venkatapathy Raju, J Srinath
Fall of wickets:1-0, 2-31, 3-59
Bowling:DeFreitas 9-3-40-0, Jarvis 10-0-49-2, Reeve 10-0-37-0, Lewis 9-0-26-1, Emburey 8-0-49-0, Gooch 2-0-13-0

ENGLAND

G A Gooch*	lbw	b Kapil Dev	4
A J Stewart†	c Yadav	b Kapil Dev	91
R A Smith	c & b Prabhakar		16
M W Gatting		b Kumble	30
N H Fairbrother	not out		46
G A Hick	run out		13
D A Reeve	lbw	b Prabhakar	2
C C Lewis	not out		8
Extras (B1, LB8, W3, NB2)			14
Total (6 wickets, 48 overs)			**224**

Did not bat:J E Emburey, P A J DeFreitas, P W Jarvis
Fall of wickets:1-29, 2-85, 3-145, 4-161, 5-200, 6-203
Bowling:Kapil Dev 10-1-36-2, Prabhakar 10-0-43-2,
Srinath 10-0-47-0, Venkatapathy 8-1-35-0, Kumble 10-0-54-1

ENGLAND WON BY 4 WICKETS
Match Award:V G Kambli

2nd One-Day International

Chandigarh   Jan 21
Umpires:R V Ramani, V K Ramaswamy
Toss:India

ENGLAND

G A Gooch*	c Tendulkar	b Srinath	7
A J Stewart†	c Azharuddin	b Kapil Dev	7
R A Smith	lbw	b Kumble	42
M W Gatting	c & b Srinath		0
N H Fairbrother	lbw	b Venkatapathy	7
G A Hick		b Kapil Dev	56
D A Reeve	not out		33
C C Lewis	not out		16
Extras (LB13, W13, NB4)			30
Total (6 wickets, 50 overs)			**198**

Did not bat:DeFreitas, Jarvis
Fall of wickets:1-19, 2-20, 3-22, 4-49, 5-132, 6-153
Bowling:Kapil Dev 10-2-40-2, Prabhakar 8-0-30-0, Srinath
10-2-34-2, Tendulkar 3-0-16-0, Venkatapathy 9-0-28-1,
Kumble 10-0-37-1

INDIA

N S Sidhu	c Reeve	b DeFreitas	76
M Prabhakar	c Reeve	b Lewis	36
V G Kambli	c & b Jarvis		9
M Azharuddin*	lbw	b Defreitas	1
P K Amre	not out		24
Kapil Dev	not out		16
Extras (LB3, W5, NB6)			14
Total (5 wickets, 45.1 overs)			**201**

Did not bat:Yadav†, Kumble, Venkatapathy, Srinath
Fall of wickets:1-79, 2-99, 3-148, 4-161, 5-195
Bowling:DeFreitas 10-1-31-2, Jarvis 10-1-43-1, Reeve 6.1-0-33-1, Lewis 10-0-47-1, Salisbury 8-1-42-0, Gatting 1-0-2-0

INDIA WON BY 5 WICKETS
Match Award:N S Sidhu

3rd One-Day International

Bangalore   Feb 26
Umpires:V K Ramaswamy, M R Singh
Toss:India

ENGLAND

R A Smith	c More	b Srinath	29
A J Stewart†	lbw	b Srinath	14
G A Hick	c Amre	b Prabhakar	56
M W Gatting		b Srinath	7
N H Fairbrother	run out		5
G A Gooch*		b Prabhakar	45
C C Lewis	c Tendulkar	b Srinath	19
D A Reeve	not out		13
P A J DeFreitas	c Prabhakar	b Srinath	2
P W Jarvis	c Azharuddin	b Kapil Dev	1
D E Malcolm	not out		0
Extras (LB15, W4, NB8)			27
Total (9 wickets, 48 overs)			**218**

Fall of wickets:1-42, 2-65, 3-79, 4-102, 5-157, 6-185, 7-210,
8-213, 9-218
Bowling:Kapil Dev 8-1-27-1, Prabhakar 10-0-50-2, Srinath
9-1-41-5, Venkatapathy 10-0-46-0, Kumble 10-1-39-0

INDIA

M Prabhakar	run out		0
N S Sidhu	c Gooch	b DeFreitas	40
V G Kambli	c Stewart	b Jarvis	33
S R Tendulkar	c Hick	b Lewis	3
M Azharuddin*	lbw	b Jarvis	1
P K Amre	c Hick	b Jarvis	16
Kapil Dev	c Gooch	b Malcolm	32
K S More†	lbw	b Jarvis	0
A R Kumble		b Jarvis	24
J Srinath	c Hick	b Malcolm	2
Venkatapathy Raju	not out		1
Extras (LB6, W3, NB1)			18
Total (41.4 overs)			**170**

Fall of wickets:1-3, 2-61, 3-66, 4-67, 5-100, 6-114, 7-115, 8-160, 9-166

Bowling:Malcolm 9-1-47-2, DeFreitas 8-0-27-1, Lewis 10-0-32-1, Jarvis 8.4-1-35-5, Reeve 6-0-25-0

ENGLAND WON BY 48 RUNS
Match Award:P W Jarvis & J Srinath

4th One-Day International

Jamshedpur   Mar 1
Umpires:L Narasimhan, C S Sathe
Toss:England

INDIA

N S Sidhu	c DeFreitas	b Malcolm	18
M Prabhakar	c Blakey	b DeFreitas	2
V G Kambli	run out		23
S R Tendulkar		b Jarvis	24
M Azharuddin*	c Fairbrother	b Lewis	23
Kapil Dev	not out		15
P K Amre	c gooch	b Jarvis	19
S A Ankola	run out		2
K S More†	not out		1
Extras (LB6, W3, NB1)			10
Total (7 wickets, 26 overs)			**137**

Did not bat:Kumble, Srinath
Fall of wickets:1-11, 2-46, 3-51, 4-96, 5-99, 6-122, 7-127
Bowling:DeFreitas 4-0-17-1, Malcolm 6-0-17-1, Lewis 5-0-25-1, Reeve 6-0-32-0, Jarvis 5-0-40-2

ENGLAND

G A Gooch*	c More	b Kapil Dev	15
R A Smith	run out		17
G A Hick	c Azharuddin	b Ankola	1
N H Fairbrother	not out		53
C C Lewis	lbw	b Prabhakar	25
D A Reeve	not out		17
Extras (LB8, W5)			13
Total (4 wickets, 25.4 overs)			**141**

Did not bat:Gatting, Blakey†, DeFreitas, Jarvis
Fall of wickets:1-27, 2-33, 3-43, 4-93
Bowling:Kapil Dev 4-1-10-1, Prabhakar 5.4-0-34-1, Srinath 6-0-38-0, Ankola 6-0-28-1, Kumble 4-0-23-0

ENGLAND WON BY 6 WICKETS
Match Award:N H Fairbrother

5th One-Day International

Gwalior   Mar 4
Umpires:A V Jayaprakash, P D Reporter
Toss:India

ENGLAND

R A Smith	lbw	b Srinath	129
A J Stewart		b Kumble	33
G A Hick	c more	b Prabhakar	18
N H Fairbrother	c Maninder	b Srinath	37
C C Lewis	lbw	b Prabhakar	4
G A Gooch*	run out		1
D A Reeve	run out		3
R J Blakey†	lbw	b Srinath	0
P A J DeFreitas	not out		2
P W Jarvis		b Prabhakar	0
D E Malcolm		b Prabhakar	0
Extras (B1, LB16, W8, NB4)			29
Total (50 overs)			**256**

Fall of wickets:1-101, 2-154, 3-227, 4-246, 5-246, 6-251, 7-251, 8-256, 9-256

Bowling:Kapil Dev 9-0-39-0, Prabhakar 10-0-54-4, Srinath 10-0-41-3, Kumble 10-0-41-1, Maninder Singh 8-0-46-0, Sharma 3-0-18-0

INDIA

N S Sidhu	not out		134
M Prabhakar	lbw	b DeFreitas	0
V G Kambli	c Gooch	b Malcolm	2
M Azharuddin	c Stewart	b Malcolm	74
S R Tendulkar		b Jarvis	5
A R Sharma	run out		0
Kapil Dev*	c Hick	b Jarvis	2
K S More†	c Hick	b Malcolm	1
A R Kumble	not out		19
Extras (B2, LB9, W8, NB1)			20
Total (7 wickets, 48 overs)			**257**

Did not bat:Maninder, Srinath
Fall of wickets:1-1, 2-4, 3-179, 4-189, 5-190, 6-202, 7-205
Bowling:DeFreitas 10-0-52-1, Malcolm 10-0-41-3, Lewis 10-0-56-0, Jarvis 10-0-43-2, Reeve 6-0-37-0, Hick 2-0-18-0

INDIA WON BY 3 WICKETS
Match Award:N S Sidhu

6th One-Day International

Gwalior   Mar 5
Umpires:S K Bansal, S Venkataraghavan
Toss:India

ENGLAND

R A Smith	c Sharma	b Maninder	72
A J Stewart†	c More	b Srinath	11
G A Hick	not out		105
N H Fairbrother	c Kapil Dev	b Srinath	41
M W Gatting	c Sidhu	b Srinath	6
C C Lewis	not out		3
Extras (LB8, W17, NB2)			27
Total (4 wickets, 48 overs)			**265**

Did not bat:Gooch*, Reeve, DeFreitas, Jarvis, Malcolm
Fall of wickets:1-42, 2-158, 3-246, 4-258
Bowling:Kapil Dev 10-2-48-0, Prabhakar 9-0-52-0, Srinath 9-0-37-3, Maninder Singh 10-0-62-0

INDIA

M Prabhakar		b Jarvis	73
N S Sidhu	c Hick	b Lewis	19
V G Kambli	c Reeve	b DeFreitas	22
M Azharuddin*	not out		95
S R Tendulkar	c sub	b Lewis	34
Kapil Dev	c Reeve	b Jarvis	2
A K Sharma	c Gooch	b Jarvis	2
K S More†	not out		10
Extras (LB1, W7, NB2)			10
Total (6 wickets, 46.4 overs)			**267**

Did not bat:Kumble, Maninder Singh, Srinath
Fall of wickets:1-41, 2-99, 3-166, 4-245, 5-251, 6-253
Bowling:Malcolm 8-0-56-0, Lewis 10-1-51-2, Jarvis 10-0-39-3, Reeve 8.4-0-64-0, DeFreitas 10-0-56-1

INDIA WON BY 4 WICKETS
Match Award: M Azharuddin

Other Matches

ENGLAND XI V DELHI
Faridabad   Jan 3-5
Delhi 286   (H Sharma 88, P W Jarvis 3-61,
              C C Lewis 3-70)
         140-2 dec (A K Sharma 61*, Bantoo Singh 50*)
England XI 194 (M A Atherton 59, Kirti Azad 6-30)
         63-3 (Ghyas 2-17)
Match Drawn

ENGLAND XI V PRESIDENT'S XI
Lucknow   Jan 8-10
President's XI 223 (V G Kambli 61 ret hrt, N R Mongia 55,
              J P Taylor 5-46)
         107-1 (N S Sidhu 57*)
England XI 307 (M W Gatting 115, G A Gooch 77,
         P A J DeFreitas 45, N D Hirwani 4-78)
Match Drawn

ENGLAND XI V INDIAN U25 XI
Cuttack   Jan 21-23
England XI 408-4 dec (R A Smith 149*,
         G A Gooch 102 ret hrt, M W Gatting 41)
         146-2 dec (M A Atherton 80*)
Indian U25 XI 273 (A Kuresia 103, G K Pande 54,
         D E Malcolm 3-3, I D K Salisbury 3-77
         53-1 (J V Paranjpe 23*, S S Dighe 23*)
Match Drawn

ENGLAND XI V REST OF INDIA
Vishakhapatnam   Feb 5-7
England XI 253 (R A Smith 82, R J Blakey 63*,
         J E Emburey 53, V Prasad 3-39)
         150-2 (N H Fairbrother 78*)
Rest of India 345 (S V Manjrekar 96, J V Parnjpe 64,
         S R Tendulkar 61, P C R Tufnell 4-95,
         I D K Salisbury 3-54)
Match Drawn

FIRST CLASS TOUR AVERAGES

BATTING

Name	M	I	NO	Runs	HS	Ave
R A Smith	6	10	2	416	149*	52.00
M W Gatting	6	11	2	423	115	47.00
G A Hick	6	11	1	407	178	40.70
G A Gooch	5	8	1	278	102*	39.71
P C R Tufnell	6	6	5	36	22*	36.00
J P Taylor	3	3	2	36	17*	36.00
M A Atherton	4	8	1	238	80*	34.00
N H Fairbrother	5	8	1	216	83	30.85
C C Lewis	6	9	1	232	117	29.00
D A Reeve	2	3	1	43	21*	21.50
J E Emburey	3	4	0	86	53	21.50
A J Stewart	7	13	1	230	74	19.16
I D K Salisbury	4	5	1	75	28	18.75
P A J DeFreitas	3	4	0	70	45	17.50
R J Blakey	3	5	1	70	63*	17.50
P W Jarvis	3	5	0	21	8	4.20
D E Malcolm	5	5	2	6	4*	2.00

BOWLING

Name	O	M	Runs	W	Ave
G A Gooch	5	3	2	2	1.00
P W Jarvis	94.2	25	245	9	27.22
G A Hick	105.5	20	277	9	30.77
J P Taylor	65.4	11	217	7	31.00
D E Malcolm	112	26	321	10	32.10
I D K Salisbury	87	11	362	9	40.22
C C Lewis	142	27	391	9	43.44
P C R Tufnell	187.1	30	604	11	54.90
J E Emburey	101	23	277	3	92.33
M W Gatting	4	0	19	0	-
D A Reeve	13	3	33	0	-
P A J DeFreitas	63	13	194	0	-

England in Sri Lanka

The Test

Sinhalese Sports Club, Colombo   Mar 13-18
Umpires:K T Francis, T M Samarasinghe
Toss:England

ENGLAND	First Innings		
R A Smith		b Muralitharan	128
M A Atherton	lbw	b Ramanayake	13
M W Gatting	c Jayasuriya	b Muralitharan	29
G A Hick	c Tillekeratne	b Muralitharan	68
A J Stewart*†	c Tillekeratne	b Warnaweera	63
N H Fairbrother		b Warnaweera	18
C C Lewis	run out		22
J E Emburey	not out		1
P W Jarvis	lbw	b Warnaweera	0
P C R Tufnell	lbw	b Muralitharan	1
D E Malcolm	c Gurusinha	b Warnaweera	13
Extras (B5, LB3, W1, NB15)			24
Total			380

Fall of wickets:1-40, 2-82, 3-194, 4-316, 5-323, 6-358, 7-366, 8-366, 9-367
Bowling:Ramanayake 17-2-66-1, Gurusinha 5-1-12-0, Warnaweera 40.1-11-90-4, Hathurusinghe 8-2-22-0, Muralitharan 45-12-118-4, Jayasuriya 12-1-53-0, Ranatunga 3-0-11-0

SRI LANKA	First Innings		
R S Mahanama	c Smith	b Emburey	64
U C Hathurusinghe	c Stewart	b Lewis	59
A P Gurusinha	st Stewart	b Tufnell	43
P A De Silva	c Stewart	b Jarvis	80
A Ranatunga*	c Stewart	b Lewis	64
H P Tillekeratne	not out		93
S T Jayasuriya	c Atherton	b Lewis	4
A M De Silva†	c Gatting	b Emburey	9
C P H Ramanayake	c Lewis	b Jarvis	1
M Muralitharan		b Lewis	19
K P J Warnaweera		b Jarvis	1
Extras (B2, LB13, W2, NB15)			32
Total			469

Fall of wickets:1-99, 2-153, 3-203, 4-330, 5-339, 6-349, 7-371, 8-376, 9-459
Bowing:Malcolm 25-7-60-0, Jarvis 25.5-1-76-3, Lewis 31-5-66-4, Tufnell 33-5-108-1, Emburey 34-6-117-2, Hick 8-0-27-0

ENGLAND	Second Innings		
R A Smith		b Jayasuriya	35
M A Atherton	c Tillekeratne	b Gurusinha	2
M W Gatting	c Tillekeratne	b Warnaweera	18
G A Hick	c Ramanayeke	b Warnaweera	26
A J Stewart*†	c Mahanama	b Warnaweera	3
N H Fairbrother	run out		3
C C Lewis	c Jayasuriya	b Muralitharan	45
J E Emburey		b Gurusinha	59
P W Jarvis	st A De Silva	b Jayasuriya	3
P C R Tufnell	c A De Silva	b Warnaweera	1
D E Malcolm	not out		8
Extras (B4, LB2, W1, NB18)			25

Total: 228
Fall of wickets:1-16, 2-38, 3-83, 4-91, 5-96, 6-130, 7-153, 8-173, 9-188
Bowling:Ramanayeke 3-0-16-0, Gurusinha 6-2-7-2, Warnaweera 25-4-98-4, Muralitharan 16-3-55-1, Jayasuriya 16-3-46-2

SRI LANKA	Second Innings		
R S Mahanama	c Stewart	b Lewis	6
U C Hathurusinghe	c Stewart	b Tufnell	14
A P Gurusinha		b Emburey	29
P A De Silva	c Jarvis	b Emburey	7
A Ranatunga*	c Gatting	b Tufnell	35
H P Tillekeratne	not out		36
S T Jayasuriya	not out		6
Extras (B1, LB2, NB 6)			9
Total (5 wickets)			142

Did not bat:A M De Silva†, C P H Ramanayeke, M Muralitharan, K P J Warnaweera
Fall of wickets:1-8, 2-48, 3-61, 4-61, 5-136
Bowling:Malcolm 3-1-11-0, Jarvis 8-2-14-0, Lewis 8-1-21-1, Tufnell 7.4-1-34-2, Emburey 14-2-48-2, Hick 2-0-11-0

SRI LANKA WON BY 5 WICKETS

England suffered their first defeat at the hands of Sri Lanka who in turn recorded only their fourth win in 43 Tests. Smith's first Test 100 abroad was not backed up by his colleagues who succumbed to the off spin of Warnaweera and Muralitharan. The loss completed a miserable tour of the sub-continent.

1st One Day International

Khetterama Stadium, Colombo   Mar 10
Umpires:K T Francis, S P Onnudurai
Toss:Sri Lanka

SRI LANKA

U C Hathurusinghe	lbw	b Emburey	43
R S Mahanama	c Hick	b Malcolm	7
A P Gurusinha	c DeFreitas	b Jarvis	5
P A De Silva	c &	b Reeve	34
A Ranatunga*	c Stewart	b Lewis	36
H P Tillekeratne	not out		66
S T Jayasuriya	not out		34
Extras (B3, LB4, W10, NB8)			25
Total (5 wickets, 47 overs)			**250**

Did not bat:A M De Silvat, R S Kalpage, C P H
Ramanayeke, G P Wickremasinghe
Fall of wickets:1-16, 2-33, 3-101, 4-109, 5-180
Bowling:Malcolm 7-1-32-1, Lewis 9-0-40-1, Jarvis 9-0-57-1,
DeFreitas 3-0-25-0, Emburey 10-1-42-1, Reeve 9-1-47-1

ENGLAND

R A Smith	c &	b Wickrem'ghe	8
A J Stewart*†	lbw	b Ramanayeke	5
G A Hick	c Mahanama	b Hathurus'ghe	31
N H Fairbrother	lbw	b Jayasuriya	34
M W Gatting		b Kalpage	1
C C Lewis		b Kalpage	16
D A Reeve	c Ranatunga	b Kalpage	16
P A J DeFreitas	c Ranaunga	b Wickrem'ghe	21
J E Emburey	st A De Silva	b Jayasuriya	10
P W Jarvis	not out		16
D E Malcolm	run out		2
Extras (LB10, W4, NB1)			15
Total (36.1 overs)			**170**

Fall of wickets:1-7, 2-9, 3-67, 4-70, 5-99, 6-103, 7-120, 8-
137, 9-152
Bowling:Ramnayeke 7-0-25-1, Wickremasinghe 6.1-1-21-
2, Hathurusinghe 6-0-28-1, Gurusinha 2-0-7-0, Kalpage 8-
0-34-3, Jayasuriya 7-0-45-2

SRI LANKA WON BY 80 RUNS
Match Award:H P Tillekeratne

2nd One-Day International

Tyronne Fernando Stadium, Moratuwa   Mar 20
Umpires:B C Cooray, T M Samarasinghe
Toss:Sri Lanka

ENGLAND

C C Lewis	c Raman'yeke	b Wickrem'ghe	8
R A Smith	st A De Silva	b Jayasuriya	31
G A Hick	lbw	b Kalpage	34
N H Fairbrother	c A De Silva	b Jayasuriya	1
A J Stewart*†	lbw	b Tillekeratne	14
M W Gatting	lbw	b P De Silva	2
D A Reeve		b Jayasuriya	21
J E Emburey	c Raman'yeke	b Jayasuriya	20
I D K Salisbury	not out		2
P W Jarvis	c A De Silva	b Jayasuriya	4
J P Taylor		b Jayasuriya	1
Extras (B2, LB9, W3, NB6)			20
Total (48.5 overs)			**180**

Fall of wickets:1-23, 2-77, 3-85, 4-111, 5-114, 6-125, 7-168,
8-172, 9-177
Bowling:Ramanayeke 4-0-20-0, Wickremasinghe 8-0-23-1,
Gurusinha 4-0-21-0, Hathurusinghe 2-0-13-0, Kalpage 10-
0-27-1, Jayasuriya 9.5-0-29-6, P A De Silva 7-1-22-1,
Tillekeratne 4-0-14-1

SRI LANKA

R S Mahanama	c Stewart	b Salisbury	29
U C Hathurusinghe	c &	b Salisbury	33
A P Gurusinha	not out		35
P A De Silva	not out		75
Extras (B1, LB2, W2, NB6)			11
Total (2 wickets, 35.2 overs)			**183**

Did not bat:A Ranatunga*, H P Tillekeratne, S T
Jayasuriya, A M De Silvat, R S Kalpage, C P H
Ramanayeke, G P Wickremasinghe
Fall of wickets:1-66, 2-68
Bowling:Lewis 7-1-13-0, Jarvis 4-0-22-0, Taylor 3-0-20-0,
Emburey 6-0-29-0, Salisbury 4-0-36-2, Hick 6.2-1-36-0,
Reeve 5-0-24-0

SRI LANKA WON BY 8 WICKETS
Match Award:S T Jayasuriya

England 'A 'in Australia

ENGLAND A V AUSTRALIAN CAPITAL TERRITORY

Canberra   Feb 2-4
England A   379-7 dec (M D Moxon 123, R C Russell 67,
           J Bull 3-81)
A C T   65   (Illott 4-12, Caddick 4-14)
           361-7 (N J Speak 120, P Solway 104,
           S Maxwell 53*)
Match Drawn

ENGLAND A V TASMANIA

Launceston   Feb 8-10
England A   420-9 dec (M N Lathwell 175, G P Thorpe 96,
           C D Matthews 4-110, D Castle 3-105)
           92-1 dec (M A Roseberry 37*, M D Moxon 37*)
Tasmania   159-0 dec (D F Hills 77*, N C P Courtenay 73*)
           288-5 (J Cox 115, D F Hills 109)
Match Drawn

ENGLAND A V AUSTRALIAN CRICKET ACADEMY

Melbourne   Feb 14-17
England A   220 (P J Prichard 77, P E McIntyre 3-85)
           286 (G D Lloyd 124, G P Thorpe 63,
           P J Prichard 43, S H Cook 4-54)
A C A   231 (D F Hills 66, M J Slater 43, G S Blewett 43
           P M Such 7-82)
           194 (M G Bevan 53, M J Slater 41,
           A R Caddick 4-46, P M Such 4-62)
England A won by 81 runs

ENGLAND A V QUEENSLAND
Caloundra   Feb 20-22
England A 287-9 dec (D J Capel 80*, M D Moxon 57,
          G P Thorpe 45, S G Law 3-45,
          M S Kasprowicz 3-64)
          104-3 dec (M N Lathwell 40)
Queensland 296-7 dec (T J Barsby 78, M L Hayden 66,
          D M Wellham 42*)
Match Drawn

ENGLAND A V SOUTH AUSTRALIA
Adelaide   Feb 26-Mar 1
England A 152 (D A Reeves 4-54)
          225 (M D Moxon 62, P E McIntyre 6-43)
South Australia
          308-8 dec (J D Siddons 74, D S Webber 55,
          J A Brayshaw 49, D J Capel 4-72)
          70-3 (P M Such 3-36)
South Australia won by 7 wickets

ENGLAND A V NEW SOUTH WALES
Sydney   Mar 4-7
England A 238 (M N Lathwell 103, G D Lloyd 60, D A
          Freedman 6-89, G R J Matthews 4-40)
          208 (R C Russell 51*, G D Lloyd 41,
          W J Holdsworth 5-47, D A Freedman 4-59)
N S W   421-6 dec
          (M G Bevan 170, R Chee Quee 90,
          T H Bayliss 52, A C Gilchrist 47,
          A R Caddick 3-68)
          26-0
New South Wales won by 10 wickets

ENGLAND A V WESTERN AUSTRALIA
Perth   Mar 14-17
England A 293 (G P Thorpe 97, T C Middleton 42, C
          McDonald 6-36, B A Reid 3-58)
          300-5 dec (G D Lloyd 105, G P Thorpe 67, R C
          Russell 58*, D Spencer 3-76)
Western Australia
          192 (M Goodwin 59, M C Illott 3-21,
          D J Millns 3-58)
          141 (A R Caddick 5-38, M C Illott 3-46)
England A won by 260 runs

FIRST CLASS TOUR AVERAGES
BATTING

Name	M	I	NO	Runs	HS	Ave
G P Thorpe	3	5	1	215	96	53.75
M D Moxon	3	6	2	194	62	48.50
M N Lathwell	4	7	0	332	175	47.42
G D Lloyd	2	4	1	140	60	46.66
M C Illott	2	3	2	38	23*	38.00
M A Roseberry	3	6	1	129	39	25.80
D J Millns	3	5	1	91	30	22.75
D J Capel	4	6	1	109	80*	21.80
R C Russell	4	6	1	103	51*	20.60
P J Prichard	2	4	0	48	34	12.00
T C Middleton	4	8	0	88	21	11.00
D G Cork	3	4	0	28	22	7.00
P M Such	3	5	2	18	11*	6.00
A R Caddick	2	3	0	16	16	5.33
J Boiling	2	3	1	9	5*	4.50

BOWLING

Name	O	M	Runs	W	Ave
A R Caddick	61	18	143	5	28.60
D J Capel	87.2	8	249	6	41.50
P M Such	106.2	21	271	6	45.16
D G Cork	54.3	11	164	3	54.66
J Boiling	87	19	232	4	58.00
M C Illott	76	21	187	2	93.50
D J Millns	74.5	10	265	1	265.00
G P Thorpe	2	0	6	0	-

The Australian Cricket Board ruled that England A's matches against Australian Capital Territory, the Australian Cricket Academy and a Western Australia XI were not first class.

South Africa v India

1ST TEST
Kingsmead, Durban   Nov 13-17, 1992
South Africa 254 (K C Wessels 118, J N Rhodes 41, A R
          Kumble 3-43)
          176-3 (A C Hudson 55, S J Cook 43)
India   277 (P K Amre 103, K S More 55,
          B M McMillan 3-52)

Match Drawn
The first Test between the countries proved to be an undramatic return to the fold for the South Africans due to the loss of the fourth day's play for bad weather. Cook had the distinction of being out to the first ball of the match whilst making his Test debut, although Wessels steadied the ship by becoming the first player to score 100's in Tests for different countries. Television also gained its first dismissal when Tendulkar was given run out following a video replay.

2ND TEST
Wanderers Stadium, Johannesburg   Nov 26-30
South Africa 292 (B M McMillan 98, J N Rhodes 91, M
          Prabhakar 4-90)
          252 (A C Hudson 53, D J Richardson 50,
          A R Kumble 6-53)
India   227 (S R Tendulkar 111, B M McMillan 4-74)
          A A Donald 3-78)
          141-4 (A Jajeda 43)

Match Drawn

3RD TEST
St George's Park, Port Elizabeth   Dec 26-29
India   212 (M Azharuddin 60, A A Donald 5-55,
          B M McMillan 3-52)
          215 (Kapil Dev 129, A A Donald 7-84)
South Africa 275 (W J Cronje 135, A C Hudson 52,
          Venkatapathy Raju 3-73)
          155-1 (K C Wessels 95*)

South Africa won by 9 wickets
Not even a defiant eighth Test century by Kapil Dev could deny South Africa a long awaited Test win, thanks largely to the pace bowling of Allan Donald who recorded match figures of 12-139.

4TH TEST
Newlands, Cape Town   Jan 2-6, 1993
South Africa   360 (J N Rhodes 86, B M McMillan 52,
                D J Cullinan 46, A R Kumble 3-101)
                130-6 dec (J Srinath 4-33)
India 276   (S R Tendulkar 73, M Prabhakar,
                S V Manjrekar 46, C R Matthews 3-32)
                29-1
Match Drawn

TEST AVERAGES
BATTING

South Africa	M	I	NO	Runs	HS	Ave
J N Rhodes	4	7	1	275	91	45.83
K C Wessels	4	8	1	295	118	42.14
W J Cronje	3	6	1	207	135	41.40
B M McMillan	4	6	1	194	98	38.80
India						
Kapil Dev	4	5	0	202	129	40.40
P K Amre	4	6	1	169	103	33.80
S R Tendulkar	4	6	0	202	111	33.66
A Jajeda	3	5	1	99	43	24.75

BOWLING

South Africa	O	M	Runs	W	Ave
A A Donald	175	49	394	20	19.70
C R Matthews	109	44	190	9	21.11
B M McMillan	155	55	307	13	23.61
W J Cronje	56.4	28	71	3	23.66
India					
S R Tendulkar	7	2	14	1	14.00
A R Kumble	254.3	87	467	18	25.94
J Srinath	138.5	30	313	12	26.08
R J Shastri	31	4	74	2	37.00

1ST ONE-DAY INTERNATIONAL
Newlands, Cape Town   Dec 7, 1992
India 184 (50 overs)
          (A Jajeda 48, W V Raman 47, W J Cronje 5-32)
South Africa 185-4 (49.3 overs)
          (P N Kirsten 56, K C Wessels 43)
South Africa won by 6 wickets
Match Award: W J Cronje

2ND ONE-DAY INTERNATIONAL
St George's Park, Port Elizabeth   Dec 9
India 147 (49.4 overs)
          (B M McMillan 4-32)
South Africa 148-4 (46.4 overs)
          (D J Callaghan 45*)
South Africa won by 6 wickets
Match Award: B M McMillan

3RD ONE-DAY INTERNATIONAL
Centurion Park, Verwoerdburg   Dec 11
South Africa 214-5 (50 overs)
          (A C Hudson 87)
India 215-6 (49.1 overs)
          (W V Raman 113, C R Matthews 3-56)
India won by 4 wickets
Match Award: W V Raman

4TH ONE-DAY INTERNATIONAL
Wanderers Stadium, Johannesburg   Dec 13
India 161-9 (50 overs)
          (M Azharuddin 49, A A Donald 3-27)
South Africa 165-4 (48.3 overs)
          (K C Wessels 45, J N Rhodes 42*)
South Africa won by 6 wickets
Match Award: J N Rhodes

5TH ONE-DAY INTERNATIONAL
Springbok Park, Bloemfontein   Dec 15
India 207-4 (50 overs)
          (M Azharuddin 86*)
South Africa 208-2 (47.2 overs)
          (A C Hudson 108, K C Wessels 55)
South Africa won by 8 wickets
Match Award: A C Hudson

6TH ONE-DAY INTERNATIONAL
Kingsmead, Durban   Dec 17
South Africa 216-8 (50 overs)
          (K C Wessels 78, P N Kirsten 44,
          Kapil Dev 3-23)
India 177   (47.5 overs)
          (M Azharuddin 41, M W Pringle 3-51)
South Africa won by 39 runs
Match Award: K C Wessels

7TH ONE-DAY INTERNATIONAL
Buffalo Park, East London   Dec 19
South Africa 203-8 (50 overs)
          (K C Wessels 57, W J Cronje 55, Venkatapathy
          Raju 3-37, M Prabhakar 3-43)
India 204-5 (47.2 overs)
          (P K Amre 84*)
India won by 5 wickets
Match Award: P K Amre

Australia v West Indies 1992-3

1ST TEST
Woolloongabba, Brisbane   Nov 27-Dec 1, 1992
Australia   293 (A R Border 73, D C Boon 48,
             C L Hooper 4-75)
             308 (D C Boon 111, M E Waugh 60,
             Ambrose 5-66)
West Indies 371 (K L T Arthurton 157*, B C Lara 58,
             C L Hooper 47, B A Reid 5-112)
             133-8 (R B Richardson 66, C J McDermott
             4-35)
Match Drawn

2ND TEST
Melbourne Cricket Ground   Dec 26-30
Australia   395 (M E Waugh 112, A R Border 110,
             D C Boon 46, C A Walsh 4-91)
             196 (D R Martyn 67*, M A Taylor 42,

I R Bishop 3-45)
West Indies 233 (K L T Arthurton 71, B C Lara 52,
 J C Adams 47, C J McDermott 4-66,
 M G Hughes 3-51)
 219 (P V Simmons 110, R B Richardson 52,
 S K Warne 7-52)
Australia won by 139 runs
The West Indian fallibility against spin re-surfaced when leg spinner Shane Warne sent the visitors plummeting to defeat after having stood at 144-1 with Phil Simmons striking his maiden Test century.

3RD TEST
Sydney Cricket Ground   **Jan 2-6, 1993**
Australia 503-9 dec (S R Waugh 100, GRJ Matthews 79,
 D C Boon 76, A R Border 74,
 C L Hooper 3-137)
 117-0 (D C Boon 63*, M A Taylor 46*)
West Indies 606 (B C Lara 277, R B Richardson 109,
 J C Adams 77*, M G Hughes 3-76)
Match Drawn
Border became only the second batsman to reach 10,000 Test runs after Sunil Gavaskar, achieving the feat in his 136th Test. It was an equally memorable match for Brian Lara who not only hit his maiden Test century but his final run tally was the highest individual score between the two countries.

4TH TEST
Adelaide Oval   **Jan 23-26**
West Indies 252 (B C Lara 52, J R Murray 49*,
 P V Simmons 46, D L Haynes 45,
 M G Hughes 5-64)
 146 (R B Richardson 72, T B A May 5-9,
 C J McDermott 3-66)
Australia 213 (MG Hughes 43, S R Waugh 42,
 C E L Ambrose 6-74)
 184 (J L Langer, T B A May 42*,
 C E L Ambrose 4-46, C A Walsh 3-44)
West Indies won by 1 run
Curtly Ambrose became the fourth West Indian to take 10 wickets in a Test against Australia and in doing so led his side to the narrowest Test win in history. Australia, yet again, had victory snatched from them after McDermott and May had put on 40 runs to bring them within one shot of an epic win. Unfortunately for the hosts the shot turned out to be a thin edge by McDermott off Walsh which sealed their fate.

5TH TEST
W A C A Ground, Perth   **Jan 30-Feb 1**
Australia 119 (D C Boon 44, C E L Ambrose 7-25)
 178 (D C Boon 52, I R Bishop 6-40)
West Indies 322 (P V Simmons 80, K L T Arthurton 77,
 R B Richardson 47, M G Hughes 4-71,
 C J McDermott 3-85)
West Indies won by an innings and 25 runs
West Indies completed their fifth successive win over Australia, thanks largely to Ambrose who, on the first afternoon, claimed seven wickets for one run in the space of 32 balls. His 33 wickets in 5 Tests equalled the record for a series between the two countries. Allan Border recorded the first pair of his first class career.

TEST AVERAGES
BATTING

Australia	M	I	NO	Runs	HS	Ave
D C Boon	5	10	2	490	111	61.25
T B A May	1	2	1	48	42*	48.00
M E Waugh	5	9	0	340	112	37.77
G R J Matthews	2	3	0	109	79	36.33
A R Border	5	9	0	228	100	25.33
West Indies						
B C Lara	5	8	0	466	277	58.25
K L T Arthurton	5	8	1	365	157*	52.14
J C Adams	3	4	1	148	77*	49.33
R B Richardson	5	8	0	380	109	47.50
P V Simmons	5	8	0	283	110	35.37

BOWLING

Australia	O	M	Runs	W	Ave
T B A May	20.5	4	50	7	7.14
M E Waugh	22	3	84	4	21.00
B A Reid	53	9	151	7	21.57
M G Hughes	145.2	30	432	20	21.60
M R Whitney	23	6	59	2	29.50
West Indies					
C E L Ambrose	260.3	77	542	33	16.42
I R Bishop	201	39	480	23	20.87
K C G Benjamin	18	2	54	2	27.00
C A Walsh	175.1	42	467	12	38.91
C L Hooper	170.5	29	438	10	43.80

World Series Cup (Australia 1992-3)

1ST MATCH
W A C A Ground, Perth   **Dec 4**
West Indies 197 (50 overs)
 (B C Lara 59, Wasim Akram 4-46)
Pakistan 199-5 (49.2 overs)
 (Javed Miandad 59*)
Pakistan won by 5 wickets
Match Award:Wasim Akram

2ND MATCH
W A C A Ground, Perth   **Dec 6**
Australia 160-7 (50 overs)
 (M E Waugh 36)
West Indies 164-1 (38.3 overs)
 (D L Haynes 81*, P V Simmons 43*)
West Indies won by 9 wickets
Match Award:P V Simmons

3RD MATCH
Sydney Cricket Ground   **Dec 8**
Australia 101-9 (30 overs)
 (P V Simmons 3-11, C E L Ambrose 3-18)
West Indies 87 (29.3 overs)
 (P R Reiffel 3-14)
Australia won by 14 runs
Match Award:M A Taylor

4TH MATCH
Bellerive Oval, Hobart   **Dec 10**
Australia   228-7 (50 overs)
        (D M Jones 53, M A Taylor 46)
Pakistan   228-9 (50 overs)
        (Salim Malik 64, Asif Mujtaba 56*,
        C J McDermott 4-42)
Match Tied
Match Award:Asif Mujtaba

5TH MATCH
Adelaide Oval   **Dec 12**
West Indies   177-7 (42 overs)
        (R B Richardson 76*, Wasim Akram 3-38)
Pakistan   173 (41.5 overs)
        (Ramiz Raja 52, Aamir Sohail 41,
        C L Hooper 3-31)
West Indies won by 4 runs
Match Award:C L Hooper

6TH MATCH
Adelaide Oval   **Dec 13**
Pakistan   195-6 (47 overs)
        (Inzamam-ul-Haq 60*, Asif Mujtaba 45)
Australia   196-2 (45 overs)
        (M A Taylor 78, D M Jones 48, D C Boon 40)
Australia won by 8 wickets
Match Award:M A Taylor

7TH MATCH
Melbourne Cricket Ground   **Dec 15**
Australia   198-8 (50 overs)
        (M E Waugh 57, D R Martyn 40,
        C E L Ambrose 3-25)
West Indies   194 (50 overs)
        (B C Lara 74, R B Richardson 61,
        M E Waugh 5-24)
Australia won by 4 runs
Match Award:M E Waugh

8TH MATCH
Sydney Cricket Ground   **Dec 17**
West Indies   214-9 (50 overs)
        (D L Haynes 96, Waqar Younis 3-29)
Pakistan   81 (48 overs)
        (P V Simmons 4-3)
West Indies won by 133 runs
Match award:P V Simmons

9TH MATCH
Woolloongabba, Brisbane   **Jan 9**
Pakistan   71 (23.4 overs)
        (I R Bishop 5-25)
West Indies   72-1 (19.2 overs)
        (D L Haynes 25*)
West Indies won by 9 wickets
Match Award:I R Bishop

10TH MATCH
Woolloongabba, Brisbane   **Jan 10**
West Indies   197-9 (50 overs)
        (C L Hooper 56, P R Reiffel 3-33)
Australia   190 (49 overs)
        (M E Waugh 54, I A Healy 41)
West Indies won by 7 runs
Match Award:C L Hooper

11TH MATCH
Melbourne Cricket Ground   **Jan 12**
Australia   212-6 (50 overs)
        (D M Jones 84, D C Boon 64)
Pakistan   180-7 (50 overs)
        (Ramiz Raja 40, Javed Miandad 40)
Australia won by 32 runs
Match Award:D M Jones

12TH MATCH
Sydney Cricket Ground   **Jan 14**
Australia   260-8 (50 overs)
        (S R Waugh 64, M A Taylor 58, D C Boon 50
        Waqar Younis 3-55)
Pakistan   237-6 (50 overs)
        (Ramiz Raja 67, Asif Mujtaba 47*, Javed
        Miandad 41, Inzamam-ul-Haq 40)
Australia won by 23 runs
Match Award:S R Waugh

WORLD SERIES CUP - FINAL TABLE

	P	W	L	Td	Pts	
Australia	8	5	2	1	11	Qlfy for final
West Indies	8	5	3	-	10	Qlfy for final
Pakistan	8	1	6	1	3	

1ST FINAL
Sydney Cricket Ground   **Jan 16**
West Indies 239-8 (50 overs)
        (B C Lara 67, C L Hooper 45)
Australia   214 (49.3 overs)
        (M E Waugh 51, C E L Ambrose 5-32)
West Indies won by 25 runs

2ND FINAL
Melbourne Cricket Ground   **Jan 18**
Australia   147 (47.3 overs)
        (C E L Ambrose 3-26)
West Indies   148-6 (47 overs)
        (B C Lara 60, C L Hooper 59*)
West Indies won by 4 wickets
Man of Finals:C E L Ambrose

WORLD SERIES CUP
BATTING AVERAGES

Name	M	I	NO	Runs	HS	Ave
Inzamam-ul-Haq (Pk)	8	8	2	224	60 *	37.33
R B Richardson (WI)	10	9	2	255	76 *	36.42
D L Haynes (WI)	10	10	2	292	96	36.50
C L Hooper (WI)	10	8	1	237	59 *	33.85
B C Lara (WI)	10	10	0	331	74	33.10
Ramiz Raja (Pk)	7	7	0	225	67	32.14
(Qualification:4 completed innings)						

BOWLING AVERAGES

Name	O	M	Runs	W	Ave
P V Simmons (WI)	46	15	110	11	10.00
C E L Ambrose (WI)	79.5	13	241	18	13.38
M E Waugh (Aus)	35.3	0	159	9	17.66
C L Hooper (WI)	80.2	3	328	15	21.86
K C G Benjamin (WI)	55	4	190	8	23.75
I R Bishop (WI)	61.4	4	215	9	23.88
(Qualification:8 wickets)					

Sri Lanka v New Zealand 1992

1ST TEST
Tyronne Fernando Stadium, Moratuwa   Nov 27-Dec 2
New Zealand 288 (K R Rutherford 105, C Z Harris 56,
Liyanage 4-82)
195-5 (K R Rutherford 53, B R Hartland 52,
J G Wright 42)
Sri Lanka   327-6 dec (R S Mahanama, P A De Silva 62,
A P Gurusinha 43)
Match Drawn
*Not only was the match affected by unsettled weather, but
prior to the game five members of the original touring side
returned home following a bomb blast in Colombo which led to
a shortened tour itinerary.*

2ND TEST
Sinhalese Sports Club, Colombo   Dec 6-9
Sri Lanka   394 (R S Mahanama 109, H P Tillek'tne 93,
A Ranatunga 76, M B Owens 4-101)
70-1 (R S Mahanma 29)
New Zealand 102 (K P J Warnaweera 4-25,
Muralitharan 3-22)
361 (M D Crowe 107, A C Parore 60,
J G Wright 50, M Muralitharan 4-134)
Sri Lanka won by 9 wickets

TEST AVERAGES
BATTING

Sri Lanka	M	I	NO	Runs	HS	Ave
R S Mahanama	2	3	0	291	153	97.00
H P Tillekeratne	2	2	0	94	93	47.00
A Ranatunga	2	2	0	79	76	39.50
A P Gurusinha	2	3	1	79	43	39.50
New Zealand						
K R Rutherford	2	4	0	196	105	49.00
M D Crowe	2	4	0	137	107	34.25
J G Wright	2	4	0	133	50	33.25
C Z Harris	2	4	1	84	56	28.00

BOWLING

Sri Lanka	O	M	Runs	W	Ave
M Muralitharan	52.1	8	156	7	22.28
K P J Warnaweera	107	37	209	9	23.22
D K Liyanage	64.5	16	174	7	24.85
S D Anurasiri	88	27	154	6	25.66
New Zealand					
M B Owens	53	11	200	7	28.57
M L Su'a	53	13	126	4	31.50
G E Bradburn	40.4	5	142	3	47.33
D J Nash	18	2	62	1	62.00

1ST ONE-DAY INTERNATIONAL
Khetterama Stadium, Colombo   Dec 4
New Zealand 166-9 (50 overs)
(R S Kalpage 3-29)
Sri Lanka   41-2 (10.2 overs)
(C Pringle 2-15)
No result

2ND ONE-DAY INTERNATIONAL
P Saravanamuttu Stadium, Colombo   Dec 12
New Zealand 190-7 (50 overs)
(B R Hartland 54, D J Nash 40*,
S T Jayasuriya 3-33)
Sri Lanka   192-2 (37.4 overs)
(R S Mahanama 84*, P A De Silva 43*)
Sri Lanka won by 8 wickets
Match Award:R S Mahanama

New Zealand v Pakistan 1992-3

THE TEST
Trustbank Park, Hamilton   Jan 2-5
Pakistan   216 (Javed Miandad 92, M L Su'a 5-73,
D K Morrison 3-42)
174 (Inzamam-ul-Haq 75,
D K Morrison 5-41)
New Zealand 264 (M J Greatbatch 133, B R Hartland 43,
Waqar Younis 4-59, Wasim Akram 3-66,
Mushtaq Ahmed 3-87)
93 (Waqar Younis 5-22,Wasim Akram 5-45)
Pakistan won by 33 runs

1ST ONE-DAY INTERNATIONAL
Basin Reserve, Wellington   Dec 26
Pakistan   158-8 (48 overs)
(Ramiz Raja 50, Javed Miandad 46)
New Zealand 108 (39.3 overs)
(Wasim Akram 5-19)
Pakistan won by 50 runs
Match Award:Wasim Akram

2ND ONE-DAY INTERNATIONAL
McLean Park, Napier   Dec 28
Pakistan   136-8 (42 overs)
(Salim Malik 39)
New Zealand 137-4 (37.4 overs)
(M D Crowe 47*)
New Zealand won by 6 wickets
Match Award:M D Crowe

3RD ONE-DAY INTERNATIONAL
Eden Park, Auckland   Dec 30
Pakistan   139 (47.4 overs)
(Watson 4-27)
New Zealand 140-4 (42.4 overs)
(M D Crowe 57*)
New Zealand won by 6 wickets
Match Award:M D Crowe

New Zealand v Australia

1ST TEST
Lancaster Park, Christchurch Feb 25-28
Australia   485 (A R Border 88, M A Taylor 82,
                 J L Langer 63, S R Waugh 62, I A Healy 54)
New Zealand 182 (K R Rutherford 57, S K Warne 3-23)
                 243 (K R Rutherford 102, M G Hughes 4-62.
                 S K Warne 4-63)
Australia won by an innings and 60 runs

2ND TEST
Basin Reserve, Wellington   Mar 4-8
New Zealand 329 (M D Crowe 98, J G Wright 72,
                 M J Greatbatch 61)
                 210-7 (T E Blain 51)
Australia   298 (S R Waugh 75, M A Taylor 50,
                 D K Morrison 7-89)
Match Drawn

3RD TEST
Eden Park, Auckland   Mar 12-16
Australia   139 (D K Morrison 6-37)
                 285 (D R Martyn 74, A R Border 71
                 D C Boon 53)
New Zealand 224 (K R Rutherford 43,
                 S K Warne 15-12-8-4)
                 201-5 (K R Rutherford 53*
New Zealand won by 5 wickets

TEST AVERAGES
BATTING

New Zealand	M	I	NO	Runs	HS	Ave
K R Ruther ford	3	6	1	298	102	59.60
J G Wright	3	6	1	237	72	47.40
M D Crowe	3	6	0	186	98	31.00
T E Blain	2	4	1	91	51	30.33
M J Greatbatch	3	6	0	126	61	21.00

Australia	M	I	NO	Runs	HS	Ave
A R Border	3	4	0	189	88	47.25
S R Waugh	3	4	0	178	75	44.50
M G Hughes	3	4	1	117	45	39.00
D R Martyn	1	2	0	75	74	37.50
M A Taylor	3	4	0	148	82	37.00

BOWLING

New Zealand	O	M	Runs	W	Ave
D K Morrison	114.2	29	288	17	16.94
W Watson	67	26	150	7	21.42
M B Owens	47	12	112	4	28.00
D N Patel	70	13	263	8	32.87

Australia	O	M	Runs	W	Ave
S K Warne	159	73	256	17	15.05
C J McDermott	125	36	326	13	25.07
M G Hughes	132.2	38	349	13	26.84
M E Waugh	15	5	27	1	27.00

1ST ONE-DAY INTERNATIONAL
Carisbrook, Dunedin   Mar 19
Australia   258-4 (50 overs)
                 (M A Taylor 78, M E Waugh 60
                 D M Jones 52)
New Zealand 129 (42.2 overs)
                 (A I C Dodemaide 4-20)
Australia won by 129 runs
Match Award:A C I Dodemaide

2ND ONE-DAY INTERNATIONAL
Lancaster Park, Christchurch   Mar 21-22
New Zealand 196-8(45 overs)
                 (T E Blain 41, P R Reiffel 4-38)
Australia   197-9 (44.3 overs)
                 (M E Waugh 57, D C Boon 55)
Australia won by 1 wicket
Match Award:P R Reiffel

3RD ONE-DAY INTERNATIONAL
Basin Reserve, Wellington   Mar 24
New Zealand 214 (50 overs)
                 (M D Crowe 91*)
Australia   126 (37.2)
                 (M A Taylor 50, G R Larsen 3-17)
New Zealand won by 88 runs
Match Award:M D Crowe

4TH ONE-DAY INTERNATIONAL
Trust Bank Park, Hamilton   Mar 27
Australia   247-7 (50 overs)
                 (M E Waugh 108, D M Jones 64
                 D K Morrison 3-35)
New Zealand 250-7 (49.4 overs)
                 (M D Crowe 91, J W Wilson 44*)
New Zealand won by 3 wickets
Match Award:M D Crowe

5TH ONE-DAY INTERNATIONAL
Eden Park, Auckland   Mar 28
Australia   232-8 (50 overs)
                 (M E Waugh 83, R T Latham 5-32)
New Zealand 229-8 (50 overs)
                 (M J Greatbatch 68)
Australia won by 3 runs
Match Award:M E Waugh

West Indies v Pakistan

1ST TEST
Queen's Park Oval, Port of Spain   Apr 16-18
West Indies   127 (Ata-ur-Rehman 3-28)
                 382 (D L Haynes 143*, B C Lara 96,
                 R B Richardson 68, Wasim Akram 4-75)
Pakistan   140 (Aamir Sohail 55, I R Bishop 5-43,
                 C E L Ambrose 4-34)
                 165 (Hooper 5-40)
West Indies won by 204 runs

2ND TEST

Kensington Oval, Bridgetown   **Apr 23-27**

West Indies   455 (D L Haynes 125, P V Simmons 87,
                  K L T Arthurton 56, B C Lara 51,
                  Waqar Younis 4-132)
                  29-0

Pakistan   221 (Basit Ali 92*, C A Walsh 4-56)
                  262 (Javed Miandad 43,
                  W K M Benjamin 3-30)

West Indies won by 10 wickets

3RD TEST

Antigua Recreation Ground, St John's   **May 1-6**

West Indies   438 (C L Hooper 178*, P B Richardson 52,
                  Waqar Younis 5-105)
                  153-4 (D L Haynes 64*,Waqar Younis 4-23)

Pakistan   326 (Inzamam-ul-Haq 123,
                  Asif Mujtaba 59, A C Cummins 4-54)

Match drawn

LEADING TEST AVERAGES

BATTING

West Indies	M	I	NO	Runs	HS	Ave
D L Haynes	3	6	3	402	143*	134.00
C L Hooper	3	5	2	231	178 *	77.00
B C Lara	3	5	0	216	96	43.20
P V Simmons	3	6	1	189	87	37.80
R B Richardson	3	5	0	158	68	31.60
Pakistan						
Basit Ali	3	5	1	222	92 *	55.50
Inzamam-ul-Haq	3	5	0	172	123	34.40
Asif Mujtaba	3	5	0	143	59	28.60
Nadim Khan	1	1	0	25	25	25.00
Javed Miandad	3	5	0	120	43	24.00

BOWLING

West Indies	O	M	Runs	W	Ave
C A Walsh	80	19	207	12	17.25
W K M Benjamin	56	16	138	8	17.25
I R Bishop	46.5	14	127	7	18.14
A C Cummins	30	5	89	4	22.25
Pakistan					
Waqar Younis	98.5	12	385	19	20.26
Aamir Sohail	9	2	44	2	22.00
Wasim Akram	108.1	17	358	9	39.77
Aamir Nazir	22	1	90	2	45.00

1ST ONE-DAY INTERNATIONAL

Sabina Park, Kingston   **Mar 23**

Pakistan   223-6 (50 overs)
                  (Aamir Sohail 87, Inzamam-ul-Haq 50)

West Indies   224-6 (44 overs)
                  (B C Lara 114, Aamir Sohail 3-42)

West Indies won by 4 wickets
Match award:B C Lara

2ND ONE-DAY INTERNATIONAL

Queen's Park, Port of Spain   **Mar 26**

Pakistan   194-7 (45 overs)
                  (Aamir Sohail 47, Javed Miandad 41)

West Indies   196-5 (41 overs)
                  (B C Lara 95, Aamir Nazir 3-43)

West Indies won by 5 wickets
Match Award:B C Lara

COOPERS & LYBRAND
RATINGS
(as at September 1st, 1993)

TEST BATSMEN

1	D L Haynes	West Indies	835
2	G A Gooch	England	819
3	R B Richardson	West Indies	781
4	D C Boon	Australia	722
5	Salim Malik	Pakistan	706
6	B C Lara	West Indies	700
7	S R Tendulkar	India	699
8	M D Crowe	New Zealand	655
9	Javed Miandad	Pakistan	644
10	A R Border	Australia	628
	H P Tillekeratne	Sri Lanka	628
12	R A Smith	England	611
13	P A De Silva	Sri Lanka	603
14	V G Kambli	India	597
15	M E Waugh	Australia	594
16	M A Atherton	England	583
17	A Ranatunga	Sri Lanka	569
	R S Mahanama	Sri Lanka	569
19	A J Stewart	England	567
20	S R Waugh	Australia	563
21	P V Simmons	West Indies	560
22	M A Taylor	Australia	559
23	D M Jones	Australia	558
24	N S Sidhu	India	556
25	K R Rutherford	New Zealand	555

TEST BOWLERS

1	Waqar Younis	Pakistan	903
2	C E L Ambrose	West Indies	885
3	A R Kumble	India	828
4	I R Bishop	West Indies	810
5	S K Warne	Australia	771
6	M G Hughes	Australia	725
7	A A Donald	South Africa	679
8	A R C Fraser	England	674
9	Wasim Akram	Pakistan	669
10	B A Reid	Australia	654
11	T B A May	Australia	650
12	C A Walsh	West Indies	613
13	Kapil Dev	India	611
14	C J McDermott	Australia	602
15	D K Morrison	New Zealand	588
16	W K M Benjamin	West Indies	583
17	M Prabhakar	India	562
18	P R Reiffel	Australia	557
19	P A J DeFreitas	England	531
20	K P J Warnaweer	Sri Lanka	455
21	P C R Tufnell	England	449
22	D E Malcolm	England	428
23	M R Whitney	Australia	424
24	B P Patterson	West Indies	416
25	M Muralitharan	Sri Lanka	410

3RD ONE-DAY INTERNATIONAL
Queen's Park, Port of Spain   Mar 27
West Indies   259-4 (45 overs)
               (P V Simmons 80*, D L Haynes 68,
               R B Richardson 46)
Pakistan   261-3 (43.1 overs)
               (Inzamam-ul-Haq 90*, Asif Mujtaba 45*)
Pakistan won by 7 wickets
Match award:Inzamam-ul-Haq

4TH ONE-DAY INTERNATIONAL
Amos Vale, St Vincent   Mar 30
Pakistan   186-9 (50 overs)
               (Basit Ali 60)
West Indies   148 (44.3 overs)
               (Wasim Akram 4-18)
Pakistan won by 38 runs
Match Award:Basit Ali

5TH ONE-DAY INTERNATIONAL
Bourda, Georgetown   Apr 3
Pakistan   244-6 (50 overs)
               (Basit Ali 57, Inzamam-ul-Haq 53)
West Indies   244-5 (50 overs)
               (D L Haynes 82, C L Hooper 69*)
Match tied
Match Award:C L Hooper

Sri Lanka v South Africa

1ST ONE-DAY INTERNATIONAL
(Abandoned without a ball being bowled due to bad weather)

2ND ONE-DAY INTERNATIONAL
Colombo   Sept 2
South Africa   222-7 (50 overs)
               (A C Hudson 48, J N Rhodes 43, S T
               Jarasuriya 4-53)
Sri Lanka   98 (34 overs)
               (B M McMillan 3-12, F de Villiers 3-15)
South Africa won by 124 runs

3RD ONE-DAY INTERNATIONAL
Colombo   Sept 5
Sri Lanka   198-9 (50 overs)
               (P A De Silva 61, R S Mahanama 41)
South Africa   154 (46.1 overs)
               (R P Snell 51, C Ramanayake 4-17)
Sri Lanka won by 44 runs

1ST TEST
Moratuwa   Aug 25-30
Sri Lanka   331 (H P Tillekeratne 92, A A Donald 5-69)
               300-6 (dec) (A Ranatunga 131)
South Africa   267 (A C Hudson 90, M Muralitharan 5-
               104)
               251-7 (J N Rhodes 101*)
Match Drawn

ISAAC VIVIAN ALEXANDER RICHARDS

Born: St John's, Antigua 7.3.1952
Played for: Leeward Islands 1971-1992 (captain since 1982), Somerset 1974-1986, Glamorgan 1990-1993.
Test debut: v India 22.1.1974 (Karnataka Stadium, Bangalore). Captain from 1985-1991 (50 Tests).

Test Batting

M	In	NO	runs	avge	100	50	Ct
121	182	12	8,540	50.24	24	45	122

v Australia: M 34, Runs 2,266, Ave 44.43
v England: M 36, Runs 2,869, Ave 62.37
v India: M 28, Runs 1,927, Ave 50.71
v New Zealand: M 7, Runs 387, Ave 43.00
v Pakistan: M 16, Runs 1,091, Ave 41.96

Test Bowling

Runs	Wkts	Ave	BB
1,964	32	61.38	2-17

One-day Batting

M	In	NO	runs	avge	100	Ct
187	167	24	6,721	47.00	11	101

One-day Bowling

Runs	Wkts	Ave	BB
4,228	118	35.83	6-41

Britannic Assurance County Championship

FINAL TABLE
Last year's position in brackets

		P	W	L	D	Bt	Bl	Pts
1	Middlesex (11)	17	11	1	5	37	59	272
2	Worcester (17)	17	9	4	3	32	52	236
3	Glamorgan (14)	17	9	5	3	32	55	231
4	Northants (3)	17	8	4	5	35	59	222
5	Somerset (9)	17	8	7	2	26	59	213
6	Surrey (13)	17	6	6	5	40	60	196
7	Nottingham (4)	17	6	3	7	34	56	194
8	Kent (2)	17	6	4	7	40	54	190
9	Leicestershire (8)	17	6	5	6	23	61	180
10	Sussex (7)	17	5	7	5	42	54	176
11	Essex (1)	17	4	6	7	44	55	163
12	Yorkshire (16)	17	5	4	8	21	56	157
13	Hampshire (15)	17	4	5	8	39	47	150
14	Lancashire (12)	17	4	8	5	38	48	150
15	Derbyshire (5)	17	4	7	6	33	50	147
16	Warwickshire (6)	17	4	8	5	24	49	137
17	Gloucester (10)	17	3	10	4	24	56	128
18	Durham (18)	17	2	10	5	29	52	113

SEASON'S STATISTICS
Double Hundreds

247	C C Lewis	for Notts v Durham
236*	C L Hooper	Kent v Glamorgan
229	J E Morris	Derby v Gloucs
225*	P J Pritchard	Essex v Sussex
224*	I V A Richards	Glamorgan v Middx
214*	A Dale	Glamorgan v Middx
200*	A R Border	Australia v England
200	RJ Bailey	Northants v Sussex

Fastest Century
93 mins M P Maynard for Glam v Aus
First to 1000 runs
H Morris (Glamorgan) 1st July
First (and only) to 2000 runs
Graham Gooch (Essex) 20th September
Highest Partnerships

425*	Dale/Richards (4th)	Glamorgan v Middx
332*	Border/S Waugh (5th)	Australia v England
321	Gatting/Rampra (3rd)	Middx v Yorkshire
313	Hall/C Wells (2nd)	Sussex v Cambs
302*	Morris/Cork (5th)	Derby v Gloucs
301	Lewis/French (7th)	Notts v Durham

Most Wickets in a Match
14-169 M C J Ball for Gloucs v Somerset
Highest Score in an Innings
653-4 Australia v England (Headingly)
Highest Match Aggregate
1,806 Sussex v Essex (Hove)
Lowest Score
68 Notts v Surrey (Oval)
Leading Run-scorer
G A Gooch (Essex) 2023
Leading Wicket-taker
S L Watkin
Leading Catcher
J D Carr (Middx) 32
Leading Wicketkeeper
64 dismissals R C Russell (Gloucs)

Even if four days is an awful long time to skip off work to watch a cricket match, the extension of the four-day principle is surely having a good effect on county cricket. Just the record of Middlesex is a fair indicator; their 11 victories in a season is more than they have ever managed in 11 previous county championship wins. In fact, the overall percentage of games finished was encouragingly close to 70% which is way higher a figure than the three day games could ever muster.

Middlesex's win owes much to their two spinners; between them Tufnell and Emburey took 127 wickets in the chase for the title. The batsmen tended to share it around with not one Middlesex player reaching 1000 runs in county championship matches. Gatting, as ever, was the bolster, but the surprise was Emburey, whose batting is all bottom hand and shuffle and doesn't it just work. Emburey hit 638 runs in championship matches at an average of 49.07.

Durham, sadly, had another unhappy season winning only two matches and finishing bottom of the table for the second successive year. They were deficient both with bat and ball; take Bainbridge out of the averages and their top batsman mustered an average of 34.87 (Larkins) and their best bowler, discounting Betts who bowled just six overs, one of 29.94 (Cummins). When Botham bowed out, his run total was 384 in 16 innings and he had taken a mere 13 wickets. Botham's performance did not help them win matches, but it did give them a share of the limelight. Next summer, Durham run the risk of being bottom again and anonymous.

Finally, spare a thought for Sussex. I don't know the last time a county scored 591 runs in their first innings and lost the match. It certainly doesn't happen a lot. Sussex did it in a remarkable game against Essex at Hove that produced a record 1,806 runs. It's little wonder they lost the NatWest final just moments after. They must have been utterly bewildered.

1993 FINAL AVERAGES - ALL FIRST-CLASS MATCHES

BATTING	M	I	NO	Runs	HS	Ave	BOWLING	O	M	Runs	W	Ave	Best
D C Boon (Aus)	14	23	4	1437	164*	75.63	N G Cowans (Mx)	81	16	234	16	14.62	4-43
M E Waugh (Aus)	16	25	6	1361	178	71.63	Wasim Akram (Lnc)	409.2	93	1137	59	19.27	8-68
D R Martyn (Aus)	12	15	3	838	138*	69.83	K M Curran (Nth)	458	123	1293	67	19.29	7-47
S R Waugh (Aus)	16	21	8	875	157*	67.30	J E Emburey (Mx)	719.4	226	1401	71	19.73	8-40
K J Barnett (Dby)	16	24	5	1223	168	64.36	A P Igglesden (Kt)	438.5	111	1068	54	19.77	6-58
C J W Athey (Sx)	17	30	5	1600	137	64.00	M P Bicknell (Sy)	502.2	137	1341	67	20.01	6-43
G A Gooch (Ex)	19	35	3	2023	159*	63.21	C E L Ambrose (Nth)	543.4	150	1207	59	20.45	6-49
C L Hooper (Kt)	16	24	2	1304	236*	59.27	C White (Yk)	130	36	310	15	20.66	3-9
M L Hayden (Aus)	13	21	1	1150	151*	57.50	Mushtaq (Sm)	694.3	212	1773	85	20.85	7-91
A P Wells (Sx)	18	27	2	1432	144	57.28	D J Capel (Nth)	117.4	37	252	12	21.00	3-15
M W Gatting (Mx)	16	24	4	1132	182	56.60	W Benjamin (Leics)	281.3	81	702	32	21.93	7-83
G A Hick (Wo)	18	30	2	1522	187	54.35	A E Warner (Dby)	322.5	76	900	41	21.95	5-27
T S Curtis (Wo)	19	32	3	1553	127	53.55	S K Warne (Aus)	765.4	281	1698	75	22.64	5-61
N Hussain (Ex)	20	35	5	1604	152	53.46	Waqar Younis (Sy)	449.4	89	1407	62	22.69	6-42
M J Slater (Aus)	17	28	4	1275	152	53.12	A R C Fraser (Mx)	532.4	131	1388	61	22.75	7-40
J E Morris (Dby)	18	29	1	1461	229	52.17	S L Watkin (Glm)	766.4	173	2098	92	22.80	5-71
J E Emburey (Mx)	17	21	7	730	123	52.14	D J Millns (Leics)	184.3	51	584	25	23.36	5-21
R J Bailey (Nth)	18	30	5	1282	200	51.28	C L Cairns (Nts)	411.5	74	1242	53	23.43	6-70
M A Earlham (Kt)	12	16	3	666	85	51.23	C A Walsh (Glc)	528.2	119	1516	64	23.68	5-59
P R Pollard (Nts)	19	32	3	1463	180	50.44	P C R Tufnell (Mx)	688.4	189	1529	64	23.89	8-29
M P Speight (Sx)	13	22	1	1009	184	48.04	T J Zoehrer (Aus)	126.1	33	335	14	23.92	3-16
J P Crawley (Lnc)	20	34	3	1474	187*	47.54	D A Reeve (Wk)	284.1	108	528	22	24.00	3-38
I V A Richards (Glm)	17	32	6	1235	224*	47.50	N A Mallender (Sm)	329.5	102	772	32	24.12	5-49
V P Terry (Ham)	19	33	2	1469	174	47.38	P J Newport (Wc)	546.5	135	1454	60	24.23	6-63
J D Carr (Mx)	17	24	6	848	192*	47.11	A D Mullally (Leics)	528.1	141	1506	62	24.29	7-72
R A Smith (Ham)	17	29	2	1253	191	46.40	M C J Ball (Glc)	157.3	35	439	18	24.38	8-46
A R Border (Aus)	16	21	3	823	200*	45.72	E E Hemmings (Sx)	683.2	208	1541	63	24.46	7-31
A D Brown	19	34	3	1382	150*	44.58	K Benjamin (Wc)	283.5	42	911	37	24.62	6-70
M P Maynard (Glm)	19	32	1	1378	145	44.45	C Penn (Kt)	142	39	296	12	24.66	4-12
R T Robinson (Nts)	18	30	4	1152	139*	44.30	G J Parsons (Leics)	490.1	151	1111	45	24.68	3-23
M A Atherton (Lnc)	19	32	1	1364	137	44.00	M N Bowen (Nth)	147.5	30	554	22	25.18	4-124
J E R Galian	11	19	3	702	141*	43.87	G D Rose (Sm)	324.3	62	1090	43	25.34	6-83
C L Cairns (Nts)	15	23	1	962	93	43.72	P Bainbridge (Dh)	333.1	76	1021	40	25.52	5-53
A S Rollins (Dby)	7	13	4	392	85	43.55	R K Illingworth (Wc)	645	219	1404	55	25.52	6-28
M R Benson (Kt)	15	23	2	913	107	43.47	J P Taylor (Nth)	646.5	191	1789	69	25.92	6-82
P D Bowler (Dby)	17	29	3	1123	153*	43.19	M A V Bell (Wk)	212.1	52	649	25	25.96	7-48
G D Hodgson (Glc)	14	27	2	1079	166	43.16	K D James (Ham)	323.2	84	942	36	26.16	4-33
D J Bicknell (Sy)	19	35	2	1418	190	42.97	K E Cooper (Glc)	502.4	149	1233	47	26.23	5-83
N J Llong (Kt)	18	27	5	943	116*	42.86	K P Evans (Nts)	265.3	69	660	25	26.40	6-67
G Chapple (Lnc)	8	13	7	256	109*	42.66	D Gough (Yk)	507.3	115	1517	57	26.61	7-42
M D Moxon (Yks)	19	33	2	1317	171*	42.48	A R Caddick (Sm)	541	115	1678	63	26.63	9-32
P Johnson (Nts)	16	27	1	1099	187	42.26	M G Field-Buss (Nts)	307.3	112	748	28	26.71	6-42
M A Taylor (Aus)	15	25	2	972	124	42.26	T B A May (Aus)	562.5	156	1429	53	26.96	5-89
D I Gower (Ham)	16	28	1	1136	153	42.07	J I D Kerr	109.1	15	405	15	27.00	3-47
A J Stewart (Sy)	16	28	1	1094	127	40.51	A A Donald (Wk)	268.1	59	811	30	27.03	7-98
A J Lamb (Nth)	18	28	1	1092	172	40.44	P W Jarvis (Yk)	267.4	62	705	26	27.11	4-51
K R Brown (Mx)	18	24	6	725	88*	40.27	M W Alleyne (Glc)	246.3	50	707	26	27.19	3-25
H Morris (Glm)	19	35	2	1326	134*	40.18	T A Munton (Wk)	334.2	112	740	27	27.40	7-41
P J Prichard (Ex)	19	36	3	1319	225*	39.97	R G Twose (Wk)	102.2	16	302	11	27.45	4-85
A Dale (Glm)	20	38	1	1472	214*	39.78	M A Robinson (Yk)	514	130	1346	49	27.46	9-37
D L Haynes (Mx)	15	24	4	793	115	39.65	P J Hartley (Yk)	351.4	91	1027	37	27.75	5-51
A J Moles (Wk)	19	34	3	1228	117	39.61	S D Thomas (Glm)	141.3	21	556	20	27.80	5-76
A N Aymes (Ham)	19	29	11	709	107*	39.38	J E Benjamin (Sy)	624.2	153	1783	64	27.85	6-19
K Greenfield (Sx)	8	12	3	353	107	39.22	J H Childs (Ex)	709	207	1729	62	27.88	6-37
A J Hollioake (Sy)	5	9	0	352	123	39.11	F D Stephenson (Sx)	397	77	1155	41	28.17	5-55
M Watkinson (Lnc)	19	30	4	1016	107	39.07	P M Such (Ex)	812	197	2148	76	28.26	6-67
R J Harden (Sm)	18	32	3	1133	132	39.06	D W Headley (Kt)	439.4	106	1191	42	28.35	7-79
W Larkins (Dh)	17	30	3	1045	151	38.70	C M Tolley (Wc)	442.5	115	1194	42	28.42	5-55
M R Ramprakash (Mx)	17	24	1	883	140	38.39	M J McCague (Kt)	298.1	67	888	31	28.64	5-33
I A Healy (Aus)	16	20	7	499	102*	38.38	A L Penberthy (Nth)	171	43	522	18	29.00	5-37

AXA Equity & Law League

		P	W	L	Tie	NR	Pts
1	Glamorgan (16)	17	13	2	0	2	56
2	Kent (5)	17	12	3	0	2	52
3	Surrey (4)	17	11	4	0	2	48
4	Sussex (11)	17	10	5	1	1	44
5	Northants (13)	17	9	5	1	2	42
6	Lancashire (11)	17	8	5	1	3	40
7	Durham (8)	17	8	7	0	2	36
8	Middlesex (1)	17	7	6	2	2	36
9	Yorkshire (15)	17	8	8	0	1	34
10	Derbyshire (13)	17	7	8	0	2	32
11	Warwickshire (8)	17	7	8	0	2	32
12	Essex (2)	17	7	8	1	1	32
13	Gloucester (8)	17	5	9	1	2	26
14	Leics (18)	17	5	10	0	2	24
15	Hampshire (3)	17	4	9	0	4	24
16	Worcs (7)	17	4	10	1	2	22
17	Notts (17)	17	4	12	0	1	18
18	Somerset (5)	17	2	12	0	3	14

1	C L Hooper	Kent	70	40	20	125	255
2	F D Stephenson	Sussex	30	90	0	60	180
3	J P Stephenson	Essex	50	50	0	70	170
4	H Morris	Glam	60	0	10	80	150
5	R P Lefebvre	Glam	0	50	25	65	140
	C L Cairns	Notts	25	50	0	65	140
7	P D Bowler	Derby	70	0	0	65	135
8	Wasim Akram	Lancs	5	70	0	55	130
	C J Adams	Derby	55	5	15	55	130
10	M R Ramprakash	Middx	50	15	0	60	125

*Players received points as follows:15pts for 100 runs,4 wickets,
4 catches; 10pts for 75+ runs, 3 wickets, 3 catches; 5pts for 50+
runs, 2 wickets, 2 catches. In addition, the match scorers
nominate the 3 best performers who receive 15, 10 & 5pts.*

It was a good September for the one-day game; first the NatWest final took the nails back to the quick (and beyond if you came from Sussex), then the AXA Equity & Law League played its best card last with the top two teams sharing the lead with equal points and meeting on the last day of the competition. Glamorgan, having its best summer since 1969 and Kent, in the doldrums elsewhere, looking to salvage something from the summer.

However, if you looked to form then Kent might just have had the edge, if only for the presence in their side of Carl Hooper. In the county championship game that preceded the final, Hooper had put the Glamorgan bowlers to the sword with 236 unbeaten and languidly struck runs, his highest yet for the county.

Glamorgan, though, if their bowlers had been knocked about a bit by Hooper, had Vivian Richards to fall back upon. If Hooper could stroke, Richards could thump; and if Hooper wanted the trophy, Richards was desperate for it.

As it came about, desperation won. Hooper played well enough to confirm his position as the winner of the sponsor's individual awards for the league, but lost his wicket at the very moment he needed to stay and the Kent total of 200 was always accessible even if the wicket was a mite playful.

Morris bolstered the Glamorgan innings after a shaky start, but Richards, in his farewell for the county, was destined to be there at the end. It was an innings of two halves; Richards missing the transition of playing himself in - simply going from dreadful to powerful somewhere around his thirtieth run. He was even caught off a no-ball in the first phase of his innings, which must have led Kent to believe that if Richards was not a friend of the Gods, he knew somebody who was.

Glamorgan duly won by four wickets with two and a bit overs in hand. Along the way this summer, they also equalled the Middlesex record of 12 Sunday league wins in a row.

Benson and Hedges Cup

(all matches over 55 overs)

Of the £614,000 sponsorship money, £93,445 is distributed in prize money: preliminary round winners £900, 1st round winners £1,200, losing quarter-finalists £7,500, losing semi-finalists £7,500, runners-up £15,000, the champions £30,000.

PRELIMINARY ROUND   APRIL 27

GLOUCESTER V DERBYSHIRE   Bristol
Gloucester 198-7 (after 55 overs)
    (B C Broad 58, R J Scott 44, D G Cork 2-39,
              F A Griffith 2-48)
Derbyshire 198-5 (55 overs)
    (P D Bowler 92, K J Barnett 40)
Derbyshire won by losing fewer wickets
Gold Award:P D Bowler

GLAMORGAN V KENT   Canterbury
Glamorgan 236-7 (55 overs)
    (M P Maynard 89, H Morris 44,
             M J McCague 3-39)
Kent 132 (49.4 overs)
    (N R Taylor 42, S R Barwick 4-15)
Glamorgan won by 104 runs
Gold Award:M P Maynard

ESSEX V SCOTLAND   Forfar
Scotland 106-8
    (J D Love 44, M C Ilott 5-21, G A Gooch 2-11)
Essex 107-1 (29.3 overs)
    (J P Stephenson 50*, G A Gooch 41)
Essex won by 9 wickets
Gold Award:M C Ilott

DURHAM V MINOR COUNTIES   Hartlepool
Minor Counties 156-8 (55 overs)
    (I Cockbain 33, P Bainbridge 3-24
             S J E Brown 2-32)
Durham 157-4 (53.5 overs)
    (W Larkins 42, I T Botham 35*)
Durham won by 6 wickets
Gold Award:A R Fothergill

HAMPSHIRE V COMB. UNIS   Southampton
Combined Universities 177-7 (55 overs)
    (J N Snape 52, J P Crawley 41)
Hampshire 178-1 (50 overs)
    (T C Middleton 91*, D I Gower 41)
Hampshire won by 9 wickets
Gold Award:T C Middleton

FIRST ROUND   MAY 11

DERBYSHIRE V MIDDLESEX   Derby
Derbyshire 253-8 (55 overs)
    (C J Adams 58, J E Morris 57, A R C Fraser 3-50)
Middlesex 239-9 (55 overs)
    (D L Haynes 60, M A Roseberry 58, J D Carr 41)
Derbyshire won by 14 runs
Gold Award:C J Adams

SUSSEX V GLAMORGAN   Cardiff
Sussex 263-7 (55 overs)
    (D M Smith 55, A P Wells 53, F D Stephenson 43,
             A Dale 3-37)
Glamorgan 230 (52.2 overs)
    (M P Maynard 57, F D Stephenson 3-48)
Sussex won by 33 runs
Gold Award:I D K Salisbury

NORTHANTS V YORKSHIRE   Headingley
Northamptonshire 211-9 (55 overs)
    (N A Felton 62, A J Lamb 54, M A Robinson 3-51)
Yorkshire 177 (52.1 overs)
    (M D Moxon 52, R B Richardson 52,
             D J Capel 3-54)
Northamptonshire won by 34 runs
Gold Award:N A Felton

LEICESTER V WARWICKSHIRE   Leicester
Leicester 206-8 (55 overs)
    (P E Robinson 70, B F Smith 43, P A Smith 3-42)
Warwickshire 206 (55 overs)
    (A J Moles 63, A R K Pierson 3-42)
Leicester won by losing fewer wickets
Gold Award:P E Robinson

DURHAM V HAMPSHIRE   Stockton
Durham 196-5 (55 overs)
    (W Larkins 110*)
Hampshire 197-7 (54.1 overs)
    V P Terry 79, A C Cummins 3-36)
Hampshire won by 3 wickets
Gold Award:W Larkins

LANCASHIRE V SURREY   The Oval
Lancashire 236 (54.1 overs)
    (N H Fairbrother 87, M P Bicknell 3-27
             Waqar 2-27)
Surrey 230 (55 overs)
    (G P Thorpe 103, A J Stewart 95,
             I D Austin 3-40)
Lancashire won by 6 runs
Gold Award:N H Fairbrother

SOMERSET V NOTTS   Trent Bridge
Nottinghamshire 279-6 (55 overs)
    (P R Pollard 80, P Johnson 59)
Somerset 283-9 (55 overs)
    (N A Folland 83, M N Lathwell 77,
             R J Harden 49, G W Mike 4-44)
Somerset won by 1 wicket
Gold Award:M N Lathwell

WORCESTER V ESSEX   Worcester
Essex 115 (53.3 overs)
    (R K Illingworth 3-21)
Worcestershire 117-1 (32.1 overs)
    (G A Hick 62*)
Worcester won by 9 wickets
Gold Award:G A Hick

QUARTER FINALS   MAY 25

LEICESTERSHIRE V WORCS   Leicester
Leicestershire 205-9 (55 overs)
        (N F Briers 58)
Worcestershire 150 (48.2 overs)
        (G A Hick 82, V J Wells 4-37
        W K M Benjamin 2-13)
Leicestershire won by 55 runs
Gold Award:W K M Benjamin

DERBYSHIRE V SOMERSET   Taunton
Derbyshire 69-0 (20.3 overs)
**Match Abandoned. Derbyshire won 6-3 in a bowl-out
on May 26**

LANCASHIRE V SUSSEX   Hove
Sussex 178-7 (55 overs)
        (C W J Athey 61*)
Lancashire 182-5 (52 overs)
        (Wasim Akram 46)
Lancashire won by 5 wickets
Gold Award:Wasim Akram

NORTHANTS V HAMPSHIRE   Southampton
Hampshire 223-7 (55 overs)
        (V P Terry 76)
Northants 227-3 (53.4 overs)
        (N A Felton 73, R J Bailey 45)
Northants won by 7 wickets
Gold Award:N A Felton

SEMI-FINALS   JUNE 8

LANCS V LEICESTERSHIRE   Leicester
Lancashire 218-6 (55 overs)
        (N H Fairbrother 64*, G J Parsons 3-21)
Leicestershire 108 (40 overs)
        (Wasim Akram 5-10, A A Barnett 3-43)
Lancashire won by 110 runs
Gold Award:N H Fairbrother

DERBY V NORTHANTS   Derby
Northants 210 (53.2 overs)
        (A J Lamb 60, R J Bailey 51, D E Malcolm 3-23,
        D G Cork 3-46)
Derbyshire 214-2 (51.3 overs)
        (K J Barnett 61, C J Adams 53*, J E Morris 48*
        P D Bowler 45)
Derbyshire won by 8 wickets
Gold Award:J E Morris

THE FINAL
DERBYSHIRE V LANCASHIRE
LORDS, JULY 10

DERBYSHIRE

			Min	Bls
K J Barnett*		b Akram	19	44	41
P D Bowler	lbw	b DeFreitas	4	7	5
J E Morris	c Hegg	b Watkinson	22	55	37
C J Adams		b Watkinson	11	23	12
T J O'Gorman	c Hegg	b DeFreitas	49	98	77
D G Cork	not out		92	136	124
F A Griffith	c Hegg	b DeFreitas	0	1	1
K M Krikken†	not out		37	40	35
Extras (B1, LB11, W1, NB5)			18		
Total (6 wickets, 55 overs, 207 mins)			**252**		

Did not bat:A E Warner, D E Malcolm, O H Mortensen
Fall of wickets: 1-5(Bowler), 2-32(Barnett), 3-61(Morris), 4-66(Adams), 5-175(O'Gorman), 6-175(Griffith)
Bowling: **Austin** 11-2-47-0, **DeFreitas** 11-2-39-3, **Wasim Akram** 11-0-65-1, **Watkinson** 11-2-44-2, **Barnett** 11-0-45-0

LANCASHIRE

			Min	Bls
M A Atherton		c & b Griffith	54	143	111
S P Titchard	c Adams	b Warner	0	7	4
N J Speak		b Mortensen	42	79	85
N H Fairbrother*		not out	87	118	85
G D Lloyd	lbw	b Warner	5	9	12
Wasim Akram		c & b Warner	12	14	13
M Watkinson		b Cork	10	19	12
P A J DeFreitas	c Krikken	b Griffith	16	12	10
I D Austin	not out		0	2	1
Extras (LB11, W3, NB6)			20		
Total (7 wickets, 55 overs, 208 mins)			**246**		

Did not bat: W K Hegg†, A A Barnett
Fall of wickets:1-9(Titchard), 2-80(Speak), 3-150(Atherton), 4-159(Lloyd), 5-184(Wasim Akram), 6-218(Watkinson), 7-243(DeFreitas)
Bowling: **Malcolm** 11-0-53-0, **Warner** 11-1-31-3, **Cork** 11-1-50-1, **Mortensen** 11-0-41-1, **Griffith** 11-0-60-2

On the day that Holland upset the odds against an England XI in Haarlem (not the England XI of course even if there were six test players included), Derbyshire upset the Lancashire applecart with a six run victory at Lords. Any side that included Fairbrother was justified in considering themselves favourites and the Lancashire captain almost stole the match with a magnificent 87 taken from just 85 balls. Yet in a final also noted for fielding errors and a Wasim Akram beamer that had the recipient, Chris Adams, threatening revenge off the pitch, the day was stolen by the 22 year old Dominic Cork. Having never before struck even 50 in a limited overs match, Cork hit a vital 92 runs at a time when Derby were looking in anything but a happy position and the match shaping to be over by tea. Warner stole the bowling honours and even Fairbrother couldn't save the day.

NatWest Trophy

(All matches played over 60 overs)

FIRST ROUND
(played June 22)

BUCKINGHAM V LEICESTER Marlow
Leicester 298-9 (60 overs)
    (T J Boon 117)
Buckingham 214-8 (60 overs)
    (S Burrow 57*, J D R Benson 3-13
Leicester won by 75 runs
Match Award: T J Boon

CHESHIRE V NOTTS Warrington
Notts 208-9 (60 overs)
    (C L Cairns 64)
Cheshire 146 (55.3 overs)
    (C L Cairns 4-18)
Notts won by 62 runs
Match Award: C L Cairns

DEVON V DERBYSHIRE Exmouth
Derby 266-7 (60 overs)
    (T G J O'Gorman 68* K J Barnett 60)
Devon 133 (43.4 overs)
    (D G Cork 4-18)
Derbyshire won by 133 runs
Match Award: D G Cork

GLAMORGAN V OXFORDSHIRE Swansea
Glamorgan 322-5 (60 overs)
    (I V A Richards 162*)
Oxford 191-5 (60 overs)
    (D A J Wise 68)
Glamorgan won by 131 runs
Match Award: I V A Richards
Richards' score was the highest ever by a Glamorgan batsman
in any one-day competition.

GLOUCESTER V HERTFORDSHIRE Bristol
Gloucester 274-9 (60 overs)
    (M W Alleyne 73, M Jahangir 4-57)
Hertford 164 (57.5 overs)
    (M R Gouldstone 68*)
Gloucester won by 110 runs
Match Award: M W Alleyne

KENT V MIDDLESEX Canterbury
Kent 282-7 (60 overs)
    (C L Hooper 62, M R Benson 60)
Middlesex 116 (36 overs)
    (M J McCague 5-26)
Kent won by 166 runs
Match Award: M J McCague

NORFOLK V WARWICKSHIRE Norwich
Warwicks 285-9 (60 overs)
    (D P Ostler 104)
Norfolk 142 (53.3 overs)
    (N M K Smith 5-17)
Warwicks won by 143 runs
Match Award: D P Ostler

NORTHANTS V LANCASHIRE Northants
Lancashire 178-7 (60 overs)
    (M Watkinson 60*)
Northants 181-4 (56.5 overs)
    (R J Bailey 96 *)
Northants won by 6 wickets
Match Award: R J Bailey

SCOTLAND V WORCESTER Edinburgh
Worcester 238-8 (60 overs)
    (G A Hick 51)
Scotland 162-7 (60 overs)
Worcester won by 76 runs
Match Award: G A Hick

SHROPSHIRE V SOMERSET Telford
Somerset 301-4 (60 overs)
    (M N Lathwell 103, R J Harden 65)
Shropshire 185 (59.4 overs)
    (J B R Jones 66)
Somerset won by 116 runs
Match Award: M N Lathwell

STAFFORDSHIRE V HAMPSHIRE Stone
Staffs 165 (59.1 overs)
    (C A Connor 3-21)
Hants 166-3 (44.5 overs)
    (R A Smith 105*)
Hants won by 7 wickets
Match Award: R A Smith

SUFFOLK V ESSEX Bury St Edmunds
Essex 251-9 (60 overs)
    (J P Stephenson 84, Salim Malik 74)
Suffolk 130 (48.2 overs)
    (P J Caley 54*, Salim Malik 4-25)
Essex won by 121 runs
Match Award: Salim Malik

SURREY V DORSET The Oval
Dorset 163 (58.5 overs)
    (J J E Hardy 73)
Surrey 164-0 (28.4 overs)
    (A J Stewart 104*, D J Bicknell 54*)
Surrey won by 10 wickets
Match Award: A J Stewart

SUSSEX V WALES Hove
Sussex 257-7 (60 overs)
    (K Greenfield 96*, C W J Athey 92)
Wales 143-6 (60 overs)
Sussex won by 114 runs
Match Award: K Greenfield

WILTSHIRE V DURHAM Trowbridge
Durham 320-5 (60 overs)
    (S Hutton 95, P Bainbridge 82,
    I T Botham 55)
Wiltshire 217-8 (60 overs)
    (I K Smith 73)
Durham won by 103 runs
Match Award: S Hutton

YORKSHIRE V IRELAND   **Headingley**
Yorkshire   272-4 (60 overs)
           (A A Metcalfe 77, M D Moxon 63)
Ireland   187-5 (60 overs)
           (S J S Warke 64)
Yorkshire won by 85 runs
Match Award: A A Metcalfe

SECOND ROUND (July 7)
ESSEX V NORTHANTS   **Chelmsford**
Essex   286-5 (60 overs)
           (P J Pritchard 92, J P Stephenson 90)
Northants   290-5 (57.5 overs)
           (A J Lamb 124*, M B Loye 65)
Northants won by 5 wickets
Match Award: A J Lamb

GLAMORGAN V DURHAM   **Cardiff**
Durham   245-5 (60 overs)
           (W Larkins 75, P W G Parker 73*)
Glamorgan   248-3 (57.1 overs)
           (M P Maynard 101)
Glamorgan won by 7 wickets
Match Award: M P Maynard

GLOUCESTER V YORKSHIRE   **Bristol**
Gloucester   241-3 (60 overs)
           (B C Broad 114*)
Yorkshire   243-8 (59.4 overs)
           (R B Richardson 90)
Yorkshire won by 2 wickets
Match Award: B C Broad

LEICESTER V SURREY   **Leicester**
Leicester   129 (46.5 overs)
           (Waqar Younis 3-18)
Surrey   131-3 (32.1 overs)
Surrey won by 7 wickets
Match Award: A W Smith

NOTTS V SOMERSET   **Trent Bridge**
Notts   203 (55.4 overs)
           (C L Cairns 71)
Somerset   204-7 (57.5 overs)
           (N A Folland 63)
Somerset won by 3 wickets
Match Award: C L Cairns

SUSSEX V HAMPSHIRE   **Hove**
Hants   248-4 (60 overs)
           (R A Smith 104*, V P Terry)
Sussex   252-1 (58.5 overs)
           (D M Smith 123, C W J Athey 107*)
Sussex won by 9 wickets
Match Award: D M Smith
*Smith and Athey shared a 1st wicket stand of 248 to set a new
NatWest record.*

WARWICKS V KENT   **Edgbaston**
Kent   262-9 (60 overs)
           (M A Earlham 58*, A A Donald 4-69)
Warwicks   265-5 (59.3 overs)
           (D A Reeve 72*)
Warwicks won by 5 wickets
Match Award: D A Reeve

WORCESTER V DERBYSHIRE   **Worcester**
Derby   244-9 (60 overs)
           (C J Adams 93, J E Morris 71)
Worcester   245-6 (57.2 overs)
           (T S Curtis 82)
Worcester won by 4 wickets
Match Award: T S Curtis

QUARTER-FINALS (July 27-28)
GLAMORGAN V WORCESTER   **Swansea**
Glamorgan   279-9 (60 overs)
           (M P Maynard 84, S P James 68)
Worcester   175 (50.5 overs)
           (A Dale 3-53)
Glamorgan won by 104 runs
Match Award: M P Maynard
Maynard's second award in this year's competition.

SOMERSET V SURREY   **Taunton**
Somerset   230-9 (60 overs)
           (M P Bicknell 4-35)
Surrey   187 (56.5 overs)
           (G P Thorpe 58, A R Caddick 5-30)
Somerset won by 43 runs
Match Award: Mushtaq Ahmed

NORTHANTS V SUSSEX   **Northampton**
Sussex   230-9 (60 overs)
           (N G B Cook 3-53)
Northants   190 (55.2 overs)
           (A J Lamb 71)
Sussex won by 40 runs
Match Award: F D Stephenson

WARWICKS V YORKSHIRE   **Headingley**
Warwicks   245 (59.4 overs)
           (J D Ratcliffe 105)
Yorkshire   224 (59.2 overs)
           (R J Blakey 75, P A Smith 4-37)
Warwicks won by 27 runs
Match Award: J D Ratcliffe

SEMI-FINALS (August 10)
SOMERSET V WARWICKS   **Taunton**
Warwicks   252-8 (60 overs)
           (D P Ostler 58)
Somerset   200 (56.3 overs)
           (N A Folland 61, Reeve 3-37)
Warwicks won by 52 runs
Match Award: D P Ostler
*This was the fifth occasion in this competition that Somerset
has been knocked out at the Semi-final stage.*

SUSSEX V GLAMORGAN   **Hove**
Glamorgan   220 (60 overs)
           (M P Maynard 84, A C S Pigott 3-23)
Sussex   224-7 (59.2 overs)
           (A Wells 106*, S L Watkin 3-43)
Sussex won by 3 wickets
Match Award: A Wells
*Although M P Maynard did not win the match award on this
occasion, the Glamorgan batsman had already collected two
such awards in this year's competition and his batting record
was Played 4, Runs 336, Not outs 0, Average 84.00.*

THE FINAL
SUSSEX V WARWICKSHIRE
LORDS, SEPTEMBER 4

SUSSEX

			Min	Bls	
D M Smith	run out		124	236	179
C W J Athey	c Piper	b Munton	0	6	2
M P Speight	c Piper	b Reeve	50	81	51
A P Wells*		b N Smith	33	67	69
F D Stephenson	c N Smith	b Twose	3	9	9
N J Lenham	lbw	b Reeve	58	66	51
K Greenfield	not out		8	7	7
Extras (LB11, W18, NB 16)			45		
Total (6 wickets, 60 overs, 236 mins)			321		

Fall of Wickets: 1-4(Athey), 2-107(Speight), 3-183(Wells), 4-190(Stephenson), 5-309(Lenham), 6-321(Smith)

Bowling: Small 12-0-71-0, **Munton** 9-0-67-1, **P Smith** 7-0-45-0, **Reeve** 12-1-60-2, **N Smith** 12-1-37-1, **Twose** 8-1-30-1

WARWICKSHIRE

			Min	Bls	
A J Moles	c Moores	b Pigott	2	19	7
J D Radcliffe		b Stephenson	13	15	17
D P Ostler	c Smith	b Salisbury	25	67	47
P A Smith	c Moores	b Stephenson	60	111	100
Asif Din	c Speight	b Giddins	104	145	106
D A Reeve*	not out		81	107	85
R G Twose	not out		2	8	1
Extras (B3, LB13, W13, NB6)			35		
Total (5 wickets, 60 overs, 240 mins)			322		

Fall of wickets: 1-18(Ratcliffe), 2-18(Moles), 3-93(Ostler), 4-164(P Smith), 5-306(Asif Din)

Bowling: Giddins 12-0-57-1, **Stephenson** 12-2-51-2, **Pigott** 11-0-74-1, **Salisbury** 11-0-59-1, **Greenfield** 7-0-31-0, **Lenham** 7-0-34-0

If you'd have watched just half a day's cricket at Lords and had to rush off elsewhere, it would not have been difficult to believe, when you heard the final score, that you had never been there at all, but dozed off in the back garden and dreamt that David Smith and Lenham and, above all, Speight had made such terrible mischief with the Warwickshire attack that they had set a record total for a NatWest final of 321-6. So secure did it all look that the rosy-red cheeks of the Sussex faithful confirmed that they had enjoyed a celebratory drink or two before even the lunchtime tray was uncovered.

Warwickshire did not aid their cause when Mole edged a Pigott ball into Moore's gloves and Radcliffe missed the line of a straight drive to leave them at 18-2 after five overs, but thereafter Ostler, Smith and Asif Din, who swept and cut and swiped a wonderful 104 runs in 106 balls, pulled Warwickshire back. Dermot Reeve all but finished the job, scoring 13 of 15 runs needed in the final over. Twose slashed the last ball of the match over gulley for two and Warwick had achieved a famous victory. The bowling wasn't always brilliant, the fielding didn't always sparkle, but for sheer excitement, it was a match difficult to top.

NATWEST TROPHY RECORDS

HIGHEST TEAM TOTALS

413-4	Somerset v Devon	1990
404-3	Worcester v Devon	1987
392-5	Warwicks v Oxon	1984
386-5	Essex v Wiltshire	1988
372-5	Lancs v Gloucester	1990

HIGHEST TOTAL IN A FINAL

322-5	Warwicks v Sussex	1993
321-6	Sussex v Warwicks	1993
317-4	Yorkshire v Surrey	1965

LOWEST TOTAL IN A FINAL

118	Lancs v Kent	1974

HIGHEST TOTAL BATTING SECOND
(to lose)

326-9	Hants v Leicester	1987

(to win)

322-5	Warwicks v Sussex	1993

HIGHEST SCORE

206	A I Kallicharran (Warwicks v Oxon)	1984
177	C G Greenidge (Hants v Glamorgan)	1975
172*	G A Hick (Worcs v Devon)	1987
165	V P Terry (Hants v Berkshire)	1985
162*	C J Tavaré (Somerset v Devon)	1990
162*	I V A Richards (Glamorgan v Oxon)	1993

FASTEST HUNDRED

36 balls	G D Rose (Somerset v Devon)	1990

MOST RUNS IN TOTAL

2287	G A Gooch (av 53.18)	

BEST BOWLING

8-21	M A Holding (Derby v Sussex)	1988
8-31	D L Underwood (Kent v Scotland)	1987

CHEAPEST BOWLING

12-9-3-1	J D Simmons (Lancs v Suffolk)	1985

DEAREST BOWLING

12-0-106-2	D A Gallop (Oxon v Warwicks)	1984

MOST WICKETS IN TOTAL

81	G G Arnold	(av 14.85)

MOST MAN OF THE MATCH AWARDS

9	G A Gooch	1973-92
8	C H Lloyd	1969-86
8	C L Smith	1980-91

Australia 1992-93
Sheffield Shield

QUEENSLAND V WESTERN AUSTRALIA
Woolloongabba, Brisbane   Oct 21-24

W Australia	370 (D R Martyn 133*, G R Marsh 121, J L Langer 40, D Tazelaar 3-78)
	184 (D R Martyn 112, J L Langer 45, S C Storey 5-55)
Queensland	221 (I A Healy 49, P J T Goggin 46, B A Reid 4-58)
	283 (M L Hayden 63, A R Border 53, S G Law 41, T M Alderman 4-55)

Western Australia won by 50 runs
Points:Q'd 0, WA 5.8

QUEENSLAND V SOUTH AUSTRALIA
Woolloongabba, Brisbane   Nov 6-9

S Australia	178 (J A Brayshaw 49, D Tazelaar 4-39, C J McDermott 4-48)
	246 (G S Blewett 50, C J McDermott 4-64)
Queensland	485-7 dec (P J T Goggin 120, M L Hayden 77, S G Law 69, I A Healy 53*, T J Barsby 49, D J Hickey 4-120)

Queensland won by an innings and 61 runs
Points:Q'd 6, SA 0

NEW SOUTH WALES V VICTORIA
Sydney Cricket Ground   Nov 6-9

NSW	377-8 dec (M A Taylor 102, M E Waugh 88, M G Bevan 68, T H Bayliss 64, M G Hughes 6-83)
	179-7 (G R J Matthews 54, M A Taylor 42)
Victoria	547-9 dec (W N Phillips 205, S P O'Donnell 67, A I C Dodemaide 53, S K Warne 52, D S Lehman 49, P C Nobes 42, M R Whitney 4-122, S R Waugh 3-90)

Match Drawn
Points:NSW 0, Victoria 2

WESTERN AUSTRALIA V NEW SOUTH WALES
WACA Ground, Perth   Nov 14-17

W Australia	159 (T J Zoehrer 61, J L Langer 58, P J S Alley 5-43, M R Whitney 5-43)
	286 (G R Marsh 47, W S Andrews 40, M R Whitney 3-72)
NSW	220 (T H Bayliss 52, M E Waugh 46, B P Julian 4-50, B A Reid 3-89)
	229-5 (G R J Matthews 65*, B E McNamara 45*)

New South Wales won by 5 wickets
Points:WA -0.2pts, NSW 6 pts

VICTORIA V QUEENSLAND
St Kilda Cricket Ground   Nov 20-23

Queensland	222-9 dec (A R Border 71, M L Hayden 51, M G Hughes 3-51)
	144-9 dec (P J T Goggin 45, A I C Dodemaide 3-41)
Victoria	195 (P C Nobes 70, A R Border 5-46)
	95-9 (G J Rowell 5-31, M S Kasprowicz 4-42)

Match Drawn
Points:Vic 0, Q'd 2

SOUTH AUSTRALIA V TASMANIA
Adelaide Oval   Nov 20-23

S Australia	368-7 dec (T J Nielsen 109, J C Scuderi 100*, G A Bishop 50, S Young 3-50)
	268-2 dec (N R Fielke 74, J A Brayshaw 73*, J D Siddons 69*, G S Blewett 43)
Tasmania	298-6 dec (D C Boon 60, R T Ponting 56, R J Tucker 49*, D J Hickey 3-75)
	123 (N C P Courtney 43, T B A May 5-42)

South Australia won by 215 runs
Points:SA 6, Tas 0

TASMANIA V NEW SOUTH WALES
Bellerive Oval, Hobart   Nov 27-30

Tasmania	403 (R J Tucker 104, N C P Courtney, M G Farrell 53*, D F Hills 48, S Young 43, W J Holdsworth 4-108)
	211-6 dec (D F Hills 87, J Cox 73, M R Whitney 3-55)
NSW	272 (M J Slater 138, C D Matthews 4-75, C R Miller 4-93)
	287-7 (S M Small 88, P A Emery 62*, C D Matthews 3-97)

Match Drawn
Points:Tas 2, NSW 0

VICTORIA V WESTERN AUSTRALIA
St Kilda Cricket Ground   Dec 4-7

W Australia	212 (J L Langer 70, D R Martyn 51, S K Warne 5-49, D W Fleming 3-45)
	337-3 (D R Martyn 116*, G R Marsh 101, J L Langer 44)
Victoria	352 (S K Warne 69, D S Lehmann 60, A I C Dodemaide 50, B P Julian 5-84, T J Zoehrer 3-66)

Match Drawn
Points:Vic 2, WA 0

NEW SOUTH WALES V QUEENSLAND
Sydney Cricket Ground   Dec 11-14

Queensland	447 (S C Storey 103, S G Law 79, P J T Goggin 68, B E McNamara 4-68)
	256-9 dec (T J Barsby 123, G R Robertson 6-104, D A Freedman 3-72)
NSW	382 (T H Bayliss 107, B E McNamara 98*, M J Slater 61, G R Robertson 48, D Tazelaar 3-63, M S Kasprowicz 3-70, G J Rowell 3-101)
	247-6 (M J Slater 72, B E McNamara 55*, S M Small 45, B N J Oxenford 4-70)

Match Drawn
Points:NSW 0, Q'd 2

WESTERN AUSTRALIA V SOUTH AUSTRALIA
WACA Ground, Perth   Dec 11-14

S Australia	409 (J A Brayshaw 77, J D Siddons 67, N R Fielke 55, P R Sleep 47, T M Alderman 4-99, M P Atkinson 3-97)
	284-6 dec (J D Siddons 189*, P R Sleep 44*)
W Australia	304-6 dec (J L Langer 96, M R J Veletta 68, G R Marsh 49, P R Sleep 4-59)
	392-7 (G R Marsh 138, J L Langer 110, T M Moody 71)

Western Australia won by 3 wickets
Points:WA 6, SA 2

SOUTH AUSTRALIA V NEW SOUTH WALES
Adelaide Oval   Dec 18-21

NSW   399-5 dec (M E Waugh 164, M A Taylor 63,
             G R J Matthews 53)
             204-7 dec (M J Slater 82, T B A May 4-66)
S Australia 215 (J C Scuderi 44, G R J Matthews 4-25,
             P J S Alley 3-68)
             379 (T J Nielsen 84, G S Blewett 71, J C
             Scuderi 50, N R Fielke 48, P J S Alley 3-68)

New South Wales won by 9 runs
Points:SA 0, NSW 6

WESTERN AUSTRALIA V TASMANIA
WACA Ground, Perth   Dec 18-21

W Australia 417 (D R Martyn 139, T J Zoehrer 52, J L
             Langer 43, M P Atkinson 43, P T McPhee
             4-96, C D Matthews 3-94)
             268-9 (M P Atkinson 52*, B P Julian 51, S
             Young 5-88)
Tasmania   457-9 dec (D F Hills 138, D J Buckingham
             60, N C P Courtney 58, T M Alderman 3-
             95, P A Capes 3-105)

Match Drawn
Points:WA 0, Tas 2

TASMANIA V VICTORIA
Bellerive Oval, Hobart   Dec 31-Jan 3

ictoria   417-7 dec (P C Nobes 145, G J Allardice
             116, S P O'Donnell 59, D M Jones 56)
             196-3 dec (D M Jones 72*, D S Lehmann
             52)
Tasmania   204 (M N Atkinson 45, D J Buckingham 41,
             N D Maxwell 5-46, A I C Dodemaide 3-51)
             332-8 (N C P Courtney 88, J Cox 64, R J
             Tucker 50, N D Maxwell 4-107)

Match Drawn
Points:Tas 0, Vic 2

SOUTH AUSTRALIA V QUEENSLAND
Adelaide Oval   Jan 8-11

S Australia 333 (D S Webber 135, J D Siddons 75, D
             Tazelaar 4-89, M S Kasprowicz 3-76)
             310 (D S Webber 77, N R Fielke 57, D
             Siddons 53)
Queensland   335-7 dec (M L Hayden 161*, D M
             Wellham 56, P R Sleep 4-80)
             43-1 (M L Hayden 35*)

Match Drawn
Points:SA 0, Q'd 2

WESTERN AUSTRALIA V VICTORIA
WACA Ground, Perth   Jan 8-11

W Australia 440 (G R Marsh 129, M P Lavender 103,
             T M Moody 54)
Victoria   265 (S P O'Donnell 62, D S Berry 57,
             J Angel 6-71)
             457-7 (A I C Dodemaide 123,
             S P O'Donnell 99, N D Maxwell 64*,
             L D Harper 58)

Match Drawn
Points:WA 2, Vic 0

TASMANIA V SOUTH AUSTRALIA
Bellerive Oval, Hobart   Jan 15-18

Tasmania   454 (D J Buckingham 161*, M G Farrell 74,
             S Young 60, D F Hills 55, R T Ponting 50)
S Australia 271 (D S Webber 43)
             314-6 (D S Webber 89, G A Bishop 56,
             J D Siddons 56)

Match Drawn
Points:Tas 2, SA 0

QUEENSLAND V TASMANIA
Woolloongabba, Brisbane   Jan 21-24

Queensland   168 (M L Hayden 46, T J Cooley 4-49)
             162 (P T McFee 5-48)
Tasmania   335 (J Cox 137*, D J Buckingham 51,
             M S Kasprowicz 6-59)

Tasmania won by an innings and 5 runs
Points:Q'd 0, Tas 6

NEW SOUTH WALES V TASMANIA
Sydney Cricket Ground   Jan 27-30

Tasmania   292 (R T Ponting 125, G D McGrath 5-79)
             295-9 dec (D F Hills 101, R T Ponting 69,
             G R J Matthews 5-61)
NSW   338 (M J Slater 79, M G Bevan 7)

Match Drawn
Points:NSW 2, Tas 0

QUEENSLAND V VICTORIA
Woolloongabba, Brisbane   Jan 28-31

Queensland   201 (N D Maxwell 3-31)
             321-7 dec (M L Hayden 112, T J Barsby 81)
Victoria   155 (C G Rackemann 4-24)
             156 (M S Kasprowicz 5-61)

Queensland won by 211 runs
Points:Q'd 6, Vic 0

NEW SOUTH WALES V WESTERN AUSTRALIA
Sydney Cricket Ground   Feb 3-6

W Australia 467 (T M Moody 78, B P Julian 75, S
             Herzberg 57, T H Bayliss 4-64)
             168 (Matthews 8-52)
NSW   452 (M J Slater 124, M G Bevan 103)
             186-4 (M G Bevan 44*)

New South Wales won by 7 wickets
Points:NSW 6, WA 2

VICTORIA V SOUTH AUSTRALIA
Melbourne Cricket Ground   Feb 3-6

Victoria 406-8 dec (D S Lehmann 112, W N Phillips 91)
             201-7 dec (M T Elliott 66)
S Australia 278-7 dec (J D Siddons 100, T J Nielsen 63*)
             306-8 (G S Blewett 69, J A Brayshaw 65)

Match Drawn
Points:Vic 2, SA 0

QUEENSLAND V NEW SOUTH WALES
Woolloongabba, Brisbane   Feb 26-28

Queensland   172 (D R Kingdon 47, G J Rowell 40, B E
             McNamara 3-46)
             349 (D M Wellham 111*, S G Law 84)
NSW   174 (S M Small 51, C G Rackemann 5-75)
             147 (S M Small 47)

Queensland won by 200 runs
Points:Q'd 6, NSW 2

VICTORIA V TASMANIA
Melbourne Cricket Ground   Feb 26-Mar 1

Victoria	225 (D S Lehmann 69, S Young 5-56)
	292-8 dec (P C Nobes 146*)
Tasmania	297 (R J Tucker 120, S Young 76, D W Fleming 4-47, A I C Dodemaide 3-80)
	217-9 (R T Ponting 64, J Cox 51)

Match Drawn
Points:Vic 0, Tas 2

SOUTH AUSTRALIA V VICTORIA
Adelaide Oval   Mar 5-8

S Australia	362 (G S Blewett 119, J A Brayshaw 91, T J Nielsen 64, C Howard 3-71, N D Maxwell)
	274 (J A Brayshaw 110, P R Sleep 41, D W Fleming 7-90)
Victoria	365-8 dec (W N Phillips 122, S P O'Donnell 86, D M Jones 67, B N Wigney 4-73)
	261-7 (P C Nobes 102, W N Phillips 65, D M Jones 46, P E McIntyre 3-102)

Match Drawn
Points:SA 0, Vic 2

WESTERN AUSTRALIA V QUEENSLAND
WACA Ground, Perth   Mar 5-8

Queensland	381 (S G Law 116, P W Anderson 63, M L Hayden 49, B P Julian 5-103)
	233 (D R Kingdon 59, B P Julian 4-82)
W Australia	298 (M W McPhee 59, M R J Veletta 55, T M Moody 45, M S Kasprowicz 5-64)
	318-3 (T M Moody 124, G R Marsh 107)

Western Australia won by 7 wickets
Points;WA 6, Q'd 2

NEW SOUTH WALES V SOUTH AUSTRALIA
Sydney Cricket Ground   Mar 11-14

S Australia	317 (J D Siddons 197, W J Holdsworth 7-81, G D McGrath 3-62)
	163 (J C Scuderi 57*, G D McGrath 5-36)
NSW	393-9 dec (M G Bevan 130, G R J Matthews 75, B E McNamara 49)
	88-1 (M J Slater 48*)

New South Wales won by 9 wickets
Points:NSW 6, SA 0

TASMANIA V WESTERN AUSTRALIA
Bellerive Oval, Hobart   Mar 11-14

W Australia	321 (T J Zoehrer 136, B P Julian 87, C D Matthews 4-77)
	299 (M R J Veletta 104, T M Moody 71)
Tasmania	370-7 dec (R T Poning 107, D F Hills 57, N C P Courtney 56, S Young 50*)
	190-6 (R T Ponting 100*)

Match Drawn
Points:Tas 2, W A 0

TASMANIA V QUEENSLAND
Bellerive Oval, Hobart   Mar 18-21

Queensland	290 (T J Barsby 100, M L Hayden 82)
	210 (D M Wellham 74, C D Matthews 5-72)
Tasmania	339 (D F Hills 110, D J Buckingham 61, S Young 53, G J Rowell 4-95)
	162-4 (D F Hills 50, C G Rackemann 3-51)

Tasmania won by 6 wickets
Points:Tas 6, Q'd 0

VICTORIA V NEW SOUTH WALES
Melbourne Cricket Ground   Mar 18-21

NSW	182 (M J Slater 53, C Howard 4-43)
	351-8 dec (M J Slater 143, M G Bevan 65, P A Emery 58, N D Maxwell 4-79, D W Fleming 3-100)
Victoria	258 (S P O'Donnell 58, L D Harper 53, M T Elliott 52, G R J Matthews 6-76)
	217 (S P O'Donnell 86, D S Lehmann 84, W J Holdsworth 7-52)

New South Wales won by 58 runs
Points:Vic 2, NSW 5.6

SOUTH AUSTRALIA V WESTERN AUSTRALIA
Adelaide Oval   Mar 18-21

W Australia	323-5 dec (M R J Veletta 104*, M W McPhee 59, T J Zoehrer 51*)
	235-9 dec (G R Marsh 50, J L Langer 40, P R Sleep 7-79)
S Australia	334-8 dec (J D Siddons 108, J A Brayshaw 82, G S Blewett 80, T M Moody 4-44)
	226-1 (G S Blewett 112*, M P Faull 56)

South Australia won by 9 wickets
Points:SA 6, WA 0

SHEFFIELD SHIELD - FINAL TABLE 1992-3

	P	W	L	D	Pts
New South Wales	10	5	1	4	33.6
Queensland	10	3	4	3	26
Tasmania	10	2	1	7	22
Western Australia	10	3	4	4	21
South Australia	10	2	4	4	14
Victoria	10	0	2	8	12

SHEFFIELD SHIELD FINAL
NEW SOUTH WALES V QUEENSLAND
Sydney Cricket Ground   Mar 26-30

Queensland	311 (S G Law 142, T J Barsby 51, M L Love 42, G D McGrath 4-64)
	75 (W J Holdsworth 7-41, G D McGrath 3-28)
N S W	341 (G R J Matthews 78, M J Slater 69, S M Small 40, P W Jackson 3-91)
	46-2 (A C Gilchrist 20*)

New South Wales won by 8 wickets

AUSTRALIAN FIRST CLASS AVERAGES 1992-3
BATTING (Excl visiting players)

Name	M	I	NO	Runs	HS	Ave
J D Siddons (SA)	11	20	2	1190	197	66.11
M E Waugh (NSW/A)	9	16	2	883	200 *	63.07
D R Martyn (WA/A)	10	18	3	921	139	61.40
M J Slater (NSW)	10	19	2	1019	143	59.94
M L Hayden (Q)	14	26	2	1249	161 *	52.04
M G Bevan (NSW)	12	21	4	875	170	51.47

BOWLING (Excl visiting players)

Name	O	M	Runs	W	Ave
M G Hughes (V)	347.2	77	954	43	22.18
C G Rackemann (Q)	257.3	45	774	33	23.45
T B A May (SA/A)	224.3	63	544	23	23.65
G D McGrath (NSW)	216.0	54	598	25	23.92
M S Kasprowicz (Q)	435.1	100	1231	51	24.13
G R Robertson (NSW)	59.0	11	176	7	25.14

New Zealand 1992-93
Shell Trophy

OTAGO V AUCKLAND
Sunnyvale, Dunedin   **Nov 26-28**
Otago   193 (I S Billcliff 51, D K Morrison 4-62)
     33-0 (R N Hoskin 22*)
Auckland   105 (N A Mallender 4-21)
Match Drawn
Points:Ot 4, Auck 0

WELLINGTON V CANTERBURY
Basin Reserve, Wellington   **Nov 26-28**
Canterbury   288-6 dec (R T Latham 134, D J Murray 47,
     M J Sears 3-58)
     52-0 dec (D J Murray 30*)
Wellington   78-3 dec (G P Burnett 34*)
     261-9 (M H Austen 85, G P Burnett 79)
Match Drawn
Points:Well 0, Cant 4

NORTHERN DISTRICTS V CENTRAL DISTRICTS
Smallbone Park, Rotorua   **Nov 26-28**
C Districts   177 (R G Twose 85, M N Hart 4-20, S A
     Thomson 3-34, R P de Groen 3-45)
     152-5 (R K Brown 51*, T E Blain 46*)
N Districts   256-8 dec (D J White 110, B S Oxenham 50)
Match Drawn
Points:N D 4, C D 0

CENTRAL DISTRICTS V OTAGO
Queen Elizabeth Park, Masterton   **Dec 3-5**
Otago   106 (D N Askew 4-40)
     86-8 (R G Twose 3-18, D N Askew 3-25)
C Districts   125 (N A Mallender 5-41, A J Gale 3-9)
Match Drawn
Points:C D 4, Ot 0

CANTERBURY V NORTHERN DISTRICTS
Lancaster Park, Christchurch   **Dec 3-5**
N Districts   250 (B A Pocock 130, B A Young 58, S J
     Roberts 4-62, R M Ford 4-65)
     155 (S A Thomson 80*, S J Roberts 4-30)
Canterbury   249 (R T Latham 88, R P de Groen 4-51)
     132-7 (R T Latham 52, S A Thomson 3-1)
Match Drawn
Points:Cant 0, N D 4

AUCKLAND V WELLNGTON
Eden Park, Auckland   **Dec 3-5**
Auckland   136 (G R Larsen 3-30, P W O'Rourke 3-35)
     247-6 dec (M J Clark 64)
Wellington   153 (W Watson 5-40, R J Drown 3-55)
     145-6 (R T Hart 49, M H Austen 41)
Match Drawn
Points:Auck 0, Well 4

AUCKLAND V CENTRAL DISTRICTS
Eden Park, Auckland   **Dec 10-12**
C Districts   177 (S W J Wilson 42, D K Morrison 5-40)
     113-6 (C D Ingham 42*, W Watson 3-44)
Auckland   168 (A P O'Dowd 85, D J Leonard 6-68)
Match Drawn
Points:Auck 0, C D 4

NORTHERN DISTRICTS V WELLINGTON
Trust Bank Park, Hamilton   **Dec 10-12**
Wellington   296 (G P Burnett 53, J D Wells 52, E B
     McSweeney 45, G R Larsen 43, S A
     Thomson 3-36, M N Hart 3-68)
N Districts   72-1 (S A Thomson 19*)
Match Drawn
Points:N D 2, Well 2

CANTERBURY V OTAGO
Lancaster Park, Christchuch   **Dec 11-13**
Otago   131 (P W Dobbs 45, S J Roberts 4-51)
     318 (J W Wilson 78, R N Hoskin 65, N A
     Mallender 62*, S J Roberts 5-75)
Canterbury   319 (S P Fleming 94, D J Murray 80, E J
     Marshall 4-80, J W Wilson 3-80)
Match Drawn
Points:Cant 4, Ot 0

CANTERBURY V AUCKLAND
Lancaster Park, Christchuch   **Dec 29-31**
Canterbury   300-7 dec (B Z Harris 82, L K Germon 60)
Auckland   293 (J G Wright 118, T J Franklin 46, M W
     Priest 3-37, R G Petrie 3-69, S J Roberts 3-73)
Match Drawn
Points:Cant 4, Auck 0

WELLINGTON V CENTRAL DISTRICTS
Basin Reserve, Wellington   **Dec 29-31**
C Districts   143 (P W O'Rourke 4-26)
     275 (D J Leonard 61, S W J Wilson 45)
Wellington   219-6 dec (M H Austen 79, D J Leonard 3-64)
     127-6 (S W Duff 3-50)
Match Drawn
Points:Well 4, C D 0

OTAGO V NORTHERN DISTRICTS
Molyneux Park, Alexandra   **Dec 29-31**
Otago   124 (R P de Groen 7-50, D F Potter 3-35)
     205 (P W Dobbs 77, D J Nash 40, R P de
     Groen 6-49)
N Districts   139 (G E Bradburn 48, A J Gale 4-12)
     105 (N A Mallender 5-30, A J Gale 3-13)
Match Drawn
Points:Ot 12, N D 4

OTAGO V WELLINGTON
Carisbrook, Dunedin   **Jan 5-7**
Wellington   283 (G R Larsen 93*, E B McSweeney 84, M P
     Speight 48, N A Mallender 4-22)
     66-2 dec (M P Speight 49)
Otago   114 (H T Davis 4-45)
     152-8 (P W Dobbs 59)
Match Drawn
Points:Ot 0, Well 4

CENTRAL DISTRICTS V CANTERBURY
Horton Park, Blenheim   **Jan 5-7**
C Districts   277 (S W Duff 62, R G Twose 56, T E Blain
     47, C L Cairns 3-40)
     237-3 dec (M W Douglas 102*, T E Blain 63*)
Canterbury   236 (C L Cairns 79, A J Alcock 3-43)
     209-8 (D J Murray 65, P D Unwin 3-73, S W
     Duff 3-86)
Match Drawn
Points:C D 4, Cant 0

AUCKLAND V NORTHERN DISTRICTS
Eden Park, Auckland　　　　　**Jan 5-7**
N Districts　367-7 dec (D J White 155, B A Young 138)
Auckland　　170 (R P de Groen 5-39)
　　　　　　178 (T J Franklin 56, M N Hart 5-37)
Auckland won by 7 wickets
Points:N D 0, Auck 16

OTAGO V CANTERBURY
Carisbrook, Dunedin　　　　　**Feb 4-6**
Canterbury　42 (J W Wilson 4-15, A J Gale 4-17)
　　　　　　153 (C L Cairns 58, A J Gale 4-50)
Otago　　　104 (M A Hastings 4-30, M B Owens 3-18)
　　　　　　95-7 (J M Paul 24*)
Otago won by 3 wickets
Points:Ot 16, Cant 0

WELLINGTON V CENTRAL DISTRICTS
Basin Reserve, Wellington　　　**Feb 4-6**
C Districts　117 (M W Douglas 62, G J Mackenzie 5-41)
　　　　　　162 (C D Ingham 40, H T Davis 4-40)
Wellington　122 (R G Twose 4-42, D N Askew 3-30)
　　　　　　160-7 (D N Askew 4-54)
Wellington won by 3 wickets
Points:Well 16, C D 0

SHELL TROPHY - FINAL TABLE 1992-3
	P	W	L	D	Pts
Northern Districts	8	3	2	3	62
Otago	8	2	2	4	40
Auckland	8	2	1	5	36
Wellington	8	1	0	7	34
Central Districts	8	1	2	5	24
Canterbury	8	0	2	6	12

NORTHERN DISTRICTS V OTAGO
Trust Bank Park, Hamilton　　　**Feb 12-15**
Otago　　　139 (D S McHardy 50, S B Doull 5-46)
　　　　　　309-9 dec (K R Rutherford 60, P W Dobbs, D
　　　　　　J Nash 42, G E Bradburn 5-56)
N Districts　215 (B S Oxenham 49, D J Nash 3-31, A J Gale
　　　　　　3-42, J W Wilson 3-46)
　　　　　　81-1 (B A Pocock 40*)
**Match Drawn. Northern Districts win Shell Trophy by
virtue of first innings lead.**

NEW ZEALAND FIRST CLASS AVERAGES 1992-3
BATTING
Name	M	I	NO	Runs	HS	Ave
M D Crowe (W/NZ)	7	14	1	803	163	61.76
J G Wright (Auc/NZ)	17	13	1	580	118	48.33
S A Thomson (ND)	9	13	2	515	167	46.81
D J Murray (C)	8	14	2	548	106 *	45.66
B A Young (ND)	9	12	2	406	138 *	40.60
R T Latham (C/NZ)	7	12	1	440	134	40.00

BOWLING
Name	O	M	Runs	W	Ave
N A Mallender	156.4	49	280	26	10.76
A J Gale	216.5	79	408	30	13.60
W Watson	289.3	99	579	34	17.02
R G Twose	123.4	35	284	16	17.75
J W Wilson	270.0	84	587	33	17.78
M N Hart	310.0	89	622	34	18.29

Croquet

British Open

Hurlingham Club, West London   Jul 18-25

OPEN SINGLES
Quarter-finals
R Bamford (RSA) bt R Fulford (GBR)
C Clark (GBR) bt A Westerby (NZL)
S Mulliner (GBR) bt D Goacher (GBR)
D Maugham (GBR) bt J Walters (GBR)
Semi-finals
R Bamford bt S Mulliner
D Maugham bt C Clark
Final
R Bamford bt D Maugham
OPEN DOUBLES
Final
Fulford/Clark bt Mulliner/Aspinall

Men's & Women's Championships

Cheltenham   June 15-20

MEN'S SINGLES
Final
R L Bamford bt C D Clark
WOMEN'S SINGLES
Final
D Root bt F Ramsome
MIXED DOUBLES
Final
D Goacher/F Ramsome bt J Haslam/D Root

British Masters

(formerly Presidents Cup)

Hurlingham   Sept 16-19

MASTERS' CHAMPIONSHIP
Final
D Maugham bt D Goacher

Eastern Championship

Colchester   Jul 10-12

FINAL
R Fulford bt C D Clark

Northern Championship

Bowdon, Cheshire   Aug 27-30

FINAL
S Mulliner bt Ms D Cornelius

McRobertson Shield

(The World Team Championship)

Moama, Australia   Mar 23-Apr 6

Phase One
Great Britain & Ireland bt New Zealand 6-2
(1 unfinished)
Great Britain & Ireland bt Australia 6-3
Great Britain & Ireland bt USA 9-0
New Zealand bt Australia 6-1 (2 unfinished)
New Zealand bt USA 8-0 (1 unfinished)
Final
Great Britain & Ireland bt New Zealand 17-3
(1 unfinished)

SIXTH SENSE

In the French Championships at La Rochelle in August, Englishman Robert Fulford completed an unbelievable **four sextuple peels** in the course of winning the title. Sextuple peels require the player not only to take one ball right the way round in turn, but in the process to knock the second ball through the final six hoops. The sextuple peel was not achieved until 1970 and most top-class players would be grateful for one a season........

Angostura Masters

Hurlingham   Sept 18-19

Final Standings

1	D Maugham	13 wins
2	D Goacher	12
3	R Bamford	11
4	C Clarke	10
	R Fulford	10
	C Irwin	10

Curling

World Championships

Geneva, Switzerland

MEN'S TEAMS
Qualifying
(Games won & lost)

Canada	7-2	Norway	4-5
Scotland	7-2	Sweden	4-5
Switzerland	5-4	Australia	4-5
USA	5-4	Germany	3-6
Denmark	5-4	France	1-8

Tie Breakers
Switzerland 8 USA 6
USA 7 Denmark 3
Semi-finals
Canada 6 USA 5
Scotland 9 Switzerland 2
Final
Canada 8 Scotland 4 (D Smith/Connal/P Smith/Hay)

MEN'S INDIVIDUAL
Champion
Russ Howard   Canada

WOMEN'S TEAM
Qualifying

Germany	8-1	Japan	3-6
Sweden	7-2	Switzerland	3-6
Canada	7-2	USA	2-7
Norway	6-3	England	2-7
Scotland	6-3	Finland	1-8

Tie Breakers
Norway 6 Scotland 5
USA 6 England 1
Semi-finals
Germany 5 Norway 3
Canada 10 Sweden 7
Final
Canada 5 Germany 3

WOMEN'S INDIVIDUAL
Champion
Sandra Peterson   Canada

European Championships

Perth   Dec 13

MEN
Semi-finals
Germany 3 Scotland 2
Sweden 9 Switzerland 2
Final
Germany 4 Sweden 3
WOMEN
Semi-final
Scotland 9 Germany 7
Sweden 8 Norway 6
Final
Sweden 9 Scotland 3

World Junior Championships

Grindelwald, Switzerland   Mar 20-27

MEN'S TEAM
1 Sweden
2 Germany
3 Scotland (Wilson/Murdoch/Burnett/Strawhorn)
WOMEN'S TEAM
1 Scotland (Hay/Brown/Pegg/Wilkie)
2 USA
3 Switzerland

Scottish Championships

Perth

Men's Team
Perth (D Smith/Connal/P Smith/Hay) bt
Stranraer(McMillan/Brown/Muirhead/McIntyre)
Women's Team
Stranraer (Cannon/Milne/Herd/Richardson) bt
Kirkcaldy (Muirhead/Scott/Brown/Moffat)

English Championships

Kinross, Perthshire   Feb 25-28

MEN'S INDIVIDUAL
Final Positions
1 Alistair Burns
2 Martyn Deakin
3 Eric Laidler
MEN'S TEAM
Final
Burns/Atherton/Hardie/Watt bt
Deakin/Bowyer/Richardson/Copperwheat
WOMEN'S INDIVIDUAL
Final Positions
1 Sally Gray
2 Venetia Scott
3 Jacqueline Ambridge
WOMEN'S TEAM
Final
Gray/Johnston/Manson/Bowman bt
Scott/Reed/Davison/Laidler

Cycling

The Tour de France celebrated its 90th year in 1993, but it wasn't marked by the most auspicious competition. Miguel Induráin had his name all over the trophy long before the first peloton was formed and though the Swiss Tony Rominger whittled away at the Spaniard's early lead, Induráin's dominance was never seriously threatened. In 1992 'Big Mig' as he has been dubbed, became the first Spaniard ever to do the Giro-Tour double. In 1993 it was more of the same. In 1994, the Tour returns fleetingly to Britain, through Sussex and Kent (where the roadcleaners will look on in horror if the continentals apply their practice of whitewashing the route, to England), but whether there will be anyone then confident enough to take on the Spaniard remains to be seen.

In Britain in 1993, Leeds played host to the seventh round of the World Cup, which saw a slight upset when Alberto Volpi broke away from his compatriot and World Cup leader Maurizio Fondriest to claim victory. "The team's only tactics was to get in all the breaks," said the Italian, by way of explaining his win. Unfortunately his tactics may have included less straightforward methods. Volpi's sample was later tested positive for banned substances; he was dropped from the Italian world championship team and his career is threatened. Fondriest, in third place, consolidated his overall World Cup lead.

There was no such drama in the Kellogg's Tour of Britain, which the Australian Phil Anderson took by the scruff of the neck in the opening stage, and held onto the lead for the next four days. It was disappointing that no Britons attached themselves to the 13 strong breakaway group in that first stage from Portsmouth to Bath. When they arrived at the regency town, the leading pack had established a ten minute gap. Even over four more days, that was simply too big a gap to bridge. There was a British success in the Milk Race when south London professional, Chris Lillywhite held off Norway's Ole Simonsen by just 20 seconds. It was the closest and quickest Milk Race on record.

Graeme Obree and Chris Boardman's feats dominated the summer; even Induráin had to struggle to compete with the media coverage, particularly the French sporting daily LÉquipe, which went into raptures when the Scot broke the world hour record. (See Landmarks) Boardman's Olympic victory began it all and for the past year and a half Britain's amateurs - or rather Boardman and Obree - have given British cycling more attention than it has ever enjoyed. The sport has long been due a higher profile and now it should have it. In August, Obree rode the world championships as a professional (Hamar was the first world championships where amateurs and pros race together) and Boardman signed terms with France's leading team GAN, winning his first event with them, the Eddy Merckx Grand Prix. Boardman took the precaution of consulting Sean Yates before agreeing to sign. "He asked me what I thought he should do," said Yates, "And I said that he should go for it. That he didn't want to look back later and wonder what might have happened." So Boardman lines up in 1994 alongside Greg Lemond. The future is compelling.

World Track Championships
Hamar, Norway   Aug 17-28

Competing in his first major championship, the 27 year old Scot Graeme Obree brought sniggers of derision from among the Norwegian crowd when he wheeled his homemade bike into the Olympic hall. The laughter was short-lived; Obree, hunched up and riding an unheard of 110 inch gear, twice broke the 4,000m pursuit world record on his way to a stunning world championship victory. In the final, Obree took three seconds out of the Frenchman and former world record holder, Philippe Ermenault, to round off a sensational year for British amateur cycling.

If there was a disappointment, it was that Obree and Chris Boardman (the past and present holder of the world one hour record) met in the semi-final, not the final. In the qualifying rounds, they were both overshadowed by Ermenault who improved his own record to 4:23.283 to be the fastest qualifier. Obree, on his 'washing-machine' bike was the next fastest, almost a second behind the Frenchman. With Boardman third fastest, it meant that the two Britons had to face each other next. Ermenault, in the other semi-final had yet another Briton to contend with, Shaun Wallace.

The Frenchman comfortably dealt with Wallace, but could not have expected his world record to have such a short tenure. Obree knocked more than half a second off it, taking the record down to 4:22.668, as he left the Olympic champion trailing in his wake. Boardman paid due credit to his conqueror - "Awesome" - and if the Frenchman was not already demoralised, he was in the final. This time, Obree took an even bigger chunk off the record (almost two seconds) and while Ermenault posted a respectable 4:23.785 it was no match. Obree, who looked as if he had given his all in the semi-final, found yet more in the bank. "I didn't expect the world record again," admitted Obree, "I wasn't sure if my legs would be tired from yesterday's effort....I think I am getting close to my limit now".

MEN
4000M PURSUIT
Qualifying Times:

1	P Ermenault	FRA	4:23.283 WR
2	G Obree	GBR	4:24.321
3	C Boardman	GBR	4:24.719
4	S Wallace	GBR	4:26.832
5	J Lehmann	GER	4:27.518
6	R Saprykin	RUS	4:29.306
7	T Scmidt	GER	4:29.785
8	A Bach	GER	4:29.892

Semi-finals (Group A qualifiers)
G Obree 4:22.688 WR bt C Boardman 4:25.052
P Ermenault 4:24.462 bt S Wallace 4:30.997

Final
G Obree 4:20.894 WR bt P Ermenault 4:23.785

Final Splits	Obree	Ermenault
1000m	1:08.773	1:09.237
2000m	2:11.734	2;13.952
3000m	3;15.812	3:18.849
4000m	4:20.894	4:23.784

SPRINT
Quarter-finals
G Neiwand AUS 10.999, 11.362 bt F Colas FRA 2-0
M Hubner GER 10.754, 10.751 bt J Fielder GER 2-0
M Nothstein USA 11.004, 11.087 bt D Hill AUS 2-0
E Pokorny GER 11.064, 11.246 bt F Rousseau FRA 2-0
Semi-finals
G Neiwand 10.907, 11.181 bt E Pokorny 2-0
M Hubner 10.808, 11.044 bt M Nothstein 2-0
Final
Gary Neiwand 10.899, 10.815 bt
Michael Hubner 10.721   2-1

1000M TIME TRIAL
Final Positions

1	Florian Rousseau	FRA	1:03.393
2	Shane Kelly	AUS	1:03.494
3	Jens Glucklich	GER	1:04.042
4	C Meidlinger	AUT	1:04.255
5	J Andrews	NZL	1:04.352
6	E Hartwell	USA	1:04.420
14	Robert Hayles	GBR	1:05.895

4000M TEAM PURSUIT
Semi-finals
Germany 4:08.185 bt Denmark 4:10.300
Australia 4:06.129 bt Russia 4:10.976

40KM POINTS RACE
Final Placings
1	Etieene De Wilde	BEL	26pts
2	Eric Magnin	FRA	17
3	Vasili Iakovlev	UKR	13
4	V Kravchenko	KZK	9
5	B Walton	CAN	5
6	J-B Peterson	DEN	0

KEIRIN
Final Placings
1	Gary Neiwand	AUS	10.997
2	Marty Nothstein	USA	
3	Toshimasa Yoshioka	JPN	

MOTOR PACED
Final Placings
1 Jens Veggerby   DEN   85pts
  (pacer: Bruno Walrave, HOL)
2 Roland Konigshofer AUT 75
  (pacer: Karl Igl, AUT)
3 Carsten Podlesch GER   46
  (pacer: Dieter Durst, GER)

TANDEM SPRINT
Semi-finals
Paris/Chiappa ITA 10.623, 10.503 bt Drcmanek/Hargas (TCH) 2-0
Pate/Day AUS 10.720 bt Raasch/Nagel GER
disqualified
Final
Frederico Paris/Roberto Chiappa 11.016 bt
Stephen Pate/Danny Day

WOMEN
3000M PURSUIT
Semi-finals Group A
R Twigg USA 3:39.361 bt S Samokhvalova RUS 3:42.773
M Clignet FRA 3:40.079 bt J Longo-Ciprelli FRA 3:41.893
Final
Rebecca Twigg 3:37.347 bt Marion Clignet 3:39.214

POINTS RACE
Final Placings
1	Ingrid Haringa	HOL	27pts
2	Sv Samokhvalova	RUS	16
3	Jessica Grieco	USA	14
4	K Werckx	BEL	12
5	B Erdinganz	SUI	10
6	N Even	FRA	10

SPRINT
Semi-finals
T Dubnicoff CAN bt G Enioukhina (RUS) withdrew
I Haringa HOL 11.809, 11.978 bt N Even FRA 12.353 2-1
Final
Tanya Dubnicoff 11.871, 11.953 bt Ingrid Haringa HOL 2-0

World Amateur Championships

MEN
ROAD RACE (184km)
1	Jan Ullrich	GER	4:13:09
2	Kaspars Ozers	LAT	st
3	Lubor Tesar	TCH	st
41	M Stephens	GBR	

100KM TEAM TRIAL
1	Italy (Brasi/Contri/Fina/Salvato)	2 001.88
2	Germany	2 014.07
3	Switzerland	2 0247.1
12	Great Britain	2 0626.2
	(Boardman/Jennings/Lillistone/Longbottom)	

WOMEN
ROAD RACE (92km)
1	Leontien Van Moorsel	HOL	2:21:20
2	J Longo-Ciprelli	FRA	st
3	L Charameda	USA	+4

50KM TEAM TIME TRIAL
1	Russia	1 0631.6
	(Sokolova/Bubenkova/Kolisseva/Polhanova)	
2	USA	1 0932.2
3	Italy	1 0934.7

World Professional Road Race (257.6km)
Oslo   Aug 29
1	Lance Armstrong	USA	6:17:10
2	Miguel Induráin	ESP	+19
3	Olaf Ludwig	GER	st
4	Johan Museeuw	BEL	st
5	Maurizio Fondriest	ITA	st
6	A Tchmil	MOL	st
7	D-O Lauritzen	NOR	st
8	G Rué	FRA	st
9	B Riis	DEN	st
10	F Maassen	HOL	st
11	M Giovannetti	ITA	st
60	S Way	GBR	+18:54

National Track Championships

Leicester   Jul 23-31

MEN

4000M TEAM PURSUIT
Final
North Wirral Velo-Kodak (Chris Boardman/Simon Lillistone/Paul Jennings/Jon Walshaw) 4:22.77 bt Team Haverhill (Adrian Allen/Andrew Forbes/Rob Hayles/Bryan Steel) 4:30.68

50KM POINTS RACE
Final Placings

1	Simon Lillistone	North Wirral	54pts
			1:04:22.51
2	Spencer Wingrave	Neilson-Tivoli	23
3	Richard Craven	Loughborough	7

20KM RACE
Final Placings

1	Chris Newton	Middridge	24:36.25
2	Adrian Allen	Haverhill	
3	Rod Ellingworth	Delta	

1000M SPRINT
Final
Stewart Brydon (Edinburgh) 11.296, 11.336 bt Gary Hibbert 2-0

KILOMETRE TIME TRIAL
Final Placings

1	Robert Hayles	Haverhill	1:07.533
2	Anthony Stirrat	Edinburgh	1:08.286
3	Steve Paulding	Edinburgh	1:09.004

OMNIUM
Final Placings

1	Gary Coltman	Team Raleigh
2	Anthony Stirrat	Edinburgh
3	Russell Williams	Geoffrey Butler-Lusso

TANDEM SPRINT
Final
Peter Boyd/Gary Hibbert 11.162, 11.114 bt Marco Librizzi/John Saysell 2-0

WOMEN

KILOMETRE TIME TRIAL
Final Placings

1	Sally Timmins	Team Raleigh	117.866
2	Sally Boyden	Askern	119.283
3	Maxine Johnson	Oundle	119.527

3000M PURSUIT
Final
Sally Timmins (Team Raleigh) 4:02.479 bt Sarah Phillips (Deeside) 4:08.117

SPRINT
Final
Sally Boyden (Askern) 13.392, 13.341 bt Gillian Danson (Ratae) 2-0

Herne Hill Meeting

29 May
1 Hour Attempt
Graeme Obree 49.38km *British record & 6th best all-time*
International Sprint
Michael Hubner GER bt Jens Fiedler GER 11.98
Invitation Kierin
Jens Fiedler
Golden Wheel 22.5km
Tony Doyle

Oxford Uni 25m Road Race

29 May

1	Chris Boardman (North Wirral)	45.57	*BR*
2	Stuart Dangerfield (Leo RC)	48:35	
3	Chris Ball (Antelope RT)	49:20	

National 25m Title

Redruth   June 6

1	Chris Boardman	48:45
2	Graeme Obree	48:55
3	Paul Jennings	52:00

National 100m Title

Almondsbury   Aug 1
Men

1	Gethin Butler	RT Italia	3:44:45
2	Pete Longbottom	North Wirral	3:47:06
3	John French	Leo RC	3:51:29

Women

1	Yvonne McGregor	Bradford	4:15:18
2	Leigh Lamont	Antelope	4:21:46
3	Ann Plant	Lakes RC	4:26:55

Tour de France
July 3-25

Date	Stage	Route (distance)	Winner(Team)		Race Leader
Jul 3	Prologue	Le Puy du Fou (6.8km)	**Miguel Induráin (Banesto)**	ESP	Induráin
Jul 4	1	Lucon-Les Sables d'Olonne (208km)	**Mario Cipollini (GB-MG)**	ITA	Induráin
Jul 5	2	Les Sables d'Olonne-Vannes (227km)	**Wilfried Nellisen (TVM)**	BEL	Nellisen
Jul 6	3	Vannes-Dinard (189km)	**D Abdoujaparov (Lampre)**	UZB	Nellisen
Jul 7	4	Dinard-Avranches (82.5km)*	**GB-MG**		Cipollini
Jul 8	5	Avranches-Evreux (226km)	**Jesper Skibby (TVM)**	DEN	Nellisen
Jul 9	6	Evreux-Amiens (158km)	**Johan Bruyneel (ONCE)**	BEL	Cipollini
Jul 10	7	Peronne-Chalons sur Marne (199km)	**Bjarne Riis (Ariostea)**	DEN	Museeuw
Jul 11	8	Chalons sur Marne-Verdun (184km)	**Lance Armstrong (Motorola)**	USA	Museeuw
Jul 12	9	Lac de Madine (61km)**	**Miguel Induráin (Banesto)**	ESP	Induráin
Jul 14	10	Villard de Lans-Serre Chevalier (204km)	**Tony Rominger (Clas)**	SUI	Induráin
Jul 15	11	Serre Chevalier-Isola 2000 (180km)	**Tony Rominger (Clas)**	SUI	Induráin
Jul 16	12	Isola 2000-Marseilles (287km)	**Fabio Roscioli (Carrera)**	ITA	Induráin
Jul 17	13	Marseilles-Montpellier (182km)	**Olaf Ludwig (Telekom)**	GER	Induráin
Jul 18	14	Montpellier-Perpignan (218km)	**Pascal Lino (Festina)**	FRA	Induráin
Jul 19	15	Perpignan-Andorra (231km)	**Oliverio Rincón (Amaya)**	COL	Induráin
Jul 21	16	Andorra-Saint Lary Soulan (230km)	**Zenon Jaskula (GB-MG)**	POL	Induráin
Jul 22	17	Tarbes-Pau (190km)	**Claudio Chiappucci (Carrera)**	ITA	Induráin
Jul 23	18	Orthez-Bordeaux (199.5km)	**D Abdoujaparov (Lampre)**	UZB	Induráin
Jul 24	19	Bretigny sur Orge-Montlhery (48km)**	**Tony Rominger (Clas)**	SUI	Induráin
Jul 25	20	Viry Chatillon-Paris (196.5km)	**D Abdoujaparov (Lampre)**	UZB	Induráin

* Team Time Trial ** Individual Time Trial

FINAL CLASSIFICATION

Rider	Team/Country	Time	Rider	Team/Country	Time
1. **Miguel Induráin**	**Banesto/ESP**	**95:57:09**	22 Laurent Madouas	Castorama/FRA	41:26
2. Tony Rominger	Clas/SUI	at 4:59	23 Frederico Echave	Clas/ESP	42:25
3 Zenon Jaskula	GB-MG/POL	5.48	24 Robert Millar	TVM/GBR	44:20
4 Alvaro Mejia	Motorola/COL	7:29	25 Udo Bolts	Telekom/GER	44:35
5 Bjarne Riis	Ariostea/DEN	16:26	26 Javier Mauleon	Clas/ESP	45:18
6 Claudio Chiappucci	Carrera/ITA	17:18	27 Raul Alcala	WordPerfect/MEX	47:40
7 John Bruyneel	ONCE/BEL	18:04	28 Thierry Claveyrolat	Gan/FRA	49:21
8 Andy Hampsten	Motorola/USA	20:14	29 Giancario Perini	Mobili-Sidi/ITA	52:02
9 Pedro Delgado	Banesto/ESP	23:57	30 Fernando Escartín	Clas/ESP	53:09
10 Vladimir Poulnikov	Carrera/UKR	25:29	31 Bo Hamburger	TVM/DEN	53:42
11 Gianni Faresin	Mobili-Sidi/ITA	29:05	32 R Gonzalez Arrieta	Festina/ESP	57:57
12 Antonio Martin	Amaya/ESP	29:51	*Others included*		
13 Sean Roche	Carrera/IRL	29:53	41 Alex Zulle	ONCE/SUI	1:18:58
14 Roberto Conti	Ariostea/	30:05	43 Pascal Lino	Festina/FRA	1:19:53
15 Jean-Philippe Dojwa	Festina/FRA	30:24	50 Johan Museeuw	GB-MG/BEL	1:35:45
16 Oliverio Rincón	Amaya/COL	33:19	76 Djamolidine Abdoujaparov		
17 Alberto Elli	Ariostea/ITA	33:29		Lampre/UZB	2:03:33
18 Jon Unzaga	Clas/ESP	38:09	84 Phil Anderson	Motorola/AUS	2:10:45
19 Richard Virenque	Festina/FRA	38:12	88 Sean Yates	Motorola/GBR	2:16:38
20 Gianni Bugno	Gatorade/ITA	40:08	126 Prudencio Induráin	Banesto/ESP	2:53:49
21 Franco Vona	GB-MG/ITA	40:39	*dnf s included* Laurent Fignon, Mario Cipollini		

Giro D'Italia
(Tour of Italy)

May 23-June 13, 1993
STAGE WINNERS:

1 (leg1)	Moreno Argentin (Mecair)	ITA
1 (leg2)	Maurizio Fondriest (Lampre)	ITA
2	Adriano Baffi (Mercatone Uno)	ITA
3	Piotr Ugrumov (Mecair)	EST
4	Fabio Beldato (GB-MG)	ITA
5	Dmitri Konyshev (Jolly Club)	RUS
6	Guido Bontempi (Carrera)	ITA
7	Bjarne Riis (Ariostea)	DEN
8	Adriano Baffi (Mercatone Uno)	ITA
9	Giorgio Furlan (Ariostea)	ITA
10	Miguel Induráin (Banesto)	ESP
11	Fabiano Fontanelli (Navigare)	ITA
12	Dmitri Konyshev (Jolly Club)	RUS
13	Moreno Argentin (Mecair)	ITA
14	Claudio Chiappucci (Carrera)	ITA
15	Davide Cassani (Ariostea)	ITA
16	Fabio Baldato (GB-MG)	ITA
17	Marco Saligari (Ariostea)	ITA
18	Adriano Baffi (Mercatone Uno)	ITA
19	Miguel Induráin (Banesto)	ESP
20	Massimo Ghirotto (Mobili-Sidi)	ITA

FINAL CLASSIFICATION

1	Miguel Induráin (Banesto)	ESP	98:09:44
2	Piotr Ugrumov (Mecari)	EST	at 0:58
3	Claudio Chiappucci (Carrera)	ITA	5:27
4	Massimiliano Lelli (Ariostea)	ITA	6:09
5	Pavel Tonko (Lampre)	RUS	7:11
6	Moreno Argentin (Mecair)	ITA	9:12
7	Vladimir Poulnikov (Carrera)	UKR	11:30
8	Mauirizio Fondriest (Lampre)	ITA	12:53
9	Stephen Roche (Carrera)	IRL	13:31
10	Zenon Jaskula (GB-MG)	POL	13:41

Points winner:Adriano Baffi
Best climber:Claudio Chiappucci

Vuelta a España
(Tour of Spain)

Apr 26-May 16
STAGE WINNERS

1	Alex Zulle (ONCE)	SUI
2	Alfonso Gutiérrez (Artlach)	ESP
3	Laurent Jalabert (ONCE)	FRA
4	Jena-Paul Van Poppel (Festina)	HOL
5	Marino Alonso (Banesto)	ESP
6	Alex Zulle (ONCE)	SUI
7	Laurent Jalabert (ONCE)	FRA
8	Jean-Paul Van Poppel (Festina)	HOL
9	D Abdouzhaparov (Lampre)	UZB
10	J C Gonzalez Salvador (Eldor)	ESP
11	Tony Rominger (Clas)	SUI
14	Tony Rominger (Clas)	SUI
15	Dag-Otto Laurizten (TVM)	NOR
16	Jesus Montoya (Amaya)	ESP
17	Oliverio Rinçon (Amaya)	COL
18	Sergei Outschakov (Lampre)	UKR
19	Tony Rominger (Clas)	SUI
20	D Abdouzhaparov (Lampre)	UZB
21	Alex Zulle (ONCE)	SUI

FINAL CLASSIFICATION

1	Tony Rominger (Clas)	SUI	96:07:03
2	Alex Zulle (ONCE)	SUI	+29
3	L Cubiño (Amaya)		+8:54
4	Oliverio Rinçon (Amaya)	COL	+9:54
5	Jesus Montoya (Amaya)	ESP	+10:27
15	Robert Millar (TVM)	GBR	+34:52

TOUR OF LOMBARDY Oct, 1992
Final Placings

1	Tony Rominger	SUI	6:07:50
2	Claudio Chiappucci	ITA	+ 41
3	Davide Cassani	ITA	+2:50
37	Sean Yates	ENG	+28:34

TOUR OF VALENCIA Mar
Final Placings

1	J Gorospe	ESP	23:31.51
2	S Della Santa	ITA	+6
3	M Induráin	ESP	+21

PARIS-NICE CLASSIC Mar
Final Placings

1	Alex Zulle	SUI	29:7:45
2	L Bezault	FRA	+41
3	P Lance	FRA	+1:07
39	R Millar	GBR	
61	S Yates	GBR	+19.37

TOUR OF SWEDEN June 20-24
Final Placings

1	Phil Anderson	AUS	28:34:50
2	F Moreau	FRA	+23
3	L Armstrong	USA	+1:06
96	S Yates	GBR	+4:22

TOUR OF SWITZERLAND June 15-24
Final Placings

1	M Saligari	ITA	44:23:15
2	R Jaermann	SUI	+2:17
3	F Escartin	ESP	+2:24

TOUR OF GALICIA Aug 9-13
Final Placings

1	Andy Hampsten (Motorola)	USA	21:50:58
2	Della Santa (Mapei)		+1:03
3	Mejia (Motorola)		+2:56

TOUR OF BURGOS Jul 31-Aug 5
Final Placings

1	Luadenlino Cubiño (Amaya)		22:36:13
2	Raul Alcala (WordPerfect)		+32
3	L Dufaux (ONCE)		+43

TOUR OF PORTUGAL Aug 1-15
Final Placings

1	Joaquim Gomes (Feirense)	POR	55:34:32
2	Vitor Gamito (Sicasal)	POR	+1:43
3	Luis Espinosa (Artiach)	COL	+2:14

GRAND PRIX EDDY MERCKX (62km) Sept 12

1	Chris Boardman	GBR	1:16:38
2	Pascal Lance	FRA	+1:02
3	Jelle Nijdam	HOL	+2:09
10	Graeme Obree	GBR	+3:39

Boardman's first professional race for GAN. Obree crashed

World Cup Series

Milan - San Remo (297km)

Mar 20

1	Maurizio Fondriest (Lampre)	ITA	7:25:37
2	L Gelfi (Eldor)		+4
3	Max Sciandri (Motorola)	ITA	+9

Tour of Flanders (263km)

Apr 4

1	Johan Museeuw (GB-MG)	BEL	6:33:00
2	F Maassen (WordPerfect)	HOL	st
3	D Bottaro (Mecair)	ITA	+22

Paris - Roubaix (267.5km)

Apr 11

1	Gilbert Duclos-Lassalle (Gan)	FRA	6:25:20
2	F Ballerini (GB-MG)	ITA	st
3	Olaf Ludwig (Telekom)	GER	+2:09

Liége - Bastogne - Liége

(261km)   Apr 18

1	Rolf Sorenseon (Carrera)	DEN	7:14:08
2	Tony Rominger (Clas)	SUI	+1
3	Maurizio Fondriest (Lampre)	ITA	+21

Amstel Gold (249km)

Apr 25

1	Rolf Jaerman (Ariostea)	SUI	6:40:04
2	Gianni Bugno (Gatorade)	ITA	st
3	J Heppner (Telekom)		+1:02

San Sebastian Classic

(238Km)   Aug 7

1	Claudio Chiappucci (Carrera)	ITA	5:47:51
2	Gianni Faresin (ZG Mobili)`	ITA	+2
3	Alberto Volpi (Mecair)	ITA	+24

Leeds International Classic (143.8m)

Aug 15

1	Alberto Volpi (Mecair)	ITA	5:41:22
2	Jesper Skibby (TVM)	DEN	+3
3	Maurizio Fondriest (Lampre)	ITA	st
4	Max Sciandri (Motorola)	ITA	st
5	Lance Armstrong (Motorola)	USA	+36

Zurich Classic (239k)

Aug 23

1	Maurizio Fondriest (Lampre)	ITA	6:23:38
2	Charly Mottet (Novémail)	FRA	st
3	Bruno Cenghialta (Ariostea)	ITA	st

QUOTES

"If they can't win themselves, they'd rather see a foreigner take the stage than another British professional. I'm sick to the back teeth of Bananas"

Rob Holden, on the tactics of the Banana team during the Milk Race.

"I've often been on a saddle for over 350km at a time. If, the minute I get off a saddle they say, 'Alfredo, do it', I will do it"

Italian coach, Alfredo Martini, suggesting that research which claims that cycling causes impotence is not all it's cracked up to be.

"As I said after Obree's record, I am capable of doing better and of achieving 53.2km. I would need a budget of half a million Swiss francs (around £200,000) and three months of preparation. I no longer have any scruples about beating the record. When it belonged to Moser, it would have been embarrassing because he is my master"

Swiss star Tony Rominger, on Obree's record.

"My world is in ruins. I am incredulous. I don't know how they could have found that substance in my urine"

Alberto Volpi, on testing positive following his Leeds Classic victory

"It's impossible. Volpi is a professional who knows what he is doing"

Mecair team leader

Milk Race

May 30-June 12

PROLOGUE: Tunbridge Wells 2.3m
1	Rob Holden	GBR	5:11.01
2	Henk Vogels	AUS	5:16.88
3	Keith Reynolds	GBR	5:18.74

STAGE ONE: Kent circuit 117m
1	Frank Hoej	DEN	4:28:30
2	Henk Vogels	AUS	st
3	Chris Lillywhite	GBR	st

STAGE TWO: Eastbourne-Portsmouth 103.4m
1	Nicholai Bo Larsen	DEN	3:36:53
2	Martin Van Der Steen	HOL	st
3	Kim Marcussen	DEN	st

STAGE THREE: Thames Ditton-Welwyn GC 98.6m
1	Matthew Postle	GBR	3:31:06
2	Mark Rendell	NZL	+2
3	Ben Luckwell	GBR	+32

STAGE FOUR: Luton-Bury St Edmunds 85.6m
1	Martin Van Steen	HOL	3:04:04
2	Paul Konings	HOL	st
3	Willie Englebrecht		st

STAGE FIVE: Cambridge-Milton Keynes 72.9m
1	Christian Anderson	DEN	2:33:28
2	Martin Van Steen	HOL	st
3	Simeon Hempsall	GBR	st

STAGE SIX: Stratford-Leicester 103m
1	Ben Luckwell	GBR	3:47:40
2	Martin Van Steen	HOL	st
3	John Charlesworth	GBR	st

STAGE SEVEN: Great Malvern circuit 74m
1	Christian Andersen	DEN	2:40:31
2	Conor Henry	IRL	st
3	Henk Vogels	AUS	+2

STAGE EIGHT: Birmingham-Llandudno 125m
1	Patrick Jonker	AUS	4:40:55
2	Jacek Mickiewicz	POL	+12
3	Grant Rice	AUS	st

STAGE NINE: Wrexham-Rotherham 120m
1	Mark Walsham	GBR	5:04:52
2	Mark McKay	GBR	st
3	Jørgen Pettersen	NOR	st

STAGE TEN: Sheffield-Liverpool
1	Alexandre Nadobenko	KZK	4:33:29
2	Gary Beneke	RSA	st
3	John Charlesworth	GBR	st

STAGE ELEVEN: Liverpool-Salford Quays 85.6m
1	Jacek Mickiewicz	POL	3:06:37
2	Milan Erzen	SLO	st
3	Christian Andersen	DEN	st

STAGE TWELVE: Manchester circuit 50m
1	Alexandre Nadobenko	KZK	1:39:46
2	Rob Holden	GBR	st
3	Damian McDonald	AUS	st

FINAL OVERALL
1	Chris Lillywhite	GBR	43:19:38
2	Ole Simensen	NOR	+20
3	Danil Kovar	TCH	+25

Team Winner
Norway
King of the Mountains
Mark McKay

Points
Martin Van Sheen
Combine
Brian Smith

Kellogg's Tour

STAGE ONE: Portsmouth - Bath 105.3m
1	Phil Anderson (Motorola)	AUS	4:33:01
2	Wladimir Belli (Lampre)	ITA	st
3	Bo-Andre Namtvedt (Subaru)	NOR	st

STAGE TWO: Cardiff - Swansea 117.4m
1	Serge Baguet (Lotto)	BEL	4:57:40
2	Maarten Den Bakker (TVM)	HOL	st
3	Maurizio Fondriest (Lampre)	ITA	+34

STAGE THREE: Newport - Coventry 123.5m
1	Dag-Otto Lauritzen (TVM)	NOR	4:29:57
2	Jan Svoroda (Lampre)		+47
3	Eddy Schurer (TVM)		st

STAGE FOUR: Birmingham - Manchester 113.3m
1	Peter de Clerq (Lotto)	BEL	4:58:52
2	Eugeny Berzin (Mecair)	RUS	st
3	Jan Svoroda (Lampre)		+1:57

STAGE FIVE: Bradford - Liverpool 109m
1	Eric de Clerq (La William)	BEL	4:38:26
2	Hendrick Redant (Collstrop)	BEL	+24
3	Thierry Claveyrolat (Gan)		+26

FINAL OVERALL
1	Phil Anderson (Motorola)	AUS	23:45:34
2	Wladimir Belli (Lampre)	ITA	+4
3	Bo-Andre Namtvedt (Subaru)	NOR	+8
26	Chris Lillywhite (Banana)	GBR	+12:58

Tour de France Féminin

Jul 25-Aug7
Overall
1	Leontien Van Moorsel	HOL	33:24:25
2	Marion Clignet	FRA	+8:29
3	Heidi Van de Vijver	BEL	+9:27

TOUR POSTSCRIPT

Manx cyclist Marie Purvis became the first British
woman to win a stage of the Tour de France
Féminin, when she came home 55 seconds clear
of the field on the eleventh stage from Le Fontanil
to Vaujany. Not so happy was the Frenchwoman
Marion Clignet who finished second. Clignet
failed a drugs test at a track meeting in Spain
and was still awaiting her punishment
when we last heard.

Cyclo-cross
World Championships

Cova, Italy   Jan 31

Professional Title (17m)

1	Dominique Arnould	FRA	1:03:17
2	Mike Kluge	GER	+9
3	W De Vos	HOL	+16
17	Steve Douce	GBR	+3:59
24	C Young	GBR	+6.19
28	N Craig	GBR	+7:54

Amateur Title

1	Henrik Djernis	DEN	46:21
2	Ralf Berner	GER	+6
3	Daniele Pontoni	ITA	st
46	Roger Hammond	GBR	+3:34
48	S Blunt	GBR	+3:49
49	J Norfolk	GBR	+3:51
51	G Foord	GBR	+3:59

British Championship

Wolverhampton   Jan 3

Final Placings

1	Steve Douce	Saracen	1:10:05
2	David Baker	Raleigh	+39
3	Peter Stevenson	Middridge	1:12

Cycle Speedway
World Cup

Salisbury, Australia   Mar 6

Final

1	England	47

(Craig Harcourt 13, Dave Hemsley 13, Mark Hammersley 11, Steve Paver 10, Dean Webb dnr)

2	Australia	43
3	Wales	42
4	European Team	26

World Masters

Individual Final

1	Tony Herd	AUS	19
2	Dave Hemsley	GBR	19

(Herd wins after tie-breaker)

3	Craig Harcourt	GBR	16
4	Norman Venson	GBR	16

(after tie-breaker)

Australia v Great Britain Test Series

Australia   Mar 7-19

Match 1

Murray Bridge   *Mar 7*

Australia	73
Great Britain	102

Match 2

Salisbury   *Mar 8*

Australia	84
Great Britain	94

Match 3

Salisbury   *Mar 15*

Australia	76
Great Britain	97

Match 4

Findon   *Mar 16*

Australia	80
Great Britain	98

Match 5

Findon   *Mar 19*

Australia	94
Great Britain	82

Great Britain win the series 4-1

Home International Series

Match 1

Great Blakenham, Suffolk   *Jul 3*

England	51
Wales	36
Scotland	33
Ireland	33

Match 2

Thurrock, Essex   *Jul 4*

Wales	45
England	43
Scotland	36
Ireland	32

Match 3

Newport, Gwent   *Jul 10*

Scotland	42
Ireland	40
England	40
Wales	35

Match 4

Wednesfield, W Midlans   *Jul 11*

England	49
Scotland	39
Wales	35
Ireland	33

Mountain Bikes
World Championships

Métabief, France   Sep 18-19
CROSS-COUNTRY
Men

1	H Djernis	DEN	2:56:53
2	M Gerritsen	HOL	+5:18
3	J Ostergaard	DEN	+5:35
10	B Clarke	GBR	+11:28
34	N Craig	GBR	+19:10
36	T Gould	GBR	+19:57
49	R Thackeray	GBR	+27:12

Women

1	P Pezzo	ITA	2:43:04
2	J Longo	FRA	+1:19
3	R Matthews	USA	+7:31
22	D Murrell	GBR	+33:43
31	S Roberts	GBR	+39:19
40	S Cartmel	GBR	+49:56

DOWNHILL
Men

1	M King	USA	4:44.4
2	P Caramellino	ITA	+0.8
3	M Rockwell	USA	+2.4

Women

1	G Bonazzi	ITA	5:34.9
2	K Sonier	USA	+3.1
3	M Giove	USA	+7.6
22	D Morrell	GBR	+1:2
34	S Roberts	GBR	+1:40
36	A Smith	GBR	+1:47
47	T Harcastle	GBR	+2:34

National Cross-country Championships

Pro-Elite Men (30m)

1	David Baker	Raleigh	2:05:35
2	Gary Foord	Scott	+1
3	N Craig	Diamond Back	+1:24

Pro-Elite Women (24m)

1	Caroline Alexander	Louis Garneau	2:00:11
2	Deb Morrell	Formula One	+4:34
3	Sally Timmins	Raleigh	+4:58

Darts

Embassy World Professional

Lakeside CC, Frimley Green Jan 1-9

MEN
2nd Round
Best of 5 sets, dart average given in brackets

Steve Beaton	ENG	3	(32.03)
Dennis Priestley(1)	ENG	1	(31.09)
Eric Bristow	ENG	0	(28.47)
Bob Anderson(8)	ENG	3	(29.96)
Ronnie Sharp	SCO	1	(29.61)
Alan Warriner(5)	ENG	3	(31.33)
Albert Anstey	CAN	0	(29.69)
Wayne Weening	AUS	3	(31.31)
Jann Hoffman	DEN	1	(28.85)
Mike Gregory(2)	ENG	3	(30.52)
Martin Phillips	WAL	0	(30.00)
Bobby George	ENG	3	(30.42)
Raymond Barneveld	HOL	2	(28.89)
John Lowe(6)	ENG	3	(28.99)
Kevin Spiolek	ENG	3	(28.83)
Phil Taylor(3)	ENG	1	(29.31)

Quarter-finals *Best of 7 sets*

Steve Beaton	4	(32.43)
Bob Anderson	1	(30.46)
Alan Warriner	4	(30.27)
Wayne Weenin	1	(28.95)
Mike Gregory	2	(31.13)
Bobby George	4	(31.07)
John Lowe	4	(29.75)
Kevin Spiolek	3	(28.82)

Semi-finals *Best of 9 sets*

Steve Beaton	2	(30.62)
Alan Warriner	5	(30.08)
Bobby George	3	(30.17)
John Lowe	5	(30.70)

Final *Best of 11 sets*

Alan Warriner	3	(27.44)
John Lowe	6	(27.99)

Winmau World Masters

Park Inn Hotel, London   Dec 11-12, 1992
Men's: Dennis Priestley (ENG)
Women's: Leanne Maddock (WAL)
Youth: Leanne Maddock (WAL)

EMBASSY GOLD CUP
Trentham Gardens, Stoke Oct 31, 1992
Men's Singles: Dennis Priestley (ENG)
Men's Doubles: Alan Taylor & Ian Long

Women's Singles: Louise Perry (ENG)
Women's Doubles: Tammy Montgomery & Val Windle (ENG)

BRITISH OPEN CHAMPIONSHIPS
Men's: Dennis Priestley (ENG)
Women's: Sandra Greatbatch (WAL)
Men's Pairs: Reg Harding & Rod Howick
Women's Pairs: Sandra Greatbatch & Rhian Speed(WAL)

BRITISH MATCHPLAY CHAMPIONSHIP
Haven Holiday Centre, Great Yarmouth Oct 20, 1992
Men's: Ronnie Baxter (ENG)

MEDITERRANEAN OPEN
Men's: Paul Williams (ENG)
Women's: Maggie Sutton
Men's Pairs: Dave Jenner & Tom Wilson
Women's Pairs: Melanie Kench & Val Windle
Mixed: Paul Wright & Nancy Grundy

BRITISH INTERNATIONAL CHAMPIONSHIP
Lakeside CC, Frimley Green Apr 3-4
Men: 1. England   4pts
      2. Scotland   1pt
      3. Wales   1pt
Women's: 1. England   3pts
        2. Wales   2pts
        3. Scotland   1pt

BRITISH INTER-COUNTY CHAMPIONSHIP
Men's Premier Div: Lancashire
Women's Premier Div: Yorkshire
Men's Scottish Div: Ayrshire
Women's Scottish Div: Grampian
Best Player Award: Men-Steve Beaton (Wiltshire)
                Women-Donna Robertson (Highland)

BDO SPORT'S PERSONALITY AWARDS
Men (Player): Steve Beaton (Wiltshire)
Women (Player): Leanne Maddock (Gwent)
Men (Official): Michael Getty
Women (Official): Vi Alderman

THE LAST DARTS

News that Englebert Humperdinck has become the chairman of the new World Darts Council will undoubtedly thrill the darts world. Englebert has, apparently, been a darts fan for years. It is even suggested that the original lyrics to his most famous song went:
'I wonder should I throw my darts away
We only had one more game to play
Then I saw you out the corner of my eye
A little girl alone and so shy
I had the last darts with you........

Equestrianism

The Whitaker's, Michael and John in that order, held the top two rankings in the showjumping world at the end of September, but silver remained the most popular currency in equestrian circles at championships (ask Ian Stark about it). The showjumping team came closest at Gijon where they missed gold by 1.92 faults to the Swiss team. Germany took an early lead, but slumped badly in the second round as all three of Switzerland's top riders went clear, Stefan Lauber on Lugano taking a measure of luck along the way, as his horse clouted three of the fences, but did not dislodge a bar. It made it all the more exasperating when Dollar Girl and Nick Skelton brushed the final fence and earned a penalty. Even though both Whitakers went clear, the title was lost. In the individual event, the placings were even closer, with Switzerland's Willi Melliger, on the second day, hanging on to the overnight lead he had established. Midnight Madness went clear over a formidable course, but it wasn't enough to catch Melliger.

Tina Gifford claimed Britain's second silver of the summer when she finished less than two points behind Jean-Lou Bigot in the European 3-day Event. Gifford, daughter of racehorse trainer Josh, only came into the team two weeks before the event, when Karen Dixon's Get Smart was injured. Ginny Leng, chasing a fourth European title, saw it slip away when Welton Houdini refused one of the cross-country fences. Leng led on the dressage and went clear on the jumping, and but for that would have won gold. It proved an up and down year for Leng, who won Badminton, remarried (to become Elliot), but lost her sponsor, Citibank.

The sport suffered tragically this year when three riders were killed in three weeks in horse trials. Following the death of Mark Holliday, the British Horse Society set up a working party to examine safety, but two more riders have died since then.

Show Jumping

European Championships

Gijon, Spain   Jul 29-Aug 1

Individual
1 Willi Melliger   SUI   8.83 faults
  (Quinta C)
2 Michel Roberts   FRA   8.91
  (Miss San Patrignano)
3 Michael Whitaker GBR   9.33
  (Everest Midnight Madness)
8 John Whitaker   GBR   18.11
  (Everest Gammon)

Team
1 Switzerland   19.23
2 Great Britain 21.15
3 France   29.88
4 Germany   31.96
5 Holland   36.57

Volvo World Cup

AARHUS, DENMARK
Oct 4
1 Jos Lansink   HOL 20pts
  (Optiebeurs Libero)
2 Lisa Jacquin   USA 17
  (For the Moment)
3 Gerd Wiltfang   GER 15
  (Warsum)

OSLO, NORWAY
Oct 10
1 Jan Tops   HOL 20pts
  (Abbeville la Silla)
2 Meredith Michaels   USA 17
  (Quick Star)
3 Hauke Luther   GER 15
  (Gaylord)

HELSINKI, FINLAND
Oct 24
1 Piet Raymakers   HOL 20pts
   (Rinnetou Z)
2 Hauke Luther   GER 17
   (Gaylord)
3 Joe Turi   GBR 15
   (Waysider)

MILLSTREET, IRELAND
Oct 31
1 Jessica Chesney   IRL 20pts
   (Diamond Exchange)
2 Francis Connors   IRL 17
   (Spring Elegance)
3 Peter Postelmans   BEL 15
   (Brandy)

AMSTERDAM, HOLLAND
Nov 15
1 Piet Raymakers   HOL 20pts
   (Rinnetou Z)
2 Ludger Beerbaum   GER 17
   (Almox Rush On)
3 Jan Tops   HOL 15
   (Abbeville La Silla)

BERLIN, GERMANY
Nov 21
1 René Tebbel   GER 20pts
   (Optiebeurs Landmann)
2 Hauke Luther   GER 17
   (Gaylord)
3 Franke Sloothaak   GER 15
   (Gina Ginelli)

BOURDEAUX, FRANCE
Dec 6
1 Roger Yves Bost   FRA 20pts
   (Norton de Rhuys)
2 Peter Charles   IRL 17
   (Royal Chocolate)
3 Eric Navet   FRA 15
   (Waiti Quito de Baussy)

GENEVA, SWITZERLAND
Dec 13
1 Philippe Lejeune   BEL 20pts
   (Roby Foulards Shogoun)
2 Stefan Lauber   SUI 17
   (Lugana)
3 L McNaught-Mändli   SUI 15
   (Panok Revanche B)

OLYMPIA, LONDON
Dec 19
1 Ludger Beerbaum   GER 20pts
   (Almox Ratina Z)
2 Peter Charles   IRL 17
   (Royal Chocalate)
3 Thomas Frühmann   AUT 15
   (Böckmann's Genius)

MECHELEN, BELGIUM
Dec 29
1 Rodrigo Pessoa   BRA 20pts
   (Loro Piana Special Envoy)
2 Hubert Bourdy   FRA 17
   (SP Razzia de l'Ain)
3 Eric Navet   FRA 15
   (Waiti Roxanne)

DORTMUND, GERMANY
Mar 14
1 Dirk Hafemeister   GER 20pts
   (PS Priamos)
2 Markus Beerbaum   GER 17
   (Almox Poker)
3 L McNaught-Mändli   SUI 15
   (Panok Pirol B)

PARIS, FRANCE
Mar 21
1 Nick Skelton   GBR 20pts
   (Everest Major Wager)
2 Michael Whitaker   GBR 17
   (Everest Midnight Madness)
3 Dirk Hafemeister   GER 15
   (PS Priamos)

'S-HERTOGENBOSCH, HOLLAND
Mar 28
1 Piet Raymakers   HOL 20pts
   (Rinnetou Z)
2 L McNaught-Mändli   SUI 17
   (Pirol)
3 George Lindemann   USA 15
   (Avalon)

WORLD CUP FINAL
Göteborg, Sweden   *Apr 8-12*
1 Ludger Beerbaum   GER 8 pens
   (Almox Ratina Z)
2 John Whitaker   GBR 10.5
   (Everest Grannusch/Everest Milton)
3 Michael Matz   USA 12.5
   (Rhum)

Nations' Cup

ROME, ITALY
Apr 27-May 1
1 Germany   4 pens
2 Great Britain   12
(Skelton, M Whitaker, Clarke, J Whitaker)
3 Holland   16

KISKUNHALAS, HUNGARY
Apr 29-May 2
1 Great Britain   16 pens
(Stockdale, Hatkins, Revan, Dye)
2 Czech Republic   21
3 Switzerland   22.75

HICKSTEAD, UK
May 20-23
1 Great Britain   8 pens
  (*Skelton, M Whitaker, Broome, J Whitaker*)
2 Holland   20
3 Germany   20

ST GALL, SWITZERLAND
June 10-13
1 France   4 pens
2 Spain   4
  France won on a jump-off
3 Great Britain   4.50
  (*Skelton, M Whitaker, Broome, J Whitaker*)

GERA
June 17-20
1 Denmark   20
2 Germany   24
3 Ireland   24.25

3 AACHEN, GERMANY
Jun 29-Jul 4
1 Switzerland   4.25
2 Holland   8.25
3 Great Britain   8.75
  (*M Whitaker, Armstrong, Broome, J Whitaker*)

DRAMMEN, NORWAY
Jul 1-4
1 Holland   8
2 Great Britain   8
  (*Edgar, Lucas, Funnell, Billington*)
3 Germany   8
Final positions decided by a jump-off

OBERANVEN, LUXEMBOURG
Jul 8-11
1 Switzerland   0
2 USA   8
3 Germany   12

FALSTERBO, SWEDEN
Jul 8-11
1 Holland   4
2 Sweden   8
3 Switzerland   8

LA BAULE, FRANCE
Jul 15-18
1 France   16
2 Germany   16
3 Belgium   20
France won on a jump-off

DUBLIN
Aug 3-7
1 USA   8
2 Great Britain   16
  (*Broome, M Whitaker, Edgar, Billington*)
3 Germany   16

ROTTERDAM, HOLLAND
Aug 20
1 Holland   4 faults
2 Germany   4
  Holland won in a jump-off
3 France   4.25

CALGARY, CANADA
Sept 13
1 France   9
2 Great Britain   12.25
  (*Skelton, M Whitaker, R Smith, J Whitaker*)
3 Germany   16

SAN MARINO
Sept 17
1 Germany   4
2 Holland   12
3 France   20

LINZ, AUSTRIA
Sept 23-26
1 Germany   8.75
2 Austria   12
3 Switzerland   12

LANAKEN, BELGIUM
Sept 23-26
1 Switzerland   4
2 France   12
2 Germany   12
2 Holland   12

NATIONS' CUP STANDING
After 20 events of 24
1 Germany   36.00pts
2 Holland   29.50
3 Switzerland   28.00
3 Great Britain   28.00
5 France   27.50
6 Denmark   11.50
7 USA   10.00
7 Ireland   10.00
7 Spain   10.00
10 Belgium   8.50

Grand Prix

MILL STREET INTERNATIONAL
Cork, Ireland   *Oct 31-Nov 1*
1 M Whitaker   GBR
  (Henderson Monsanta)
2 N Pessoa   BRA
  (Loro Piana Elastique)

MAASTRICHT, HOLLAND
Nov 5-8
1 Michael Whitaker   GBR 28.41s
  (Henderson Midnight Madness)
2 Piet Ratmakers   HOL 28.77
  (Rinnetou Z)
3 Jenny Zoer   HOL 30.51
  (Dolcevita)

VIENNA, AUSTRIA
Nov 5-9
1 Kurt Gravemeier   GER   30.89s
   (Wum)
2 Ludger Beerbaum   GER   31.65
   (Almox Rasman)
3 Hugo Simon   AUT
   (Apricot)

BREMEN, GERMANY
Nov 15-18
1 John Whitaker   GBR   4.00pts
   (Henderson Milton)
2 Jos Lansink   HOL   5.10
   (Optiebeurs Egano)
3 Evelyne Blaton   GER
   (Optiebeurs Careful)

ZUIDLAREN, HOLLAND
Nov 20-22
1 Michael Whitaker   GBR   29.76s
   (Henderson Midnight Madness)
2 Albert Voorn   HOL   30.11
   (Goldano)
3 Nelson Pessoa   BRA
   (Loro Piana Elastique)

FRANKFURT, GERMANY
Dec 3-6
1 Jos Lansink   HOL   38.39s
   (Optiebeurs Egano)
2 John Whitaker   GBR   39.04
   (Henderson Milton)
3 Evelyne Biston   BEL   46.76
   (Optiebeurs Care)

PORTE DE VERSAILLES, FRANCE
Dec 11-13
1 John Whitaker   GBR
   (Henderson Milton)
2 Michael Whitaker   GBR
   (Henderson Midnight Madness)
3 Jos Lansink   HOL
   (Optiebeurs Egano)

OLYMPIA, LONDON
Dec 16-20
1 Michael Whitaker   GBR   29.64s
   (Everest Midnight Madness)
2 Ludger Beerbaum   GER   30.32
   (Almox Ratina Z)
3 Hervé Godignon   FRA   30.44
   (Akai Quidam de Revel)

ZURICH, SWITZERLAND
Mar 25-28
1 Hauke Luther   GER   31.74s
   (Gaylord)
2 Hugo Simon   AUT   32.08
   (Apricot)
3 Geoff Billington   GBR
   (Rhapsody)

CAEN, FRANCE
Apr 2-4
1 Michael Whitaker   GBR   37.73s
   (Everest My Messieur)
2 Otto Becker   GER   37.83
   (Herrmann's Paledo)
3 John Whitaker   GBR   37.95
   (Everest Gammon)

ROME, ITALY
Apr 27-May 1
1 Jean Vangeenberghe   BEL   36.23
   (Osta Carpets Quenn)
2 Michel Robert   FRA
   (San Patrignano Nonix CFE)
3 Michael Whitaker   GBR
   (Everest Midnight Madness)

HICKSTEAD, UK
May 20-23
1 Michael Whitaker   GBR   0 (44.27 secs)
   (Everest Midnight Madness)
2 Emile Hendrix   HOL   0 (48.85)
   (Anadolu Arabian)
3 Edouard Couperie   FRA   4
   (Quat'Sous)

ST GALL, SWITZERLAND
June 10-13
1 Nick Skelton   GBR   0 (37.92 secs)
   (Everest Dollar Girl)
2 Michael Whitaker   GBR   0 (38.12)
   (Everest Two Steps)
3 Jan Tops   HOL   0 (42.16)
   (Top Gun La Silla)

AACHEN, GERMANY
June 29-Jul 4
1 J-C Vangeenberghe   BEL
   (Osta Carpets)
1 Michael Whitaker   GBR
   (Everest Midnight Madness)
3 Hervé Godignan   FRA
   (Twist du Valon)

DRAMMEN, NORWAY
Jul 1-4
1 Carsten-Otto Nagel   GER
   (Franziska)
2 Beat Grandjean   SUI
   (Sir Archy)
3 Beat Mändli   SUI
   (Galant XVIII)

OBERANVEN, LUXEMBOURG
Jul 8-11
1 Beezie Patton   USA
   (French Rapture)
2 Stefan Lauber   SUI
   (Corado)
3 Pedro Sanchez Aleman   ESP

FALSTERBO, SWEDEN
Jul 8-11
1 Beat Mändli   SUI
  (Galant XVIII)
2 Philippe Guerdal   SUI
  (Cornado Fier)
3 Dirk Hafemeister   GER
  (PS Priamos)

LA BAULE, FRANCE
JUl 15-18
1 Franke Sloothaak   GER
  (San Patrignano W)
2 Gianni Govoni   ITA
  (Imperial King)
3 Leslie Lenehan   USA
  (Gem Twist)

DUBLIN, IRELAND
Aug 7
Kerrygold International GP
1 Michael Whitaker   GBR
  (Everest Monsanta)
2 Eddie Macken   IRL
  (Schalkhaar)
3 John Ledingham   IRL
  (Kilbala)

ROTTERDAM
Aug 19-22
1 Ludger Beerbaum   GER
  (Almox Rush On)
2 Hugo Simon   AUT
  (Apricot)
3 Ludo Philippaerts   BEL
  (Trudo Darco)

CALGARY, CANADA
Sept 13
1 Nick Skelton   GBR
  (Everest Dollar Girl)
2 Hugo Simon   AUT
  (Apricot)
3 Stefan Lauber   SUI
  (Lugana II)

SAN MARINO
Sept 19
Pavarotti International
1 Eric Navet   FRA
  (Waito Roxane de Gruchy)
2 Sven Harmsen   HOL
  (Sovjet Look)
3 Michel Robert   FRA
  (Miss San Patrignano)

LINZ, AUSTRIA
Sept 23-26
1 Peter Erikson   SWE
  (Robin Z)
2 Jan-Wout van der Schans HOL
  (Capuccino)
3 Andrea Fuchs   SUI
  (Warlock)

LANAKEN, BELGIUM
Sept 23-26
1 Holgaer Hetzel   GER
  (St Ludwig's Gip)
2 Jos Lansink   HOL
  (Olympic Concorde)
3 George Lindemann   USA
  (Starlet)

Wembley, England

Oct 6-11
Derby
1 Michael Whitaker   GBR   33.59s
  (Henderson My Messieur)
2 John Whitaker   GBR   36.11
  (Henderson Gammon)
3 David Broome   GBR   41.58
  (Ancit Countryman)

Royal Show, UK

Stoneleigh, Warwicks   Jul 6
Penquest Compeition
1 John Whitaker   GBR
  (Everest Hopscatch)
2 Liz Edgar   GBR
  (Everest Ashes)
3 M Lanni   ITA
  (Ultra)

Everest National Championship
1 John Whitaker
  (Everest Hopscotch)
2 M McCourt
  (Lapaz)
3 Tony Maguire
  (Dun Corteiga)

Hickstead, UK

Jul 11
King George V Gold Cup
1 Nick Skelton   GBR
  (Everest Limited Edition)
Queen Elizabeth II Cup
1 Tina Cassan   GBR
  (Bond Xtra)

Hickstead, UK

Aug 28
Silk Cut Speed Derby
1 Capt John Ledingham   IRL
  (Castlepollard)
2 Francis Connor   IRL
  (Belarus Diamond Express)
3 Capt John Ledingham   IRL
  (Garrann)

WORLD JUMPING RANKINGS
For the period Sept 20, 1992 - Sept 19 1993

1	Michael Whitaker	GBR	4851.1
2	John Whitaker	GBR	4569.3
3	Ludger Beerbaum	GER	3615.9
4	Jos Lansink	HOL	3458.7
5	Eric Navet	FRA	2925.3
6	Nick Skelton	GBR	2664.5
7	Michael Matz	USA	2384.7
8	Willi Melliger	SUI	2380.6
9	Michel Robert	FRA	2357.4
10	Piet Raymakers	HOL	2353.3
11	Franke Sloothaak	GER	2162.7
12	Hugo Simon	AUT	2123.7
13	Rodrigo Pessoa	BRA	2030.0
14	Hervé Godignon	FRA	1988.4
15	Lesley McNaught-Mändli	SUI	1983.0
16	Leslie Leneham	USA	1981.5
17	Ludo Philippaerts	BEL	1832.4
18	Tim Grubb	USA	1818.4
19	Beezie Patton	USA	1803.1
20	Stefan Lauber	SUI	1772.9
21	René Tebbel	GER	1758.2
22	Thomas Fuchs	SUI	1648.8
23	Roger-Yves Bost	FRA	1637.0
24	Jan Tops	HOL	1461.6
25	Debbie Shaffner Stephens	USA	1460.6
Also			
68	Maria Edgar	GBR	591.0
80	Geoff Billiington	GBR	546.0
83	David Broome	GBR	525.0

Dressage
Volvo World Cup Final (1992-3)

's-Hertogenbosch   Mar 25-28
1 Monica Theodorescu GER 30pts
  (Ganimedes TecRent)
2 Sven Rothenberger   GER 27.5
  (Ideaal)
3 Isabell Werth   GER 25
  (Fabienne)

Volvo World Cup (1993-94)

Schoten, Belgium   June 4-6
1 Anky van Grunsven HOL 77.29
  (Olympic Bonfire)
2 Nicole Uphoff   GER 74.87
  (Hermann's Grand Gilbert)
3 Gyula Dalloz   HUN 72.41
  (Aktion)

Grands Prix

STUTTGART, GERMANY
Grand Prix   Oct 22-25
1 Nicole Uphoff   GER 1669pts
  (Grand Gilbert)
2 Monica Theodorescu GER 1668
  (Ganimedes TecRent)
3 Isabell Werth   GER 1618
  (Fabienne)

AMSTERDAM, HOLLAND
Freestyle to Music   Nov 12-15
1 Monica Theodorescu GER 78.03pts
  (Ganimedes TecRent)
2 Nicole Uphoff   GER 74.43
  (Grand Gilbert)
3 Sven Rothenberger   GER 72.15
  (Attention)

Grand Prix
1 Monica Theodorescu GER 1634pts
  (Ganimedes TecRent)
2 Sven Rothenberger   GER 1587
  (Ideaal)
3 Michael Klimke   GER 1576
  (Chan)

BERLIN, GERMANY
Grand Prix   Nov 12-15
1 Monica Theodorescu GER 1624pts
  (Ganimedes TecRent)
2 Nicole Uphoff   GER 1613
  (Grand Gilbert)
3 Sven Rothenberger   GER 1608
  (Attention)

FRANKFURT, GERMANY
Grand Prix   Dec 3-6
1 Sven Rothenberger   GER 1674pts
  (Andiamo)
2 Monica Theodorescu GER 1673
  (Grunox TecRent)
3 Isabell Werth   GER 1664
  (Fabienne)

NEUMÜNSTER, GERMANY
Freestyle to Music   Feb 18-21
1 Monica Theodorescu GER 81.01pts
  (Ganimedes TecRent)
2 Nicole Uphoff   GER 75.77
  (Hermann's Grand)
3 Sven Rothenberger   GER 75.66
  (Ideaal)

Grand Prix
1 Sven Rothenberger   GER 1586pts
  (Attention)
2 Karin Rehbein   GER 1581
  (Donnerhall)
3 Heike Kemmer   GER 1554
  (Nicholas)

PARIS BERCY, FRANCE
Freestyle to Music   *Nov 15-18*
1 Sven Rothenberger GER 75.42pts
  (Ideaal)
2 Isabell Werth   GER 75.22
  (Fabienne)
3 Gina Cappelmann   GER 72.66
  (Cyprys)

DORTMUND, GERMANY
Grand Prix *Mar 11-14*
1 Isabell Werth   GER 1714
  (Maedler Gigolo)
2 Monica Theodorescu GER 1690
  (Grunox TecRent)
3 Sven Rothenberger GER 1636
  (Andiamo)

PARIS BERCY, FRANCE
Grand Prix *Mar 17-20*
1 Sven Rothenberger GER 1622
  (Ideaal)
2 Gina Capellmann   GER 1562
  (Cyprys)
3 Isabell Werth   GER 1558
  (Fabienne)

'S-HERTOGENBOSCH, HOLLAND
Grand Prix *Mar 25-28*
1 Sven Rothenberger GER 1647
  (Andiamo)
2 Anky van Grunsven HOL 1647
  (Olympic Bonfire)
3 Karin Rehbein   GER 1573
  (Donnerhall)

GOODWOOD, ENGLAND
Grand Prix *Apr 30-May 2*
1 Sven Rothenberger GER 1616
  (Andiamo)
2 Kyra Kyrklund   FIN 1609
  (Edinburg)
3 Gina Capellmann   GER 1599
  (Cyprys)

SCHOTEN, BELGIUM
June 4-6
1 Anky van Grunsven HOL 1671
  (Olympic Bonfire)
2 Nicole Uphoff   GER 1593
  (Hermann's Grand Gilbert)
3 Gina Cappelmann-L GER 1529
  (Cyprys)

Three-Day Eventing
European Championships
Achselschwang, Germany   Sept 10-12

Individual
1 Jean-Lou Bigot   FRA 87.95
  (Twist la Beige)
2 Tina Gifford   GBR 89.8
  (Song and Dance Man)
3 Eddy Stibbes   HOL 93
  (Bahlua)
7 Ginny Leng   GBR 106.8
  (Welton Houdini)

Teams
1 Sweden   347.15
2 France   347.70
3 Irland   375.90
4 Germany   403.65
5 Italy   617.30
6 Spain   672.75
Great Britain did not complete a team.

LOUGHANMORE, IRELAND
Oct 2-5
1 David O'Connor   USA 40.80pts
  (On a Mission)
2 David Foster   IRL 47.40
  (Grey Prospect)
3 Karen Lende   USA 51.40
  (Biko)

BOEKLO, HOLLAND
Oct 8-11
1 Joerg Bodenmueller SUI 48.80
  (Oree de la Brasserie)
2 Nick Burton   GBR 60.75
  (Bertie Blunt)
3 A van Spaendonck HOL 61.00

LE LIONS D'ANGIERS, FRANCE
Oct 15-18
1 Jean Teulere   FRA 59.20
  (Tobi de Marillet)
2 Philippe Mull   FRA 62.80
  (Roy de Boulay)
3 Eddy Stibbe   HOL 63.00
  (Bristol's Autumn)

PAU, FRANCE
Oct 22-25
1 Andrew Nicholson NZL 63.60
  (Optimisti)
2 Viva Guerin-Pollas DEN 65.80
  (Orak de la Touche)
3 Gilles Pons   FRA 65.80
  (Nirvana Loutares)

EUROPEAN CONTINENTAL CUP FINAL
Compiegne, France Jun 3-6
1 Marie C Duroy   FRA 66.60
  (Yarlande Summer Song)
2 Frédéric de Romblay FRA 68.95
  (Rosendael)
3 Karen Dixon   GBR 71.00
  (Too Smart)

SAUMUR, FRANCE
Apr 29-May 2
1 Dider Seguret   FRA 60.35
  (Coeur de Rocker)
2 Ian Stark   GBR 68.40
  (Stanwick Ghost)
3 Jean-Marc Favereau FRA 72.00
  (Suzon de Vaillac)

BADMINTON MITSUBISHI, UK
May 6-9
1 Virginia Leng   GBR 43.00
  (Welton Houdini)
2 Blyth Tait   NZL 44.80
  (Ricochet)
3 Tanya Cleverly   GBR 48.20
  (Watkins)
4 Victoria Latta   NZL 50.00
  (Chief)
5 Anna Hermann   SWE 54.40
  (Mr Punch)
6 Marie-Christine Duroy FRA 55.85
  (Quart du Placineau)
7 William Fox-Pitt   GBR 56.25
  (Chaka)
8 Charlotte Hollingsworth GBR 56.60
  (The Cool Customer)
9 Nick Burton   GBR 57.00
  (Bertie Blunt)
10 Helen Bell   GBR 57.70
  (Troubleshooter)

PUNCHESTOWN, IRELAND
May 21-24
1 Karen Lende   USA 40.45
  (Shannon)
2 Mary Thompson   GBR 41.20
  (Star Appeal)
3 Karen Lende   USA 45.00
  (Enniskerry)

WINDSOR, UK
May 27-30
1 Andrew Hoy   AUS 55.60
  (Snow Gun)
2 Pippa Nolan   GBR 57.20
  (Merry Gambler)
3 Ian Stark   GBR 58.00
  (Dear Hardy)

LAND ROVER FEI WORLD 3-DAY EVENT RANKINGS
As at 1 Oct 1993

1	Andrew Nicholson	NZL	290
2	Bruce Davidson	USA	283
3	Marina Loheit	GER	246
4	Virginia Leng	GBR	194
5	Pippa Nolan	GBR	194
6	Kristina Gifford	GBR	192
7	Anna Hermann	SWE	192
8	Mark Todd	NZL	188
9	Marie-Christine Duroy	FRA	185
10	Ian Stark	GBR	183

BREDA, GERMANY
May 28-31
1 Katie Parker   GBR 42.60
  (Percy Trebyan)
2 Jean Teulere   FRA 43.60
  (Rodosto)
3 Maren Sorgenfrei   GER 45.80
  (Chanell)

COMPIEGNE, FRANCE
June 3-6
1 Jorg Bodenmuller   SUI 50.20
  (Fancy Hill)
2 Vicky Latta   NZL 54.40
  (Home Run)
3 Marina Loheit   GER 60.60
  (Jelly Lorum)

BRAMHAM TOYOTA, UK
June 10-13
1 Kristina Gifford   GBR 61.20
  (General Jock)
2 Pippa Nolan   GBR 64.00
  (Cartoon II)
3 Carolyne Ryan-Bell   GBR 64.80
  (Hooray Henry II)

BURGHLEY, UK
Sept 2-5
1 Stephen Bradley   USA 50.2
  (Sassy Reason)
2 Mark Todd   NZL 56.8
  (Just An Ace)
3 Andrew Nicholson   NZL 57.15
  (Spinning Rhombus)

BLENHEIM AUDI, UK

Sept 16-19
Individual

1	Pippa Nolan (Metronome)	GBR	42.8
2	Ginny Leng (Welton Romance)	GBR	45.05
3	Bruce Davidson (Squelch)	USA	53.8

Team

1	Great Britain	166.25

Calor Gas
Gatcombe Horse Trials

Gatcombe Park   Aug 13-15

Final Placings

1	David O'Connor (Lighter Than Air)	USA	46
2	Vicky Latta (Chief)	NZL	48
3	Mark Todd (Just An Ace)	NZL	52
4	Virginia Leng (Welton Houdini)	GBR	53
5	Stephen Bradley (Sassy Reason)	USA	54
6	Mary Thompson (King Boris)	GBR	54

Endurance Riding
European Championships

Southwell, Notts   Sept 5

1	J Thomas (Main Ring Egyptian Khalifa)	GBR
2	C Nelson (Janos)	SWE
3	C Brown (King Minos)	GBR

Fencing

World Championships

Essen, Germany   *July 1-11*

MEN

Foil: 1 Alexander Koch GER
2 Sergy Golubitsky UKR
3 Philippe Omnès FRA
Ewe Römer GER
60 Donnie McKenzie GBR

Team 1 Germany
2 Italy
3 Poland

Epee: 1 Pavel Kolobkov RUS
2 Arnd Schmitt GER
3 Ivan Kovacs HUN
Olivas Peña ESP
36 Quentin Berriman GBR

Team 1 Italy
2 France
3 Germany

Sabre: 1 Grigory Kirienko RUS
2 Bence Szabo HUN
3 Steffen Wiesinger GER
Toni Terenzi ITA
32 James Williams

Team 1 Hungary
2 Italy
3 Germany

WOMEN

Foil: 1 Francesca Bortolozzi ITA
2 Aida Mohamed HUN
3 Simone Bauer GER
Zita Funkenhauser GER
41 Fiona McIntosh

Team 1 Germany
2 Romania
3 Italy

Epee: 1 Oksana Ermakova EST
2 Laura Chiesa ITA
3 Sophie Moresée FRA
Helena Elinder SWE
100 Charlotte Read

Team 1 Hungary
2 Germany
3 Ukraine

Note: Though we do not have exact placings, no British team featured in the top eight in any weapon.

British Championships

MEN

Foil: 1 Lauren Harper (Salle Boston)
2 Nick Bell (Salle Paul)
3 N Payne
D McFarlane (both Salle Paul)

Epee: 1 Steven Paul (Salle Paul)
2 John Llewelyn
3 Quentin Berriman

Sabre 1 Amin Zahir
2 Kirkham Zavieh

3 Paul Hoenigman & Steven Lawrence

WOMEN

Foil: 1 Fiona McIntosh (Salle Paul)
2 Sara Mawby (Salle Paul)
3 C Smith (Salle Boston) & F Cowen (Much Wendlock)

Epee: 1 Nicola Cain
2 Tomlinson
3 Goodall & Cox

Sabre: 1 Sue Bennett (BAG)
2 Fiona McIntosh (Salle Paul)
3 Lynne Boeneisza (Bath) & Tracey Richards (Worcester)

Martini '93

Mar 6

Men's Epee
1 Robert Felisiak GER
2 Marius Strazalka GER
3 Paul Maroto ESP
Fernando Peña ESP
20 Steven Paul GBR
32 M Corish GBR

Birmingham International

Birmingham, England   *Apr 10-11*

MEN

Foil: 1 Lauren Harper
2 Donnie McKenzie
3 Tony Bartlett
Guenigalt

Epee: 1 Pollard
2 S Paul
3 J Chalmers
Shindler

Sabre: 1 N Fletcher
2 M Hoenigman
3 Slade & Saba

Corble Cup

May 1

Men's Sabre
1 Vilmos Szabo (ROM)
2 Christian Eich (GER)
3 Kirkham Zavieh (GBR)
Hannes Hradez (AUT)

Cole Cup

Men's Sabre
1 James Williams
2 Ian Williams
3 Hall
Paul Hoenigman

Golf

It's not so much of a big deal, is it, winning a Ryder Cup? It never used to be, because Britain never won it. A little success, though, is a dangerous thing and Europe having won a couple of times recently, you start believing it's going to happen every time. Against the Americans it's just that much more important. It's no accident that in no other competition does a European team gel so well. For the Americans, it's become so important that Tom Watson, who's won a bit in his time, reckoned that he'd not felt that good about anything in golf. Still, look on the bright side. At least we don't have to look at those Ryder Cup sweaters for another two years. Designed by Jeff Banks and costing £800, the only people who could afford them were golfers and their families.

Britain's richest golfer (by a distance) had something of an ordinary year. Mind, it comes to something when an ordinary year takes in a second in one of the 'majors' and third in another and leaves you only a couple of points clear at the head of the Sony rankings. Faldo has topped those rankings now for well over a year and, at the beginning of the calendar year, had a lead over Fred Couples of over seven points. Nick Price, Bernhard Langer and, most forcefully, Greg Norman have made inroads into that lead.

Peter Baker, following his Ryder Cup performance, is everyone's new favourite. Corey Pavin must have felt like Jim Meade when he was playing Baker in the Cup. Who was Jim Meade? Jim Meade was playing the 16th at Tilgate Forest golf club when his ball went into the rough. As Meade bent down to pick it up, a ball driven from the 17th tee bounced off a tree and hit Meade in the head. As Meade got up a second ball, driven from the 16th this time, hit him in the back. That's how Pavin must have felt.

At the Belfry, Baker was simply living up to the prophesy of Faldo, who said something like he'd be the next Faldo. Baker won two European Tour events as well, which secured his place in the team and his bank balance. The amount of money on the tours these days is almost unbelievable. Even a modest European tournament can earn the winner £100,000 and the US Tour events attract even greater funding.

The richest golfer in the world, though, is undoubtedly Prince Abdul Hakeem of the Brunei. Mr Prince, as his caddie calls him, earns his money from his country's oil wells and earns even more than Faldo. In Gleneagles, for a golf tournament, he showed what the whim of the rich can mean. Unhappy with the mustard being served at the Gleneagles Hotel, he dispatched his jet, a Gulfstream 4, to London to fetch mustard to his taste. There, what do you think of that, Nick?

To help prepare our golfers for such fame and fortune, Merrist Wood College, associated with Kingston University has been runnning an HND course in 'Golf-course Studies'. The students, who are only accepted if they have 'A' levels and a nine handicap, or less. What do they do on this course? They play golf. They also learn about club design (that's the clubs that you play with) and how to manage a golf club (that's the building). There are 40 places this year and wouldn't you want one of them.

What else? Colin Montgomerie was rude about the Moroccan Open and got fined £1,000 and Mark Roe dumped a plate of spaghetti on Russell Claydon's head at the French Open (well, a nearby Pizzeria) and got fined £100. Montgomerie, you suspect, would rather have eaten the spaghetti. They discovered that playing golf can lower the risk of heart disease and an assistant golfer in Coral Springs, Florida played 440 holes in 12 hours. The most surreal story comes from California where Cannuck's Sportsmens Memorials takes the ashes of cremated sports enthusiasts and puts them in the shafts of golf clubs and things. How would you like to be remembered sir, as a one iron or a sand wedge? Equally bizarre, but less disturbing is the Bering Sea Ice Classic which is played annually at Nome in Alaska. Last year, 64 people paid $50 each to play in the tournament in a snowstorm. The course is only six holes long, the balls are orange, the turf is artificial and the holes are coffee cans and everybody, but everybody loses their balls in the snow. Oh, and I should say, there is no such thing as an unplayable lie and you are penalised three shots if you hit a polar bear. "I don't know that the touring pros could handle it," said the tournament founder Elliott Staples. "This is a tough course. People at Pebble Beach don't know tough."

QUOTES

"This is the greatest feeling I have ever had and I didn't even hit a shot"
Tom Watson, after the third and final day's play in the Ryder Cup.

"I'm not nervous, the only thing that scares me these days is the Americans' dress sense"
Mark James, during the Ryder Cup.

"Even a blind pig finds an acorn occasionally"
Ian Woosnam, after a rare putting success during the Open.

"He hits divots further than I hit my drives"
David Feherty, after partnering John Daly in the Open.

"Greg Norman will be the toast of Sandwich tonight"
Radio Five

"The guy who set the pin on the 9th green must have been born with a spanner in his head"
Ian Woosnam at the European Open.

"I'll take a two stroke penalty, but I'm damned if I'm going to play the ball where it lies"
Elaine Johnson, after her tee shot hit a tree and bounced into her bra.

"My mother told me there would be days like this"
Jeff Sluman, after being beaten 8 & 7 by Nick Faldo in the World Matchplay.

"I have lost all my growing-up years. I haven't lived a normal life. I think it was a mistake"
Seve Ballesteros

"What I said is, that he looks like a bulldog licking piss off a nettle"
David Feherty denying he said Colin Montgomerie looked like "a warthog that's been stung by a wasp".

The Ryder Cup

DAY 1 Europe, for all its success in the past few Ryder Cups, has never won the opening foursomes, nor did it again. Torrance and James lost five holes in a row to lose the first match and Ballesteros and Olazábal succumbed to Kite and Love in the third. It was the Spaniards' first ever defeat in the foursomes. Woosnam and Langer, though, had a resounding victory over Azinger and Stewart and that, combined with Faldo and Montgomerie's defeat of Floyd and Couples guaranteed it to be level at lunch. In the fourballs, Bernard Gallacher introduced Peter Baker, pairing him with Woosnam. The tyro took to it, overshadowing the Welshman as they took a point off the US twosome of Gallagher and Janzen. "Peter played all the golf, played fantastic" acknowledged Woosnam, "I just had a stroll this afternoon." Langer without Woosnam, was not so successful and the German and Barry Lane, another Ryder Cup novice, tumbled 4 & 2 to the pairing that Tom Watson called "the pillars of the US team", Wadkins and Pavin. Inspiration served Ballesteros and Olazábal. They responded to the call and produced some sparkling golf to oust Love and Kite. Between them, they were 11 under par. But Ballesteros was occasionally wayward from the tee and warnings were being posted for the next day. The evening closed before Faldo and Montgomerie could finish their match against Azinger and Couples. In the gathering darkness, Faldo pitched in on the 17th to square the match. "He's so mechanical, he plays in the dark even when it's light," said Gallacher. Faldo had already made birdies at the 13th, 14th and 15th to give Gallacher cause for such praise. The Britons squared the 18th the next morning, so the score at the end of the first eight matches was one point in Europe's favour.

DAY 1 SCORES

FOURSOMES
Europe scores are given first

Sam Torrance/Mark James v
Lanny Wadkins/Corey Pavin
Scores: 5 4 4 5 3 4 3 5 5 4 5 4 4 3 5 - - -
              4 4 5 5 4 3 3 4 4 3 4 3 4 4 5 - - -
USA won by 4 & 3

Ian Woosnam/Bernhard Langer v
Paul Azinger/Payne Stewart
Scores: 4 3 4 4 3 4 2 4 4 4 4 3 4 - - - - -
              5 5 5 3 4 5 2 5 4 5 4 3 C - - - - -
Europe won 7 & 5

Seve Ballesteros/José-Maria Olazábal v
Tom Kite/Davis Love III
Scores: 4 4 4 5 4 4 2 4 4 3 4 3 4 3 5 3 5 -
              4 3 4 4 5 3 3 4 4 2 4 3 3 3 5 4 5 -
USA won by 2 & 1

Nick Faldo/Colin Montgomerie v
Ray Floyd/Fred Couples
Scores: 4 4 4 4 4 4 3 4 4 4 4 3 5 2 4 - - -
              5 4 3 5 4 4 3 4 5 2 4 4 4 3 5 - - -
Europe won by 4 & 3

FOURBALLS
Europe scores first

Ian Woosnam/Paul Baker v
Jim Gallagher jr/Lee Janzen
Scores: 4 3 3 5 4 4 3 4 4 4 3 3 4 2 4 4 5 3
              4 3 4 4 4 4 3 4 4 3 4 3 4 3 4 4 5 4
Europe won by 1 hole

Bernhard Langer/Barry Lane v
Lanny Wadkins/Corey Pavin
Scores: 4 4 4 5 4 3 2 3 4 4 4 3 4 3 4 4 - -
              4 3 4 4 3 4 2 4 4 4 3 3 3 3 4 3 - -
USA won 4 & 2

Nick Faldo/Colin Montgomerie v
Paul Azinger/Fred Couples
Scores: 3 3 4 5 3 4 2 3 4 4 4 3 3 2 4 4 4 -
              3 3 4 4 4 3 3 3 4 3 4 3 4 2 4 3 5 -
Match Halved

Seve Ballesteros/José-Maria Olazabal v
Davis Love III/Tom Kite
Scores: 4 3 4 3 3 3 3 4 3 2 3 3 3 2 4 - - -
              3 4 4 4 4 3 2 4 4 4 3 3 4 3 4 - - -
Europe won by 4 & 3

MATCH POSITION AFTER DAY ONE: EUROPE 4 1/2 USA 3 1/2

DAY 2 For half a day, it looked as if Europe might not even bother with the final day singles. They had gone out before lunch and inflicted a 3-1 defeat on the Americans. Faldo had continued the momentum of the previous day, by holing from 10 feet at the 18th in the fourballs held over from the previous day. That secured a half to ensure that Europe went a point ahead. Faldo and Montgomerie continued the mood with a 3 & 2 win over Wadkins & Pavin. Langer and Woosnam just got the better of Couples and Azinger, while Ballesteros and Olazábal took on and beat Love and Kite. Ballesteros, though, was not happy with his game and requested to be dropped from the afternoon fourballs. His driving throughout the foursomes had been wildly erratic, but the Spaniards had saved hole after hole. With Langer also rested for the fourth session, the European fourballs had a slightly raw look about them. Peter Baker, playing alongside Woosnam, was outstanding and proved that you don't have to have been there before to know how to do it. They took apart the pairing of Couples and Azinger 6 & 5. That was the only satisfaction for Europe during the afternoon. Faldo and Montgomerie had a close encounter with Beck and Cook. The Americans took a one shot lead at the eighth and then every remaining hole was halved, an unlikely occurrence in fourballs. At the 18th, Faldo had a chance to put pressure on the Americans when he putted first, but his miss and the failure of Montgomerie to chip in gave the match to the Americans. James and Rocca had no sort of chance against Pavin and Gallagher, but Olazábal and Haeggman came back from four down to within two shots after the Spaniard holed from the bunker on the 16th. Both the Europeans played superb shots at the 17th and were shaping up to take that hole as well, until Stewart, who had not had the best of Ryder Cups till this point, made the perfect pressure putt and that was that.

DAY 2 SCORES
FOURSOMES

Europe scores are given first

Nick Faldo/Colin Montgomerie v
Lanny Wadkins/Corey Pavin
Scores: 4 4 5 5 4 4 2 4 4 4 4 3 4 2 5 4
          4 4 5 5 4 4 2 5 4 3 5 5 4 3 5 4
Europe won by 3 & 2

Bernhard Langer/Ian Woosnam v
Fred Couples/Paul Azinger
Scores: 4 4 4 4 4 4 3 4 4 4 4 4 4 3 5 3 5
          4 4 4 5 4 4 3 4 4 3 4 4 5 3 5 4 5
Europe won by 2 & 1

Paul Baker/Barry Lane v
Ray Floyd/Payne Stewart
Scores: 4 4 5 4 5 4 3 4 4 3 4 3 5 3 5 4
          4 4 4 4 4 3 4 3 4 4 3 4 3 5 4
USA won 3 & 2

Seve Ballesteros/José Maria Olazábal v
Davis Love III/Tom Kite
Scores: 3 4 4 4 4 4 3 5 5 3 5 2 4 3 5 3 5
          4 4 4 5 4 5 3 4 3 4 4 3 3 3 5 5 5
Europe won 2 & 1

FOURBALL

Nick Faldo/Colin Montgomerie v
John Cook/Chip Beck
Scores: 3 4 4 4 4 3 3 5 4 4 4 3 4 3 4 4 5 4
          3 4 4 4 4 2 4 4 4 4 3 4 3 4 4 5 3
USA won 2 holes

Mark James/Constantino Rocca v
Corey Pavin/Jim Gallagher
Scores: 4 4 4 5 3 4 3 3 4 4 5 3 3 3
          4 3 4 4 2 3 3 4 3 4 3 4 3
USA won by 5 & 4

Ian Woosnam/Paul Baker v
Fred Couples/Paul Azinger
Scores: 4 4 3 5 3 3 3 3 4 4 2 3
          4 3 4 4 4 4 3 4 4 5 4 3 4
Europe won by 6 & 5

José Maria Olazábal/Joakim Haeggman v
Ray Floyd/Payne Stewart
Scores: 4 4 5 5 4 4 3 3 3 3 4 3 3 3 4 3 4
          4 3 4 4 4 3 3 3 5 3 4 3 3 3 4 4 4
USA won 2 & 1

MATCH POSITION AFTER DAY TWO: EUROPE 8 $\frac{1}{2}$ USA 7 $\frac{1}{2}$

DAY 3 A European hit the shot of the day. Nick Faldo, at the 16th, hit a hole in one. It was only the second time in Ryder Cup history that it had been achieved. Most else on the final day belonged to the Americans. They were always close enough, providing they could generate an extra surge towards the end of the day. The team charge happened and the European dream evaporated. Woosnam had held his own early; the first time in Ryder Cup competition that he hadn't lost his singles. The second match home was more crucial. Lane had held a three hole lead with five to play. When they came to the 18th, it was all square and Lane was under intense pressure. He bunkered his drive, hit the bunker shot in the water and Beck took a match the Americans must have already put in the 'lost' bag. With James and Langer left trailing by Stewart and Kite, and Baker playing magnificently against Pavin it became obvious where those points were going and the decision began to hinge on two or three matches. Europe took one of them as Haeggman beat Cook on the final hole when the American found water. There was no one else to cheer for. One by one the Europeans succumbed. Even Ballesteros could not find any of the enchantment of old to pull one back. The Spaniard was beaten 3 & 2 by Jim Gallagher, having lost three of the first four holes. His compatriot, Olazábal, lost the 12th, 13th and 14th holes and could never quite get them back against the canny old Floyd and Constantino Rocca cut the most tragic figure of the day (make that the year) when he went from one up with two to play to one down and nothing to play. So, when Faldo in the final match against Azinger made that ace, it didn't matter at all. The ship was sunk and all the eagles in the world wouldn't refloat it.

DAY 3 SCORES
SINGLES
Europe scores are given first
Sam Torrance and Lanny Wadkins withdrew
Torrance had an injured foot
Treated as match halved
Ian Woosnam v Fred Couples
Scores:　4 4 4 5 4 4 3 5 4 3 3 3 4 3 5 4 5 4
　　　　　3 5 4 5 4 4 3 5 4 4 4 3 3 3 4 4 5 4
Match halved

Barry Lane v Chip Beck
Scores:　5 4 4 4 4 4 2 4 3 4 4 4 3 4 4 5 5 5
　　　　　4 4 5 5 3 4 4 4 4 4 5 3 4 3 3 4 5 4
USA won by 1 hole

Colin Montgomerie v Lee Janzen
Scores:　4 4 4 5 4 3 4 3 4 4 4 3 4 4 3 4 5 4
　　　　　5 5 4 4 4 4 3 3 4 4 4 3 4 2 4 4 5 4
Europe won by 1 hole

Paul Baker v Corey Pavin
Scores:　5 4 4 5 4 4 3 3 4 3 3 3 4 2 5 4 5 3
　　　　　4 5 4 5 4 4 3 4 3 4 4 2 4 3 5 3 5 4
Europe won by 2 holes

Joakim Haeggman v John Cook
Scores:　4 4 4 5 4 4 3 3 4 4 4 5 4 3 4 4 5 4
　　　　　4 4 4 5 4 4 3 4 4 4 4 4 4 3 4 4 5 6
Europe won by 1 hole

FINAL POSITION : EUROPE 13 USA 15

Mark James v Payne Stewart
Scores:　5 4 4 4 4 4 3 4 5 4 4 3 3 2 4 4 - -
　　　　　4 3 4 4 3 4 3 3 4 4 4 3 5 3 4 4 - -
USA won 3 & 2

Constantino Rocca v Davis Love III
Scores:　4 4 5 4 4 4 3 C 4 4 4 4 2 4 4 6 5
　　　　　4 4 4 4 5 4 4 3 4 4 4 3 4 3 5 4 4
USA won by 1 hole

Seve Ballesteros v Jim Gallagher jr
Scores:　5 5 5 6 4 5 3 5 4 4 4 3 4 3 4 4 - -
　　　　　4 3 5 5 4 6 3 4 4 3 4 4 4 3 4 4 - -
USA won 3 & 2

José-Maria Olazábal v Ray Floyd
Scores:　5 4 5 5 3 3 3 4 4 4 3 3 5 3 4 4 4 C
　　　　　4 4 4 5 4 4 3 4 3 4 4 2 3 2 5 4 5 W
USA won by 2 holes

Bernhard Langer v Tom Kite
Scores:　4 4 5 4 4 5 3 4 4 4 4 4 3 4 3 5 - - -
　　　　　4 4 4 5 4 5 4 3 3 2 3 4 4 3 3 - - -
USA won 5 & 3

Nick Faldo v Paul Azinger
Scores:　5 3 5 5 3 4 3 4 4 3 5 3 5 1 5 4 4 4
　　　　　4 4 5 4 4 4 3 5 4 4 4 3 4 2 4 4 5 3
Match halved

Solheim Cup (Europe v USA)

Dalmahoy, Scotland   Oct 2-4, 1992

"You could put any one of us in the European team and make it stronger," said American Beth Daniel on the eve of the second Solheim Cup. No sooner had Daniels removed her foot from her mouth than she was watching the unsurprising effects of her put-down. On the first day foursomes, the Europeans took an advantage that was never lost. If they ever needed motivation, Daniel had supplied it.

If it was motivation from Daniel, it was inspiration from Laura Davies who, paired with Alison Nicholas returned the first victory in the first match of the foursomes on Friday. Lottie Neumann and Helen Alfredsson followed up with a second and at the end of the first day, the European team had an unexpected lead. On Saturday, Davies and Nicholas won again, but by the end of the day, the lead remained a slight one of just one point. Sunday was altogether a different story, hope turned to expectation in a major way. Daniel, who was watching on the sidelines, must have felt her words come back to haunt her. Again, it was Davies who set the tone.

Against the 20 year old Brandie Burton, Davies found herself all square at the turn. In four holes, from the 11th to the 14th, the West Byfleet golfer then produced unassailable golf. A birdie at each, achieved with a 25 ft putt at the 14th, left Burton reeling and at the 16th, needing to win the hole to survive, she lost it and the match. Helen Alfredsson followed up with two singles wins out of two when she beat Danielle Ammaccapane, but arguably the best victory of the day belonged to Trish Johnson. Just a week earlier, Patty Sheehan had won the British Open to become the first golfer ever to capture both the American and British titles in the same summer. Johnson, though, was not intimidated and scored a fine 2 & 1 success. Thereafter, it was all downhill; Sweden Catrin Nilsmark sinking the match-winning putt on the 16th green as she defeated Meg Mallon 3 & 2.

Europe team names given first

FOURSOMES
Fri, Oct 2
Laura Davies/Alison Nicholas bt Betsy King/Beth Daniel 1 hole
Liselotte Neumann/Helen Alfredsson bt Pat Bradley/Dottie Mochrie 2 & 1
Florence Descampe/Trish Johnson lost to **Danielle Ammaccapane/Meg Mallon** 1 hole
Dale Reid/Pam Wright halved with Patty Sheehan/Juli Inkster

Europe 2.5 USA 1.5

FOURBALLS
Sat, Oct 3
Davie/Nicholas bt Sheehan /Inkster 1 hole
Johnson/Descampe halved with Brandie Burton/Deb Richard
Wright/Reid lost to **Mallon/King** 1 hole
Alfredsson/Neumann halved with Bradley/Mochrie

Europe 4.5 USA 3.5

SINGLES
Sun, Oct 4
Davies bt Burton 4 & 2
Alfredsson bt Ammaccapane 4 & 3
Johnson bt Sheehan 2 & 1
Nichols lost to **Inkster** 3 & 2
Descampe lost to **Daniel** 3 & 1
Wright bt Bradley 4 & 3
Catrin Nilsmark bt Mallon 3 & 2
K Douglas lost to **Richard** 7 & 6
Neumann bt King 2 & 1
Reid bt Mochrie 3 & 2

FINAL SCORE
Europe 11.5 USA 6.5

The 122nd Open Championship

Royal St George, Sandwich   July 15-18

267	**Greg Norman (AUS)**	**66 68 69 64**
	(£100,000)	
269	Nick Faldo (ENG)	69 63 70 67
	(£80,000)	
270	Bernhard Langer (GER)	67 66 70 67
	(£67,000)	
272	Corey Pavin (USA)	68 66 68 70
	Peter Senior (AUS)	66 69 70 67
	(£50,500 each)	
274	Ernie Els (SAF)	68 69 69 68
	Paul Lawrie (ENG)	72 68 69 65
	Nick Price (ZIM)	68 70 67 69
	(£33,166 each)	
275	Scott Simpson (USA)	68 70 71 66
	Fred Couples (USA)	68 68 72 69
	Wayne Grady (AUS)	74 68 64 69
	(£25,500 each)	
276	Payne Stewart (USA)	71 72 70 63
	(£21,500)	
277	Barry Lane (ENG)	70 68 71 68
	(£20,500)	
278	Mark Calcavecchia (USA)	68 73 71 68
	Tom Kite (USA)	72 70 68 68
	Mark McNulty (ZIM)	67 71 71 69
	Gil Morgan (USA)	70 68 70 70
	Jose Rivero (ESP)	68 73 67 70
	Fuzzy Zoeller (USA)	66 70 71 71
	John Daly (USA)	71 66 70 71
	(£15,214 each)	
279	Peter Baker (ENG)	70 67 74 68
	Jesper Parnevik (SWE)	68 74 68 69
	Howard Clark (ENG)	67 72 70 70
	(£10,000 each)	
280	Mark Roe (ENG)	70 71 73 66
	David Frost (SAF)	69 73 70 68
	Rodger Davis (AUS)	68 71 71 70
	(£8,400 each)	
281	Malcolm Mackenzie (ENG)	72 71 71 67
	Yoshinori Mizumaki (JPN)	69 69 73 70
	Des Smyth (IRE)	67 74 70 70
	Larry Mize (USA)	67 69 74 71
	Mark James (ENG)	70 70 70 71
	Ian Pyman* (ENG)	68 72 70 71
	Seve Ballesteros (ESP)	68 73 69 71
	(£7,225 each)	
282	Jean Van de Velde (FRA)	75 67 73 67
	Paul Broadhurst (ENG)	71 69 74 68
	Wayne Westner (SAF)	67 73 72 70
	Ray Floyd (USA)	70 72 67 73
	Howard Twitty (USA)	71 71 67 73
	(£6,180)	
283	Rocco Mediate (USA)	71 71 72 69
	Carl Mason (ENG)	69 73 72 69
	Andrew Magee (USA)	71 72 71 69
	Greg Turner (NZL)	67 76 70 70
	Duffy Waldorf (USA)	68 71 73 71
	Paul Moloney (AUS)	70 71 71 71
	Anders Sorensen (DEN)	69 70 72 72
	Christy O'Connor Jr. (IRE)	72 68 69 74
	Darren Clarke (NIR)	69 71 69 74
	(£5,327 each)	
284	John Huston (USA)	68 73 76 67
	Steve Elkington (AUS)	72 71 71 70
	Lee Janzen (USA)	69 71 73 71
	(£4,850 each)	
285	Ian Garbutt (ENG)	68 75 73 69
	Stephen Ames (TRI)	67 75 73 70
	Miguel Angel Jimenez (ESP)	69 74 72 70
	Ian Woosnam (WAL)	72 71 72 70
	Sam Torrance (SCO)	72 70 72 71
	Frank Nobilo (NZL)	69 70 74 72
	Manuel Piñero (ESP)	70 72 71 72
	(£4,356 each)	
286	Paul Azinger (USA)	69 73 74 70
	Tom Lehman (USA)	69 71 73 73
	Vijay Singh (FIJ)	69 72 72 73
	Craig Parry (AUS)	72 69 71 74
	(£4,025 each)	
287	Ross Drummond (SCO)	73 67 76 71
	Olle Karlsson (SWE)	70 71 73 73
	Jamie Spence (ENG)	69 72 72 74
	(£3,850 each)	
288	James Cook (ENG)	71 71 74 72
	Magnus Sunesson (SWE)	70 73 73 72
	William Guy (SCO)	70 73 73 72
	Tom Pernice (USA)	73 70 70 75
	(£3,675 each)	
289	Mike Miller (SCO)	73 68 76 72
	Tom Purtzer (USA)	70 70 74 75
	Ian Baker-Finch (AUS)	73 69 67 80
	(£3,516 each)	
290	Dan Forsman (USA)	71 70 76 73
	Peter Fowler (AUS)	74 69 74 73
	Peter Mitchell (ENG)	73 70 72 75
	Mike Harwood (AUS)	72 70 72 76
	(£3,500 each)	
292	Mikael Krantz (SWE)	77 66 72 77
	(£3,500)	
293	Rocky Willison (ENG)	73 70 74 76
	(£3,500)	

Denotes Amateur

Greg Norman - Hole by Hole Details

Hole	1	2	3	4	5	6	7	8	9	out	10	11	12	13	14	15	16	17	18	in	Total
Round 1	6	3	3	4	3	4	4	4	4	35	4	4	4	3	4	3	2	3	4	4	66
Round 2	4	3	3	4	5	2	5	4	4	34	4	3	3	3	5	4	3	5	4	34	68
Round 3	3	4	3	4	4	3	5	4	4	34	4	2	4	4	5	5	3	4	4	35	69
Round 4	3	4	2	4	4	3	5	4	3	31	4	3	3	4	4	4	2	5	4	33	64
Par	4	4	3	4	4	3	5	4	4	35	4	3	4	4	5	4	3	4	4	35	70
Yardage	441	376	210	468	421	155	530	418	389	3408	339	216	365	443	507	466	163	425	468	3452	6860

It was a championship of championships, this one. Gene Sarazen, who has been around a few years (well, 91 actually), reckoned it was the best he had ever seen. Greg Norman, who won it playing superb golf, pointed out how good it felt to win when everyone was there and all of them playing well. Norman has flattered to deceive, where the Majors are concerned, for most of his golfing life. For a golfer who has ranked in the world's top half dozen seemingly for ever, to have only one Major, his 1986 win in the Open, was scant reward. That 1986 season had become apocryphal for Norman; he had led going into the last round in all four of the majors.

Payne Stewart had started as one of the favourites, but even a record-equalling 63 on his final round could only draw him back to twelfth placing. Nick Price stayed closer to the leaders, but was never quite able to get in a blow. Bernhard Langer, playing like a Masters champion, had a marvellous start and reached halfway for the competition in 133 shots, which would have looked good, except that Nick Faldo was doing even better. Faldo's second round of 63, like Stewart later, equalled the much-equalled Open record and left the Englishman one shot clear. The third round did not unshuffle the pack and the golf on that final round left everybody buzzing. "I never missed a shot all day. Every drive and every iron was perfect," said Norman. "I only screwed up on that one little putt on the 17th, but that was probably the kick I needed. I hit two really super shots down to the 18th." Norman was not being arrogant, simpy telling it how it was. Though Faldo played fine golf, he was never able to reach Norman playing this kind of game.

Final Scores (cont.)
The following did not make the cut:

144			Gary Evans (ENG)	67 78	José Manuel Carriles (ESP)	76 73
Katsuyoshi Tomori (JPN)	71 73		Bill Malley (USA)	74 71	Brian Watts (USA)	72 77
Eoghan O'Connell (IRE)	74 70		John Cook (USA)	73 72	Brad Faxon (USA)	70 97
Billy Andrade (USA)	70 74		**146**		Roger Chapman (RNG)	73 76
Tony Johnstone (ZIM)	72 72		Sandy Lyle (SCO)	70 76	Gordon Brand Jr. (SCO)	70 79
Davis Love III (USA)	70 74		Richard Boxall (ENG)	71 75	Peter Smith (SCO)	75 74
Constantino Rocca (ITA)	71 73		De Wet Basson (SAF)	72 74	Mark Davis (ENG)	74 75
David Edwards (USA)	76 68		Jeff Sluman (USA)	74 72	**150**	
Chip Beck(USA)	73 71		Robert Karlsson (SWE)	74 72	Terry Price (AUS)	72 78
Philip Talbot (ENG)	70 74		Paul Way (ENG)	72 74	Gary Orr (SCO)	72 78
Tom Watson (USA)	71 73		Mats Hallberg (SWE)	69 77	Benoit Telleria (FRA)	73 77
Fulton Allem (SAF)	73 71		Robert Lee (ENG)	72 74	**151**	
Colin Montgomerie (SCO)	74 70		**147**		Larry Rinker (USA)	78 73
Gary Player (SAF)	73 71		Noamichi Ozaki (JPN)	70 77	Paul Eales (ENG)	73 78
Jack Nicklaus (USA)	69 75		Joakim Haeggman (SWE)	73 74	Andrew Sherbourne (ENG)	73 78
Robert Allenby (AUS)	69 75		David Gilford (ENG)	72 75	Anthony Nash (ENG)	70 81
Donnie Hammond (USA)	69 75		Jim Gallagher Jr. (USA)	73 74	**152**	
Glen Day (USA)	67 77		Tze Ming Chen (TPE)	73 74	Graham Farr (WAL)	73 79
145			Mark O'Meara (USA)	71 76	Peter Scott (ENG)	73 79
Steven Richardson (ENG)	72 73		José Maria Olazabal (ESP)	73 74	**153**	
Lanny Wadkins (USA)	72 73		**148**		Stephen Dundas* (SCO)	76 77
Ben Crenshaw (USA)	70 75		Per-Ulrik Johansson (SWE)	69 79	**155**	
Paul McGinley (IRE)	73 72		Steve Pate (USA)	79 69	Ricky Kawagishi (JPN)	79 76
Eduardo Romero (ARG)	73 72		Takaaki Fukuzawa (JPN)	73 75	Mitch Voges* (USA)	80 75
Craig Cassells (ENG)	68 77		Stephen Field (ENG)	72 76	**156**	
Retief Goosen (SAF)	69 76		Brendan McGovern (IRE)	74 74	Noboru Sugai (JPN)	74 82
Martin Gates (ENG)	72 73		Paul Leonard* (IRE)	74 74	**158**	
Vincente Fernandez (ARG)	73 72		Michael Welch* (ENG)	74 74	Simon Griffith* (ENG)	77 81
Jeff Maggert (USA)	72 73		**149**		**159**	
Anders Forsbrand (SWE)	71 74		Mike Clayton (AUS)	72 77	Nico Van Rensburg (SAF)	82 77
			David Feherty (NIR)	77 72	*150 professionals and 6 amateurs*	
			Tony Jacklin (ENG)	73 76	*began the tournament.*	

The US Masters
Augusta National Course, Augusta, Georgia   Apr 8-11

FINAL SCORES

277	**Bernhard Langer (GER)** ($306,000)	**68 70 69 70**
281	Chip Beck (USA) ($183,600)	72 71 73 69
283	John Daly (USA) ($81,600)	70 71 73 69
283	Steve Elkington (AUS) ($81,600)	71 70 71 71
283	Tom Lehman (USA) ($81,600)	67 75 73 68
283	Lanny Wadkins (USA) ($81,600)	69 72 71 71
284	Dan Forsman (USA) ($54,850)	69 69 73 73
284	José Maria Olazabal (ESP) ($54,850)	70 72 74 68
285	Brad Faxon (USA) ($47,600)	71 70 72 72
285	Payne Stewart (USA) ($47,600)	74 70 72 69
286	Seve Ballesteros (ESP) ($34,850)	74 70 71 71
286	Ray Floyd (USA) ($34,850)	68 71 74 73
286	Anders Forsbrand (SWE) ($34,850)	71 74 75 66
286	Corey Pavin (USA) ($34,850)	67 75 73 71
286	Scott Simpson (USA) ($34,850)	72 71 71 72
286	Fuzzy Zoeller (USA) ($34,850)	75 67 71 73
287	Mark Calcavecchia (USA) ($24,650)	71 70 74 72
287	Jeff Sluman (USA) ($24,650)	71 72 71 73
287	Howard Twitty (USA) ($24,650)	70 71 73 73
287	Ian Woosnam (WAL) ($24,650)	71 74 73 69
288	Russ Cochran (USA) ($17,000)	70 69 73 76
288	Fred Couples (USA) ($17,000)	72 70 74 72
288	Sandy Lyle (SCO) ($17,000)	73 71 71 73
288	Jeff Maggert (USA) ($17,000)	70 67 75 76
288	Larry Mize (USA) ($17,000)	67 74 74 73
288	Mark O'Meara (USA) ($17,000)	75 69 73 71
289	Nolan Henke (USA) ($12,350)	76 69 71 73
289	Hale Irwin (USA) ($12,350)	74 69 74 72
289	Jack Nicklaus (USA) ($12,350)	67 75 76 71
289	Joey Sindeler (USA) ($12,250)	72 69 76 72

290: Bruce Lietzke (USA), Andrew Magee (USA), Greg Norman (AUS).
291: Bob Gilder, Phil Mickelson, Gene Sauers, Craig Stadler (all USA).
292: Jay Haas (USA).
293: Keith Clearwater (USA), John Cook (USA), Nick Faldo 71-76-79-67(GBR), Lee Janzen (USA), Ted Schulz (USA), Duffy Waldorf (USA).
294: Jay Don Blake (USA), Joe Ozaki (JPN), Jumbo Ozaki (JPN), Craig Parry (AUS), Tom Watson (USA).
295: Gil Morgan, Brett Ogle (both USA).
296: Colin Montgomerie (SCO), David Peoples (USA).
298: Ian Baker-Finch (AUS), David Edwards (USA), Davis Love III (USA).
299: Charles Coody, Gary Hallberg (both USA).
301: John Huston (USA).
302: Gary Player (RSA).
303: Billy Andrade (USA).
Those who failed to make the cut included: 148 Paul Azinger, Ben Crenshaw (both USA); 151 Tom Kite (USA); 152 Arnold Palmer (USA); 153 Nick Price (ZIM); 77 Curtis Strange (USA) - completed 1 rd.

Eight years after he won his first Masters title, Bernhard Langer slipped on the green jacket for a second time. Langer thus became the fifth European in six years to take the title, but not before a couple of old pros revived memories of the day when it would have been heresy for a green jacket to be worn by anyone east of Maine. Arnold Palmer, all of 63, but hardly creaking, began his first round with three successive birdies. If he tailed off a touch towards the end of the day (finishing with a two over par 74), Nicklaus most surely did not. With six jackets already crowding the wardrobe, the 53 year old Nicklaus looked in search of a seventh. It wasn't only birdies that he was piling up; at the 15th Nicklaus claimed an eagle and, there he was, at the end of the day sharing the leaderboard on 67 with Janzen, Lehman, Pavin and Mize. The perfect conditions of day one, gave way to the predicted storm. Play had started an hour early, but when the rains came there was still an hour to play. Nicklaus had lost only a little ground at that point (he was 1 over for the 13 holes he played) but was to lose touch in the morning. Jeff Maggert, who has yet to win a tournament, found himself briefly top of the board. Faldo had a disaster. At the short 12th, he carded a quadruple bogey and waved goodbye to any chance of a third Masters. His 76 left him down in the pack. Langer, six under with two holes to play when they wrapped up for the day, was threatening the lead. He took it soon enough. Maggert's third round 75 looked good compared to Faldo's awful 79, but it paled alongside Langer's three under par 69. At the start of the final day, the German was four shots clear. Forsman worried Langer with an outward 33 on the final round, but at the 12th he emulated Faldo's seven and that was that. Beck came within two shots, but no closer and, in the brilliant evening sunshine, Langer tried on his new jacket.

The US Open
Baltusrol, Springfield, New Jersey   Apr 8-11

FINAL SCORES

272	**Lee Janzen (USA)** ($290,000)	**67 67 69 69**
274	Payne Stewart (USA) ($145,000)	70 66 68 70
277	Paul Azinger (USA) ($78,556)	71 68 69 69
277	Craig Parry (AUS) ($78,556)	66 74 69 68
278	Scott Hoch (USA) ($48,730)	66 72 72 68
278	Tom Watson (USA) ($48,730)	70 66 73 69
279	Ernie Els (RSA) ($35,481)	71 73 68 67
279	Ray Floyd (USA) ($35,481)	68 73 70 68
279	Fred Funk (USA) ($35,481)	70 72 67 70
279	Nolan Henke (USA) ($35,481)	72 71 67 69
280	John Adams (USA) ($26,249)	70 70 69 71
280	David Edwards (USA) ($26,249)	70 72 66 72
280	Nick Price(ZIM) ($26,249)	71 66 70 73
280	Loren Roberts (USA) ($26,249)	70 70 71 69
280	Jeff Sluman (USA) ($26,249)	71 71 69 69
281	Barry Lane (ENG) ($21,576)	74 68 70 69
281	Mike Standly (USA) ($26,249)	70 69 70 72
281	Fred Couples (USA) ($26,249)	68 71 71 71
282	Ian Baker-Finch (AUS) ($18,071)	70 70 70 72
282	Dan Forsman (USA) ($18,071)	73 71 70 68
282	Tom Lehman (USA) ($18,071)	71 70 71 70
282	Corey Pavin (USA) ($18,071)	68 69 75 70
282	Blaine McCallister (USA) ($18,071)	68 73 73 68
282	Steve Pate (USA) ($18,071)	70 71 71 70

283: Chip Beck, Mark Calcavecchia, John Cook, Wayne Levi , Rocco Mediate (all USA), Joe Ozaki (JPN), Ken Perry, Curtis Strange (both USA).
284: Robert Allenby (AUS), John Daly, Mike Donald (both USA), Steve Elkington (AUS), Davis Love III, Steve Lowery, Craig Stadler, Greg Twiggs, Billy Andrade, Bob Gilder (all USA), Colin Montgomerie (SCO), Jumbo Ozaki (JPN), Lee Rinker (USA).
285: Rick Fehr, Mark McCumber, Larry Nelson, Scott Simpson, Mark Brooks, Brian Claar (all USA).
286: Fulton Allem (RSA), Michael Christie, Keith Clearwater, Bob Estes, Vance Heafner, Edward Kirby (all USA), Sandy Lyle (SCO), Jeff Maggert, Kirk Triplett (both USA), Ian Woosnam (WAL).
287: Jay Don Blake, Joel Edwards, Mike Hulbert, Hale Irwin (all USA), Arden Knoll (CAN), Mike Smith (USA).
288: Brad Faxon, Steve Gotsche, Fuzzy Zoeller, Justin Leonard (all USA).
289: Nick Faldo 70-74-73-72 (ENG), Peter Jordan, Jack Nicklaus, Grant Waite, Duffy Waldorf (all USA).
290: Jay Haas (USA), Tony Johnstone (ZIM), Barney Thompson, Mark Wiebe (both USA).
291: Wayne Grady (AUS), Ted Schulz (USA).
292: Steve Stricker (USA).
294: Stephen Flesch (USA).
295: John Flannery, Doug Weaver (both USA).
297: Robert Wrenn (USA).
298: Robert Gamez (USA).
Those who failed to make the cut included: 145 Tom Kite (USA), Bernhard Langer (GER), Vijay Singh (FIJ); 147 Larry Mize (USA), Greg Norman (AUS); 148 Seve Ballesteros (ESP), David Frost (RSA), José Maria Olazabal; 149 Anders Forsbrand (SWE), David Gilford (GBR).

Thoughts of a grand slam do not linger long at the best of times. Packed full of medication for a bad neck, Masters winner Langer did not enjoy even the briefest fancy. The injury curtailed his swing and a first round 74 left him eight shots adrift of the leaders Hoch, Sindelar and Parry. Tony Jacklin, who won at Hazeltine in 1970, is the only Briton to have won this title in the last 70 years, but Faldo, Lyle and Woosnam managed to extend their dream at least past the first round, as each played a par 70. Tomorrow, being another day, their hopes went the way of Langer's. Faldo hit seven at the seventh which was pleasing symmetry, but little else. Woosnam saved his seven for the 18th, but both found themselves, along with Lyle, signing 74s on their scorecards. Barry Lane was the best of British, adding a secure second round of 68 to his earlier 74. It was Lane's first tournament in the US since he won the world assistants' championship in Orlando in 1983. However, Lane was still some way back from Lee Janzen who, despite a bogey on the last, was pulling everyone along with a pair of 67s for a two stroke lead at halfway. Janzen, if not as raw as Lane in this company, was still very much a novice and Payne Stewart, just two shots adrift, could have been excused for thinking he was the favourite. Stewart might have done better, however, if he had kept his confidence to himself; the Gods tend not to like that sort of thing. To be fair to Janzen, he didn't really need any divine intervention. A third round of 69 gave him a one stroke lead going in to the last. The 28 year old extended that to two strokes; saving his best of the day for the 18th, when he placed his third shot six feet from the pin. Lane remained easily the best Briton, his 16= placing earning him an automatic entry into the 1994 Masters.

The US PGA

Inverness, Toledo, Ohio   Aug 12-15

FINAL SCORES

272	**Paul Azinger (USA)**	**69 66 69 68**
	won play-off on second hole.	
	($300,000)	
272	Greg Norman (AUS)	68 68 67 69
	($155,000)	
273	Nick Faldo (ENG)	68 68 69 68
	($105,000)	
274	Vijay Singh (FIJ)	68 63 73 70
	($90,000)	
276	Tom Watson (USA)	69 65 70 72
	($75,000)	
277	John Cook (USA)	72 66 68 71
	($47,812)	
277	Bob Estes (USA)	69 66 69 73
	($47,812)	
277	Dudley Hart (USA)	66 68 71 72
	($47,812)	
277	Nolan Henke (USA)	72 70 67 68
	($47,812)	
277	Scott Hoch (USA)	74 68 68 67
	($47,812)	
277	Hale Irwin (USA)	68 69 67 73
	($47,812)	
277	Phil Mickelson (USA)	67 71 69 70
	($47,812)	
277	Scott Simpson (USA)	64 70 71 72
	($47,812)	
278	Steve Elkington (AUS)	67 66 74 71
	($25,000)	
278	Brad Faxon (USA)	70 70 65 73
	($25,000)	
278	Bruce Fleisher (USA)	69 74 67 68
	($25,000)	
278	Gary Hallberg (USA)	70 69 68 71
	($25,000)	
278	Lanny Wadkins (USA)	65 68 71 74
	($25,000)	
278	Richard Zokol (CAN)	66 71 71 70
	($25,000)	
279	Jay Haas (USA)	69 68 70 72
	($18,500)	

279	Eduardo Romero (ARG)	67 67 74 71
	($18,500)	
281	Lee Janzen (USA)	70 68 71 72
	($14,500)	
281	Jim McGovern (USA)	71 67 69 74
	($14,500)	
281	Frank Nobilo (NZL)	69 66 74 72
	($14,500)	
281	Gene Sauers (USA)	68 74 70 69
	($14,500)	
281	Greg Twiggs (USA)	70 69 70 72
	($14,500)	
281	Ian Woosnam (WAL)	70 71 68 72
	($14,500)	

282: Peter Jacobsen, Billy Mayfair, Loren Roberts (all USA).
283: Mark Calcavecchia, Davis Love III, Mark McCumber (all USA), Fulton Allem (RSA), Fred Couples, Mike Hulbert, Stu Ingraham, Wayne Levi (all USA), Craig Parry (AUS), Nick Price (ZIM), Hal Sutton, Tom Wargo, Fuzzy Zoeller (all USA).
284: Fred Funk, D A Weibring, Russ Cochran, Dan Forsman, John Huston, Payne Stewart (all USA), Joe Ozaki (JPN).
285: John Daly, Hubert Green, Andrew McGee, Jeff Maggert (all USA), Peter Senior (AUS).
286: Rick Fehr, Tom Kite, Larry Nelson (all USA), Sandy Lyle (SCO), José Maria Olazabal (ESP).
287: Michael Allen, Ben Crenshaw, Donnie Hammond, Jeff Sluman, Mike Standly (all USA).
288: Ian Baker-Finch (AUS).
289: Mark Wiebe (USA).
290: Bob Ford, Rocco Mediate (both USA).
292: Steve Pate (USA)
294: Kevin Burton (USA), Barry Lane (ENG).
295: Bob Borowicz (USA).
296: John Adams (USA).
Those who failed to make the cut included: 144 Ray Floyd, Jack Nicklaus (both USA), Bernhard Langer (GER); 145 Wayne Grady (AUS), Corey Pavin, Curtis Strange (both USA); 146 Larry Mize.

Lanny Wadkins, without a 1993 win to his credit but with 21 on the all-time list, was the early trailblazer with an opening 67. Barry Lane was two shots behind and the favourites, Greg Norman and Nick Faldo were just a shot further back. Lyle showed glimpses of old glory with a 69, but Nick Price probably sacrificed any hope of a successful defence of his title when he shot a 74. He did have something of a revival with a second day 66. Having finished in the top three in 15 of his last 30 tournaments, Price certainly wasn't going to be giving this one away. However, Friday did not belong to an African, but a Polynesian. Vijay Singh floated through a round of 63 to break the course record and take a two stroke lead. For 13 holes, Faldo had been as flawless as Singh. On the 14th, he recovered from a terrible position to claim par; on the 15th, again terribly sited after his drive, he took a seven and lost ground. Ominously, Azinger, with three tournament victories already this year (but never yet a major), took a 66 to move into sixth place. It hotted up literally on the Saturday with the temperature over 90 degrees and the field squeezed together as if drawing breath for a final charge. Norman ended the day one stroke ahead of Irwin, Watson, Azinger, Estes, Wadkins and Singh, with Faldo, Simpson and Hart one more in arrears. Consistency told the tale of the final day. Between them, Azinger, Norman and Faldo shot nothing better than 67, nor worse than 69 for 12 rounds of golf. It was fitting that they should end the last day separated by one shot. That was enough to leave Faldo out of the play-off; a birdie putt that whispered past the hole on the 16th the culprit. Norman came close to emulating Walter Hagen, who in 1924 was the last man to double the PGA and the Open, but it was Azinger who found the spark when it mattered. Four birdies in the last seven holes took him to a play-off, which the American duly won on the second.

SONY RANKINGS

As at October 3, 1993

1	Nick Faldo	ENG	21.11
2	Greg Norman	AUS	18.68
3	Bernhard Langer	GER	17.81
4	Nick Price	ZIM	15.78
5	Paul Azinger	USA	15.61
6	Fred Couples	USA	14.34
7	Ian Woosnam	WAL	12.32
8	Tom Kite	USA	10.16
9	José-Maria Olazábal	ESP	9.81
10	David Frost	RSA	9.66
11	Payne Stewart	USA	9.57
12	Davis Love III	USA	9.51
13	John Cook	USA	9.38
14	Masashi Ozaki	JPN	9.02
15	Corey Pavin	USA	8.94
16	Colin Montgomerie	SCO	8.05
17	Steve Elkington	AUS	7.97
18	Mark McNulty	ZIM	7.45
19	Vijay Singh	FIJ	7.44
20	Lee Janzen	USA	7.09
21	Seve Ballesteros	ESP	6.93
22	Mark O'Meara	USA	6.93
23	Chip Beck	USA	6.56
24	Ray Floyd	USA	6.45
25	Peter Senior	AUS	6.16
26	Tom Watson	USA	6.11
27	Rodger Davis	AUS	6.01
28	Ernie Els	RSA	5.97
29	Craig Parry	AUS	5.81
30	Frank Nobilo	AUS	5.76
31	Mark James	ENG	5.73
32	Sandy Lyle	SCO	5.68
33	Bruce Lietzke	USA	5.65
34	Larry Mize	USA	5.62
35	Rocco Mediate	USA	5.52
36	Ronan Rafferty	IRL	5.49
37	Gordon Brand jr	SCO	5.46
38	Sam Torrance	SCO	5.37
39	Constantino Rocca	ITA	5.36
40	Tony Johnstone	ZIM	5.31
41	David Edwards	USA	5.28
42	Fuzzy Zoeller	USA	5.13
43	Scott Simpson	USA	5.00
44	Steven Richardson	USA	4.93
45	Barry Lane	ENG	4.85
46	David Gilford	ENG	4.80
47	Dan Forsman	USA	4.74
48	Mark Calcavecchia	USA	4.73
49	Nolan Henke	USA	4.72
50	Anders Forsbrand	SWE	4.67
51	Brad Faxon	USA	4.65
52	Wayne Westner	RSA	4.60
53	Robert Allenby	AUS	4.54
54	Jeff Sluman	USA	4.52
55	Craig Stadler	USA	4.45

56	Ben Crenshaw	USA	4.43
57	Jim Gallagher jr	USA	4.42
58	Eduardo Romero	ARG	4.41
59	Joakim Haeggman	SWE	4.40
60	Tom Lehman	USA	4.38
61	David Feherty	NIR	4.38
62	Naomichi Ozaki	JPN	4.37
63	Fulton Allem	RSA	4.34
64	Ian Baker-Finch	AUS	4.33
65	Phil Mickelson	USA	4.29
66	Brett Ogle	AUS	4.29
67	Gil Morgan	USA	4.26
68	Peter Baker	ENG	4.26
69	Duffy Waldorf	USA	4.25
70	Jeff Maggert	USA	4.16
71	John Huston	USA	4.12
72	Rick Fehr	USA	4.04
73	Jay Haas	USA	4.02
74	Lanny Wadkins	USA	3.99
75	Steve Pate	USA	3.95
76	Tsun'ki Nakajima	JPN	3.84
77	Jesper Parnevik	SWE	3.81
78	Todd Hamilton	USA	3.65
79	Andrew Magee	USA	3.64
80	D A Weibring	USA	3.63
81	Joey Sindelar	USA	3.62
82	Billy Andrade	USA	3.60
83	Mark Roe	ENG	3.60
84	Paul Broadhurst	ENG	3.55
85	José Rivero	ESP	3.53
86	Masashito Kuramoto	JPN	3.43
87	Mark Brooks	USA	3.37
88	Tze-Chung Chen	TPE	3.36
89	John Daly	USA	3.32
90	Roger Mackey	AUS	3.31
91	Russ Cochran	USA	3.28
92	Retief Goosen	RSA	3.27
93	Mark McCumber	USA	3.24
94	Keith Clearwater	USA	3.23
95	Hale Irwin	USA	3.22
96	Scott Hoch	USA	3.19
97	Per-Ulrik Johansson	SWE	3.12
98	Jamie Spence	ENG	3.11
99	Jay Don Blake	USA	3.05
100	Robert Karlsson	SWE	3.00
	Howard Twitty	USA	3.00
	Darren Clarke	ENG	3.00

Volvo European Tour 1992-3

Date	Tournament	Venue	Winner	Score	1st Prize	Runner(s)-up	Margin
Oct 1 -4	Mercedes German Masters	Stuttgarter GC Stuttgart	**Barry Lane** (England)	272 (-16)	£100,000	Davis/Langer Woosnam	2
Oct 8 -11	Honda Open	Gut Kaden Hamburg	**Bernhard Langer** (Germany)	273 (-15)	£75,000	Darren Clarke	3
Oct 8 -11	Toyota World Matchplay	Wentworth Club	**Nick Faldo** (England)	8 & 7	£160,000	Jeff Sluman	
Oct 15 -18	Alfred Dunhill Cup	Old Course St Andrews	**England**	2-0	£300,000 (team)	Scotland	
Oct 15 -18	UAP European U 25 Championship	La Prieure France	**Paul Lawrie** (Scotland)	272	£14,160	Pierre Fulke J E Dahlstrom	1
Oct 22 -25	Iberia Madrid Open	Puerto de Hierro Madrid	**David Feherty** (Northern Ireland)	272 (-16)	£66,660	Mark McNulty	4
Oct 29 Nov 1	Volvo Masters	Valderrama Sotogrande	**Sandy Lyle** (Scotland)	287 (+3)	£110,000	C Montgomerie	pl-off (1st)
Nov 5 -8	World Cup of Golf	La Moraleja Madrid	**USA**	548 (team)	$248,000 (team)	Sweden	1
Dec 17 -20	Johnnie Walker World Ch'pionship	Tryall, Jamaica	**Nick Faldo** (England)	274 (-6)	$550,000	Greg Norman	pl-off (1st)
Jan 14 -17	Madeira Island Open	Santa Cruz Funchal	**Mark James** (England)	281 (-7)	£41,000	Paul Broadhurst Gordon Brand	3
Jan 28 -31	Dubai Desert Classic	Emirates GC Dubai	**Wayne Webster** (South Africa)	274 (-14)	£66,660	Retief Goosen	2
Feb 4 -7	Johnnie Walker Classic	Singapore Island CC	**Nick Faldo** (England)	269 (-11)	£91,660	C. Montgomerie	1
Feb 11 -14	Turespaña Iberia Open de Canarias	Golf del Sur	**Mark James** (England)	275 (-13)	£58,330	De Wet Basson	6
Feb 18 -21	Moroccan Open	Golf Royal de Agadir	**David Gilford** (England)	279 (-9)	£62,500	Stephen Ames Jamie Spence	1
Feb 25 -28	Turespaña Masters Open de Andalucia	Novo Sancti Petri, Cadiz	**Andrew Oldcorn** (England)	285 (-3)	£58,330	Ed'rdo Romero	1
Mar 4 -7	Turespaña Open Mediterrania	El Saler Valencia	**Frank Nobilo** (New Zealand)	279 (-9)	£66,660	David Feherty Gordon Brand	1
Mar 11 -14	Turespaña Iberia Open de Balaeres	Santa Ponsa	**Jim Payne** (England)	277 (-11)	£50,000	Anders Gillner	pl-off (1st)
Mar 18 -21	Portuguese Open	Vila Sol Algarve	**David Gilford** (England)	275 (-13)	£41,660	Jorge Berendt	pl-off (1st)
Mar 25 -28	Kronenbourg Open	Gardagolf nr. Verona, Italy	**Sam Torrance** (Scotland)	284 (-4)	£33,330	Mike Miller	1
Apr 1 -4	Open V33 du Grand Lyon	Lyon GC Villette d'Anthon	**Constantino Rocca** (Italy)	267 (-21)	£41,660	J. Haeggman G. Hjertstedt Paul McGinley	6
Apr 15 -18	Roma Masters	Castelgandolfo Rome	**J. Van de Velde** (France)	281 (-7)	£50,000	Greg Turner	pl-off (3rd)
Apr 22 -25	Heineken Open	OsunaMontanya nr. Barcelona	**Sam Torrance** (Scotland)	201* (-15)	£50,000	Jay Townsend	3
Apr 29 May 2	Air France Cannes Open	Cannes Mougins	**Rodger Davis** (Australia)	271 (-13)	£66,660	Mark McNulty	pl-off (1st)
May 6 -9	Benson & Hedges International Open	St Melion Plymouth	**Paul Broadhurst** (England)	276 (-12)	£91,660	J-M. Olazabal Mark James	2

Date	Tournament	Venue	Winner	Score	1st Prize	Runner(s)-up	Margin
May 13 -19	Peugeot Open de España	RAC de España Madrid	**Joak. Haeggman** (Sweden)	275 (-13)	£83,330	Ernie Els Nick Faldo	2
May 20 -23	Lancia Martini Italian Open	Modena nr. Bologna	**Greg Turner** (New Zealand)	267 (-21)	£73,392	Jose Coceres	1
May 28 -31	Volvo PGA Championship	The Wentworth Club, Surrey	**Bernhard Langer** (Germany)	274 (-14)	£116,660	Brand Jr/Nobilo Montgomerie	6
Jun 3 -6	Dunhill British Masters	Woburn, Bucks	**Peter Baker** (England)	266 (-22)	£100,000	Carl Mason	7
Jun 10 -13	Honda Open	Gut Kaden Hamburg	**Sam Torrance** (Scotland)	278 (-10)	£83,330	Ian Woosnam John Rystrom Paul Broadhurst	4-way pl-off (1st)
Jun 17 -20	Jersey European Airways Open	La Moye Jersey	**Ian Palmer** (South Africa)	268 (-20)	£50,000	Sam Torrance	2
Jun 24 -27	Peugeot Open de France	National GC Paris	**Constant. Rocca** (Italy)	273 (-11)	£83,330	Paul McGinley	pl-off (1st)
Jul 1 -4	Carroll's Irish Open	Mount Juliet CC Kilkenny	**Nick Faldo** (England)	276 (-12)	£96,630	J-M Olazabal	pl-off (1st)
Jul 10 -13	Bell's Scottish Open	Gleneagles Hotel Perthshire	**Jesper Parnevik** (Sweden)	271 (-9)	£100,000	Payne Stewart	5
Jul 22 -25	Heineken Dutch Open	Noordwijkse Leiden	**C Montgomerie** (Scotland)	281 (-7)	£108,330	José Coceres J. Van de Velde	1
Jul 29 Aug 1	Scandinavian Masters	Forsgårdens G C nr Goteburg	**Peter Baker** (England)	278 (-10)	£108,330	A Forsbrand	Play-off (2nd)
Aug 5 -8	BMW International Open	Munchen Nord Eichenried	**Peter Fowler** (Australia)	267 (-21)	£83,330	Ian Woosnam	3
Aug 12 -15	Hohe Brüke Austrian Open	Colony Club Gutenhof, Himberg	**Ronan Rafferty** (N Ireland)	274 (-14)	£41,660	A Sörensen	Play-off (1st)
Aug 19 -22	Murphy's English Open	Forest of Arden Warwicks	**Ian Woosnam** (Wales)	269 (-19)	£100,000	C Rocca	2
Aug 26 -29	Volvo German Open	Hubbelrath Dusseldorf	**Bernhard Langer** (Germany)	269 (-19)	£108,330	Baker/Allenby Montgomerie	5
Sept 2 -5	Canon European Masters	Crans-sur-Sierre Switzerland	**BarryLane** (England)	270 (-18)	£102,960	M A Jiménez Seve Ballesteros	1
Sept 9 -12	GA European Open	Uckfield, Sussex	**Gordon Brand Jr** (Scotland)	275 (-13)	£100,000	Phillip Price Ronan Rafferty	7
Sept 16 -19	Trophée Lancôme	St Nom la Breteche Paris	**Ian Woosnam** (Wales)	267 (-13)	£91,500	Sam Torrance	

Toyota World Matchplay

West Course, Wentworth   Oct 8-11

FIRST ROUND

Jeff Sluman (USA) bt Vijay Singh (FIJ)	4 & 3
Ian Woosnam (WAL) bt Norio Suzuki (JPN)	8 & 6
Greg Norman (AUS) bt Brad Faxon (USA)	1 hole
Mark O'Meara (USA) bt Anders Forsbrand (SWE) @37th	

First round losers collect £22,500

SECOND ROUND

Jeff Sluman bt Seve Ballesteros (ESP)	2 holes
Ian Woosnam bt José Maria Olazabal (ESP)	8 & 7
Nick Price (ZIM) bt Greg Norman	retd
Nick Faldo (ENG) bt Mark O'Meara	5 & 3

Second round losers collect £27,500

SEMI-FINALS

Jeff Sluman bt Ian Woosnam	3 & 2
Nick Faldo bt Nick Price	2 & 1

3RD/4TH PLAY-OFF

Nick Price bt Ian Woosnam	4 & 3

3rd place collects £50,000, 4th place £40,000

FINAL

Nick Faldo bt Jeff Sluman	8 & 7

1st place collects £160,000, 2nd £100,000

Alfred Dunhill Cup

The Old Course, St Andrews   Oct 15-18

1ST ROUND - DAY 1

Group 1
USA bt New Zealand 3-0
Fred Couples (70) bt Frank Nobilo (75)
Davis Love III (70) bt Grant Waite (76)
Tom Kite (71) bt Greg Turner (73)

Ireland bt Korea 2-1
Philip Walton (77) bt Cho Chui-Sang (80)
Christy O'Connor jn (77) bt Park Nam-Sin (Disq)
Ronan Rafferty (74) lost to Choi Sang-Ho (72)

Group 2
Spain bt Italy 2-1
Miguel Angel Jiménez (69) bt Guiseppe Cali (77)
José Rivero (77) lost to Constantino Rocca (74)
José Maria Olazabal (76) bt Silvio Grappasonni (76) pl-off 1st hole

England bt Japan 2-1
Steven Richardson (70) bt Mashahiro Kuramoto (72)
David Gilford (76) bt Nobumitsu Yuhara (76) pl-off 1st hole
Jamie Spence (77) lost to Hiroshi Makino (70)

Group 3
Scotland bt Canada 3-0
Gordon Brand jr (75) bt Danny Mijovic (81)
Colin Montgomerie (71) bt Brent Franklin (72)
Sandy Lyle (71 bt Richard Zokol (74)

Sweden bt France 2-1
Robert Karlsson (77) lost to Jean Van de Velde (73)
Per-Ulrik Johansson (75) bt Thomas Levet (77)
Anders Forsbrand (74) bt Marc Farry (75)

Group 4
Australia bt Germany 2-0
Greg Norman (72) tied with Bernhard Langer (72)
Rodger Davis (78) bt Heinz-Peter Thül (81)
Ian Baker-Finch (75) bt Torsten Giedeon (81)

South Africa bt Thailand 3-0
John Bland (78) bt Santi Sophon (80)
Ernie Els (77) bt Boonchu Ruangkit (82)
David Frost (78) bt Thaworn Wiratchant (85)

FIRST ROUND - DAY 2
Group 1
USA bt Korea
Couples (70) bt Park Nam-Sin (78)
Kite (70) bt Choi Sang-Ho (74)
Davis Love III (72) bt Cho Chui-Sang (79)

New Zealand bt Ireland
Nobilo (67) bt Rafferty (68)
Waite (70) bt Walton (72)
Turner (74) lost to O'Connor (68)

Group 2
Japan bt Spain 3-0
Yuhara (72) bt Jiménez (77)
Makino (71) bt Rivero (76)
Kuromoto (71) bt Olazabal (72)

England bt Italy 2-1
Spence (71) lost to Rocca (70)
Gilford (71) bt Cali (74)
Richardson (70) bt Grappasonni (78)

Group 3
Scotland bt France 3-0
Brand (75) bt Farry (78)
Montgomerie (71) bt Levet (78)
Lyle (70) bt Van de Velde (71)

Canada bt Sweden 3-0
Franklin (71) bt Karlsson (75)
Zokol (72) bt Forsbrand (74)
Mijovic (74) bt Johansson (75)

Group 4
Australia bt Thailand 3-0
Norman (69) bt Ruangkit (76)
Baker-Finch (74) bt Sophon (78)
Davis (73) bt Wiratchant (78)

Germany bt South Africa 2-1
Langer (72) bt Bland (77)
Giedeon (72) lost to Frost (69)
Thül (75) bt Els (75) pl-off 1st hole

1ST ROUND - DAY 3
Group 1
New Zealand bt Korea 2-1
Nobilo (75) lost to Choi Snag-Ho (73)
Turner (70) bt Park Nam-Sin (76)
Waite (72) bt Cho Chui-Sang (72) pl-off 2nd hole

Ireland bt USA 2-1
O'Connor (69) bt Couples (73)
Walton (72) bt Davis Love III (74)
Rafferty (71) lost to Kite (70)

Group 2
Italy bt Japan 2-0
Rocca (70) bt Makino (74)
Cali (71) tied with Kuramoto (71)
Grappasonni (75) bt Yuhara (75) pl-off 1st hole

Spain bt England 2-1
Olazabal (70) bt Spence (72)
Jiménez (73) bt Richardson (77)
Rivero (73) lost to Gilford (69)

Group 3
Sweden v Scotland 2-1
Karlsson (71) bt Brand (75)
Johansson (74) lost to Montgomerie (70)
Forsbrand (70) bt Lyle (74)

Canada bt France 2-1
Mijovic (73) bt Van de Velde (75)
Franklin (73) bt Farry (76)
Zokol (75) lost to Levet (73)

Group 4
Germany bt Thailand 2-1
Giedeon (79) lost to Wiratchant (77)
Langer (72) bt Ruangkit (77)
Thül (76) bt Sophon (76) pl-off 1st hole

Australia bt South Africa 2-0
Baker-Finch (74) bt Frost (75)
Davis (75) tied with Bland (75)
Norman (67) bt Els (70)

SEMI-FINALS
England bt USA 2-1
Gilford (69) bt Couples (70)
Richardson (68) bt Davis Love III (71)
Spence lost to Kite (71)

Scotland bt Australia 2-1
Montgomerie (68) bt Baker-Finch (72)
Lyle (69) bt Davis (73)
Brand (73) lost to Norman (68)

FINAL
England bt Scotland 2-0
Richardson (71) bt Brand (73)
Spence (69) tied with Montgomerie (69)
Gilford (71) bt Lyle (74)
*The winners collect £100,000 per player; runners-up £50,000
per player.*

Walker Cup

Edina, Minnesota   Aug 18-19

Singles, Day 1
British players first
I Pyman lost to A Doyle   1 hole
M Stanford bt D Berganio   3 & 2
D Robertson bt J Sigel   3 & 2
P Harrington lost to T Herron   1 hole
P Page lost to D Yates   2 & 1
S Cage halved with K Mitchum
R Russell lost to T Dempsey   2 & 1
R Burns lost to J Leonard   4 & 3
V Phillips bt B Gay   2 & 1
B Dredge lost to J Harris   4 & 3
Foursomes
Pyman/Cage lost to Doyle/Leonard   4 & 3
Stanford/Harrington lost to Berganio/Dempsey   3 & 2
Dredge/Phillips lost to Sigel/Mitchum   3 & 2
Russell/Robertson lost to Harris/Herron   1 hole
Singles, Day 2
D Robertson lost to A Doyle   4 & 3
I Pyman lost to J Harris   3 & 2
S Cage lost to D Yates   2 & 1
P Page lost to J Sigel   5 & 4
P Harrington halved with B Gay
V Phillips lost to T Herron   3 & 2
R Russell lost to K Mitchum   4 & 2
R Burns bt D Berganio   1 hole
M Stanford lost to J Leonard   5 & 4
B Dredge lost to T Dempsey   3 & 2

Match result: USA 19, Great Britain & Ireland 5

English Amateur Championships

Saunton   Aug

Final
David Fisher (Stoke Poges) bt Richard Bland (Bramshott
Hill) 3 & 1

Scottish Amateur Championships

Royal Darnoch   Aug

Final
Dean Robertson (Cochrane Castle) bt Raymond Russell
(Longniddry) by 2 holes

Welsh Amateur Championships

Southerndown   Aug

Final
Bradley Dredge bt Matthew Ellis (Wrexham) 3 & 1

US PGA Tour 1992/3

Excluding Majors

Date	Tournament	Venue	Winner	Score	1st Prize	Runner(s)-up	Margin
Oct 1 -4	Buick Southern Open (3 rds)		Gary Hallberg (USA)	206	$126,000	Jim Gallagher jr	1
Oct 8 -11	Las Vegas Invitational (5 rds)		John Cook (USA)	334	$234,000	David Frost	2
Oct 15 -18	Walt Disney World Oldsmobile GC		John Huston (USA)	262	$180,000	Mark O'Meara	3
Oct 22 -25	H-E-B Texas Open		Nick Price (ZIM)	263	$162,000	Steve Elkington	pl-off
Oct 29 Nov 1	Tour Championship		Paul Azinger (USA)	276	$360,000	Lee Janzen Corey Pavin	3
Nov 5 -8	Amocentel Championship	Mount Pleasant South Carolina	Don Pooley (USA)	268 (-20)	$115,000	Gil Morgan	1
Nov 12 -15	Lincoln Mercury Kapalua Intern'l	Kapalua Maui, Hawaii	Davis Love III (USA)	275	$150,000	Mike Hulbert	1
Nov 20 -22	Franklin Funds Shootout (best ball-3 rds)	Sherwood CC Thousand Oaks California	Davis Love III/ Tom Kite	191 (-25)	$125,000 each	Couples/Floyd Price/Brown Irwin/Lietzke	1
Nov 28 -29	The Skins Game (cash per hole)	Bighorn GC Palm Desert CA	Payne Stewart (USA)	-	$220,000	Fred Couples ($210k)	-
Dec 3 -6	The JCPenney Classic (M/F)	Tarpon Springs Florida	Dottie Mochrie/ Dan Forsman	264 (-20)	$110,000 each	Beth Daniel/ Davis Love III	4
Jan 7 -10	Infiniti Tournament of Champions	La Costa CC Carlsbad, CA	Davis Love III (USA)	272	$144,000	Tom Kite	1
Jan 14 -17	United Airlines Hawaiian Open	Waialae CC Honolulu, HI	Howard Twitty (USA)	269	$216,000	Joey Sindelar	4
Jan 21 -24	Northern Telecom Open	Tucson Golf Res. Tucson, AZ	Larry Mize (USA)	271	$198,000	Jeff Maggert	2
Jan 28 -31	Phoenix Open	Scottsdale Arizona	Lee Janzen (USA)	273	$180,000	Andrew McGee	2
Feb 4 -7	AT&T Pebble Beach National Pro-Am	Pebble Beach California	Brett Ogle (USA)	276	$225,000	Billy Ray Brown	3
Feb 10 -14	Bob Hope Chrysler Classic (5 rds)	La Quinta California	Tom Kite (USA)	325	$198,000	Rick Fehr	6
Feb 18 -21	Buick Invitational of California	Torrey Pines GC La Jolla, CA	Phil Mickelson (USA)	278	$180,000	Dave Rummells	4
Feb 25 -28	Nissan Los Angeles Open (3 rds)	Riviera CC Pacific Palisades	Tom Kite (USA)	206	£180,000	Dave Barr	3
Mar 4 -7	Doral Ryder Open	Miami Florida	Greg Norman (AUS)	265	$252,000	Paul Azinger Mark McCumber	4

Date	Tournament	Venue	Winner	Score	Prize	Runner(s)-up	
Mar 11 -14	Honda Classic (3 rds)	Weston Hills CC Ft Lauderdale	Fred Couples (USA)	207	$198,000	Robert Gamez	pl-off
Mar 18 -21	The Nestlé Invitational	Bay Hill CC Orlando Florida	Ben Crenshaw (USA)	282	$180,000	Rocco Mediate Vijay Singh Davis Love III	2
Mar 25 -28	The Players Championship	Sawgrass Ponte Vedra, FL	Nick Price (ZIM)	270	$450,000	Bernhard Langer	5
Apr 1 -4	Freeport-McMoran Classic	English Turn CC New Orleans	Mike Standly (USA)	281	$180,000	Russ Cochran Payne Stewart	1
Apr 8 -11	Deposit Guaranty Golf Classic	Hattiesburg CC Hattiesburg, MS	Greg Craft (USA)	267	$54,000	Morris Hatalsky Tad Rhyan	1
Apr 15 -18	MCI Heritage Golf Classic	Hilton Head Isl. South Carolina	David Edwards (USA)	273	$202,500	David Frost	2
Apr 22 -25	Kmart Greater Greensboro Open	Forest Oaks CC Greensboro, NC	Rocco Mediate (USA)	281	$270,000	Steve Elkington	pl-off
Apr 29 May 2	Shell Houston Open	The Woodlands Texas	Jim McGovern (USA)	199	$234,000	John Huston	pl-off
May 6 -9	Bellsouth Classic	Atlanta CC Marietta, GA	Nolan Henke (USA)	271	$216,000	Mark Cal'vecchia	2
May 13 -16	GTE Byron Nelson Golf Classic	Las Colinas Irving, Texas	Scott Simpson (USA)	270	$216,000	Billy Mayfair Corey Pavin D Awiebring	1
May 20 -23	Kemper Open	Avenel Potomac, MD	Grant Waite (USA)	275	$234,000	Tom Kite	1
May 27 -30	Southwestern Bell Colonial	Colonial CC Ft Worth, TX	Fulton Allem (RSA)	264	$234,000	Greg Norman	1
June 3 -6	Memorial Tournament	Muirfield Vill. Dublin, Ohio	Paul Azinger (USA)	274	$252,000	Corey Pavin	1
June 10 -13	Buick Classic	Westchester CC Rye, New York	Vijay Singh (FIJ)	280	$180,000	Mark Wiebe	pl-off
June 24 -27	Canon Greater Hartford Open	River Highlands Cromwell, CT	Nick Price (ZIM)	271	$180,000	Dan Forsman Roger Maltbie	1
July 1 -4	Sprint Western Open	Cog Hill GC Lemont, IL	Nick Price (ZIM)	269	$216,000	Greg Norman	5
July 8 -11	Anheuser-Busch Golf Classic	Kingsmill GC Williamsburg	Jim Gallagher jr (USA)	269	$198,000	Chip Beck	2
July 22 -25	The New England Classic	Pleasant Vly GC Sutton, MA	Paul Azinger (USA)	268	$180,000	Jay Delsing Bruce Fleisher	4
July 29 Aug 1	Federal Express St Jude Classic	Southwind Memphis, TN	Nick Price (ZIM)	266	$198,000	Rick Fehr Jeff Maggert	3
Aug 5 -8	Buick Open	Warwick Hills Grand Blanc, MI	Larry Mize (USA)	272	$180,000	Fuzzy Zoeller	1
Aug 19 -22	The International	Castle Pines GC Castle Rock, Co	Phil Mickelson (USA)	-	$234,000	Mark Calcavecchia (Stapleford comp)	-

Aug 26 -29	NEC World Series of Golf	Firestone CC Akron, Ohio	Fulton Allem (RSA)	270 (-10)	$360,000	Stadler/Price/ Gallacher	5
Sept 2 -5	Greater Milwaukee Open	Tuckaway CC Franklin, WI	Billy Mayfair (USA)	270	$180,000	M Calcavecchia Ted Schulz	pl-off
Sept 9 -12	Canadian Open	Glen Abbey GC Oakville, Ontar.	David Frost (RSA)	279	$180,000	Fred Couples	1
Sept 16 -19	Hardee's Golf Classic	Oakwood CC Coal Valley, IL	David Frost (RSA)	259	$180,000	Payne Stewart DA Weibring	7
Sept 23 -26	B C Open	En-Jolie GC Endicott, NY	Blaine McCallister (USA)	271	$144,000	Denis Watson	1

US PGA Seniors Tour

Sep 28-Oct 4	Vantage Championships	Jim Colbert(USA)	134	$202,500
Oct 5-11	Raley's Senior Gold Rush	Bob Charles (NZL)	208	$75,000
Oct 12-15	Transamerica Senior GC	Bob Charles (NZL)	200	$75,000
Oct 19-25	Ralphs Senior Classic	Ray Floyd (USA)	195	$90,000
Oct 26-Nov 1	Kaanapali Classic	Tommy Aaron (USA)	199	$75,000
Nov 2-8	Ko Olina Senior Invitational	Chi Chi Rodriguez (USA)	206	$75,000
Jan 4-10	Infiniti Tournmt of Champs	Al Geiberger (USA)	280	$52,500
Jan 30-31	The Skins Game	Arnold Palmer (USA)	-	$190,000
Feb 1-7	Royal Caribbean Classic	Jim Colbert (USA)	199	$112,500
Feb 8-14	The Challenge	Mike Hill (USA)	204	$75,000
Feb 15-21	GTE Suncoast Classic	Jim Albus (USA)	206	$75,000
Feb 24-28	The Chrysler Cup	Tom Weiskopf (USA)	202	$55,000
Mar 1-7	GTE West Classic	Al Geiberger (USA)	198	$75,000
Mar 8-14	Vantage at the Dominion	J C Sead (USA)	215	$52,000
Mar 15-21	Gulfstream Aerospace Int	Ray Floyd (USA)	194	$82,500
Mar 22-28	Doug Sanders Celeb Classic	Bob Charles	208	$75,000
Mar 29-Apr 4	The Tradition	Tom Shaw (USA)	269	$127,500
Apr 12-18	PGA Seniors Championship	Tom Wargo (USA)	275	$110,000
Apr 19-25	Muratec Reunion Pro-Am	Dave Stockton (USA)	211	$75,000
Apr 26-May 2	Las Vegas Classic	Gibby Gilbert (USA)	204	$105,000
May 6-9	Liberty M Legends of Golf	Harold Henning (RSA)	204	$250,000
May 10-16	Paine Webber Invitational	Mike Hill (USA)	204	$82,500
May 17-23	Bell Atlantic Classic	Bob Charles (NZL)	204	$97,500
Mat 24-30	Cadillac NFL Classic	Lee Trevino (USA)	209	$127,500
May 31-June 6	Nynex Commemorative	Bob Wynn (USA)	203	$82,500
June 7-13	Southwestern Bell Classic	Dave Stockton (USA)	204	$105,000
June 14-20	Burnet Classic	Chi Chi Rodriguez (USA)	201	$157,500
June 21-27	Ford Players Champ'ship	Jim Colbert (USA)	278	$180,000
June 28-July 4	Kroger Classic	Simon Hobday (ZIM)	202	$127,500
July 5-11	US Senior Open	Jack Nicklaus (USA)	278	$135,330
July 12-18	Amertech Open	George Archer (USA)	133	$90,000
July 19-25	First of America Classic	George Archer (USA)	199	$82,500
July 26-Aug 1	Northville Long Island Cl	Ray Floyd (USA)	208	$82,500
Aug 2-8	Bank of Boston Classic	Bob Betley (USA)	204	$112,500
Aug 9-15	Franklin Quest Champ'ship	Dave Stockton (USA)	197	$75,000
Aug 19-22	GTE Northwest Classic	Dave Stockton (USA)	200	
Aug 26-29	Bruno's Memmorial Classic	Bob Murphy (USA)	203	
Sept 2-5	Quicksilver Classic	Bob Charles (NZL)	207	
Sept 9-12	GTE North Classic	Bob Murphy (USA)	134	
Sept 16-19	Bank One Classic	Gary Player (RSA)	202	
Sept 23-26	Nationwide Champs	Lee Trevino (USA)	205	$142,500

Ben Hogan/Nike Tour

1-4/10	Sonoma County	John Flannery	199	$25,000
8-11/10	Bakersfield Opn	Tom Garner	205	$30,000
15-18/10	Fresno Open	Mike Springer	206	$30,000
19-21/2	Nike Yuma	Ron Streck	201	$27,000
4-7/3	Monterrey	Olin Browne	276	$36,000
18-21/3	Louisiana	R W Eaks	273	$27,000
26-28/3	Panama City	Mike Schuchart	208	$27,000
4/4	South Texas	Doug Martin	287	$27,000
15-18/4	Nike Shreveport	Sonny Skinner	278	$27,000
23-25/4	Central Georgia	Sean Murphy	205	$27,000
29/4-2/5	South Carolina	Hugh W Royer	273	$27,000
6-9/5	Nike Greenville	Sean Murphy	271	$27,000
13-16/5	Knoxville Open	Tim Conley	261	$31,500
21-23/5	Miami Valley	Emlyn Aubrey	202	$31,500
3-6/6	Nike Dominion	Angel Franco	272	$31,500
10-13/6	Cleveland Open	Stan Utley	271	$49,500
18-20/6	Connecticut Opn	D B Stockton jr	204	$27,000
24-27/6	New England Cl	John Morse	278	$27,000
1-4/7	White Rose Cl	Curt Byrum	270	$36,000
11/7	Hawkeye Open	D B Stockton jr	200	$27,000
15-18/7	Dakota Dunes	Alan Pate	260	$31,500
22-25/7	Greater Ozarks	Tommy Tolles	271	$31,500
29/7-1/8	Mississippi Gulf	Jim Furyk	206	$27,000
6-8/8	Permian Basin	F Langham	202	$27,000
12-15/8	New Mexico	Chris Patton	262	$31,500
19-22/8	Wichita Open	David Duval	271	
26-19/8	Texarkana Open	H Royer III	267	
2-5/9	Tri-City Open	D Jurgensen	207	
16-19/9	Utah Classic	Sean Murphy	204	
24-26/9	Boysie Open	Tommy Moore	199	$36,000

Australasian PGA Tour 1992/3

Winners Australian unless stated.

Date	Tournament	Venue	Winner	1st Prize
Oct 15-18	Perak Masters	Perak GC, Ipoh, Malaysia	Robert Allenby	$27,000
Oct 22-25	Dunhill Malaysian Masters	Selangor GC, Kuala Lumpur	Terry Price	$79,200
Oct 29-Nov 1	Pioneer Singapore PGA C'ship	Singapore Island Country Club	Terry Gale	$27,000
Nov 5-8	Air NZ Shell Open	Grange GC, Auckland	Nick Price (ZIM)	$41,418
Nov 12-15	Eagle Blue Open Golf C'ship	Royal Adelaide GC	Brett Ogle	$27,000
Nov 19-22	Ford Australian PGA C'ship	Concord GC, Sydney	Craig Parry	$54,000
Nov 26-29	Heineken Australian Open	The Lakes GC	Stephen Elkington	$144,000
Dec 3-6	Johnnie Walker Classic	Royal Melbourne GC	Robert Allenby	$126,000
Dec 10-13	Coolum Classic	Hyatt Regency, Coolum	Rodger Davis	$36,000
Jan 21-24	Optus Players Championship	Royal Melbourne GC	Robert Allenby	$54,000
Jan 28-31	Heineken Classic	Vines Resort	Peter Senior	$54,000
Feb 11-14	AMP NZ Open	Paraparaumu Beach GC	Peter Fowler	$40,673
Feb 18-21	Microsoft Australian Masters	Huntingdale GC, Melbourne	Bradley Hughes	$130,572
Feb 25-28	Canon Challenge	Castle Hill CC, Sydney	Michael Campbell	$45,000
Mar 4-7	Epson Singapore Open	Tanah Merah CC	Paul Moloney	$101,880

Women's European Tour

WEETABIX WOMEN'S BRITISH OPEN
Woburn - Dukes Course   Aug 12-15

275	**Karen Lunn (AUS)**	71 69 68 67
(-17)	**(£50,000)**	
283	Brandie Burton (USA)	75 70 68 70
	(£32,000)	
286	Kathryn Marshall (SCO)	73 71 69 73
	(£21,000)	
287	Li Wen-Lin (CHN)	70 71 74 72
	Jane Geddes (USA)	76 75 72 64
	(£14,350 each)	
289	Patty Sheehan (USA)	75 70 72 72
	(£10,500)	
290	Laura Davies (ENG)	69 76 75 70
	Marie Laure de Lorenzi (FRA)	73 77 72 68
	Suzanne Strudwick (ENG)	72 71 73 74
	Catrin Nilsmark (SWE)	76 71 74 69
	(£7,300 each)	
291	Alison Nicholas (ENG)	74 73 70 74
	(£5,400)	
293	Trish Johnson (ENG)	72 75 77 69
	Dale Reid (SCO)	76 75 74 68
	Carin Hjalmarsson (SWE)	77 74 68 74
	Helen Alfredsson (SWE)	77 71 74 71
	(£4,670 each)	
294	S Gronberg Whitmore (SWE)	76 70 79 69
	Karina Orum (DEN)	75 72 73 74
	Sarah Gautrey (AUS)	76 75 69 74
	(£4,180 each)	
295	Claire Duffey (ENG)	75 76 71 73
	Rae Hast (ENG)	77 71 72 75
	(£3,880 each)	
296	Janet Soulsby (ENG)	76 75 73 72
	Cindy Figg-Currier	75 75 72 74
	(£3,685 each)	
297	Gillian Stewart (SCO)	74 75 76 72
	Patricia Meunier* (FRA)	73 76 77 71
	Joanne Morley* (ENG)	77 74 74 72
	Valerie Michaud (FRA)	79 73 70 75
	(£3,505 each)	

298 Tania Abitbol (FRA) Frederica Dassau (ITA) Xonia Wunsch-Ruiz (ESP) Debbie Hanna (NIR) Kim Cathrein (USA) Asa Gottmo (SWE) Nikki Buxton* (ENG) (£3,145 each); 299 Liselotte Neumann (SWE) Shani Waugh (AUS) Caroline Hall (ENG) (£2,740 each); 300 Karine Espinasse (FRA), Florence Descampe (BEL), Anna-Carin Jonasson* (SWE), Lauren Cowan (AUS), (£2,470 each); 301 Corinne Dibnah (AUS), Karen Weiss (USA), Stephanie Dallongeville(FRA), (£2,245 each); 302 Susan Moon (USA), Dianne Patterson (USA), Catriona Lambert* (SCO) (£2,065 each); 303 Corinne Soules (FRA); 304 Lynette Brooky* (NZL), Veronique Palli (FRA); 305 Regine Lautens (SUI), Sonja Van Wyk (RSA), Mary Grace Estuesta (PHI), Sarah Burnell* (ENG), Tracy Loveys (ENG), Sarah Bennett (ENG); 306 Mandy Sutton (ENG), Helen Wadsworth (WAL); 307 Kelly Leadbetter (USA); 309 Diane Barnard (ENG), Charlotta Sorenstam* (SWE;, 310 Debbie Petrizzi (USA); 311 Mette Hageman (HOL)
* denotes amateur

Date	Tournament	Venue	Winner	Score	1st Prize	Runner(s)-up	Margin
Jan 14 -17	World Ladies Classic	Kelab Putra GC Malaysia	**Karen Lunn** (Australia)	286 (-2)	£45,000	S Mendiburu	Play off
Apr 29 May 2	Ford Golf Classic	Woburn GC England	**Frederica Dassau** (Italy)	289 (-7)	£10,500	Annika Sorenstam	1
May 29 -31	Holiday Inn Leiden Ladies Open	Rijswijk GC Holland	**Corinne Dibnah** (Australia)	214 (-2)	£8,250	Annika Sorenstam	1
June 24 -27	BMW European Masters	Golf de Bercuit Belgium	**Helen Dobson** (England)	283 (-9)	£22,500	M L de Lorenzi & Dale Reid	1
July 1 -4	Hennessy Ladies Cup	Köln GC Germany	**Liselotte Neumann** (Sweden)	280 (-8)	£30,000	Laura Davies	Play off
July 8 -11	European Ladies Golf Classic	Sagmühle GC Germany	**Mardi Lunn** (Australia)	287 (-1)	£15,000	Annika Sorenstam	1
Aug 19 -22	IBM Ladies Open	Haninge GC Sweden	**Lora Fairclough** (England)	280 (-12)	£15,000	Corinne Dibnah	5
Sept 2 -5	Waterford Dairies English Open	Tytherington GC Macclesfield	**Laura Davies** (England)	277 (-11)	£9,000	M L de Lorenzi	1
Sept 16 -19	BMW Ladies' Open	Lignano GC Italy	**Amaya Arruti** (Spain)	270 (-18)	£15,750	Annika Sorenstam	2

LADIES' BRITISH OPEN (AMATEUR)

145	**Janice Moodie (Windyhill)**	**74 71**
148	Catriona Lambert (North Berwick)	75 73
	Sarah Burnell (Burnham & Berrow)	73 75
	Kirsty Speak (Clitheroe)	73 75
149	Lisa Walton (Calcot Park)	76 73
150	Patricia Meunier (France)	76 74
	Iben Tinning (Denmark)	74 76

Matchplay Final
Kirsty Speak bt Catriona Lambert 3&2

GIRLS' BRITISH OPEN (AMATEUR)

69	**Filippa Helmerson (Sweden)**
72	Georgina Simpson (Cleckheaton and District)
73	Sara Beautell (Spain)

GIRLS' BRITISH OPEN TEAM CHAMPIONSHIPS

1. Spain
2. Sweden
3. Italy

SPALDING
ORDER OF MERIT
As at Sept 30, 1993

			(£)
1 (17)	Karen Lunn	AUS	66,266
2 (1)	Laura Davies	ENG	54,938
3 (-)	Annika Sorenstam	SWE	49,927
4 (7)	Liselotte Neumann	SWE	39,530
5 (36)	Helen Dobson	ENG	37,633
6 (6)	Marie L de Lorenzi	FRA	37,479
7 (3)	Corinne Dibnah	AUS	33,883
8 (23)	Lora Fairclough	ENG	27,125
9 (14)	Dale Reid	SCO	25,007
10 (47)	Mardi Lunn	AUS	23,495
11 (26)	L Maritz-Atkins	RSA	22,707
12 (24)	Federica Dassau	ITA	22,562
13 (36)	Alison Nicholas	ENG	22,055
14 (39)	Kathryn Marshall	SCO	21,763
15 (41)	Li Wen-Lin	CHN	20,175
16 (5)	Catrin Nilsmark	SWE	19,984
17 (15)	Carin Hjalmarsson	SWE	19,189
18 (58)	Pamela Wright	SCO	18,900
19 (-)	Amaya Arruti	ESP	18,579
20 (4)	Trish Johnson	ENG	17,452

SOLHEIM CUP 1994
SELECTION STANDINGS
As at Sept 30, 1993

1 (-)	Annika Sorenstam	SWE	363.00
2 (1)	Laura Davies	ENG	362.50
3 (8)	Marie L de Lorenzi	FRA	204.00
4 (22)	Lora Fairclough	ENG	170.00
5 (5)	Alison Nicholas	ENG	153.00
6 (11)	Dale Reid	SCO	143.50
7 (18)	Helen Dobson	ENG	138.00
8 (15)	Federica Dassau	ITA	135.50
9 (2)	Trish Johnson	ENG	133.50
10 (13)	Liselotte Neumann	SWE	130.00
11 (6)	Catrin Nilsmark	SWE	118.50
12 (16)	Lisa Hackney	ENG	108.00
13 (39)	Carin Hjalmarsson	SWE	97.50
14 (17)	Helen Wadsworth	WAL	92.00
15 (-)	Amaya Arruti	ESP	90.00
16 (23)	Pamela Wright	SCO	80.00
17 (79)	Mette Hageman	HOL	74.00
18 (4)	Helen Alfredsson	SWE	73.50
19 (37)	Kathryn Marshall	SCO	72.00
20 (50)	Janet Soulsby	ENG	71.00

FINAL MONEY TABLE 1992

			£ stlg
1	Laura Davies	ENG	66,333
2	Helen Alfredsson	SWE	55,900
3	Corinne Dibner	AUS	53,211
4	Trish Johnson	ENG	51,805
5	Catrin Nilsmark	SWE	35,728
6	Marie Laure de Lorenzi	FRA	34,921
7	Liselotte Neumann	SWE	34,201
8	Alison Nicholas	ENG	31,584
9	Kitrina Douglas	ENG	31,511
10	Sandrine Mendiburu	FRA	26,896

Greyhound Racing

Major Events

DAILY MIRROR/SPORTING LIFE DERBY

Wimbledon	460m	June 26
1 (3) Ringa Hustle	5/2	
2 (1) Sullane Castle	7/1	
3 (6) Hypnotic Stag	7/2	
4 (2) Greenane Squire	15/8F	
5 (4) Lassa Java	7/2	
6 (5) Ceader Mountain	50/1	

Trainer: Meek   1st Prize: £40,000
Ringa Hustle, eliminated in the semi-finals last year, made amends by leading throughout this year's Derby.

FOSTERS GOLD CUP

Wimbledon	660m	Jan 23
Winner	*Trainer*	*1st Prize*
Squire Delta	**Coleman**	**£30,000**

LADBROKES GOLDEN JACKET

Crayford	714m	Feb 20
Heavenly Lady	**Mullins**	**£5,000**

RACING POST ARC

Walthamstow	475m	Mar 6
Bonney Seven	**Coleman**	**£5,000**

MAX THOMAS PALL MALL

Oxford	450m	Mar 20
Sullane Castle	**Saunders**	**£5,000**

WENDY FAIR BLUE RIBAND

Wembley	490m	April 15
Hypnotic Stag	**Coleman**	**£7,500**

BBC TELEVISION TROPHY

Wimbledon	820m	April 21
Heavenly Lady	**Mullins**	**£6,000**

DAILY MIRROR/SPORTING LIFE NATIONAL

Hall Green	474m	Mar 31
Arfur Daley	**Meadows**	**£5,000**

COURAGE GREYHOUND OLYMPIC

Hove	515m	April 15
Hypnotic Stag	**Coleman**	**£3,000**

READING MASTERS

Reading	465m	May 1
Im His	**Jordon**	**£20,000**

REGAL SCOTTISH DERBY

Shawfield	500m	May 15
New Level	**Williams**	**£20,000**

REGENCY

Hove	710m	May 22
Trans Domino	**Thomas**	**£5,000**

COURAGE PRODUCE STAKES

Bristol	480m	June 12
Cortman Jasper	**Meek**	**£5,000**

MEL ATTREED CHAMPION STAKES

Romford	575m	July 16
Westmead Surprise	**Savva**	**£10,000**

WEY PLASTICS WINNER

Wimbledon	480m	Jul 24
Pearls Girl	**Sykes**	**£6,000**

KENT ST LEGER

Ramsgate	640m	Jul 31
Heavenly Lady	**Mullins**	**£4,000**

PETERBOROUGH DERBY

Peterborough	420m	Aug 7
Gentle Warning	**McGee**	**£8,000**

TODAY'S BEST BET

All the inside information in the world couldn't compare with the betting opportunity on offer at the Waikato track, Wellington, New Zealand in January. For two races on the card, the Tote continued to accept bets for almost three minutes after the races were over. On one race, 36 bets were laid on a tricast which paid out £3,000. Some punters though obviously smelled a rat. Determined not to be caught out, 153 of them actually placed their bets on the *wrong* dogs, even though they had just seen the races run.

Gymnastics

"It felt like I was competing in Russia," said Grigory Misutin, the former world champion from Russia. As well it might, for seven of the top eight in the men's all round category came from the former Soviet states. There were exceptions to the dominance of the new republics and one of them was a 25 year old from Shropshire, Neil Thomas, who did what no other Briton before him has done and won a medal at these championships. Thomas earned it for his floor routine and a measure of his achievement was that, in sharing second place, he was equal on scores with Vitaly Scherbo, the six-time gold medallist from Barcelona. Eddie van Hoof, Thomas's coach, even suggested that his charge would have won the gold had he completed the final tumble in his routine. Called Le Thomas (I kid you not) and invented by our Shropshire lad, it was to wrap up the section. But Thomas failed to gain sufficient height, changed his mind somewhere mid-flight and missed a twist out. He still landed perfectly enough for silver, the gold stayed with Misutin.

The women's competition was dominated by the American Shannon Miller, who took advantage of the retirement of many of the former Soviet stars to win three of the four disciplines. She withdrew from the vault, with a stomach illness, and so sacrificed an attempt to become the first gymnast to make a clean sweep of the titles.

Last year's Rhythmic Gymnastics world championships turned out to be the epitaph for the young Russian Oksana Kostina. Kostina, who took all the titles, was killed in a car crash in February (see Obituary). She was 19.

World Championships

Birmingham   April 12-18

MEN
ALL ROUND

1 **Vitaly Scherbo**   BLS   56.174
   (Floor: 9.325, P Horse: 9.350, Rings: 9.125,
   Vault: 9.537, P Bars: 9.462, H Bar: 9.375)
2 Sergei Charkov   RUS   55.625
   (9.200, 9.075, 9.375, 9.150, 9.450, 9.375)
3 Andreas Wecker   GER   55.450
   (9.175, 9.275, 9.500, 9.225, 9.250, 9.025)
4 Ivan Ivankov   BLS   55.425
   (9.000, 9.275, 9.325, 9.375, 9.250, 9.200)
5 Dmitri Karbonenko   RUS   55.275
   (9.300, 9.350, 8.875, 9.525, 9.375, 8.850)
6 Valeri Liukin   KZK   55.225
   (8.925, 9.225, 9.350, 9.350, 9.100, 9.275)

APPARATUS
Floor

1 **Grigori Misutin**   UKR   **9.400**
2 Neil Thomas   GBR   9.350
3 Vitaly Scherbo   BLS   9.350
Pommell Horse
1 **Gil Su Pae**   PRK   **9.750**
2 Andreas Wecker   GER   9.425
3 Karoly Schupkegel   HUN   9.400

Rings
1 **Yuri Chechi**   ITA   **9.625**
2 Andreas Wecker   GER   9.575
3 Ivan Ivankov   BLS   9.500
Vault
1 **Vitaly Scherbo**   BLS   **9.612**
2 Chang Feng Chih   TPE   9.487
3 Ok-ryul Yoo   KOR   9.418
Parallel Bars
1 **Vitaly Scherbo**   BLS   **9.600**
2 Igor Korobchinski   UKR   9.525
3 Valeri Belenki   FIG   9.475
High Bars
1 **Sergei Charkov**   RUS   **9.450**
2 Marius Gherman   ROM   9.375
3 Zoltan Supola   HUN   9.350

WOMEN
All round

1 **Shannon Miller**   USA   **39.062**
   (Vault: 9.787, Asym.bars: 9.825, Beam: 9.625, Floor: 9.825)
2 Gina Gogean   ROM   39.055
   (9.718, 9.812, 9.725, 9.800)
3 Tatiana Lisenko   UKR   39.011
   (9.824, 9.725, 9.712, 9.750)

4 Dominique Dawes USA 38.830
(9.493, 9.762, 9.775, 9.800)
5 Oxana Fabrichnova RUS 38.630
(9.643, 9.712, 9.750, 9.525)
6 Rozalia Galieva UZB 38.554
(9.599, 9.775, 9.575, 9.637)

APPARATUS
Vault
1 Yelena Piskoun BLS 9.762
2 Lavinia Milosovici ROM 9.737
3 Oksana Chusovitina UZB 9.718
Asymmetric Bars
1 Shannon Miller USA 9.887
2 Dominique Dawes USA 9.800
3 Andrea Cacovean ROM 9.787
Beam
1 Lavinia Milosovici ROM 9.850
2 Dominique Dawes USA 9.725
3 Gina Gogean ROM 9.650
Floor
1 Shannon Miller USA 9.787
2 Gina Gogean ROM 9.737
3 Natalia Bobrova RUS 9.712

European Junior Championships

Geneva May 14-16
MEN
ALL ROUND
1 Evgueni Jukov RUS 54.650
APPARATUS
Floor
1 Jon Melisanidis GRE 9.250
Pommel Horse
1 Marius Urzica ROM 9.600
Rings
1 Jury Gotov RUS 9.150
Vault
1 Murat Canbas TUR 9.387
Parallel Bars
1 Evgueni Jukov RUS 9.275
High Bars
1 Bernd Lill GER 9.225
1 Alexander Selk NED 9.225

WOMEN
ALL ROUND
1 Elodie Lussac FRA 39.100

APPARATUS
Vault
1 Michal Shahaf ISR 9.700
Asymmetric Bars
1 Nadia Hatagan ROM 9.812
1 Andrea Cacovean ROM 9.812
1 Elodie Lussac FRA 9.812
Beam
1 Elodie Lussac FRA 9.837
Floor
1 Elodie Lussac FRA 9.875

Japan-USA Championships

Hamamatsu, Japan Mar 27
MEN
All Round
1 Japan 218.350

DTB-Pokal

Stuttgart Dec 5-6
MEN
All Round
1 Vitaly Scherbo BLS 58.6000
Floor
1 Igor Korobchinski UKR 9.800
1 Vitaly Scherbo BLS 9.800
Pommel Horse
1 Andreas Wecker GER 9.875
1 Vitaly Scherbo BLS 9.875
Ring
1 Andreas Wecker GER 9.900
Vault
1 Vitaly Scherbo BLS 9.850
Parallel Bars
1 Andreas Wecker GER 9.850
High Bars
1 Ralf Buechner GER 9.900

WOMEN
All Round
1 Svetlana Boguinskaia BLS 39.475
Vault
1 Lavinia Milosovici ROM 9.900
Asymmetric Bars
1 Lavinia Milosovici ROM 9.900
1 Svetlana Boguinskaia BLS 9.900
Beam
1 Tatiana Lisenko UKR 9.925
Floor
1 Tatiana Lisenko UKR 9.950

Swiss Cup

Zurich Nov 29
Mixed
All Round
1 Svetlana Boguinskaia/
Vitaly Scherbo BLS 78.750
2 Tatiana Lisenko/
Igor Korobchinski UKR 78.450
3 Chiara Ferrazzi/
Valeri Belenki AZE 76.875

Memorial Arthur Gander

Chiasso, Switzerland Dec 2
MEN
All Round
1 Vitaly Scherbo BLR 58,900
WOMEN
All Round
1 Svetlana Boguinskaia BLR 39,325

Chunichi Cup

Nagoya, Japan   Nov 26-29
MEN
All Round
| 1 Yutaka Aihara | JPN | 58.10 |

Floor
| 1 Yukio Iketani | JPN | 9.750 |

Pommel Horse
| 1 Gil Su Pae | PRK | 9.900 |

Rings
| 1 Ivan Ivankov | BLS | 9.700 |

Vault
| 1 Joo Hyung Lee | KOR | 9.568 |
| 1 Yutaka Aihara | JPN | 9.568 |

Parallel Bars
| 1 Hikaru Tanaka | JPN | 9.762 |

High Bars
| 1 Yutaka Aihara | JPN | 9.775 |

WOMEN
All Round
| 1 Lavinia Milosovici | ROM | 39.374 |

Vault
| 1 Lavinia Milosovici | ROM | 9.990 |

Asymmetric Bars
| 1 Gwang Suk Kim | PRK | 9.975 |

Beam
| 1 Lyudmila Stovbchataya | UKR | 9.887 |

Floor
| 1 Christina Bontas | ROM | 9.887 |
| 1 Lyudmila Stovbchataya | UKR | 9.887 |

Nomura Tokyo Cup

Yokohama, Japan   Dec 3-6
MEN
Floor
| 1 Ok Youl You | KOR | 9.725 |

Vault
| 1 Gil Su Pae | PRK | 9.837 |

Rings
| 1 Ivan Ivankov | BLS | 9.675 |

Pommel Horse
| 1 Yutaka Aihara | JPN | 9.700 |

High Bars
| 1 Rustanu Sharipov | UKR | 9.750 |

English Championships

Liverpool   Sept 18-19
Men's Artistic
1 M Campbell	53.15
2 C Heap	51.40
3 P Bowler	51.20

Women's Artistic
1 J Brady	36.775
2 K Szymko	36.925
3 K Hackman	35.575

Rhythmic
1 A McKenzie	33.925
2 L Southwick	33.275
3 A Deehan	32.900

Rhythmic Gymnastics

European Championships

Bucharest May 20-23
Team Results
1 Bulgaria	108.900
2 Rumania	108.700
3 Ukraine	108.500

All Round
| 1 Olgar Gontar | BLR | 38.125 |

Ribbon
| 1 Olga Gontar | BLS | 9.650 |

Rope
| 1 Yana Baiychina | RUS | 9.700 |

Ball
| 1 Olga Gontar | BLS | 9.675 |

Group - Multiple
1 Russia	38.900
2 Bulgaria	38.750
3 Spain	38.500

Group - Hoop & Clubs
| 1 Bulgaria | 19.575 |
| 1 Russia | 19.575 |

Group - Rope
| 1 Russia | 19.550 |

European Cup

Malaga   June 26-27
All Round
1 Maria Petrova	BUL	38.700
2 Larissa Lukyanenko	BLS	38.550
3 Carolina Pascual	ESP	37.975

Hoop
1 Maria Petrova	BUL	9.800
2 LarissaLukyanenko	BLS	9.775
3 Amina Zaripova	RUS	9.575

Ball
1 Larissa Lukyanenko	BLS	9.800
2 Maria Petrova	BUL	9.750
3 Tatiana Ogrizko	BLS	9.550

Clubs
1 Larissa Lukyanenko	BLS	9.800
2 Carolina Pascual	ESP	9.600
3 Carmen Acedo	ESP	9.500

Ribbon
1 Maria Petrova	BUL	9.800
2 Larissa Lukyanenko	BLS	9.775
3 Carolina Pascual	ESP	9.575

Medico Cup

Feldkirch, Austria   May 1-2

All Round
1 Maria Petrova   BUL   37.150
Hoop
1 Maria Petrova   BUL   9.425
Ball
1 Maria Petrova   BUL   9.500
Clubs
1 Amina Zaripova   RUS   9.450
Ribbons
1 Amina Zaripova   RUS   9.500

VIIIth International RSG

Nouvain-La-Neuve, Belg.   Mar 26-28

All Round
1 Cindy Stollenberg   BEL   36.800
Clubs
1 Cindy Stollenberg   BEL   9.300
Ribbon
1 Cindy Stollenberg   BEL   9.200
Ball
1 Andrea Szalay   HUN   9.300
1 Marina Vinogradova   RUS   9.300
Hoop
1 Andrea Szalay   HUN   9.300

Team Results
1 Russia   107.00
2 Canada   103.20
3 Germany   102.80

19th Tournoi International De Grs

Corbeil-Essonnes, France   May 14-16

All Round
1 Larissa Lukianenko   BLS   37.900
2 Maria Petrova   BUL   37.650
3 Ekater Serebryanskaya   UKR   36.775
Hoop
1 Larissa Lukianenko   BLR   9.600
1 Maria Petrova   BUL   9.600
Ball
1 Maria Petrova   BUL
Clubs
1 Larissa Lukianenko   BLR   9.500
1 Maria Petrova   BUL   9.500
Ribbon
1 Maria Petrova   BUL   9.625

Handball

Men's World Championship

Stockholm, Sweden   Mar 16-21

Group 1 (Final Standings)

	P	W	D	L	GF	GA	Pts
France	5	4	0	1	115	103	8
Switzerland	5	3	0	2	122	118	6
Spain	5	2	1	2	105	101	5
RCS	5	2	1	2	104	110	5
Romania	5	2	0	3	105	110	4
Egypt	5	1	0	4	100	109	2

Group 2 (Final Standings)

	P	W	D	L	GF	GA	Pts
Russia	5	4	1	0	131	98	9
Sweden	5	4	0	1	108	101	8
Germany	5	2	2	1	100	100	6
Iceland	5	2	0	3	103	114	4
Denmark	5	1	1	3	102	117	3
Hungary	5	0	0	5	104	118	0

Classification Matches
11/12: Hungary 29 Egypt 25
9/10: Denmark 27 Romania 23
7/8: RCS 22 Iceland 21
5/6: Spain 29 Germany 26
3/4: Sweden 26 Switzerland 19
Final
Russia 28 France 19
Russia are World Champions

Top Scorers
1 Marc Baumgartner SUI
2 Jozsef Eles HUN
3 Yoon Kyung-Shin KOR

Top Goalkeepers
1 Rico Lorenzo ESP
2 Tomas Svesson SWE
3 Mats Olsson SWE

Europa Cup

May 30

Men's
Champions Cup
Badel 1862 Zagreb CRO 40
SG Wallau-Massenheim GER 39

Cup-Winner's Cup
Olympique Marseille Vitrolles FRA 46
Fotex Veszprem HUN 43

IHF Cup
Teka Santander ESP 46
TSV Bayer Dormagen GER 44

Women's
Champions Cup
Hypobank Südstadt AUT 40
Vasaa Budapest HUN 25

Cup-Winner's Cup
TV Giessen-Lützellinden GER 48
Rostelmash Rostov/Don RUS 43

IHF Cup
Rapid Fem. Bucuresti ROM 50
CSL Dijon FRA 40

Junior World Championships
Women

Bulgaria   Sept 7-12

Classification Matches
11/12: Austria 34 Japan 33
9/10: Germany 24 Sweden 26
7/8: Poland 14 Ukraine 32
5/6: Romania 33 Belarus 29
3/4: Denmark 27 Korea 28
Final
Russia 24 Bulgaria 17

Men

Egypt   Sept 7-12

Classification Matches
11/12: Argentina 33 Poland 29
9/10: Spain 24 Portugal 22
7/8: Romania 29 Norway 30
5/6: Hungary 26 Sweden 28
3/4: Israel 21 Russia 20
Final
Denmark 19 Egypt 22

Hockey

Unhappy at the lack of success from a jaded team, Britain's men's team sacked its manager, Bernie Cotton and coach, Norman Hughes. They were replaced by one man; David Whitaker, who last graced the international stage as coach to the gold medal team of 1988, and who took over the helm of the England team also. The golden touch was still apparent in Whitaker's first match when England beat Germany, but the Olympic champions had more important matters on their agenda than helping England exorcise a few ghosts. They went straight on to the Champions' Trophy in Kuala Lumpur, the competition for the top six teams in the world. Although they won all their round-robin matches, Germany came apart under the pressure of Australia's fast counter-attacking play and succumbed 4-0.

Dennis Hay also retired as coach of the British women's team, but left on a somewhat different note to Cotton and Hughes, having taken the women to an Olympic bronze medal in Barcelona. His replacement was Bristol university lecturer, Sue Slocombe, who is not averse to a drop of success herself having steered England to a European Cup success in 1991, whilst at Clifton.

In the Leagues, still in their infancy, the talent has already tended to polarise to the leading clubs and the danger is that it will become a London franchise with the odd game against the provincials to calm unrest. Hounslow continued to be the main culprit in this respect; League champions and HA Cup winners, they have been so dominant in the latter that they have lost a match in over three years. Ironically, this has been achieved with a team over half of whom hail from the north of England where top-level hockey comes a poor second to whippet racing.

Hounslow and Teddington (who qualify for the European Cup Winners Cup by dint of Hounslow's chase for glory in the Champions' Cup) are in the powerful position of having a strong European fixture list to compensate for a sometimes mediocre League. With the rolling substitution law (similar to basketball) meaning that up to 16 players can be used in one game, the danger is that the top clubs could cream off even more of the talent widening the gap still further between the league haves and have-nots.

The women's situation could not be more different. Since the National League was inaugurated in 1989/90, the English women have won a European gold and the British team Olympic bronze. Not only that, but success has followed in European competitions as well. The women's league now has just eight teams playing both home and away; this competitive and geographically sound league structure has been part and parcel of the women's success.

Men's Hockey

Champions Trophy

Kuala Lumpur, Malaysia   July 3-11

Pool Matches
3rd July 1993
Netherlands 2 Malaysia 1
Germany 2 Spain 0
Australia 2 Pakistan 1

4th July 1993
Spain 1 Malaysia 2
Pakistan 2 Germany 3

5th July 1993
Australia 0 Netherlands 1

6th July 1993
Spain 1 Australia 5
Germany 4 Malaysia 1
Netherlands 1 Pakistan 3

7th July 1993
Malaysia 2 Pakistan 2

8th July 1993
Netherlands 0 Spain 0
Australia 1 Germany 3

9th July 1993
Pakistan 2 Spain 0
Malaysia 2 Australia 4
Germany 3 Netherlands 2

Ranking: 1. Germany 10 pts - 2. Australia 6 pts - 3.
Pakistan 5pts (+2) - 4. Netherlands 5 pts (+1) - r.
Malaysia 3 pts - 6. Spain 1 pt

Final Play-Offs
11th July 1993
5th/6th Spain 5 Malaysia 3
3rd/4th Netherlands 6 Pakistan 2
Final   Australia 4 Germany 0

Intercontinental Cup

Poznan, Poland   Aug
7th/8th
Canada 1 Malaysia 1
Canada won 8-7 on penalties
5th/6th
Belgium 0 South Africa 1
Semi-finals
Korea 1 Argentina 0
Spain 3 India 2
3rd/4th
India 3 Argentina 2
Final
Korea 1 Spain 0

Four Nations Tournament

Hamburg, Germany   Sept 2-5

Pakistan 2 Germany 1
Australia 2 Holland 2
Australia 3 Germany 2
Pakistan 2 Holland 0
Australia 3 Pakistan 1
Holland drew with Germany
Final Standings: 1 Australia 5pts, 2 Pakistan 4pts, 3
Holland 2pts, Germany 1pt

World Junior Cup

Terrassa, Spain   Sept

MEN
Final
Germany 3 Pakistan 1
3rd/4th
Australia 3 Holland 1
5th/6th
England 3 Argentina 1
7th/8th
Spain 3 Cuba 2
WOMEN
Final
Australia 1 Argentina 2
3rd/4th
Germany 2 Korea 2
(Germany won 3-2 on penalties)
9th/10th
England 1 Kenya 0
11th/12th
Scotland 3 Trinidad & Tobago 1

Pizza Express National Hockey League

DIVISION 1

		P	W	D	L	GF	GA	Pts
1	Hounslow	17	16	0	1	58	14	48
2	Southgate	17	13	2	2	54	24	41
3	Old Loughtonians	17	11	4	2	42	22	37
4	Havant	17	11	2	4	43	23	35
5	Firebrands	17	9	5	3	33	27	32
6	Stourport	17	9	3	5	31	31	30
7	Teddington	17	7	4	6	33	24	25
8	St Albans	17	7	4	6	29	43	25
9	Slough	17	6	4	7	23	28	22
10	East Grinstead	17	6	3	8	38	31	21
11	Bournville	17	6	1	10	22	33	19
12	Cannock	17	6	1	10	25	39	19
13	Bromley	17	4	6	7	25	26	18
14	Trojans	17	4	6	7	25	29	18
15	Welton	17	4	5	8	19	33	17
16	Canterbury	17	4	3	10	26	39	15
17	Neston	17	1	2	14	15	45	5
18	Surbiton	17	0	3	14	26	56	3

DIVISION 2

1	Reading	17	15	1	1	48	9	46
2	Indian Gymkhana	17	13	3	1	43	11	42
3	Guildford	17	14	0	3	46	17	42
4	Barford Tigers	17	10	3	4	27	20	33
5	Beeston	17	9	2	6	24	19	29
6	Brooklands	17	8	3	6	32	27	27
7	Isca	17	7	4	6	27	22	25
8	Doncaster	17	8	1	8	24	27	25
9	Cambridge City	17	8	1	8	27	34	25
10	Harleston Magpies	17	7	1	9	27	37	22
11	Richmond	17	6	2	9	29	26	20
12	Harborne	17	5	4	8	27	28	19
13	Cheltenham	17	5	2	10	15	26	17
14	Warrington	17	4	5	8	22	37	17
15	Chelmsord	17	4	2	11	19	33	14
16	Brean	17	4	1	12	10	38	13
17	Old Kingstonians	17	3	3	11	11	23	12
18	Lyons	17	2	4	11	20	44	10

Top Scorers

P Osborn	Reading	25
R Welsh	Southgate	21
I Jennings	Guildford	20
R Thompson	Hounslow	20
N Thompson	Old Loughtonians	20

The Royal Bank of Scotland Cup

Final Rounds Only

Round Five
Beeston 1 Slough 0
Canterbury 1 Cannock 3
East Grinstead 3 Sheffield 0
Guildford 2 Stourport 2
(Guildford win 5-3 on strokes)
Hampstead & W 3 Northampton 0
Harleston Magpies 1 Hounslow 6
ISCA 0 Teddington 1
Reading 6 Indian Gymkhana 2

Round Six
Reading 1 Beeston 0
Hampstead 0 East Grinstead 1
Guildford 1 Teddington 1
(Teddington won 4-3 on strokes)
Cannock 1 Hounslow 2

Semi-Finals
Hounslow 3 East Grinstead 1
Reading 1 Teddington 1

The Final
(Milton Keynes   May 2)
Hounslow 4   Teddington 1

INDOOR CLUB CHAMPIONSHIP
Crystal Palace   *Jan 22*
Quarter-Finals
Blackheath 3 Welton 7
East Grinstead 6 Harbourne 3
St Albans 4 Stourport 5
Old Loughtonians 5 Firebrands 3

Semi-Finals
Welton 3 East Grinstead 3
(East Grinstead won 3-2 on penalty strokes)
Stourport 3 Old Loughtonians 4

The Final
East Grinstead 6 Old Loughtonians 3

NORWICH UNION COUNTY CHAMPIONSHIPS
Cannock HC Apr 17-18
Quarter-Finals
Staffordshire 5 Hampshire 2
Cheshire 4 Durham 0
Yorkshire 2 Cambridgeshire 0
Middlesex 3 Essex 2

Semi-Finals
Cheshire 2 Yorkshire 1
Oxfordshire 3 Middlesex 0

The Final
Staffordshire 3 Cheshire 2

YOUTH CUP FINALS
Birmingham May 3
U18
Kingston Grammar School 2 RGS High Wycombe 0
U16
St Georges College 2 Simon Langton GS 0

Women's Hockey

Champions Trophy

Amsterdam   Aug 28-29

Standings after pool matches

1	Australia	10pts
2	Holland	7
3	Korea	6
4	Germany	4
5	Great Britain	3
6	Spain	0

5th/6th

Spain 1   Great Britain 0

3rd/4th

Germany 2   Korea 1

Final

Holland 1   Australia 1

Australia won 4-2 on penalties

TYPHOO TEA CUP

Birmingham   Oct 3

England 1   Spain 0

HOME COUNTRIES INTERNATIONALS

Cardiff   Apr 23-25

England 0   Ireland 0
Scotland 4   Wales 0

England 0   Wales 0
Scotland 2   Ireland 2

England 1   Scotland 3
Wales 0   Ireland 4

Final Table

1	Scotland	5
2	Ireland	4
3	England	2
4	Wales	1

FOUR NATIONS TOURNAMENT

Glasgow   June 25-27

England 0   Germany 1
Scotland 2   France 0

England 3   France 1
Scotland 0   Germany 0

England 1   Scotland 1
Germany 3   France 0

SOUTH AFRICAN TOUR

Cape Town   July 17

England 0   South Africa 3

Port Elizabeth   July 25

England 0   South Africa 2

Johannesburg   July 30

England 2   Zimbabwe 0

Johannesburg   July 31

England 1   South Africa 0

National League

DIVISION 1

1	Ipswich	11	9	1	1	23	7	28
2	Hightown	11	9	0	2	20	4	27
3	Slough	11	8	1	2	24	8	25
4	Sutton Coldfield	11	7	1	3	19	7	22
5	Clifton	11	5	1	5	12	9	16
6	Ealing	11	4	3	4	9	9	15
7	Balsam Leicester	11	4	2	5	13	16	14
8	Chelmsford	11	3	4	4	14	22	13
9	Wimbledon	11	3	2	6	11	25	11
10	Pickwick	11	3	1	7	8	17	10
11	Doncaster	11	1	3	7	4	12	6
12	Exmouth	11	0	1	10	4	25	1

DIVISION 2

1	Trojans	9	7	1	1	15	3	22
2	Bracknell	9	6	2	1	14	6	20
3	Blueharts	9	6	1	2	16	8	19
4	Bradford Swithenb'k	9	6	0	3	14	10	18
5	Sherwood	9	5	2	2	12	7	17
6	Sunderland Bedans	9	4	1	4	9	9	13
7	Harleston Magpies	9	3	3	3	12	10	12
8	Colwall	9	1	1	7	10	20	4
9	Cambridge City	9	1	0	8	2	18	3
10	Yate	9	0	1	8	3	16	1

AEWHA Cup

Quarter-Finals

Ealing 1   Wimbledon 0
FP Sutton Coldfield 4   Exmouth 0
Ipswich 2   Chelmsford 1
Balsam Leicester 5   St Albans 0

Semi-Finals

Ipswich 2   Ealing 2
(Ealing won 5-3 after penalties)
Balsam Leicester 0   FP Sutton Coldfield 0
(Leicester won 4-2 after pens)

The Final

Stantonbury, M Keynes   May 16

Balsam Leicester 1   Ealing 0

Horse Racing

There it was, top of the television rankings for sport with over 15 million people tuning in - to an event that didn't take place. It's amazing how much more compelling the non-event was than the event itself. It was brilliant and bewildering viewing with Peter O'Sullevan obviously as brilliantly bewildered as the rest of us. Though the race was clearly not going to count, O'Sullevan didn't know how to handle it and, in a ding-dong battle between reality and reflex, O'Sullevan's reflex was the overwhelming winner and (though he did mention the race would be void) nevertheless felt compelled to call it as if it was the real thing. Anybody walking into the room two minutes after the start would have thought it was a cracking good race.

Afterwards, the working reflexes dropped and the emotional reflexes came up. It was fair enough for John White to be near to tears or Jenny Pitman to feel roused, but everyone else wanted a piece of the emotional bandwagon. I mean, have you ever seen Brough Scott so angry? He was on the emotional high ground before you could say, "They're off".

Ken Brown, the starter, became the first villain of the piece and, according to *The Observer*, the most hated man in Britain, which rated the crime of letting a load of horses stand too near a bit of tape quite highly. Brown, to argue for his corner, had to contend with 60m of tape (the longest on a racecourse in Britain) and it would contradict nature for it to rise with anything other than lethargy.

Ken Evans, the recall man, was the next culprit. Evans had 12 seconds to wave his flag before goodness knows how many tons of horseflesh descended on him, but insisted he did, all the same. As we read everywhere, Evans earned just £28 a day to do his job, which is not very much. He did, though, have a lawyer acting for him at the enquiry. On £28 a day, he did well to manage that.

The bookmakers were roused, complaining that they had lost their profits on the £75 million + that we were supposed to have put on the race. That makes thirty-bob for every man, woman and child in the country; could they be exaggerating perchance? They didn't lose as much as they might have because a lot of people, apparently, didn't reclaim their betting stakes. They'll probably do it when they next go back into a bookies - for next year's Grand National.

So who do you blame? Well, from the 34 page report produced by the Inquiry, it looks like there's going to be a second recall man for next year. Thinking about it, you could have one every furlong. That would cost 36 x £28 = £1008, which is much cheaper than installing anything more modern.

Other things did happen in the last twelve months, but thankfully with not quite the same impact. The Jockey Club relinquished control of the sport handing over to the British Horserace Board in June. The Jockey Club did not induce tears at its departure. The BHB has inherited a host of problems; money, to whip or not to whip and drugs, to name but a few.

The latter generated more than a few good stories, not least the Jockey club's announcement, on February 25 1993, that a horse, Flash of Straw, had been positive as long ago as August, 1992. In no other sport would the governing body sit on such information for so long. Flash of Straw and Martin Pipe's hurdler, Her Honour, found positive in February, reawoke the drugs controversy. Adding fuel to the fire came the *On The Line* BBC TV programme where an unidentified doper, later revealed to be ex-jockey Dermot Browne, talked of the ease in drugging runners. In this instance, the drugs controversy was all about 'stopping' horses, but racing still allows you to use drugs to assist horses to run faster too. Or, at least to train harder.

More edifying was the appearance of Zafonic in April at Newmarket. The French horse looked superb and broke the 47 year old course record as he hacked up. Pat Eddery could have read the Sunday papers while it was all happening. At Epsom, Eddery experienced a somewhat different feeling on Tenby. As short as 2/5, in the days preceding the event, Tenby could never even make his presence felt. Commander-in-Chief won and Henry Cecil, who trains them both, got through another two packets of cigarettes.

By the end of September, Michael Roberts, who must have been looking forward to this season like no other, could have felt a bit like the Grand National starter . Stood down for 10 days in the middle of the season, he got stood down from his retainer for Sheikh Mohammed at the end of it. Frankie Dettori started off no better, being refused a licence by the Royal Hong Kong Jockey Club to race there. He found the silver lining when he slipped into the saddle of Roberts' old job.

Lester Piggott continued to amaze. Having broken a rib and fractured his clavicle at the Breeders' Cup event in October last, he returned this summer to show no ill-effects. He even smiled once. Desert Orchid showed he is a old toughie as well, following an operation for a twisted gut that put him in intensive care, he came out almost as straight as new - but he didn't get his other bits back. You think they'd do that now he's retired, wouldn't you? Peter Scudamore, who didn't have to worry about such things, retired in April. He went as you'd expect, without any great fuss. His record speaks for itself.

THE LIFE AND RIDING TIMES OF PETER SCUDAMORE

Born: Hereford, June 13,1958 **Apprenticeship:** Michael Scudamore, Willie Stephenson, Dennis Holmberg, Jim Bolger and David Nicholson **First ride:** Stellemon(unplaced), Leics - flat, Aug 18, 1975 **First winner:** Rolyat, Devon & Exeter, Aug 31, 1978 **Main retaining stables:** David Nicholson (1978-86), Fred Winter (1986-88), Martin Pipe (1986-93) **Champion Jockey:** 1981-82 (shared with John Francome), 1985-86, 1986-87, 1987-88, 1988-89, 1990-91, 1991-92 **Career wins:** 1,677 (record) **Most winners in a season:** 221 (record) **Final Ride:** Sweet Duke, Ascot, Apr 7 1993 **Good horses ridden:** Broadsword, Burrough Hill Lad, Corbière, Very Promising, Gaye Brief, Royal Vulcan, Half Free, Pearlyman, Celtic Shot, Beau Ranger **Good races won:** Champion Hurdle - Celtic Shot (1986) & Granville Again (1993), Queen Mother champion Chase - Pearlyman (1987, Hennessy Gold Cup - Strands of Gold (1988) & Chatam (1991), Mackeson Gold Cup - Pegwell Bay (1988)

QUOTES

"You must stop this race. What are you doing? My bloody horse has already gone one circuit, I don't want to win the National like this"

> Jenny Pitman, trainer of Esha Ness, in the weighing room halfway through the non-race.

"This race is not actually taking place"

> Aintree racecourse commentator

"Stewards Enquiry"

> Aintree public address system

"I could see there were only a few horses round, but I thought the others had fallen or something"

> John White, rider of Esha Ness, 'winner' of the void race.

"I saw not one flag. There were a few people waving their arms. There were two cones at the Chair and a man wandering around as if it was a Sunday school picnic"

> John Bradbourne, jockey of Interim Lib.

"It wouldn't happen in a point-to-point in Ireland. In a little backward country like Ireland, and I mean that in the nicest possible way......"

> John Upson, trainer of one of the Grand National favourites, Zeta's Lad, opening his mouth before his brain was in the saddle.

"It's the worst thing to happen in the sport since the suffragette Emily Davidson was killed throwing herself in front of the King's horse, Aboyeur in the 1907 Derby"

> Richard Pitman, TV commentator and former jockey.

"It wouldn't be too difficult to have a flashing light saying 'Jockeys Stop', most jockeys can read"

> Bill Smith, former jockey.

"Stories that some 300 million people saw this humiliation of a British institution are silly.....I would estimate the total world audience at not more than 25 million"

> Paul Fox, in the *Daily Telegraph,* getting something into perspective.

"I've come all the way from Stoke for this pigging crap"

> A punter at Aintree

"Starter cocked it up....Aintree cocked it up....Jockey Club cocked it up....Now we step in. *Sun* to run the National on computer"

> *Sun* newspaper

"So much for the luck of the Irish"

> Alan Ruddock, a journalist, had a tricast on the National, picking Esha Ness, Cahervillahow and Romany King to finish in that order. They did, but instead of £3,000 he got his money back.

"I was f***ing good there, wasn't I?"

> Lester Piggott to Richard Hannon, after winning on the trainer's Geisway at Goodwood.

Flat Racing

The Classics
The money shown is for 1st prize unless stated otherwise

MADAGANS 1000 GUINEAS
3 year old fillies (1m)
Newmarket, Apr 29
Sayyedati (9-0)   Walter Swinburn
C E Brittain   4/1   £39,446

2000 GUINEAS
3 year old colts + fillies (1m)
Newmarket, May 1
Zafonic (9-0)   Pat Eddery
A Fabre in France   5/6   £40,890

EVER READY DERBY
3 year old colts + fillies (1m 4f)
Epsom Downs, June 2
Commander in Chief (9-0) Michael Kinane
H R A Cecil   15/2   £168,489

ENERGIZER OAKS (1m 4f)
3 year old fillies (1m 4f)
Epsom Downs, June 5
Intrepidity (9-0)   Michael Roberts
A Fabre in France   5/1   £55,000

COALITE ST LEGER
3 year old colts + fillies (1m 6f)
Doncaster, Sept 11
Bob's Return (9-0)   Philip Robinson
M H Tompkins   3/1   £72,230

Group 1

EVER READY CORONATION CUP (1m 4f)
4+ (1m 4f)
Epsom Downs, June 3
Opera House (5-9-0)   Michael Roberts
M R Stoute   9/4   £31,212

ST JAMES'S PALACE (1m)
3 c + f (1m)
Royal Ascot, June 15
Kingmambo (9-0)   Cash Asmussen
F Boutin in France   2/5   £43,253

CORONATION STAKES
3 f (1m)
Royal Ascot, June 16
Gold Splash (9-0)   C Mosse
Mrs C Head in France   100/30   £40,740

GOLD CUP
4+ (2m 4f)
Royal Ascot, June 17
Drum Taps (7-9-2)   Frankie Dettori
Lord Huntingdon   13/2   £39,853)

CORAL-ECLIPSE
3+ (1m 2f)
Sandown Park, Jul 3
Opera House (5-9-7)   Michael Kinane
M R Stoute   9/2   £55,260

JULY CUP
3+ (6f)
Newmarket, Jul 8
Hamas (4-9-6)   Willie Carson
P T Walwyn   33/1   £39,414

KING GEORGE VI & QUEEN ELIZABETH DIAMOND
3+ (1m 4f)
Ascot, Jul 24
Opera House (5-9-7)   Michael Roberts
M R Stoute   8/1   £100,546

SUSSEX
3+ (1m)
Goodwood, Jul 28
Bigstone (3-8-13)   D Boeuf
E Lellouche in France   14/1   £29,935

JUDDMONTE INTERNATIONAL (1m 2f)
3+ f (1m 2f)
York, Aug 17
Ezzoud (4-9-6)   Walter Swinburn
M R Stoute   28/1   £57,665

ASTON UPTHORPE YORKSHIRE OAKS
3+ f (1m 4f)
York, Aug 18
Only Royale (4-9-7)   Ray Cochrane
L M Cumani   10/1   £28,882

KEENELAND NUNTHORPE
2+ (5f)
York, Aug 19
Lochsong (5-9-3)   Frankie Dettori
I A Balding   10/1   £32,104

HAZLEWOOD FOODS SPRINT CUP
2+ (6f)
Haydock Park, Sept 4
Wolfhound (4-9-9)   Michael Roberts
J H M Gosden   7/2   £30,059

FILLIES' MILE
2F (1m)
Ascot, Sept 25
Fairy Heights (2-8-10)   Cash Asmussen
N Callaghan   11/1   £93,420

QUEEN ELIZABETH II
3+ (1m)
Ascot, Sept 25
Bigstone (3-9-0)   Pat Eddery
E Lellouche in France   100/30   £194,280

SHADWELL STUD CHEVELEY PARK
2F (6F)
Newmarket, Sept 29
Prophecy (2-8-11)   Pat Eddery
J Gosden   12-1   £73,122

NEWGATE STUD MIDDLE PARK
2C (6f)
Newmarket, Sept 30
First Trump (2-9-0)   Michael Hills
G Wragg   6/1   £91,233

Group 2

GARDNER MERCHANT MILE
4+ (1m)
Sandown Park, Apr 23
Alhijaz (4-9-6)   Willie Carson
J L Dunlop   6/1   £13,125

JOCKEY CLUB STAKES
4+ (1m 4f)
Newmarket, Apr 30
Zinaad (4-8-9)   Walter Swinburn
M R Stoute   3/1   £12,446

TOTE DANTE
3 (1m 2f)
York, May 12
Tenby (9-0)   Pat Eddery
H R A Cecil   1/3   £22,412

POLO MINTS YORKSHIRE CUP
3+ (1m 6f)
York, May 13
Assessor (4-9-0)   Richard Quinn
R Hannon   9/1   £18,024

JUDDMONTE LOCKINGE
3+ (1m)
Newbury, May 14
Swing Low (4-9-0)   Lester Piggott
R Hannon   12/1   £14,448

UB GROUP TEMPLE
3+ (5f)
Sandown Park, May 31
Paris House (4-9-7)   John Carroll
J Berry   9/2   £13,125

QUEEN ANNE
3+ (1m)
Royal Ascot, June 15
Alfiora (4-9-2)   Michael Kinane
C E Brittain   20/1   £19,817

KING EDWARD VII
3 c + g (1m 4f)
Royal Ascot, June 15
Beneficial (8-8)   Michael Hills
G Wragg   11/4   £21,825

PRINCE OF WALES'S
3+ (1m 2f)
Royal Ascot, June 15
Placerville (3-8-4)   Pat Eddery
H R A Cecil   11/2   £21,422

RIBBLESDALE
3f (1m 4f)
Royal Ascot, June 17
Thawakib (8-8)   Willie Carson
J L Dunlop   5/2   £22,199
KING'S STAND
3+ (5f)
Royal Ascot June 18
Elbio (6-9-3)   Walter Swinburn
P J Makin   12/1   £22,472

HARDWICKE
4+ (1m 4f)
Royal Ascot, June 18
Jeune (4-8-9)   Ray Cochrane
G Wragg   7/2   £21,069

PRINCESS OF WALES'S
3+ (1m 4f)
Newmarket, Jul 6
Desert Team (3-8-1)   Willie Carson
J S Bolger in Ireland 10/1   £13,965

FALMOUTH
3+ f (1m)
Newmarket, Jul 7
Niche (3-8-6)   Lester Piggott
R Hannon   13/8   £14,178

RICHMOND
2 c + g (6f)
Goodwood, Jul 28
First Trump (8-11)   Michael Hills
G Wragg   100/30   £10,902

VODAFONE NASSAU (1m 2f)
3+ F (1m 2f)
Goodwood, Jul 31
Lyphard's Delta (3-8-6) Willie Ryan
H R A Cecil   10/1   £19,221

IBN BEY GEOFFREY FREER (1m 5f)
3+ (1m 5f)
Newbury, Aug 14
Azzilfi (3-8-5)   Willie Carson
J L Dunlop   5/1   £14,895

GREAT VOLTIGEUR (1m 4f)
3 c + g (1m 4f)
York, Aug 17
Bob's Return (8-9)   Philip Robinson
M H Tompkins   16/1   £17,160

SCOTTISH EQUITABLE GIMCRACK (6f)
2 c + g (6f)
York, Aug 18
Turtle Island (9-5)   John Reid
P W Chapple-Hyam 5/2   £20,871

LOWTHER STAKES
2 f (6f)
York, Aug 19

Velvet Moon (8-11)	Alan Munro	
P F I Cole	10/1	£14,191

TRIPLEPRINT CELEBRATION MILE
3+ (1m)
Goodwood, Aug 28

Swing Low (4-9-3)	John Reid	
R Hannon	10/1	£13,460

LAURENT PERRIER CHAMPAGNE
2 c + g (7f)
Doncaster, Sept 10

Shepton Mallet (9-0)	John Reid	
P W Chapple-Hyam	11/10	£1,140

TRIPLEPRINT FLYING CHILDERS
2 (5f) Doncaster, Sept 11

Imperial Ballwick (8-6)	John Williams	
M D I Usher	12/1	£9,336

ROKEBY FARMS MILL REEF
2 (6f)
Newbury, Sept 18

Polish Laughter (8-11)	Walter Swinburn	
B Hanbury	4/1	£29,030 (total)

ROYAL LODGE
2 c + g (1m)
Ascot, Sept 25

Mister Baileys (8-10)	Frankie Dettori	
M Johnson	100/30	£59,940 (total)

1992 Group 2

CHEVELEY PARK STUD SUN CHARIOT
3+ f 1m 2f
Newmarket, Oct 3 1992

Red Slippers (3-8-8)	Frankie Dettori	
L M Cumani	6/4	£12,539

CHALLENGE
3+ (7f)
Newmarket, Oct 15 1992

Selkirk (4-9-3)	Ray Cochrane	
I A Balding	5/6	£13,057

Group 3

SHADWELL STUD NELL GWYN
3 f (7f)
Newmarket, Apr 13

Niche (9-0)	Lester Piggott	
R Hannon	11/1	£21,691

EARL OF SEFTON E.B.F.
3+ (1m 1f)
Newmarket, April 14

Ezzoud (4-8-10)	Walter Swinburn	
M R Stoute	5/1	£7,991

CRAVEN
3 c + g (1m)
Newmarket, April 15

Emperor Jones (8-9)	Ray Cochrane	
J H M Gosden	14/1	£8,496

GAINSBOROUGH STUD FRED DARLING
3 f (7f)
Newbury, Apr 16

Sueboog (9-0)	Walter Swinburn	
C E Brittain	5/2	£8,716

SINGER & FRIEDLANDER GREENHAM
3 c + g (7f)
Newbury, Apr 17

Inchinor (9-0)	Frankie Dettori	
R Charlton	7/2	£8,302

LANES END JOHN PORTER E.B.F.
4+ (1m 4f)
Newbury, Apr 17

Linpac West (7-8-12)	Frankie Dettori	
C W C Elsey	25/1	£7,557

TGI FRIDAY'S GORDON RICHARDS EBF
4+ (1m 2f)
Sandown, Apr 24

Ruby Tiger (6-8-12)	Richard Quinn	
P F I Cole	9/2	£7,971

THRESHER CLASSIC TRIAL
3 (1m 2f)
Sandown Park, Apr 24

True Hero (8-11)	Ray Cochrane	
J H M Gosden	7/1	£10,890

INSULPAK SAGARO E.B.F.
4+ (2m)
Ascot, Apr 28

Roll a Dollar (7-8-12)	Brian Rouse	
D R C Elsworth	12/1	£9,938

PALACE HOUSE
3+ (5f)
Newmarket, May 1

Paris House (4-8-10)	John Carroll	
J Berry	9/1	£7,488

DALHAM CHESTER VASE
3 (1m 4f)
Chester, May 4

Armiger (8-11)	Pat Eddery	
H R A Cecil	4/6	£12,435

ORMONDE E.B.F.
4+ (1m 5f)
Chester, May 6

Shambo (6-9-2)	Michael Roberts	
C E Brittain	7/1	£11,459

ALPINE (DOUBLE GLAZING) DERBY TRIAL
3 (1m 3f)
Lingfield, May 8

Bob's Return (9-0)	Philip Robinson	
M H Tompkins	14/1	£12,524

TATTERSALLS MUSIDORA
3 f (1m 3f)
York, May 11
Marillette (8-10)   Pat Eddery
JH M Gosden   5/1   £8,914

DUKE OF YORK
3+ (6f)
York, May 13
Hamas (4-9-0)   Willie Carson
P T Walwyn   14/1   £8,147

CEMENTONE BEAVER HENRY II E.B.F.
4+ (2m)
Sandown Park, May 31
Brier Creek (4-8-10)   Michael Roberts
J H M Gosden   7/2   £9,821

BRIGADIER GERARD
4+ (1m 2f)
Sandown Park, June 1
Red Bishop (5-8-10)   Michael Roberts
J H M Gosden   5/4   £7,283

DIOMED
3+ (1m)
Epsom Downs, June 2
Enharmonic (6-9-7)   Frankie Dettori
Lord Huntingdon   12/1   £8,095

COVENTRY
2 (6f)
Royal Ascot, June 15
Stonehatch (8-13)   John Reid
P W Chapple-Hyam   evens   £9,936

QUEEN MARY
2 f (5f)
Royal Ascot, June 16
Risky (8-8)   Walter Swinburn
R Hannon   11/2   £10,468

QUEEN'S VASE
3 (2m)
Royal Ascot, June 16
Infrasonic (8-11)   Pat Eddery
A Babre in France   3/1   £12,843

JERSEY
3 (7f)
Royal Ascot, June 16
Ardkinglass (9-1)   Willie Ryan
H R A Cecil   10/1   £15,064

NORFOLK
2 (5f)
Royal Ascot, June 17
Turtle Island (8-13)   John Reid
P W Chapple-Hyam   3/1   £8,999

CORK AND ORRERY
3+ (6F)
Royal Ascot, June 17
College Chapel (3-8-10) Lester Piggott
M V O'Brien in Ireland 7/2   £15,145

VAN GEEST CRITERION
3+ f (7f)
Newmarket, June 26
Inchinor (3-8-12)   Richard Quinn
R Charlton   7/1   £7,620

LANCASHIRE OAKS
3+ f (1m 4f)
Haydock Park, Jul 3
Rainbow Lake (3-8-4)   Willie Ryan
H R A Cecil   11/8   £7,164

HILLSDOWN CHERRY HINTON
2 f (6f)
Newmarket, Jul 6
Lemon Souffle (8-9)   Lester Piggott
R Hannon   5/4   £5,855

SJB GROUP JULY STAKES
2 c + g (6f)
Newmarket, Jul 7
First Trump (8-10)   Michael Hills
G Wragg   9/2   £5,745

TENNENTS SCOTTISH CLASSIC
3+ (1m 2f)
Ayr, Jul 19
River North (3-8-6)   Kevin Darley
Lady Herries   100/30   £7,422

PRINCESS MARGARET
2 f (6f)
Ascot, Jul 24
A Smooth One (8-8)   John Reid
R Hannon   12/1   £6,116

**FEDERATION BREWERY LCL PILLS LAGER
BEESWING**
3+ (7f)
Newcastle, Jul 26
Eurolink Thunder (3-8-7) Ray Cochrane
J L Dunlop   5/1   £7,842

GORDON
3 (1m 4f)
Goodwood, Jul 27
Right Win (8-10)   John Reid
R Hannon   3/1   £7,356

LANSON CHAMPAGNE VINTAGE
2 (7f)
Goodwood, Jul 29
Mister Baileys (8-11)   Dean McKeown
M Johnston   13/8   £7,359

KING GEORGE
3+ (1m)
Goodwood, Jul 29
Lochsong (5-8-11)   Frankie Dettori
I A Balding   13/8   £7,888

TIFFANY GOODWOOD CUP
3+ (2m)
Goodwood, Jul 29
Sonus (4-9-3)   Pat Eddery
J H M Gosden   4/1   £10,180

MOLECOMB
2 (5f)
Goodwood, Jul 30
Risky (8-12)   Walter Swinburn
R Hannon   4/9   £7,359

BURTONWOOD BREWERY ROSE OF LANCASTER
3+ (1m 2f)
Haydock Park, Aug 7
Knifebox (5-9-7)   Michael Roberts
J H M Gosden   11/10   £7,405

GARDNER MERCHANT HUNGERFORD
2 c+f (7f)
Newbury, Aug 13
Inchinor (3-8-11   Frankie Dettori
R Charlton   2/1   £9,348

SUNSET BOULEVARD SOLARIO
2 (7f)
Sandown, Aug 20
Island Magic (8-11)   Keiran Fallon
Mrs J R Ramsden   2/1   £8,062

BUTLINS SOUTHCOAST WORLD PRESTIGE
3+ (7f)
Goodwood, Aug 27
Glatisant (8-9)   Michael Hills
G Wragg   1/2   £6,477

BONUSPRINT SEPTEMBER
3+ (1m 3f)
Kempton Park, Sept 4
Spartan Shareef (4-9-3)   Alan Munro
C E Brittain   5/1   £9,577

WORTHINGTON BEST BITTER PARK HILL
3+ f (1m 6f)
Doncaster, Sept 8
Anna of Saxony (4-9-3)   Frankie Dettori
J H M Gosden   8/1   £8,070

MAY HILL
2 f (1m)
Doncaster, Sept 9
Hawajiss (8-8)   Walter Swinburn
M R Stoute   5/2   £6,506

KIVETON PARK
3+ (1m)
Doncaster, Sept 9
Swing Low (4-9-7)   John Reid
R Hannon   7/2   £8,139

DONCASTER CUP
3+ (2m 2f)
Doncaster, Sept 9
Assessor (4-9-7)   Richard Quinn
R Hannon   5/4   £7,338

ABTRUST SELECT
3+ (1m 2f)
Goodwood, Sept 10
Knifebox (5-9-3)   Michael Roberts
J H M Gosden   6/4   £7,911

HOOVER CUMBERLAND LODGE
3+ (1m 4f)
Ascot, Sept 23
Prince of Andros (3-8-6) Frankie Dettori
D Loder   9/4   £28,080

DIADEM
3 (6f)
Ascot, Sept 25
Catrail (3-8-11)   Michael Roberts
J Gosden   10/11   £41,580 (total)

1992 Races

SUPREME
3+ (7f)
Goodwood, Oct 2 1992
Hazaam (3-8-9)   Walter Swinburn
M R Stoute   7/1   £5,726

JOCKEY CLUB CUP
3+ (2m)
Newmarket, Oct 3 1992
Further Flight (6-9-3)   Michael Hills
B W Hills   4/6   £6,454

PRINCESS ROYAL
3+ f (1m 4f)
Ascot, Oct 10 1992
Cunning (3-8-9)   Frankie Dettori
L M Cumani   8/13   £10,256

CORNWALLIS
2 (5f)
Ascot, Oct 10 1992
Up and At 'em (8-13)   B Coogan
J G Coogan in Ireland   11/2   £8,209

ROCKFEL
2 f (7f)
Newmarket, Oct 16 1992
Yawl (8-8)   Darryll Holland
B W Hills   9/4   £5,136

VODAFONE HORRIS HILL
2 c + f (7f)
Newbury, Oct 22 1992
Beggarman Thief (8-12) Ray Cochrane
J H M Gosden   5/1   £9,559

CASTROL ST SIMON
3+ (1m 4f)
Newbury, Oct 24 1992
Up Anchor (3-8-4)   Alan Munro
P F I Cole   25/1   £7,497

Major Handicaps

WILLIAM HILL LINCOLN HANDICAP
3+ (1m)
Doncaster, Mar 27
High Premium (5-8-8) **Keiran Fallon**
J R Ramsden   16/1   £14,550

ROYAL HUNT CUP
3+ (1m)
Ascot, June 16
Imperial Ballet (4-8-12) Pat Eddery
H Cecil   20/1   £12,940

NORTHUMBERLAND PLATE
3+ (2n 119y)
Newcastle, June 26
Highflying (7-7-11)   **J Fanning**
G M Moore   7/1   £21,300

SCHWEPPES GOLDEN MILE
3+ (1m)
Goodwood, Jul 29
Philidor (4-8-4)   **N Kennedy**
J M P Eustace   13/2   £19,680

STEWARDS CUP
3+ (6f)
Goodwood, Jul 31
King's Signet (4-9-10) **Willie Carson**
J H M Gosden   16/1   £51,175

AYR GOLD CUP
3+ (6f)
Ayr Sep 18
Hard to Figure (7-9-6) **Ray Cochrane**
R J Hodges   12/1   £50,427

Overseas Races
(Group One or equivalent)

France

DUBAI POULE D'ESSAI DES POULICHES
3F (1m)
Longchamp, May 16
Madeleine's Dream (3-9-2) Cash Asmussen
F Boutin in France   49/10   £119,474

PRIX LUPIN
3 (1m 2f 110y)
Longchamp, May 16
Hernando (3-9-2)   **Cash Asmussen**
F Boutin in France   32/10   £59,507

PRIX SAINT-ALARY
3F (1m 2f)
Longchamp, May 23
Intrepidity (3-9-2)   **T Jarnet**
F Boutin   8/10   £61,302

PRIX D'ISPAHAN
3+ (1m 1f 55y)
Longchamp, May 30

Arcangues (5-9-2)   **T Jarnet**
A Fabre in France   66/10   £59,737

PRIX JEAN PRAT
3 (1m 1f 55y)
Longchamp, May 30
Le Balafre (3-92)   **O Peslier**
N Clement in France 57/10   £59,737

PRIX DU JOCKEY CLUB
3 (1m 4f)
Chantilly, June 6
Hernando (3-9-2)   **Cash Asmussen**
F Boutin in France   2/1   £298,686

PRIX DE DIANE
3F (1m 2f 110y)
Chantilly, June 13
Shemaka (3-9-2)   **G Mosse**
A de Royer-Dupre in France 66/10   £167,264

GRAND PRIX DE PARIS
3 (1m 2f)
Longchamp, June 27
Fort Wood (3-9-2)   **S Guillot**
A Fabre in France   11/2   £179,211

PRIX DU HARAS DE FRESNAY
3 (1m)
Deauville, Aug 15
Sayyedati (3-8-8)   **Walter Swinburn**
C E Brittain   23/10   £119,474

PRIX MORNY
2 (6f)
Deauville, Aug 22
Coup de Genie (2-8-8) **Cash Asmussen**
F Boutin in France   7/10   £119,474

PRIX DU MOULIN
3+ (1m)
Longchamp, Sep 5
Kingmambo (3-8-11)   **Cash Asmussen**
F Boutin in France   27/10   £107,527

PRIX VERMEILLE
3 (1m 4f)
Longchamp, Sept 12
Intrepidity (3-9-2)   **T Jarnet**
A Fabre in France   5/2   £119,474

PRIX DE LA SALAMANDRE
2 (7f)
Longchamp, Sept 12
Coup de Genie (2-8-8) **Cash Asmussen**
F Boutin in France   2/5   £59,737

Germany

BAYERISCHES ZUCHTRENNAN
3+ (1m 2f)
Munich, Aug 1
Market Booster (4-9-2) **Michael Kinane**
D K Weld in Ireland   £114,286

GROSSER PREIS VON BADEN
3 (7f 110y)
Baden-Baden
Lando (3-8-9)   A Tylicki
H Jentzsch in Germany   £122,449

Hong Kong

HONG KONG INVITATIONAL BOWL
3+ (7f)
Sha Tin, Apr 18
Glan Kate (6-8-11)   C Black
W Shoemaker in America   £173,060

HONG KONG INVITATIONAL CUP
3+ (1m 1f)
Sha Tin, Apr 18
Romanee Conti (4-8-11) G Childs
P J & P M Vela in NZ   £222,506

Ireland

AIRLIE/COOLMORE IRISH 2000 GUINEAS
3 (1m)
Curragh, May 15
Barathea (3-9-0)   Michael Roberts
L M Cumani   4/7   £122,581

IAWS IRISH 1000 GUINEAS
3F (1m)
Curragh, May 22
Nicer (3-9-0)   Michael Hills
B W Hills   8/1   £121,505

BUDWEISER IRISH DERBY STAKES
3 (1m4f)
Curragh, June 26
Commander In Chief (3-9-0)   Pat Eddery
H Cecil   4/7   £368,280

KILDANGAN STUD IRISH OAKS
3 (1m 4f)
Curragh, Jul 10
Wemyss Bight (3-9-0) Pat Eddery
A Fabre in France   9/2   £121,505

HEINZ '57 PHOENIX STAKES
2 (6f)
Leopardstown, Aug 8
Turtle Island (2-9-0)   John Reid
P Chapple-Hyam   7/4   £91,935

GUINNESS CHAMPION STAKES
3+ (1m 2f)
Leopardstown, Sept 11
Muhtarrum (4-9-4)   Willie Carson
J H M Gosden   7/1   £90,645

Italy

PREMIO PRESIDENTE DELLA REPUBBLICA
3+ (1m 2f)
Capanelle, May 16
Great Palm (4-9-2)   Alan Munro
P Cole   £49,311

OAKS D'ITALIA
3F (1m 4f)
San Siro, May 23
Bright Generation (3-8-11)   Alan Munro
P Cole   £76,208

DERBY ITALIANO
3 (1m 4f)
Capannelle
White Muzzle (3-9-2) John Reid
P Chapple-Hyam   £179,312

GRAN PREMIO DE MILANO
3+ (1m 4f)
San Siro, June 20
Platini (4-9-6)   Mark Rimmer
B Schutz in Germany   £112,070

United States

BREEDERS' CUP SPRINT
Gulfstream Park, Oct 31
3+ (6f dirt)
Thirty Slews (5-9-0)   E Delahoussaye
B Baffert in America   £267,380

BREEDERS' CUP JUVENILE
2F (1m 110y dirt)
GP, Oct 31
Eilza (2-8-7)   P Valenzuela
A Hassinger jr in America   £267,380

BREEDERS' CUP DISTAFF
3+ (1m 1f dirt)
GP, Oct 31
Paseana (5-8-11)   C McCarron
R McAnally in America   £367,780

BREEDERS' CUP MILE
3+ (1m turf)
GP, Oct 31
Lure (3-8-10)   M Smith
C McGaughey in America   £267,380

BREEDERS' CUP JUVENILE (C & G)
2C & G (1m 110y)
GP, Oct 31
Gilded Time (2-8-10) C McCarron
D Vienna in America   £269,380

BREEDERS' CUP TURF
3+ (1m 4f turf)
GP, Oct 31
Fraise (4-9-0)   P Valenzuela
W Mott in America   £534,759

BREEDERS' CUP CLASSIC
3+ (1m 2f dirt)
GP, Oct 31
A P Indy (3-8-9)   E Delahoussaye
N Drysdale in America   £829,787

FLAT LEADERS
As at Oct 8
The % refers to winners from runners
The prize money given is win only

Top Trainers

		Wins	£	%
1	R Hannon	161	1,145,959	15
2	H R A Cecil	86	1,127,600	24
3	M R Stoute	61	1,034,853	16
4	J H M Gosden	93	908,670	24
5	J L Dunlop	84	644,483	18
6	J Berry	126	519,823	17
7	G Wragg	33	419,516	19
8	C E Brittain	32	392,380	8
9	P W Chapple-Hyam	49	392,273	23
10	I A Balding	48	375,699	15
11	R Charlton	40	341,309	16
12	M H Tomkins	24	337,513	10
13	Lord Huntingdon	38	322,087	16
14	M Johnson	67	301,318	14
15	A Fabre	3	293,011	21
16	P F I Cole	52	276,137	14
17	E Lellouche	2	273,980	100
18	L M Cumani	35	224,529	14
19	D R Loder	45	198,170	25
20	B Hanbury	35	196,628	17

Top Jockeys

		1st	2nd	3rd	Total
1	Pat Eddery	152	122	75	744
2	K Darley	135	125	100	782
3	L Dettori	125	106	109	782
4	T Quinn	110	103	91	780
5	G Duffield	108	85	91	675
6	W Carson	107	84	104	746
7	M Roberts	101	83	106	653
8	J Reid	96	99	62	674
9	J Carroll	86	75	68	567
	W Ryan	86	76	72	583
11	W Swinburn	84	66	73	514
12	R Cochrane	80	96	78	662
13	M Hills	77	86	67	550
14	D McKeown	67	63	53	460
	A Munro	67	75	60	584
16	D Holland	58	49	53	455
	Paul Eddery	58	45	59	529
18	J Williams	57	46	54	560
19	R Hills	56	56	45	404
20	J Quinn	54	78	63	695

National Hunt

MACKESON GOLD CUP
Handicap Chase (2m 110y)
Cheltenham, Nov 14
Tipping Tim (7-10-10)   Carl Llewellyn
N Twiston-Davies   11/2F   £12,108

H & T WALKER GOLD CUP
H'cap chase (2m 3f 110y)
Ascot, Nov 21
Deep Sensation (7-11-2) Declan Murphy
J Gifford   11/2   £10,272

HENNESSY GOLD CUP
H'cap chase (3m 2f 110y)
Newbury, Nov 28
Sibton Abbey (7-10-0)   Adrian Maguire
F Murphy   40/1   £13,645

WILLIAM HILL HANDICAP HURDLE
(2m 110y)
Sandown, Dec 5
Valfinet (5-10-2)   Jon Lower
M C Pipe   5/4F   £7,800

TRIPLEPRINT GOLD CUP
H'cap Chase (2m 5f)
Cheltenham, Dec 12
Another Coral (9-11-4)   Richard Dunwoody
D Nicholson   11/2   £12,003

YOUNGMANS LONG WALK HURDLE
(2m 3f 110y)
Ascot, Dec 19
Vagog (7-11-7)   Mark Foster
M C Pipe   15/2   £8,674

SGB HANDICAP CHASE
(3m 110y)
Ascot, Dec 19
Captain Dibble (7-10-1) Carl Llewellyn
N A Twiston-Davies   7/1   £7,281

TRIPLEPRINT FELTHAM NOVICES' CHASE
(3m)
Kempton Park, Dec 26
Dakyns Boy (7-11-7)   Peter Scudamore
N A Twiston-Davies   9/2   £7,286

KING GEORGE VI CHASE
(3m)
Kempton Park, Dec 26
The Fellow (7-11-10)   Adam Kondrat
F Doumen in France   Evens F   £16,842

BONUSPRINT CHRISTMAS HURDLE
(2m)
Kempton Park, Dec 27
Mighty Mogul (5-11-7)   Richard Dunwoody
D Nicholson   3/1   £11,894

MITSUBISHI SHOGUN NEWTON CHASE
(2m 4f)
Haydock, Jan 9
Gold Options (11-11-10) Lorcan Wyer
J G Fitzgerald   14/1   £11,300

BARING SECURITIES TOLWORTH HURDLE
(2m 110y)
Sandown, Jan 9
Sun Surfer (5-11-7)   Carl Llewellyn

ANTHONY MILDMAY, PETER CAZALET
MEMORIAL HANDICAP CHASE
(3m 5f 110y)
Sandown, Jan 9
Rushing Wild (8-10-1)   Peter Scudamore
M C Pipe   Evens F   £4,260

MITSUBISHI SHOGUN NEWTON CHASE
(2m 4f)
Haydock, Jan 9
Gold Options (11-11-10) Lorcan Wyer
J G FitzGerald   14/1   £11,300

BIC RAZOR LANZAROTE HANDICAP HURDLE
(2m)
Kempton, Jan 23
Tomahawk (6-10-0)   Declan J Murphy
P G Murphy   12/1   £15,500

WYKO POWER TRANSMISSION HURDLE
(2m 5f 110yd)
Cheltenham, Jan 30
Muse (6-11-8)   Paul Holley
D R C Elsworth   11/4   £9,322

FOOD BROKERS FINESSE HURDLE
(2m 1f)
Cheltenham, Jan 30
Major Bugler (11-0)   Adrian Maguire
G B Balding   13/2   £2397

GREAT YORKSHIRE HANDICAP CHASE
(3m)
Doncaster, Jan 30
Young Hustler (6-10-0)   D Bridgwater
N A Twiston-Davies   9/2   £5,955

AGFA DIAMOND HANDICAP CHASE
(3m 110yds)
Sandown, Feb 6
Country Member (8-10-7) Luke Harvey
Andrew Turnell   100/30   £7,129

SCILLY ISLES NOVICES' CHASE
(2m 4f 110yd)
Sandown, Feb 6
Young Hustler (6-11-6)   Carl Llewellyn
N A Twiston-Davies   5/2   £7,233

JOHN HUGHES GRAND NATIONAL TRIAL
(3m 5f 110yds)
Chepstow, Feb 6
Fiddlers Pike (12-10-0)   Mrs R Henderson
Mrs R G Henderson   7/2   £2,660

TOTE GOLD TROPHY
(2m 110yds)
Newbury, Feb 13
King Credo (8-10-0)   Adrian Maguire
 S Woodman   10/1   £12,802

PERSIAN WAR PREMIER NOVICES'S HURDLE
(2m 4f 110yds)
Chepstow, Feb 20
High Altitude (5-11-9)   N Bentley
G M Moore   11/4   £2,367

TOTE EIDER HANDICAP CHASE
(4m 1f)
Newcastle, Feb 20
Into the Red (9-10-0)   N Williamson
J White   3/1   £3,843

THE RACING POST HANDICAP CHASE
(3m)
Kempton, Feb 27
Zeta's Lad (10-10-10)   John White
John R Upson   11/1   £10,590

GREENALLS GOLD CUP
(3m 4f 110yds)
Haydock, Feb 27
Party Politics (9-11-7) Carl Llewellyn
N A Gaselee   16/1   £9,458

SUNDERLANDS IMPERIAL CUP
(2m 110yds)
Sandown, Mar 13
Olympian (6-10-0)   Peter Scudamore
M C Pipe   6/4   £6,138

SMURFIT CHAMPION HURDLE CHALLENGE TROPHY
(2m 110yds)
Cheltenham, Mar 16
Granville Again (7-12-0)Peter Scudamore
 M C Pipe   13/2   £31,706

TRAFALGAR HOUSE SUPREME NOVICES'S HURDLE
(2m 110yds)
Cheltenham, Mar 16
Montelado (6-11-8)   Charlie Swan
P J Flynn in Ireland   5/1   £11,167

WATERFORD CASTLE ARKLE CHALLENGE TROPHY
(2m)
Cheltenham, Mar 16
Travado (7-11-8)   Jamie Osborne
N J Henderson   5/1   £15,120

RITZ CLUB NATIONAL HUNT HANDICAP CHASE
(3m 1f)
Cheltenham, Mar 16
Givus a Buck (10-10-8)   Paul Holley
D R C Elsworth   11/2   £8,491

AMERICAN EXPRESS GOLD CARD HANDICAP HURDLE
(3m 2f)
Cheltenham, Mar 16
Fissure Seal (7-11-4)   Charlie Swan
H de Bromhead in Ireland 14/1   £6,245

SUN ALLIANCE NOVICES'S CHASE
(3m 1f)
Cheltenham, Mar 17
Young Hustler (6-11-4)   Peter Scudamore
N A Twiston-Davies   9/4   £15,560

SUN ALLIANCE NOVICES'S HURDLE
(2m 5f)
Cheltenham, Mar 17
Gaelstrom (6-11-2)   Carl Llewellyn
N A Twiston-Davies   16/1   £11,244

QUEEN MOTHER CHAMPION CHASE
(2m)
Cheltenham, Mar 17
Deep Sensation (8-12-0) Declan Murphy
J T Gifford   11/1   £23,725

MILDMAY OF FLETE CHALLENGE CUP
(2m 4f 110yds)
Cheltenham, Mar 17
Sacre D'Or (8-11-0)   Graham McCourt
N Tinkler   7/1   £7,638

DAILY EXPRESS TRIUMPH HURDLE
(2m 1f)
Cheltenham, Mar 18
Shawiya (10-9)   Charlie Swan
M J P O'Brien in Ireland 12/1   £12,783

TOTE CHELTENHAM GOLD CUP
(3m 2f 110yds)
Cheltenham, Mar 18
Jodami (8-12-0)   Mark Dwyer
P Beaumont   8/1   £37,132

TETLEY   BITTER   MIDLANDS   NATIONAL HANDICAP CHASE
(4m 2f)
Uttoxeter, Mar 20
Mister Ed (10-10-3)   D Morris
R Curtiss   25/1   £8,804

MARTELL CUP
(3m 1f)
Aintree, Apr 1
Docklands Express (11-11-5) Jamie Osborne
K C Bailey   6/4   £11,493

GLENLIVET ANNIVERSARY HURDLE
(2m 110yds)
Aintree, Apr 1
Titled Dancer (10-9)   **J Shortt**
J G Coogan in Ireland   9/2   £9,254

MUMM MELLING CHASE
(2m 4f)
Aintree, Apr 2
Deep Sensation (8-11-10) Declan Murphy
J T Gifford   7/4   £15,130

MARTELL AINTREE HURDLE
(2m 4f)
Aintree, Apr 3
Morley Street (9-11-7)   **Graham Bradley**
G B Balding   6/1   £11,135

MARTELL AINTREE HANDICAP CHASE
(2m)
Aintree, Apr 3
Boutzdaroff (11-10-7)   **Mark Dwyer**
J G FitzGerald   9/1   £8,607

STAKIS SCOTTISH NATIONAL HANDICAP CHASE
(4m 1f)
Ayr, Apr 17
Run for Free (9-11-10)   **Mark Perrett**
M C Pipe   6/1   £11,200

**EDINBURGH WOOLLEN MILL'S FUTURE
CHAMPION NOVICES' CHASE**
(2m 4f)
Ayr, Apr 17
Cab on Target (7-11-8)   **Peter Niven**
Mrs M Reveley   4/9   £7,129

WHITBREAD GOLD CUP
H'cap Chase (3m 5f 110y)
Sandown, Apr 24
Topsham Bay (10-10-1)   **Richard Dunwoody**
D H Barons   10/1   £21,400

The compilation of these results was

made possible by the invaluable

RACEFORM GUIDE

NATIONAL HUNT 1992-3
Top Trainers

		Wins	£	%
1	M Pipe	194	807,156	25.2
2	D Nicholson	100	492,420	27.3
3	N Twiston-Davies	76	451,838	23.8
4	G Richards	104	327,758	22.6
5	J Gifford	49	286,086	16.3
6	J G Fitzgerald	62	261,064	22.8
7	Mrs M Reveley	90	250,257	26.4
8	N J Henderson	53	242,916	18.3
9	G B Balding	38	212,439	13.0
10	K C Baily	57	170,176	18.8
11	P Beaumont	19	162,641	17.9
12	A Turnell	37	161,357	23.5
13	D Elsworth	18	133,167	15.6
14	J Upson	31	132,386	16.6
15	M D Hammond	51	128,041	18.7
16	Mrs J Pitman	36	117,194	14.9
17	M H Easterby	39	114,745	17.0
18	F Murphy	23	105,273	16.3
19	Capt T Forster	29	95,681	13.4
20	D H Barons	16	94,994	7.5

Top Jockeys

		1st	2nd	3rd	Total
1	R Dunwoody	173	121	89	741
2	P Scudamore	129	75	47	419
3	A Maguire	124	117	98	723
4	P Niven	108	62	52	386
5	J Osborne	102	71	61	503
6	G McCourt	70	62	61	432
7	N Doughty	69	36	33	263
8	C Llewellyn	68	43	50	414
9	M Dwyer	61	58	47	317
10	C Grant	58	56	49	419
11	M Fitzgerald	54	51	50	428
12	S McNeil	51	36	47	388
13	Peter Hobbs	51	49	37	319
14	L Wyer	45	39	31	260
15	D J Murphy	45	38	42	302
16	B Storey	44	33	47	342
17	N Williamson	41	56	36	325
18	D Bridgwater	39	41	42	356
19	T Reed	33	26	36	226
20	J Railton	33	32	24	240

Ice Hockey

Olympic Qualifying Tournament

Sheffield   Sept

A single team qualifies for Group B at the Winter Olympics in Lillehammer in February.

Pool Matches

Great Britain 2 Poland 2
Slovakia 7 Japan 2
Japan 4 Great Britain 2
Latvia 6 Poland 2
Poland 4 Slovakia 4
Great Britain 4 Latvia 8
Slovakia 7 Latvia 1
Poland 6 Japan 4
Latvia 7 Japan 1
Great Britain 1 Slovakia 7

	P	W	D	L	F	A	Pts
SLO	4	3	1	0	25	8	7
LAT	4	3	0	1	22	14	6
POL	4	1	2	1	14	16	4
JPN	4	1	0	3	11	22	2
GBR	4	0	1	3	9	21	1

World Championship

Pool A

Munich & Dortmund,   Apr 18-May 2
Germany

GROUP A

Italy 2	Russia 2
Sweden 1	Austria 0
Canada 2	Switzerland 0
Russia 4	Austria 2
Sweden 1	Canada 4
Switzerland 0	Italy 1
Italy 2	Sweden 6
Switzerland 0	Russia 6
Austria 0	Canada 11
Switzerland 5	Austria 1
Russia 2	Sweden 5
Canada 11	Italy 2
Sweden 4	Switzerland 6
Russia 1	Canada 3
Austria 1	Italy 1

Prelim Table		W	D	L	F	A	Pts
1 CAN	5	5	0	0	31	4	10
2 SWE	5	3	0	2	17	14	6
3 RUS	5	2	1	2	15	12	5
4 ITA	5	1	2	2	8	20	4
5 SUI	5	2	0	3	11	14	4
6 AUT	5	0	1	4	4	22	1

GROUP B

Norway 0	Germany 6
USA 1	Czech Repub 1
Finland 2	France 0
Czech Repub 5	Germany 0
Finland 1	USA 1
Germany 5	France 3
Czech Repub 2	Norway 0
USA 6	France 1
Norway 0	Finland 2
Germany 3	Finland 1
Czech Repub 6	France 2
USA 3	Norway 1
Finland 1	Czech Repub 3
Germany 6	USA 3
France 4	Norway 5

Prelim Table							
1 TCH	5	4	1	0	17	4	9
2 GER	5	4	0	1	20	12	8
3 USA	5	2	2	1	14	10	6
4 FIN	5	2	1	2	7	7	5
5 NOR	5	1	0	4	6	17	2
6 FRA	5	0	0	5	10	24	0

Quarter Finals

Sweden 5	USA 2
Germany 1	Russia 5
Canada 5	Finland 1
Czech Repub 7	Italy 1

Relegation

Switzerland 1	France 3
Norway 2	Austria 6

Semi Finals

Sweden 4	Czech Repub 3
Russia 7	Canada 4

Relegation

Switzerland 2   Norway 5
(Switzerland relegated to Pool B for 1994 championship)

Place 3/4

Czech Repub 5   Canada 1

Final

Sweden 1   Russia 3

Final Standing

1	Russia	7	Finland
2	Sweden	8	Italy
3	Czech Repub	9	Austria
4	Canada	10	France
5	Germany	11	Norway
6	USA	12	Switzerland

Pool B

Eindhoven, Holland   Mar 25-Apr 4

There is only one group in Pool B

Poland 3	Great Britain 4
Denmark 5	Bulgaria 1
Japan 8	Romania 1
Netherlands 15	China 1

Romania 2	Holland 4
China 1	Poland 21
Romania 2	Holland 4
Denmark 0	Great Britain 4
Bulgaria 1	Japan 7
Poland 13	Romania 0
Japan 4	Great Britain 5
Holland 14	Bulgaria 0
Romania 5	China 3
Poland 7	Denmark 3
Great Britain 10	Bulgaria 0
Denmark 13	China 0
Holland 5	Japan 3
Bulgaria 2	Poland 13
Holland 2	Great Britain 3
Romania 3	Denmark 4
China 3	Japan 8
Japan 1	Poland 7
Great Britain 10	Romania 4
China 4	Bulgaria 3
Japan 3	Denmark 9
Poland 7	Netherlands 1
Bulgaria 2	Romania 5
Great Britain 14	China 0

Final Table

1	GBR	7	7	0	0	50	13	14
2	POL	7	6	0	1	71	12	12
3	HOL	7	5	0	2	47	20	10
4	DEN	7	4	0	3	38	24	8
5	JPN	7	3	0	4	34	31	6
6	ROM	7	2	0	5	20	44	4
7	CHN	7	1	0	6	12	79	2
8	BUL	7	0	0	7	9	58	0

Great Britain promoted into Pool A 1994
Bulgaria relegated into Pool C 1994

Pool C

Ljubljana & Bled, Slovenia   Mar 12-21

GROUP A

DPR Korea 2	Hungary 20
Ukraine 16	Korea 1
Latvia 26	Belgium 3
Korea 8	Israel 5
Belgium 2	Ukraine 37
DPR Korea 0	Latvia 4
Belgium 5	Korea 3
Israel 0	Latvia 32
Ukraine 15	DPR Korea 2
Belgium 8	Israel 1
Korea 4	DPR Korea 7
Latvia 5	Ukraine 5
Korea 0	Latvia 27
Israel 0	Ukraine 29
DPR Korea 7	Belgium 1

Prelim Table

1	UKR	5	4	1	0	102	10	9
2	LAT	5	4	1	0	94	8	9
3	PRK	5	3	0	2	30	26	6
4	BEL	5	2	0	3	19	74	4
5	KOR	5	1	0	4	16	60	2
6	ISR	5	0	0	5	8	91	0

GROUP B

South Africa 2	Hungary 20
Kazakhstan 14	Spain 0
Australia 2	Slovenia 15 .
Hungary 1	Kazakhstan 7
Spain 0	Slovenia 12
Australia 9	South Africa 3
Kazakhstan 23	Australia 1
Hungary 6	Spain 5
Slovenia 29	South Africa 0
Spain 3	Australia 4
South Africa 0	Kazakhstan 32
Hungary 2	Slovenia 14
Spain 10	South Africa 3
Australia 3	Hungary 7
Slovenia 4	Kazakhstan 0

Prelim Table

1	SLO	5	5	0	0	74	4	10
2	KZK	5	4	0	1	76	6	8
3	HUN	5	3	0	2	36	31	6
4	AUS	5	2	0	3	19	51	4
5	ESP	5	1	0	4	18	39	2
6	RSA	5	0	0	5	8	100	0

Semi Finals

Ukraine 3	Kazakhstan 2
Slovenia 1	Latvia 5

Place 3/4

Kazakhstan 7	Slovenia 3

Final

Ukraine 0	Latvia 3

Final Standing

1 Latvia
2 Ukraine
3 Kazakhstan
4 Slovenia
5 Hungary, DPR Korea, Australia, Belgium
9 Korea
10 Spain

Latvia promoted into Pool B 1994
Israel & S Africa relegated into qualification games 1994

World Junior Championship
Pool A

Gävle, Sweden   Dec 26-Jan 4

USA 0	Canada 3
Sweden 4	Germany 2
Russia 16	Japan 0
Finland 5	Czechoslovakia 2
Canada 5	Sweden 4
Finland 7	Japan 0
Germany 0	Russia 4
Czechoslovakia 6	USA 5
Russia 1	Canada 9
Sweden 7	Czechoslovakia 2
Finland 11	Germany 0
USA 12	Japan 2
Czechoslovakia 1	Russia 1
Sweden 20	Japan 1
Germany 3	USA 4

Canada 3	Finland 2	
Canada 5	Germany 2	
Russia 1	Finland 1	
Japan 2	Czechoslovakia 14	
Sweden 4	USA 2	
Finland 2	Sweden 9	
USA 4	Russia 2	
Japan 1	Canada 8	
Germany 3	Czechoslovakia 6	
USA 5	Finland 3	
Czechoslovakia 7	Canada 4	
Germany 6	Japan 3	
Russia 1	Sweden 5	

Final Table

1	CAN	7	6	0	1	37	17	12
2	SWE	7	6	0	1	53	15	12
3	TCH	7	4	1	2	38	27	9
4	USA	7	4	0	3	32	23	8
5	FIN	7	3	1	3	31	20	7
6	RUS	7	2	2	3	26	20	6
7	GER	7	1	0	6	16	37	2
8	JPN	7	0	0	7	9	83	0

Canada Champions, Japan relegated into Pool B 1994

Pool B

Hamar & Lillehammer, Norway   Dec 27-Jan 5

Norway 9	Holland 0
Switzerland 5	Italy 1
France 5	Romania 2
Poland 3	Austria 6
Romania 1	Norway 9
Austria 1	Switzerland 7
France 3	Italy 6
Holland 4	Poland 3
Norway 5	Italy 0
Switzerland 11	Holland 0
France 1	Austria 2
Poland 5	Romania 3
Holland 3	France 5
Romania 1	Switzerland 1
Austria 0	Norway 7
Poland 0	Italy 9
Italy 7	Romania 3
Switzerland 6	France 4
Holland 1	Austria 7
Poland 1	Norway 7
Austria 9	Romania 1
Norway 4	Switzerland 5
Italy 6	Holland 1
France 4	Poland 3
Romania 5	Holland 1
Switzerland 4	Poland 2
Italy 3	Austria 1
Norway 8	France 4

Final Table

1	SUI	7	6	1	0	39	13	13
2	NOR	7	6	0	1	49	11	12
3	ITA	7	4		2	23	18	9
4	AUT	7	4	0	3	26	23	8
5	FRA	7	3	0	4	26	30	6
6	POL	7	1	1	5	17	28	3
7	ROM	7	1	1	5	16	37	3
8	HOL	7	1	0	6	10	46	2

Switzerland promoted into Pool A 1994
Holland relegated into Pool C 1994

Pool C

Odense & Esbjerg, Denmark   Dec 30-Jan 3

GROUP A

DPR Korea 1 Ukraine 16; Spain 1 Hungary 8; Hungary 5
DPR Korea 5; Spain 0 Ukraine 13; Ukraine 9 Hungary 2;
DPR Korea 3 Spain 3.

Prelim Table

1	UKR	3	3	0	0	38	3	6
2	HUN	3	1	1	1	15	15	3
3	PRK	3	0	2	1	9	24	2
4	SPA	3	0	1	2	4	24	1

GROUP B

Denmark 9 Bulgaria 1; Great Britain 7 Korea 1; Korea 4
Denmark 9; Great Britain 5 Bulgaria 6; Bulgaria 5 Korea 5

Prelim Table

1	DEN	3	2	1	0	23	10	5
2	BUL	3	1	1	1	12	17	3
3	GBR	3	1	1	1	15	12	3
4	KOR	3	0	1	2	10	21	1

7/8th place

Spain 13	Korea 2

5/6th place

Great Britain 4	DPR Korea 2

3/4th place

Hungary 15	Bulgaria 4

Final

Ukraine 8	Denmark 3

Final Standing

1	Ukraine	5	Great Britain
2	Denmark	6	DPR Korea
3	Hungary	7	Spain
4	Bulgaria	8	Korea

Ukraine promoted into Pool B 1994
Korea relegated into Qualification games 1994

European Junior Championship

Pool A

Nowy-Targ & Oswiecim, Poland   April 2-9

GROUP A

Czech Repub 15	Italy 1
Finland 5	Germany 0
Italy 0	Finland 4
Germany 0	Czech Repub 12
Czech Repub 6	Finland 2
Germany 1	Italy 1

Prelim Table

1	TCH	3	3	0	0	33	3	6
2	FIN	3	2	0	1	11	6	4
3	GER	3	0	1	2	1	18	1
4	ITA	3	0	1	2	2	20	1

GROUP B

Russia 7	Poland 1
Sweden 13	Norway 1
Poland 1	Sweden 14
Norway 2	Russia 9
Russia 2	Sweden 7
Poland 5	Norway 5

Prelim Table

1	SWE	3	3	0	0	34	4 6
2	RUS	3	2	0	1	18	10 4
3	NOR	3	0	1	2	8	27 1
4	POL	3	0	1	2	7	26 1

Play off round

Finland 2	Russia 2
Czech Repub 18	Norway 0
Sweden 7	Germany 1
Czech Repub 0	Russia 4
Germany 2	Norway 4
Sweden 6	Finland 4
Russia 15	Germany 0
Norway 1	Finland 5
Czech Repub 1	Sweden 2

Relegation games

Poland 6	Italy 8
Italy 4	Poland 9
Italy 7	Poland 10

Final Standing

1	SWE	5	5	0	0	35	9	10
2	RUS	5	3	1	1	32	11	7
3	TCH	5	3	0	2	37	8	6
4	FIN	5	2	1	2	18	15	,5
5	NOR	5	1	0	4	8	47	2
6	GER	5	0	0	5	3	43	0
7	POL	3	2	0	1	25	19	4
8	ITA	3	1	0	2	19	25	2

Sweden European Junior Champion 1993
Italy relegated into Pool B 1994

Pool B

Bucharest, Romania   Mar 18-28

Switzerland 4	Hungary 2
Denmark 2	Great Britain 1
Austria 2	Spain 2
Romania 1	France 4
Spain 3	Denmark 4
France 3	Austria 1
Great Britain 2	Switzerland 9
Romania 1	Hungary 8
Denmark 2	France 4
Switzerland 11	Spain 2
Austria 3	Hungary 4
Romania 6	Great Britain 3
France 1	Switzerland 6
Denmark 1	Hungary 3
Great Britain 4	Austria 7
Romania 4	Spain 5
Denmark 2	Austria 3
Hungary 3	France 1
Spain 4	Great Britain 5
Switzerland 11	Romania 1
Spain 2	Hungary 10

Great Britain 0	France 14
Romania 7	Denmark 2
Austria 0	Switzerland 12
France 12	Spain 0
Hungary 10	Great Britain 2
Austria 6	Romania 3
Switzerland 5	Denmark 0

Final Standing

1	SUI	7	7	0	0	58	8	14
2	HUN	7	6	0	1	40	14	12
3	FRA	7	5	0	2	39	13	10
4	AUT	7	3	1	3	22	30	7
5	ROM	7	2	0	5	23	39	4
6	DEN	7	2	0	5	13	26	4
7	SPN	7	1	1	5	18	48	3
8	GBR	7	1	0	6	17	52	2

Switzerland promoted into Pool A 1994
Great Britain relegated into Pool C 1994

Pool C

Riga, Latvia   Mar 22-28

GROUP A

Holland 3	Lithuania 7
Lithuania 1	Slovenia 8
Slovenia 7	Holland 0

Prelim Table

1	SLO	2	2	0	0	15	1 4
2	LIT	2	1	0	1	8	11 2
3	HOL	2	0	0	2	3	14 0

GROUP B

Bulgaria 0	Slovakia 39
Slovakia 5	Ukraine 2
Ukraine 29	Bulgaria 1

Prelim Table

1	SVK	2	2	0	0	44	2 4
2	UKR	2	1	0	1	31	6 2
3	BUL	2	0	0	2	1	68 0

GROUP C

Latvia 10	Estonia 4
Estonia 3	Belarus 6
Belarus 3	Latvia 2

Prelim Table

1	BLS	2	2	0	0	9	5 4
2	LAT	2	1	0	1	12	6 2
3	EST	2	0	0	2	7	16 0

Play offs 7-9

Holland 4	Estonia 7
Bulgaria 3	Holland 7
Estonia 22	Bulgaria 0

Play offs 4-6

Lithuania 1	Latvia 5
Ukraine 19	Lithuania 1
Latvia 4	Ukraine 6

Play offs 1-3

Slovenia 3	Belarus 3
Slovakia 9	Slovenia 0
Belarus 4	Slovakia 1

Final Standing

1	BLS	2	1	1	0	7	4
2	SVK	2	1	0	2	10	4
3	SLO	2	0	1	1	3	12
4	UKR	2	2	0	0	25	5
5	LAT	2	1	0	1	3	12
6	LIT	2	0	0	2	2	24
7	EST	2	2	0	0	29	4
8	HOL	2	1	0	1	11	10
9	BUL	2	0	0	2	3	29

Belarus promoted into Pool B 1994
Bulgaria relegated into Qualification for Pool C 1994

Asian/Oceania Junior Championship
Seoul, Rep. of Korea   Mar 6-12

Korea 26	Australia 1
Kazakhstan 13	China 0
Korea 0	Kazakhstan 11
Japan 43	Australia 0
Japan 11	China 0
Kazakhstan 57	Australia 0
Korea 3	China 1
Kazakhstan 7	Japan 0
Korea 2	Japan 11
China 25	Australia 0

Final Standing

1	KZK	4	4	0	0	88	0	8
2	JPN	4	3	0	1	65	9	6
3	KOR	4	2	0	2	31	24	4
4	CHN	4	1	0	3	26	27	2
5	AUS	4	0	0	4	1	151	0

European Women's Championship
Pool A
Esbjerg, Denmark   Mar 24-27

GROUP A

Norway 5	Switzerland 2
Finland 17	Switzerland 1
Norway 3	Finland 9

Prelim Table

1	FIN	2	2	0	0	25	4	4
2	NOR	2	1	0	1	8	10	2
3	SUI	2	0	0	2	3	22	0

GROUP B

Denmark 4	Germany 6
Sweden 10	Germany 3
Denmark 0	Sweden 6

Prelim Table

1	SWE	2	2	0	0	16	3	4
2	GER	2	1	0	1	9	14	2
3	DEN	2	0	0	2	4	12	0

5th place

Denmark 1	Switzerland 4

3rd place

Norway 6	Germany 3

Final

Finland 8	Sweden 2

Finland European Champion 1993
Finland, Sweden, Norway, Germany, Switzerland participants of the Women's World Championship 1994

Pool B
Kiev, Ukraine   Mar 22-27

Latvia 4	France 3
Ukraine 0	Czech Repub 3
Czech Repub 1	Latvia 3
Great Britain 1	Ukraine 0
Great Britain 2	France 7
Ukraine 1	Latvia 0
Latvia 3	Great Britain 0
France 2	Czech Repub 3
Czech Repub 1	Great Britain 1
France 1	Ukraine 0

Final Standing

1	LAT	4	3	0	1	10	5	6
2	TCH	4	2	1	1	8	6	5
3	FRA	4	2	0	2	13	9	4
4	GBR	4	1	1	2	4	11	3
5	UKR	4	1	0	3	1	5	2

Latvia promoted into Pool A 1995

European Cup
Düsseldorf,   Dec 26-30, 1992

GROUP 1

EG Düsseldorf 8	Rouen HC 2
Dynamo Moscow 6	Jokerit Helsinki 0
Dynamo Moscow 5	Rouen HC 0
EG Düsseldorf 0	Jokerit Helsinki 3
EG Düsseldorf 1	Dynamo Moscow 3
Jokerit Helsinki 4	Rouen HC 2

Prelim Table

1	Dynamo Moscow	RUS	3	3	0	0	14	1	6
2	Jokerit Helsinki	FIN	3	2	0	1	7	8	4
3	Düsseldorfer EG	GER	3	1	0	2	9	8	2
4	Rouen HC	FRA	3	0	0	3	4	17	0

GROUP 2

Malmö IF 5	Unia Oswiecim 0
Lions Mediolanum 4	SC Bern 3
Unia Oswiecim 2	SC Bern 1
Lions Mediolanum 2	Malmö IF 3
Unia Oswiecim 3	Lions Mediolanum 8
Malmö IF 5	SC Bern 1

Prelim Table

1	Malmö IF	SWE	3	3	0	0	13	6	6
2	Mediolanum	ITA	3	2	0	1	14	9	4
3	Unia Oswiecim	POL	3	1	0	2	5	14	2
4	SC Bern	SUI	3	0	0	3	5	11	0

3/4th Play off

Lions Mediolanum 2	Jokerit Helsinki 4

Final

Malmö IF 4	Dynamo Moscow 3

Final Standing

1	Malmö IF	SWE
2	Dynamo Moscow	RUS
3	Jokerit Helsinki	FIN
4	Lions Mediolanum	ITA

Malmö IF European Champions 1992/3

British Results
Heineken League

PREMIER DIVISION

1	Cardiff	36	28	6	2	319	187	58
2	Murrayfield	36	20	14	2	299	267	42
3	Nottingham	36	19	15	2	256	236	40
4	Whitley	36	18	17	1	262	286	37
5	Bracknell	36	15	17	4	190	194	34
6	Billingham	36	14	18	4	275	303	32
7	Humberside	36	15	20	1	193	232	31
8	Fife	36	15	20	1	193	232	31
9	N & Peterboro	36	14	21	1	238	272	29
10	Durham	36	12	22	2	201	232	26

DIVISION ONE

1	Basingstoke	32	28	3	1	389	146	57
2	Sheffield	32	22	6	4	300	186	48
3	M Keynes	32	17	9	6	262	192	40
4	Swindon	32	13	15	4	230	254	30
5	Romford	32	12	16	4	221	239	28
6	Slough	32	12	16	4	207	234	28
7	Telford	32	11	16	5	233	242	27
8	Medway	32	10	20	2	194	255	22
9	Lee Valley	32	3	27	2	195	483	8

Heineken Championships

QUARTER FINALS

1	Cardiff	6	6	0	0	52	24	12
2	Humberside	6	3	2	1	34	36	7
3	Whitley	6	2	3	1	44	44	5
4	Bracknell	6	0	6	0	23	49	0
5	Nottingham	6	5	1	0	52	24	10
6	Murrayfield	6	5	1	0	54	33	10
7	Billingham	6	2	4	0	30	44	4
8	Fife	6	0	6	0	21	56	0

The Roll of Honour

The Grand Slam Cardiff Devils
Heineken Championships Cardiff Devils
Premier Division Cardiff Devils
Benson and Hedges Cup Cardiff Devils
Division One Basingstoke Beavers
Capital Foods Scottish Cup Murrayfield Racers
Castle Eden Cup Humberside Seahawks
Southern Cup Cardiff Devils
Tyne Tees Trophy Billingham Bombers
English League Division One Solihull Barons
Autumn Trophy Milton Keynes Kings
Essex Radio Midweek League Romford Raiders
Scottish League Division One Paisley Pirates
English Conference League Bradford Bulldogs
British Junior (U-16) Champions Durham Mosquitoes

American Results
National Hockey League

CLARENCE CAMPBELL CONFERENCE

Norris Division

		GP	W	L	T	GF	GA	Pts	%
1	Chicago	84	47	25	12	279	230	106	.631
2	Detroit	84	47	28	9	369	280	103	.613
3	Toronto	84	44	29	11	288	241	99	.589
4	St Louis	84	37	36	11	288	278	85	.506
5	Minnesota	84	36	38	10	272	293	82	.488
6	Tampa Bay	84	23	54	7	245	332	53	.315

Smythe Division

1	Vancouver	84	46	29	9	346	278	101	.601
2	Calgary	84	43	30	11	322	282	97	.577
3	Los Angeles	84	39	35	10	338	340	88	.524
4	Winnipeg	84	40	37	7	322	320	87	.518
5	Edmonton	84	26	50	8	242	337	60	.357
6	San Jose	84	11	71	2	218	414	24	.143

PRINCE OF WALES CONFERENCE

Adams Division

1	Boston	84	51	26	7	332	268	109	.649
2	Quebec	84	47	27	10	351	300	104	.619
3	Montreal	84	48	30	6	326	280	102	.607
4	Buffalo	84	38	36	10	335	297	86	.512
5	Hartford	84	26	52	6	284	369	58	.345
6	Ottawa	84	10	70	4	202	395	24	.143

Patrick Division

1	Pittsburgh	84	56	21	7	367	268	119	.708
2	Washington	84	43	34	7	325	286	93	.554
3	NY Islanders	84	40	37	7	335	297	87	.518
4	New Jersey	84	40	37	7	308	299	87	.518
5	Philadelphia	84	36	37	11	319	319	83	.494
6	NY Rangers	84	34	39	11	304	308	79	.470

Stanley Cup

Montreal   June

Montreal Canadiens 4 Los Angeles Kings 1

QUICKIES

Durham Wasps v Romford in April was abandoned with 3 minutes 27 seconds left because Romford had no players left. They'd all either been dismissed or sent to the sin-bin.

Great Britain have had their best season ever thanks to the fact that most of the team are not Great Britons at all, but Canadians. Watch for a new trend though. Hull have brought in a couple of Ukrainians. You wait, they'll be naturalised before you can say Pool A.

Judo

It was a year of administrative disruption for judo with both the men's and women's team managers losing their jobs. Arthur Mapp was for 11 years the men's team manager, Roy Inman had charge of the women's team for 15 years. Mapp resigned in November and later accepted a payment of £4,000 as redundancy. Inman, whose resignation was surprising given the success of the women's squad, left at the same time, but a month later found his licence revoked as well, for alleged "financial irregularities". The affair dragged on into the summer, with Inman countering the BJA's accusations with his own claims, eventually receiving his licence back and taking them to an industrial tribunal for 'constructive dismissal'. The whole affair was injudiciously handled and gave the sport an image of one in disarray. Threats exchanged between Elvis Gordon and his former coach, Malcolm Abbotts, at the British Open in Birmingham hardly added to the general edification. The women's team rose above such shenanigans enjoying yet more success. Inman, it should be said, based in a church hall in Hatton Cross, had built the team up from scratch since he began in 1977. Nicola Fairbrother was the star of Athens, but there were two silvers and two bronzes to celebrate as well.

European Championships

Athens   April 29- May 2

Men

-60kg	1 Huseinov Nazim	AZE
	2 Khasain Bisoultanov	RUS
	3 Pavel Botev	BUL
	3 Nigel Donohue	GBR
-65kg	1 Sergey Kosmynine	RUS
	2 Vsevolod Zelzoni	LAT
	3 Tudor Lazarenko	MLD
	3 Udo Quellmalz	GER
	5 Jean-Paul Bell	GBR
-71kg	1 Vladimir Dgebounaze	GEO
	2 Tarlan Poladov	AZE
	3 Jorma Korhonen	FIN
	3 Patrick Rosso	FRA
-78kg	1 Darcel Yandzi	FRA
	2 Sosso Liparteliani	GEO
	3 Johan Laats	BEL
	3 Alexxey Timochkine	RUS
-86kg	1 Pascal Tayot	FRA
	2 Apti Magomadov	MOL
	3 Alex Smeets	HOL
	3 Olg Maltsev	RUS
-95kg	1 Stephane Traineau	FRA
	2 Thomas Etlinger	AUT
	3 Leonid Svirid	BLS
	3 Antal Kovacs	HUN
+95kg	1 David Khakhaleichvili	GEO
	2 David Douillet	FRA
	3 Rafal Kubacki	POL
	3 Frank Moller	GER
Open	1 David Khakhaleichvili	GEO
	2 Harry Van Bameveld	BEL
	3 Evgenyi Petchourov	RUS
	3 Henry Stohr	GER

Women

-48kg	1 Jana Perlberg	GER
	2 Tatyana Kouvchinova	RUS
	3 Martine Dupond	FRA
	3 Hülya Senyurt	TUR
-52kg	1 Almudena Munoz	ESP
	2 Cecile Nowak	FRA
	3 Elise Summers	GBR
	3 Alessandro Giungi	ITA
-56kg	1 Nicola Fairbrother	GBR
	2 Tanya Munzinger	GER
	3 Anita Kubica	POL
	3 Nicole Flagothier	BEL
-61kg	1 Arad Yael	ISR
	2 Gella Vandecaveye	BEL
	3 Diane Bell	GBR
	3 Catharine Fleury	FRA
-66kg	1 Alice Dubois	FRA
	2 Chloe Cowan	GBR
	3 Claudia Zwiers	HOL
	3 Omanuele Pierantozzi	ITA
-72kg	1 Laetitia Meignan	FRA
	2 Ulla Werbrouck	BEL
	3 Kate Howey	GBR
	3 Karin Kienhuis	HOL
+72kg	1 Monique Van Der Lee	HOL
	2 Svetlana Goundarenko	RUS
	3 Elina Lupino	FRA
	3 Beata Maksymow	POL
Open	1 Raquel Barrientos	ESP
	2 Elina Lupino	FRA
	3 Eva Granjcz	HUN
	3 Beata Maksymow	POL

European Team Championships

Leonding, Austria   Oct 24-25 1992

Men

1   France
2   Germany
3   Great Britain
3   Russia

Women

1   France
2   Netherlands
3   Russia
3   Great Britain

World Junior Championships

Buenos Aires   Oct 8-11

Men

-60kg	1 Ryuji Sonoda	JPN
	2 B Hernandez Reyes	CUB
	3 Hyuk Kim	KOR
	3 Sebastian Hampel	GER
	5 James Johnson	GBR
-65kg	1 Ian Freeman	GBR
	2 Henrique Guimares	BRA
	3 Ralf Akoto	GER
	3 Mikios Illyes	HUN
-71kg	1 Patrick Reiter	AUT
	2 Tekehisa Iwakawa	JPN
	3 Daniel Kingston	GBR
	3 Tino Buchholz	GER
-78kg	1 Darcel Yandzi	FRA
	2 Dong-Nik Yun	KOR
	3 Marcus Dawson	USA
	3 Alexandru Ciupe	ROM
-86kg	1 Masaru Tanabe	JPN
	2 Nicolas Gill	CAN
	3 Ghislain Lemaire	FRA
	3 Young-Ho Han	KOR
-95kg	1 Chung-Suk Lee	KOR
	2 Antal Kovacs	HUN
	3 Sven Helbing	GER
	3 Elton Fiebig	BRA
+95kg	1 Ralf Koser	GER
	2 Jerome Lorenzini	FRA
	3 Yoshinharu Makishi	JPN
	3 Pascal De Groof	BEL

Women

-48kg	1 Ying-Hua Yang	CHN
	2 Atsuko Nagai	JPN
	3 Phillipa Gemmill	GBR
	3 A Savon Carmenety	CUB
-52kg	1 Chun-Hong Zhao	CHN
	2 Hitomi Yamaguchi	JPN
	3 Cheryl Peel	GBR
	3 Salima Souakri	ALG
-56kg	1 Karen Roberts	GBR
	2 Nancy Van Stokkum	HOL

	3 Karine Paillard	FRA
	3 Hye-Suk Kim	KOR
-61kg	1 Hyun-Hee Jean	KOR
	2 Deborah Gravenstejn	HOL
	3 Severine Vandenhende	FRA
	3 Zsuzsanna Nagy	HUN
-66kg	1 Chiu-Ping Chen	TPE
	2 S Van Crombrugge	BEL
	3 Yu-Jing Nie	CHN
	3 Natsuko Sano	JPN
-72kg	1 Saki Yoshida	JPN
	2 Carine Varlez	FRA
	3 Ylenia Scapin	ITA
	3 Cindy Sneevliet	NED
+72kg	1 Yuan Hua	CHN
	2 Noriko Anno	JPN
	3 Marlene Ivars	FRA
	3 Stacey Smith	GBR

European Junior Championships

Jerusalem   Nov 23- 26 1992

Men

-60kg	1 Douma	FRA
	2 Luukkainen	FIN
	3 Soultanov	RUS
	3 Jamie Johnson	GBR
-65kg	1 Ian Freeman	GBR
	2 Malinski	ISR
	3 Zelaniy	LAT
	3 Leon	ESP
-71kg	1 Schieicher	AUT
	2 Lewak	POL
	3 Daniel Kingston	GBR
	3 Savtchichkina	RUS
-78kg	1 Yandzi	FRA
	2 Arens	HOL
	3 Ciupe	ROM
	3 Hoffmann	GER
-86kg	1 Haranauskas	LTU
	2 Lemaire	FRA
	3 Biro	HUN
	3 Bogdasarov	RUS
-95kg	1 Helbing	GER
	2 Munteanu	ROM
	3 Teunissen	HOL
	3 Etlinger	AUT
+95kg	1 Magomadov	RUS
	2 Braidotti	ITA
	3 De Groof	BEL
	3 Koser	GER

Women

-48kg	1 Chirinovva	RUS
	2 Phillipa Gemmill	GBR
	3 Jossinet	FRA
	3 Kuchazewska	POL
-52kg	1 Krause	POL
	2 Cheryl Peel	GBR
	3 Eineck	GER
	3 Nedellec	FRA
-56kg	1 Van Stokkum	HOL
	2 Clement	BEL

	3 Karen Roberts	GBR
	3 Kobes	TUR
-61kg	1 Gravenstijn	HOL
	2 Vandenhendel	FRA
	3 Alvanez	ESP
	3 Yazic	TUR
-66kg	1 Spacek	AUT
	2 Charve	FRA
	3 Sakizligil	TUR
	3 Henriques	POR
-72kg	1 Varlez	FRA
	2 Graco	GER
	3 Horvath	HUN
	3 Migurel	ESP
+72kg	1 Harteveld	HOL
	2 Darnoziotou	GRE
	3 Grigoras	ROM
	3 Barrientos	ESP

British Open Championships

Birmingham   April 1993

Men

-60kg	1 Richard Trautmann	GER
	2 Nigel Donohue	GBR
	3 Guy Fogel	ISR
	3 John Newton	GBR
	5 J Morrisson	GBR
-65kg	1 Tsuyoshi Uchida	JPN
	2 Heiko Seiditz	GER
	3 David Somerville	GBR
	3 Jean-Paul Bell	GBR
	5 Julian Davis	GBR
	5 Matt Ruff	GBR
-71kg	1 Danny Kingston	GBR
	2 Ian Freeman	GBR
	3 Steve Ravenscroft	GBR
	3 Micael Riquin	FRA
	5 Billy Cusack	GBR
-78kg	1 Ryan Birch	GBR
	2 Oren Smadja	ISR
	3 Alvara Paseyro	FRA
	3 Guy Nahon	FRA
-86kg	1 David Southby	GBR
	2 Carlos Matt	BRZ
	3 Bernd Pirpamer	GER
	3 Timo Peltola	FIN
-95kg	1 Fabrice Guenet	FRA
	2 Joseph Guiller	BRZ
	3 Bjorni Fridriksson	ICE
	3 V Heyer	GER
+95kg	1 Henry Stohr	GER
	2 H Watanabe	JPN
	3 Igor Mullar	LUX
	3 Elvis Gordon	GBR
	5 Nick Kokotaylo	GBR

Women

-48kg	1 Kazui Nagai	JPN
	2 Joyce Heron	GBR
	3 Sandine Dardillac	FRA

	3 Phillipa Gemmill	GBR
-52kg	1 Elise Summers	GBR
	2 Marjo Vilhola	FIN
	3 Alison Gordon	GBR
	3 Annika Mutanen	FIN
-56kg	1 Nicola Fairbrother	GBR
	2 Debbie Allan	GBR
	3 Magalie Baton	FRA
	3 Meglimi Yabushita	JPN
	5 Ceri Richards	GBR
-61kg	1 Diane Bell	GBR
	2 Yael Arad	ISR
	3 Kasumi Izumi	JPN
	3 Mayulie Cazenove	FRA
	5 Rosie Felton	GBR
-66kg	1 Yukiko Abe	JPN
	2 Chloe Cowan	GBR
	3 C Janisson	FRA
	3 Rowen Sweatman	GBR
	5 P Reed	GBR
-72kg	1 Kate Howey	GBR
	2 Josie Horton	GBR
	3 Sabrina Greco	GER
	3 Jeanne Veilex	FRA
+72kg	1 Sandra Koppen	GER
	2 Anne Akerblom	FIN
	3 Sharon Lee	GBR
	3 Heba Rashid	EGY
	5 Michelle Rogers	GBR

Korfball

European Cup (for clubs)

Caustrop Rauxal, Germany   Jan 9-10

Deetos (HOL) 24	Kólin (TCH) 9
Armsikopi (ARM) 7	Catba (BEL) 25
Grün-Weisz (GER) 19	Bourges (FRA) 5
ISEF (POR) 16	Nomads (GBR) 18

Kólin 18	Bourges 8
Armsikopi 7	ISEF 12
Deetos 12	Grün-Weisz 9
Catba 23	Nomads 3

7th/8th place

ISEF 13	Bourges 8

5th/6th place

Armsikopi 13	Kólin 9

3rd/4th place

Grün-Weisz 9	Nomads 8

1st/2nd place

Deetos 10	Catba 9

Inter-Counties Championships
1 Surrey
2 London
3 Kent
4 Middlesex

National League 1992-3

Premier Division

	P	W	D	L	GF	GA	Pts
1 Vultrix 1	12	8	3	1	175	138	19
2 Nomads 1	12	8	1	3	182	144	17
3 Croydon 1	12	7	2	3	163	153	16
4 Mitcham 1	11	6	1	4	147	140	13
5 Bec 1	12	4	2	5	139	155	10
6 Vultrix 2	12	2	0	10	129	160	4
7 Trojans	11	1	1	9	117	162	3

Mitcham v Trojans match declared void

Division 1

	P	W	D	L	GF	GA	Pts
1 Crystal Palace	12	7	2	3	133	113	16
2 Nomads 2	12	7	0	5	129	112	14
3 Borough Green	12	6	2	4	129	134	14
4 Kingfisher 1	12	6	0	6	115	100	12
5 Kwiek	12	5	2	5	126	135	12
6 Mitcham 2	12	5	1	6	126	126	11
7 Scorpians	12	2	1	9	102	152	5

Division 2

	P	W	D	L	GF	GA	Pts
1 Invicta	12	12	0	0	169	69	24
2 Croydon 2	12	10	0	2	147	75	20
3 Bec 2	12	6	1	5	111	120	13
4 Sheffield	12	5	2	5	108	103	12
5 Kingfisher 2	12	4	1	7	110	133	9
6 Woking	12	3	0	9	86	107	6
7 Norwich	12	0	0	12	61	185	

BKA Cup Final
Vultrix 16   Mitcham 8

Lacrosse

Women's World Cup

Edinburgh, Scotland   Aug 7-14

Qualifying rounds
Day 1
Scotland 13 Japan 5
England 5 Australia 4
Wales 23 Czech Republic 2
USA 14 Canada 0
Day 2
Australia 14 Wales 2
Japan 2 USA 19
Canada 7 Scotland 7
Czech Republic 0 England 25
Day 3
Japan 4 Canada 13
Wales 0 England 12
Australia 22 Czech Republic 0
USA 15 Scotland 1
Day 4
USA 17 Czech Republic 2
Scotland 2 Australia 12
Wales 6 Canada 7
England 23 Japan 1

Classification matches
7/8th: Japan 20 Czech Republic 3
5/6th: Scotland 15 Wales 2

Semi-finals
United States 6 Australia 5
England 8 Canada 2

3/4th Play-off
Australia 14 Canada 3

Final
United States 4 England 1

Home Internationals

England 11 Scotland 4
England B 3 Wales 5 *(Eng B played as A side were on tour)*
Scotland 10 Wales 5

COUNTY CHAMPIONSHIP
Final
Middlesex 2 Surrey 1

CLUBS AND COLLEGES TOURNAMENT

SAC Cup
Centaurs 5 Banbury 0

Carlton Berry Cup
Edinburgh Thistles 3 Beckenham Beetles 2

Len Smith Cup (mixed)
Weybridge 3 Pendley 2

Men's Events

SOUTH OF ENGLAND FINALS

Senior Flags
Kenton 22 Motspur Park 6
Intermediate Flags
Beckenham 10 Hillcroft II 8
Minor Flags
Hitchin II 11 Oxford University 8

NORTH OF ENGLAND FINALS

Senior Flags
Heaton Mersey 13 Timperley 9
Junior Flags
Stockport 17 Poynton 5

IROQUOIS CUP
(North v South)

Heaton Mersey 12 Kenton 4

Modern Pentathlon

World Championships

Darmstadt, Germany   Aug 8

FINAL STANDINGS

The figure in brackets show the overall position of Phelps throughout the day.

		Shoot	Fence	Swim	Run	Ride	Total
1 Richard Phelps	GBR	880 (4)	1268 (6)	1165 (2)	1342 (2)	1100 (1)	5755
2 Laszlo Fabian	HUN	1120	1236	1105	1234	974	5669
3 Sebastien Deleigne	FRA	940	1216	1120	1327	1055	5658
4 Alessandro Conforto	ITA	1090	1116	1045	1276	1024	5551
5 Per Nyqvist	SWE	910	1184	1180	1267	1010	5551
6 Christophe Ruer	FRA	760	1324	1105	1324	1010	5523
7 Myung-Gun Kim	KOR	940	1224	1105	1180	1070	5519
8 Cesare Toraldo	ITA	940	1292	1045	1159	1040	5476
9 Mike Gostigian	USA	760	1272	1120	1246	1064	5462
10 Ismo Marjunen	FIN	790	1176	1180	1258	1040	5444
11 Stefan Asenov	BUL	790	1264	1150	1162	1061	5427
12 Sergio Salazar	MEX	820	1228	910	1306	1100	5364

British Open Championships
(includes Junior championships)

Stowe & Bedford   June 25-26

FINAL STANDINGS

1 Richard Phelps	SPA	1054	1316	895	1300	1058	5623
2 Greg Whyte	IND	1027	1368	1000	1183	1031	5609
3 James Greenwell (J)	IND	1027	1188	955	1120	1082	5372
4 Graham Brookhouse	SPA	946	1248	1075	1132	965	5366
5 Shawn Morgan	ARM	919	1340	820	1237	1034	5350
6 Simeon Robbie	OU	865	1184	1030	1111	1070	5260
7 David Sweeting	SEA	676	1224	1045	1120	1073	5138
8 Paul Sell	ARM	919	1244	925	886	1037	5011

Teams: 1 Spartan (Phelps/Brookhouse/Kinsey 4686)   15,675
   2 Army (Morgan/Brookfield 4946/Paddon 4934)   15,230
   3 OU (Robbie/Egan 4909/Crowdie 4602)   14,771

The International Union for the Modern Pentathlon, following pressure from the International Olympic Committee which threatened the participation of the Modern Pentathlon in future Olympics, amended the format of the sport. For the first time, this year's world championships was competed for over a single day (rather than five or three days as previously). There was a necessary reduction in the duration of disciplines: the shoot became 20 shots on a turning target; in the fencing, each bout was reduced to a minute (though each competitior still meets every other); the swimming was over 300m; the run 4000m; and the ride was 12 obstacles negotiated in a single minute. Each participant has just 20 minutes to become acquainted with a horse they have never before ridden. In Darmstadt, Richard Phelps became the first Briton ever to win a world or Olympic title. *See Landmarks*. The British championships was competed for over two days.

Motor Cycling

It was a summer dominated by one event; the tragic crash of Wayne Rainey on the 11th lap of the Italian Grand Prix at Misano on September 6th. Rainey, who had won the three previous world championships and was clear by 11 points in this one, was leading the race when the accident happened. On cornering, the rear of Rainey's bike slid away from him, the tyre gripped again and threw him over the handlebars. The American, who was airlifted to a clinic in nearby Cesena, was diagnosed to have broken his back at the sixth vertebra. Paralysed from the waist down, Rainey was transferred to a hospital in Los Angeles. At both hospitals, though, the prognosis was the same, that Rainey's chances of ever walking again were zero.

Rainey's crash cast a long shadow over the sport. It was a manifestation of every rider's fears and if such a crash could happen to the very best rider, what chance did the rest have? Ironically, the final round of the world championship was held a week later at Monterey in California, where Rainey lives, his new home overlooking the track.

Kenny Roberts, a former world champion and Rainey's team manager was shattered. Luca Cadalora, his Yamaha teammate did not want to race in Monterey until Rainey convinced him to. Kevin Schwantz, who inherited the title, admitted feeling "lost and empty". Such events put trophies in perspective. Rainey, however, eschewed self-pity. If you want an exit line, Rainey's will be written into the folk-lore of the sport. "I was in the lead, I was on the gas. What could be a better way to go out?"

Australian GP

Eastern Creek, Sydney   Mar 28

500CC

1.	Kevin Schwantz (Suzuki)	USA	46:21.885	25pts
			(avge 95.70mph)	
2.	Wayne Rainey (Yamaha)	USA	+03.118	20
3.	Doug Chandler (Cagiva)	USA	+06.111	16
4.	Daryl Beattie (Honda)	AUS	+12.430	13
Also				
10.	Niall Mackenzie (Yamaha)	GBR		6
16.	Sean Emmett (Yamaha)	GBR		-
22.	A Scott (Yamaha)	GBR		-

250CC

1.	Tetsuya Harada (Yamaha)	JPN	43:57.049	25pts
			(avge 93.29mph)	
2.	John Kocinski (Suzuki)	USA	+00.030	20
3.	Max Biaggi (Honda)	ITA	+06.160	16

125CC

1.	Dirk Raudies (Honda)	GER	42:58.125	25pts
			(avge 89.82mph)	
2.	Kazuto Sakata (Honda)	JPN	+12.995	20
3.	Herri Torrentegui (Aprilia)	ESP	+25.981	16

Malaysian GP

Shah Alam   Apr 4

500CC   (31 laps - 67.47m)

1.	Wayne Rainey (Yamaha)	USA	44:54.102	25pts
			(avge 90.163mph)	
2.	Daryl Beattie (Honda)	AUS	+06.145	20
3.	Kevin Schwantz (Suzuki)	USA	+18.367	16
4.	Mick Doohan (Honda)	AUS	+20.973	13
5.	Alex Criville (Honda)	ESP	+21.715	11
6.	Shinichi Itoh (Honda)	JPN	+29.770	10
Also				
8.	Niall Mackenzie (Yamaha)	GBR	+1:04.514	8
12.	John Reynolds (Yamaha)	GBR		4

Points after 2 rounds: **Rainey 45,** Schwantz 41, Beattie 33, Chandler 23, Criville 21, Barros 20 - GB:Mackenzie 14, Reynolds 4, Emmett 2

250CC   (29 laps - 63.12m)

1.	Nobuatsu Aoki (Honda)	JPN	42:36.014	25pts
			(avge 88.903mph)	
2.	Tetsuya Harada (Yamaha)	JPN	+00.327	20
3.	Tadayuki Okada (Honda)	JPN	+04.154	16
4.	Doriano Romboni (Honda)	ITA	+17.065	13
5.	John Kocinski (Suzuki)	USA	+17.284	11
6.	Helmut Bradl (Honda)	GER	+28.439	10

Points after 2 rounds: **Harada 45,** Aoki 36, Kocinski 31, Okada 29, Romboni 22, Bradl 18

125CC (29 laps - 63.12m)

1.	**Dirk Raudies (Honda)**	GER	45:16.181	25pts
			(avge 83.660mph)	
2.	Kazuto Sakata (Honda)	JPN	+07.743	20
3.	Takeshi Tsujimura (Honda)	JPN	+10.188	16
4.	Noboru Ueda (Honda)	JPN	+11.779	13
5.	Ralf Waldmann (Aprilia)	GER	+15.188	11
6.	Masafumi Ono (Honda)	JPN	+20.120	10

Points after 2 rounds: **Raudies 50,** Sakata 40, Torrentegui 23, Tsujimura 23, Ono 23, Ueda 21

Japanese GP

Suzuka   Apr 18

500CC (21 laps - 76.472m)

1.	**Wayne Rainey (Yamaha)**	USA	46:12.307	25pts
			(avge 99.304mph)	
2.	Kevin Schwantz (Suzuki)	USA	+00.086	20
3.	Daryl Beattie (Honda)	AUS	+00.287	16
4.	Shinichi Itoh (Honda)	JPN	+01.782	13
5.	Alex Criville (Honda)	ESP	+22.532	11
6.	Alex Barros (Suzuki)	BRA	+22.819	10
Also				
13.	Niall Mackenzie (Yamaha)	GBR	+1:18.044	3
15.	Sean Emmett (Yamaha)	GBR	+1:46.827	1
18.	Kevin Mitchell (Yamaha)	GBR	+	-
21.	A Scott (Yamaha)	GBR		-

Points after 3 rounds: **Rainey 70,** Schwantz 61, Beattie 49, Itoh 32, Criville 32, Barros 30 - GB:Mackenzie 17, Reynolds 4, Emmett 3

250CC (19 laps - 69.189m)

1.	**Tetsuya Harada (Yamaha)**	JPN	42:24.209	25pts
			(avge 97.901mph)	
2.	Tadayuki Okada (Honda)	JPN	+00.655	20
3.	Doriano Romboni (Honda)	ITA	+20.524	16
4.	Nobuatsu Aoki (Honda)	JPN	+20.571	13
5.	Jean-P Ruggia (Aprilia)	FRA	+20.622	11
6.	Helmut Bradl (Honda)	GER	+24.510	10

Points after 3 rounds: **Harada 70,** Aoki 49, Okada 49, Kocinski 38, Romboni 38, Bradl 28

125CC (18 laps - 65.547m)

1.	**Dirk Raudies (Honda)**	GER	42:32.095	25pts
			(avge 92.461)	
2.	Kazuto Sakata (Honda)	JPN	+02.744	20
3.	Takeshi Tsujimura (Honda)	JPN	+03.149	16
4.	Akira Saito (Honda)	JPN	+03.720	13
5.	Norboru Ueda (Honda)	JPN	+04.356	11
6.	Ralf Waldmann (Aprilia)	GER	+04.403	10
Also				
16.	Neil Hodgson (Honda)	GBR		-

Points after 3 rounds: **Raudies 75,** Sakata 60, Tsujimura 39, Ueda 32, Torrentegui 28, Ono 26

Spanish GP

Jerez   May 2

500CC (27 laps - 74.16m)

1.	**Kevin Schwantz (Suzuki)**	USA	47:39.627	25pts
			(avge 93.361mph)	
2.	Wayne Rainey (Yamaha)	USA	+01.664	20
3.	Alex Criville (Honda)	ESP	+12.280	16
4.	Mick Doohan (Honda)	AUS	+26.514	13
5.	Luca Cadalora (Yamaha)	ITA	+47.828	11
6.	Daryl Beattie (Honda)	AUS	+54.886	10
Also				
7.	Niall Mackenzie (Yamaha)	GBR	+1:02.335	9
9.	Sean Emmett (Yamaha)	GBR	+1:1.312	7

Points after 4 rounds: **Rainey 90,** Schwantz 86, Beattie 59, Criville 48, Doohan 35, Itoh 32 - GB:Mackenzie 26, Emmett 10, Reynolds 5

250CC (26 laps - 71.413m)

1.	**Tetsuya Harada (Yamaha)**	JPN	46:22.519	25pts
			(avge 92.394mph)	
2.	Max Biaggi (Honda)	ITA	+04.717	20
3.	Jean-P Ruggia (Aprilia)	FRA	+04.908	16
4.	John Kocinski (Suzuki)	USA	+13.943	13
5.	Helmut Bradl (Honda)	GER	+24.745	11
6.	Wilco Zeelenburg (Aprilia)	HOL	+32.284	10

Points after 4 rounds: **Harada 95,** Okada 55, Aoki 49, Kocinski 49, Biaagi 47, Romboni 43

125CC (23 laps - 63.174m)

1.	**Kazuto Sakata (Honda)**	JPN	43:17.138	25pts
			(avge 87.567mph)	
2.	Ralf Waldmann (Aprilia)	GER	+00.602	20
3.	Takeshi Tsujimura (Honda)	JPN	+13.620)	16
4.	Herri Torrentegui (Aprilia)	ESP	+18.260	13
5.	Noboru Ueda (Honda)	JPN	+20.314	11
6.	Oliver Petrucciani (Aprilia)	SUI	+22.190	10

Points after 4 rounds: **Sakata 85,** Raudies 75, Tsujimura 55, Ueda 43, Waldmann 41, Torrentegui 41

Austrian GP

Salzburgring   May 16

500CC (29 laps - 122.82m)

1.	**Kevin Schwantz (Suzuki)**	USA	38:15.613	25pts
			(avge 119.604mph)	
2.	Mick Doohan (Honda)	AUS	+00.493	20
3.	Wayne Rainey (Yamaha)	USA	+04.892	16
4.	Alex Barros (Suzuki)	BRA	+04.954	13
5.	Luca Cadalora (Yamaha)	ITA	+16.550	11
6.	Shinichi Itoh (Honda)	JPN	+22.595	10
Also				
11.	Niall Mackenze (Yamaha)	GBR	+1:17.920	5
14.	John Reynolds (Yamaha)	GBR		2

Points after 5 rounds: **Schwantz 111,** Rainey 106, Beattie 68, Doohan 55, Criville 48, Barros 43 - GB:Mackenzie 31, Emmett 10, Reynolds 5

250CC (26 laps - 68.37m)

1.	**Doriano Romboni (Honda)**	ITA	35:48.648	25pts
	(avge 114.567)			
2.	Loris Capirossi (Honda)	ITA	+00.050	20
3.	Helmut Bradl (Honda)	GER	+00.407	16
4.	Loris Reggiani (Aprilia)	ITA	+14.888	13
5.	Max Biaggi (Honda)	ITA	+15.051	11
6.	Tetsuya Harada (Yamaha)	JPN	+15.105	10

Points after 5 rounds: **Harada 105**, Romboni 71, Kocinski 60, Okada 58, Bradl 55, Aoki 49

125CC (24 laps - 63.118)

1.	**Takeshi Tsujimura (Honda)**	JPN	36:19.800	25pts
	(avge 104.241)			
2.	Kazuto Sakata (Honda)	JPN	+00.012	20
3.	Dirk Raudies (Honda)	GER	+00.158	16
4.	Ezio Gianola (Honda)	ITA	+00.509	13
5.	Akira Saito (Honda)	JPN	+04.141	11
6.	Martin Baumann (Honda)	AUT	+04.240	10

German GP

Hockenheim   June 13

500CC (laps -   m)

1.	**Daryl Beattie (Honda)**	AUS	36:05.476	25pts
	(avge 128.58mph)			
2.	Kevin Schwantz (Suzuki)	USA	+00.083	20
3.	Shinichi Itoh (Honda)	JPN	+00.536	16
4.	Alex Criville (Honda)	ESP	+05.936	13
5.	Wayne Rainey (Yamaha)	USA	+28.054	11
6.	Doug Chandler (Cagiva)	USA	+48.349	10
Also				
9.	Niall Mackenzie (Yamaha)	GBR		7
17.	John Reynolds (Yamaha)	GBR		-

Points after 6 rounds: **Schwantz 131**, Rainey 117, Beattie 93, Criville 61, Itoh 58, Doohan 55 - GB:Mackenzie 38, Emmet 10, Reynolds 5

250CC (16 laps - 67.485m)

1.	**Doriano Romboni (Honda)**	ITA	33:53.776	25pts
	(avge 119.456mph)			
2.	Loris Capirossi (Honda)	ITA	+00.090	20
3.	Helmut Bradl (Honda)	GER	+00.384	16
4.	Max Biaggi (Honda)	ITA	+02.346	13
5.	Loris Reggiani (Aprilia)	ITA	+02.411	11
6.	Tetsuya Harada (Yamaha)	JPN	+02.537	10

Points after 6 rounds: **Harada 115**, Romboni 93, Biaggi 71, Capirossi 68, Bradl 68, Kocinski 62

125CC (15 laps - 63.267m)

1.	**Dirk Raudies (Honda)**	GER	34:45.987	25pts
	(avge 109.187mph)			
2.	Kazuto Sakata (Honda)	JPN	+08.807	20
3.	Takeshi Tsujimura (Honda)	JPN	+08.943	16
4.	Akira Saito (Honda)	JPN	+09.160	13
5.	Ralf Waldmann (Aprilia)	GER	+09.169	11
6.	Ezio Gianola (Honda)	ITA	+09.834	10
Also				
24.	Neil Hodgson (Honda)	GBR		-

Points after 6 rounds: **Sakata 125**, Raudies 116, Tsujimura 96, Waldmann 59, Ueda 48, Torrontegui 47

Dutch GP

Assen   June 26

500CC (20 laps - 75.13m)

1.	**Kevin Schwantz (Suzuki)**	USA	41:35.943	25pts
	(avge 108.361mph)			
2.	Mick Doohan (Honda)	AUS	+00.829	20
3.	Alex Criville (Honda)	ESP	+13.518	16
4.	Doug Chandler (Cagiva)	USA	+13822	13
5.	Wayne Rainey (Yamaha)	USA	+18.063	11
6.	Shinichi Itoh (Honda)	JPN	+34.405	10
Also				
8.	Niall Mackenzie (Yamaha)	GBR	+56.672	8
10.	John Reynolds (Yamaha)	GBR	+1:14.408	6
16.	Sean Emmett (Yamaha)	GBR		-
19.	Kevin Mitchell (Yamaha)	GBR		-

Points after 7 rounds: **Schwantz 156**, Rainey 128, Beattie 93, Criville 77, Doohan 75, Itoh 68

250CC (18 laps - 67.62m)

1.	**Loris Capirossi (Honda)**	ITA	38:26.004	25pts
	(avge 105.558mph)			
2.	Tetsuya Harada (Yamaha)	JPN	+03.917	20
3.	John Kocinski (Suzuki)	USA	+04.680	16
4.	Jean-P Ruggia (Aprilia)	FRA	+05.578	13
5.	Helmut Bradl (Honda)	GER	+09.391	11
6.	Loris Reggiani (Aprilia)	ITA	+14.448	10

Points after 7 rounds: **Harada 135**, Romboni 96, Bradl 82, Capirossi 81, Kocinski 80, Biaggi 60

125CC (17 laps - 63.86m)

1.	**Dirk Raudies (Honda)**	GER	39:08.938	25pts
	(avge 97.871mph)			
2.	Kazuto Sakata (Honda)	JPN	+09.790	20
3.	Martin Baumann (Honda)	AUT	+10.374	16
4.	Mark Stief (Honda)	GER	+11.958	13
5.	Hans Spaan (Honda)	HOL	+12.104	11
6.	P Oetti (Aprilia)	GER	+12.173	10
Also				
15.	Neil Hodgson (Honda)	GBR	+1:12.316	1

Points after 7 rounds: **Sakata 145**, Raudies 141, Tsujimura 96, Waldmann 59, Saito 53, Torrontegui 49 - GB:Hodgson 5

European GP

Catalunya, Spain   July 4

500CC (25 laps - 73.70m)

1.	**Wayne Rainey (Yamaha)**	USA	45:58.314	25pts
	(avge 96.185mph)			
2.	Mick Dohan (Honda)	AUS	+03.898	20
3.	Kevin Schwantz (Suzuki)	USA	+18.992	16
4.	Daryl Beattie (Honda)	AUS	+46.625	13
5.	Alex Barros (Suzuki)	BRA	+55.799	11
6.	Niall Mackenzie (Yamaha)	GBR	+55.806	10
Also				
11.	Jerry McWilliams (Yamaha)	GBR	+1:49.221	5
12.	Sean Emmett (Yamaha)	GBR		4

Points after 8 rounds: **Schwantz 172**, Rainey 153, Beattie 106, Doohan 95, Criville 77, Itoh 68 - GB:Mackenzie 56, Emmett 14, Reynolds 12, McWilliams 5

250CC (23 laps - 67.80m)

1.	**Max Biaggi (Honda)**	ITA	**43:09.388**	**25pts**
			(avge 94.263mph)	
2.	Tadayuki Okada (Honda)	JPN	+02.601	20
3.	Alberto Puig (Honda)	ESP	+03.58	16
4.	Nobuatsu Aoki (Honda)	JPN	+03.655	13
5.	Jean-P Ruggia (Aprilia)	FRA	+03.814	11
6.	Carlos Cardus (Honda)	ESP	+06.489	10

Points so far after 8 rounds: **Harada 135**, Romboni 96, Bradl 87, Biaggi 85, Capirossi 81, Kocinski 80, Okada 78

125CC (22 laps - 64.85m)

1.	**Noboru Ueda (Honda)**	JPN	**43:33.091**	**25pts**
			(avge 89.347mph)	
2.	Ralf Waldmann (Aprilia)	GER	+00.061	20
3.	Akira Saito (Honda)	JPN	+00.085	16
4.	Herri Torrontegui (Aprilia)	ESP	+00.224	13
5.	Dirk Raudies (Honda)	GER	+01.571	11
6.	J Martinez (Honda)	ESP	+22.513	10
Also				
19.	Neil Hodgson (Honda)	GBR	-	

Points after 8 rounds: **Raudies 152**, Sakata 145, Tsujimura 103, Waldmann 79, Ueda 73, Saito 69 - GB:Hodgson 5

San Marino GP

Mugello, San Marino — July 19

500CC (23 laps - 74.91m)

1.	**Mick Doohan (Honda)**	AUS	**44:02.712**	**25pts**
			(avge 102.051mph)	
2.	Kevin Schwantz (Suzuki)	USA	+09.953	20
3.	Wayne Rainey (Yamaha)	USA	+31.701	16
4.	Shinichi Itoh (Honda)	JPN	+35.893	13
5.	Luca Cadalora (Yamaha)	ITA	+46.598	11
6.	Daryl Beattie (Honda)	AUS	+57.000	10
Also				
8.	Niall Mackenzie (Yamaha)	GBR	+1:27.893	8
13.	Jerry McWilliams (Yamaha)	GBR		3
17.	David Jefferies (Yamaha)	GBR	-	

Points after 9 rounds: **Schwantz 192**, Rainey 169, Doohan 120, Beattie 116, Itoh 81, Criville 77 - GB:Mackenzie 64, Emmett 14, Reynolds 12, McWilliams 8

250CC (21 laps - 68.40m)

1.	**Loris Capirossi (Honda)**	ITA	**41:05.271**	**25pts**
			(avge 99.883mph)	
2.	Loris Reggiani (Aprilia)	ITA	+00.118	20
3.	Tetsuya Harada (Yamaha)	JPN	+04.837	16
4.	Jean-P Ruggia (Aprilia)	FRA	+04.859	13
5.	Max Biaggi (Honda)	ITA	+14.364	11
6.	Tadayuki Okada (Honda)	JPN	+14.376	10

Points after 9 rounds: **Harada 151**, Capirossi 106, Romboni 96, Biaggi 96, Bradl 96, Okada 88

125CC (20 laps - 65.14m)

1.	**Dirk Raudies (Honda)**	GER	**41:28.495**	**25pts**
			(avge 94.240mph)	
2.	Kazuto Sakata (Honda)	JPN	+10.949	20
3.	Akira Saito (Honda)	JPN	+11.797	16
4.	Ralf Waldmann (Aprilia)	GER	+11.875	13
5.	Carlos Giro (Aprilia)	ESP	+11.933	11
6.	Noboru Ueda (Honda)	JPN	+14.153	10

Points after 9 rounds: **Raudies 177**, Sakata 165, Tsujimura 110, Waldmann 92, Saito 85, Ueda 83 - GB:Hodgson 5

British GP

Donington — Aug 1

500CC (30 laps - 74.95m)

1.	**Luca Cadalora (Yamaha)**	ITA	**47:45.630**	**25pts**
			(avge 94.155mph)	
2.	Wayne Rainey (Yamaha)	USA	+03.312	20
3.	Niall Mackenzie (Yamaha)	GBR	+21.898	16
4.	Carl Fogarty (Cagiva)	GBR	+22.238	13
5.	Shinichi Itoh (Honda)	JPN	+36.151	11
6.	Daryl Beattie (Honda)	AUS	+36.394	10
Also				
9.	John Reynolds (Yamaha)	GBR	+1:16.010	7
11.	James Haydon (Yamaha)	GBR	+1:24.715	5
14	Ron Haslam (Yamaha)	GBR	+1:34.590	2

Points after 10 rounds: **Schwantz 192**, Rainey 189, Beattie 126, Doohan 120, Itoh 92, Cadalora 84 - GB:Mackenzie 80, Reynolds 19, Emmett 14, Fogarty 13, McWilliams 8, Haydon 5, Haslam 2

250CC (27 laps - 67.45m)

1.	**Jean-P Ruggia (Aprilia)**	FRA	**43:05.248**	**25pts**
			(avge 93.930mph)	
2.	Loris Capirossi (Honda)	ITA	+03.266	20
3.	Loris Reggiani (Aprilia)	ITA	+19.510	16
4.	Pier Chili (Yamaha)	ITA	+35.138	13
5.	Tadayuki Okada (Honda)	JPN	+49.614	11
6.	Max Biaggi (Honda)	ITA	+1:14.134	10

Points after 10 rounds: **Harada 151**, Capirossi 126, Biaggi 106, Ruggia 104, Okada 99, Romboni 96, Bradl 96

125CC (26 laps - 64.96m)

1.	**Dirk Raudies (Honda)**	GER	**44:21.938**	**25pts**
			(avge 87.845mph)	
2.	Kazuto Sakata (Honda)	JPN	+08.150	20
3.	Ralf Waldmann (Aprilia)	GER	+10.760	16
4.	Oliver Petrucciani (Aprilia)	SUI	+18.532	13
5.	Akira Saito (Honda)	JPN	+19.056	11
6.	Noboru Ueda (Honda)	JPN	+19.543	10
Also				
10.	Neil Hodgson (Honda)	GBR	+34.128	6

Points after 10 rounds:**Raudies 202**, Sakata 185, Tsujinura 118, Waldmann 108, Saito 96, Ueda 93 - GB:Hodgson 11

Italian GP

Misano — Sept 5

500CC

1.	**Luca Cadalora (Yamaha)**	ITA	**45:59.165**	**25pts**
			(avge 96.32mph)	
2.	Mick Doohan (Honda)	AUS	+00.358	20
3.	Kevin Schwantz (Suzuki)	USA	+07.658	16
4.	John Kocinski (Cagiva)	USA	+15.941	13
5.	Alex Barros (Suzuki)	BRA	+41.777	11
6.	Alex Criville (Honda)	ESP	+42.064	10
Also				
9.	Niall McKenzie (Yamaha)	GBR		

Points after 11 rounds: **Schwantz 219**, Rainey 214, Doohan 156, Beattie 145, Cadalora 129

250CC

1. **Jean-P Ruggia (Aprilia)**   FRA   43:39.138   25pts
          (avge 94.820 mph)
2. Loris Capirossi (Honda)   ITA   +10.425   20
3. Loris Reggiani (Aprilia)   ITA   +24.452   16

Points after 11 rounds: **Harada 161**, Capirossi 157, Ruggia 129, Biaggi 126, Reggiani 122

125CC

1. **Dirk Raudies (Honda)**   GER   42:30.722   25pts
          (avge 89.840 mph)
2. Kazuto Sakata (Honda)   JPN   +15.874   20
3. P Oetti (Aprilia)   GER   +16.466   16

Points after 11 rounds: **Raudies 247**, Sakata 230, Tsujimura 147, Waldmann 119, Saito 117

US GP

Monterey   Sept 12

500CC

1. **John Kocinski (Cagiva)**   USA   48:17.165   25pts
2. Alex Barros (Suzuki)   BRA   +6.375   20
3. Luca Cadalora (Yamaha)   ITA   +10.489   16
4. Kevin Schwantz (Suzuki)   USA   +18.265   13
5. Daryl Beattie (Honda)   AUS   +19.493   11
6. Shinichi Itoh (Honda)   JPN   +37.292   10

Also

8. Niall Mackenzie (Yamaha)   GBR   +42.851   8

Final Championship positions: **1 Schwantz 232**, 2 Rainey 214, 3 Doohan 156, 4 Beattie 156, 5 Cadalora 145, 6 Itoh 119, 7 Criville 104, 8 Barros 100 , 9 Mackenzie 95

250CC

1. **Loris Capirossi (Honda)**   ITA   46:04.505   25pts
2. Doriano Romboni (Honda)   ITA   +1.381   20
3. Loris Reggiani (Aprilia)   ITA   +3.803   16
4. Alberto Puig (Honda)   ESP   +3.881   13

Final Championship positions: **1 Capirossi 182**, 2 Harada 172, 3 Reggiana 138, 4=Romboni & Ruggia 129, 5=Baggia & Bradl 126

125CC

1. **Dirk Raudies (Honda)**   GER   45:40.444   25pts
2. K Sakata (Honda)   JPN   +0.142   20
3. R Waldmann (Aprilia)   GER   +3.527   16

Final Championship positions: 1 Raudies 272, 2 Sakata 250, 3 Tsujimura 157

HEAT Supercup

ROUND 1

Oulton Park   May 15-16

TT Superbike

1st Leg	2nd Leg
1 James Whitnam	1 James Whitnam
2 Rob McElnea	2 Steve Hislop
3 David Jeffries	3 Brian Morrison

250CC
1 James Haydon
2 Paul Brown
3 Graeme Thompson

125CC
1 Kevin Mawdsley
2 Fernando Mendes
3 Patrick Corrigan

Sidecar
1 Webster/Simmons
2 Fisher/Butler
3 Robinson/Graham

Supersport 600
Abandoned

Superteen
1 Lee Masters
2 Douglas Cowie
3 Jonathan Peacock

ROUND 2

Donington Park   June 19-20

TT Superbike

1st Leg	2nd Leg
1 Carl Fogarty	1 Carl Fogarty
2 James Whitnam	2 James Whitnam
3 Steve Hislop	3 Rob McElnea

250CC
1 Paul Brown
2 Darren Dixon
3 Nigel Bosworth

125CC
1 Robin Appleyard
2 Steve Patrickson
3 Kevin Mawdsley

Sidecar
1 Webster/Simmons
2 Abbott/Tailford
3 Brindley/Hutchinson

Supersport 600
1 Jim Moodie
2 Ian Simpson
3 Phil Borley

Superteen
1 Jonathan Peacock
2 Tim Smith
3 Lee Humphries

ROUND 3

Snetterton   Jul 17-18

TT Superbike

1st Leg	2nd Leg
1 Jim Moodie	1 James Whitnam
2 Steve Hislop	2 Steve Hislop
3 Rob McElnea	3 Jim Moodie

250CC
1 Nigel Bosworth
2 Paul Brown
3 Steve Sawford
125CC
1 Mick Lofthouse
2 Robin Appleyard
3 Chris Palmer
Sidecar
1 Gray/Pointer
2 Robinson/Graham
3 Wright/Woodhead
Supersport 600
1 Jim Moodie
2 Ian Simpson
3 Mike Edwards
Superteen
1 Tim Smith
2 Jonathan Peacock
3 Damion Baily

ROUND 4
Cadwell Park   Jul 24-25
TT Superbike

1st Leg	2nd Leg
1 James Whitnam	1 James Whitnam
2 Rob McElnea	2 Rob McElnea
3 Brian Morrison	3 Brian Morrison

250CC
1 James Haydon
2 Ron Haslam
3 David Rawlins
125CC
1 Mick Lofthouse
2 Robin Appleyard
3 Chris Palmer
Sidecar
1 Webster/Simmons
2 Abbott/Tailford
3 Smith/Hopkinson
Supersport 600
1 Mike Edwards
2 Jim Moodie
3 Phil Borley
Superteen
1 Tim Smith
2 Jonathan Peacock
3 Torquil Patterson

ROUND 5
Brands Hatch   Sept 4-5
TT Superbike

1st Leg	2nd Leg
1 James Whitnam	1 James Whitnam
2 Jim Moodie	2 Ray Stringer
3 Ray Stringer	3 Brian Morrison

250CC
1 Ian Newton
2 Nigel Bosworth
3 Steve Sawford
125CC
1 Robin Appleyard
2 Mick Lofthouse
3 Kevin Mawdsley

Sidecar
1 Abbott/Tailford
2 Dixon/Hetherington
3 Brindley/Whiteside
Supersport 600
1 Phil Borley
2 Jim Moodie
3 Ian Simpson
Superteen
1 Jonathan Peacock
2 Lee Masters
3 Damion Baily

ROUND 6
Mallory Park   Sept 18-19
TT Superbike

1st Leg	2nd Leg
1 Jim Moodie	1 Jim Moodie
2 Ray Stringer	2 Michael Rutter
3 Steve Hislop	3 Matt Llewellyn

Final Standings
1 Whitnam 174, 2 Moodie 154, 3 Stringer 136, 4 McElnea 128, 5 Morrison 109, 6 Hislop 91
250CC
1 James Haydon
2 Nigel Bosworth
3 Paul Brown
Final Standings
1 Brown 95, 2 Hayden 84, 3 Bosworth 79, 4 Sawford 76 5 Patterson 54.5, 6 McConnachie 45
125CC
1 Kevin Mawdsley
2 Mick Lofthouse
3 Chris Palmer
Final Standings
1 Appleyard 82, 2 Palmer 75, 3 Lofthouse 74, 4 Mawdsley 70, 5 Patrickson 69, 6 Brown 67
Sidecar
1 Abbott/Tailford
2 Webster/Simmons
3 Brindley/Whiteside
Supersport 600
1 Phil Borley
2 Jim Moodie
3 Ian Simpson
Final Standings
1 Moodie 91, 2 Simpson 77, 3 Edwards 72, 4 Borley 70, 5 Heal 44, 6 Duffus 40
Superteen
1 Jonathan Peacock
2 Damion Baily
3 Gary Walker
Final Standings
1 Peacock 109, 2 Smith 83, 3 Humphries 69, 4 Baily 68, 5 Walker 55, 6 Bristow 48

Motor Racing

It was a landmark year for motor racing with Nigel Mansell becoming the first man ever to follow a Formula One title with an Indy Car championship (*See Landmarks)*; Alain Prost retiring after a fourth world championship and a record 51 grand prix victories; and Damon Hill, in his F1 baptismal season winning a hattrick of races.

The year began on a more downbeat note as Fisa threatened to ban the Williams team because it had handed its team sheet in too late. It was part and parcel of an internecine squabble about Williams Renault being too dominant for the sport's good. There was talk of lead weights in cars (can you imagine it, Damon Hill a 33-year-old carrying 11-7); of a "technological freeze" whereby no-one anywhere was allowed to think of anything that might improve performance if they didn't all think of it together; or of banning active suspensions and traction-control systems. They settled on the third, or rather decided that active suspensions and the like were already banned and there was talk of retrogressive action against the infringers. It was all hardly designed to enhance the profile of the sport.

When racing started, Prost cruised home in the South African Grand Prix and everyone began to panic again. When Mansell had a winning debut in Australia, it made things no better. Formula One could sense the eyes of the media and the public fixing on Indy Car events across the pond.

In Britain, certainly, attention was more and more directed west as Mansell, apart from a nasty knock in Phoenix, began to mark out a clear track to the Indy Car title. He won five races on his way to the crown; at Queensland, West Allis, Brooklyn, London (New Hampshire) and Nazareth. It was the same number as Michael Andretti had won last season, but Andretti didn't take the title. This year, Andretti did a Mansell in reverse, joining the F1 circuit. It was a catastrophe. Driving for McLaren, he hit more cars than he missed in the first few weeks and eventually bowed out before the season ended.

Damon Hill drew the British focus back on F1 in August when he finally won a grand prix. Hill came good in Budapest, after failing narrowly at the British and German events. In Germany, Hill found cruel luck, puncturing with only a couple circuits left and a clear lead.

Hill graduated from Formula 3 racing a few years back (he finished 9th, 5th & 3rd in 1987-88-89) and last year's F3 winner, Rubens Barrichello, made the transition a deal quicker joining the Jordan-Hart team for this year's championship. Kelvin Burt must wonder what life has in store having taking this year's F3 title.

It was a good year too for Juan Manuel Fangio as the retirement of Prost meant that his record of five championships will continue for a good while longer. Fangio, now 81, admitted this year that he never bothered to get a driving licence till he was 50. If ever he was stopped by the police in his heyday, they would instantly recognise him and wave him on. Chancellor of the Exchequer, Kenneth Clarke has a driving licence, but we're not sure if he should have. Clarke came last in the Commons v Lords motor racing championship complaining of a burnt-clutch. They have an excuse for everything, don't they, politicians.

QUOTES

"Someone hit me at about 40 or 50 mph up the back as I was turning into the corner. I went to see the stewards who said it was a sporting accident, but I didn't see it that way at all"

Nigel Mansell, after crashing with Ayrton Senna in his final F1 race.

It's a new life, a New Year and Formula One is history'

Nigel Mansell, in January

"Although I do not have the gift of the gab and am completely charmless, I just persevere. I never give up"

Damon Hill

"My father will be up there dancing"

Damon Hill, following his Italian Grand Prix victory.

"It was obvious from the first four races that he could win and cut the mustard"

Frank Williams in praise of Damon Hill.

"In some ways it is a boring track, but there is a certain crazy thrill to hurtling along at over 200mph on a narrow track between rows of trees. It is like riding a bullet"

Damon Hill talking kindly about the Hockenheim circuit in Germany before the race. He wasn't in such a good mood afterwards.

"Like I say to everybody, it's a learning curve and I think we're going up the curve quite quickly"

Nigel Mansell before the first Indy Car championship race in Surfers' Paradise, Australia.

"I don't remember anyone going through a test that fast"

Tom Binford, chief track steward at the Indianapolis 500 circuit, watching Mansell do his test.

"It's one of the five most special moments of my life. Three of them were watching the births of my children, then came the Formula One title and now this"

Nigel Mansell comparing like and not-so-like.

Formula 1, 1993

South African Grand Prix

Kyalami   Mar 14

Laps:72 x 4.261km   Total distance:306.763km
1 **Alain Prost FRA (Williams-Renault)   1:38:45.082**
                                            (186.385 kmh)

2 Ayrton Senna BRA (McLaren-Ford)   at 1:19.824
3 Mark Blundell GBR (Ligier-Renault)   1 lap
4 Christian Fittipaldi BRA (Minardi-Ford)   1 lap
5 J J Lehto FIN (Sauber)   2 laps
6 Gerhard Berger AUT (Ferrari)   3 laps
7 Derek Warwick GBR (Footwork-Honda)   3 laps
Pole position:Prost
Fastest lap:1:19.492 (192.970 kmh)
Race leaders:Senna 1-23, Prost 24-72
It was as if Prost had never been away. After a sabbatical
from the sport, the Frenchman took up from where he left
off. Comfortably the most successful Grand Prix driver in
history, Prost clocked up his 45th GP victory with an
effortless win, finishing almost a lap clear of Senna. A
Mansell-less summer looked less barren for Brits when
Blundell, on his debut in the Ligier-Renault car, stepped
on the podium for the first time. Warwick almost scored
points too, only missing out when he took a spin on the
final lap. Damon Hill, a debutant in the Williams team,
did not have an auspicious opener. The 32 year old spun
on his first lap and collided with Alessandro Zanardi's
Lotus-Ford on his 17th.
WORLD CHAMPIONSHIP STANDINGS
Drivers: Prost 10pts, Senna 6, Blundell 4, Fittipaldi 3, Lehto 2,
Berger 1.
Constructors: Williams 10, McLaren 6, Ligier 4, Minardi 3,
Sauber 2, Ferrari 1.

Brazilian Grand Prix

Interlagos   Mar 28

Laps:71 x 4.325km   Total distance:307.075km
1 **Ayrton Senna BRA (McLaren-Ford)   1:51:15.485**
                                        (165.601 kmh)

2 Damon Hill GBR (Williams-Renault)   at 16.625
3 Michael Schumacher GER (Benetton-Ford)   45.436
4 Johnny Herbert GBR (Lotus-Ford)   46.557
5 Mark Blundell GBR (Ligier Renault)   52.127
6 Alessandro Zanardi ITA (Lotus-Ford)   1 lap
7 Philippe Alliot FRA (Larrousse Lamborghini) 1 lap
8 Jean Alesi FRA (Ferrari)   1 lap
9 Derek Warwick GBR (Footwork-Honda)   2 laps
10 Erik Comas FRA (Larrousse Lamborghini)   2 laps
11 Michele Alboreto ITA (Lola-Ferrari)   3 laps
12 Luca Badoer ITA (Lola-Ferrari)   3 laps
Pole position:Prost
Race leaders: Prost 1-28, Senna 29-36, Hill 37-41, Senna 42-
71
At Kyalami, a thunderstorm broke just as the race finished
and had little effect on proceedings. At Interlagos, the
clouds rolled over earlier and heavy rain poured onto the
track after just 28 of the 71 laps. Prost was the most
auspicious casualty, spinning off the track as he
attempted to avoid a collision with Fittipaldi's Minardi-

Ford. Prost was not the only driver to suffer when the
rains came and, for the first time, a pace car was used to
slow the drivers while the debris was removed from the
track. Thereafter, the race was Senna's. While Hill
adopted a conservative approach, after his disasters in
Kyalami, Senna, on wet tyres, sped through the puddles.
Herbert, in fourth, equalled his best-ever GP performance
and Blundell again scored points. Andretti, like Hill in his
first GP season, had his second shunt in a row. This time it
was a spectacular first lap crunch with Berger's Ferrari.
WORLD CHAMPIONSHIP STANDINGS
Drivers:Senna 16, Prost 10, Hill & Blundell 6, Schumacher 4,
Herbert & Fittipaldi 3, Lehto 2, Berger & Zanardi 1.
Constructors: McLaren & Williams 16, Ligier 6, Benetton &
Lotus 4, Minardi 3, Sauber 2, Ferrari 1.

Grand Prix of Europe

Donington Park, UK   Apr 11

Laps:76 x 4.023km   Total distance:305.748km
1 **Ayrton Senna BRA (McLaren-Ford)   1:50:45.570**
                                        (165.600 kmh)

2 Damon Hill GBR (Williams-Renault)   at 1:23.199
3 Alain Prost FRA (Williams-Renault)   1 lap
4 Johnny Herbert GBR (Lotus-Ford)   1 lap
5 Riccardo Patrese ITA (Benetton-Ford)   2 laps
6 Fabrizio Barbazza ITA (Minardi-Ford)   2 laps
7 Christian Fittipaldi BRA (Minardi-Ford)   3 laps
8 Alessandro Zanardi ITA (Lotus-Ford)   3 laps
9 Erik Comas FRA (Larrousse-Lamborghini)   4 laps
10 Rubens Barrichello BRA (Jordan-Hart)   6 laps
11 Michele Alboreto ITA (Lola-Ferrari)   6 laps
Pole position:Prost
When it rains, watch Senna, appears to be the maxim.
Although the McLaren-Ford may not match the
capabilities of the Williams-Renault cars of Hill and Prost,
Senna's expertise brought off another scintillating victory.
Prost came into the pits seven times throughout the race
in a forlorn attempt to get his tyres right as the rain came
and went and came and went again. Senna took just four
stops as he more adeptly adjusted to conditions. Herbert
was the most daring, coming in just once, staying on the
faster slicks as long as possible. Hill accelerated along his
learning curve with a second successive second place,
while Andretti must have entertained a few nostalgic
thoughts about his IndyCar career as he notched up his
third successive shunt - as in Kyalami, on the first lap.
WORLD CHAMPIONSHIP STANDINGS
Drivers: Senna 26, Prost 14, Hill 12, Blundell & Herbert 6,
Schumacher 4, Fittipaldi 3, Lehto & Patrese 2, Berger, Barbazza
& Zanardi 1.
Constructors: Williams & McLaren 26, Lotus 7, Ligier &
Benetton 6, Minardi 4, Sauber 2, Ferrari 1.

San Marino Grand Prix
Imola   Apr 25

Laps:61 x 5.040km   Total distance:307.440km
1   **Alain Prost FRA (Williams-Renault)   1:33:20.413**
(196.538 kmh)
2   Michael Schumacher GER (Benetton-Ford)   at 32.410
3   Martin Brundle GBR (Ligier-Renault)   1 lap
4   J J Lehto FIN (Sauber)   2 laps
5   Philippe Alliot FRA (Larrousse-Lamborghini) 2 laps
6   Fabrizio Barbazza ITA (Minardi-Ford)   2 laps
7   Luca Badoer ITA (Lola-Ferrari)   3 laps
8   Johnny Herbert GBR (Lotus-Ford)   4 laps
9   Aguri Suzuki JPN (Footwork-Honda)   7 laps
Pole position:Prost
Fastest lap:Prost 1:26.128 (210.663 kmh)
Race leaders:Hill 1-11, Prost 12-61
Senna, seeking a hattrick of wins, was one of 18 drivers
who failed to cross the finish line. Senna, after a
combative start to the race, was eventually forced to
retire. His car was travelling at 300kmh when the
hydraulics failed. Hill retired on lap 21, when the
Williams-Renault suffered braking problems, Warwick
got just eight laps further before he retired, Mark
Blundell span off on the first lap and Johnny Herbert saw
his Lotus engine blow up - though with just three laps to
go, the Briton was classified as eighth. Prost did not have
a trouble-free day, but handled the rainy conditions
much more happily than he did at Donington and ran
out a comfortable winner.
WORLD CHAMPIONSHIPS STANDINGS
*Drivers: Senna 26, Prost 24, Hill 12, Schumacher 10, Blundell
& Herbert 6, Lehto 5, Brundle 4, Fittipaldi 3, Patrese, Alliot &
Barbazza 2, Berger & Zanardi 1. **Constructors:** Williams 36,
McLaren 26, Benetton 12, Ligier 10, Lotus 7, Minardi &
Sauber 5, Larrousse 2, Ferrari 1.*

MICHAEL ANDRETTI'S NOTEBOOK

Mar 14 (Kyalami) Stalled at start, clutch problems,
then drove into the back of a car. Race over lap 4.
Mar 28 (Intelagos) Collided with Berger's Ferrari
at start, spun into crash barrier. Race ended lap 1.
Apr 11(Donington) Drove into back of
Wendlinger's Sauber at start. Race over both cars.
Apr 26(Imola) Brakes locked and came off the
track. Race over lap 32.
May 23(Monaco) Drove into the back of car on the
first lap. Stopped for repairs then finished the
race.
July 11(Silverstone) Came off the track on lap 1.
Race over.
July 25(Hockenheim) Crashed into Berger's
Ferrari and damaged steering. Race over lap 5.

Andretti had previously won 27 times from 145
starts on the Indy Car circuit in the United States
and was Champion in 1991. He commuted from
the US to compete on the F1 circuit, but quit F1
prematurely on Sept 17 to return to the US.

Spanish Grand Prix
Montmelo, nr Barcelona   May 9

Laps:65 x 4.747km   Total distance:308.555km
1   **Alain Prost FRA (Williams-Renault)   1:32:27.685**
(200.227 kmh)
2   Ayrton Senna BRA (McLaren-Ford)   at 16.873
3   Michael Schumacher GER (Benetton-Ford)   27.125
4   Riccardo Patrese ITA (Benetton-Ford)   1 lap
5   Michael Andretti USA (McLaren-Ford)   1 lap
6   Gerhard Berger AUT (Ferrari)   2 laps
7   Mark Blundell GBR (Ligier-Renault)   2 laps
8   Christian Fittipaldi BRA (Minardi-Ford) 2 laps
9   Erik Comas FRA (Larrousse-Lamborghini)   2 laps
10 Aguri Suzuki JPN (Footwork-Honda)   2 laps
11 Thierry Boutsen BEL (Jordan-Hart)   3 laps
12 Rubens Barrichello BRA (Jordan-Hart)   3 laps
13 Derek Warwick GBR (Footwork-Honda)   3 laps
14 Alessandro Zanardi ITA (Lotus-Ford)   5 laps
Pole position:Prost
Fastest lap:Schumacher 1:20.989 (211.006 kmh) *New
Record*
Race leaders:Hill (Laps 1-10), Prost (Laps 11-65)
Hill was combative for 40 of the 65 laps, before engine
failure put him out of the race. It left Prost clear and
apparently unworried. Yet in the later stages of the race,
a rear wheel on the Frenchman's Williams-Renault
FW15C worked loose and, retrospectively, Senna was
kicking himself for taking a precautionary pit-stop for a
tyre-change. That stop left Prost 50 seconds ahead and
able to protect his car during the latter part of the race. Of
the Brits, Brundle spun off after 11 laps when a rear tyre
punctured and Herbert lasted just two laps, withdrawing
as his Lotus-Ford continued to have suspension troubles.
WORLD CHAMPIONSHIP STANDINGS
*Drivers: Prost 34, Senna 32, Schumacher 14, Hill 12, Blundell
& Herbert 6, Lehto & Patrese 5, Brundle 4, Fittipaldi 3, Alliot,
Barbazza Andretti & Berger 2, Zanardi 1.
Constructors: Williams 46, McLaren 34, Benetton 19, Ligier
10, Lotus 7, Minardi & Sauber 6, Larrousse 2, Ferrari 2.*

Monaco Grand Prix
Monte Carlo   May 23

Laps:78 x 3.328km   Total distance:259.584km
1   **Ayrton Senna BRA (McLaren-Ford)   1:52:10.947**
(138.837 kmh)
2   Damon Hill GBR (Williams-Renault)   at 52.118
3   Jean Alesi FRA (Ferrari)   1:3.362
4   Alain Prost FRA (Williams-Renault)   1 lap
5   Christian Fittipaldi BRA (Minardi-Ford) 2 laps
6   Martin Brundle GBR (Ligier-Renault)   2 laps
7   Alessandro Zanardi ITA (Lotus-Ford)   2 laps
8   Michael Andretti USA (McLaren-Ford)   2 laps
9   Rubens Barrichello BRA (Jordan-Hart)   2 laps
10 Andrea De Cesaris ITA (Tyrrell-Yamaha)   2 laps
11 Fabrizio Barbazza ITA (Minardi-Ford)   2 laps
12 Philippe Alliot FRA (Larrousse-Lamborghini) 3 laps
13 Karl Wendlinger AUT (Sauber)   4 laps
14 Gerhard Berger AUT (Ferrari   8 laps
Pole position:Prost
Fastest lap:Prost 1:23.604 (143.304 kmh)
Race leaders:Prost 1-11, Schumacher 12-32, Senna 33-78
It was a race all about record wins; Senna seeking a
record-breaking sixth Monaco success, Prost a record

equalling fifth, and Damon Hill, hoping to protect his father's place in the record-books (Graham Hill won five to set the record) by snatching the race from the leading players. Hill tried gamely, surviving a collision with Berger's Ferrari en route; Prost drove brilliantly after suffering a ten-second penalty for anticipating the start and later stalling twice in the pit-lane; but it was Senna's day. The 33 year old Brazilian inherited the lead on lap 33, when Schumacher's Benetton erupted in smoke and flames. Thereafter, only a tyre-change on lap 52 threatened his superiority (his lead dipped to just 9 seconds). Senna's victory, his third of the summer, also took him back to the top of the drivers' championship.

WORLD CHAMPIONSHIP STANDING
Drivers:Senna 42, Prost 37, Hill 18, Schumacher 14, Blundell & Herbert 6, Lehto, Patrese Brundle & Fittipaldi 5, Alesi 4, Alliot Andretti Barbazza & Berger 2, Zanardi 1.
Constructors:Williams 55, McLaren 44, Benetton 19, Ligier 11, Lotus & Minardi 7, Ferrrari 6, Sauber 5, Larrousse 2.

Canadian Grand Prix
Montreal   June 13

Laps:69 x 4.43km   Total distance:305.67km
1 **Alain Prost FRA (Williams-Renault)   1:36:41.822**
                                    (189.667 kmh)
2 Michael Schumacher GER (Benetton-Ford) at 14.527
3 Damon Hill GBR (Williams-Renault)   52.685
4 Gerhard Berger AUT (Ferrari)   1 lap
5 Martin Brundle GBR (Ligier-Renault)   1 lap
6 Karl Wendlinger AUT (Sauber)   1 lap
7 J J Lehto FIN (Sauber)   1 lap
8 Erik Comas FRA (Larrousse-Lamborghini)   1 lap
9 Christian Fittipaldi BRA (Minardi-Ford)   2 laps
10 Johnny Herbert GBR (Lotus-Ford)   2 laps
11 Alessandro Zanardi ITA (Lotus-Ford)   2 laps
12 Thierry Boutsen BEL (Jordan-Hart)   2 laps
13 Aguri Suzuki JPN (Footwork-Honda)   3 laps
14 Michael Andretti USA (McLaren-Ford)   3 laps
15 Luca Badoer ITA (Lola-Ferrari)   4 laps
16 Derek Warwick GBR (Footwork-Honda)   4 laps
17 Ukyo Katayama JPN (Tyrrell-Yamaha)   5 laps
18 Ayrton Senna BRA (McLaren-Ford)   7 laps
Pole position:Prost
Fastest lap:Schumacher 1:21.500 (195.681 kmh)
Hill started better than his teammate, but allowed Prost to pass him on lap six. From that point on, Prost was unharried. At the back end of the race Senna threatened to put the Frenchman under pressure only to be forced into retirement with an alternator failure. Schumacher took second despite stalling twice at the start and dropping down to seventh. Hill, meanwhile, took third despite a near-record for the slowest tyre-change in the nineties - an avoidable 17 seconds. Berger continued the Ferrari revival; they have taken third and fourth in successive GPs. Not quite the old days, yet.
WORLD CHAMPIONSHIP STANDINGS
Drivers:Prost 47, Senna 42, Hill 22, Schumacher 20, Brundle 7, Blundell & Herbert 6, Lehto Patrese Fittipaldi & Berger 5, Alesi 4, Alliot Barbazza &Andretti 2, Zanardi & Wendlinger 1.
Constructors:Williams 69, McLaren 44, Benetton 25, Ligier 13, Ferrari 9, Lotus & Minardi 7, Sauber 6, Larrousse 2.

French Grand Prix
Magny-Cours   July 4

Laps:79 x 4.25km   Total distance:300km
1 **Alain Prost FRA (Williams-Renault)   1:38:35.241**
                                    (186.231 kmh)
2 Damon Hill GBR (Williams-Renault)   at 0.342
3 Michael Schumacher GER (Benetton-Ford)   21.209
4 Ayrton Senna BRA (McLaren-Ford)   32.405
5 Martin Brundle GBR (Ligier-Renault)   33.795
6 Michael Andretti USA (McLaren-Ford)   1 lap
7 Rubens Barrichello BRA (Jordan-Hart)   1 lap
8 Christian Fittipaldi BRA (Minardi-Ford)   1 lap
9 Philippe Alliot FRA (Larrousse-Lamborghini) 1 lap
10 Riccardo Patrese ITA (Benetton-Ford)   1 lap
11 Thierry Boutsen BEL (Jordan-Hart)   2 laps
12 Aguri Suzuki JPN (Footwork-Honda)   2 laps
13 Derek Warwick GBR (Footwork-Honda)   2 laps
14 Gerhard Berger AUT (Ferrari)   2 laps
15 Andrea De Cesaris ITA (Tyrrell-Yamaha)   4 laps
16 Erik Comas FRA (Larrousse-Lamborghini)   6 laps
Pole position:Hill
Fastest lap:Schumacher 1:19.256 (193.045 kmh)
Race leaders:Hill 1-26, Prost 27-72
Prost showed rare emotion as he crossed the line to register his sixth victory at his native GP, taking a French flag from a supporter and waving it exuberantly. For once, Prost had not taken pole position; a brake problem had hindered his preparation and the honour went instead to Hill. There the Briton stayed until a tyre change on lap 27. Again Hill suffered, braking to avoid a collision with Andretti. Prost drove hard for two laps before his own pit stop. He returned to the track still ahead of Hill, and they proceeded, almost in tandem (and with Hill apparently under team instructions not to challenge for victory), for the first Williams 1-2 of the season. Given that last year Mansell and Patrese gave the Williams team three 1-2s in the first three races, this season's progress has been almost modest.
WORLD CHAMPIONSHIP STANDINGS
Drivers:Prost 57, Senna 45, Hill 28, Schumacher 24, Brundle 9, Blundell & Herbert 6, Lehto Patrese Fittipaldi & Berger 5, Alesi 4, Andretti 3, Alliot & Barbazza 2, Zanardi & Wendlinger 1.
Constructors:Williams 85, McLaren 48, Benetton 29, Ligier 15, Ferrari 9, Lotus & Minardi 7, Sauber 6, Larrousse 2.

British Grand Prix
Silverstone   July 11

Laps:59 x 5.226km   Total distance:308.334km
1 **Alain Prost FRA (Williams-Renault)   1:25:38.189**
                                    (216.030 kmh)
2 Michael Schumacher GER (Benetton-Ford) at 7.660
3 Riccardo Patrese ITA (Benetton-Ford)   1:17.482
4 Johnny Herbert GBR (Lotus-Ford)   1:18.407
5 Ayrton Senna BRA (McLaren-Ford)   1 lap
6 Derek Warwick GBR (Footwork-Honda)   1 lap
7 Mark Blundell GBR (Ligier-Renault)   1 lap
8 J J Lehto FIN (Sauber)   1 lap
9 Jean Alesi FRA (Ferrari)   1 lap
10 Rubens Barrichello BRA (Jordan-Hart)   1 lap
11 Philippe Alliot FRA (Larrousse-Lamborghini) 2 laps
12 Christian Fittipaldi BRA (Minardi-Ford) 2 laps

13 Ukyo Katayama JPN (Tyrrell-Yamaha)   4 laps
14 Martin Brundle GBR (Ligier-Renault)   6 laps
Pole position:Prost
Fastest lap:Damon Hill 1:22.515 (228.002 kmh)
Ráce leaders:Hill 1-42, Prost 43-57
In just his eleventh Grand Prix, Hill almost achieved his
first victory. Although there was still some racing to be
done, Hill was leading and favoured for victory, ahead of
Prost, when his smoking engine signalled the worst. The
Briton pulled out, after 42 laps, and left Prost with his
50th Grand Prix victory. Senna had tried early to thwart
Prost's progress, but the power of the Williams engine
took the Frenchman through; Schumacher had tried later
to catch him (assisted by the introduction of the security
car), but the gap never dropped below four seconds.
Prost thus recorded his fifth success in six races; a run
that beginning to resemble that of Mansell a year past.

WORLD CHAMPIONSHIP STANDINGS
Drivers:Prost 67, Senna 47, Schumacher 30, Hill 28, Patrese
Brundle & Herbert 9, Blundell 6, Lehto Fittipaldi & Berger 5,
Alesi 4, Andretti 3, Alliot & Barbazza 2, Zanardi Wendlinger
& Warwick 1.
Constructors:Williams 95, McLaren 50, Benetton 39, Ligier
15, Lotus 10, Ferrari 9, Minardi 7, Sauber 6, Larrousse 2,
Footwork 1.

German Grand Prix
Hockenheim   July 25

Laps:45 x 6.815km Total distance:306.675kmh
1 Alain Prost FRA (Williams-Renault)   1:18:40.885
                                            ((233.861 kmh))
2 Michael Schumacher GER (Benetton-Ford) at 16.664
3 Mark Blundell GBR (Ligier-Renault)   59.349
4 Ayrton Senna BRA (McLaren-Ford)   1:08.229
5 Riccardo Patrese ITA (Benetton-Ford)   1:31.516
6 Gerhard Berger AUT (Ferrari)   1:34.754
7 Jean Alesi FRA (Ferrari)   1:35.841
8 Martin Brundle GBR (Ligier-Renault)   1 lap
9 Karl Wendlinger GER (Sauber)   1 lap
10 Johnny Herbert GBR (Lotus-Ford)   1 lap
11 Christian Fittipaldi BRA (Minardi-Ford) 1 lap
12 Philippe Alliot FRA (Larrouse-Lamborghini) 1 lap
13 Thierry Boutsen BEL (Jordan-Hart)   1 lap
14 Pierluigi Martini (Minardi-Ford)   1 lap
15 Damon Hill GBR (Williams-Renault)   2 laps
16 Michele Alboreto ITA (Lola BMS-Ferrari) 2 laps
17 Derek Warwick GBR (Footwork-Honda)   3 laps
Pole position: Prost
Fastest Lap: Schumacher 1:41.859 (240.862kmh)
Race leaders: Hill 1-7, Prost 8-9, Hill 10-43, Prost 44-45
Poor Hill, the gap twixt cup and lip diminishes with
every race. On his 43rd lap, with the race in his pocket, a
rear tyre on the Briton's Williams did not so much
puncture as shred. Prost had earlier been the recipient of
a cruel stop-go penalty when he took the escape road at
the chicane to avoid Brundle's spinning Ligier. Brundle,
too, incurred a penalty. At that stage the Frenchman was
ahead of Hill. The penalty reversed positions and they
did not change again until Hill's demon struck again.
Senna, who spun off at the chicane on lap one, recovered
from 26th position to finish fourth.

WORLD CHAMPIONSHIP STANDINGS
Drivers:Prost 77, Senna 50, Schumacher 36, Hill 28, Patrese
11, Blundell 10, Brundle & Herbert 9, Berger 6, Lehto &
Fittipaldi 5, Alesi 4, Andretti 3, Alliot & Barbazza 2, Zanardi
Wendlinger & Warwick 1.
Constructors:Williams 105, McLaren 53, Benetton 47, Ligier
19, Ferrari, Lotus 10, Minardi 7, Sauber 6, Larrousse 2,
Footwork 1.

Hungarian Grand Prix
Budapest   Aug 15
Laps:77 x 3.968km   Total distance:305.536km
1 Damon Hill GBR (Williams-Renault)   1:47:39.098
                                          (170.292kmh)
2 Riccardo Patrese ITA (Benetton-Ford) 1:11.195
3 Gerhard Berger AUT (Ferrari)   1:18.042
4 Derek Warwick GBR (Footwork-Honda)   1 lap
5 Martin Brundle GBR (Ligier-Renault)   1 lap
6 Karl Wendlinger AUT (Sauber)   1 lap
7 Mark Blundell GBR (Ligier-Renault)   1 lap
8 Philippe Alliot FRA (Larrousse-Lamborghini) 2 laps
9 Thierry Boutsen BEL (Jordan)   2 laps
10 U Katayama JPN (Tyrrell-Yamaha)   5 laps
11 Andrea de Cesaris ITA (Tyrrell-Yahama) 5 laps
12 Alain Prost FRA (Williams-Renault)   7 laps
Pole Position: Prost
Fastest lap: Prost 1:19.633 (179.383kmh)
Alain Prost, three times a winner here and in pole
position, was favoured to secure his fourth world
championship with a 52nd grand prix win. But Prost had
one of those days. The Frenchman stalled at the start and
was relegated to the back of the grid. He flew through the
field into fourth place, but then a broken rear wing
caused a lengthy pit-stop and that was that. He could be
relieved, though, that it was Hill, shaking off his demons,
who finally won a grand prix. It meant that Prost's 27
point lead in the title race remained intact. For Hill, it
was a euphoric day. "I thought of my dad," he said, "Of
him telling me to keep concentrating." Hill was
unfortunate in one sense; he scored his first win on the
day that Linford Christie won the world 100m title and
Nick Faldo just missed out in the US PGA, so he didn't
quite make back-page headlines.
WORLD CHAMPIONSHIP STANDINGS
Drivers: Prost 77, Senna 50, Hill 38, Schumacher 36, Patrese
17, Brundle 11, Blundell, & Berger 10, Herbert 9, Lehto &
Fittipaldi 5, Alesi & Warwick 4, Andretti 3, Alliot
,Wendlinger & Barbazza 2, Zanardi 1.
Constructors:Williams 115, McLaren & Benetton 53,, Ligier
21, Ferrari 14,Lotus 10, Sauber & Minardi 7, Footwork 4,
Larrousse 2.

Belgian Grand Prix
Spa-Francorchamps   Aug 29
Laps:44 x 6.940km   Total distance:305.360km
1 Damon Hill GBR (Williams-Renault)   1:24:32.124
                                          (217.795kmh)
2 Michael Schumacher GER (Benetton-Ford) 3.668
3 Alain Prost FRA (Williams-Renault)   14.988
4 Ayrton Senna BRA (McLaren-Ford)   1:39.763
5 Johnny Herbert GBR (Lotus-Ford)   1 lap
6 Riccardo Patrese ITA (Benetton-Ford) 1 lap

7	Martin Brundle GBR (Ligier-Renault)	1 lap
8	Michael Andretti USA (McLaren-Ford)	1 lap
9	J-J Lehto FIN (Sauber)	1 lap
10	Gerhard Berger AUT (Ferrari)	2 laps
11	Mark Blundell GBR (Ligier-Renault)	2 laps
12	Philippe Alliot FRA (Larrousse-Lamborghini)	2 laps
13	Luca Badoer ITA (Lola-Ferrari)	2 laps
14	Michele Alboreto ITA (Lola-Ferrari)	3 laps
15	U Katayama JPN (Tyrrell-Yamaha)	4 laps

Pole position: Prost
Fastest lap: Prost 1:51.095 (225.990kmh)

Hill, having broken the spell, found a second victory following hard on the heels of the first. It was nothing like as facile a victory as Budapest. On one of the faster circuits, Hill had a humdinger of a drive-off against Schumacher and Prost. Hill's victory assured Williams of yet another constructors' championship and notched up a 50th grand prix win for Renault.

WORLD CHAMPIONSHIP STANDINGS
Drivers: Prost 81, Senna 53, Hill 48, Schumacher 42, Patrese 18, Brundle & Herbert 11, Blundell & Berger 10, Lehto & Fittipaldi 5, Alesi & Warwick 4, Andretti 3, Alliot, Wendlinger & Barbazza 2, Zanardi 1.
Constructors:Williams 129, Benetton 60, McLaren 56,, Ligier 21, Ferrari 14,Lotus 12, Sauber & Minardi 7, Footwork 4, Larrousse 2.

Italian Grand Prix

Monza   Sept 12

Laps:53 x 5.8km   Total distance:307.4km

1	**Damon Hill GBR (Williams-Renault)**	**1:17:7.509**
		(239.144kmh)
2	Jean Alesi FRA (Ferrari)	40.012
3	Michael Andretti USA (McLaren-Ford)	1 lap
4	Karl Wendlinger AUT (Sauber)	1 lap
5	Riccardo Patrese ITA (Benetton-Ford)	1 lap
6	Erik Comas FRA (Larrousse-Lamborghini)	2 laps
7	Pierluigi Martini ITA (Minardi-Ford)	2 laps
8	Christian Fittipaldi BRA (Minardi-Ford)	2 laps
9	Philippe Alliot FRA (Larrousse-Lamborghini)	2 laps
10	Luca Badoer ITA (Lola-Ferrari)	2 laps
11	P Lamy POR (Lotus-Ferrari)	4 laps
12	Alain Prost FRA (Williams-Renault)	5 laps
13	Andrea de Cesaris ITA (Tyrrell-Yamaha)	6 laps
14	U Katayama JPN (Tyrrell-Yahama)	6 laps

Pole position: Prost
Fastest lap: Hill 1:23.575

Hill was bouncing from one peak to the next; in three races he had gone from a maiden F1 driver to a championship challenger. Indeed, after this race there really was no other possible challenger to Prost. The Frenchman, though, must have been a bit miffed. While Hill was having a little early race set-about with Senna's McLaren, Prost took control. For 48 of the 53 laps, Prost led. Hill was even signalled by the Williams pit, after recording the fastest lap, to obey instructions and follow Prost home. But, with only five laps left (around 18 miles or seven and a bit minutes), the Frenchman's engine splurted oil and that was that. Hill took over, with Alesi some distance away in second and Michael Andretti, desperate for success, getting into the frame.

Drivers: Prost 81, Hill 58, Senna 53, Schumacher 42, Patrese 20, Brundle & Herbert 11, Blundell Berger & Alesi 10, Andretti 7, Lehto Wendlinger & Fittipaldi 5, Warwick 4, Alliot & Barbazza 2, Zanardi & Comas 1.
Constructors:Williams 139, Benetton 62, McLaren 60,, Ligier 21, Ferrari 20,Lotus 12, Sauber 10, Minardi 7, Footwork 4, Larrousse 3.

Portuguese Grand Prix

Estoril   Sept 26

Laps:71 x 4.35km   Total distance:308.85km

1	**Michael Schumacher GER (Benetton-F)**	**1:32:46.309**
		(199.619kmh)
2	Alain Prost FRA (Williams-Renault)	0.982
3	Damon Hill GBR (Willliams-Renault)	8.206
4	Jean Alesi ITA (Ferrari)	1:7.605
5	Karl Wendlinger AUT (Sauber)	1 lap
6	Martin Brundle GBR (Ligier-Renault	1 lap
7	J J Lehto FIN (Sauber)	2 laps
8	Pierluigi Martini ITA (Minardi-Ford)	2 laps
9	Christian Fittipaldi BRA (Minardi-Ford	2 laps
10	Philippe Alliot FRA (Larrousse-Lamborghini)	2 laps
11	Erik Comas FRA (Larrousse-Lamborghini)	3 laps
12	Andrea de Cesaris ITA (Tyrrell-Yahama)	3 laps
13	Rubens Barrichello BRA (Jordan-Hart)	3 laps

Pole position: Hill

Schumacher, driving the spare Benetton because of handling difficulties with the first car, took a tactical shot at staying with the same tyres after an early pit stop and brought off a well-earned victory. Prost, in the faster Williams, put him under considerable pressure, but at the line the second between them was enough. Hill did a Prost, stalling on the start line and having to restart at the back. Hill came through the field to third, but this was his teammate's day. Finally, the Frenchman had put the title beyond anyone's grasp. The Frenchman wasn't exactly overwhelmed by it all; indeed, he was decidedly miserable. He had announced his retirement a few days earlier. It remains to be seen whether he will even see out the last two events.

Drivers: Prost 87, Hill 62, Senna 53, Schumacher 52, Patrese 20, Alesi & Brundle 12, Herbert 11, Blundell & Berger 10, Andretti 7, Wendlinger 7, Lehto 5, Fittipaldi 5, Warwick 4, Alliot & Barbazza 2, Zanardi & Comas 1
Constructors: Williams 149, Benetton 72, McLaren 60, Ferrari 23, Ligier & Renault 22, Lotus 12

1992 Season

Japanese Grand Prix

Suzuka   Oct 25, 1992
Laps:53 x 5.859km   Total distance:310.792km
1 **Riccardo Patrese ITA (Williams-Renault) 1:33:9.553**
(200.168 kmh)
2 Gerhard Berger AUT (McLaren Honda)   at 13.729
3 Martin Brundle GBR (Benetton-Ford)   1:15.503
4 Andrea De Cesaris ITA (Tyrrell-Ilmor)   1 lap
5 Jean Alesi FRA (Ferrari)   1 lap
6 Christian Fittipaldi BRA (Minardi-Lamb'ghini) 1 lap
Pole position:Mansell
Fastest lap:Mansell 1:40.646 (209.570 kmh)
Race leaders:Mansell 1-35, Patrese 36-53
Mansell opened up a comfortable 19 second lead before, on lap 36, allowing his teammate Patrese through. It was a concession that the Briton had apparently made to the Italian before the race. The Japanese might have been excused for thinking that such an agreement rather devalued the event. As it happened, Mansell was forced to retire anyway on the 45th lap when his engine caught fire. Brundle climbed from his sick-bed (he had food poisoning) to claim third.

Australian Grand Prix

Adelaide   Nov 8
Laps:81 x 3.778km   Total distance:306.180km
1 **Gerhard Berger AUT (McLaren-Honda) 1:46:54.786**
(179.829 kmh)
2 Michael Schumacher GER (Benetton-Ford)   at 0.741
3 Martin Brundle GBR (Benetton-Ford)   53.415
4 Jean Alesi FRA (Ferrari)   1 lap
5 Thierry Boutsen BEL (Ligier-Renault)   1 lap
6 Stefano Modena ITA (Jordan-Yamaha)   1 lap
Pole position:Mansell
Race leaders:Mansell 1-16, Patrese 17-50, Berger 51-81
It might have been a dream season for Nigel Mansell, but it wasn't a dream ending. Mansell looked to be on the way to a record 10 wins for the season when Ayrton Senna clattered straight into the backside of the Williams car and took Mansell out of the race. "He braked early..."claimed Senna, as a fuming Mansell stormed off the track. The Briton protested, but in vain. It was an unhappy ending to (maybe) his last Formula 1 outing. Patrese looked to be carrying the Williams flag to victory before mechanical troubles ended his hopes on lap 51, leaving the way open to Berger. Brundle's third place brought him points for the 11th time in 12 races.

PROST'S 51

Year	Grands Prix
1981	France, Holland, Italy
1982	South Africa, Brazil
1983	France, Belgium, Britain, Austria
1984	Brazil, San Marino, Monaco, Germany, Holland, Europe(Nuremburg) Portugal
1985	Brazil, Monaco, Britain, Austria, Italy *World Champion*
1986	San Marino, Monaco, Austria, Australia *World Champion*
1987	Brazil, Belgium, Portugal
1988	Brazil, Monaco, Mexico, France, Portugal, Spain, Australia
1989	United States, France, Britain, Italy *World Champion*
1990	Brazil, Mexico, France, Britain, Spain
1993	South Africa, San Marino, Spain, Canada, France, Britain Germany *World Champion*

Grand Prix Hierarchy: Prost 51 wins (from 192 GPs), Senna 39, Mansell 30, Stewart 27, Clark & Lauda 25, Fangio 24, Piquet 23, Moss 16, Brabham, Fittipaldi, G Hill 14. *(as at 1/10/93)*

Indy Car World Series (PPG)

The Indy Car Series comprises 16 races; 15 in north America and one in Australia(the first). In the race charts below, the drivers are given in finish positions, the numbers in brackets after the placings refer to the start grid position. The Laps column gives the position of the driver when the winner crossed the line - if the car withdrew, then it will show on which lap. If the driver was also in the final lap, the Status column shows an average speed figure. Otherwise, the Status column shows Running if the car was still racing (but not on the final lap) or the reason for withdrawal. The figure in brackets refers to the qualifying speeds.

Australian FAI Grand Prix(Race 1)

Surfers Paradise, Queensland　　　Mar 21

	Driver	Ctry	Car	Laps	Status	Awards	Pts	Total
1 (1)	Nigel Mansell	GBR	Kmart Texaco L93 Ford Cos	65	97.284(102.095)	M*AC	21	21
2 (2)	Emerson Fittipaldi	BRA	Marlboro Penske 93 Chevy V8/C	65	97.210(101.758)	AC	17	17
3 (4)	Robby Gordon	USA	Copenhagen Racing L92 Ford Cos	65	97.203(101.192)		14	14
4 (6)	Mario Andretti	USA	Kmart Texaco L93 Ford Cos	65	97.073(100.884)	AC	12	12
5 (5)	Arie Luyendyk	HOL	Target-Scotch Video L93 Ford Cos	65	96.606(100.988)	AC	10	10
6 (13)	Bobby Rahal	USA	Miller Draft R/H Chevy V8/C	64	Running	AC	8	8
7 (16)	Eddie Cheever	USA	No Drugs Penske 92 Chevy V8/B	64	Running		6	6
8 (8)	Raul Boesel	BRA	Duracell-Mobil 1 L93 Ford Cos	64	Running		5	5
9 (12)	Teo Fabi	ITA	Pennzoil Special L 93 Chevy V8/C	64	Running		4	4
10 (7)	Scott Goodyear	CAN	Mackenzie Special L93 Ford Cos	63	Running		3	3
11 (24)	Hiro Matsushita	JPN	Panasonic Special L93 Ford Cos	63	Running		2	2
12 (18)	Stefan Johansson	SWE	AMAX Metals PC 93 Ch V8/C	63	Running		1	1
Also								
21 (3)	Paul Tracy	CAN	Marlboro Penske 93 Chevy V8/C	30	Electrical		-	-

Time of Race:1:52:02.886 Margin of Victory: 5.113 Lap Leaders:Emerson Fittipaldi 1-15, Nigel Mansell 16-18, Fittipaldi 19-21, Mansell 22-29, Fittipaldi 30-44, Mansell 45-65

Nigel Mansell became only the second rookie to enjoy a victory on his debut in Indy Car following Graham Hill in 1966. The street circuit at Surfers Paradise offered few obstacles to a man who had Formula One opposition on similar tracks worldwide. Of his drive in Australia, one commentator called his performance "courageous to the point of foolhardiness." Colin Chapman once said of driving "the really good driver wins races not in the quickest time but in the slowest". This is a view obviously not shared by Mansell who continued to push himself to the limits of his ability. Disaster nearly ensued when, with the race won, he brushed one of the concrete walls. He recovered to show that even he relies on Lady Luck once in a while.

Valvoline 200(Race 2)

Phoenix, Arizona　　　Apr 4

	Driver	Ctry	Car	Laps	Status	Awards	Pts	Total
1 (2)	Mario Andretti	USA	Kmart Texaco L93 Ford Cos	200	123.847(172.294)	AC	20	32
2 (6)	Raul Boesel	BRA	Duracell-Mobil 1 L93 Ford Cos	199	Running	STP	16	21
3 (9)	Jimmy Vasser	USA	Kodalux STP L92 CH V8/A	197	Running		14	14
4 (13)	Al Unser Jr	USA	Valvoline L93 CH V8/C	197	Running	AC	12	12
5 (8)	Teo Fabi	ITA	Pennzoil Special L93 CH V8/C	196	Running	AC	10	14
6 (10)	Arie Luyendyk	HOL	Target-Scotch Video L93 Ford Cos	195	Running	AC	8	18
7 (15)	Scott Pruett	USA	Tobacco-Free USA L91 CH V8/A	194	Running	AC	6	6
8 (22)	David Kudrave	USA	Andrea Moda L92 CH V8/A	193	Running		5	5
9 (11)	Mark Smith	USA	Craftsman Penske 92 CH V8/B	192	Running		4	4
10 (17)	Hiro Matsushita	JPN	Panasonic Special L93 Ford Cos	187	Running		3	5
11 (24)	Marco Greco	BRA	Team Losi L92 CH V8/A	183	Running		2	2
12 (25)	Ross Bentley	CAN	AGFA-Rain X L92 CH V8/A	183	Running		1	1
Also								
14 (3)	Emerson Fittipaldi	BRA	Marlboro Penske 93 CH V8/C	171	Contact		-	17
16 (5)	Paul Tracy	CAN	Marlboro Penske 93 CH V8/C	161	Contact		1	1
20 (1)	Scott Goodyear	CAN	Mackenzie Special L93 Ford Cos	116	Gearbox	M	1	4

Time of Race:1:36:53.630 Margin of Victory:22.378 Lap Leaders:Mario Andretti 1-10, Paul Tracy 11-161, Emerson Fittipaldi 162-171, Andretti 172-200

Mansell missed the second race of the series after connecting with the wall in practice at the Phoenix International Raceway. After being airlifted to hospital, Mansell was banned by doctors from the race which was won by Newman-Haas team-mate Andretti. Mansell said of his first experience of oval racing "I suppose it's a case of welcome to the club. I'm mega disappointed." Meanwhile Andretti became the oldest race winner at the sprightly age of 53 years and 34 days, ending a long barren streak for the former F1 world champion.

Toyota Grand Prix of Long Beach(Race 3)

Long Beach, California   Apr 18

	Driver	Ctry	Car	Laps	Status	Awards	Pts	Total
1 (2)	Paul Tracy	CAN	Marlboro Penske 93 CH V8/C	105	93.089(107.705)	AC	21	22
2 (11)	Bobby Rahal	USA	Miller DraftR/H Chevy V8/C	105	92.907(106.453)	AC	16	24
3 (1)	Nigel Mansell	GBR	Kmart Texaco L93 Ford Cos	105	92.809(108.198)	ACM	15	36
4 (7)	Teo Fabi	ITA	Pennzoil Special L93 CH V8/C	105	92.332(106.875)	AC	12	26
5 (18)	Roberto Guerrero	COL	Budweiser King L93 Chevy V8/C	104	Running	AC	10	10
6 (23)	Robbie Buhl	USA	MI-JACK L92 Chevy Indy V8/A	104	Running		8	8
7 (15)	Scott Pruett	USA	Tobacco Free USA L91 Chevy V8/A	103	Running		6	12
8 (12)	Danny Sullivan	USA	Molson L93 Chevy V8/C	103	Running		5	5
9 (10)	Eddie Cheever	USA	No Drugs Penske 92 Chevy V8/B	103	Running		4	10
10 (14)	Mark Smith	USA	Craftsman Penske 92 Chevy V8/B	103	Running		3	7
11 (19)	Arie Luyendyk	HOL	Target-Scotch Video L93 Ford Cos	103	Running		2	20
12 (9)	Raul Boesel	BRA	Duracell-Mobil L93 Ford Cos	102	Electrical		1	22
Also								
13 (3)	Emerson Fittipaldi	BRA	Marlboro Penske 93 Chevy V8/C	102	Running		-	17
18 (6)	Mario Andretti	USA	Kmart Texaco L93 Ford Cos	94	Electrical		-	32

Time of Race:1:47:36.418 Margin of Victory:12.658 Lap Leaders:Nigel Mansell 1-4, Paul Tracy 5-35, Mansell 36-42, Tracy 43-60, Mansell 61-73, Tracy 74-105

Indianapolis 500(Race 4)

Speedway, Indianapolis   May 30

	Driver	Ctry	Car	Laps	Status	Awards	Pts	Total
1 (9)	Emerson Fittipaldi	BRA	Marlboro Penske 93 Chevy V8/C	200	157.207(220.150)		20	37
2 (1)	Arie Luyendyk	HOL	Target-Scitch Video L93 Ford Cos	200	157.168(223.967)		17	37
3 (8)	Nigel Mansell	GBR	Kmart Texaco L93 Ford Cos	200	157.149(220.255)		14	50
4 (3)	Raul Boesel	BRA	Duracell-Mobil L93 Ford Cos	200	157.142(222.379)		12	34
5 (2)	Mario Andretti	USA	Kmart Texaco L93 Ford Cos	200	157.133(223.414)		11	43
6 (11)	Scott Brayton	USA	Amway/Byrd's L93 Ford Cos	200	157.117(219.637)		8	8
7 (4)	Scott Goodyear	CAN	Mackenzie Financial L93 Ford Cos	200	157.099(222.344)		6	10
8 (5)	Al Unser Jr	USA	Valvoline L93 Chevy V8/C	200	157.070(221.773)		5	17
9 (17)	Teo Fabi	ITA	Pennzoil Special L93 Chevy V8/C	200	156.968(220.514)		4	30
10 (24)	John Andretti	USA	AJFoyt/Copenhagen L92 Ford Cos	200	156.964(221.746)		3	3
11 (6)	Stefan Johansson	SWE	AMAX Metals PC 93C V8/C	199	Running		2	3
12 (23)	Al Unser	USA	Budweiser king L93 Chevy V8/C	199	Running		1	1
Also								
30 (7)	Paul Tracy	CAN	Marlboro Penske 93 Chevy V8/C	94	Contact		-	22

Time of Race:3:10:49.860 Margin of Victory:2.862 Lap Leaders:Raul Boesel 1-17, Stephan Gregoire 18, Kevin Cogan 19-22, Al Unser 23-31, Mario Andretti 32-46, Arie Luyendyk 47-57, Unser 58-63, John Andretti 64-65, Robby Gordon 66-67, Scott Goodyear 68-69, Nigel Mansell 70-91, M Andretti 92-128, Mansell 129-130, Luyendyk 131-132, Al Unser Jr 135-151, M Andretti 152-168, Goodyear 169-171, M Andretti 172, Boesel 173, M Andretti 174, Mansell 175-184, Emerson Fittipaldi 185-200

Watched by 450,000 spectators Mansell narrowly lost a thrilling race after being jumped by Fittipaldi when the pace car pulled off with 15 laps to go. With the field condensed after a yellow flag, Mansell was caught cold and had to battle against the field and the concrete to come through in third place. Nevertheless he had gone a long way to convince a sceptical American public that he could race competitively on oval circuits, claiming the distincion of being the first rookie to complete the 500 miles since 1970.

Miller Genuine Draft 200(Race 5)

West Allis, Wisconsin   June 6

	Driver	Ctry	Car	Laps	Status	Awards	Pts	Total
1 (7)	Nigel Mansell	GBR	Kmart Texaco L93 Ford Cos	200	110.970(160.414)	ACS	20	70
2 (1)	Raul Boesel	BRA	Duracell-Mobil L93 Ford Cos	200	110.961(165.752)	M	18	52
3 (2)	Emerson Fittipaldi	BRA	Marlboro Penske 93 Chevy V8/C	200	110.894(161.057)	AC	14	51
4 (9)	Bobby Rahal	USA	Miller Draft L93 Chevy V8/C	200	110.743(157.912)	AC	12	36
5 (18)	Al Unser Jr	USA	Valvoline L93 Chevy V8/C	198	Running	AC	10	27
6 (6)	Scott Brayton	USA	Amway-N'West Air L93 Ford Cos	198	Running		8	16
7 (10)	Roberto Guerrero	COL	Budweiser King L93 Chevy V8/C	198	Running	AC	6	16
8 (13)	Jimmy Vasser	USA	Kodalux-STP L92 Chevy V8/A	196	Running		5	19
9 (14)	Teo Fabi	ITA	Pennzoil Special L93 Chevy V8/C	195	Running		4	34
10 (8)	Robby Gordon	USA	Copenhagen Racing L93 Ford Cos	193	Running		3	17

11 (21)	Willy T Ribbs	USA	Cosby-Service L92 Ford Cos	193	Running	2	2
12 (15)	Olivier Grouillard	FRA	Eurosport-M'boro L92 Chevy V8/A	191	Running	1	1

Also

18 (5)	Mario Andretti	USA	Kmart Texaco L93 Ford Cos	176	Running	-	43
20 (4)	Paul Tracy	CAN	Marlboro Penske 93 Chevy V8/C	141	Contact	-	22

Time of Race:1:48:08.245 Margin of Victory:0.514 Lap Leaders:Raul Boesel 1-45, Scott Goodyear 46-75, Robby Gordon 76, Mike Groff 77, Goodyear 78-82, Paul Tracy 83-115, Gordon 116-119, Tracy 120-141, Boesel 142-181, Nigel Mansell 182-200
Being in the lead in an Indy Car race guarantees you nothing. With 2 laps remaining the ubiquitous pace car emerged to test the resolve of Mansell. "I learned a very painful lesson in Indianapolis on the re-start there. I wasn't going to let that happen again." Mansell survived a late assault by Boesel to record his first oval win on the 1 mile track having had to carve his way through the field to achieve it.

ITT Automotive Detroit Grand Prix(Race 6)
Detroit, Michigan   June 13

Driver	Ctry	Car	Laps	Status	Awards	Pts	Total
1 (10) Danny Sullivan	USA	Molson L93 Chevy V8/C	77	83.116(104.356)	ACS	21	26
2 (11) Raul Boesel	BRA	Duracell-Mobil L93 Ford Cos	77	82.972		16	68
2 (9) Mario Andretti	USA	Kmart Texaco L93 Ford Cos	77	82.932(104.486)	AC	14	57
4 (6) Andrea Montermini	ITA	Moda-Agip-ETI L92 Chevy V8/A	77	82.911(104.823)		12	12
5 (5) Bobby Rahal	USA	Miller Draft R/H Chevy V8/C	77	82.908(104.962)	AC	10	46
6 (7) Al Unser Jr	USA	Valvoline L93 Chevy V8/C	77	82.796(104.723)	AC	8	35
7 (21) Adrian Fernandez	MEX	Tecate-Amway L93 Chevy V8/C	77	82.696(102.640)	AC	6	6
8 (8) Robby Gordon	USA	AJFoyt-Copenhagen L93 Ford Cos	77	82.046(104.553)		5	22
9 (3) Paul Tracy	CAN	Marlboro Penske 93 Chevy V8/C	76	Tyre		4	26
10 (22) Scott Goodyear	CAN	Mackenzie Special L93 Ford Cos	76	Running		3	13
11 (24) Mike Groff	USA	Miller Draft L1 Sp R/H Chevy V8/C	75	Running		2	2
12 (25) Willy T Ribbs	USA	Cosby-Service Spl L93 Ford Cos	75	Running		1	3

Also

15 (1) Nigel Mansell	GBR	Kmart Texaco L93 Ford Cos	68	Contact	M	1	71
23 (2) Emerson Fittipaldi	BRA	Marlboro Penske 93 Chevy V8/C	37	Contact		-	51

Time of Race:1:56:43.678 Margin of Victory:12.206 Lap leaders:Emerson Fittipaldi 1-12, Paul Tracy 13-38, Bobby Rahal 39-46, Tracy 47, Danny Sullivan 48-77
Oval walls and Nigel Mansell have become synonymous whether he is clipping them or ploughing into them. His latest brush with concrete forced him to slide off the track and out of contention. Sullivan recorded his 17th career victory having been pushed hard by team-mate Al Unser Jr whose challenge was effectively finished after picking up a penalty for striking a traffic cone.

Budweiser/G I Joe's 200(Race 7)
Portland, Oregon   June 27

Driver	Ctry	Car	Laps	Status	Awards	Pts	Total
1 (2) Emerson Fittipaldi	BRA	Marlboro Penske 93 Chevy V8/C	102	96.312(115.069)	AC	21	72
2 (1) Nigel Mansell	GBR	Kmart Texaco L93 Ford Cos	102	96.255(115.266)	ACSM	17	88
3 (4) Paul Tracy	CAN	Marlboro Penske 93 Chevy V8/C	102	96.179(114.008)	AC	14	40
4 (15) Bobby Rahal	USA	Miller Draft Sp L93 Chevy V8/C	101	Running	AC	12	58
5 (9) Al Unser Jr	USA	Valvoline L93 Chevy V8/C	101	Running	AC	10	45
6 (5) Mario Andretti	USA	Kmart Texaco L93 Ford Cos	101	Running		8	65
7 (11) Raul Boesel	BRA	Duracell-Mobil L93 Ford Cos	100	Running		6	74
8 (10) Robby Gordon	USA	AJFoyt Copenhagen L93 Ford Cos	100	Running		5	27
9 (12) Mike Groff	USA	Miller Draft R/H-Chevy V8/C	100	Running		4	6
10 (14) Arie Luyendyk	HOL	Target-Scotch Video L93 Ford Cos	99	Running		3	40
11 (22) Jimmy Vasser	USA	Kodalux-STP L92 Chevy V8/A	99	Running		2	21
12 (16) Scott Goodyear	CAN	Mackenzie Special L93 Ford Cos	98	Fuel		1	14

Time of Race:2:03:54.620 Margin of Victory:4.359 Lap leaders:Nigel Mansell 1-27, Emerson Fittipaldi 28-33,Mario Andretti 34, Fittipaldi 35-48, Mansell 49-52, Fittipaldi 53-102
Fittipaldi, the veteran Brazilian and former F1 world champion, won his second race of the series amid fluctuating weather conditions which forced a flurry of pit stops. Mansell again showed his pedigree to retain his series lead, though higher honours were denied him when he slid off the track on lap 27 and dropped to fourth. However, as the sun came out, a full course yellow flag set up a sprint over the final 10 laps, though the experience of Fittipaldi was sufficient to keep him ahead of the pack.

Budweiser Grand Prix of Cleveland(Race 8)

Cleveland, Ohio   July 11

	Driver	Ctry	Car	Laps	Status	Awards	Pts	Total
1 (1)	Paul Tracy	CAN	Marlboro Penske 93 Chevy V8/C	85	127.913(144.139)	ACM	22	62
2 (3)	Emerson Fittipaldi	BRA	Marlboro Penske 93 Chevy V8/C	85	Running	AC	16	88
3 (2)	Nigel Mansell	GBR	Kmart Texaco L93 Ford Cos	85	Running	AC	14	102
4 (4)	Stefan Johansson	SWE	AMAX Metals PC 93 Chevy V8/C	84	Running	DH	12	15
5 (11)	Mario Andretti	USA	Kmart Texaco L93 Ford Cos	84	Running	AC	10	75
6 (20)	Robby Gordon	USA	AJFoyt/Copenhagen L93 Ford Cos	84	Running	DH	8	35
7 (12)	Raul Boesel	BRA	Duracell-Mobil L93 Ford Cos	84	Running	DH	6	80
8 (9)	Teo Fabi	ITA	Pennzoil Special L93 Chevy V8/C	84	Running		5	39
9 (13)	Brian Till	USA	No Drugs Penske 92 Chevy V8/B	83	Running	DH	4	4
10 (15)	Arie Luyendyk	HOL	Target-Scotch Video L93 Ford Cos	83	Running		3	43
11 (17)	Olivier Grouillard	FRA	Eurosport-M'boro L92 Chevy V8/A	82	Running	DH	2	3
12 (21)	Hiro Matsushita	JPN	Panasonic Special L93 Ford Cos	81	Running		1	6

Time of Race:1:34:27.254 Margin of Victory:18.090 Lap Leaders:Nigel Mansell 1-14, Paul Tracy 15-30, Mansell 31, Tracy 32-60, Mansell 61, Tracy 62-85

Paul Tracy, the Canadian who has led more laps in the series than any other driver, turned his pole position to full advantage to claim his second victory of the season. Mansell had squeezed his way into the lead at the start, avoiding a multiple collision on the first hairpin that accounted for local favourite Bobby Rahal and Roberto Guerrero. Mansell again lost the lead following a re-start, with Tracy dominating the remainder of the 2.369 mile, 10 turn temporary road course to set up a Penske one-two to close the gap on Mansell in the championship.

Molson Indy Toronto(Race 9)

Toronto, Ontario   July 18

	Driver	Ctry	Car	Laps	Status	Awards	Pts	Total
1 (2)	Paul Tracy	CAN	Marlboro Penske 93 Chevy V8/C	103	96.510(109.544)	AC	21	83
2 (1)	Emerson Fittipaldi	BRA	Marlboro Penske 93 Chevy V8/C	103	96.326(109.997)	ACM	17	105
3 (4)	Danny Sullivan	USA	Molson L93 Chevy V8/C	103	96.310(109.286)	AC	14	40
4 (3)	Bobby Rahal	USA	Miller Draft R/H Chevy V8/C	103	96.301(109.331)	AC	12	70
5 (7)	Al Unser Jr	USA	Valvoline L93 Chevy V8/C	103	96.294(109.033)	AC	10	55
6 (12)	Robby Gordon	USA	AJFoyt/Copenhagen L93 Ford Cos	103	95.854(108.459)		8	43
7 (6)	Raul Boesel	BRA	Duracell-Mobil L93 Ford Cos	103	95.854(109.162)		6	86
8 (13)	Mario Andretti	USA	Kmart Texaco L93 Ford Cos	102	Running		5	80
9 (10)	Scott Goodyear	CAN	Mackenzie Special L93 Ford Cos	102	Running		4	18
10 (14)	Roberto Guerrero	COL	Budweiser King L93 Chevy V8/C	102	Running		3	19
11 (17)	Jimmy Vasser	USA	Kodalux STP L92 Ford Cos	101	Running		2	23
12 (15)	Bertrand Gachot	BEL	CAPA L92 Ford Cosworth	101	Running		1	1
Also								
20 (9)	Nigel Mansell	GBR	Kmart Texaco L93 Ford Cos	55	Wastegate		-	102

Time of Race:1:53:58.951 Margin of Victory:13.023 Lap Leaders:Emerson Fittipaldi 1-15, Paul Tracy 16-38, Fittipaldi 39-72, Tracy 73-103

The Canadians turned out in force to will home driver Paul Tracy on to his second successive victory Amid interruptions caused by yellow flags, Fittipaldi took the lead in the championship after claiming second place and seeing Mansell retire. A struggling Mansell was forced to retire after only 55 laps with smoke billowing from his car - the result of a broken wastegate valve. Mansell never got to grips with the bumpy 1.78 mile Exhibition Place street circuit crashing twice in qualifying and practice.

Marlboro 500(Race 10)

Brooklyn, Michigan   Aug 1

	Driver	Ctry	Car	Laps	Status	Awards	Pts	Total
1 (2)	Nigel Mansell	GBR	Kmart Texaco L93 Ford Cos	250	188.203(233.462)	ACS	21	123
2 (1)	Mario Andretti	USA	Kmart Texaco L93 Ford Cos	250	188.018(234.275)	ACSM	17	97
3 (3)	Arie Luyendyk	HOL	Target-Scotch Video L93 Ford Cos	249	Running	AC	14	57
4 (4)	Raul Boesel	BRA	Duracell-Mobil L93 Ford Cos	248	Running	DH	12	98
5 (6)	Scott Goodyear	CAN	Mackenzie Special L93 Ford Cos	247	Running	DH	10	28
6 (8)	Teo Fabi	ITA	Pennzoil Special L93 Ch V8/C	246	Running	AC	8	47
7 (11)	Roberto Guerrero	COL	Budweiser King L93 Ch V8/C	245	Running	AC	6	25
8 (17)	Al Unser Jr	USA	Valvoline L93 Chevy V8/C	245	Running		5	60
9 (16)	Bobby Rahal	USA	Miller Draft L93 Ch V8/C	243	Running		4	74

10 (13)	Willy T Ribbs	USA	Cosby-Service L93 Ford Cos	243	Running	DH	3	6
11 (7)	Scott Brayton	USA	Amway-N'west Air L93 Ford Cos	241	Running	DH	2	18
12 (19)	David Kudrave	USA	Moda-Agip L92 Ch V8/A	239	Running	DH	1	6

Also

13 (15)	Emerson Fittipaldi	BRA	Marlboro Penske 93 Chevy V8/C	237	Running		-	105
19 (5)	Paul Tracy	CAN	Marlboro Penske 93 Chevy V8/C	114	Engine		-	83

Time of Race:2:39:24.131 Margin of Victory:9.434 Lap Leaders:Mario Andretti 1-27, Nigel Mansell 28-82, Arie Luyendyk 83, Mansell 84-250

Prior to the race Mansell had created a storm by making an official protest to the circuit's chief steward. "When a circuit is this bumpy, it is not bad to drive at 160mph, but it is unacceptable at 230mph. I'm not happy and I'm not shy about expressing my opinion." He was somewhat more mellow after completing what he described as "the greatest victory of my career", which took him back to the top of the championship. It was also a triumph for the Newman-Haas team, which recorded a one-two on the circuit owned by their great rival Roger Penske. Mansell, suffering from acute nausea, amended his view of the track when he said afterwards, "This is a fantastic circuit. It stands alone."

New England 200(Race 11)
London, New Hampshire   Aug 8

	Driver	Ctry	Car	Laps	Status	Awards	Pts	Total
1 (1)	Nigel Mansell	GBR	Kmart Texaco L93 Ford Cos	200	130.148(169.247)		21	144
2 (4)	Paul Tracy	CAN	Marlboro Penske 93 Chevy V8/C	200	130.138(167.788)		17	100
3 (13)	Emerson Fittipaldi	BRA	Marlboro Penske 93 Chevy V8/C	200	129.953(`64.096)		14	119
4 (5)	Roberto Guerrero	USA	Budweiser King L93 Chevy V8/C	199	Running		12	37
5 (14)	Robby Gordon	USA	AJFoyt/Copenhagen L93 Ford Cos	199	Running		10	53
6 (7)	Scott Brayton	USA	Amway-N'west Air L93 Ford Cos	198	Running		8	26
7 (9)	Bobby Rahal	USA	Miller Draft L93 Chevy V8/C	197	Running		6	80
8 (15)	Al Unser jr	USA	Valvoline L93 Chevy V8/C	197	Running		5	65
9 (11)	Jimmy Vasser	USA	Kodalux-STP L92 Ford Cos	194	Running		4	27
10 (21)	Brian Till	USA	No Drugs PC92 Chevy V8/C	194	Running		3	7
11 (16)	Mike Groff	USA	Miller Draft R/H Chevy V8/C	194	Running		2	8
12 (19)	Olivier Grouillard	FRA	Eurosport-M'boro L92 Chevy V8/A	192	Running		1	4

Also

20 (6)	Mario Andretti	USA	Kmart Texaco L93 Ford Cos	137	Contact		-	97
21 (2)	Raul Boesel	BRA	Duracell-Mobil L93 Ford Cos	120	Contact		-	98

Time of Race: 1:37:33.033 Lap Leaders:Nigel Mansell 1-40, Paul Tracy 41-68, Mansell 69-94, Tracy 95-196, Mansell 197-200

If life really does begin at 40, then Nigel Mansell should look forward to enjoying himself even more. On his 40th birthday he wrenched the lead from Tracy with only 4 laps remaining to lift him 25 points clear of Fittipaldi in the drivers' championship. After a race-long battle with the two Penske Chevrolets, Mansell took advantage of a late full course yellow flag to keep in touch and ultimately pass Tracy and Fittipaldi with a succession of dashing moves to round off a well timed win.

Texaco/Havoline 200(Race 12)
Elkhart Lake, Wisconsin   Aug 22

	Driver	Ctry	Car	Laps	Status	Awards	Pts	Total
1 (1)	Paul Tracy	CAN	Marlboro Penske 93 Chevy V8/C	50	118.408(134.072)	AC/M	22	122
2 (2)	Nigel Mansell	GBR	Kmart Texaco L93 Ford Cos	50	117.875(133.516)	AC/STP	16	160
3 (10)	Bobby Rahal	USA	Miller Draft R/H Chevy V8/C	50	117.643(131.450)	AC	14	94
4 (4)	Raul Boesel	BRA	Duracell-Mobil L93 Ford Cos	50	117.248(133.059)	DH	12	110
5 (5)	Emerson Fittipaldi	BRA	Marlboro Penske 93 Chevy V8/C	50	117.248(132.985)	AC	10	129
6 (15)	Eddie Cheever	USA	Menard Immobiliser L92 Ford Cos	50	116.270(130.536)	DH	6	32
7 (13)	Scott Brayton	USA	Amway-N'west Air L93 Ford Cos	49	Running	DH	6	32
8 (16)	Teo Fabi	ITA	Pennzoil Special L93 Chevy V8/C	49	Running		5	52
9 (11)	Arie Luyendyk	HOL	Target-Scotch Video L93 Ford Cos	49	Running	AC	4	61
10 (7)	Scott Goodyear	CAN	Mackenzie Special L93 Ford Cos	49	Running	DH	3	31
11 (14)	Christian Danner	GER	Moda Trop L92 Chevy V8/A	49	Running		2	2
12 (22)	Willy T Ribbs	USA	Cosby-Service L93 Ford Cos	48	Running	DH	1	7

Also

15 (3)	Mario Andretti	USA	Kmart Texaco L93 Ford Cos	47	Engine		-	97
25 (6)	Al Unser jr	USA	Valvoline L93 Chevy V8/C	21	Gearbox		0	65

Time of Race: 1:41:20.689 Margin of Victory: 27.459 secs Lap Leaders: Paul Tracy 1-50

Nigel Mansell's hopes of recording a hattrick of victories were dashed by Paul Tracy who led from start to finish in the 200 mile race. Tracy, returning from a crash in practice which had left him with neck and ankle injuries, strengthened his grip on third place in the 16 race championship with his fourth win of the season.

Molson Indy Vancouver(Race 13)
Vancouver   Aug 29

Driver	Ctry	Car	Laps	Status	Awards	Pts	Total
1 (5) Al Unser	USA	Valvoline L93 Chevy V8/C	102	91.794(109.604)	AC	20	85
2 (2) Bobby Rahal	USA	Miller Draft L93/Chevy V8/C	102	91.638(110.171)	AC/STP	17	111
3 (11)Stefan Johansson	SWE	AMAX Metals PC 93 Chevy V8/C	102	91.318(108.644)	DH	14	29
4 (1) Scott Goodyear	CAN	Mackenzie Special L93 Ford Cos	102	91.205(110.293)	M/DH	13	44
5 (14)Mario Andretti	USA	Kmart Texaco L93 Ford Cos	102	91.143(108.229)	AC	10	107
6 (3) Nigel Mansell	GBR	Kmart Texaco L93 Ford Cos	101	Running	AC	8	168
7 (10)Emerson Fittipaldi	BRA	Marlboro Penske 93 Chevy V8/C	101	Running	AC	6	135
8 (9) Teo Fabi	ITA	Pennzoil Special L93 Chevy V8/C	101	Running		5	57
9 (8) Raul Boesel	BRA	Duracell-Mobil L93 Ford Cos	101	Running	DH	4	114
10 (15)Danny Sullivan	USA	Molson L93 Chevy V8/C	100	Running		3	43
11 (18)Roberto Guerrero	USA	Budweiser King L93 Chevy V8/C	100	Running		2	39
12 (22)Hiro Matsushita	JPN	Panasonic Special L93 Ford Cos	96	Running	DH	1	7
Also							
13 (4) Paul Tracy	CAN	Marlboro Penske 93 Chevy V8/C	93	Running		0	122

Time of Race: 1:49:52.452 Margin of Victory: 11.199 secs Lap Leaders: Scott Goodyear 1-13, Paul Tracy 14, Bobby Rahal 15-64, Al Unser jr 65-102

Another flirtation with the concrete almost cost Mansell dear in Vancouver. He was plagued by handling problems for most of the race and dropped back to 11th position after brushing the wall midway through the 102 lap event. However his closest contender for the title, Fittipaldi, could make little headway on a circuit that provided Al Unser with his first win of the championship.

Pioneer Electronics 200(Race 14)
Lexington, Ohio   Sept 12

Driver	Ctry	Car	Laps	Status	Awards	Pts	Total
1 (5) Emerson Fittipaldi	BRA	Marlboro Penske 93 Chevy V8/C	89	118.113(118.113)	AC	21	156
2 (15)Robby Gordon	USA	AJFoyt/Copenhagen L93 Ford Cos	89	101.975(116.084DH/STP	16	69
3 (5) Scott Goodyear	CAN	Mackenzie Special L93 Ford Cos	89	101.918(117.177)	DH	14	58
4 (4) Raul Boesel	BRA	Duracell-Mobil L93 Ford Cos	89	101.911(117.209)	DH	12	126
5 (8) Arie Luyendyk	HOL	Target-Scotch Video L93 Ford Cos	89	101.898(116.582)	AC	10	71
6 (14)Bobby Rahal	USA	Miller Draft R/H Chevy V8/C	89	101.700(116.274)	AC	8	119
7 (10)Mario Andretti	USA	Kmart Texaco L93 Ford Cos	89	101.443(116.464)	AC	6	113
8 (6) Al Unser jr	USA	Valvoline L93 Chevy V8/C	89	101.368(117.177)	AC	5	90
9 (18)Scott Brayton	USA	Amway-Northwest L93 Ford Cos	88	Running	DH	4	36
10 (9) Jimmy Vasser	USA	Kodalux-STP L92 Ford Cos	88	Running		3	30
11 (22)Willy T Ribbs	USA	Cosby-Service L93 Ford Cos	88	Running	DH	2	9
12 (1) Nigel Mansell	GBR	Kmart Texaco L93 Ford Cos	87	Running	M	2	170
Also							
25 (2) Paul Tracy	CAN	Marlboro Penske 93 Chevy V8/C	21	Contact		0	122

Time of Race: 1:58:59.188 Margin of Victory: 16.217 secs Lap Leaders: Paul Tracy 1-20, Emerson Fittipaldi 21-89

Emerson Fittipaldi's authoritative drive showed that the title race was not going to be handed on a platter to Mansell, who struggled to record a points finish. The Briton, racing amid growing speculation that he was to leave the Indy Car circuit, was left fuming after the race following a first lap collision. He complained that he had been "chopped into" by Penske rival Paul Tracy which had dented any hopes of victory whilst allowing the second placed Brazilian to narrow the championship lead to 14 points..

Bosch
Spark Plug Grand Prix(Race 15)
Nazareth, Pennsylvania   September 19

Driver	Ctry	Car	Laps	Status	Awards	Pts	Total
1 (1) Nigel Mansell	GBR	Kmart Texaco L93 Ford Cos	200	158.685	AC	21	191
2 (10)Scott Goodyear	CAN	Mackenzie Special L93 Ford Cos	200	158.015	DH/STP	16	74
3 (4) Paul Tracy	CAN	Marlboro Penske 93 Chevy V8/C	198	Running	AC	14	136
4 (9) Robby Gordon	USA	AJFoyt/Copenhagen L93 Ford Cos	198	Running	DH	12	81
5 (2) Emerson Fittipaldi	BRA	Marlboro Penske 93 Chevy V8/C	198	Running	AC	10	166
6 (5) Bobby Rahal	USA	Miller Draft R/H Chevy V8/C	196	Running	AC	8	127
7 (14)Stefan Johansson	SWE	AMAX Metals PC 93 Chevy V8/C	196	Running	DH	6	35
8 (8) Arie Luyendyk	HOL	Target-Scotch Video L93 Ford Cos	195	Running	AC	5	76

9 (3) Ralf Boesel	BRA	Duracell-Mobil L93 Ford Cos	194	Running		4	130
10 (15)Eddie Cheever	USA	Budweiser L93 Chevy V8/C	192	Running		3	21
11 (11)Teo Fabi	ITA	Pennzoil Special L93 Chevy V8/C	191	Running		2	59
12 (19)Mark Smith	USA	Craftsman Panske 92 Chevy V8/B	189	Running	DH	1	8

Also

25 (7) Al Unser jr	USA	Valvoline L93 Chevy V8/C	75	Engine		0	90

Time of Race: 1:15:37.273 Margin of Victory: 19.042 secs Lap Leaders: Nigel Mansell 1, Emerson Fittipaldi 2-10, Paul Tracy 11-46, Nigel Mansell 47-200

All caution was tossed to the wind as Nigel Mansell not only won the fastest race on a one-mile oval in Indy Car history, but with it became the 1993 champion. Mansell has become accustomed to stretching the feats of racing performance, and to his remarkable list of achievements can be added the fact that he is the first man to win the championship the year after bringing home the World Formula One title. He scorched around the three cornered circuit, lapping in under 20 seconds, taking the lead from Tracy on the 47th lap and never relinquishing the advantage. Fittipaldi faded in the closing stages as Mansell roared home 19 seconds ahead of Scott Goodyear and over a lap ahead of the rest of the field. For a man who is as emotionally complex as Mansell, his delight manifested itself in a manner that many of his followers could relate to "I've been teetotal for 14 years but I don't care. I'm going to get drunk tonight. I'm going to drink like there's no tomorrow."

Makita 300 (Race 16 and last)
Monterey, California   October 3

Driver	Ctry	Car	Laps	Status	Awards	Pts	Total
1 (2) Paul Tracy	CAN	Marlboro Penske 93 Chevy V8/C	84	106.303(112.232)	AC	21	157
2 (1) Emerson Fittipaldi	BRA	Marlboro Penske 93 Chevy V8/C	84	105.841(112.296)	ACM	17	183
3 (5) Arie Luyendyk	HOL	Target-Scotch Video L93 Ford Cos	84	105.529(111.433)	AC	14	90
4 (9) Scott Goodyear	CAN	Mackenzie Special L93 Ford Cos	84	105.257(111.282)	DH	12	86
5 (12)Al Unser jr	USA	Valvoline L93 Ch V8/C	84	105.104(110.758)	AC	10	100
6 (7) Stefan Johansson	SWE	AMAX Metals PC 93 Chevy V8/C	83	Running	DH	8	43
7 (10)Bobby Rahal	USA	Miller Draft L93 Ch V8/C	83	Running	AC	6	133
8 (11)Teo Fabi	ITA	Pennzoil Special L93 Ch V8/C	83	Running		5	64
9 (6) Mario Andretti	USA	Kmart Texaco L93 Ford Cos	83	Running		4	117
10 (14)Robby Gordon	USA	AJFoyt/Copenhagen L93 Ford Cos	83	Running	DH	3	84
11 (13)Raul Boesel	BRA	Duracell-Mobil L93 Ford Cos	82	Running	DH	2	132
12 (24)Adrian Fernandez	MEX	Conseca-Galles L93 Ch V8/C	82	Running		1	7

Also

23 (3) Nigel Mansell	GBR	Kmart Texaco L93 Ford Cos	71	Contact		0	191

Time of Race: 1:44:58.169 Margin of Victory: 27.491 secs Lap Leaders: Paul Tracy 1-26, Emerson Fittipaldi 27-29, Paul Tracy 30-84

It was not the season's end he would have wished for, but for Nigel Mansell the serious business had already been done. The only real problem was whether he would have any trouble picking up the PPG Cup at the banquet after the race. Mansell had two accidents and his right wrist was heavily strapped.

Final Championship Positions: 1 Nigel Mansell GBR 191pts, 2 Emerson Fittipaldi BRA 183, 3 Paul Tracy CAN 157, 4 Bobby Rahal USA 133, 5 Raul Boesel BRA 132, 6 Mario Andretti USA 117, 7 Al Unser jr USA 100, 8 Arie Luyendyk HOL 90, 9 Scott Goodyear CAN 86, 10 Robby Gordon USA 84.

Formula 3 Championship

ROUND 1
Silverstone   Mar 21
  1 Kelvin Burt (Reynard)   GBR
  2 Paul Evans (Reynard)   GBR
  3 Andre Ribeiro (Dallara)   BRA
Kelvin Burt was disqualified for contact with Ribeiro's car then reinstated

ROUND 2
Thruxton   *Apr 4*
  1 Marc Goossens (Reynard)   BEL
  2 Kelvin Burt (Reynard)   GBR
  3 Pedro de la Rosa (Dallara)   ESP
Goossens was disqualified, for impeding Ribeiro, then reinstated

ROUND 3
Brands Hatch   Apr 18
  1 Kelvin Burt (Reynard)   GBR
  2 Andre Ribeiro (Dallara)   BRA
  3 Jeremie Dufour (Dallara)   FRA

ROUND 4
Donington   May 2-3
  1 Warren Hughes (Dallara)   GBR
  2 Kelvin Burt (Reynard)   GBR
  3 Pedro de la Rosa (Dallara)   ESP

ROUND 5
Brands Hatch (Indy Circuit)   May 16
  1 Kelvin Burt (Reynard)   GBR
  2 Marc Goossens (Reynard)   BEL
  3 Oliver Gavin (Dallara)   GBR

ROUND 6
Silverstone   May 31
  1 Oliver Gavin (Dallara)   GBR
  2 Warren Hughes (Dallara)   GBR
  3 Kelvin Burt (Reynard)   GBR

ROUND 7
Oulton Park   June 12
  1 Oliver Gavin (Dallara)   GBR
  2 Marc Goossens (Reynard)   BEL
  3 Warren Hughes (Dallara)   GBR

ROUND 8
Donington   June 26-27
  1 Oliver Gavin (Dallara)   GBR
  2 Warren Hughes (Dallara)   GBR
  3 Andre Ribeiro (Reynard)   BRA

ROUND 9
Silverstone   Jul 9-10
  1 Oliver Gavin (Dallara)   GBR
  2 Warren Hughes (Dallara)   GBR
  3 Ricardo Rosset (Dallara)   BRA

ROUND 10
Donington   Jul 17-18
  1 Kelvin Burt (Dallara)   GBR
  2 Marc Goossens (Dallara)   BEL
  3 Oliver Gavin (Dallara)   GBR
Burt and Goossens switched to the more competitive Dallara chassis

ROUND 11
Snetterton   Aug 7-8
  1 Kelvin Burt (Dallara)   GBR
  2 Marc Goossens (Dallara)   BEL
  3 Ricardo Rosset (Dallara)   BRA

ROUND 12
Pembrey   Aug 21-22
  1 Oliver Gavin (Dallara)   GBR
  2 Kelvin Burt (Dallara)   GBR
  3 Marc Goossens (Dallara)   BEL

ROUND 13
Silverstone   Sept 4-5
  1 Kelvin Burt (Dallara)   GBR
  2 Ricardo Rosset (Dallara)   BRA
  3 Andre Ribeiro (Dallara)   BRA
This victory clinched the F3 Championship for Burt

ROUND 14
Silverstone   Oct 2-3
  1 Kelvin Burt (Dallara)   GBR
  2 Marc Goossens (Dallara)   BEL
  3 Oliver Gavin (Dallara)   GBR

Rallying

World Rally Championship

MONTE CARLO RALLY
Jan 21-27
Winner
Didier Auriol/Bernard Ocelli   FRA
Toyota Celica Turbo   6:13:43

SWEDISH RALLY
Feb 12-14
Winner
Mats Jonsson/Lars Backman   SWE
Toyota Celica Turbo   4:49:05

RALLYE DE PORTUGAL
Mar 3-6
Winner
François Delecour/Daniel Grataloup FRA
Ford Escort RS Cosworth   6:20:37

TRUST BANK SAFARI RALLY
Apr 8-12
Winner
Juha Kankkunen/Juha Piironen   FIN
Toyota Celica Turbo 4WD   3:54

TOUR DE CORSE RALLYE DE FRANCE
May 2-4
Winner
François Delecour/Daniel Grataloup FRA
Ford Escort RS Cosworth   6:14:41

ACROPOLIS RALLY
May 30-June 1
Winner
Miki Biaision/Tiziano Siviero   ITA
Ford Escort RS Cosworth   6:54:35

RALLY YPF ARGENTINA (RA)
Jul 14-17
Winner
Juha Kankkunen/Nicky Grist   FIN
Toyota Celica Turbo 4WD   5:32:31

ROTHMANS RALLY OF NEW ZEALAND
Aug 5-8
Winner
Colin McCrae/Derek Ringer   GBR
Subaru Legacy 4WD   6:12:31

1000 LAKES RALLY
Aug 27-29
Winner
Juha Kankkunen/Nicky Grist   FIN
Toyota Celica Turbo 4WD   4:23:51

TELECOM RALLY AUSTRALIA
Sept 18-21
Winner
Juha Kankkunen/Nicky Grist   FIN
Toyota Celica Turbo 4WD   5:19:58

Peugeot GTI Challenge

BRECKLAND FOREST RALLY
Feb 13
Winner
Nick Elliott/Dave Price   Peugeot 205GTI

GLIDDONS SOMERSET STAGES
Mar 14
Winner
Phil Brown/Nick Beech   Peugeot 205GTI

IMBER STAGES RALLY
Apr 11-12
Winner
Mark Lawn/Steve Harris   Peugeot 205GTI

DONINGTON PARK RACE
Apr 25
Winner
David Higgins   Peugeot 205GTI

PLAINS RALLY
May 8
Winner
Rudi Lancaster/Paul Spooner   Peugeot 205GTI

JOHN HARRISON DUKERIES RALLY
June 5
Winner
Ashley Field/D Broadhurst   Peugeot 309GTI

JIM CLARK MEMORIAL RALLY
July 10
Winner
Andy Knight/Mike Corner   Peugeot 309GTI

YELLOW BRICK ROAD RALLY
Aug 14-15
Winner
Ben Howlett/Simon Howlett   Peugeot 309GTI

TOUR OF FLANDERS
Sept 11-12
Winner
Ryan Champion/M Douglas   Peugeot 205GTI

Final Standings

1	Paul Richardson	Ripon	205GTI	96pts
2	Justin Dale	Andover	205GTI	94
3	Ashley Field	Mansfield	309GTI	91
4	Mike Reed	Hull	205GTI	80
5	Ben Howlett	Sudbury	309GTI	73

*After mid-season point the top five drivers in the championship
are promoted to Peugeot Masters series.*

Mobil/*Top Gear* Rally Series

VAUXHALL RALLY OF WALES
Mar 20-21
Winner
Richard Burns/Robert Reid   Subaru Legacy

PIRELLI INTERNATIONAL
Apr 17-18
Winner
Richard Burns/Robert Reid   Subaru Legacy

PERTH SCOTTISH INTERNATIONAL
June 4-6
Winner
Richard Burns/Robert Reid   Subaru Legacy
Championship positions after 3 rounds
1 Richard Burns   75pts

VILLAGE HOMES ULSTER RALLY
Jul 30-31
Winner
Malcolm Wilson/Bryan Thomas   Escort Cosworth
Championship positions after 4 rounds
1 Malcolm Wilson   81
2 Richard Burns   75

Mintex National Rally Series

Driver Overall		Pts
1 Douglas Watson-Clark	Ford Escort	112
2 Christopher Mellors	Ford Sierra	111
3 David Mann	Toyota Cecilia	111
4 Murray Grierson	MG Metro 6R4	107
5 Martin Rowe	Ford Sierra	105
6 Steve Petch	Ford Sierra	100
7 Gordon Smith	Ford Sierra	76
8 Steve Smith	Lancia Delta	69
9 Marcus Dodd	Ford Sapphire	57
10 Panny Mallory	Ford Escort	56

Karting

CIK World Championship
(250 Formula E)

Points are awarded to the first 12 finishers in both Pre-Finals and Finals as follows: 1st-15, 2nd-12, 3rd-10, 4th-9, 5th-8...down to 12th-1. All six races count in deciding the world champion.

Osterreichring, Austria
June 19-20

Pre-Final			Final		
1 Stuart Mead	(GBR)		1 Chris Stoney	GBR	
2 Simon Cullen	GBR		2 Martin Hines	GBR	
3 Perry Grondstra	HOL		3 Peter Gray	GBR	
4 Chris Stoney	GBR		4 Phil Glencross	GBR	
5 Martin Hines	GBR		5 Simon Cullen	GBR	
6 Dave Buttigieg	GBR		6 Perry Grondstra	HOL	

Val de Vienne, France
Aug 14-15

Pre-Final			Final		
1 Martin Hines	GBR		1 Perry Grondstra	HOL	
2 Perry Grondstra	HOL		2 Martin Hines	GBR	
3 Poul Petersen	DEN		3 Poul Petersen	DEN	
4 Phil Glencross	GBR		4 Chris Stoney	GBR	
5 Trevor Roberts	GBR		5 Trevor Roberts	GBR	
6 Chris Stoney	GBR		6 Stuart Mead	GBR	

Knockhill, Scotland
Sept 5

Pre-Final			Final		
1 Perry Grondstra	HOL		1 Perry Grondstra	HOL	
2 Martin Hines	GBR		2 Martin Hines	GBR	
3 Ricky Doyle	GBR		3 Stuart Mead	GBR	
4 Peter Gray	GBR		4 Gary Tupper	GBR	
5 Poul Petersen	DEN		5 Ricky Doyle	GBR	
6 Gary Tupper	GBR		6 Peter Gray	GBR	

FINAL PLACINGS
1 Perry Grondstra	HOL	74Pts
(World Champion)		
2 Martin Hines	GBR	71
3 Chris Stoney	GBR	40
4 Peter Gray	GBR	36
5 Poul Petersen	DEN	33
6 Stuart Mead	GBR	32

Netball

International Matches

ENGLAND V NEW ZEALAND
1st Test
Wembley Arena   *Nov 7*
England 34 New Zealand 62

2nd Test
G Mex Centre, Manchester   Nov 12
England 26 New Zealand 60

3rd Test
Granby Halls, Leicester   Nov 14
England 33 New Zealand 58

ENGLAND V JAMAICA
1st Test
Kingston, Jamaica   Apr
England 56 Jamaica 39

2nd Test
Kingston, Jamaica   Apr
England 41 Jamaica 36

3rd Test
Kingston, Jamaica   Apr
England 44 Jamaica 38

HOME INTERNATIONALS
Cardiff   Jan 16
Wales 25 England 42
Guildford   Feb 6
England 69 Republic of Ireland 12
Rivermead, Berkshire   Feb 20
England 63 Scotland 13
Belfast   Mar 27
N Ireland 30 England 65

WORLD YOUTH CUP
Suva, Fiji   Dec

3/4th Play Off
Cook Islands 51 England 50
Final
New Zealand 44 Australia 40

Domestic Fixtures

NATIONAL CLUBS' KNOCKOUT
Wembley, London   Nov 7

2nd Round
Oaksway 7 Wirral 1
Weston Park 7 Grasshoppers 2
Chevrons 8 Dudley Leisure 4
Hirondelles 9 Essex Wanderers 7
Hertford Hornets 6 Leeds Athletic 4
Aquila 13 Sarnians 0
YWCA 8 Wallsend 4
Clan 8 Pessimists 4
Quarter-Finals
Weston Park 9 Oaksway 5
Hirondelles 10 Chevrons 6

Hertford Hornets 5 Aquila 8
Clan 9 YWCA 6
Semi-Finals
Hirondelles 10 Weston Park 9
Aquila 5 Clan 4
Final
Hirondelles 8 Aquila 7

National League

DIVISION 1

	P	W	D	L	GF	GA	Pts
1 Linden	7	5	2	0	359	299	31
2 New Cambell	7	5	1	1	319	261	29
3 BICC	7	4	1	2	285	266	25
4 Toucans	7	4	0	3	278	249	23
5 Aquila	7	3	0	4	294	292	19
6 Harborne	7	3	0	4	327	330	19
7 Academy	7	2	0	5	257	298	15
8 Henley	7	0	0	7	228	352	7

DIVISION 2

	P	W	D	L	GF	GA	Pts
1 Hertford Hornets	7	6	0	1	358	291	31
2 Tongham	7	5	0	2	392	289	27
3 OPA	7	5	0	2	386	295	27
4 Vauxhall Golds	7	5	0	2	324	274	27
5 Crawley Sports	7	4	0	3	268	323	22
6 YWCA	7	2	0	5	354	385	15
7 Weston Park	7	1	0	6	290	308	11
8 Kestrel	7	0	0	7	172	379	2

English Counties League

DIVISION 1

	P	W	D	L	GF	GA	Pts
1 Surrey	7	6	0	1	438	370	31
2 Essex Met	7	5	0	2	379	302	27
3 Bedfordshire	7	5	0	2	324	290	27
4 Birmingham	7	5	0	2	367	371	27
5 Hampshire North	7	3	0	4	335	341	19
6 Middlesex	7	2	0	5	274	302	15
7 Hertfordshire	7	1	0	6	327	386	11
8 Kent	7	1	0	6	321	392	11

DIVISION 2

	P	W	D	L	GF	GA	Pts
1 Mid Hampshire	7	6	0	1	297	266	31
2 East Essex	7	6	0	1	318	293	31
3 West Yorkshire	7	5	0	2	281	234	27
4 Humberside	7	3	0	4	304	293	19
5 Cheshire	7	3	0	4	317	315	19
6 Nottinghamshire	7	2	0	5	286	307	15
7 Gloucestershire	7	2	0	5	266	306	15
8 Northamptonshire	7	1	0	6	254	309	11

INTER-COUNTY CHAMPIONSHIP
Winner: Essex Met

INTER-REGIONAL CHAMPIONSHIP
Winner: East Region

Orienteering

World Cup 1992

Cumulative totals from eight World Cup events

Men

1	Joakim Ingelsson	SWE	179
2	Martin Johansson	SWE	173
3	Petter Thoresen	NOR	158
4	Allan Mogensen	DEN	157
5	Håvard Tveite	NOR	151
6	Keijo Parkkinen	FIN	149
7	Björnar Valstad	NOR	143
8	Thomas Bührer	SUI	143
9	Arto Rautiainen	SWE	138
10	Vladimir Alexeev	RUS	138

Women

1	Marita Skogum	SWE	190
2	Jana Cieslarova	TCH	176
3	Yvette Hague	GBR	168
4	Anette Nilsson	SWE	168
5	Annika Zell	SWE	162
6	Eija Koskivaara	FIN	162
7	Ragnhild B Andersen	NOR	160
8	Annika Viilo	FIN	152
9	Anna Bogren	SWE	151
10	Hanne Sandstad	NOR	145

Junior World Championships

Men

1	Tellesbo Odin	NOR	70:50
2	Norgaard Torren	DEN	72:41
3	Tolkko Tommi	FIN	72:54

Women

1	Anttila Liisa	FIN	58:03
2	Norgaard Tenna	DEN	59:37
3	Dolezalova Hana	TCH	59:57

World Cup Ski-Orienteering

Men

1	Vidar Benjaminsen	NOR	187
2	Lars Lystad	NOR	173
3	Harald Svergja	NOR	168
4	Anssi Juutilainen	FIN	162
5	Vesa Mäkipää	FIN	162
6	Kjetil Ulven	NOR	160
7	Raino Pesu	FIN	159
8	Markku Järvinen	FIN	154
9	Ivan Kuzmin	RUS	152
10	Andreas Edvardsen	NOR	144

Women

1	Arja Nuolioja	FIN	197
2	Riitta Karjalainen	FIN	189
3	Hilde G. Pedersen	NOR	184
4	Sanna Savolainen	FIN	176
5	Pepa Milusheva	BUL	162
6	Kristin Hasle	NOR	153
7	Mervi Anttila	FIN	152
8	Mia Karvanen	FIN	146
9	Maret Vaher	EST	139
10	Valborg Madslien	NOR	138

British Championships

Brown Clee Hill, Shropshire   June 24

Men's Individual

1	David Peel	Clydeside	94.13
2	Martin Bagness	Warrior	95.40
3	Alistair Landels	S Yorkshire	95.56

Women's Individual

1	Heather Monro	Cambridge Uni	72.09
2	Claire Bolland	Edinburgh Uni	74.05
3	Sarah Hague	Merseyside	75.14

Jan Kjellstrom Festival

Hampshire, England   April 9-12

Men's Individual

1	Steven Hale	Oktyr (SWE)	168.55
2	Thomas Buehrer	Sutoc (SUI)	169.06
3	Jon Musgrave	Maroc	177.09

Women's Individual

1	Heather Monro	Cambridge Uni	137.29
2	Sarah Hague	Merseyside	143.03
3	Wendy Smallwood	S Yorkshire	147.45

British Night Championships

Chelwood Vachery, East Grinstead   Feb. 27

Men's Individual 10.0k

1	Ulrik Staugaard	Thames Valley	76.59
2	Ifor Powel	Wrekin Orienteers	80.05
3	Mark Saunders	Bristol Orienteers	80.32

Women's Individual 6.5k

1	Heather Monro	Cambridge Uni	62.54
2	Christine Robinson	Sth London	76.25
3	Alice Bedwell	Bristol Orienteers	78.04

Sweden's men's team, which includes many of the world's best orienteers withdrew from international competitions against Austria and Italy at the beginning of the year after a seventh young orienteer in three years, Melker Karlsson, died in November last year. Tests were carried out to try and discover the causes of the deaths and a strain of virus known as TWAR was thought, at one point, to be responsible. However, the TWAR virus has now been ruled out, but they are no closer to identifying any other cause for the deaths.

Polo

European 8-Goal Championship

St Moritz   Jul 31
Final
England 11   Italy 3

British Open Championship
(Davidoff Gold Cup)

Cowdray Park   Jul 18

Final
Alcatel 9   Ellerston Black 8
After a sudden death play-off

Cowdray Challenge Cup

Cowdray Park
Final
Maple Leaf 5   Alcatel 2

Coronation Cup

Guards Polo Club   Jul 25

England 8   Chile 3

Queen's Cup

Windsor   June 6

Final
Black Bears 10   Ellerston White 8

Alfred Dunhill Cup

Windsor   June 6

Final
Maple Leaf 11   Labegorce 6

Prince of Wales' Trophy

Royal Berkshire Club   May

Final
Maple Leaf 8   Franmen 5

Warwickshire Cup

Cirencester   June 27

Final
Ellerston White 14   Black Bears 10

Silver Jubilee Cup

Hurlingham
Canada 7   Hurlingham PA 5

Universities 1993

June 13

Oxford 10   Cambridge 2

Captain & Subaltern Tournament

Tidworth's Fisher Ground   Aug 8

Household Cavalry 7   Foot Guards 4

Racketball

Men's British Singles Championship

Bromley Town Club   Nov 27-29
2nd Round
S Martin (Wycombe) bt D Best (Bromley) 3-0
D Fan (Berks) bt R Bridger (Berks) 3-0
N Millington (Derby) bt J Gibbons (Bromley) 3-0
E Sommers (Howdon) bt S Stabler (Bromley) 3-0
A Trowell (Bromley) bt R Sutherland (Bromley) 3-0
P Gregory (Sutton) bt S Bateman (Bromley) 3-0
A Rayner (Lingfield) bt A Stabler (Bromley) 3-0
M Parker (New Malden) bt B Abbott(Bromley) 3-1
Quarter-Finals
Martin bt Fan 3-0
Sommers bt Millington 3-2
Bateman bt Trowell 3-0
Parker bt Stabler 3-0
Semi-Finals
Martin bt Sommers 3-1
Bateman bt Parker 3-1
Final
Bateman bt Martin 3-1 (15-11, 15-4, 15-17, 15-11)

Women's British Singles Champs

Bromley Town Club   Nov 28-29
1st Round
B Dryhurst (Images) bt S Ferrier (Coulsdon) 3-0
L Hodgins (Bromley) bt J Liddelow (Arrow) 3-0
S Downhill (Wycombe) bt S Gowers (Coulsdon) 3-0
K Gregory (Sutton) bt H Doyle (Bromley) 3-0
Y Cobb (Coulsdon) bt D Weston (Sutton) 3-0
C Round (Aberdeen) bt D Guthrie (Bromley) 3-0
D Readshaw (Sutton) bt A Duffen 3-0
M Newell (Arrow) bt J Mills (Bromley) 3-0
Quarter-Finals
Dryhurst bt Hodgins 3-0
Downhill bt Gregory 3-0
Round bt Cobb 3-0
Newell bt Readshaw 3-0
Semi-Finals
Dryhurst bt Downhill 3-0
Newell bt Round 3-0
Final
Newell bt Dryhurst 3-2 (15-8, 4-15, 15-8, 9-15, 15-10)

British Men's Veterans

Bromley Town Club   Nov 28-29
Quarter-Finals
D Reeve (Essex) bt B Davies (Bromley) w/o
P Cripps (Lingfield) bt P Amato (Howdon) 3-1

B Tutin (Purley) bt N Nicolaou (Essex) w/o
K Baker (Bromley) bt J Prowse (Bexley) 3-1
Semi-Finals
Reeve bt Cripps 3-1
Baker bt Tutin 3-0
Final
Reeve bt Baker 3-0 (15-8, 15-6, 15-8)

British Women's Veterans

Bromley Town Club   Nov 28-29
Quarter-Finals
B Dryhurst (Images) bt J Shenton (Lingfield) 3-0
Y Cobb (Coulsdon) bt D Guthrie (Bromley) 3-0
L Hodgins (Bromley) bt B Gaskell (Bromley) 3-0
C Round (Aberdeen) bt M Gill (Bromley) 3-0
Semi-Finals
Dryhurst bt Guthrie 3-1
Round bt Hodgins 3-0
Final
Dryhurst bt Round 3-0 (15-11, 15-9, 15-7)

British Men's Vintage
Final
P Hoade (H Wycombe) bt S Holt (Bromley) 3-0
(15-11, 15-11, 15-10)

British Women's Vintage
Final
G Saunders (Bromley) bt F Jesseman (Lingfield) 3-0
(15-9, 15-4, 15-3)

Rackets

World

Championship

Queen's Club   Jan 23
Final
J S Male bt N P A Smith 6-5, 15-7, 12-15, 5-4, 10-15, 8-15, 15-17, 11-15, 15-10, 15-12, 15-2, 15-4

Lacoste Open Championships

Queen's   Feb 14
Final
N P A Smith Bt S M Hazell 15-9, 15-11, 15-8, 18-16
Under 24 Singles
A Robinson bt G Barker 9-15, 15-5, 15-11, 15-8
Under 24 Doubles
G Barker/A Robinson bt P le Marchand/K Walker 15-4, 15-2, 18-14, 15-5
Under 24 Singles
C Dandy bt P le Marchand 15-12, 15-8, 8-15, 7-15, 15-10
Over 40 Singles
W R Boone bt D V Watkins 15-6, 15-2, 15-0

Lacoste British Open Doubles

Queen's   Apr 25
Final
J A N Prenn/J S Male bt W R Boone/N P A Smith 18-17, 15-12, 15-1, 15-12
Over 40 Doubles
W R Boone/D M Norman bt R Gracey/M Smith 11-15, 17-14, 15-2, 15-3
Over 50 Doubles
R Gracey/M Smith bt T Milligan/C Palmer-Tomkinson 15-1, 15-12, 15-2

Amateur Rackets

Championships

Queen's   Mar 17
Singles Final
J S Male bt W R Boone 15-12, 15-1
Doubles Final
J A N Prenn/J S Male bt W R Boone/T Cockroft 11-15, 11-15, 15-0, 15-7, 15-12, 15-1

Henderson Pro

Championships

Eton College   Jan 31
Singles
N P A Smith bt S M Hazell 15-0, 15-6, 18-14

NOEL BRUCE CUP
Queen's   Nov 15
Eton bt Harrow 4-0

Real Tennis

World Championship

New York   Mar 8
Final
Wayne Davis (AUS) bt Lachie Deuchar (AUS) 7-6

George Wimpey British Open

Queen's   Nov 29
Final
J P Snow GBR bt C Bray GBR 6-2, 6-2, 6-3
Under 24 Open Singles
N Wood bt A Lyons 6-4, 1-6, 6-4, 6-2
Under 21 Open Singles
R Gunn bt J Dawes 6-0, 6-4
Over 40 Open Singles
C J Ronaldson bt K Sheldon 6-2, 6-1
Over 50 Open Singles
M McMurrugh bt J D Ward 6-3, 3-6, 6-4
Open Doubles
W F Davies/L Deuchar (walk-over)

Amateur Championships

Singles Final
J P Snow bt N Pendrigh 6-5, 6-0, 6-2
Doubles Final
J P Snow/M McMurrugh bt T D J Warburg/I Snell 6-2, 6-1, 6-3

BRITISH PROFESSIONAL DOUBLES
Queen's   Jan 17
Sheldon/Devine bt Howell/Bray 5-6, 6-5, 6-1

EUROPEAN OPEN DOUBLES
W F Davies/L Deuchar bt N P Snow/I Wood 5-6, 6-1, 6-4, 5-6, 6-4

BRITISH PROFESSIONAL SINGLES
Holyport   May 11
L Deuchar bt R Fahey 6-5, 6-1, 6-4

AUSTRALIAN OPEN
Melbourne   Aug 15
Fahey AUS bt Snow GBR 6-0, 6-4, 6-5

FRENCH OPEN
Bordeaux   Nov 18
Men
Snow GBR bt Fahey AUS 3-6, 6-5, 5-6, 6-5, 6-4
Women
K Allen GBR bt A Cockcroft GBR 6-3, 6-3

COUPE DE BOURDEAUX
Bordeaux   Apr 28
Snow GBR bt Prats FRA 6-0, 6-3, 6-0

INTER CLUB CHAMPIONSHIP - THE FIELD TROPHY
Petworth bt Seacourt 5-0

Women's World Championships

Bordeaux   May 9-10
Final
Jones GBR bt Cornwallis GBR 5-6, 6-2, 6-3
Doubles final
Cornwallis/Lumley GBR bt Jones/Garside GBR

British Women's Open

Seacourt, Hayling Island   May 2
Singles final
P Lumley bt A Garside 6-3, 6-0
Doubles final
S Jones/A Garside bt P Lumley/C Cornwallis 3-6, 6-4, 6-1

SEACOURT SILVER RACKET
Seacourt   Feb 16
Final
Latham bt Warburg 6-4, 6-2

ERNST & YOUNG CLUB HANDICAP
Queen's   Nov 9
Singles Final
Cambridge 8   Manchester 6
Doubles Final
Leamington 6   Oratory 5

NATIONAL HANDICAP
Happell bt Owens 8-4

Rowing

There was a suspension of disbelief in Barcelona when the Searle brothers won their gold medal, so rapidly did they make up ground over the last few hundred metres of the race to overtake their rival siblings, the Abbagnale brothers of Italy. In Roudnice, at the World Championships, they took (or had imposed) a different strategy and produced another dazzling performance. At the start, on a wet, grey Czechoslovakian day, the Searle brothers were unready for the off, Jonny Searle even had his hand in the air. But there was no call back and the brothers Searle were last away and still last as they came to the 1,000m mark. Then came the dazzling. Over the next 500m the Searle brothers, coxed as ever by Garry Herbert, covered the water five seconds faster than anyone else in the race. They went literally from last to first. The Abbagnales, with seven world titles to their credit, could have seen nothing like it. They hung on for second, but the Searles had won their first world title.

Peter Haining became Britain's first ever singles sculls' gold medallist when he took the lightweight crown; the women's lightweight coxless four won gold; and as sure as rivers flow, there was Redgrave with Pinsent to add another world title. Those four golds made it Britain's most successful world championships ever.

Elsewhere, Cambridge took the boat race in a time that probably would have been a race record with more favourable tides. Cambridge thus checked the extraordinary recent record of Oxford (until this year, 16 wins in the last 17 races). At Henley, three crews were warned for abusive language and one of them was a school boat, Kingston Grammar, which used to be a posh school.

World Championships

Roudnice, Czech Republic   Aug 30-Sept 5
Each event has an A and B final, with six boats in the A race.
Placings given over six therefore refer to B final positions. For
example, a 14 placing means eighth in the B final.

MEN

Single Sculls

1	Derek Porter	CAN	6:59.03
2	Vaclav Chalupa	TCH	7:00.56
3	Thomas Lange	GER	7:04.35

Double Sculls

1	Lamarque/Barathay	FRA	6:24.69
2	Thonsen/Bjonness	NOR	6:28.42
3	Uhrig/Handle	GER	6:29.03

Quads

1	Germany	5:43.99
	(Steiner/Hajek/Volkert/Willms)	
2	Ukraine	5:46.25
3	Italy	5:47.07
14	Great Britain	6:03.33
	(Walters/Pooley/Brown/Hall-Craggs)	

Coxless Pairs

1	Redgrave/Pinsent	GBR	6:36.98
2	Kirchhoff/Sennewald	GER	6:38.51
3	Zvegelj/Cop	SLO	6:39.58

Coxed Pairs

1	Great Britain	7:01.50
	(Searle J/Searle G/Herbert)	
2	Italy	7:03.59
	(Abbagnale C/Abbagnale G/Di Capua)	
3	Germany	7:04.96

Coxless Fours

1	France	6:04.54
2	Poland	6:06.63
3	USA	6:08.50
5	Great Britain	6:12.18
	(Obholzer/Manners/Foster/Hunt-Davies)	

Coxed Fours

1	Romania	6:14.44
2	Czech Republic	6:17.50
3	Germany	6:17.78
9	Great Britain	6:38.92
	(MacLennan/Peel/Stewart/Dillon/Ellison)	

Eights

1	Germany	5:37.08
2	Romania	5:39.33
3	USA	5:41.47
6	Great Britain	5:45.92
	(Cross/Cracknell/Walker/Singfield/Behrens/ Phelps/Cassidy/Parish/Thomas)	

Disabled Fixed Seat

1 D Irvine	GBR	6:41.12

Disabled Sliding Seat

1 M Briggs	AUS	5:03.03
2 G Spenser	GBR	5:13.79
5 N Davis	GBR	6:03.34

MEN'S LIGHTWEIGHT

Single Sculls

1 Peter Haining	GBR	7:05.34
2 Stephen Hawkins	AUS	7:06.66
3 Pepijn Aardewijn	HOL	7:07.70

Double Sculls

1 Lynagh/Hick	AUS	6:20.64
2 Michael & Markus Gier	SUI	6:20.73
3 S Posito/Pittino	ITA	6:21.94

Coxless Pairs

1 Climent/Molina	ESP	6:39.41
2 Mitiouchev/Ustinov	RUS	6:40.77
3 Vogt/Fahrig	GER	6:40.79
9 Williams/Baker	GBR	6:53.33

Coxless Fours

1 USA		6:03.27
2 Switzerland		6:03.99
3 Italy		6:04.59

Coxed Fours

1 Austria		5:49.30
2 Italy		5:51.00
2 Germany		5:51.00
5 Great Britain		5:55.22
(Sinton/Long/Elmitt/Whitelaw)		

Eights

1 Canada		5:39.17
2 Denmark		5:41.25
3 Italy		5:41.53
5 Great Britain		5:44.99
(Everington/Helm/Butt/Watson/Strange		
McNiven/Lemon/Partridge/Denkin)		

WOMEN

Single Sculls

1 Jana Thieme	GER	7:26.00
2 Marnie McBean	CAN	7:27.42
3 Trine Hansen	DEN	7:28.14

Double Sculls

1 Lawson P/Lawson B	NZL	7:03.42
2 Koppen/Boron	GER	7:05.61
3 Oronova/Kamenova	BUL	7:07.26

Quads

1 China		6:21.07
2 Germany		6:24.31
3 USA		6:33.98

Coxless Pairs

1 Gosse/Cortin	FRA	7:24.74
2 Toogood/Davies	AUS	7:27.21
3 McCagg E/McCagg M	USA	7:27.65
4 Turvey/Batten	GBR	7:31.71

Coxless Fours

1 China		6:42.06
2 USA		6:42.72
3 Canada		6:43.92

Eights

1 Romania		6:18.88
2 USA		6:20.42
3 Germany		6:21.52

WOMEN'S LIGHTWEIGHT

Single Sculls

1 Michele Darville	CAN	7:47.14
2 Laurien Vermulst	HOL	7:51.37
3 Mette Bloch	DEN	7:52.52
9 Sue Kay	GBR	8:00.27

Double Sculls

1 Wiebe/Miler	CAN	6:59.74
2 Fei Li/Fang Wang	CHN	7:01.33
3 Rip/Meliesje	HOL	7:01.66
6 Mangan/Corless	GBR	7:16.22

Coxless Fours

1 Great Britain		6:45.30
(Brownless/Hall/Dryden/Williams)		
2 Canada		6:48.87
3 USA		6:49.47

Lucerne Rotsee Regatta

Lucerne, Switzerland   Jul 9–11

MEN

Double Sculls

1 Germany	6:25.27

Coxless Pairs

1 Great Britain	7:02.95
(Redgrave/Pinsent)	

Coxless Fours

1 Croatia	6:03.29

Coxed Fours

1 Germany	6:12.81
7 Great Britain (Dillon)	
9 Great Britain (Stanhope)	

Quadruple Sculls

1 Germany	5:45.59
7 Great Britain	

Eights

1 Holland	5:33.55
6 Oxford University	

LIGHTWEIGHT MEN

Single Sculls

1 P Haining	7:08.42

Double Sculls

1 Australia	6:32.51
14 Great Britain	
(Lees/Collins)	

Coxless Pairs

1 Spain	6:55.03
4 Great Britain	
(Williams/Baker)	

Coxless Fours

1 Great Britain	6:10.16
(NCRA)	

Quadruple Sculls

1 Germany	5:53.29
(Mainzer)	
6 Great Britain	

Eights

1 Denmark	5:42.63
2 Great Britain	5:43.07

WOMEN
Double Sculls
 1 Potsdam   7:04.17
Coxless Pairs
 1 France   7:24.75
Great Britain (Batten/Turvey) disqualified
Quadruple Sculls
 1 Germany   6:28.45
Coxless Fours
 1 Germany   6:54.37
 3 Great Britain   6:52.69
Eights
 1 Germany   6:18.96
LIGHTWEIGHT WOMEN
Single Sculls
 1 Vermault (HOL)   7:54.74
 5 Key (GBR)
 9 Appelboom (GBR)
Double Sculls
 1 Holland   7:20.93
 4 Great Britain
   (Mangan/Corless)
Coxless Fours
 1 Great Britain   6:53.02

World Cup

FINAL STANDINGS

Men's Single Sculls

1 Vaclav Chalupa	TCH	69
2 Martin Hansen	DEN	46
3 Nikolae Taga	ROM	42

Women's Single Sculls

1 Annelies Bredael	BEL	65
2 Maria Brandin	SWE	61
3 Ellisabetha Lipa	ROM	53

QUOTES

"I'm lucky if my aunt recognises me"

Steve Redgrave, on how things haven't changed since he won his third Olympic gold medal.

"If a woman is capable, people call her bossy. If a man is capable, they call him assertive. I'm not bossy, I'm assertive. I have to have the guys under my thumb, whether it is telling them to pick up their dirty clothes or keeping them away from a bridge"

Samantha Bentham, Oxford boat race cox.

"Ergomax is definitely a psychological boost. You feel better for it"

James Behrens, president of Cambridge, explaining the benefits of Creatine, which purports to aid muscle function. According to the Behrens dictum, whether it actually does or not is irrelevant.

"When eight people form a unit, the boat gets its own energy. You're compelled by that energy. I know it sounds like hocus pocus, but the boat *flew*"

Jon Bernstein, Cambridge oarsman.

"Hatred is what you need. Contempt implies complacency"

Daniel Topolski, former Oxford coach, on sports psychology

"We each know what the other is thinking and we know we are both trying as hard as we can. We know how stupidly competitive we are. And we trust each other."

Jonny Searle on the advantages of your partner being your brother.

"I'm going to eat, drink and even shower with my medal on. It's staying round my neck"

Peter Haining, after winning a gold medal at the world championships.

Henley Regatta

Finals only
THAMES CUP
Notts County bt Isis A   6:22
TEMPLE CUP
Oxford Brookes University bt TCD (IRL)   6:33
WYFOLD CUP
London B bt Leander   6:55
BRITANNIA CUP
Harvard (USA) bt Goldie   7:05
DOUBLE SCULLS
Kittoe/Redpath bt Hopkins/Pollecutt 7:32
SILVER GOBLETS
Redgrave/Pinsent bt Coventry/Clayton 7:22
DIAMOND SCULLS
T Lange (GER) bt V Chalupa (TCH)   7:39
WOMEN'S SCULLS
M Brandin (SWE) bt A Braedel (BEL)
PRINCESS ELIZABETH CUP
Brisbane (AUS) bt Eton   6:38
QUEEN MOTHER CUP
Tideway/Notts County bt Goldie/Notts County 6:36
VISITOR'S CUP
Kings Chester bt University of London   7:03
STEWARDS' CUP
Leander bt Dortmund (GER) 6:44
LADIES' PLATE
Brown Uni (USA) bt Notts County/London   6:14
PRINCE PHILIP CUP
Leander/Molesey bt Molesey/Uni of London   7:10
FAWLEY CUP
Walton/Burton/Leander bt Windsor Boys   6:51
GRAND CHALLENGE CUP
Dortmund (GER) bt Cambs Uni/Uni of London   6:11
*Steven Redgrave brought his Henley medal tally to 12 when he
shared victory in the Silver Goblets with Matthew Pinsent and
when then drafted into the winning crew for the
Stewards Cup*

WORLD INDOORS

*At Cambridge, Mass in February, this event was held
over 2000m on Concept II ergometers*

Men's Open

1	M Siejkowski	GER	7:24.0
2	J Kovan	USA	7:30.6
3	R Tozer	GBR	7:30.8

Lightweight Men

1	P Aardewijn	HOL	7:51.4

Senior Men (40-49)

1	A Ripley	GBR	7:55.0
2	K Helmudt	DEN	7:57.3
3	R Uttley	GBR	7:58.2

Women's Open

1	H Cortin	FRA	8:32.4

Lightweight Women

1	A-M Dryden	GBR	8:56.1

GB National Championships

Strathclyde Park   Jul 16-19
MEN
Single Sculls
1	L Fletcher	7:41.20
2	A Larkman	7:44.87
3	S Allpass	7:47.31

Double Sculls
1	Molesey	6:49.79
	(Hopkins/Pollicut)	
2	Leander	6:51.24
3	Thames	6:57.28

Coxed Pairs
1	City of Oxford	7:58.72
	(Graham/Edge/Smallman-Smith)	
2	Thames Tradesman A	8:02.45
3	Staines	8:06.06

Coxless Pairs
1	Cambridge 99	7:08.78
	(Layton/Weller)	
2	Notts County	7:10.10
3	Notts & Union	7:12.75

Coxed Fours
1	Notts County	6:38.75
2	Bedford	6:48.70
3	Kingston	6:52.07

Coxless Fours
1	Notts County (Wilson)	6:40.79
2	Notts County (Dunne)	6:45.49
3	London	6:45.83

Eights
1	Notts County	6:00.91
2	Upper Thames	6:08.80
3	Agecroft	6:15.01

WOMEN
Single Sculls
1	G Batten	8:12.91
2	K Thomas	8:20.55
3	G Lindsay	8:23.75

Double Sculls
1	Notts County	7:43.92
	(Hart/Batten)	
2	Staines	7:51.01
3	Thames	8:02.23

Coxless Pairs
1	Thames T/Tideway Sc	8:05.58
	(O'Malley/Hopkins)	
2	Norwich	8:08.33
3	Cambridge University	8:13.82

Coxless Fours
1	Staines	7:54.15
2	Bedford	7:58.71
3	Glasgow University	7:59.02

Quadruple Sculls
1	Thames B	7:11.63
2	Thames C	7:13.63
3	Thames A	7:17.05

Eights
1 Cambridge University 6:56.63
2 Staines 7:01.40
3 Bedford 7:01.86
LIGHTWEIGHT MEN
Single Sculls
1 M Chmiel 7:41.94
Double Sculls
1 London RC 6:42.14
(Booth/Haining)
Coxless Pairs
1 London RC 7:11.59
(Williams/Baker)
Quadruple Sculls
1 Thames 6:42.32
Coxless Fours
1 London 6:40.99
Eights
1 Notts & Union 6:29.63
LIGHTWEIGHT WOMEN
Single Sculls
1 N Ashcroft 8:41.30
Double Sculls
1 Clyde 8:00.76
(McGarvey/McIntosh)
Coxless Pairs
1 Thames Tradesmen 8:34.69
(Burford/Brown)
Coxless Fours
1 Thames Tradesmen 7:34.42

The Boat Race

Putney-Mortlake　　　　Mar 27

Cambridge bt Oxford 3¹/₂ lengths
Times (Cambridge 1st)
Mile 3:31 (=record) to 3:36
Hammersmith Bridge 6:21 (rec) to 6:29
Chiswick Steps 10:12 (rec) to 10:21
Barnes Bridge 14:04 to 14:16
Finish 17:00 to 17:11

Goldie bt Isis 9 lengths
17:07 (rec)

Head of the River

Mar 20
1 RV Munster von 1882 17:02.31
2 Molesey I 17:10.10
3 Leander I 17:16.25

Rugby League

It's been a year dominated by money, with clubs labouring under deficits such that Widnes were prepared to release Jonathan Davies to Warrington, without a transfer fee (though he did go on the market in January at £50,000) simply because they could not afford the Welshman's wages bill. Warrington, too, are hardly in the pink. At the start of the year, that club was labouring under a long-term debt of £487,000. As average gates in the championship generate just £30,000, such debts are not easily shifted. In mid-summer, Hull were prepared to sell their best players to make ends meet. With their gates down by an average 1,000 a week last season, they saw the sale of £1,300,000 of players as the only get-out. There was a bit of money around, for Bradford managed to rustle up £245,000 for Featherstone's Paul Newlove. That didn't please Featherstone greatly. They had valued him at £750,000, but the game's tribunal thought otherwise. At Nottingham, such numbers might as well refer to the grains of sand used to tee-up the ball at penalties, for all the difference it makes. When you get a gate of 109, as Nottingham City did against Workington early last season, the financial discussions are more likely to concern raffles or car boot sales or other possible earners.

The season was dominated by Wigan, the club completing the Stones Bitter Championship and the Challenge Cup double for the fourth consecutive year. They lose their coach, John Monie, for this season, but it remains to be seen whether that will prevent them chalking up a fifth.

It will be a season without Ellery Hanley, who announced his retirement, and a season when John Gallacher comes south. Gallacher, once lauded as the best rugby union full-back in the world, has had a turbulent time since switching codes. He joins London Crusaders.

QUOTES

"What else could it be - a duck?"

Lawyer Tom Hughes to Shona Martyn, editor of Australian *HQ Magazine*.
Hughes was referring to a picture of rugby player Andrew Ettingshausen's penis which was shown in the magazine. The player sued when the picture, taken in the showers after a game, was published. Ettingshausen won what became known as the 'Pecker in the Paper' case and was awarded £190,000 damages.

"League is a fabulous game, but if I knew what I know now, I would never have left Pontypool"

Dave Bishop, former rugby union scrum half.

"If we had the name of the company on our shirts like the Poms have British Coal on theirs, I would be tearing it off"

Bobby Fulton, Australian coach, after the decision to close 31 pits.

"We were beaten and you don't do laps of honour when you're beaten"

Martin Offiah, on refusing to join teammates on a lap of honour after the World Cup final

World Cup Final

Wembley   Oct 24, 1992

Great Britain 6	**Australia 10**
Goals: Fox 3	*Try: S Renouf*
	Goals: Meninga 3

According to coach Malcolm Reilly, Great Britain were one mistake away from beating the Australians. That error was John Devereux's missed tackle in the 67th minute that enabled Steve Renouf to go over for the only try of the game. It was a defensively tight match, in which Britain's potentially match-winning wings had no running opportunities. The home team came back strongly in the final ten minutes and, by way of a consolation, Australian coach Bobby Fulton reckoned that this team was 30 points better than the 1982 Lions, but they still lost this match.

Great Britain: Lydon (Tait 48), Hunte, Connolly (Devereux 41), Schofield, Offiah, Edwards, Fox, Ward (Skerrett 52), Dermott, Platt, Betts, Clarke, Hanley (Eyres 75

Australia: Brasher, Carne, Renouf, Meninga, Hancock, Fittler, Langer, Lazarus, S Walters, Sargent (Cartwright 63), Sironen (Gillespie 41), Lindner, Clyde (Walters 44)

OTHER AUSTRALIAN MATCHES

Oct 9, 1992

Huddersfield 2	**Australia 66**

Oct 14

Sheffield E 22	**Australia 52**

Oct 18

Cumbria 0	**Australia 44**

BRITISH COAL TEST MATCHES

Swansea   Nov 28

Wales 11	**England 26**

France   Dec 13

France 18	**Wales 19**

Carcassonne, France   Mar 7

France 6	**Great Britain 48**

Headingley   Apr 2

Great Britain 72	**France 6**

This was the largest international win in rugby league history.

JOHN SMITH'S KIWI TOUR

Swansea   Oct 3

Wales 19	**New Zealand 24**

RUSSIAN TOUR OF SOUTH AFRICA

Johannesburg   Nov 13, 1992

South Africa 26	**Russia 30**

Cape Town   Nov 18

Western Province 22	**Russia 12**

Pretoria   Nov 20

South Africa 19	**Russia 22**

FIJI IN PAPUA NEW GUINEA

Port Moresby, PNG   June 19

Papua New Guinea 35	**Fiji 24**

NEW ZEALAND V AUSTRALIA

1st Test
Auckland   June 20

Australia 14	**New Zealand 14**

2nd Test
Palmerston   June 25

Australia 16	**New Zealand 8**

3rd Test
Brisbane   June 30

Australia 16	**New Zealand 4**

COCA-COLA WORLD SEVENS

Sydney   Feb 5-7

Quarter-finals

Canterbury 20	Illawarra 10
Manly 18	St George 10
Easts 26	Papua New Guinea 10
Western Samoa 24	Canberra 16

Semi-finals

Manly 22	Canterbury 16
Easts 32	Western Samoa 14

Final

Easts 18	Manly 12

WORLD CLUB CHALLENGE

Wigan   Oct 10, 1992

Wigan 8	**Brisbane Broncos 22**

Stones Bitter
Premiership

First Round

St Helens 34	Halifax 25
Bradford N 6	Castleford 19
Widnes 10	Leeds 22
Wigan 40	Warrington 5

Semi-finals

Wigan 25	Castleford 8
St Helens 15	Leeds 2

Final

St Helens 10	Wigan 4

DIVISIONAL PREMIERSHIP
First Round

Dewsbury 22	Batley 18
Keighley C 34	Hunslet 6
Ryedale York 31	Whitehaven 6
Workington 44	Doncaster 14

Second Round

Featherstone 46	Ryedale York 8
Huddersfield 10	Workington 24
Oldham 14	Dewsbury 14
Rochdale H 26	Keighley C 18

Second Round replay

Dewsbury 20	Oldham 18

Semi-finals

Featherstone 35	Dewsbury 12
Rochdale 16	Workington T 30

Final

Featherstone 20	Workington 16

Stones Bitter Championship

DIVISION 1

		P	W	D	L	Dg	Gls	Trs	Pts	Dg	Gls	Trs	Pts	Pts
1	Wigan	26	20	1	5	6	123	123	744	3	48	57	327	41
2	St Helens	26	20	1	5	6	95	109	632	7	57	56	345	41
3	Leeds	26	14	2	10	3	80	108	595	5	72	93	521	30
4	Bradford N	26	15	-	11	5	78	98	553	4	65	75	434	30
5	Widnes	26	15	-	11	1	80	97	549	2	76	73	446	30
6	Castleford	26	14	1	11	-	94	89	544	5	68	65	401	29
7	Halifax	26	13	-	13	1	88	95	557	3	73	89	505	26
8	Warrington	26	12	1	13	11	68	85	487	10	68	76	450	25
9	Hull	26	10	1	15	1	64	63	381	3	86	90	535	21
10	Sheffield E	26	10	1	15	5	66	67	405	1	100	106	625	21
11	Leigh	26	9	2	15	8	63	69	410	2	94	110	630	20
12	Wakefield	26	8	2	16	3	53	74	405	5	81	92	535	18
13	Salford	26	9	-	17	4	69	89	498	1	108	127	725	18
14	Hull	26	7	-	19	3	61	49	321	5	87	105	599	14

DIVISION 2

		P	W	D	L	Dg	Gls	Trs	Pts	Dg	Gls	Trs	Pts	Pts
1	Featherstone R	28	24	1	3	-	128	185	996	2	55	60	352	49
2	Oldham	28	20	1	7	5	122	126	753	3	76	87	503	41
3	Huddersfield	28	15	-	13	9	82	98	565	4	82	95	548	30
4	Rochdale H	28	14	-	14	4	91	109	622	3	90	106	607	28
5	London C	28	12	2	14	2	76	95	534	6	82	98	562	26
6	Swinton	28	10	-	18	5	58	72	409	4	82	117	636	20
7	Carlisle	28	6	3	19	2	68	79	454	5	100	129	721	15
8	Bramley	28	7	1	20	4	46	58	328	4	104	130	732	15

DIVISION 3

		P	W	D	L	Dg	Gls	Trs	Pts	Dg	Gls	Trs	Pts	Pts
1	Keighley C	24	21	-	3	5	146	155	917	4	38	52	288	42
2	Workington T	24	19	-	5	3	134	141	835	5	38	39	237	38
3	Dewsbury	24	18	-	6	10	88	133	718	7	48	47	291	36
4	Ryedale York	24	17	-	7	5	109	131	747	7	52	56	335	34
5	Whitehaven	24	16	-	8	4	94	126	696	4	54	54	328	32
6	Batley	24	16	-	8	-	60	97	508	4	40	46	268	32
7	Hunslet	24	14	-	10	6	82	96	554	2	78	85	498	28
8	Doncaster	24	14	-	10	2	91	95	564	7	67	82	469	28
9	Highfield	24	6	-	18	8	47	52	331	5	135	160	915	12
10	Barrow	24	5	-	19	-	64	87	476	5	94	108	625	10
11	Chorley	24	5	-	19	7	47	54	317	9	104	141	781	10
12	Blackpool G	24	4	-	20	8	43	52	302	2	132	173	958	8
13	Nottingham C	24	1	-	23	7	27	30	181	4	152	206	1132	2

Silk Cut
Challenge Cup

Preliminary Round

Widnes 62	Swinton 14
Batley 20	Blackpool G 10
Wigan 40	Hull 2

First Round

Warrington 6	Castleford 21
Bradford N 28	Workington Town 18
Chorley B 6	Batley 20
Dewsbury 4	Wigan 20
Featherstone 22	St Helens 24
Halifax 66	Carlisle 16
Huddersfield 66	Nottingham City 1
Hull KR 30	Bramley 0
Hunslet 27	Ryedale York 22
Keighley C 86	Highfield 0
Leeds 54	Barrow 18
Oldham 54	London C 6
Rochdale H 34	Doncaster 13
Salford 12	Wakefield T 20
Sheffield E 32	Leigh 5
Whitehaven 8	Widnes 20

Second Round

Wigan 23	St Helens 3
Castleford 34	Hunslet 16
Hull KR 30	Keighley C 28
Leeds 68	Rochdale H 6
Oldham 20	Huddersfield 17
Sheffield 6	Widnes 52
Wakefield T 18	Bradford N 20
Halifax 50	Batley 20

Third Round

Leeds 12	Castleford 8
Halifax 18	Wigan 19
Hull KR 4	Widnes 4
Oldham 4	Bradford N 42

Third Round Replay

Widnes 16	Hull KR 11

Semi-Finals

Central Park, Wigan   *Mar 13*
Leeds 4   Widnes 39

Elland Road, Leeds   *Mar 27*
Bradford N 6   Wigan 15

THE FINAL
Wembley   *May 1*
77,684
Wigan 20   **Widnes 14**

Regal Trophy

Preliminary Round

Chorley 10	Sheffield E 38
St Helens 44	Huddersfield 18
Wakefield T 90	Highfield 12
Swinton 12	Hull KR 32

First Round

Wigan 52	Carcassonne 0
Batley 6	Hunslet 13
Bradford N 70	Barrow 10
Bramley 12	Carlisle 16
Doncaster 4	Workington T 30
Halifax 76	Nottingham C 6
Hull 22	Dewsbury 16
Hull KR 48	Whitehaven 4
Leigh 32	Keighley C 24
London C 30	Wakefield T 0
Oldham 22	Castleford 40
Rochdale H 32	Catalan XIII 16
St Helens 15	Leeds 14
Salford 14	Featherstone R 18
Warrington 31	Sheffield E 16
Widnes 46	Ryedale York 4

Second Round

Warrington 12	Bradford N 12
Castleford 54	Carlisle 0
Featherstone 8	St Helens 25
Hull 28	Halifax 14
Hull KR 0	Wigan 18
Hunslet 12	Workington T 34
Leigh 16	London C 6
Widnes 30	Rochdale H 2

Second Round replay

Bradford N 9	Warrington 6

Third Round

St Helens 8	Castleford 12
Hull 24	Leigh 14
Workington 12	Wigan 24
Bradford N 21	Widnes 10

Semi-Finals

Central Park, Wigan   *Jan 2*
Wigan 19   Hull 4

Valley Parade, Bradford   *Jan 9*
Bradford N 19   Castleford 12

THE FINAL
Elland Road, Leeds   *Jan 23*
Bradford N 8   **Wigan 15**

Rugby Union

What a difference winning makes. Had the Lions won in New Zealand it would have been described as a vintage year. Had England won an unprecedented third grand slam, it would have been an historic year. But neither came about and the year was more memorable for its moments than for any continuing theme.

England, the dominant force in northern hemisphere rugby for the past two years almost conceded those grand slam hopes in the first game. If Webb had struck his goal rather than the ball bouncing off the posts into the arms of an alert, but extremely fortunate Hunter, who can say how the match would have developed. Mathematically, the difference between a converted try and a goal was more than enough, as England won by only a single point. Anyway, it was all incidental three weeks later.

Rory Underwood contributed at least two unforgettable moments to the year; one saw him skirting the fringes of the All Blacks defence in Wellington to score for the Lions, the other had him dillying and dallying while Ieuan Evans hacked the ball past him for the only try of the Wales-England match. Who'd have guessed that England would stumble over what had looked an easy hurdle. Yet Wales played in that one game as well as they have for a few seasons, tackling with venom. Unfortunately, the venom was on ration, for after that suprise win, they tumbled to miserable defeats against both Scotland and Ireland.

Scotland would have had a half decent season were it not for Stuart Barnes. The Bath stand-off reintroduced himself to the English back line (he had been a long time away) in dazzling fashion. Short legs, he may have, but don't they just move. The Championship went, technically, to the final game. Yet, because of the introduction of goal difference to settle it, France had effectively got the title in the bag. They duly beat Wales and England duly beat.....but they didn't, did they? Ireland were there to be rolled over, but they had had enough of rolling over. A fiery Irish performance stopped England in their tracks; 17-3, they didn't get a look in. In Ireland, the party is probably still going.

Although they didn't win anything this year, 16 of those Englishmen found themselves on the plane to New Zealand. In the second and third Tests, 11 of them featured in the Lions side, a record. One didn't, though. Will Carling, England's captain and the only serious opposition to Gavin Hastings as Lions captain, was dropped for the last two Tests.

Money figured highly on the annual agenda, as it is bound to until the game decides to go fully professional and there were welcome commitments for the next three years from sponsors, Pilkington (club rugby) and Famous Grouse (Scottish rugby), while Nike (using most of the England pack) put out a series of ads that upset a lot of people.

And an old financial sore was exposed when Tom Brown was granted an unprecedented pardon. Brown, a Bristol player and England international in the twenties, was banned from Union when he was accused of having his expenses met, on a trip north, by the Rugby League. Brown's family were grateful for the pardon. Brown, though, has been dead these past thirty or more years.

The Lions Tour

For two-thirds of this series, the Lions could with some justification claim dominance. In the Christchurch encounter, a dubious try just one minute into the match when Evans and Bunce went down with the ball together and an arguable last minute penalty gave the All Blacks the match. The Lions felt aggrieved, but they had glorious recompense in the second match when the New Zealanders found their reputation in tatters. Jason Leonard, a loosehead prop brought in as a tight-head, earned many of the plaudits going, as the Englishman gave much needed stability to the Lions set pieces. It was all down to the wire now, with the match in Auckland settling the series. The Lions, after such a demonstrative win, should have been favourites and looked that way for the first quarter of the match as Gibbs touched down for a 23rd minute try that was to give the Lions a 10-0 lead. But All Black reputations are not easily buried and, exhibiting a commitment and cohesion missing from their game previously, they took control of the game. The Lions, on the other hand, quickly tired, as without clean ball from the line-out, they struggled to make an impression. Long before the All Blacks made it numerically secure, the game looked beyond redemption for the Lions.

1ST TEST

Christchurch   June 12

New Zealand 20   **British Lions 18**

Try: Bunce   *PG: Hastings 6*

PG: Fox 5

New Zealand: Timu, Clarke, Bunce, Little (Cooper 79), Tuigamala, Fox, Strachan, Dowd, Fitzpatrick*, Brown, I Jones, R Brooke, Joseph M Jones, Z Brooke

British Lions: G Hastings*, Evans, Guscott, Carling, R Underwood, Andrew, Morris, Popplewell, Milne, Burnell, Bayfield, Reed, Clarke, Winterbottom, Richards

Scoring Sequence

1m	Bunce try	NZ 5	Lions 0
10m	Hastings penalty	NZ 5	Lions 3
17m	Hastings penalty	NZ 5	Lions 6
22m	Fox penalty	NZ 8	Lions 6
35m	Hastings penalty	NZ 8	Lions 9
40m	Foz penalty	NZ 11	Lions 9
43m	Fox penalty	NZ 14	Lions 9
48m	Hastings penalty	NZ 14	Lions 12
51m	Fox penalty	NZ 17	Lions 12
53m	Hastings penalty	NZ 17	Lions 15
71m	Hastings penalty	NZ 17	Lions 18
79m	Fox penalty	NZ 20	Lions 18

2ND TEST

Wellington   June 26

New Zealand 7   **British Lions 20**

Try: Clarke   *Try: Underwood*

Conv: Fox   *PG: Hastings 4*

                   DG: Andrew

New Zealand: Timu, Kirwan, Bunce, Clarke, Tuigamala, Fox, Preston, Dowd, Fitzpatrick, Brown, R Brooke, Cooksley, M Jones, Z Brooke

British Lions: G Hastings, Evans, Guscott, Gibbs, R Underwood, Andrew, Morris, Popplewell, Moore, Leonard, Johnson, Bayfield, Clarke, Winterbottom, Richards

ScoringSequence

12m	Clarke try	NZ 5	Lions 0
12m	Fox conversion	NZ 7	Lions 0
30m	Hastings penalty	NZ 7	Lions 3
35m	Hastings penalty	NZ 7	Lions 6
40m	Andrew dropped gl	NZ 7	Lions 9
48m	Hastings penalty	NZ 7	Lions 12
60m	Underwood try	NZ 7	Lions 17
71m	Hastings penalty	NZ 7	Lions 20

3RD TEST

Auckland   Jul 3

New Zealand 30   **British Lions 13**

Tries: Bunce, Preston   *Try: Gibbs*

      Fitzpatrick

Conv: Fox 3

PG: Fox 3

New Zealand: Timu, Kirwan, Stensness, Bunce, Tuigamala, Fox, Preston, Dowd, Fitzpatrick, Brown, R Brooke, I Jones (Cooksley 20), J Joseph, M Jones (Z Brooke 73), Pene

British Lions: G Hastings, Evans, Guscott, Gibbs, R Underwood, Andrew, Morris, Popplewell, Moore, Leonard, Johnson, Bayfield, Clarke, Winterbottom, Richards

Scoring Sequence

19m	Hastings penalty	NZ 0	Lions 3
23m	Gibbs try	NZ 0	Lions 8
24m	Hastings conversion	NZ 0	Lions 10
27m	Bunce try	NZ 5	Lions 10
28m	Fox conversion	NZ 5	Lions 10
32m	Fitzpatrick try	NZ 12	Lions 10
33m	Fox conversion	NZ 14	Lions 10
44m	Fox penalty	NZ 17	Lions10
52m	Hastings penalty	NZ 17	Lions 13
59m	Fox penalty	NZ 20	Lions 13
67m	Preston try	NZ 25	Lions 13
68m	Fox conversion	NZ 27	Lions 13
75m	Fox penalty	NZ 30	Lions 13

Five Nations Championship

Rugby Union

Five Nations Championship

Murrayfield Jan 16
Scotland 15 **Ireland 3**
Tries: Stark, Stanger *PG: Malone*
Scotland: G Hastings*, Stanger, S Hastings, Shiel, Stark,
Chalmers, Armstrong, Watt, Milne, Burnell, Reed,
Cronin, Turnbull, Weir, Morrison
Ireland: Wilkinson, Geoghegan, Cunningham, Danaher,
Wallace, Malone, Bradley*, Popplewell, Smith, McCarthy,
Johns, Costello, Lawlor, Mannion, McBride

Twickenham Jan 16
England 16 **France 15**
Try: Hunter *Tries: Saint-André (2)*
Conv: Webb *Conv: Camberabero*
PG: Webb (3) *PG: Camberabero*
England: Webb, Hunter, Carling*, Guscott, Underwood,
Andrew, Morris, Leonard, Moore, Probyn, Bayfield,
Johnson, Teague, Clarke, Winterbottom
France: Lafond, Saint-André, Sella (Mesnel), Lacroix
(Ougier), Hontas, Camberabero, Hueber, Amary, Tordo*,
Seigne, Benazzi, Roumat, Benetton, Cecillon, Cabannes

Cardiff Arms Park Feb 7
Wales 10 **England 9**
Try: Evans *PG: Webb (2)*
Conv: Jenkins *DG: Guscott*
PG: Jenkins
Wales: Rayer, I Evans*, Hall, Gibbs, Proctor, Jenkins,
Jones, R Evans, Meek, Williams-Jones, Llewellyn,
Copsey, Lewis, Davies, Webster
England: Webb, Hunter (de Glanville), Carling*, Guscott,
Underwood, Andrew, Morris, Leonard, Moore, Probyn,
Bayfield, Johnson, Teague, Clarke, Winterbottom

Parc des Princes Feb 7
France 11 **Scotland 3**
Try: Lacroix *PG: Hastings*
PG: Camberabero (2)
France: Lafond, Saint-André, Sella, Lacroix, Hontas,
Camberabero, Hueber, Armary, Tordo, Seigne, Benazzi,
Roumat, Benetton, Cecillon*, Cabannes
Scotland: Hastings*, Stanger, Hastings, Shiel, Start,
Chalmers, Armstrong, Wright, Milne, Burnell, Reed,
Cronin, Turnbull, Weir, Morrison

Lansdowne Road Feb 20
Ireland 6 **France 21**
PG: Malone(2) *Tries: Saint-André, Sella*
Conv: Camberabero
PG: Camberabero(2)
DG: Camberabero
Ireland: Clarke, Geoghegan, Cunningham, Danaher
(Glennon), Wallace, Malone, Bradley*, Popplewell,
Kingston, Clohessy, Johns, Francis, O'Hara, Galwey,
McBride.
France: Lafond, Saint-André, Sella, Lacroix, Hontas,
Camberabero, Hueber, Armary, Tordo*, Seigne, Benazzi,
Roumat, Benetton, Cecillon, Cabannes.

Murrayfield Feb 20
Scotland 20 **Wales 0**
Try: Turnbull
PG: Hastings(5)
Scotland: G Hastings*, Stanger, S Hastings, Shiel, Stark,
Chalmers, Armstrong, Wright, Milne, Burnell, Reed,
Cronin, Turnbull, Weir, Morrison.
Wales: Rayer, I Evans*, Hall, Gibbs, Proctor, Jenkins,
Jones, R Evans, Meek, Williams-Jones, Llewellyn,
Copsey, Lewis, Davies, Webster.

Cardiff Arms Park March 6
Wales 14 **Ireland 19**
Try: Evans *Try: Robinson*
PG: Jenkins(3) *Conv: Elwood*
PG: Elwood (3)
DG: Clarke
Wales: Rayer, I Evans*(Clement), Hall, Gibbs, Walker,
Jenkins, Jones, R Evans, Meek, Williams-Jones, Llewellyn,
Copsey, Lewis, Davies, Webster
Ireland: Clarke, Wallace, Cuningham, Danaher,
Geoghegan, Elwood, Bradley*, Popplewell, Kingston,
Clohessy, Johns, Galwey, O'Hara, Robinson, McBride

Twickenham March 6
England 26 **Scotland 12**
Tries: Guscott *PG: Hastings(3)*
R Underwood *DG: Chalmers*
Conv: Webb
PG: Webb (3)
England: Webb, T Underwood, Carling*, Guscott, R
Underwood, Barnes, Morris, Leonard, Moore, Probyn,
Bayfield, Dooley, Teague, Clarke, Winterbottom
Scotland: G Hastings*, Stanger, S Hastings(Logan), Shiel,
Stark, Chalmers (Townsend), Armstrong, Wright, Milne,
Burnell, Reed, Cronin, Turnbull, Weir, Morrison

Lansdowne Road March 20
Ireland 17 **England 3**
Try: Galwey *PG: Webb*
PG: Elwood(2)
DG: Elwood(2)
Ireland: Clarke, Wallace, Cunningham, Danaher,
Geoghegan, Elwood, Bradley*, Popplewell, Kingston,
Clohessy, Johns, Galwey, O'Hara, Robinson, McBride
England: Webb, T Underwood, Carling*, Guscott, R
Underwood, Barnes, Morris, Leonard, Moore, Probyn,
Bayfield, Dooley, Teague, Clarke, Winterbottom

Parc des Princes March 20
France 26 **Wales 20**
Tries: Benetton (2) *Try: Walker*
Lafond *Conv: Jenkins*
PG: Lacroix(3) *PG: Jenkins*
France: Lafond, Saint-Andre, Sella, Lacroix, Hontas,
Mesnel, Hueber, Armary, Tordo*, Seigne, Benazzi,
Roumat, Benetton, Cecillon, Cabannes
Wales: Clement, I Evans*, N Davies, Gibbs, Walker,
Jenkins, T J B Moon, R Evans (J Davies), Lamerton,
Williams-Jones, Llewellyn, P Davies, Perego (Arnold),
Lewis, Webster.

318

QUOTES

"The lads are absolutely disgusted. I wouldn't like to be in his shoes when he's recaptured"

> Andy Curtis, organiser of the Little Hey prison team, on the fleet-footed full-back Mitchell Douglas, who took the opportunity, on an away game, to go missing. Little Hey, the first prison side to play league games, were already under-strength as their best player, scrum-half Chris Rankin, was considered too big a security risk for away games.

"He was by no means athletic, in fact a bit lumpy, but made an excellent second row forward"

> Chris McCooey, recalling Bill Clinton's rugby days at Oxford, where he played for the second team.

"We were hoping to keep that a secret.......a week in Lourdes"

> Gerry Murphy, Ireland's coach explaining the transformation of the Irish team that defeated England in the Five Nations.

"The Irish treat you like royalty before and after the game and kill you to pieces during it"

> England prop, Jeff Probyn, after that Ireland game.

"I was so excited, I stuck my finger in my mouth. At that moment, my mental age was 11"

> Franck Mesnel, explaining what it felt like to be recalled to the French team.

"As a rugby junkie, New Zealand has given me most of my best fixes"

> Ian McGeechan, coach to the Lions team.

"Top man, top job"

> Gareth Chilcott, former England prop praising Jason Leonard after the second Test against the All Blacks.

"Well, it's better than being called a plonker"

> Leonard, on being praised.

"Like a Porsche passing a Lada"

> Tony Underwood's description of his brother Rory running round All Black wing, John Kirwan, en route to scoring for the British Lions in the second Test.

"It's a fair swop, he gets my daughter and I get tickets to the international matches"

> Mike Carter, whose daughter became engaged to England winger Tony Underwood.

"Last year's speaker used language unsuitable for women and her presence would have embarrassed the men"

> The reason given why Kate Don, secretary of Market Overton rugby club, couldn't attend the Rutland rugby club's dinner. Yes, they move with the times in Rutland.

British International Matches

(excluding Five Nations Championship)

South Africa in England

Twickenham	Nov 14
England 33	**South Africa 16**
Tries: Carling,	*Try: Strauss*
Guscott, Morris	*Conv: Botha*
Underwood	*PG: Botha (2)*
Conv: Webb (2)	*DG: Botha*
PG: Webb (3)	

England: Webb, T Underwood, Carling*, Guscott, R
Underwood, Andrew, Morris, Leonard, Moore, Ubogu,
Bayfield, Dooley, Teague, Clarke, Winterbottom
South Africa: van Rensberg, Small, Gerber, Müller,
Olivier, Botha*, Wright, Styger, Hills, Andrews, Hattingh,
Malan, Strauss, Richter, Smit

OTHER MATCHES

Leicester	*Nov 4*
Midland Div 9	**South Africa 32**

Bristol	*Nov 7*
England B 16	**South Africa 20**

Leeds	*Nov 10*
Northern Div 3	**South Africa 19**

Australia in Ireland & Wales (& a little bit of England)

Lansdowne Rd, Dublin	Oct 31
Ireland 17	**Australia 42**
Try: Wallace	*Tries: Campese, McKenzie, Little,*
PG: Russell (4)	*Kelaher, Horan*
	Conv: Roebuck (4)
	PG: Roebuck (3)

Ireland: Staples, Geoghegan, Danaher*, Cunningham,
Wallace, Russell, Aherne, Popplewell, Murphy,
McCarthy, Galwey, Johns, Robinson, Lawler, Hamilton
Australia: Roebuck, Campese, Little, Horan, Carozza,
Lynagh*, Slattery, Crowley, Kearns, McKenzie, McCall,
Eales, Ofahengaue, Gavin, Wilson

Cardiff Arms Park	Nov 21
Wales 6	**Australia 23**
PG: Stephens	*Tries: Wilson, McCall, Campese*
	Conv: Roebuck
	PG: Roebuck (2)

Wales: Rayer, Evans*, Hall, Gibbs, Proctor, Stephens, R
Jones, Griffiths, Jenkins, Williams-Jones, Llewellyn,
Copsey, Lewis (Reynolds 74), Davies, Webster
Australia: Roebuck, Campese, Little, Horan, Carozza,
Kahl, Slattery, Crowley, Kearns*, McKenzie, McCall,
Morgan, Ofahengaue, Gavin, Wilson (Coker 56)

OTHER MATCHES

Lansdowne Rd	*Oct 17*
Leinster 11	**Australia 38**

Cork	*Oct 21*
Munster 22	**Australia 19**

Ravenhill, Belfast	*Oct 24*
Ulster 11	**Australia 35**

Galway	*Oct 27*
Connacht 6	**Australia 14**

Swansea	*Nov 4*
Swansea 21	**Australia 6**

Cardiff Arms Park	*Nov 7*
Wales B 11	**Australia 24**

Neath	*Nov 11*
Neath 8	**Australia 16**

Llanelli	*Nov 14*
Llanelli 13	**Australia 9**

Ebbw Vale	*Nov 17*
Monmouthshire 9	**Australia 19**

Bridgend	*Nov 24*
Welsh Students 6	**Australia 37**

Twickenham	*Nov 28*
Barbarians 20	**Australia 30**

Canada in England

Wembley	Oct 17
England 26	**Canada 13**
Tries: Hunter 2	*Try: Graf*
Guscott	*Conv: Rees*
Winterbottom	*PG: Rees 2*
PG: Webb 2	

England: Webb, Hunter, Carling, Guscott, T Underwood,
Andrew, Morris, Leonard, Olver, Ubogu, Bayfield,
Dooley, Wyan, Winterbottom, Richards
Canada: Stewart, Gray, Williams, Stuart, Lougheed, Rees,
Graf, Evans (Wirachowski 49), Svoboda, Jackart, Knauer,
Hadley, Gordon, MacKinnon, McKenzie

**MOST CAPPED PLAYERS
BY POSITION**
As at Oct 1, 1993

Full Back	Serge Blanco	FRA	81
Wing	Rory Underwood	ENG	63
Centre	Philippe Sella	FRA	81
Fly-half	Rob Andrew	ENG	53
Scrum-half	Gareth Edwards	WAL	63
Prop	Phil Orr	IRL	59
Hooker	Colin Deans	SCO	52
Lock	Willie John McBride	IRL	80
Flanker	Fearghus Slattery	IRL	65

*Serge Blanco is also the most capped international player
of all-time with a total of 93 caps (12 as a winger). These
figures include Lions caps and as accurate as at 31.3.93*

A INTERNATIONALS

Melrose, Scotland	*Dec 19*
Scotland 22	**Italy 17**
Lansdowne Rd, Dublin	*Dec 28*
Ireland 13	**Scotland 22**
Leicester	*Jan 15*
England 29	**France 17**
Bath	*Feb 3*
England 59	**Italy 0**
S'Hertogenbosh, HOL	*Feb 6*
Holland 12	**Wales 57**
Richmond	*Mar 5*
England 66	**Spain 5**
Newport	*Mar 5*
Wales 28	**Ireland 29**
Donnybrook, Dublin	*Mar 19*
Ireland 18	**England 22**
Aberdeen	*Mar 20*
Scotland 19	**France 29**

U-21 MATCHES

Newcastle	*Oct 14*
England 39	**Ireland 28**
Donnybrook, Dublin	*Oct 28*
Ireland 22	**Wales 11**
Murrayfield	*Jan 15*
Scotland 3	**Ireland 18**
Dijon	*Feb 5*
France 67	**Scotland 9**
Edinburgh	*Feb 19*
Scotland 8	**Wales 16**
	May 1
England 31	**French Armed Forces 3**

Other International Matches

SOUTH AFRICA IN FRANCE
1st Test

Stade Gerlaud, Lyons	Oct 17
France 15	**South Africa 20**
Tries: Penaud (2)	*Tries: Gerber, Small*
Conv: Viars	*Conv: Botha (2)*
PG: Viars	*PG: Botha*
	DG: Botha

2nd Test

Parc des Princes, Paris	Oct 24
France 29	**South Africa 16**
Tries: Roumat, Penaud	*Try: Gerber*
Conv: Lacroix (2)	*Conv: Botha*
PG: Lacroix (5)	*PG: Botha (2)*
	DG: Botha

Bordeaux	*Oct 3*
French Select XV 24	**South Africa 17**
Pau	*Oct 7*
Aquitaine 22	**South Africa 29**
Toulouse	*Oct 10*
Midi-Pyrenées 15	**South Africa 18**
Marseilles	*Oct 13*
Provence-C. d'Azur 12	**South Africa 41**
Béziers	*Oct 20*
Languedoc 15	**South Africa 36**
Tours	*Oct 28*
French Universities 18	**South Africa 13**
Stade du Nord	*Oct 31*
French Barbarians 25	**South Africa 20**

BEDISLOE CUP

Dunedin, NZ	*Jul 17*
New Zealand 25	**Australia 10**

SOUTH AFRICA IN AUSTRALIA
1st Test

Sydney FG	Jul 31	
Australia 12	**South Africa**	**19**
PG: Roebuck 4	*Tries: Small 2, Müller*	
	Conv: van Rensburg 2	

2nd Test

Brisbane	Aug 14
Australia 28	**South Africa**
Tries: Little 2	*Tries: Stransky*
Horan	*Olivier*
Conv: Roebuck 2	*Conv: Stransky 2*
PG: Roebuck 3	*PG: Stransky 2*

3rd Test

Sydney FG	Aug 21
Australia 19	**South Africa 12**
Try: Horan	*Tries: Small, Piennar*
Conv: Roebuck	*Conv: Stransky*
PG: Roebuck 4	

Fira Championship

GROUP A POOL 1

Brussels	*Oct 11*
Belgium 11	**Russia 17**
Villeneuve sur Lot	*Oct 18*
France 76	**Russia 12**
Moscow	*Oct 25*
Russia 18	**Germany 15**
Brussels	*Nov 1*
Belgium 9	**Morocco 11**
Stuttgart	*Nov 15*
Germany 13	**Belgium 10**
Soissons	*Mar 21*
France 38	**Belgium 6**
Casablanca	*Apr 17*
Morocco 23	**Germany 3**
Moscow	*May 15*
Russia 24	**France 34**
Hanover	*May 30*
Germany 27	**France 71**

FINAL TABLE

	P	W	D	L	F	A	Pts
France	4	4	0	0	219	57	12
Russia	4	3	0	1	71	118	10
Morocco	4	2	0	2	62	70	8
Germany	4	1	0	3	58	122	6
Belgium	4	0	0	4	36	79	4

GROUP A POOL 2

Rome	*Oct 1*
Italy 22	**Romania 3**
Tunis	*Jan 30*
Tunisia 8	**Spain 20**
Madrid	*Feb 14*
Spain 0	**Italy 52**
Leno	*Mar 27*
Italy 51	**Tunisia 8**
Lisbon	*Apr 3*
Portugal 13	**Romania 41**
Coimbra	*Apr 17*
Portugal 11	**Italy 33**
Tunis	*Apr 24*
Tunisia 14	**Portugal 10**
Bucharest	*May 8*
Romania 51	**Tunisia 0**
Lisbon	*May 16*
Portugal 15	**Spain 37**
Bucharest	*May 30*
Romania 33	**Spain 15**

FINAL TABLE

	P	W	D	L	F	A	Pts
Italy	4	4	0	0	158	22	12
Romania	4	3	0	1	128	50	10
Spain	4	2	0	2	72	108	8
Tunisia	4	1	0	3	30	132	6
Portugal	4	0	0	4	49	125	4

HONG KONG SEVENS
Final
Western Samoa 14   Fiji 12

World Cup Sevens

Murrayfield, Edinburgh   Apr 16-18

POOL A
Fiji 42 Latvia 0; S.Africa 28 Japan 5; Wales 33 Romania
7; Fiji 28 Japan 17; Latvia 5 Romania 22; S.Africa 36
Wales 14; Fiji 40 Romania 0; Japan 7 Wales 35; Latvia 5
S.Africa 47; Fiji 21 Wales 17; Romania 0 S.Africa 38;
Japan 21 Latvia 14; Fiji 19 S.Africa 26; Wales 36 Latvia
14; Romania 15
Japan 17

POOL B
New Zealand 49 Holland 7; France 22 USA 7; Ireland 21
Korea 12; New Zealand 19 USA 5; Holland 12 Korea 28;
France 9 Ireland 1;
New Zealand 46 Korea 0; USA 0 Ireland 38;
Holland 14 France 26; New Zealand 24 Ireland 7; Korea
14 France 0; USA 31 Holland 0;
New Zealand 19 France 5; Ireland 45 Holland 0;
Korea 26 USA 19

POOL C
Australia 28 Taiwan 0; Scotland 15 Tonga 7; Argentina
17 Italy 7; Australia 7 Tonga 10;
Taiwan 14 Italy 15; Scotland 10 Argentina 14;
Australia 40 Italy 0; Tonga 17 Argentina 5;
Taiwan 5 Scotland 36;Australia 40 Argentina 5;
Italy 12 Scotland 21; Tonga 52 Taiwan 0;
Australia 26 Scotland 14; Argentina 26 Taiwan 5
Italy 7 Tonga 31

POOL D
England 40 Hong Kong 5; W.Samoa 47 Spain 0;
Canada 21 Namibia 7; England 31 Spain 0;
Hong Kong 19 Namibia 17; W.Samoa 28 Canada 14;
England 24 Namibia 5;Spain 12 Canada 5;
Hong Kong 7 W.Samoa 43; England 33 Canada 0;
Namibia 0 W.Samoa 47; Spain 26 Hong Kong 5;
England 28 Canada 35 Hong Kong 7;
Namibia 26 Spain 21

POOL E
Ireland 17 W.Samoa 0; Tonga 7 Fiji 14;
Fiji 14 W.Samoa 12; Ireland 14 Tonga 12
W.Samoa 42 Tonga 7;Fiji 31 Ireland 7

POOL F
Australia 7 S.Africa 5; England 21 New Zealand 12;
England 14 S.Africa 7; New Zealand 42 Australia 0;
S.Africa 31 New Zealand 14;Australia 21 England 12

1st Semi Final RWC Plate
Argentina 24 Korea 0
2nd Semi Final RWC Plate
Spain 10 Wales 7
RWC PLATE FINAL
Argentina 19 Spain 12
1st Semi Final RWC Bowl
Scotland 14 France 7
2nd Semi Final RWC Bowl
Japan 14 Canada 0
RWC BOWL FINAL
Japan 33 Scotland 19
1st Semi Final Melrose Cup
England 21 Fiji 7
2nd Semi Final Melrose Cup
Australia 21 Ireland 19
MELROSE CUP FINAL
England 21 Australia 17

NATIONAL LEAGUE
DIVISION 1

		P	W	D	L	GF	GA	Pts
1	Bath	12	11	0	1	335	97	22
2	Wasps	12	11	0	1	186	118	22
3	Leicester	12	9	0	3	220	116	18
4	Northampton	12	8	0	4	215	150	16
5	Gloucester	12	6	0	6	173	151	12
6	London Irish	12	6	0	6	175	223	12
7	Harlequins	12	5	1	6	197	187	11
8	Orrell	12	5	0	7	175	183	10
9	London Scottish	12	3	1	8	192	248	7
10	Saracens	12	3	0	9	137	180	6
11	West Hartlepool	12	3	0	9	149	236	6
12	Rugby	12	1	0	11	104	368	2

DIVISION 2

		P	W	D	L	GF	GA	Pts
1	Newcastle Gos	12	10	0	2	241	106	20
2	Waterloo	12	10	0	2	228	138	20
3	Wakefield	12	8	1	3	186	123	17
4	Nottingham	12	8	0	4	249	145	16
5	Sale	12	7	1	4	237	102	15
6	Moseley	12	6	2	4	184	150	14
7	Bedford	12	6	2	4	186	183	14
8	Rosslyn Park	12	5	0	7	209	199	10
9	Richmond	12	5	0	7	204	196	10
10	Blackheath	12	4	2	6	142	231	10
11	Coventry	12	3	0	9	192	236	6
12	Fylde	12	0	3	9	108	290	3
13	Morley	12	0	1	11	107	374	1

DIVISION 3

		P	W	D	L	GF	GA	Pts
1	Otley	11	8	1	2	274	118	17
2	Havant	11	8	1	2	185	93	17
3	Exeter	11	8	1	2	247	169	17
4	Redruth	11	7	2	2	175	125	16
5	Sheffield	11	7	0	4	208	134	14
6	Leeds	11	7	0	4	228	220	14
7	Liverpool St.H	11	5	0	6	203	130	10
8	Clifton	11	4	2	5	206	175	10
9	Aspatria	11	3	1	7	170	308	7
10	Askeans	11	3	0	8	132	300	6
11	Broughton Park	11	2	0	9	136	217	4
12	Plymouth A	11	0	0	11	130	305	0

ADT COUNTY CHAMPIONSHIP

AREA NORTH
League 1

		P	W	D	L	GF	GA	Pts
1	Lancashire	3	3	0	0	72	27	6
2	Yorkshire	3	2	0	1	74	39	4
3	Northumberland	3	2	0	1	74	39	4
4	Cumbria	3	0	0	3	8	80	0

League 2

		P	W	D	L	GF	GA	Pts
1	Durham	3	3	0	0	47	16	6
2	Warwickshire	3	2	0	1	58	44	4
3	Leicestershire	3	1	0	2	33	39	2
4	North Midlands	3	0	0	3	21	60	0

League 3

		P	W	D	L	GF	GA	Pts
1	Cheshire	3	3	0	0	101	15	6
2	Notts,Lincs,Derby	3	3	0	0	101	15	16
3	East Midlands	3	1	0	2	37	122	2

AREA SOUTH
League 1

		P	W	D	L	GF	GA	Pts
1	Cornwall	3	3	0	0	36	31	6
2	Middlesex	3	2	0	1	97	33	4
3	Hampshire	3	1	0	2	37	47	2
4	Surrey	3	0	0	3	22	81	0

League 2

		P	W	D	L	GF	GA	Pts
1	Gloucestershire	3	3	0	0	76	41	6
2	Kent	3	2	0	1	68	30	4
3	Devon	3	1	0	2	39	56	2
4	Hertfordshire	3	0	0	3	24	80	0

League 3

		P	W	D	L	GF	GA	Pts
1	Dorset & Wilts	3	3	0	0	65	28	6
2	Buckingham	3	2	0	1	49	41	4
3	Sussex	3	1	0	2	56	39	2
4	Berkshire	3	0	0	3	25	87	0

League 4

		P	W	D	L	GF	GA	Pts
1	Somerset	2	1	0	1	46	24	2
2	Eastern Counties	2	1	0	1	34	35	2
3	Oxfordshire	2	1	0	1	35	56	2

Final *17 April 1993*

Lancashire 9   Yorkshire 6

MIDDLESEX SEVENS
Final
Wasps 26   Northampton 24

Women's Rugby

NATIONAL LEAGUE
Division 1

		P	W	D	L	GF	GA	Pts
1	Saracens	14	13	0	1	569	59	26
2	Wasps	14	12	1	1	292	75	25
3	Richmond	14	10	1	3	268	75	21
4	Clifton	14	5	1	8	106	203	11
5	Lampeter	14	5	0	9*	128	173	10
6	Blackheath	14	4	0	10	131	303	8
7	Waterloo	14	4	0	10	91	366	8
8	Leeds	14	1	1	12	26	357	3

(*defaulted 2 fixtures)

Division 2

		P	W	D	L	GF	GA	Pts
1	Cardiff	12	11	0	1	339	58	22
2	Eton Manor	12	10	0	2	238	81	20
3	Richmond II	12	6	1	5	205	159	13
4	Medway	11	4	1	6*	127	85	9
5	Bury	11	4	0	7*	50	218	8
6	Sale	10	3	0	7	49	147	6
7	Northampton	10	0	0	10	36	296	0

(*defaulted a fixture)

The Pilkington Cup

Third Round
Clifton 3 Exeter 19
Coventry 14 Nottingham 28
Harlequins 72 Blackheath 3
London Scottish 11 Leicester 20
Morley 10 Tynedale 6
Moseley 9 Fylde 6
Newcastle Gosforth 13 Gloucester 10
Orrell 20 Sale 3
Redruth 16 London Welsh 7
Richmond 22 Wakefield 25
Rosslyn Park 10 Wasps 37
Rugby 27 Bedford 14
Saracens 20 Bristol 15
Tabard 13 Northampton 50
West Hartlepool 13 London Irish 8
Waterloo 9 Bath 8
Fourth Round
Harlequins 47 Wakefield 18
Northampton 33 Newcastle Gosforth 3
Nottingham 3 Leicester 28
Redruth 3 Exeter 8
Rugby 5 Moseley 11
West Hartlepool 21 Moreley 3
Wasps 18 Saracens 17
Waterloo 8 Orrell 3
Quarter Final
Leicester 76 Exeter 0
Northampton 37 Moseley 15
Waterloo 14 Harlequins 21
West Hartlepool 9 Wasps 15
Semi Final
Leicester 28 Northampton 6
Wasps 13 Harlequins 14
Final
Harlequins 16 Leicester 23

Provincial Insurance Cup

Sixth Round Results
(London & South West Divisions)
Chipping Sodbury 0 Stow-on-the-Wold 7
Datchworth 5 Tring 0
Hitchin 10 Barnet 0
Tredworth 25 Chosen Hill Former Pupils 12
(Northern & Midland Divisions)
Old Anselmians 47 Wigston 24
Old Centrals 11 Kidderminster Carolians 18
Phoenix Park 9 Old Northamptonians 11
Windermere 5 Fleetwood 9
Quarter Finals
Hitchin 8 Datchworth 0
Tredworth 5 Stow-on-the-Wold 0
Old Anselmians 9 Kidderminster Carolians 15
Old Northamptonians 12 Fleetwood 17
Semi Finals
Kidderminster Carolians 10 Hitchin 19
Tredworth 5 Fleetwood 24
Final
Hitchin 7 Fleetwood 13

Scottish League

DIVISION 1

	P	W	D	L	F	A	Pts
1 Melrose	13	12	0	1	326	134	24
2 Edinburgh Acad.	13	9	1	3	269	156	19
3 Gala	13	9	1	3	275	171	18
4 Currie	13	8	0	5	218	242	16
5 Jed-Forest	13	7	0	6	206	185	14
6 Boroughmuir	11	6	0	5	208	162	12
7 Hawick	12	5	1	6	197	199	11
8 Heriot's FP	13	5	0	8	295	285	10
9 Stirling County	13	5	0	8	179	208	10
10 Watsonians	13	5	0	8	196	277	10
11 Kelso	13	5	0	8	711	345	10
12 Selkirk	13	4	1	8	194	316	9
13 Glasgow High	13	4	0	9	291	295	8
14 Dundee HSFP	12	3	0	9	142	269	6

Welsh League

DIVISION 1

	P	W	D	L	F	A	Pts
1 Llanelli	22	19	1	2	901	254	39
2 Cardiff	22	18	0	4	636	260	36
3 Swansea	22	17	0	5	548	326	34
4 Neath	22	13	0	9	448	359	26
5 Pontypridd	22	11	2	9	400	353	24
6 Bridgend	22	11	1	10	402	400	23
7 Newport	22	11	0	11	513	512	22
8 Pontypool	22	10	0	12	489	508	20
9 Aberavon	22	7	0	15	271	501	14
10 Newbridge	22	6	0	16	258	536	12
11 Maesteg	22	3	1	18	278	632	7
12 South Wales Pol.	22	3	1	18	243	746	7

Irish League

DIVISION 1

	P	W	D	L	F	A	Pts
1 Young Munster	8	5	1	1	114	44	13
2 Cork Constitution	8	5	0	2	166	128	12
3 St Mary's	8	5	1	2	170	84	11
4 Greystones	8	4	1	3	132	132	9
5 Old Wesley	8	4	0	4	107	155	8
6 Dungannon	8	3	0	5	144	172	6
7 Shannon	8	2	1	5	86	75	5
8 Garryowen	8	2	0	6	132	117	4
9 Ballymena	8	2	0	5	107	148	4

Shooting

NRA Imperial Meeting

Bisley   July 16-24

The Queen's Prize
1	C Brook	295.39
2	A Ringer	294.39
3	M Millar	294.35

Land Rover Discovery Trophy
1	R Grisenthwaite	74.12
2	A Jones	74.08
3	C Whatley	74.10

Chancellor's Trophy
1	Cambridge	1,169.147
2	Oxford	1,120.107

Mackinnon Trophy
1	England	1,137.111
2	Canada	1,128.100
3	Ireland	1,127.112

University Long Range
1	London	384.43

British Pistol Club Championships

Bisley   Sept 25-26
MEN
Centre Fire
1	J Harrison	581	

Standard Pistol
1	M Gault	564	

Rapid Fire
1	J Rolfe	588	UK record

Free Pistol
1	M Gault	557	

Air Pistol
1	M Gault	578	

Standard Handgun
1	P Leatherdale	588	UK record

WOMEN
Air Pistol
1	C Page	378	

Sport Pistol
1	C Page	580	

British Open Championships

Aldersly   Feb
Men
1	C Hector	Baldock	684.8
2	N Wallace	Cambs	683.8
3	R Laws	Stirling	683.2

Women
1	T Lumm	Wandsw	477.6
2	H Jones	Brton	476.5
3	J Malcolm	Whitehds	474.6

World Cup Final - Rifle

Munich   Aug 28
60 Shots Prone Rifle
1	Jens Harskov	DEN	701.6
2	S Beliaev	KZK	699.6
3	Jonathan Stern	GBR	699.1

Clay Pigeon

BRITISH OPEN
Northampton   *Mar 7*
1	K Mayor	76/188
2	N Bailey	74/182
3	J W Cook	71/175

ENGLISH OPEN
Northampton   *Apr 4*
1	K Mayor	97/241
2	B Bradley	92/226
3	A Evans	91/223

ENGLISH OPEN - DOUBLE TRAP
Thurlaston   *Apr 10*
1	K Gill	135	179
2	J Grice	137	177
3	P Boden	133	175

ENGLISH OPEN OLYMPIC TRAP
East Yorkshire GC   *May 8-9*
1	John Grice	207 ex 225
2	James Birkett-Evans	205
3	Peter Croft	204

ENGLISH ALL ROUND OPEN
Southern Counties SG   *Apr 18*
1	Mick Howell	94
2	Andy Moon	91
3	Andy Bailey	91

EUROPEAN FITSAC CHAMPIONSHIP
Zaragoza, Spain   *Apr 29-May 2*
Men's Team
1 Great Britain
Women's Team
1 Great Britain
Women's Individual
1	Anthea Hillyer	GBR

Men's Individual
1	Duan Morley	GBR

Skiing

Alpine World Championships

Morioka-Shizukuishi, Japan   Feb 5-13

MEN

Downhill

Feb 11   Dist 2735m/Drop 733m   Snow Hard

1	Urs Lehmann	SUI	**1:32.06**	**0.00**
2	Atle Skaardal	NOR	1:32.66	7.89
3	A J Kitt	USA	1:32.98	12.09
29	Martin Bell	GBR	1:34.86	36.80
32	Graham Bell	GBR	1:34.95	37.99

Slalom

Feb 13   Drop 180m   Snow Hard

1	Kjetil Andre Aamodt	NOR	**1:40.33**	**0.00**
2	Marc Girardelli	LUX	1:40.37	0.24
3	Thomas Stangassinger	AUT	1:40.44	0.67

Giant Slalom

Feb 10   Drop 370m   Snow Hard

1	Kjetil Andre Aamodt	NOR	**2:15.36**	**0.00**
2	Rainer Salzgeber	AUT	2:16.23	5.27
3	Johan Wallner	SWE	2:17.27	11.57

SUPER G

This event was not held because of adverse weather conditions.

COMBINED

Dh Feb 5/Sl Feb 8

			Dh	Sl	Total
1	Lasse Kjus	NOR	30.84	3.38	34.44
2	Kjetil Andre Aamodt	NOR	36.09	0.00	36.09
3	Marc Girardelli	LUX	30.71	5.56	36.27

WOMEN

Downhill

Feb 11   Dist 2376m/Drop 625m   Snow hard

1	Kate Pace	CAN	1:27.38	
2	Astrid Lödemel	NOR	1:27.66	3.88
3	Anja Haas	AUT	1:27.84	6.37

Slalom

Feb 9   Drop 150m   Snow hard

1	Karin Buder	AUT	1:27.66	0.00
2	Julie Parisien	USA	1:27.87	1.46
3	Elfi Eder	AUT	1:28.65	6.89
17	Emma Carrick-Anderson	GBR	1:30.97	23.03
24	Claire de Pourtales	GBR	1:32.21	31.66

Giant Slalom

Feb 10   Drop 370m   Snow hard

1	Carole Merle	FRA	2:17.59	0.00
2	Anita Wachter	AUT	2:17.99	2.38
3	Martina Ertl	GER	2:18.70	6.62

Super G

Feb 14   Dist 2131m/Drop 565m   Snow hard

1	Katja Seizinger	GER	1:33.52	0.00
2	Sylvia Eder	AUT	1:33.68	1.57
3	Astrid Lødemel	NOR	1:34.07	5.41

Combined

Dh Feb 5/Sl Feb 4

			Points		
			Dh	Sl	Total
1	Miriam Vogt	GER	3.21	0.18	3.29
2	Picabo Street	USA	0.00	32.15	32.15
3	Anita Wachter	AUT	33.52	0.00	33.52
27	Claire de Pourtales	GBR	66.76	18.33	85.09

disq sl Emma Carrick-Anderson GBR

The weather called all the shots at the World Championships, in which not one race was run on schedule. Competition was completely cancelled for four days and though most events were rearranged the men's super giant slalom was not run - the first time ever that a world championships had ended with a race not being staged.. The International Ski Federation talked of rescheduling the event after the championships, but that failed to materialise. Even when events did go ahead, there were plenty of complaints, particularly about the wind which gusted in and made racing a lottery. None of this prevented Norway's Kjetil Andre Aamodt from dominating the men's events. He won the slalom and the giant slalom and finished second in the combined and, had they run the super G and given that he was the World Cup overall champion, he would pretty damn sure have won that too.

World Cup

Men's Downhill

GARDENA, ITALY
Dec 11   Dist 3446m/Drop 839m   Snow hard
1	William Besse	SUI	1:59.49
57	Martin Bell	GBR	2:02.91
67	Graham Bell	GBR	2:04.48

Dec 12
1	Leonard Stock	AUT	2:01.90
50	Graham Bell	GBR	2:05.38
58	Martin Bell	GBR	2:05.73
67	Ronald Duncan	GBR	2:07.46

GARMISCH-PARTENKIRCHEN, GERMANY
Jan 10   Dist 3455m/Drop 960m   Snow hard
1	Franz Heinzer	SUI	1:55.09
73	Martin Bell	GBR	2:00.01
76	Ronald Duncan	GBR	2:00.40

Jan 11   Dist. 3455m/Drop 960m   Snow hard
1	Daniel Mahrer	SUI	1:53.26
56	Martin Bell	GBR	1:57.16
65	Graham Bell	GBR	1:58.91

ST ANTON-AM-ARLBERG, AUSTRIA
Jan 16   Dist 3261m/Drop 959m   Snow hard
1	Franz Heinzer	SUI	2:03.48
49	Martin Bell	GBR	2:08.23
53	Graham Bell	GBR	2:08.93

VEYSONNAZ, SWITZERLAND
Jan 23   Dist 3347m/Drop 900m   Snow hard
1	Franz Heinzer	SUI	1:59.53
52	Martin Bell	GBR	2:03.14
65	Graham Bell	GBR	2:04.38

WHISTLER MOUNTAIN, CANADA
Jan 27   Dist 3850m/Drop 1015m   Snow hard
1	Atle Skaardal	NOR	2:10.97
39	Graham Bell	GBR	2:15.24
dns	Martin Bell	GBR	

SIERRA NEVADA, SPAIN
Mar 15   Dist 3610m/Drop 970m
1	Armin Assinger	AUT	1:55.64
29	Martin Bell	GBR	1:57.84
49	Graham Bell	GBR	1:59.75
52	Roger Walker	GBR	1:59.98

KVITFJELL, NORWAY
Mar 19   Dist 3007m/Drop 837m   Snow hard
1	Adrien Duvillard	FRA	1:42.32
48	Graham Bell	GBR	1:45.50
52	Martin Bell	GBR	1:46.08
57	Roger Walker	GBR	1:49.29

Mar 20
1	Armin Assinger	AUT	1:43.13
48	Graham Bell	GBR	1:46.28
52	Martin Bell	GBR	1:46.84
dnf	Roger Walker	GBR	

FINAL DOWNHILL STANDINGS
1	**Franz Heinzer**	**SUI**	**527**
2	Atle Skaardal	NOR	427
3	William Besse	SUI	366
4	Armin Assinger	AUT	360
5	Daniel Mahrer	SUI	343

Men's Slalom

SESTRIERE, ITALY
Nov 29   Drop 210m   Snow hard
1	Fabrizio Tescari	ITA	1:58.48

VAL D'ISERE, FRANCE
Dec 6   Drop 204m   Snow hard
1	**Tomas Fogdoe**	**SWE**	**1:34.76**

MADONNA DI CAMPIGLIO, ITALY
15 Dec   Drop 180m   Snow hard
1	**Patrice Bianchi**	**FRA**	**1:35.12**

KRANJSKA GORA, SLOVENIA
Dec 19   Drop 199m   Snow hard
1	Tomas Fogdoe	SWE	1:43.20

GARMISCH-PARTENKIRCHEN, GERMANY
Jan 9   Drop 200m   Snow hard
1	Alberto Tomba	ITA	1:38.65

LECH, AUSTRIA
Jan 17   Drop 190m   Snow hard
1	Tomas Fogdoe	SWE	1:44.36

VEYSONNAZ, SWITZERLAND
Jan 24   Drop 180m   Snow hard
1	Thomas Stangassinger	AUT	1:30.42

ARE, SWEDEN
Mar 28   Drop 188m   Snow: Hard
1	Tomas Fogdoe	SWE	1:49.69	0.00

FINAL SLALOM STANDINGS
1	**Tomas Fogdoe**	**SWE**	**545**
2	Alberto Tomba	ITA	436
3	Thomas Stangassinger	AUT	362
4	B Grstein	AUT	276
5	Kjetil Andre Aamodt	NOR	267

Men's Giant Slalom

SESTRIERE, ITALY
Nov 28   Drop 325m   Snow hard
1	Kjetil Andre Aamodt	NOR	1:48.34

Dec 13   Drop 448m   Snow hard
1	Marc Girardelli	LUX	2:46.25

KRANJSKA GORA, SLOVENIA
Dec 20   Drop 320m   Snow hard
1	Marc Girardelli	LUX	1:57.48

VEYSONNAZ, SWITZERLAND
Jan 19   Drop 400m   Snow hard
1	Michael von Grünigen	SUI	2:29.51

OPPDAL, NORWAY
Mar 23   Drop 409m   Snow hard
1	Kjetil Andre Aamodt	NOR	2:21.87

ARE, SWEDEN
Mar 27   Drop 400m   Snow hard
1	Kjetil Andre Aamodt	NOR	2:28.65	0.00

FINAL GIANT SLALOM STANDINGS
1	**Kjetil Andre Aamodt**	**NOR**	**410**
2	Alberto Tomba	ITA	381
3	Marc Girardelli	LUX	372
4	Lasse Kjus	NOR	254
5	Fredrik Nyberg	SWE	250

Men's Super G

VAL D'ISERE, FRANCE
Dec 5   *Dist 2215m/Drop 530m*   *Snow: Fresh*
1 Jan Elnar Thorsen   NOR   1:16.03
dnf Graham Bell   GBR
BAD KLEINKIRCHHEIM, AUSTRIA
Dec 22   *Dist 2670m/Drop 680m*   *Snow hard*
1 Armin Assinger   AUT   1:45.60
ST. ANTON-AM-ARLBERG, AUSTRIA
Jan 12   *Dist 2235m/Drop 630m*   *Snow hard*
1 Marc Giradelli   LUX   1:28.53
49 Martin Bell   GBR   1:34.04
dnf Graham Bell   GBR
WHISTLER MOUNTAIN, CANADA
Feb 28   *Dist 1965m/Drop 537m*   *Snow hard*
1 Günther Mader   AUT   1:20.66
37 Martin Bell   GBR   1:23.26
59 Graham Bell   GBR   1:24.68
ASPEN, USA
Mar 7   *Dist 2032m/Drop 574*   *Snow hard*
1 Kjetil Andre Aamodt   NOR   1:17.48
50 Martin Bell   GBR   1:20.24
dnf Graham Bell   GBR
KVITFJELL, NORWAY
Mar 21   *Dist 2350m/Drop 640m*   *Snow hard*
1 Kjetil Andre Aamodt   NOR   1:31.59
51 Graham Bell   GBR   1:35.08
dnf Martin Bell   GBR
ARE, SWEDEN
Mar 26   *Dist 1755m/Drop 465m*   *Snow hard*
1 Kjetil Andre Aamodt   NOR   1:07.43

SUPER G FINAL STANDINGS
1 Kjetil Andre Aamodt   **NOR**   **320**
2 Jan Einar Thorsen   NOR   270
3 Franz Heinzer   SUI   241
4 Günther Mader   AUT   227
5 Marc Girardelli   LUX   200

Women's Downhill

VAIL, USA
Dec 12   *Dist 2632m/Drop 667m*   *Snow hard Pack*
1 Miriam Vogt   GER   1:42.06
LAKE LOUISE, CANADA
Dec 19   *Dist 2602m/Drop 725m*   *Snow hard*
1 Chantal Bournissen   SUI   1:35.88
CORTINA D'AMPEZZO, ITALY
Jan 9   *Dist 2490m/Drop 723m*   *Snow hard*
1 Regina Haeusl   GER   1:28.49
Jan 15   *Snow hard*
1 Katja Seizinger   GER   1:27.35
HAUS-IM-ENNSTAL, AUSTRIA
Jan 22   *Dist 3046m/Drop 786m*   *Snow hard*
1 Chantal Bournissen   SUI   1:42.64
Feb 26   *Dist 2500m/Drop 675m*   *Snow hard*
1 Katja Seizinger   GER   1:34.41
44 Debbie Pratt   GBR   1:38.66
Feb 27   *Snow hard*
1 Anja Haas   AUT   1:34.47
46 Debbie Pratt   GBR   1:38.14

MORZINE, FRANCE
Mar 6   *Dist 2680/Drop 767m*   *Snow hard*
1 Katja Seizinger   GER   1:18.88
45 Debbie Pratt   GBR   1:24.07
HAFJELL, NORWAY
Mar 13   *Dist 3000m/Drop 692m*   *Snow hard*
1 Kate Pace   CAN   1:50.60

DOWNHILL FINAL STANDINGS
1 Katja Seizinger   **GER**   **604**
2 Regina Haeusl   GER   323
3 Kerrin Lee-Gartner   CAN   294

Women's Slalom

PARK CITY, USA
Nov 29   *Drop 150m*   *Snow hard*
1 Julie Parisien   USA   1:18.63
STEAMBOAT SPRINGS
Dec 6   *Drop 187m*   *Snow hard*
1 Pernilla Wiberg   SWE   1:35.82
MARIBOR, SLOVENIA
Jan 6   *Drop 196m*   *Snow hard*
1 Vreni Schneider   SUI   1:39.11
CORTINA D'AMPEZZO, ITALY
Jan 10   *Drop 400m*   *Snow hard*
1 Carole Merle   FRA   2:31.54
Jan 17   *Drop 160m*   *Snow hard*
1 Vreni Schneider   SUI   1:32.39
dnq for 2nd run:
    Claire de Pourtales   GBR
    Emma Carrick-Anderson GBR
HAUS-IM-ENNSTAL, AUSTRIA
Jan 24   *Drop 176m*   *Snow hard*
1 Patricia Chauvet   FRA   1:38.24
dnf 1st run:
Clarie de Pourtales GBR
Emma Carrick-Anderson GBR
HAFJELL, NORWAY
Mar 14   *Drop 178m*   *Snow hard*
1 Renate Götschl   AUT   1:38.01
VEMDALEN, SWEDEN
Mar 19   *Drop 193m*   *Snow hard*
1 Vreni Schneider   SUI   1:43.36
ARE, SWEDEN
Mar 28   *Drop 163m*   *Snow hard*
1 Vreni Schneider   SUI   1:34.05

SLALOM FINAL STANDINGS
1 Vreni Schneider   **SUI**   **490**
2 Annelise Coburger   NZL   484
3 Patricia Chauvet   FRA   402
4 Anita Wachter   AUT   272
5 Kristina Andersson   SWE   261

Women's Giant Slalom
PARK CITY, USA
Nov 28   *Drop 340m*   Snow hard
1 Ulrike Maier   AUT   2:21.87   0.00
STEAMBOAT SPRINGS, USA
Dec 5   *Drop 300m*   *Snow hard*
1 Anita Wachter   AUT   2:00.61   0.00

MARIBOR, SLOVENIA
5 Jan	Drop 390m	Snow hard		
1	Carole Merle	FRA	2:29.44	0.00

HAFJELL, NORWAY
Mar 15	Drop 370m		Snow hard	
1	Christina Meier	GER	2:22.06	

KLOEVSJOE, SWEDEN
Mar 20	Drop 304m		Snow hard	
1	Katja Seizinger	GER	2:02.71	

ARE, SWEDEN
Mar 27	Drop 400m		Snow hard	
1	Carole Merle	FRA	2:29.65	0.00

FINAL GIANT SLALOM STANDINGS

1	Carole Merle	FRA	**480**
2	Anita Wachter	AUT	396
3	Martina Ertl	GER	278
4	Ulrike Maier	AUT	252
5	Heidi Zeller	SUI	245

OVERALL WORLD CUP STANDINGS

Men

1	Marc Girardelli	LUX	1,379
2	Kjetil Andre Aamodt	NOR	1,347
3	Franz Heinzer	SUI	828
4	Günthor Mader	AUT	826
5	Alberto Tomba	ITA	817
6	Atle Skaardal	NOR	596

Women

1	Anita Wachter	AUT	1,286
2	Katja Seizinger	GER	1,266
3	Carole Merle	FRA	1,086
4	Miriam Vogt	GER	699
5	Ulrike Maier	AUT	696
6	Vreni Schneider	SUI	626

Ski Jumping

World Cup - Final Standings

1	A Goldberger	AUT	206
2	J Sakala	RCS	185
3	N Kasai	JPN	172

Nordic Skiing

World Cup - Final Standings
Women's Team

1	Norway	6,255
2	Russia	6,135
3	Italy	4,852

Men's Individual Cross-country

1	B Daehlie	NOR	696
2	V Smirnov	KZK	649
3	V Ulvang	NOR	576

British Ski Championships

(sponsored by The British Land Company)
Feb 13-20   Tignes, France

MEN
Downhill
Jan 15   *Dist 2500m/Drop 575m*   *Snow:Hard*
1. Graham Bell   GBR   1:14.10
Slalom
Jan 19   *Drop 160m*   *Snow:Hard*
1. Didier Schmidt   FRA   1:15.47
Giant Slalom
Jan 18   *Drop 300m*   *Snow:Hard*
1. Spenser Pession   GBR   1:47.94
Super G
Jan 17   *Dist 2350m/Drop 500m*   *Snow:Hard*
1. Graham Bell   GBR   1:14.57
WOMEN
Downhill
Jan 16   *Dist 2500m/Drop 575m*   *Snow:Hard*
1. Debbie Pratt   GBR   1:18.78
Slalom
Jan 19   *Drop 140m*   *Snow:Hard*
1. Emma Carrick-Anderson GBR   1:09.06
Giant Slalom
Jan 18   *Drop 300m*   *Snow:Hard*
1. Carole Moschetti   FRA   1:54.00
Super G
Jan 17   *Dist 2350m/Drop 500m*   *Snow:hard*
1. Jessika Duvillard   FRA   1:20.07

AERIALS
Men
1 Phillippe Laroche   CAN   231.79
2 Richard Cobbing   GBR   229.75
Eliminated:
32 Kevin Harbut   GBR
Women
1 Lina Tcherjazova   UZB   161.37
Eliminated:
20 Jill Curry   GBR

COMBINED

Men		Ballet	Aerl	Mgl	Total
1 Sergey Shupletsov	RUS	10.00	7.71	10.00	27.71
Women					
1 Katherina Kubenk	CAN	10.00	8.06	9.91	27.97
5 Jill Curry	GBR	7.82	7.96	10.00	25.78

Freestyle Skiing
World Championships

Alternmarkt, Austria   Mar 6-14

MOGHULS			*time*	
Men		*pts*	*pts*	*total*
1 Jean-Luc Brassard	CAN	20.50	6.07	26.57
Eliminated:				
29 Hugh Hutchison	GBR			
51 Michael Liebreich	GBR			
69 Neil Munro	GBR			
Women				
1 Stine Lise Hattestad	NOR	19.35	5.87	25.22
Eliminated:				
16 Jill Curry	GBR			

BALLET			
Men		*Pts*	
1 Fabrice Becker	FRA	29.30	
Women			
1 Ellen Breen	USA	25.50	
5 Julia Snell	GBR	22.75	
Eliminated:			
12 Vicki Simpson	GBR		
23 Jill Curry	GBR		

Snooker

Stephen Hendry did not start the season as an incumbent world champion should. By his own reckoning, at the beginning of 1993, his world number one ranking was in jeopardy. However, the 24 year old Scot could afford to forget the start and the middle of the season because, when the world championships came around at the tail end of the season, he was concentrating brilliantly. In the world championship final, played at Sheffield's Crucible Theatre for the 17th successive year, Hendry so dominated proceedings in his 18-5 victory that his opponent Jimmy White won just a single frame on the final day. It was Hendry's third world championship in four years - on each occasion defeating White in the final - and only Steve Davis, in beating John Parrott 18-3 in 1989, has won a Crucible final by a wider margin.

"I punished Jimmy's every mistake and never had any lapses of concentration. It felt awesome," said Hendry, who in collecting the £175,000 first prize took his table earnings for his career to over £3 million. Hendry equalled the event record of Davis by winning 70 frames to 24 overall. Also the three century breaks that he made in the final took his tally of such breaks in major competitions to 206 in his brief career. Davis, who held the previous record of 203 such breaks, is now 36, making him over 11 years senior to Hendry.

For Davis, after two years of purgatory, he re-emerged at least as a contender with victories in the European and British Opens in February and March. However, the six-time champion, who rebuilt his technique to correct a cue-ball alignment problem, could not sustain the recovery to Sheffield, where Alan McManus halted his progress in the last sixteen. McManus had already eliminated the undoubted Rookie of the Year Ronnie O'Sullivan, who turned professional in September 1992, while still only 16, and proceeded to win his first 38 matches, thereby eclipsing Hendry's record. Hendry had previously enjoyed 36 straight wins - though even he could not manage it that soon in his career.

Tony Drago also claimed a record; that of fastest victory in a nine frame match. Drago beat Sean Lanigan 5-0 in the 5th round of the Strachan Challenge at the White Snooker Lodge in Aldershot. Drago took just 34 minutes to complete the rout, but the record could not be ratified as the official stopwatch was not started. At the other end of the scale, in September, Cliff Thorburn (who else?) broke his own co-held record for the longest frame. Competing against Stephen O'Connor in the Regal Welsh Open at Blackpool (yes, Blackpool's in Wales now), the Canadian and O'Connor took a mere 93 minutes and 59 seconds to settle the deciding frame. Thorburn, who shared the previous record taking 88 minutes in the Rothmans in 1991 to finish a frame with Paul Gibson, lost the match 5-4, which might be God's way of saying, 'Can you go a bit quicker, please?'

THE YOUNGEST STEPHEN HENDRY
13.1.69 South Queensferry, Edinburgh

1984: Youngest ever Scottish Amateur champion
1985: Turned professional on 1st July
1986: Youngest Scottish Professional Champion
1987: Youngest player to win a world ranking event
1990: Youngest world champion
      Youngest world number one
1991: Youngest snooker millionaire
1993: Youngest three-time world champion

Managed by Ian Doyle
Career prize money earnings £3,048,011

Dave Harold, at 93, was the lowest ranked player to win a major tournament when, to the collective grief of 50 million Thais, the Stoke player took the Nescafe Asian Open. In the same competition, Jimmy White made himself the least popular man in Bangkok when he eliminated national hero James Wattana. Fifteenth ranked Dennis Taylor failed to win any of the major events, but the 1985 world champion wrote his own little bit of snooker history when he featured in the top sixteen rankings for the 17th successive season - every year since they were first compiled.

Embassy World Championship

Crucible Theatre, Sheffield   April 17 - May 3

ROUND 11		ROUND 12		ROUND 13		Q/F		S/F	
Danny Fowler	10	Stephen Hendry(1)	10						
Karl Broughton	4	Danny Fowler	1						
				Stephen Hendry	13				
Eddie Charlton	0	Darren Morgan(16)	10	Darren Morgan	4				
Les Dodd	10	Les Dodd	5			Stephen Hendry	13		
						Nigel Bond	7		
Mark Bennett	9	Nigel Bond(9)	10						
Spencer Dunn	10	Spencer Dunn	4	Nigel Bond	13				
				Gary Wilkinson	7				
Dean Reynolds	10	Gary Wilkinson(8)	10						
Dave Finbow	8	Dean Reynolds	4					Stephen Hendry	16
								Alan McManus	8
Silvino Francisco	6	Neil Foulds(5)	10						
Brian Morgan	10	Brian Morgan	5	Neil Foulds	13				
				Martin Clark	7				
Joe Johnson	6	Martin Clark(12)	10						
Karl Payne	10	Karl Payne	6			Neil Foulds	11		
						Alan McManus	13		
M Johnston-Allen	4	Alan McManus(13)	10						
Ronnie O'Sullivan	10	Ronnie O'Sullivan	7	Alan McManus	13				
				Steve Davis	11				
Dene O'Kane	5	Steve Davis(4)	10						
Peter Ebdon	10	Peter Ebdon	3						
								Stephen Hendry	**18**
Mike Hallett	7	Jimmy White(3)	10					**Jimmy White**	**5**
Joe Swail	10	Joe Swail	4						
				Jimmy White	13				
Doug Mountjoy	10	Alain Robidoux(14)	6	Doug Mountjoy	6				
Tony Chappel	2	Doug Mountjoy	10			Jimmy White	13		
						Dennis Taylor	8		
Tony Drago	10	Dennis Taylor(11)	10						
Tony Wilson	5	Tony Drago	9	Dennis Taylor	13				
				Terry Griffiths	11				
David Roe	10	Terry Griffiths(6)	10						
Nigel Gilbert	4	David Roe	6					Jimmy White	16
								James Wattana	9
Tony Jones	10	James Wattana(7)	10						
John Read	9	Tony Jones	7	James Wattana	13				
				Steve James	7				
Tony Knowles	6	Steve James(10)	10						
John Harvey Giles	10	John Harvey Giles	2			James Wattana	13		
						John Parrott	6		
Ken Doherty	4	Willie Thorne(15)	10						
Shaun Mellish	10	Shaun Mellish	6	Willie Thorne	9				
				John Parrott	13				
Peter Francisco	6	John Parrott(2)	10						
Stephen O'Connor	10	Stephen O'Connor	1						

Major Tournaments

Date	Tournament	Venue	Status	Final		S/Finalists	1stPrize
Sep 30 Oct 10	Dubai Duty Free Classic	Al Nasr Stadium	Major Ranking	John Parrott Stephen Hendry	9 8	A McManus J Wattana	£40,000
Oct 12 -25	Rothmans Grand Prix	Hexagon Reading	Major Ranking	Jimmy White Ken Doherty	10 9	A McManus T Griffith	£80,000
Oct 31 Nov 11	Benson & Hedges Championship	Glasgow	Ranking	Chris Small Alan McManus	9 1	P Lines Birch	
Nov 13 -29	Royal Liver Assurance UK Championship	Guildhall Preston	Major Ranking	Jimmy White John Parrott	16 9	A McManus S Davis	£70,000
Dec 4 -12	World Matchplay	Dome Doncaster	Sanctioned	James Wattana Steve Davis	9 4	A McManus M Clark	£70,000
Dec 12 -21	Strachan Challenge Series	Aldershot	Ranking	Joe Swail Stefan Mazrocis	9 4	R O'Sullivan Hamilton	
Jan 3 -12	Strachan Challenge Series	Sheffield	Ranking	Troy Shaw Nigel Bond	9 4	B Morgan E Henderson	
Jan 24 -31	Regal Welsh	Newport Centre	Major Ranking	Ken Doherty Alan McManus	9 7	J Wattana J Swail	£27,500
Feb 1 -6	Strachan Challenge Series - Final Stages	White Lodge Aldershot	Ranking	Tony Drago Ken Doherty	9 7	B Snaddon K Payne	
Feb 7 -14	Benson & Hedges Masters	Wembley Conference C	Sanctioned	Stephen Hendry James Wattana	9 5	A McManus J White	£110,000
Feb 16 -24	Humo European Open	Antwerp Belgium	Major Ranking	Steve Davis Stephen Hendry	10 4	A Hicks M Price	£25,000
Feb 22 Mar 6	Wikes Home Improvement British Open	Assembly Rooms, Derby	Major Ranking	Steve Davis James Wattana	10 2	J White S Hendry	£50,000
Mar 13 -20	Nescafé Asian Open	Bangkok Thailand	Major Ranking	Dave Harold Darren Morgan	9 3	P Davies J White	£30,000
Mar 23 -28	Benson & Hedges Irish Masters	Goff's Complex Co. Kildare	Sanctioned	Steve Davis Alan McManus	9 4	S Hendry J Parrott	£45,000
Apr 2 -11	International Open	Pavilions Plymouth	Major Ranking	Stephen Hendry Steve Davis	10 6	D Harold K Doherty	£25,000
Apr 17 May 3	Embassy World Championships	Crucible Sheffield	Major Ranking	Stephen Hendry Jimmy White	18 5	A McManus J Wattana	£175,000
	Matchroom League			Jimmy White Alan McManus	10		£25,000

HIGHEST BREAKS in the 1993 World Championships

144	Steve Davis
139	Nigel Bond
138	Steve James
136	Stephen Hendry
133	Terry Griffiths
129	Stephen Hendry

HIGHEST BREAKS in the 1992-3 Season

147	Peter Ebdon	UK Championships
144	Jamie Woodman	Asian Open
144	Steve Davis	Embassy World Chmps
141	Steve Davis	World Matchplay
141	John Giles	European Open

World Ranking List -1993

1 Stephen Hendry	50050.000	
2 John Parrott	44200.000	
3 Jimmy White	44050.000	
4 Steve Davis	43700.000	
5 James Wattana	41450.000	
6 Alan McManus	40400.000	
7 Willie Thorne	35600.000	
8 Terry Griffiths	35200.000	
9 Nigel Bond	35130.000	
10 Darren Morgan	34600.000	
11 Ken Doherty	33220.000	
12 Martin Clark	32960.000	
13 Steve James	30550.000	
14 Neil Foulds	30020.000	
15 Dennis Taylor	29100.000	
16 David Roe	29080.000	
17 Gary Wilkinson	28260.000	
18 Alain Robidoux	27320.000	
19 Mike Hallett	27100.000	
20 Tony Drago	26850.000	
21 Peter Ebdon	26805.625	
22 Dean O'Kane	26170.000	
23 Tony Knowles	25940.000	
24 Mark Bennett	25830.000	
25 Joe Swail	24942.500	
26 Joe Johnson	24330.000	
27 Mick Price	24220.000	
28 Dean Reynolds	24150.000	
29 Tony Jones	23160.000	
30 Doug Mountjoy	22960.000	
31 Mark Johnston-Allen	22950.000	
32 Jason Ferguson	22225.000	
33 Silvino Francisco	22010.000	
34 Eddie Charlton	21290.000	
35 Danny Fowler	20580.000	

36 Paul Davies	19376.250
37 Brian Morgan	19120.000
38 Peter Francisco	18850.000
39 Bob Chaperon	18750.000
40 Jim Wych	18600.000
41 Cliff Thorburn	18000.000
42 Jason Prince	17790.000
43 Wayne Jones	17750.000
44 Jonathan Birch	17620.000
45 Rod Lawler	17430.000
46 Les Dodd	17420.000
47 Cliff Wilson	16790.000
48 Tony Chappel	16650.000
49 Anthony Hamilton	16367.500
50 Dave Harold	16016.875
51 Tony Meo	15790.000
52 Nigel Gilbert	15520.000
53 Nick Terry	15440.000
54 Andy Hicks	15236.875
55 Ian Graham	14820.000
56 Steve Newbury	14730.000
57 Ronnie O'Sullivan	14720.000
58 Jack McLaughlin	14610.000
59 Billy Snaddon	14427.500
60 Steve Murphy	14380.000
61 Alex Higgins	14220.000
62 Eugene Hughes	14180.000
63 Dave Finbow	14067.500
64 Drew Henry	13780.000
65 John Campbell	13730.000
66 Barry West	13420.000
67 David Taylor	13375.000
68 Brady Gollan	13300.000
69 Kirk Stevens	13100.000
70 Warren King	13000.000
71 Andrew Cairns	12970.000

72 John Virgo	12900.000
73 Mark Rowing	12300.000
74 Paul McPhillips	12078.750
75 Nick Dyson	11755.000
76 Colin Roscoe	11610.000
77 Troy Shaw	11006.875
78 John Read	10935.000
79 Franky Chan	10900.000
80 Tony Wilson	10735.000
81 Paul Tanner	10638.750
82 Steve Campbell	10635.000
83 Karl Broughton	10537.500
84 Robby Foldvari	10485.000
85 Shaun Mellish	10430.000
86 Brian Rowswell	10290.000
87 Joe Grech	10270.000
88 Paul Gibson	10235.000
89 Craig Edwards	9955.000
90 Anthony Davies	9864.375
91 Mark Davies	9741.250
92 Jon Wright	9575.000
93 Robert Marshall	9465.000
94 Karl Payne	9437.500
95 Bill Oliver	9430.000
96 Steve Duggan	9400.000
97 Peter Daubney	9217.500
98 Chris Small	8940.000
99 Ken Owers	8910.000
100 Fergal O'Brien	8905.625
Others include:	
134 Ray Edmonds	5625.000
234 Alison Fisher	1963.125
259 Fred Davies	1360.000
288 Stacey Hillyard	985.625

The 1993 rankings above apply throughout the 1993/4 season.

Women's Snooker

FOTE HOTELS WORLD CHAMPIONSHIP
April
Quarter-finals
Allison Fisher 6 *frames* Sharon Dickson 1
Ann-Marie Farren 6 Tessa Davidson 4
Karen Corr 6 Sarah Smith 2
Stacey Hillyard 6 Georgina Apun 0
Semi-finals
Allison Fisher 7 Ann-Marie Farren 3
Stacey Hillyard 7 Karen Corr 2 ·
Final
Allison Fisher 9 Stacey Hillyard 3

SCOTTISH REGAL MASTERS
Nov 7-8, 1992
Semi-finals
Karen Corr 4 Mandy Fisher 0
Ann-Marie Farren 4 Allison Fisher 1
Final
Karen Corr 4 Ann-Marie Farren 3

PONTINS BRITISH OPEN CHAMPIONSHIPS
Nov 28-29, 1992
Semi-finals
Allison Fisher 3 Tessa Davidson 1
Karen Corr 3 Maria Tart 0
Final
Allison Fisher 4 Karen Corr 0

SAFFRON LADIES CLASSIC
Feb 14
Semi-finals
Tessa Davidson 3 Allison Fisher 2
Karen Corr 3 Stacey Hillyard 2
Final
Karen Corr 3 Tessa Davidson 0

PONTINS UK CHAMPIONSHIPS
Mar 20-21
Semi-finals
Tessa Davidson 3 Karen Corr 2
Stacey Hillyard 3 Sarah Smith 0
Final
Stacey Hillyard 4 Tessa Davidson 3

PONTINS BOWL
May 12-14
Semi-finals
Allison Fisher 3 Ann-Marie Farren 0
Karen Corr 3 Kim Shaw 1
Final
Allison Fisher 4 Karen Corr 3

LLANELLI CLASSIC
June
Semi-finals
Karen Corr 3 Ann-Marie Farren 1
Stacey Hillyard 3 Tessa Davidson 0
Final
Stacey Hillyard 3 Karen Corr 2

JAMES BROOKS CLASSIC
August
Semi-finals
Tessa Davidson 3 June Banks 0
Caroline Walch 3 Emma Bonney 1
Final
Tessa Davidson 3 Caroline Walch 2

CONNIE GOUGH MEMORIAL
Aug 22
Semi-finals
Kelly Fisher 3 Kim Shaw 1
Tessa Davidson 3 Stacey Hillyard 0
Final
Kelly Fisher 3 Tessa Davidson 1

WORLD RANKING LIST
As at October 1

1	Allison Fisher	Hadlow	568
2	Karen Corr	Bourne	488
3	Stacey Hillyard	Christchurch	473
4	Tessa Davidson	Bicester	457
5	Ann-Marie Farren	Nottingham	394
6	Kim Shaw	Wisbech	326
7	Mandy Fisher	Wisbech	289
8	Lynette Horsburgh	Blackpool	276
9	Sarah Smith	Sheffield	257
10	Sharon Dickson	Newport	257
11	Lisa Quick	Weston-S-M	212
12	Georgina Aplin	Royston	212
13	Kelly Fisher	Pontefract	210
14	Caroline Walch	Sunbury	205
15	Julie Gillespie	Doune	182
16	June Banks	Orpington	169
17	Lisa Gordon	Romford	133
18	Maria Tart	Hounslow	124
19	Jenny Poulter	Snodland	116
20	Helen Audus	Leeds	111
21	Maureen Seto	Canada	98
22	Carla Jolly	Reading	86
23	Theresa Carlisle	Mitcham	79
24	Debbie Reynolds	Peterborough	78
25	Nicola Binden	Bournemouth	77

Speedway

World Championship

Pocking, Germany   Aug 29

Heat 1
1 Gustafsson 2 Hamill 3 Castagna
Rise fell
Heat 2
1 Ermolenko 2 Karlsson 3 Screen 4 Jonsson
Heat 3
1 Nielsen 2 Hancock 3 Rickardsson 4 Adams
Heat 4
1 Louis 2 Havelock 3 Gollob 4 Smith
Heat 5
1 Ermolenko 2 Louis 3 Adams 4 Riss
Heat 6
1 Nielsen 2 Havelock 3 Screen
Castagna fell
Heat 7
1 Gollob 2 Rickardsson 3 Hamill 4 Karlsson
Heat 8
1 Jonsson 2 Smith 3 Gustafsson 4 Hancock
Heat 9
1 Smith 2 Screen 3 Riss 4 Rickardsson
Heat 10
1 Ermolenko 2 Gollob 3 Castagna 4 Hancock
Heat 11
1 Havelock 2 Jonsson 3 Hamill 4 Adams
Heat 12
1 Karlsson 2 Nielsen 3 Louis 4 Gustafsson
Heat 13
1 Riss 2 Karlsson 3 Havelock 4 Hancock
Heat 14
1 Castagna 2 Louis 3 Jonsson 4 Rickardsson
Heat 15
1 Ermolando 2 Smith 3 Hamill 4 Nielsen (FX)
Heat 16
1 Gustafsson 2 Gollob 3 Adams 4 Screen (FX)
Heat 17
1 Nielsen 2 Riss 3 Jonsson 4 Gollob
Heat 18
1 Smith 2 Adams 3 Karlsson 4 Castagna
Heat 19
1 Louis 2 Hamill 3 Screen 4 Hancock
Heat 20
1 Gustafsson 2 Havelock 3 Rickardsson 4 Ermolenko

Final Placings

			1	2	3	4	5	Tot
1	Sam Ermolenko	USA	3	3	3	3	0	12
2	Hans Nielsen	DEN	3	3	2	X	3	11
				after run off				
3	Chris Lewis	ENG	3	2	1	2	3	11
4	Andy Smith	ENG	0	2	3	2	3	10
5	H Gustafsson	SWE	3	1	0	3	3	10
6	Gary Havelock	ENG	2	2	3	1	2	10
7	Tomasz Gollob	POL	1	3	2	2	0	8
8	Peter Karlsson	SWE	2	0	3	2	1	8
9	Per Jonsson	SWE	0	3	2	1	1	7
10	Billy Hamill	USA	2	1	1	1	2	7

11	Gerd Riss	GER	F	0	1	3	2	6
12	A Castagna	ITA	1	F	1	3	0	5
13	Joe Screen	ENG	1	1	2	X	1	5
14	Leigh Adams	AUS	0	1	0	1	2	4
15	T Rickardsson	SWE	1	2	0	0	1	4
16	Greg Hancock	USA	2	0	0	0	0	2

England v United States

Arena-Essex   Sept 24
United States 65 (S Ermolenko 15, G Hancock 13, B Ott 12, J Larsen 12, B Hamill 10, J Cook 3, S Moran 0, D Nicol 0)
England 43 (M Loran 10, J Screeen 10, G Havelock 10, M Dugard 8, C Louis 5, D Norris 1, T Pratt 0)

World Pair Championships

Vojens, Denmark   Aug 1
Final Placings

1	Sweden	26
2	USA	23
3	Denmark	21
4	England	18

Squash

Men's World Open

Johannesburg   Nov 21-26

2nd Round

Selected results

Jansher Khan (PAK) bt Tony Hands (ENG) 3 sets to 1
Sami Elopuro (FIN) bt Chris Walker (ENG) 3 sets to 1
Peter Marshall (ENG bt Jahangir Khan (PAK) 2-2 retd
Rodney Martin (AUS) bt Del Harris (ENG) 3 sets to 1

Quarter-finals

Jansher Khan (PAK) bt Sami Elopuro 3 sets to 0
Austin Adarraga (ESP) bt Peter Marshall 3 sets to 2
Rodney Martin bt Brett Martin (AUS) 3 sets to 2
Chris Dittmar (AUS) bt Rodney Eyles (AUS) 3 sets to 0

Semi-finals

Jansher Khan bt Austin Adarraga 3 sets to 1
Chris Dittmar bt Rodney Martin 3 sets to 1

Final

Jansher Khan (PAK) bt Chris Dittmar (AUS) 15-11 15-9
10-15 15-6

Women's World Open

Johannesburg   Sept 19-25

Quarter-finals

Martine Le Moignan (ENG) bt S Horner (ENG) 9-0, 5-9, 9-
7, 10-8
S Schöne (GER) bt C Jackman (ENG) 8-10, 1-9, 9-1, 10-8,
9-6
Michelle Martin (AUS) bt S Fitzgerald (AUS) 9-7, 9-4, 9-3
E Irving (AUS) bt S Wright (ENG) 9-4, 9-1, 9-6

Semi-finals

Michelle Martin bt Martine Le Moignan 9-4, 9-0, 9-6
E Irving bt S Schöne 9-5, 8-10, 9-4, 9-6

Final

Michelle Martin bt E Irving 9-2, 9-2, 9-1

WOMEN'S WORLD TEAM CHAMPIONSHIPS

Vancouver, CAN

Semi-finals

England 1   New Zealand 2
Australia 3   Holland 0

Final

Australia 2   New Zealand 1

BRITISH OPEN

Wembley   Apr 14-19

Men's Final

Jansher Khan bt Chris Dittmar 9-6, 9-5, 6-9, 9-2

Women's Final

Michelle Martin (AUS) bt Suzanne Horner (ENG) 9-7, 9-0,
9-4

WORLD RANKINGS

Men

As at Sept 1

1	Jansher Khan	PAK	1210.947
2	Chris Dittmar	AUS	114.400
3	Rodney Martin	AUS	708.158
4	Brett Martin	AUS	643.358
5	Peter Marshall	ENG	497.713
6	Rodney Eyles	AUS	400.557
7	Ross Norman	NZL	394.942
8	Sami Elopuro	FIN	331,848
9	Chris Walker	ENG	331.748
10	Philip Whitlock	ENG	325.102
11	Tristan Nancarrow	AUS	311.925
12	Simon Parke	ENG	279.696

Women

As at May

1	Michelle Martin	AUS	13140
2	Martine le Moignan	ENG	6235
3	Suzanne Horner	ENG	5850
4	Susan Wright	ENG	5615
5	Cassandra Jackman	ENG	5325
6	Liz Irving	AUS	5287
7	Sarah Fitzgerald	AUS	4867
8	Heather Wallace	CAN	4070
9	Sabine Schöne	GER	3360
10	Lisa Opie	ENG	3355
11	Rebecca O'Callaghan	IRL	3170
12	Claire Nitch	RSA	2817

TOURNAMENT OF CHAMPIONS

New York   Apr

Final

Jansher Khan bt Chris Dittmar 15-7, 12-15, 15-4, 15-9

GUERNSEY OPEN

Kings Club, Guernsey   Mar 24-28

Women's Final

Michelle Martin (AUS) bt Liz Irving (AUS) 9-5, 9-6, 9-7

JSM SUPER SQUASH '93 TOURNAMENT

Tokyo   May 19-23

Women's Final

Michelle Martin bt Cassie Jackman (ENG) 9-3, 9-7, 9-7

HONG KONG OPEN

May 30

Men's Final

Rodney Martin (AUS) bt Chris Dittmar (AUS) 12-15,
15-13, 16-14, 15-9

Women's Final

Michelle Martin bt Liz Irving 4-9, 9-0, 6-9, 9-4, 9-3

Swimming

If your name is Franziska van Almsick, you can make a very nice living out of swimming these days. Franzi, as she is known to all and sundry in Germany, is reputed to earn £300,000 for her swimwear contracts (although such stories always confuse the period of the contract). She also picked up around £200,000 for Suchard chocolate ads, so however you add it up, she won't be worrying about the VAT on her gas bill. Van Almsick cornered much of the limelight from the European championships with six gold medals, but as all her titles were freestyle events, three of them relays, her performance hardly compares with the four individual golds, two back, one fly and one IM, of Hungary's four-time Olympic champion Kristina Egerszegi. Nick Gillingham came up trumps for Britain, although after Guttler's astounding 100m, it looked as if the Briton would be stretched in the longer event. But Gillingham continued his fine championship record and set Britain up for its best European championship since the 1958 event. The ASA, looking ahead, implemented the next stage of its development plan this year with the appointment of five RDOs - regional development officers. The hope is that the sport will be able to channel some of the vast number of leisure swimmers into competitive swimming.

European Championships   Sheffield   Jul 30-Aug 8

MEN

50m Free

1 Alexander Popov	RUS	22:27 CR
2 Christophe Kalfayan	FRA	22:39
3 Raimundas Mazulis	LIT	22:44
Mark Foster	GBR	Disq.
Mike Fibbens	GBR	Disq.

100m Free

1 Alexander Popov	RUS	49:14 CR
2 Tommy Werner	SWE	49.71
3 Pavel Khnikin	UKR	49:76
7 Mike Fibbens	GBR	50:48
B Final: 7 Alan Rapley	GBR	51:32

200m Free

1 Antti Kasvio	FIN	1:47:11
2 Evgeny Sadovy	RUS	1:47:25
3 Anders Holmertz	SWE	1:47:69

400m Free

1 Antti Kasvio	FIN	3:47:81
2 Paul Palmer	GBR	3:48:14
3 Anders Holmertz	SWE	3:48:98

1500m Free

1 Jorg Hoffmann	GER	15:13:31
2 Sebastian Wiese	GER	15:14:76
3 Igor Majcen	SLO	15:15:05

100m Breast

1 Karoly Guttler	HUN	1:01:04
2 Nick Gillingham	GBR	1:02:02
3 Vitaly Kirinchuk	RUS	1:02:48
B Final: 8 Richard Maden	GBR	1:04:71

200m Breast

1 Nick Gillingham	GBR	2:12:49 CR
2 Karoly Guttler	HUN	2:13:26
3 Andrey Korneev	RUS	2:14:20

100m Back

1 Martin Lopez-Zubero	ESP	55:03 CR
2 Vladimir Selkov	RUS	55:58
3 Martin Harris	GBR	55:75
8 Adam Ruckwood	GBR	56:68

200m Back

1 Vladimir Selkov	RUS	1:58:09 CR
2 Martin Lopez-Zubero	ESP	1:58:51
3 Emanuele Merisi	ITA	1:59:57
B Final: 1 Adam Ruckwood	GBR	2:02:16

100m Fly

1 Rafal Szukala	POL	53:41 CR
2 Denis Pankratov	RUS	53:43
3 Milos Milosevic	CRO	53:65

200m Fly

1 Denis Pankratov	RUS	1.56.25 CR
2 Franck Esposito	FRA	1:58:66
3 Chris-Carol Bremer	GER	2:00:33

200m IM

1 Jani Sievinen	FIN	2:00:70
3 Christian Keller	GER	2:01:18

400m IM

1 Tamás Darnyi	HUN	4:15:24 CR
2 Jani Sievinen	FIN	4:15:51
3 Marcel Wouda	NED	4:15:51

4x100m Free

1 Russia		3:18:80 CR
(Predkin, Pyshnenko, Sadovy, Popov)		
2 Sweden		3:19:33
3 Germany		3:20:13
7 Great Britain		3:22:37
(Fibbens, Foster, Rapley, Metcalfe)		

4x100m Medley

1 Russia		3:38:90 CR

(Selkov, Kirinchuk, Pankratov, Popov)			
2 Hungary			3:40:97
3 Great Britain			3:41:66
(Harris, Gillingham, Fibbens, Foster)			

4x200m Free

1 Russia		7:15:84
(Lepikov, Pyshnenko, Mukhin, Sadovy)		
2 Germany		7:18:53
3 France		7:19:86
5 Great Britain		7:26:48
(Palmer, Clayton, Carl, Mellor)		

WOMEN

50m Free

1 Franziska Van Almsick	GER	25:53
2 Linda Olofsson	SWE	25:67
3 Inge de Bruijn	NED	25:86

100m Free

1 Franziska Van Almsick	GER	54.57 ER
2 Martina Moravcova	SVK	55:97
3 Catherine Plewinski	FRA	56:09
6 Karen Pickering	GBR	56.44

200m Free

1 Franziska Van Almsick	GER	1:57:97 CR
2 Luminita Dobrescu	ROM	2:00:39
3 Karen Pickering	GBR	2:01:15

400m Free

1 Dagmar Hase	GER	4:10:47
2 Kerstin Kielgass	GER	4:12:18
3 Irene Dalby	NOR	4:12:51
8 Sarah Hardcastle	GBR	4:17:47

800m Free

1 Jana Kenke	GER	8:32:47
2 Irene Dalby	NOR	8:33:77
3 Olga Splichalova	TCH	8:36:59
6 Sarah Hardcastle	GBR	8:40:45

100m Breast

1 Sylvia Gerasch	GER	1:10:05
2 Svetlana Bondarenko	UKR	1:10:29
3 Elena Roudkovskaya	BLS	1:10:52
8 Jaime King	GBR	1:12:37
B Final: 5 Marie Hardiman	*GBR*	*1:12:18*

200m Breast

1 Brigitte Becue	BEL	2:31:18
2 Anna Nikitina	RUS	2:32:15
3 Marie Hardiman	GBR	2:32:48

100m Back

1 Krisztina Egerszegi	HUN	1:00:83
2 Nina Zhivanevskaya	RUS	1:01:16
3 Sandra Volker	GER	1:01:89
6 Kathy Osher	GBR	1:03:54
B Final: 1 Helen Slatter	*GBR*	*1:04:22*

200m Back

1 Krisztina Egerszegi	HUN	2:09:12
2 Lorenza Vigarani	ITA	2:11:94
3 Nina Zhivanevskaya	RUS	2:12:14
6 Kathy Osher	GBR	2:14:76
7 Joanne Deakins	GBR	2:16:02

100m Fly

1 Catherine Plewinski	FRA	1:00:13
2 Franziska Van Almsick	GER	1:00:94
3 Betina Ustrowski	GER	1:01:06
B Final: 5 Nicola Goodwin	*GBR*	*1:03:13*

200m Fly

1 Krisztina Egerszegi	HUN	2:10:71
2 Katrin Jaeke	GER	2:13:07

3 Barbara Franco	ESP	2:13:39

200m IM

1 Daniela Hunger	GER	2:15:33
2 Daria Shmeleva	RUS	2:16:90
3 Silvia Parera	ESP	2:17:06
5 Lucy Findlay	GBR	2:17:78

400m IM

1 Krisztina Egerszegi	HUN	4:39:55
2 Daria Shmeleva	RUS	4:44:91
3 Hana Cerna	TCH	4:46:37
B Final: 6 Helen Slatter	*GBR*	*4:54:90*

4x100m Free

1 Germany		3:41:69 CR
(Van Almsick, Stellmach, Kielgass, Hunger)		
2 Sweden		3:45:33
3 Russia		3:45:37
6 Great Britain		3:49:09
(Pickering, Rolph, Huddart, Bennett)		

4x100m Medley

1 Germany		4:06:91
(Volker, Gerasch, Ustrowski, Van Almsick)		
2 Russia		4:10:09
3 Great Britain		4:12:18
(Osher, King, Goodwin, Pickering)		

4x200m Free

1 Germany		8:03:12
(Kielgass, Osygus, Van Almsick, Hase)		
2 Sweden		8:08:82
3 Great Britain		8:11:11
(Hardcastle, Armitage, Huddart, Pickering)		

EUROPEAN CHAMPIONSHIPS
FINAL MEDAL TABLE

		G	S	B
1	Germany	11	5	5
2	Russia	7	8	4
3	Hungary	6	3	-
4	Finland	3	1	-
5	Great Britain	1	2	6
6	France	1	2	2
7	Spain	1	1	2
8	Belgium	1	-	-
	Poland	1	-	-
10	Sweden	-	5	2
11	Italy	-	1	1
	Norway	-	1	1
	Ukraine	-	1	1
14	Slovakia	-	1	-
	Romania	-	1	-
16	Czech Republic	-	-	2
	Netherlands	-	-	2
18	Croatia	-	-	1
	Slovenia	-	-	1
	Belarus	-	-	1
	Lithuania	-	-	1

DIVING
MEN
1m Spring

1 Peter Boehler	GER	361.74
2 Joakim Andersson	SWE	347.70
3 Borris Lietzow	GER	342.24
4 Robert Morgan	GBR	338.22
Prelim 17 Tony Ali	*GBR*	*158.52*

3m Spring

1 Jan Hempel	GER	637.77
2 Dmitri Sautin	RUS	619.59
3 Joakim Andersson	SWE	589.74
Prelim 20 Tony Ali	*GBR*	*302.64*

10m Platform

1 Dmitri Sautin	RUS	617.73
2 Robert Morgan	GBR	617.70
3 Jan Hempel	GER	607.62
Prelim 14 Tony Ali	*GBR*	*316.56*

Women
1m Spring

1 Simona Koch	GER	278.94
2 Irina Laskko	RUS	276.24
3 Vera Ilina	RUS	275.40
Prelim 19 Lesley Ward	*GBR*	*176.13*
20 Hayley Allen	*GBR*	*172.35*

3m Spring

1 Brita Baldus	GER	541.68
2 Vera Ilina	RUS	494.25
3 Simona Koch	GER	493.05
Prelim 14 Alison Roffey	*GBR*	*239.91*

10m Platform

1 Svetlana Khokhlova	RUS	434.25
2 Ute Wetzig	GER	425.61
3 Elena Jupina	UKR	411.81
11 Beth Ackroyd	GBR	304.83
Prelim 13 Hayley Allen	*GBR*	*251.40*

WATER POLO
MEN
Great Britain finished 12th
Semi-Final 'A'
Hungary 8   Romania 7
Semi-Final 'B'
Italy 10   Spain 9
3rd & 4th Place
Spain 13   Romania 12
Final
Italy 11   Hungary 9
Goal Scorers

1 Manuel Estiarte	ESP	29
2 Tibor Benedek	HUN	23
3 Dmitriy Apanasenko	RUS	19
Bogdan Giambasu	ROM	19

WOMEN
Great Britain finished in 8th place
1st Semi Final
Russia 8   Italy 6
2nd Semi Final
Holland 9   Hungary 8
Final
Holland 13   Russia 8
Goal Scorers

1 Alice Lindhout	NED	31
2 Iren Rafael	HUN	28
3 Andrea Eke	HUN	21

SYNCHRONISED SWIMMING
Solo

1 Olga Sedakova	RUS	183.781
2 Marianne Aeschbacher	FRA	178.510
3 Kerry Shacklock	GBR	178.147

Duet

1 Sedakova/Kozlova	RUS	183.936
2 Aeschbacher/Leveque	FRA	177.268
3 Shacklock/Vakil	GBR	176.298

Teams

1 Russia		178.504
2 France		175.397
3 Italy		173.304
4 Great Britain		170.913

Mycil National Championships

Sheffield   June 10-13
MEN
50m Free

1 Michael Fibbens	Barnet	22.90
2 Mark Foster	Barnet	23.15
3 Alan Rapley	Sheffield	23.19

100m Free

1 Michael Fibbens	Barent	50.55
2 Alan Rapley	Sheffield	51.05
3 Martin Carl (J)	Sheffield	51.05

200m Free

1 Paul Palmer	Lincoln	1:50.84
2 Andrew Clayton	Leeds	1:51.65
3 Martin Carl (J)	Redbridge	1:52.50

400m Free

1 Paul Palmer	Lincoln	3:55.46
2 Andrew Clayton	Leeds	3:56.03
3 Steven Mellor	Satellite	4:02.08

1500m Free

1 Graeme Smith (J)	Stockport	15:37:67
2 Ian Wilson	Sunderland	15:40:39
3 Marc Clements (J)	Portsmouth	15:48.84

50m Breast

1 Peter McGinty	Beckenham	29.89
2 Nerijus Beiga	Waltham	29.91
3 James Parrack	Leeds	29.94

100m Breast

1 Nick Gillingham	Birmingham	1:02.16
2 Richard Maden	Leeds	1:03.13
3 Ian Swift	Rotherham	1:04:31

200m Breast

1 Nick Gillingham	Birmingham	2:11.56
2 Ian Swift	Rotherham	2:17.82
3 Richard Maden	Leeds	2:18.08

50m Back

1 Martin Harris	Waltham	26.65
2 Neil Willey (J)	Barnet	26.99
3 Jamie Fleet	Waltham	27.99

100m Back

1 Martin Harris	Waltham	55.92
2 Adam Ruckwood	Birmingham	56.93
3 Neil Willey (J)	Barnet	58.26

200m Back
1 Adam Ruckwood	Birmingham	2:01.90
2 Grant Robins	Portsmouth	2:03.83
3 Jamie Fleet	Waltham	2:03.99

50m Fly
1 Mark Foster	Barnet	24.86
2 Michael Fibbens	Barnet	24.94
3 Alan Rapley	Sheffield	25.31

100m Fly
1 Michael Fibbens	Barnet	55.67
2 Kevin Crosby	Warriors	56.37
3 David Warren	Leeds	56.49

200m Fly
1 Kevin Crosby	Warriors	2:02.11
2 James Hickman (J)	Stockport	2:04.04
3 David Warren	Leeds	2:04.30

200m IM
1 Fraser Walker	Warrender	2:03.77
2 Grant Robins	Portsmouth	2:06.84
3 David Warren	Leeds	2:06.90

400m IM
1 Grant Robins	Portsmouth	4:27.28
2 David Warren	Leeds	4:28.76
3 Fraser Walker	Warrender	4:29.67

4x100m Free
1 Sheffield		3:28.81
2 Leeds		3:32.02
3 Birmingham		3:33.13

4x100m Medley
1 Waltham		3:55.89
2 Portsmouth		3:59.24
3 Birmingham		4:00.03

WOMEN

50m Free
1 Karen Pickering	Ipswich	26.40
2 Alison Sheppard	Milngavie	26.70
3 Susan Rolph	Newcastle	26.94

100m Free
1 Karen Pickering	Ipswich	56.54
2 Susan Rolph	Newcastle	27.89
3 Claire Huddart	Leeds	28.25

200m Free
1 Karen Pickering	Ipswich	2:02:59
2 Claire Huddart	Leeds	2:04.12
3 Sarah Hardcastle	Southend	2:04.27

400m Free
1 Sarah Hardcastle	Southend	4:16.04
2 Vicki Horner (J)	Newburn	4:22.16
3 Helen Billington (J)	St Helens	4:22.78

800m Free
1 Sarah Hardcastle	Southend	8:50.91
2 Elina Arter (J)	Leeds	8:58.59
3 Susan Colling (J)	Derwentside	9:00.21

50m Breast
1 Zoe Baker (J)	Sheffield	32.68
2 Karen Rake (J)	Maxwell	33.26
3 Lorraine Coombes	Southampton	33.65

100m Breast
1 Jaime King (J)	Tigersharks	1:11.55
2 Marie Hardiman (J)	Birmingham	1:11.85
3 Zoe Baker (J)	Sheffield	1:12.82

200m Breast
1 Marie Hardiman (J)	Birmingham	2:33.18
2 Jaime King (J)	Tigersharks	2:36.69
3 Helen Gorman	Nova Cent'n	2:37.69

50m Back
1 Kathy Osher	Barnet	30.00
2 Helen Slatter	Warriors	30.75
3 Alex Bennet	Nova Cent'n	31.15

100m Back
1 Kathy Osher	Barnet	1:03.90
2 Helen Slatter	Warriors	1:03.93
3 Joanne Deakins	Coventry	1:05.34

200m Back
1 Kathy Osher	Barnet	2:14.86
2 Joanne Deakins	Coventry	2:15.91
3 Helen Slatter	Warriers	2:18.56

50m Fly
1 Maxine Lock	Cardiff	29.24
2 Marion Madine	Ireland	29.26
3 Kerry Martin (J)	Stirling	29.30

100m Fly
1 Marion Madine	Ireland	1:03.27
2 Nicola Goodwin	Nova Cent'n	1:03.37
3 Louise Waller (J)	Barnet	1:03.74

200m Fly
1 Marion Madine	Ireland	2:17.05
2 Helen Jepson	Leeds	2:18.47
3 Helen Slatter	Warriors	2:19.48

200m IM
1 Lucy Findlay	Kelly Col'ge	2:19.03
2 Susan Rolph	Newcastle	2:20.63
3 Helen Slatter	Warriors	2:20.65

400m IM
1 Marie Hardiman (J)	Birmingham	4:53.28
2 Helen Slatter	Warriors	4:53.42
3 Susan Rolph	Newcastle	5:00.59

4x100m Free
1 Nova Centurion		4:00.88
2 Cardiff		4:02.23
3 Leeds		4:04.91

4x100m Medley
1 Nova Centurion		4:24.58
2 Leeds		4:27.10
3 Kirklees		4:29.44

Table Tennis

World Championships

Gothenberg, Sweden   May 11-23

MEN'S TEAM	WOMEN'S TEAM
1 Sweden	1 China
2 China	2 DPR Korea
3 Germany	3 Korea
12 England	13 England
45 Wales	46 Wales
56 Scotland	53 Scotland

MEN'S SINGLES
Final
Jean-Philippe Gatien bt Jean-Michel Saive 21-19, 17-21, 21-14, 17-21, 21-18

WOMEN'S SINGLES
Final
Hyun Jung Hwa bt Chen Jing 21-16, 21-15, 21-14

MEN'S DOUBLES
Final
Wang Tao/Lu Lin (CHN) bt Ma Wenge/Zhang Lei (CHN) 18-21, 21-12, 21-13, 21-15

WOMEN'S DOUBLES
Final
Liu Wei/Qiao Yunping (CHN) bt Deng Yaping/Qiao Hong (CHN) 21-19, 14-21, 21-17, 23-21

MIXED DOUBLES
Final
Wang Tao/Liu Wei bt Yoo Nam Kyu/Hyun Jung Hwa (KOR) 22-20, 13-21, 21-9, 21-13

World Cup

Guangzhou, China   Aug 19-22

Semi-finals
Zoran Primorac (CRO) bt Peter Karlsson (SWE) 10-21, 21-19,
21-19, 21-23, 21-17
Wang Tao (CHN) bt Huang Wenguan (CHN) 21-13, 21-15, 21-8

Final
Zoran Primorac bt Wang Tao 21-19, 16-21, 21-18, 18-21, 21-18

European Masters Cup

Hanover   Sept 11-12
Semi-finals
Jörg Rosskopf bt Jean-Paul Gatien 21-16, 12-21, 21-17, 21-19
Peter Karlsson bt Jean-Michel Saive 15-21, 21-14, 12-21, 21-15, 22-20
Final
Jörg Rosskopf bt Peter Karlsson 17-21, 23-21, 21-18, 21-17

WORLD RANKINGS

Men
As at Aug 13

			Pts
1	Jan-Ove Waldner	SWE	2085
2	Jean-Philipe Gatien	FRA	2055
3	Jean-Michel Saive	BEL	2007
4	Ma Wenge	CHN	2001
5	KimTaek Soo	KOR	1973
6	Wang Tao	CHN	1949
7	Jörgen Persson	SWE	1914
8	Jörg Rosskopf	GER	1890
9	Li Gun Sang	PRK	1884
10	Andrzej Grubba	POL	1873
11	Peter Karlsson	SWE	1870
12	Kim Song Hui	KOR	1852
	Also		
27	Carl Prean	ENG	1710
53	Alan Cooke	ENG	1593
83	Matthew Syed	ENG	1450

Women
As at Aug 13

1	Deng Yaping	CHN	2250
2	Qiao Hong	CHN	2124
3	Jung Hwa Hyun	KOR	2085
4	Li Bun Hul	PRK	1994
5	Gao Jun	CHN	1994
6	Chen Zihe	CHN	1992
7	Chen Jing	TPE	1990
8	Chai Po Wa	HKG	1962
9	Yu Sun Bok	PRK	1937
10	Jing Jun Hong	SIN	1934
11	Tang Welyi	CHN	1927
12	Zhang Qin	CHN	1911
	Also		
45	Lisa Lomas	ENG	1695
67	Alison Gordon	ENG	1523
93	Andrea Holt	ENG	1439

EUROPEAN WOMEN'S LEAGUE 1992-93
Final Ranking
1 Holland, 2 Belgium, 3= Germany & Sweden,
5= Czechoslovakia & Hungary, 7= England & Romania

JOOLA EUROPEAN MEN'S LEAGUE 1992-93
Final Ranking
1 Sweden, 2 Belgium, 3= Germany & Poland, 5= England
& France, 7 Holland, 8 Hungary

Tennis

The Championships

Wimbledon   June 21-Jul 4

MEN'S DOUBLES
Selected results from rounds 1-3; complete results from quarter-finals. Seedings in brackets.
1st Round
Bates GBR/Black ZIM bt Eltingh/Koevermans HOL (7) 6-2 6-1 6-4
L Jensen/M Jensen USA (9) bt Henman/Bailey GBR 4-6 7-6 7-6 6-3
2nd Round
Hand/Wilkinson GBR bt L Jensen/M Jensen (9) 6-4 6-7 6-3 7-6
De Jager/Ondruska RSA bt Fitzgerald AUS/Jarryd SWE (2) 6-7 6-4 6-4 7-6
3rd Round
Bates/Black bt Ferreira RSA/Stich GER (10) 7-6 4-6 4-6 7-5 6-1
Hand/Wilkinson bt Garnett/Middleton 6-4 6-7 6-3 7-6
Quarter-Finals
Woodbridge/Woodforde (1) bt Bates/Black 6-4 6-3 6-4
Kuhnen/Muller bt Deppe/Knowles 6-2 6-4 7-6
Connell/Galbraith (5) bt P McEnroe/Stark 4-6 6-3 6-7 7-6 6-4
Bergh/Talbot bt Hand/Wilkinson 6-4 6-7 4-6 6-3 6-4
Semi-Finals
Woodbridge/Woodforde (1) bt Kuhnen/Muller 6-4 6-4 6-4
Connell/Galbraith (5) bt Bergh/Talbot 6-3 6-4 6-4
Final
Woodbridge/Woodforde (1) bt Connell/Galbraith 7-5 6-3 7-6

WOMEN'S DOUBLES
1st Round
Lake/Wood GBR bt Coetzer RSA/Gorrochategui ARG (10) 6-2 2-6 6-4
Kschwendt/Probst GER bt Grunfeld/Salmon GBR 6-4 5-7 6-4
2nd Round
Lake/Wood bt Harvey-Wild USA/Weisner AUT 6-2 6-3
Maleeva BUL/Maleeva-Fragniere SUI (11) bt Durie GBR/Suire 6-1 6-3
Third Round
McNeil/Stubbs (4) AUS bt Lake/Wood 7-5 7-6
Quarter-Finals
Fernandez/Zvereva (1) bt Hetherington/Rinaldi (8) 6-1 6-2
Fernandez/Garrison-Jackson (5) bt McNeil/Stubbs (4) 7-5 7-6
Shriver/Smylie (6) bt Sanchez Vicario/Sukova (3) 6-3 6-4
Neiland/Novotna (2) bt Faull/Richardson 7-6 4-6 6-3
Semi-Finals
Fernandez/Zvereva (1) bt Fernandez/Garrison-Jackson (5) 3-6 6-1 10-8
Neiland/Novotna (2) bt Shriver/Smylie (6) 6-2 6-2

Final
Fernadez/Zvereva (1) bt Neiland/Novotna (2) 6-4 6-7 6-4

MIXED DOUBLES
1st Round
Bates/Durie GBR bt Van Emburgh USA/Sukova TCH 7-5 6-4
Adams USA/Maniokova RUS bt Macalagan/Wainwright GBR 6-2 6-1
Connell CAN/White USA (11) bt Foster/Grunfeld GBR 6-2 7-5
2nd Round
Leach/Garrison-Jackson USA (5) bt Petchey/Wood GBR 6-3 6-4
Kruger/Coetzer RSA (16) bt Bailey/Javer GBR 6-4 3-6 6-1
Third Round
Bates/Durie bt Fitzgerald/Smylie AUS 6-2 6-7 6-3
Quarter-Finals
Woodbridge/Sanchez Vicario (1) bt Bates/Durie 6-2 3-6 6-3
Nijssen/Bollegraf (12) bt Apell/Strandlund 6-2 6-3
Woodforde/Navratilova (3) bt Galbraith/Rinaldi (7) 7-6 7-6
Kratzmann/Zvereva (2) bt Connell/White (11)
Semi-Finals
Nijssen/Bollegraf (12) bt Woodbridge/Sanchez Vicario (1) 5-7 7-5 6-4
Woodforde/Navratilova (3) bt Kratzmann/Zvereva (2) 4-6 6-3 6-4
FINAL
Woodforde/Navratilova (3) bt Nijssen/Bollegraf (12) 6-3 6-4

BOY'S SINGLES FINAL
R Sabau ROM (9) bt J Syzmanski VEN (7) 6-1 6-3

GIRL'S SINGLES FINAL
N Feber BEL (1) bt R Grande ITA (7) 7-6 1-6 6-2

Wimbledon - Men's Singles

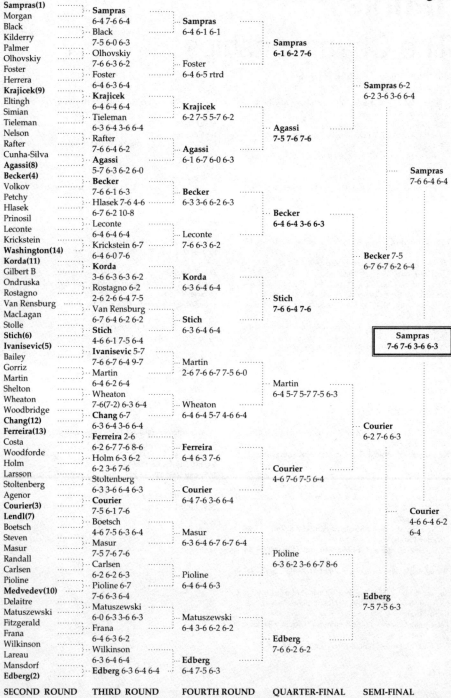

SECOND ROUND	THIRD ROUND	FOURTH ROUND	QUARTER-FINAL	SEMI-FINAL

Sampras(1)
Morgan
Black
Kilderry
Palmer
Olhovskiy
Foster
Herrera
Krajicek(9)
Eltingh
Simian
Tieleman
Nelson
Rafter
Cunha-Silva
Agassi(8)
Becker(4)
Volkov
Petchy
Hlasek
Prinosil
Leconte
Krickstein
Washington(14)
Korda(11)
Gilbert B
Ondruska
Rostagno
Van Rensburg
MacLagan
Stolle
Stich(6)
Ivanisevic(5)
Bailey
Gorriz
Martin
Shelton
Wheaton
Woodbridge
Chang(12)
Ferreira(13)
Costa
Woodforde
Holm
Larsson
Stoltenberg
Agenor
Courier(3)
Lendl(7)
Boetsch
Steven
Masur
Randall
Carlsen
Pioline
Medvedev(10)
Delaitre
Matuszewski
Fitzgerald
Frana
Wilkinson
Lareau
Mansdorf
Edberg(2)

Sampras 6-4 7-6 6-4
Black 7-5 6-0 6-3
Olhovskiy 7-6 6-3 6-2
Foster 6-4 6-3 6-4
Krajicek 6-4 6-4 6-4
Tieleman 6-3 6-4 3-6 6-4
Rafter 7-6 6-4 6-2
Agassi 5-7 6-3 6-2 6-0
Becker 7-6 6-1 6-3
Hlasek 7-6 4-6 6-7 6-2 10-8
Leconte 6-4 6-4 6-4
Krickstein 6-7 6-4 6-0 7-6
Korda 3-6 6-3 6-3 6-2
Rostagno 6-2 2-6 2-6 6-4 7-5
Van Rensburg 6-7 6-4 6-2 6-2
Stich 4-6 6-1 7-5 6-4
Ivanisevic 5-7 7-6 6-7 6-4 9-7
Martin 6-4 6-2 6-4
Wheaton 7-6(7-2) 6-3 6-4
Chang 6-7 6-3 6-4 3-6 6-4
Ferreira 2-6 6-2 6-7 7-6 8-6
Holm 6-3 6-2 6-2 3-6 7-6
Stoltenberg 6-3 3-6 6-4 6-3
Courier 7-5 6-1 7-6
Boetsch 4-6 7-5 6-3 6-4
Masur 7-5 7-6 7-6
Carlsen 6-2 6-2 6-3
Pioline 6-7 7-6 6-3 6-4
Matuszewski 6-0 6-3 3-6 6-3
Frana 6-4 6-3 6-2
Wilkinson 6-3 6-4 6-4
Edberg 6-3 6-4 6-4

Sampras 6-4 6-1 6-1
Foster 6-4 6-5 rtrd
Krajicek 6-2 7-5 5-7 6-2
Agassi 6-1 6-7 6-0 6-3
Becker 6-3 3-6 6-2 6-3
Leconte 7-6 6-3 6-2
Korda 6-3 6-4 6-4
Stich 6-3 6-4 6-4
Martin 2-6 7-6 6-7 7-5 6-0
Wheaton 6-4 6-4 5-7 4-6 6-4
Ferreira 6-4 6-3 7-6
Courier 6-4 7-6 3-6 6-4
Masur 6-3 6-4 6-7 6-7 6-4
Pioline 6-4 6-4 6-3
Matuszewski 6-4 3-6 6-2 6-2
Edberg 6-4 7-5 6-3

Sampras 6-1 6-2 7-6
Agassi 7-5 7-6 7-6
Becker 6-4 6-4 3-6 6-3
Stich 7-6 6-4 7-6
Martin 6-4 5-7 5-7 7-5 6-3
Courier 4-6 7-6 7-5 6-4
Pioline 6-3 6-2 3-6 6-7 8-6
Edberg 7-6 6-2 6-2

Sampras 6-2 6-2 3-6 3-6 6-4
Becker 7-5 6-7 6-7 6-2 6-4
Courier 6-2 7-6 6-3
Edberg 7-5 7-5 6-3

Sampras 7-6 6-4 6-4
Courier 4-6 6-4 6-2 6-4

Sampras 7-6 7-6 3-6 6-3

Wimbledon - Women's Singles

Graf(1)				
Wood	Graf			
McQuillan	6-2 6-1	Graf		
Kelesi	Kelesi	6-0 6-0		
Grossman	7-6 6-4		Graf	
McGrath	McGrath		6-1 6-4	
Stafford	6-4 1-6 6-3	McGrath		
Coetzer(14)	Stafford	6-1 6-2		Graf
Maleeva-Frag.(11)	6-3 6-2			7-6 6-1
Sawamatsu	Sawamatsu			
Arendt	6-3 6-3	Raymond		
Raymond	Raymond	7-5 6-2		
Schultz	6-2 6-3		Capriati	
Rubin	Schultz		4-6 6-3 8-6	
Smylie	4-6 6-2 6-2	Capriati		
Capriati(7)	Capriati	7-5 4-6 6-2		
Sanchez-Vicario(3)	4-6 6-3 6-2			Graf
Neiland	Sanchez-V			7-6 6-3
Wasserman	7-6 6-0	Sanchez-V		
Fendick	Fendick	6-3 6-2		
Provis	6-1 6-3		Sukova	
Brioukhovets	Brioukhovets		6-3 6-4	
Farina	7-5 6-4	Sukova		
Sukova(15)	Sukova	6-7 6-3 6-3		
Maleeva Mag.(10)	6-4 6-2			Martinez
McNeil	Maleeva Mag			6-1 6-4
White	7-6 6-4	Basuki		
Basuki	Basuki	6-4 6-2		
Kruopova	7-5 6-3		Martinez	
Paradis-Mangon	Paradis-M.		3-6 6-2 6-2	
Wiesner	6-0 6-0	Martinez		
Martinez(6)	Martinez	7-5 6-0		
Novotna(8)	7-5 6-0			Graf
Gorrochategui	Novotna			7-6 1-6 6-4
Werdel	6-0 7-5	Novotna		
Gavaldon	Werdel	6-3 6-1		
Wainwright	6-2 6-1		Novotna	
Pizzichini	Pizzichini		7-5 4-6 6-4	
Oremans	6-4 7-6	Oremans		
Field	Oremans	6-3 6-2		
Huber(9)	6-3 6-2			Novotna
Golarsa	Huber			6-4 6-3
Porwik	6-4 6-0	Huber		
Labat	Labat	6-4 6-3		
Dahlman	3-6 6-1 6-4		Sabatini	
Medvedeva	Medvedeva		7-6 6-0	
Rinaldi	1-6 6-3 6-4	Sabatini		
Sabatini(4)	Sabatini	6-1 2-6 6-4		
Fernandez M(5)	6-2 6-2			Novotna
Dragomir	Fernandez M			6-4 6-4
Garrison	6-3 6-2	Garrison		
Fernandez G	Garrison	6-0 6-1		
Appelmans	6-4 4-2(ret'd)		Zvereva	
Frankl	Appelmans		7-5 6-2	
Strnadova	6-2 6-3	Zvereva		
Zvereva	Zvereva	6-3 6-4		
Tauziat(16)	6-3 6-2			Navratilova
Javer	Tauziat			6-3 6-1
Rittner	6-1 6-2	Tauziat		
Davenport	Davenport	6-3 7-6		
Endo	6-0 7-6		Navratilova	
Hy	Hy		6-1 6-3	
Nideffer-Fairbank	6-3 6-2	Navratilova		
Navratilova(2)	Navratilova 6-0 6-4	6-1 6-0		

SECOND ROUND	THIRD ROUND	FOURTH ROUND	FIFTH ROUND	SEMI-FINAL

Australian Open - Men's Singles

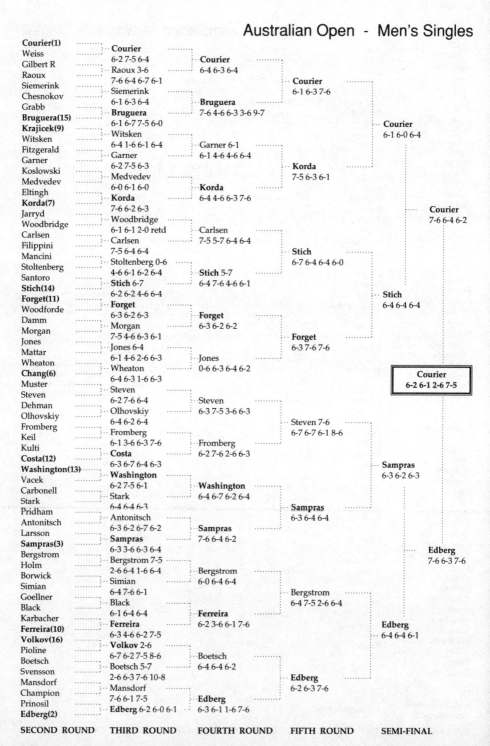

Courier(1)	**Courier**					
Weiss	6-2 7-5 6-4	**Courier**				
Gilbert R	Raoux 3-6	6-4 6-3 6-4	**Courier**			
Raoux	7-6 6-4 6-7 6-1		6-1 6-3 7-6			
Siemerink	Siemerink					
Chesnokov	6-1 6-3 6-4	**Bruguera**				
Grabb	**Bruguera**	7-6 4-6 6-3 3-6 9-7		**Courier**		
Bruguera(15)	6-1 6-7 7-5 6-0			6-1 6-0 6-4		
Krajicek(9)	Witsken					
Witsken	6-4 1-6 6-1 6-4	Garner 6-1				
Fitzgerald	Garner	6-1 4-6 4-6 6-4				
Garner	6-2 7-5 6-3		**Korda**			
Koslowski	Medvedev		7-5 6-3 6-1			
Medvedev	6-0 6-1 6-0	**Korda**				
Eltingh	**Korda**	6-4 4-6 6-3 7-6			**Courier**	
Korda(7)	7-6 6-2 6-3				7-6 6-4 6-2	
Jarryd	Woodbridge					
Woodbridge	6-1 6-1 2-0 retd	Carlsen				
Carlsen	Carlsen	7-5 5-7 6-4 6-4				
Filippini	7-5 6-4 6-4		**Stich**			
Mancini	Stoltenberg 0-6		6-7 6-4 6-4 6-0			
Stoltenberg	4-6 6-1 6-2 6-4	**Stich** 5-7				
Santoro	**Stich** 6-7	6-4 7-6 4-6 6-1				
Stich(14)	6-2 6-2 4-6 6-4			**Stich**		
Forget(11)	**Forget**			6-4 6-4 6-4		
Woodforde	6-3 6-2 6-3	**Forget**				
Damm	Morgan	6-3 6-2 6-2				
Morgan	7-5 4-6 6-3 6-1		**Forget**			
Jones	Jones 6-4		6-3 7-6 7-6			
Mattar	6-1 4-6 2-6 6-3	Jones				
Wheaton	Wheaton	0-6 6-3 6-4 6-2			**Courier**	
Chang(6)	6-4 6-3 1-6 6-3				**6-2 6-1 2-6 7-5**	
Muster	Steven					
Steven	6-2 7-6 6-4	Steven				
Dehman	Olhovskiy	6-3 7-5 3-6 6-3				
Olhovskiy	6-4 6-2 6-4		**Steven** 7-6			
Fromberg	Fromberg		6-7 6-7 6-1 8-6			
Keil	6-1 3-6 6-3 7-6	Fromberg				
Kulti	**Costa**	6-2 7-6 2-6 6-3				
Costa(12)	6-3 6-7 6-4 6-3			**Sampras**		
Washington(13)	**Washington**			6-3 6-2 6-3		
Vacek	6-2 7-5 6-1	**Washington**				
Carbonell	Stark	6-4 6-7 6-2 6-4				
Stark	6-4 6-4 6-3		**Sampras**			
Pridham	Antonitsch		6-3 6-4 6-4			
Antonitsch	6-3 6-2 6-7 6-2	**Sampras**				
Larsson	**Sampras**	7-6 6-4 6-2				
Sampras(3)	6-3 3-6 6-3 6-4				**Edberg**	
Bergstrom	Bergstrom 7-5				7-6 6-3 7-6	
Holm	2-6 6-4 1-6 6-4	Bergstrom				
Borwick	Simian	6-0 6-4 6-4				
Simian	6-4 7-6 6-1		**Bergstrom**			
Goellner	Black		6-4 7-5 2-6 6-4			
Black	6-1 6-4 6-4	**Ferreira**				
Karbacher	**Ferreira**	6-2 3-6 6-1 7-6		**Edberg**		
Ferreira(10)	6-3 4-6 6-2 7-5			6-4 6-4 6-1		
Volkov(16)	**Volkov** 2-6					
Pioline	6-7 6-2 7-5 8-6	Boetsch				
Boetsch	Boetsch 5-7	6-4 6-4 6-2				
Svensson	2-6 6-3 7-6 10-8		**Edberg**			
Mansdorf	Mansdorf		6-2 6-3 7-6			
Champion	7-6 6-1 7-5	**Edberg**				
Prinosil	**Edberg** 6-2 6-0 6-1	6-3 6-1 1-6 7-6				
Edberg(2)						

SECOND ROUND	THIRD ROUND	FOURTH ROUND	FIFTH ROUND	SEMI-FINAL

Australian Open - Women's Singles

Seles(1)
Strandlund
Grossman
Fendick
Dahlman
Stafford
Probst
Tauziat(13)
Garrison(16)
Faber
Kschwendt
Halard
Oremans
Reinach
Javer
Martinez(6)
Sabatini(3)
Baudone
Po
Hy
Demongeot
Endo
Provis
McNeil(12)
Pierce(10)
Date
Davenport
Kiene
Arendt
Fernandez G
White
Novotna(8)
Fernandez M(5)
Wang
Thoren
Sawamatsu
Meier
Helgeson
Wasserman
Maleeva-Frag.(9)
Huber(11)
Martinek
Temesvari-Trunkos
Gorrochategui
Zrubakova
Rehe
Gildemeister
Sanchez-Vicario(4)
Capriati(7)
Labat
Hack
Zvereva
Rittner
Habsudova
Monami
Maleeva K(14)
Maleeva Mag(15)
Langrova
Babel
Price
Graham
Porwik
Santrock
Graf(2)

SECOND ROUND

Seles
6-2 6-0
Fendick
6-1 7-6
Dahlman
6-1 6-2
Tauziat
6-2 4-6 6-2
Garrison
4-6 6-4 6-2
Halard
6-4 1-6 6-4
Oremans
6-1 6-1
Martinez
7-5 6-1
Sabatini
6-0 6-1
Po
6-4 6-2
Demongeot
2-6 6-2 6-2
Provis
3-6 6-1 6-1
Pierce
6-1 6-1
Davenport
7-5 6-4
Fernandez G
6-4 7-6
White
4-6 7-5 6-2
Fernandez M
7-6 6-4
Sawamatsu
6-1 7-5
Helgeson
6-3 6-3
Maleeva-Frag.
6-4 6-1
Huber
6-2 6-4
Gorrochategui
6-1 7-5
Zrubakova
6-7 6-3 8-6
Sanchez-V
6-0 6-1
Capriati
6-7 7-5 6-2
Zvereva
7-5 6-7 6-3
Rittner
6-2 7-6
Maleeva K
6-1 6-4
Maleeva Mag.
6-1 6-0
Babel
7-5 1-6 6-3
Porwick
6-3 7-5
Graf 6-1 6-1

THIRD ROUND

Seles
6-1 6-0
Tauziat
6-2 6-1
Halard
6-4 7-5
Martinez
6-3 4-6 6-4
Sabatini
6-1 6-3
Provis
6-1 6-2
Pierce
6-3 6-0
Fernandez G
7-6 3-6 7-5
Fernandez M
2-6 6-3 6-1
Maleeva-Frag.
6-2 3-6 6-4
Huber
6-2 7-5
Sanchez-V
6-1 6-3
Capriati
7-5 7-5
Maleeva K
6-1 6-1
Maleeva Mag.
6-3 6-2
Graf
6-1 Rtrd

FOURTH ROUND

Seles
6-2 6-0
Halard
6-4 6-3
Sabatini
7-5 6-3
Pierce
6-0 6-0
Fernandez M
7-5 2-6 6-2
Sanchez-V
7-5 6-2
Capriati
6-7 6-3 6-1
Graf
6-3 6-3

FIFTH ROUND

Seles
6-2 6-7 6-0
Sabatini
4-6 7-6 6-0
Sanchez
7-5 6-4
Graf
7-5 6-2

SEMI-FINAL

Seles
6-1 6-2
Graf
7-5 6-4

Seles
4-6 6-3 6-2

Australian Open
Melbourne   Jan 18-31

MEN'S DOUBLES
Selected results from 1st & 2nd rounds; complete results from 3rd round on. Seedings in brackets.
1st Round
Muller RSA/Sanchez ESP bt Woodbridge /Woodforde AUS (1) 6-7 7-6 6-2
Garnett/Middleton USA bt Adams USA/Olhovskiy RUS (12) 3-6 7-6 6-4
Jeremy Bates GBR/Schapers HOL bt Lavalle MEX/Mattar BRA 6-4 6-3
2nd Round
Edberg SWE/Siemerink HOL bt Connell CAN/Galbraith USA (9) 7-6 6-7 6-2
Camporese ITA/Krajicek HOL bt Nijssen HOL/Suk TCH (5) 7-6 6-3
Cannon USA/Melville USA bt Casal/Sanchez ESP (11) 6-4 7-6
De Jager RSA/Ondruska RUS bt Jones/Leach USA (3) 7-6 6-3
Visser RSA/Warder AUS bt Bates/Schapers 4-6 6-3 6-2
Briggs/Kronemann USA bt Davids HOL/Pimek BEL (15) 7-6 7-6
3rd Round
Muller/Sanchez bt Kinnear/Salumaa USA (16) 6-7 6-4 6-3
Kratzmann/Masur AUS (8) walked over Edberg/Siemerink
Fitzgerald AUS/Jarryd SWE bt Eltingh/Haarhuis HOL (13) 7-5 6-4
Garnett/Middleton bt Devries USA/MacPherson AUS (6) 6-4 7-6
Cannon/Melville bt Camporese/Krajicek 4-6 7-5 6-1
De Jager/Ondruska bt Ferreira/Norval RSA (14) 6-2 7-6
Visser/Warder (10) bt McEnroe/Stark USA7-6 7-6
Grabb/Reneberg USA (2) bt Briggs/Kronemann 6-4 6-4
Quarter-finals
Kratzmann/Masur (8) bt Muller/Sanchez 6-3 6-0 6-7 6-2
Fitzgerald/Jarryd (4) bt Garnett Middleton 7-5 6-3 6-4
De Jager/Ondruska bt Cannon/Melville 4-6 7-6 6-4 6-4
Visser/Warder (10) bt Grabb/Reneberg (2) 6-3 6-4 4-6 4-6 22-20
Semi-finals
Fitzgerald/Jarryd (4) bt Kratzmann/Masur (8) 7-6 6-4 6-1
Visser/Warder (10) bt De Jager/Ondruska 4-6 7-6 6-4 6-4
Final
Visser/Warder (10) bt Fitgerald/Jarryd (4) 6-4 6-3 6-4

WOMEN'S DOUBLES
1st Round
Gorrochategui ARG/Harvey USA bt Provis AUS/Reinach RSA (9) 6-2 3-6 6-1
Basuki INA/Miyagi JPN bt Collins/Pierce USA (12) 7-6 6-2
Morton AUS/Wood GBR bt Lohmann/Martinek GER 6-2 6-1
Dopper AUT/Zivec-Skulz GER bt Appelmans BEL/Demongeot FRA (14) 6-7 6-4 6-3

2nd Round
Hetherington CAN/Rinaldi USA bt Morton/Wood 7-6 6-2
Date JPN/Jaggard-Lai AUS w-o McQuillan AUS/Porwick GER (11)
3rd Round
G Fernandez USA/Zvereva BLS bt Fairbank/Richardson RSA 6-4 6-0
McNeil USA/Stubbs AUS (5) bt Gorrochategui/Harvey-Wild 6-3 7-6
M Fernandez/Garrison (4) bt Basuki/Miyagi 6-2 6-2
Fendick USA/Strnadova TCH (8) bt Labat/Tarabini ARG (15) 6-4 6-4
Hetherington/Rinaldi (6) bt Date/Jaggard-Lai 6-3 6-3
Martinez/Sanchez ESP (3) bt Maleeva BUL/Tauziat FRA (16) 6-3 3-0 retd
Shriver USA/Smylie AUS (10) bt Adams USA/Bollegraf HOL (7) 6-3 6-2
Neiland LAT/Novotna TCH (2) bt Davenport/Rubin USA 3-6 7-5 6-2
Quarter-finals
G Fernandez/Zvereva (1) bt McNeil/Stubbs (5) 6-3 6-1
Fendick/Strnadova (8) bt M Fernandez/Garrison (4) 6-2 6-2
Hetherington/Rinaldi (6) bt Martinez/Sanchez (3) 4-6 6-1 6-0
Shriver/Smylie (10) bt Neiland/Novotna 6-3 6-3
Semi-finals
G Fernandez/Zvereva (1) bt Fendick/Strnadova (8) 6-2 7-5
Shriver/Smylie (10) bt Hetherington/Rinaldi 4-6 6-1 6-0
Final
G Fernandez/Zvereva (1) bt Shriver/Smylie (10) 6-4 6-3

MIXED DOUBLES
3rd Round
Sanchez -Vicario ESP/Woodbridge AUS (1) bt Martinez/Sanchez ESP 6-1 6-1
Hetherington/Michibata CAN bt Shriver USA/Stolle AUS 7-6 3-6 6-2
Garrison Jackson/Leach USA (3) bt Miyagi JPN/Kinnear USA 4-6 7-6 9-7
Zvereva BLS/Jones USA bt Smylie/Fitzgerald AUS 6-1 3-6 6-3
Semi-finals
Sanchez-Vicario/Woodbridge (1) bt Hetherington/Michibata CAN 6-3 6-3
Garrison/Leach (3) bt Zvereva/Jones (2) 6-2 7-6
Final
Sanchez-Vicario/Woodbridge (1) bt Garrison/Leach 7-5 6-4

BOYS' SINGLES
Final
James Bailey GBR bt Steven Downs NZL 6-3 6-2

GIRLS' SINGLES
Final
Heike Rusch GER bt Andrea Glass GER 6-1 6-2

French Open
Paris   May 24-June 6

MEN'S DOUBLES
*Selected results from rounds 1-3; complete results from
quarter-finals. Seedings in brackets.*
1st Round
Motta BRA/Sanchez ESP bt Bates GBR/Black ZIM 6-2,
4-6, 6-4
Quarter-Finals
Woodbridge/Woodforde (1) bt Davids/Norval 6-2, 6-2
Goellner/Prinosil bt Kratzmann/Masur (3) 6-4, 6-4
Edberg/Korda bt Casal/Sanchez (12) 7-5, 6-1
Jensen/Jensen bt Ivanisevic/Leconte 6-7, 7-5, 6-3
Semi-Final
Goellner/Prinosil bt Woodbridge/Woodforde (1) 7-6, 6-2
Jensen/Jensen bt Edberg/Korda 7-6, 6-1
Final
Jensen/Jensen bt Goellner/Prinosil 6-4, 6-7, 6-4
WOMEN'S DOUBLES
1st Round
Oremans/Vis HOL bt Morton AUS/Wood GBR 7-5, 6-3
Third Round
Quarter-Finals
Fernandez/Zvereva (1) bt Adams/Bollegraf (8) 6-4, 3-6,
7-5
Cecchini/Tarabini bt McNeil/Stubbs (4) 6-3, 4-6, 6-3
Coetzer/Gorrochategui (13) bt Martinez/Sanchez Vicario
(3) 7-6, 3-6, 7-5
Neiland/Novotna (2) bt Maleeva/Tauziat 6-4, 7-6
Semi-Finals
Fernandez/Zvereva (1) bt Cecchini/Tarabini 7-6, 7-5
Neiland/Novotna (2) bt Coetzer/Gorrochategui 6-4, 6-7,
7-5
Final
Fernadez/Zvereva (1) bt Neiland/Novotna (2) 6-3, 7-5
MIXED DOUBLES
2nd Round
Quarter-Finals
Jensen/Schultz bt Woodbridge/Fernandez (1) 6-3, 6-2
Olhovskiy/Maniokova (11) bt Haarhuis/Hetherington
(3) 6-4, 3-6, 6-1
Fitzgerald/Smylie (6) bt Van Emburgh/Graham 6-2, 6-4
Visser/Reinach (9) bt Kratzmann/Reinach (2) 6-4, 6-4

Semi-Finals
Olhovskiy/Maniokova (11) bt Jensen/Schultz 7-6, 7-6
Visser/Reinach (9) bt Fitzgerald/Smylie (6) 6-4, 3-6, 6-2
FINAL
Olhovskiy/Maniokova (11) bt Visser/Reinach (9) 6-2, 3-
6, 6-2

BOYS' SINGLES FINAL
R Carretero ESP bt A Costa ESP (1) 6-0, 7-6

GIRLS' SINGLES FINAL
M Hingis SUI bt L Courtois BEL 7-5, 7-5

ALL-TIME
WOMEN'S
CAREER PRIZE MONEY
As at 13 Sept 1993

			US $
1	Martina Navratilova	USA	19,052,570
2	Steffi Graf	GER	12,761,510
3	Chris Evert	USA	8,896,195
4	Monica Seles	YUG	7,408,981
5	Gabriela Sabatini	ARG	6,604,102
6	Pam Shriver	USA	5,028,325
7	Helena Sukova	TCH	4,942,256
8	Arantxa Sanchez-Vicario	ESP	4,641,751
9	Zina Jackson-Garrison	USA	3,845,298
10	Hana Mandlikova	TCH	3,340,959
11	Jana Novotna	TCH	3,325,103
12	Natalia Zvereva	RUS	3,007,939
13	Mañuela Maleeva-Fragniere	BUL	2,926,652
14	Mary Joe Fernandez	USA	2,831,252
15	Wendy Turnbull	AUS	2,769,024
16	Gigi Fernandez	USA	2,382,752
17	Lori McNeil	USA	2,309,944
18	Claudia Kohde-Kilsch	GER	2,224,887
19	Larrisa Neiland	LAT	2,006,489
20	Billie Jean King	USA	1,966,487
21	Conchita Martinez	ESP	1,946,065
22	Tracy Austin	USA	1,925,415
23	Katerina Maleeva	BUL	1,880,817
24	Kathy Jordan	USA	1,592,111
25	Virginia Wade	GBR	1,542,278
26	Natalie Tauziat	FRA	1,505,935
27	Jennifer Capriati	USA	1,491,823
28	Ros Fairbank-Nideffer	AUS	1,468,692
29	Elizabeth Smylie	AUS	1,437,975
30	Evonne Goolagong	AUS	1,399,431

*Moral: If you are thinking of taking up tennis, but
don't expect to be as good as Steffi Graf, polish up your
doubles. Larrisa Neiland has been a professional for six
years and only fleetingly has she ventured into the top
ten (in 1988). Yet, mostly through her association with
Natalia Zvereva in the two-hander, she has earned a
worthwhile $2m+, with endorsements to add on.......*

French Open - Men's Singles

SECOND ROUND

- Sampras(1)
- Ondruska
- Svensson
- Sanchez
- Rostagno
- Hlasek
- Arriens
- Washington(18)
- Bruguera(11)
- Champion
- Larsson
- Oncins
- Devening
- Kuhnen
- Meligeni
- Huet
- Edberg(3)
- Krickstein
- De la Peña
- Stark
- Visconti
- Steeb
- Haarhuis
- Ferreira(15)
- Medvedev(12)
- Furland
- Wuyts
- Markus
- Woodforde
- Steven
- Goellner
- Korda(6)
- Ivanisevic(5)
- Berasategui
- Chesnokov
- Costa
- Woodbridge
- Arrese
- Rosset
- Krajicek(13)
- Novacek(14)
- Clavet
- Pescosolido
- Carlsen
- Kafelnikov
- Dosedel
- Gilbert R
- Becker(4)
- Chang(9)
- Karbacher
- Matsuoka
- Prpic
- O'Brien
- Fromberg
- Holm
- Stich(10)
- Muster(16)
- Pioline
- Gilbert B
- Prinosil
- Tarango
- Delaitre
- Charbonne
- Courier(2)

THIRD ROUND

- Sampras 7-5 6-0 6-3
- Svensson 6-3
- 6-7 5-7 6-3 6-4
- Rostagno 6-3 6-4 4-6 6-2
- Washington 7-6 6-4 6-0
- Bruguera 6-0 6-0 6-0
- Larsson 3-6 7-6 6-4 6-4
- Kuhnen 7-5 6-4 6-1
- Meligeni 7-6 7-5 6-4
- Edberg 6-3 6-1 5-7 7-5
- Stark 7-6 3-6 3-6 7-5 7-6
- Steeb 7-5 6-3 6-0
- Haarhuis 4-6 6-3 6-0 7-6
- Medvedev 6-3 6-4 6-4
- Markus 6-1 2-6 6-4 6-4
- Woodforde 6-2 6-7 6-4 3-6 6-1
- Goellner 6-3
- Korda 6-3 7-6 7-6
- Ivanisevic 6-3 6-3 6-2
- Costa 6-3 6-2 6-4
- Arrese 4-6 6-4 3-6 7-5 6-0
- Krajicek 6-2 6-3 6-1
- Novacek 6-4 6-2 4-6 6-0
- Pescosolido 6-3 1-6 6-4 6-7 6-2
- Dosedel 6-3 6-1 6-0
- Gilbert R 7-5 6-3 7-5
- Karbacher 1-6 6-3 6-4 6-2
- Prpic 6-3 6-3 2-6 6-3
- Fromberg 6-2 6-1 6-2
- Stich 6-4 6-2 7-5
- Muster 7-5 2-6 6-4 6-2
- Gilbert B 6-1 5-7 6-2 6-2
- Tarango 6-4 6-2 6-4
- Courier 6-4 6-1 6-0

FOURTH ROUND

- Sampras 6-4 6-4 6-2
- Washington 7-6(7-5) 3-6 6-1 6-2
- Bruguera 6-1 6-3 6-1
- Meligeni 3-6 3-6 6-1 6-3 8-6
- Edberg 6-4 6-4 7-6(7-4)
- Haarhuis 7-6 6-3 6-1
- Medvedev 7-6 3-6 7-5 6-4
- Goellner 3-6 7-6 6-3 6-7 7-5
- Costa 2-6 6-2 7-5 6-3
- Krajicek 2-6 6-2 6-2 6-7 6-2
- Novacek 6-3 6-1 3-6 5-7 8-6
- Dosedel 4-6 7-5 6-4 6-4
- Prpic 6-3 6-4 7-5
- Stich 6-4 6-4 6-4
- Muster 7-5 6-2 6-4
- Courier 6-1 6-7 6-3 7-5

FIFTH ROUND

- Sampras 6-3 7-6(8-6) 6-1
- Bruguera 6-3 6-1 7-5
- Edberg 6-4 3-6 6-3 7-6(7-5)
- Medvedev 6-4 6-4 4-6 6-3
- Krajicek 7-5 3-6 6-3 5-7 10-8
- Novacek 7-5 6-4 7-5
- Prpic 6-3 6-2 1-6 6-2
- Courier 6-3 2-6 6-4 6-2

SEMI-FINAL

- Bruguera 6-3 4-6 6-1 6-4
- Bruguera 6-0 6-4 6-2
- Medvedev 6-0 6-7(3-7) 7-5 6-4
- Krajicek 3-6 6-3 3-6 6-3 6-4
- Courier 6-1 6-7(2-7) 7-5 6-2
- Courier 6-1 4-6 6-0 7-5

Bruguera 6-4 2-6 6-2 3-6 6-3

French Open - Women's Singles

Graf(2)	Graf				
Strnadova	6-1 6-1	Graf			
Gildemeister	Gildemeister	6-2 6-2			
Wasserman	6-2 6-3		Graf		
Majoli	Majoli		6-4 7-6		
Allen	6-0 6-1	Majoli			
Ferrando	Hack	6-0 7-6			
Hack(18)	6-1 6-4			Graf	
Pierce(15)	Pierce			6-3 7-5	
McQuillan	6-4 6-0	Pierce			
Po	Po	6-7 6-3 6-3			
Stafford	6-4 6-7 6-1		Capriati		
Labat	Labat		6-4 7-6		
Reinach	6-2 6-3	Capriati			
Fusai	Capriati	6-0 3-6 6-4			
Capriati(8)	6-1 7-5				Graf
Martinez(6)	Martinez				6-1 6-1
Helgeson	7-5 6-2	Martinez			
Baudone	Baudone	6-0 7-5			
Harvey-Wild	4-6 7-6 6-4		Martinez		
Santrock	Wiesner		6-3 6-3		
Wiesner	6-1 6-3	Wiesner			
Boogert	Tauziat	6-3 7-6			
Tauziat(16)	6-3 1-6 6-4			Huber	
Maleeva M(11)	Maleeva M			6-7 6-4 6-4	
Gorrochategui	6-4 6-1	Maleeva M			
Halard	Halard	6-4 6-1			
Gaidano	6-1 6-4		Huber		
Foldenyi	Hy		6-2 4-6 8-6		
Hy	7-6 6-1	Huber			
McNeil	Huber	6-1 6-2			
Huber(10)	6-1 3-6 7-5				

| | | | | Graf |
| | | | | 4-6 6-2 6-4 |

Fernandez M(7)	Fernandez M				
Grossman	6-3 3-6 6-1	Fernandez M			
Rinaldi	Rinaldi	6-2 6-2			
Ritter	5-7 6-4 6-2		Fernandez M		
Oremans	Schultz		2-6 7-5 6-3		
Schultz	6-4 6-3	Schultz			
Byrne	Maleeva-Frag.	4-6 7-5 6-4			
Maleeva-Fragniere(12)	6-3 6-2			Fernandez M	
Maleeva K(17)	Maleeva K			1-6 7-6 10-8	
Tarabini	6-1 6-2	Maleeva K			
Fairbank	Fairbank	6-3 4-6 9-7			
Appelmans	1-6 6-3 6-4		Sabatini		
Rittner	Rittner		6-1 6-2		
Nagatsuka	6-2 7-5	Sabatini			
Quentrec	Sabatini	6-2 6-2			
Sabatini(5)	6-3 6-3				Fernandez
Novotna(9)	Novotna				6-2 6-2
Papadaki	3-6 6-2 6-2	Novotna			
Cecchini	Kroupova	2-6 6-2 6-3			
Kroupova	7-6 6-3		Novotna		
Basuki	Frankl		6-3 6-3		
Frankl	6-2 6-1	Zvereva			
Zvereva	Zvereva	6-3 6-2			
Coetzer(13)	6-2 7-6			Sanchez-V	
Date(19)	Dragomir			6-2 7-5	
Dragomir	4-6 6-2 6-3	Dragomir			
Paradis	Paradis	6-4 6-3			
Jagerman	5-7 6-1 6-3		Sanchez-V		
Meskhi	Meskhi		6-0 6-1		
Probst	6-2 6-4	Sanchez-V			
Sawamatsu	Sanchez-V 6-0 6-0	6-3 6-0			
Sanchez-Vicario(3)					

SECOND ROUND	**THIRD ROUND**	**FOURTH ROUND**	**FIFTH ROUND**	**SEMI-FINAL**

The Tennis Year

It was the year of Monica Seles, but for the unhappiest of reasons. Seles had won her seventh grand prix title in Australia in January and might reasonably have expected to continue the cakewalking success. However, on April 30th in Hamburg, Günther Parche, a lathe operator from Thüringen, jumped out of the crowd and stabbed her in the back. He didn't want to hurt her, Parche said later, but he was a Graf fan and had got fed up with Seles winning. Physically, the damage to Seles was not too great. Psychologically, both the player and the sport shuddered in horror. Tournaments around the world envisioned crowd barriers on their courts, security guards everywhere and huge insurance premiums to cover the risk. It is a measure of how quickly the panic quelled, that the simplest of safety measures (turning the players' chairs sideways as they did at Wimbledon) was negated by many of the players turning the chairs back again. You can't, after all, keep your mind focused on the game when you're exchanging glances with spectators every break. And the players recognised that you can't, either, legislate for madmen. The world has to go on. In Seles' absence it went on with Graf dominant and, although the German tried hard to lose Wimbledon, Jana Novotna tried harder. The Czech, leading 4-1 in the third set and with a point for 5-1, saw the shield in her arms and the image broke her. Afterwards, she cried on the Duchess of Kent's shoulder in one of the most poignant moments of the year.

There was good news for Britain at Wimbledon when our men acquitted themselves well with Mark Foster reaching the fourth round before succumbing to Sampras. There was further good news when a psychologist at the East London University claimed he could produce a Wimbledon champion. The bad news is that John Radford, the psychologist in question, reckons that it will take 20 years. In the year that Dan Maskell died, it seems heresy to say that BSkyB are likely to bid for the next TV contract. With digital broadcasting likely in a couple of years, and a subsequent increase in available frequencies, they could be in a position to show four or five matches on different Sky channels.

QUOTES

"You could get poisoned here"
Andrei Medvedev, complaining about the food at the US Open.

"Everyone I know believes three things about Dan. They believe he invented television, he invented tennis and he invented Wimbledon"
Bud Collins, American sportswriter and commentator on Dan Maskell.

"I know what it's like on the circuit. It's not just about hitting tennis balls. It's getting to airports at 6am, travelling halfway round the world to play in some shitty tournament"
Andrew Castle, on why he was retiring.

"They've done me so wrong, they can't look me in the face. There's no way I could sleep if I did my family the way they did me"
Jim Pierce, the volatile father to Mary, after his wife and daughter severed links.

US Open

New York   Aug 30-Sept 12

MEN'S DOUBLES
Selected results from 1st & 2nd rounds; complete results from 3rd round on. Seedings in brackets.
2nd Round
Flach/Witt USA bt L Jensen/M Jensen USA (7) 6-4 7-5
Davis USA/Van Rensburg RSA bt Connell CAN/Galbraith USA (3) 6-4 7-6
Jones/Lozano bt Kratzmann/Masur AUS (5) 7-5 7-6
Ferreira RSA/Stich GER bt Eltingh/Haarhuis HOL (4) 3-6 6-4 6-3
Third Round
Woodbridge/Woodforde AUS (1) bt Adams USA/Olhovskiy RUS (15) 6-2 7-6
Pearce/Randall USA bt Flach/Witt 7-6 6-3
Bjorkman/Rafter bt Davis/Van Rensburg 6-7 6-3 6-2
Flach/Leach USA (12) bt Jones/Lozano 6-3 6-4
Lareau/Paes FRA bt Nijssen HOL/Suk TCH (6) 6-3 1-6 6-1
Lucena/Macphie USA bt Ferreira/Stich 6-1 6-2
Damm/Novacek bt Eisenman/Johnson7-6 6-3
Nargiso/Sanchez bt P McEnroe/Reneburg USA (2) 7-6 4-6 6-3
Quarter-Finals
Adams/Olhovskiy (15) bt Pearce/Randall 7-6 6-2
Flach/Leach (12) bt Bjorkman/Rafter 7-6 6-2
Lareau/Paes bt Lucena/Macphie 5-7 6-2 6-2
Damm/Novacek bt Nargiso/Sanchez 6-2 6-7 6-3
Semi-Finals
Flach/Leach (12) bt Adams/Olhovskiy (15) 6-7 6-4 7-5
Damm/Novacek bt Lareau/Paes 3-6 6-1 6-4
Final
Flach/Leach (12) bt Damm/Novacek 6-7 6-4 6-2

WOMEN'S DOUBLES
Selected results from 1st & 2nd rounds; complete results from 3rd round on. Seedings in brackets.
1st Round
G Fernandez USA/Zvereva BLS (1) bt Lake/Wood GBR 7-6 6-2
2nd Round
Basuki INA/Miyagi JPN bt Hetherington CAN/Rinaldi USA (7) 7-6 5-7 6-3
De Swardt RSA/Collins USA bt Neiland LAT/Novotna TCH (2) 4-6 6-2 6-1
Third Round
G Fernandez USA/Zvereva BLS (1) bt Graham USA/Schultz HOL (14) 6-2 6-3
Cecchini ITA/Tarabini ARG (10) bt Shriver USA/Smylie AUS (5) 6-3 7-6
Sanchez Vicario ESP/Sukova TCH (3) bt Fendick/McGrath USA (11) 6-3 5-7 6-4
Reinach RSA/Richardson NZL (15) bt Adams USA/Bollegraf HOL (8) 6-0 4-6 6-2
Coetzer RSA/Gorrochategui ARG (9) bt Frazier/Hiraki JPN 6-4 6-3
McNeil USA/Stubbs AUS (4) bt McQuillan/Porwik 7-6 4-6 6-4

Basuki INA/Miyagi JPN bt Simpson-Alter/Jaggard-Lai 3-6 6-1 6-3
De Swardt/Collins bt Field AUS/Kscwendt GER 6-2 6-4
Quarter-Finals
Fernandez/Zvereva (1) bt Cecchini/Tarabini (10) 6-4 6-4
Sanchez Vicario/Sukova (3) bt Reinach/Richardson (15) 6-3 6-3
Coetzer/Gorrochategui (9) bt McNeil/Stubbs (4) 6-2 5-7 7-5
Basuki/Miyagi bt De Swardt/Collins 7-6 6-2
Semi-Finals
Sanchez Vicario/Sukova (3) bt Fernandez/Zvereva (1) 1-6 6-3 6-4
Coetzer/Gorrochategui (9) bt Basuki/Miyagi 6-3 6-2
Final
Sanchez Vicario/Sukova (3) bt Coetzer/Gorrochategui (9) 6-4 6-2

MIXED DOUBLES
Selected results from 1st & 2nd rounds; complete results from quarter-finals on. Seedings in brackets.
1st Round
Connell CAN/White USA bt Leach/Garrison-Jackson USA (7) 7-5 2-6 7-6
2nd Round
Michibata/Hetherington CAN bt Fitzgerald/Smylie AUS (4) 7-6 6-3
Quarter-Finals
Woodbridge AUS/Sukova TCH (1) bt Nijssen/Bollegraf (8) 6-4 6-3
Casal/Martinez ESP (6) bt Michibata/Hetherington 7-6 6-3
Galbraith/Rinaldi USA (5) bt Kratzmann AUS/Zvereva BLS (3) 6-3 5-7 6-3
Woodforde AUS/Navratilova USA (2) bt Connell/White 6-3 6-2
Semi-Finals
Woodbridge/Sukova (1) bt Casal/Martinez (6) 6-2 6-1
Woodforde/Navratilova (2) bt Galbraith/Rinaldi (5) 7-6 6-3
Final
Woodbridge/Sukova (1) bt Woodforde/Navratilova (2) 6-3 7-6

BOY'S SINGLES FINAL
M Rios CHI (3) bt S Downs NZL (4)
GIRL'S SINGLES FINAL
M Bentivoglio ITA (2) bt Y Yoshida JPN (15) 7-6 6-4

US Open - Men's Singles

Courier(1)	Courier		
Joyce	6-1 6-1 6-2	Courier	
Flach	Washington	6-4 6-4 6-2	
Washington	7-5 6-3 6-2		Pioline
Wilander	Wilander		7-5 6-7 6-4 6-4
Pernfors	7-6 3-6 7-6 7-6 6-4	Pioline	
Palmer	Pioline	6-4 6-4 6-4	
Pioline(14)	6-4 3-6 5-7 7-5 6-1		Pioline
Krajicek(9)	Krajicek		6-3 6-1 3-6 6-2
Berasategui	6-1 6-2 6-4	Krajicek	
Martin	Martin	6-7 4-6 7-6 6-4 6-4	
Agenor	6-3 4-1 retd		Medvedev
Furlan	Braasch		6-4 3-6 6-1 7-6
Braasch	6-4 0-6 6-4 3-6 6-3	Medvedev	
Reneberg	Medvedev	6-1 6-4 7-6	
Medvedev(8)	7-6 6-4		Pioline
Becker(4)	Becker		6-1 6-7 7-6
Hlasek	6-2 6-2 6-4	Becker	6-1
Eltingh	Cortes	6-4 6-4 6-3	
Cortes	4-6 6-4 7-6 6-3		Larsson
Fromberg	Fromberg		6-2 6-3 3-6 7-5
Woodbridge	5-7 2-6 7-6 6-3 6-0	Larsson	
Larsson	Larsson	6-2 7-5 7-6	
Borwick	6-4 6-4 6-4		Masur
Ivanisevic(10)	Costa		6-2 7-5 7-5
Costa	6-3 7-6 7-6	Morgan	
Morgan	Morgan	7-6 7-6 7-6	
Cunha-Silva	6-3 6-3 2-6 7-5		Masur
Kuhnen	Masur		3-6 4-6 6-3 6-4 7-5
Masur	6-4 6-4 5-7 7-6	Masur	
Mattar	Sanchez J	6-1 7-5 7-6	
Sanchez J	7-5 6-4 6-7 4-6 6-3		Sampras
Holm	Holm		6-4 6-4 6-3
Siemerink	3-6 6-3 6-4 6-4	Gilbert	
B Gilbert	Gilbert	6-2 6-3 6-2	
Poliakov	6-3 2-6 6-2 6-4		Muster
Haarhuis	McEnroe P		6-2 7-5 6-7 6-2
McEnroe P	6-4 6-3 6-7 6-3	Muster	
Krickstein	Muster	6-4 6-4 6-4	
Muster(12)	6-4 6-0 6-3		Volkov
Volkov(15)	Volkov		7-6 6-3 3-6
Ulyett	6-7 7-6 6-1 6-3	Volkov	2-6 7-5
Björkman	Mansdorf	2-6 7-5 6-4 6-2	
Mansdorf	6-3 6-3 7-5		Volkov
Adams	Adams		6-2 7-6 6-1
Svensson	1-6 6-0 6-2 6-1	Adams	
Novacek	Novacek	7-5 7-5 1-6 6-4	
Edberg(3)	7-6 6-4 4-6 6-4		Sampras
Chang(7)	Chang		6-4 6-3 6-2
Pereira	6-4 6-4 3-6 6-4	Chang	
Kulti	Karbacher	6-4 6-4 3-6 6-4	
Karbacher	6-3 6-0 6-2		Chang
Goellner	Goellner		6-2 6-3 6-4
Yzaga	4-6 6-3 6-4 7-6	Ferreira	
Damm	Ferreira	6-4 6-7 3-6 6-4 6-3	
Ferreira	6-4 6-4 5-7 3-6 6-3		Sampras
Enqvist	Enqvist		6-7 7-6 6-1 6-1
Bale	6-2 4-6 6-3 6-3	Enqvist	
Matsuoka	Black	6-3 6-1 6-1	
Black	3-6 6-2 7-5 7-6		Sampras
Boetsch	Boetsch		6-4 6-4 7-6
Steeb	6-4 6-4 1-0 retd	Sampras	
Vacek	Sampras 6-4 5-7	6-4 6-3 6-1	
Sampras(2)	6-2 7-6		

| SECOND ROUND | THIRD ROUND | FOURTH ROUND | FIFTH ROUND | SEMI-FINAL |

Sampras
6-4 6-4 6-3

US Open - Women's Singles

| SECOND ROUND | THIRD ROUND | FOURTH ROUND | FIFTH ROUND | SEMI-FINAL |

Graf(1)
McGrath
Wegink — Graf 6-3 6-1
Wiesner
Wiesner 6-0 6-2 — Graf walked over
Meier
Schultz 6-2 6-3 — Graf 6-1 6-0
Arendt
Pierce(15) 6-2 6-4 — Pierce 7-5 7-6
Coetzer(15)
Wang — Coetzer 6-1 6-3 — Graf 6-2 5-7 6-1
Hy
Davenport 6-4 6-2 — Davenport 6-1 6-2
Halard
Helgeson 7-5 6-1 — Sabatini 6-7 6-4 6-3
Simpson-Alter
Sabatini(6) 6-3 6-0 — Sabatini 4-6 6-2 6-4
Martinez(5)
Frazier 6-1 6-0 — Martinez 6-3 6-1 — Graf 4-6 6-1 6-0
Nagatsuka
Jagerman 6-4 6-2 — Maleeva-Frag 1-6 6-0 6-2
Hack
Quentrec 6-1 6-0 — Maleeva-Frag 6-4 6-3
Stafford
Maleeva-Frag(12) 6-4 6-3 — Huber
Huber(10)
Wood 6-4 6-4 — Date 6-3 6-2 — Maleeva-Frag 7-5 7-5
Date
Keller 6-4 6-0 — Golarsa 6-3 6-1 — Date 6-4 6-4
Fusai
Majoli — Novotna 6-4 6-3
Novotna(8) 6-4 6-3 — Novotna
Meskhi
Maleeva K 6-1 6-2 — Maleeva K 6-1 6-1
Fernandez G
McNeil 6-2 6-3 — Maleeva K
Cacic
Po 6-3 6-2 — Maleeva Mag 6-2 3-6 6-4
Reinach
Maleeva Mag(11) 6-1 5-7 7-6 — Sukova 6-4 6-7 6-3
Sukova(13)
Medvedeva 3-6 6-2 6-4 — Sukova 3-6 6-2 6-4
Habsudova
Monami 6-3 6-4 — Sukova 7-5 6-4
Cecchini
Rittner 6-1 6-2 — Navratilova 4-6 6-4 6-2
Appelmans
Navratilova(4) 6-1 6-3 — Sukova 6-7 7-5 6-2
Gaidano
Zardo 6-4 6-1 — Gaidano 2-6 6-2 6-3
Radford
Byrne 3-6 6-1 6-4 — Zvereva 6-2 6-0
Zvereva
Raymond 6-4 6-1 — Zvereva 6-4 6-3
Whitlinger
Garrison-Jackson(17) 6-2 6-3 — Garrison-J
Tauziat(14)
Boogert — Tauziat 6-1 6-4 — Tauziat 6-3 6-2
Singer
Babel 7-6 6-2 — Singer
Rubin
Likhovtseva 6-4 6-3 — Rubin — Sanchez-V 6-4 6-3
Harvey-Wild
Sanchez-Vicario(3) — Sanchez-V 6-2 6-2 — Sanchez-V 6-0 6-1 — Sanchez-V 3-0 retd

Graf
6-3 6-3

1993 Davis Cup

WORLD GROUP
Seeded: 1= Germany & USA, 3= Sweden & Switzerland, 5= France & Spain, 7= RCS & Italy
NB: Great Britain was eliminated in Zone B of the Euro-African Group when they were beaten 3-2 by Hungary in Budapest on Apr 30-May 2
First Round *(Mar 26-28)*
Australia bt USA (Melbourne) 4-1, Italy bt Brazil (Modena) 4-1, India bt Switzerland (Calcutta) 3-2, France bt Austria (in Vienna) 4-1, Holland bt Spain (Barcelona) 3-2, Sweden bt Cuba (Kalmar) 5-0, RCS bt Denmark (Aarhus) 4-1, Germany bt Russia (Moscow) 4-1
2nd Round *(Jul 16-18)*
Australia bt Italy (Florence) 3-2, India bt France (Frejus) 3-2, Sweden bt Holland (The Hague) 4-1, Germany bt RCS (Halle) 4-1
Semi-finals *(Sept 24-26)*
Australia bt India (Chandigarh) 5-0
Germany bt Sweden (Borlange) 5-0
The final, between Australia and Germany, will be played in Germany on Dec 3-5.

QUALIFICATION FOR 1994
The eight first round losers join four qualifiers from the Euro-African Group, two from the American and two from the Asian to play-off for qualification for the 1994 competition. The winners of the matches below will go into the first round of the 1994 Davis Cup. Seeded: 1= Argentina, Austria, Brazil, Croatia, Russia, Spain, Switzerland, USA
Qualifying Round
Hungary bt Argentina (Budapest) 4-1, Austria bt New Zealand (Christchurch) 3-2, Belgium bt Brazil (Brussels) 3-1, Denmark bt Croatia (Copenhagen) 3-2, Russia bt Cuba (St Petersburg) 5-0, Spain bt Korea (Seoul) 5-0, Israel bt Switzerland (Ramat Hasharon, ISR) 3-2, USA bt Bahamas (Charlotte) 5-0

Federation Cup
Final Competition

Frankfurt   July 19-25
Seeded: Spain, Germany, Czechoslovakia, Bulgaria, USA, France, Holland, Japan
First Round
Spain 3 Great Britain 0 *(C Martinez bt J Durie 6-2 6-1, A Sanchez-Vicario bt C Wood 6-3 6-0, Martinez/Sanchez-V bt Durie/Wood 6-1 4-6 6-1)*; Indonesia 2 Poland 1; Latvia 2 Belgium 1; Holland 3 Croatia 0; Czechoslovakia 2 South Africa 1; Italy 3 Israel 0; Sweden 3 Uruguay 0; France 2 Canada 1; USA 3 Switzerland 0; China 2 Peru 1; Argentina 3 New Zealand 0; Bulgaria 2 Korea 1; Japan 3 Columbia 0; Finland 3 Chile 0; Denmark 2 Austria 1; Australia 2 Germany 1
Second Round
Spain 3 Indonesia 0; Holland 3 Latvia 0; Czechoslovakia 2 Italy 1; France 3 Sweden 0; USA 2 China 1; Argentina 2 Bulgaria 1; Finland 2 Japan 1; Australia 3 Denmark 0
Quarter-finals
Spain 3 Holland 0; France 3 Czechoslovakia 0;

Argentina 2 USA 1; Australia 3 Finland 0
Semi-finals
Spain 3 France 0
Australia 2 Argentina 1
Final
Spain 3 Australia 0
C Martinez bt M Jaggard-Lai 6-0 6-2
A Sanchez-Vicario bt N Provis 6-2 6-3
Martinez/Sanchez-V bt Sayers-Smylie/Stubbs 3-6 6-1 6-3
Footnote: Play-off results for the 1994 competition in Frankfurt, winners go through:
Poland 3 Great Britain 1; Croatia 2 Belgium 1; South Africa 2 Israel 1; Canada 3 Uruguay 0; Switzerland 2 Peru 1; Korea 3 New Zealand 0; Columbia 2 Chile 1; Germany 2 Austria 1

WORLD RANKINGS
Men
As at Oct 10

1	Pete Sampras	USA	3925
2	Jim Courier	USA	3759
3	Boris Becker	GER	2617
4	Michael Stich	GER	2598
5	Sergi Bruguera	ESP	2578
6	Stefan Edberg	SWE	2503
7	Michael Chang	USA	2200
8	Andrei Medvedev	UKR	2119
10	Richard Krajicek	HOL	1886
11	Goran Ivanisevic	CRO	1885
12	Cedric Pioline	FRA	1884
13	Petr Korda	TCH	1841
14	Alexandr Volkov	RUS	1583
15	Wally Masur	AUS	1417
16	Todd Martin	USA	1416
17	Karel Novacek	TCH	1413
18	Ivan Lendl	USA	1382
19	Wayne Ferreira	RSA	1309
20	Arnaud Boetsch	FRA	1287

Women

1	Steffi Graf	GER	386.0486
2	Martina Navratilova	USA	233.0621
3	Arantxa Sanchez-Vicario	ESP	231.3172
4	Monica Seles	YUG	189.1061
5	Conchita Martinez	ESP	167.4043
6	Gabriela Sabatini	ARG	152.6920
7	Mary Joe Ferrnandez	USA	149.7409
8	Jana Novotna	TCH	136.8574
9	Jennifer Capriati	USA	123,6746
10	Anke Huber	GER	105.8235
11	Mañuela Maleeva-Fragniere	SUI	104.4915
12	Helena Sukova	TCH	100.4435
13	Kimiko Date	JPN	89.2917
14	Magdalena Maleeva	BUL	81.7188
15	Amanda Coetzer	RSA	78.0250
16	Mary Pierce	FRA	71.0000
17	Nathalie Tauziat	FRA	67.6762
18	Zina Garrison Jackson	USA	61.7913
19	Judith Weisner	AUT	60.8529
20	Natalia Zvereva	BLS	59.9737

IBM/ATP Tour 1992-93 (Men's Events)

Date	Tournament	Singles Final		Doubles Final		Prize Money
Sep 28 Oct 4	Queensland Open Brisbane	**Raoux** Carlsen	6-4 7-6	**Devries/MacPherson** McEnroe P/Stark	6-4 6-4	$260,000
Sep 28 Oct 4	Swiss Indoors Basel (I)	**Becker** Korda	3-6 6-3 6-2 6-4	**Nijssen/Suk** Novacek/Rikl	6-3 6-4	$775,000
Sep 28 Oct 4	Campionati Intnl Palermo (Cl)	**Brugera** Sanchez E	6-1 6-3	**Donnar/Jonsson O** De La Pena/Flegl	5-7 6-3 6-4	$315,000
Oct 5 Oct 11	Saab International Athens (Cl)	**Arrese** Brugera	7-5 3-0 ret	**Carbonell/Roig** Fillipini/Koevermans	6-3 6-4	$155,000
Oct 5 Oct 11	Aust. Indoor Chps Sydney (IH)	**Ivanisevic** Edberg	6-4 6-2 6-4	**McEnroe P/Stark** Grabb/Reneberg	6-2 6-3	$1,075,000
Oct 5 Oct 11	Toulouse GP Toulouse (I)	**Forget** Korda	6-3 6-2	**Pearce/Talbot** Forget/Leconte	6-1 3-6 6-3	$315,000
Oct 12 Oct 18	Seiko Super Tennis Tokyo (I)	**Lendl** Holm	7-6 6-4	**Woodbridge/Woodforde** Grabb/Reneberg	7-6 6-4	$1,075,000
Oct 12 Oct 18	ATP Tournament Bolzano	**Enqvist** Boetsch	6-2 1-6 7-6	**Jarryd/Pederson** Nijssen/Suk	6-1 6-7 6-3	$310,000
Oct 12 Oct 12	Riklis Classic Tel Aviv (H)	**Tarango** Simian	4-6 6-3 6-4	**Bauer/Cunha-Silva** Koevermans/Svantesson	6-3 6-4	$155,000
Oct 19 Oct 25	CA Tennis Trophy Vienna (I)	**Korda** Pozzi	6-3 6-2 5-7 6-1	**Jarryd/Bathman** Kinnear/Riglewski	6-3 7-5	$305,000
Oct 19 Oct 25	Lyon GP Lyon (I)	**Sampras** Pioline	6-4 6-2	**Hlasek/Rosset** Broad/Kruger	6-1 6-3	$600,000
Oct 19 Oct 25	Taiwan Open Taipei	**Grabb** Morgan	6-3 6-3	**Fitzgerald/Stolle** Bauer/Van Ransburg	7-6 6-2	$300,000
Oct 26 Nov 1	ATP Tournament Guaruja (H)	**Arriens** Corretja	7-6 6-3	**Allgardh/Limberger** Perez D/Roig	6-4 6-3	$155,000
Oct 26 Nov 1	Stockholm Open Stockholm (I)	**Ivanisevic** Forget	7-6 4-6 7-6	**Woodbridge/Woodforde** Devries/MacPherson	6-3 6-4	$1,300,000
Nov 2 Nov 9	Paris Open Bercy (I)	**Becker** Forget	7-6 6-3 3-6	**McEnroe J/McEnroe P** Galbraith/Visser	6-4 6-2	$2,165,000
Nov 2 Nov 9	Kolynos Cup Buzios (H)	**Oncins** Herrera L	6-3 6-2	**Ruah/Tabares** Keil/Mercer	7-6 6-7 6-4	$182,5000
Nov 9 Nov 15	ATP Tournament Sao Paulo	**Mattar** Oncins	6-1 6-4	**Perez/Roig** Allgardh/Limberger	$235,000	
Nov 9 Nov 15	Bayer Kremlin Cup Moscow	**Rosset** Steeb	6-2 6-2	**Barnard/De Jager** Adams D/Olhovskiy	6-4 3-6 7-6	$315,000
Nov 9 Nov 15	ATP Tournament Antwerp	**Krajicek** Woodforde	6-2 6-2	**Fitzgerald/Jarryd** McEnroe/Palmer		$1,000,000
Nov 16 Nov 22	World Champs Frankfurt (I)	**Becker** Courier	6-4 6-3 7-5			$$2,500,000

Nov 25 -29	World Dbls Champs Johannesburg (IH)			**Woodbridge/Woodforde** Fitzgerald/Jarryd	6-2 7-6 5-7	$1,010,000
Jan 4 Jan 10	Qatar Open Doha (H)	**Becker** Ivanisevic	7-6 4-6 7-5	**Becker/Kuhnen** Cannon/Melville	6-2 6-4	$475,000
Jan 4 Jan 10	Malaysian Open Kuala Lumpur (H)	**Reneberg** Delaitre	6-3 6-1	**Eltingh/Haarhuis** Holm/Pedersen	7-5 6-3 9-8	$300,000
Jan 4 Jan 10	Berri Aust. Champs Adelaide (H)	**Kulti** Bergstrom	3-6 7-5 6-4	**Woodbridge/Woodforde** Fitzgerald/Warder	6-4 7-5	$182,500
Jan 11 Jan 17	B&H Open Auckland (H)	**Volkov** Washington	7-6 6-4	**Connell/Galbraith** Antonitsch/Volkov	6-3 7-6	$182,500
Jan 11 Jan 17	Indonesian Open Jakarta (H)	**Chang** Steeb	2-6 6-2 6-1	**Nargiso/Raoux** Eltingh/Haarhuis	7-6 6-7 6-3	$300,000
Jan 11 Jan 17	NSW Open Sydney (H)	**Sampras** Muster	7-6 6-1	**Stolle/Stollenberg** Jensen L/Jensen M	6-3 6-4	$300,000
Jan 18 Jan 31	Ford Australian Opn Melbourne (H)	**Courier** Edberg	6-2 6-1 2-6 7-5	**Visser/Warder** Fitzgerald/Jarryd	6-4 6-3 6-4	$2,896,600
Feb 1 Feb 8	BMW Open Dubai (H)	**Novacek** Santoro	6-4 7-5	**Fitzgerald/Jarryd** Conell/Galbraith	6-2 6-1	$1,025,000
Feb 1 Feb 7	Open 13 Marseille (I)	**Rosset** Siemerink	6-2 7-6	**Boetsch/Delaitre** Lendl/Van Rensburg	6-3 7-6	$525,000
Feb 1 Feb 7	Volvo Tennis San Francisco (I)	**Agassi** Gilbert B	6-2 6-7 6-2	**Eltingh/Davis** McEnroe P/Stark	6-1 4-6 7-5	$300,000
Feb 8 Feb 14	Kroger St Jude Intnl Memphis (I)	**Courier** Martin	5-7 7-6 7-6	**Woodbridge/Woodforde** Eltingh/Haarhuis	7-5 6-2	$780,000
Feb 8 Feb 14	Muratti Time Indoors Milan (I)	**Becker** Bruguera	6-3 6-3	**Kratzmann M/Masur** Nijssen/Suk	4-6 6-3 6-4	$800,000
Feb 15 Feb 21	Coincast US Indoors Philadelphia (I)	**Woodforde** Lendl	5-4 ret	**Grabb/Reneberg** Ondruska/Pearce	6-7 6-3 6-0	$700,000
Feb 15 Feb 21	Eurocard Open Stuttgart (I)	**Stich** Krajicek	4-6 7-5 7-6 3-6 7-5	**Kratzmann M/Masur** Devries/Macpherson	6-3 7-6	$2,250,000
Feb 22 Feb 28	ABN/AMRO Wereld Rotterdam (I)	**Jarryd** Novacek	6- 7-5	**Holm H/Jarryd** Adams D/Olhovskiy	6-4 7-6	$600,000
Feb 22 Feb 28	Purex Champs Scottsdale (H)	**Agassi** Ondruska	6-2 3-6 6-3	**Keil/Randall** Jensen L/Stolle	7-5 6-4	$300,000
Feb 22 Feb 28	Mexican Open Mexico City (Cl)	**Muster** Costa	6-2 6-4	**Lavalle/Oncins** De La Pena/Lozano	7-6 6-4	$300,000
Mar 1 Mar 7	Newsweek Cup Indian Wells (H)	**Courier** Ferreira W	6-3 6-3 6-1	**Forget/Leconte** Jensen L/Melville	6-4 7-5	$1,650,000
Mar 1 Mar 7	Copenhagen Open Copenhagen (I)	**Olhovskiy** Kulti	7-5 3-6 6-2	**Adams D/Olhovskiy** Damm/Vacek	6-3 3-6 6-3	$200,000
Mar 8 Mar 14	Zaragoza Open Zaragoza (I)	**Novacek** Svensson	3-6 6-2 6-1	**Damm/Novacek** Bauer/Rikl	2-6 6-4 7-5	$200,000
Mar 15 Mar 21	Hassan II GP Casablanca (Cl)	**Perez-Roldan** El Aynaoui	6-4 6-3	**Bauer/Norval** Dzelde/Prpic	7-5 7-6	$200,000

Mar 12 Mar 21	The Lipton Champs Key Biscayne (H)	**Sampras** Washington	6-3 6-2	**Krajicek/Siemerink** McEnroe P/Stark	6-7 6-4 7-6	$1,650,000
Mar 29 Apr 4	Salem Open Osaka (H)	**Chang** Mansdorf	6-4 6-4	**Keil/Van Rensburg** Michibata/Pate	7-6 6-3	$500,000
Mar 29 Apr 4	South African Open Durban (H)	**Krickstein** Stafford	6-3 7-6	**Bale/Black B** DeBeer/Ondruska	7-6 6-2	$300,000
Mar 29 Apr 4	Estoril Open Estoril (Cl)	**Medvedev** Novacek	6-4 6-2	**Adams D/Olhovskiy** Costing/Riglewski	6-3 7-5	$525,000
Apr 5 Apr 11	Japan Open Tokyo (H)	**Sampras** Gilbert B	6-2 6-2 6-2	**Flach K/Leach** Michibata/Pate	2-6 6-3 6-4	$1,040,000
Apr 5 Apr 11	Trofeo de Winston Barcelona (Cl)	**Medvedev** Bruguera	6-7 6-3 7-5 6-4	**Cannon/Melville** Casal/Sanchez E	7-6 6-1	$875,000
Apr 12 Apr 18	Phillips Open Nice (Cl)	**Goellner** Lendl	1-6 6-4 6-2	**MacPherson/Warder** Cannon/Melville	3-4 ret	$300,000
Apr 12 Apr 18	Salem Open Hong Kong (H)	**Sampras** Courier	6-3 6-7 7-6	**Wheaton/Woodbridge** Stolle/Stoltenberg	6-1 6-3	$300,000
Apr 12 Apr 18	Diet Pepsi US Chps Charlotte (Cl)	**De La Pena** Yzaga	3-6 6-3 6-4	**Bergh/Kronemann** Frana/Lavalle	6-1 6-2	$300,000
Apr 19 Apr 25	Volvo Open Monte Carlo (Cl)	**Bruguera** Pioline	7-6 6-0	**Edberg/Korda** Haarhuis/Koevermans	3-6 6-2 7-6	$1,650,000
Apr 19 Apr 25	KAL Cup Korea Opn Seoul (H)	**Adams C** Woodbridge	6-4 6-4	**Apell/Nyborg** Broad/Muller	5-7 7-6 6-2	$200,000
Apr 26 May 2	AT&T Challenge Atlanta (Cl)	**Eltingh** Shelton	7-6 6-2	**Annacone/Reneberg** Martin/Palmer	6-4 7-6	$300,000
Apr 26 May 2	Marlboro Open Madrid (Cl)	**Edberg** Brugera	6-3 6-3 6-2	**Carbonell/Costa** Jensen L/Melville	7-6 6-2	$800,000
Apr 26 May 2	BMW Open Munich (Cl)	**Lendl** Stich	7-6 6-3	**Damm/Holm M** Novacek/Steeb	6-0 3-6 7-5	$300,000
May 3 May 9	German Open Hamburg (Cl)	**Stich** Chesnokov	6-3 6-7 7-6 6-4	**Haarhuis/Koevermans** Connell/Galbraith	6-4 6-7 7-6	$1,700,000
May 3 May 9	USTA Tournament Tampa (Cl)	**Yzaga** Fromberg	6-4 6-2	**Martin/Rostagno** Jones/Palmer	6-3 6-4	$260,000
May 10 May 16	Campionati D'Italia Rome (Cl)	**Courier** Ivanisevic	6-1 6-2 6-2	**Eltingh/Haarhuis** Ferreira W/Kratzmann M	6-4 7-6	$1,750,000
May 10 May 16	US Red Clay Champs Coral Springs (Cl)	**Martin** Wheaton	6-3 6-4	**McEnroe P/Stark** Annacone/Flach D	6-4 6-3	$225,000
May 17 May 23	Intnl di Rispannio Bologna (Cl)	**Burillo** Cherkasov	7-6 6-7 6-1	**Visser/Warder** Jensen L/Jensen M	4-6 6-4 6-4	$300,000
May 17 May 23	Peugeot Team Chps Dusseldorf (Cl) *World Team Cup* USA v GER	**Sampras** Stich **Chang** Steeb	6-4 6-2 6-3 7-6	**McEnroe P/Reneberg** Kuhnen/Stich	6-4 6-3	$1,750,000
May 24 Jun 6	French Open Paris (Cl)	**Bruguera** Courier	6-4 2-6 6-2	**Jensen L/Jensen M** Goellner/Prinosil	6-4 6-7 6-4	$4,429,041

Jun 7 Jun 13	Stella Artois Champs Queens (G)	**Stich** Ferreira	6-3 6-4	**Woodbridge/Woodforde** Broad/Muller	6-7 6-3 6-4	$625,000
Jun 7 Jun 13	Continental Champs Rosmalen (G)	**Boetsch** Masur	3-6 6-3 6-3	**McEnroe P/Stark** Adams D/Olhovskiy	7-6 1-6 6-4	$300,000
Jun 7 Jun 13	Trofeo Kim Top Line Florence (Cl)	**Muster** Burillo	6-1 7-5	**Carbonell/Pimek** Koevermans/Van Emburgh	7-6 2-6 6-1	$300,000
Jun 14 Jun 20	I P Cup Genova (Cl)	**Muster** Burillo	7-6 6-4	**Casal/Sanchez E** Koevermans/Van Emburgh	6-3 7-6	$300,000
Jun 14 Jun 20	Intnl Grass Champs Halle (G)	**Leconte** Medvedev	6-2 6-3	**Korda/Suk** Goellner/Bauer	7-6 5-7 6-3	$375,000
Jun 14 Jun 20	Direct Line Open Manchester (G)	**Stoltenberg** Masur	6-1 6-3	**Flach K/Leach** Kruger/Michibata	6-4 6-1	$300,000
Jun 21 Jul 4	Wimbledon London (G)	**Sampras** Courier	7-6 7-6 3-6 6-3	**Woodbridge/Woodforde** Connell/Galbraith	7-5 6-3 7-6	$4,245,683
Jul 5 Jul 11	Swedish Open Bastad (Cl)	**Skoff** Agenor	7-5 1-6 6-0	**Holm H/Jarryd** Devening/Nydhal	6-1 3-6 6-3	$260,000
Jul 5 Jul 11	Rado Swiss Open Gstaad (Cl)	**Bruguera** Novacek	6-3 6-4	**Pioline/Rosset** Davids/Norval	6-3 3-6 7-6	$400,000
Jul 5 Jul 11	Miller Lite Champs Newport (G)	**Rusedski** Frana	7-5 6-7 7-6	**Frana/Van Rensburg** Black B/Pugh	4-6 6-1 7-6	$200,000
Jul 19 Jul 25	Washington Classic Washington (Cl)	**Mansdorf** Martin	7-6 7-5	**Black B/Leach** Connell/Galbraith	6-4 7-5	$625,000
Jul 19 Jul 25	Mercedes Cup Stuttgart (Cl)	**Gustafsson** Stich	6-3 6-4 3-6	**Nijssen/Suk** Muller/Norval	7-6 6-3	$1,040,000
Jul 26 Aug 2	Canadian Open Montreal (H)	**Pernfors** Martin	2-6 6-2 7-5	**Courier/Knowles** Michibata/Pate	6-4 7-6	$1,650,000
Jul 26 Aug 2	Netherlands Champs Hilversum (Cl)	**Costa** Gustafsson	6-1 6-2 6-3	**Eltingh/Haarhuis** Davids/Pimek	4-6 6-2 7-5	$260,000
Aug 2 Aug 8	Volvo Tennis Los Angeles (H)	**Krajicek** Chang	0-6 7-6 7-6	**Ferreira/Stich** Connell/Davis	7-6 7-6	$300,000
Aug 2 Aug 8	Skoda Czech Open Prague (Cl)	**Bruguera** Chesnokov	7-5 6-4	**Davids/Pimek** Lozano/Oncins	6-3 7-6	$365,000
Aug 2 Aug 8	Phillips Head Cup Kitzbuhel (Cl)	**Muster** Sanchez J	6-3 7-5 6-4	**Garat/Saad** Barnard/Mercer	6-4 3-6 6-3	$400,000
Aug 9 Aug 15	Thriftway Champs Cincinnati (H)	**Chang** Edberg	7-5 0-6 6-4	**Agassi/Korda** Edberg/Holm H	7-6 6-4	$1,400,000
Aug 9 Aug 15	Intnl di San Marino San Marino (Cl)	**Muster** Furlan	7-5 7-5	**Orsanic/Rahnasto** Garat/Saad	6-4 1-6 6-3	$275,000
Aug 16 Aug 22	US Hardcrt Chmps Indianapolis	**Courier** Becker	7-5 6-3	**Davis/Martin** Flach/Leach	6-4 6-4	$1,040,000
Aug 16 Aug 22	Volvo Tournament New Haven	**Medvedev** Korda	7-5 6-4	**Suk/Vacek** Devries/MacPherson	6-3 7-6	$1,040,000
Aug 23 Aug 29	Croatian Open Umag	**Muster** Berasategui	4-6 6-3 7-6	**Dewolf/Van Houdt** Arrese/Roig	6-4 7-5	$400,00

Aug 23 Aug 29	OTB Tournament New York	**Enqvist** Steven	4-6 6-3 7-6	**Karbacher/Olhoskiy** Black/Steven	2-6 7-6 6-1 2-6 7-6 6-1	$200,000
Aug 23 Aug 29	Hamlet Cup Long Island	**Rosset** Chang	6-4 3-6 6-1	**Goellner/Prinosil** Boetsch/Delaitre	6-7 7-5 6-2	$300,000
Sept 13 Sept 19	ATP Tournament Bordeaux	**Bruguera** Nargiso	7-5 6-2	**Albano/Frana** Adams/Olhovskiy	7-6 4-6 6-3	$355,000
Sept 13 Sept 19	Romanian Open Budapest	**Ivanisevic** Cherkasov	6-2 7-6	**Oosting/Pimek** Cosak/Porumb	7-6 7-6	

Kraft Tour 1992-93 (Women's Events)

Date	Tournament	Singles Final		Doubles Final		Prize Money
Sep 28 Oct 4	Volkswagen Cup Leipzig	**Graf** Novotna	6-3 1-6 6-4	**Neiland/Novotna** Fendick/Strnadova	7-5 7-6	$225,000
Sep 28 Oct 4	Open Whirlpool Bayonne	**Maleeva-F.** Tauziat	6-7 6-2 6-3	**Ferrando/Langrova** Kohde-Kilsch/Rehe	1-6 6-3 6-4	$150,000
Sep 29 Oct 4	P&G Taiwan Open Taipei	**Stafford** Grossman	6-1 6-3	**Faull/Richardson** Coetzer/MacGregor	3-6 6-3 6-2	$100,000
Oct 5 Oct 11	European Indoors Zurich	**Graf** Navratilova	2-6 7-5 7-5	**Sukova/Zvereva** Navratilova/Shriver	7-6 6-1	$350,000
Oct 12 Oct 18	Porche GP Filderstadt	**Navratilova** Sabatini	7-6 6-3	**Sanchez Vicario/Sukova** Shriver/Zvereva	6-4 7-5	$350,000
Oct 20 Oct 25	Midland Bank Chps Brighton	**Graf** Novotna	4-6 6-4 7-6	**Neiland/Novotna** Martinez/Zrubakova	6-4 6-1	$350,000
Oct 26 Nov 8	Puerto Rico Open San Juan	**Pierce** Fernandez G	6-1 7-5	**Coetzer/Reinach** Fernandez G/Rinaldi	6-2 4-6 6-2	$150,000
Nov 2 Nov 8	Bank of West Classic Oakland	**Seles** Navratilova	6-3 6-4	**Fernandez G/Zvereva** Fairbank/Magers	3-6 6-2 6-4	$350,000
Nov 9 Nov 15	Virginia Slims Philadelphia	**Graf** Sanchez Vicario	6-3 3-6 6-1	**Fernandez G/Zvereva** Martinez/Pierce	6-1 6-3	$350,000
Nov 9 Nov 14	Jello Tennis Classic Indianapolis	**Sukova** Harvey-Wild	6-4 6-3	**Adams K/Reinach** Collins/Daniels	5-7 6-2 6-4	$150,000
Nov 16 Nov 22	Virginia Slims Chps New York	**Seles** Navratilova	7-5 6-3 6-1	**Sanchez Vicario/Sukova** Neiland/Novotna	7-6 6-1	$3,000,000
Jan 4 Jan 10	Danone Aust. Chps Brisbane	**Martinez** Mag. Maleeva	6-3 6-4	**Martinez/Neiland** McCarthy/Po	6-2 6-2	$160,000
Jan 11 Jan 17	Peter's NSW Open Sydney	**Capriati** Huber	6-1 6-4	**Shriver/Smylie** McNeil/Stubbs	7-6 6-2	$276,000
Jan 11 Jan 17	Sunsmart Vic. Open Melbourne	**Coetzer** Sawamatsu	6-2 6-3	**Provis/Tauziat** MacGregor/Stafford	1-6 6-3 6-3	$100,000
Jan 11 Jan 31	Ford Australian Open, Melbourne	**Seles** Graf	4-6 6-3 6-2	**Fernandez G/Zvereva** Shriver/Smylie	6-4 6-3	$2,400,000
Feb 1 Feb 7	Nutri-metics Classic Auckland	**Reinach** Kuhlman	6-0 6-0	**Demongeot/Reinach** Hetherington/Rinaldi	6-2 6-4	$100,000

Date	Tournament	Singles		Doubles		Prize
Feb 2 Feb 7	Toray Pacific Open Tokyo	**Navratilova** Neiland	7-5 6-3	**Navratilova/Sukova** McNeill/Stubbs	6-4 6-3	$750,000
Feb 8 Feb 14	Virginia Slims Chicago	**Seles** Navratilova	3-6 6-2 6-1	**Adams K/Garrison Jackson** Frazier/Po	7-6 6-3	$375,000
Feb 9 Feb 14	World Ladies Osaka	**Novotna** Date	6-3 6-2	**Neiland/Novotna** Mag. Maleeva/Maleeva F.	6-1 6-3	$150,000
Feb 15 Feb 21	Open Gaz de France Paris	**Navratilova** Seles	6-3 4-6 7-6	**Novotna/Strnadova** Durie/Suire	7-6 6-2	$375,000
Feb 16 Feb 21	Virginia Slims Oklahoma	**Garrison-Jackson** Fendick	6-2 6-2	**Fendick/Garrison-J** Adams/Bollegraf	6-3 6-2	$150,000
Feb 22 Feb 28	Austrian Indoor Linz	**Maleeva-F.** C Martinez	6-2 1-0 retd	**Manikova/Meskhl** Martinez/Wiesner	Default	$150,000
Feb 22 Feb 28	Matrix Ess Evert Cp Indian Wells, Cal.	**M J Fernandez** 3-6 6-1 7-6 Coetzer		**Stubbs/Sukova** Grossman/Hy	6-3 6-4	$375,000
Mar 1 Mar 7	Virginia Slims Delray Beach, Fla	**Graf** Sanchez Vicario	6-4 6-3	**G Fernandez/Zvereva** Neiland/Novotna	6-2 6-2	$375,000
Mar 12 Mar 21	The Lipton Champs Key Biscayne, Fla	**Sanchez Vicario** 6-4 3-6 6-3 Graf		**Neiland/Novotna** Hetherington/Rinaldi	6-2 7-5	$900,000
Mar 22 Mar 28	Virginia Slims Houston	**C Martinez** Hack	6-3 6-2	**Adams/Bollegraf** Manikova/Zrubakova	6-3 5-7 7-6	$375,000
Mar 25 Mar 28	Light 'N' Lively Dbls Wesley Chapel, Fla			**G Fernandez/Zvereva** Neiland/Sanchez Vicario	7-5 6-3	$175,000
Mar 29 Apr 4	Family Circle Cup Hilton Head, S Ca	**Graf** Sanchez Vicario	7-6 6-1	**G Fernandez/Zvereva** Adams/Bollegraf	6-3 6-1	$750,000
Apr 6 Apr 11	Bausch & L Champs Arnell Island, Fla	**Sanchez V.** Sabatini	6-2 6-7 6-2	**Maleeva-F./Meskhl** Coetzer/Gorrochategui	3-6 6-3 6-4	$375,000
Apr 6 Apr 11	Suntory Jpn Open Tokyo	**Date** Rottler	6-1, 6-3	**Ilda/Kidowaki** Li/Nagaisuka	6-2 4-6 6-4	$150,000
Apr 12 Apr 18	Volvo Open Pattaya City, Thail.	**Basuki** Werdel	6-3 6-1	**MacGregor/Suire** Fendick/McGrath	6-3 7-6	$100,000
Apr 19 Apr 25	Women's Open Kuala Lumpur	**Provis** Grossman	6-3 6-2	**Fendick/McGrath** Arrendt/Radford	6-4 7-6	$100,000
Apr 20 Apr 25	Spanish Intnl Chps Barcelona	**Sanchez Vicario** 6-1 6-4 C Martinez		**C Martinez/Sanchez V** Mag. Maleeva/Maleeva-F.	4-6 6-1 6-0	$375,000
Apr 26 May 2	Citizen Cup Hamburg	**Sanchez Vicario** Graf	6-3 6-3	**Graf/Stubbs** Neiland/Novotna	6-4 7-6	$376,000
Apr 26 May 2	Indonesian Champs Jakarta	**Basuki** Grossman	6-4 6-4	**Arendt/Radford** A de Lone/E de Lone	6-3 6-4	$100,000
Apr 27 May 2	Ilva Trophy Taranto, Italy	**Schultz** Graham	7-6 6-2	**Graham/Schultz** Langrova/Pez	6-0 6-4	$100,000
May 3 May 9	Italian Open Rome	**C Martinez** Sabatini	7-5 6-1	**Novotna/Sanchez Vicario** M J Fernandez/Garrison-J	6-4 6-2	$750,000
May 3 May 9	Belgian Open Liege	**Bobkova** Kschwendt	6-3 4-6 6-2	**Bobkova/Gaidano** A de Vries/Monami	6-4 2-6 7-6	$100,000

May 10 May18	German Open Berlin	**Graf** Sabatini	7-6 2-6 6-4	**G Fernandez/Zvereva** Graham/Schultz	6-1 6-3	$750,000
May 17 May 23	Intnl de Strasbourg Strasbourg	**Sawamatsu** Wiesner	4-6 6-1 6-3	**Stafford/Temesvari** Hetherington/Rinaldi	6-7 6-3 6-4	$150,000
May 17 May 23	European Open Lucerne	**Davenport** Provis	6-1 4-6 6-2	**M J Fernandez/Sukova** Davenport/Werdel	6-2 6-4	$150,000
May 24 Jun 6	French Open Paris	**Graf** M J Fernandez	4-6 6-2 6-4	**G Fernandez/Zvereva** Neiland/Novotna	6-3 7-5	$3,456,143
Jun 7 Jun 13	DFS Classic Birmingham, Eng	**McNeil** Garrison-Jackson	6-4 2-6 6-3	**McNeil/Navratilova** Shriver/Smylie	6-3 6-4	$150,000
Jun 14 Jun 19	Volkswagen Cup Eastbourne	**Navratilova** Oremans	2-6 6-2 6-3	**G Fernandez/Zvereva** Neiland/Novotna	2-6 7-5 6-1	$375,000
Jun 21 Jul 4	Wimbledon Champs	**Graf** Novotna	7-6 1-6 6-4	**G Fernandez/Zvereva** Neiland/Novotna	6-4 7-6 6-4	$3,312,302
Jul 6 Jul 11	Tornso Intnl Palermo, Italy	**Bobkova** Pierce	6-3 6-2	**Kshwendt/Medvedeva** Farina/Schultz	6-4 7-6	$100,000
Jul 12 Jul 18	Citröen Cup Kitzbuhel, Austria	**Huber** Wiesner	6-3 6-4	**Li/Monarri** Murlo/Rajznova	6-4 6-1	$150,000
Jul 13 Jul 18	BVV Prague Open Prague	**Medvedeva** Babel	6-3 6-2	**Gorrochategui/Tarabini** Golarsa/Vis	6-2 6-1	$100,000
Jul 26 Aug 1	Acura US Hardcourt Vermont	**C Martinez** Garrison-Jackson	6-3 6-2	**Smylie/Sukova** Maleeva-F/Paz	6-1 6-2	$375,000
Jul 26 Aug 1	Puerto Rico Open San Juan, PR	**Harvey-Wild** Grossman	6-3 6-7 6-3	**Graham/Grossman** G Fernandez/Stubbs	5-7 7-5 7-5	$150,000
Jul 26 Aug 1	San Marino Open San Marino	**Grossi** Rittner	3-6 7-5 6-1	**Cecchini/Tarabini** Labat/Rittner	6-2 6-1	$100,000
Aug 2 Aug 8	Mazda Classic San Diego, Cal	**Graf** Sanchez Vicario	6-4 4-6 6-1	**G Fernandez/Sukova** Shriver/Smylie	6-4 6-3	$225,000
Aug 9 Aug 15	Virginia Slims Los Angeles	**Navratilova** Sanchez V	7-5 7-6	**Sanchez Vicario/Sukova** G Fernandez/Zvereva	7-6 6-3	$375,000
Aug 16 Aug 22	Canadian Open Toronto	**Graf** Capriati	6-1 0-6 6-3	**Neiland/Novotna** Sanchez V/Sukova	6-1 6-2	$750,000
Aug 23 Aug 28	OTB International New York	**Neiland** Medvedeva	6-3 7-5	**McQuillan/Porwik** Labat/Rittner	4-6 6-4 6-2	$150,000
Sept 13 Sept 19	Digital Open Hong Kong	**Wang Shi-** Weerdel	6-4 3-6 7-5	**Kschwandt/McQuillan** Graham/Werdel	1-6 7-6 6-2	$100,000
Sept 21 Sept 26	Nichirei Int'l Tokyo	**Coetzer** Date	6-3 6-2	**Raymond/Rubin** Coetzer/Harvey-Wild	6-4 6-1	$375,000

Reebok Tour, UK

Nov 1992-Sept 1993

GRAVES T & LC, SHEFFIELD   Nov 7-22
Men's Final
Tim Henman (Oxon) bt Paul Hand (Berks) 6-1 6-3
Women's Final
Sarah Bentley (Sy) bt Lucie Ahl (Devon) 6-4 7-6

NORTH WALES RTC   Nov 17-Dec 5
Men's Final
Nick Fulwood (Derby) bt Paul Hand 7-5 7-6
Women's Final
S Parkhomenko (RUS) bt Valda Lake (Devon) 6-4 6-1

NOTTINGHAM TC   Dec 3-13
Men's Final
Paul Hand bt Darren Kirk (Lincs) 4-6 6-4 6-1
Women's Final
Anne Simpkin (Leics) bt S Nicholson 6-1 6-4

CORBY ITC   Dec 5-20
Men's Final
Jeffrey Hunter (Sy) bt Nicholas Gould (Avon) 7-6 7-5
Women's Final
G Coorengel bt Sarah Bentley 6-4 5-7 6-4

COVENTRY RACQUET CENTRE   Dec 11-23
Men's Final
Paul Hand bt Chris Wilkinson (Hants) 7-6 6-3
Women's Final
Jane Wood (Middx) bt G Coorengel 7-5 2-0 retd

SWANSEA CITY TC   Dec 19-Jan 10
Men's Final
Nick Fulwood bt Jeffrey Hunter 6-4 6-4
Women's Final
Valda Lake bt Anne Simpkin 6-1 7-6

DELTA SWINDON TC   Dec 19-Jan 17
Men's Final
Nick Fulwood bt Colin Beecher (Kent) 6-3 6-2
Women's Final
G Coorengel bt Lizzie Jelfs (Oxon) 6-1 6-3

PUMA WIGAN TC   Jan 9-24
Men's Final
Nick Fulwood bt Ross Matheson (West Scot) 6-4 7-6
Women's Final
G Coorengel bt Sarah Bentley 6-3 6-1

CENTRECOURT H & TC   Jan 16-31
Men's Final
Danny Sapsford (Sy) bt Andrew Richardson (Lincs)
6-3 7-5
Women's Final
S Parkhomenko bt N Egorova (RUS) 5-7 6-3 6-3

MATCHPOINT TC   Mar 29-Apr 3
Men's Final
Nick Fulwood bt Jamie Delgado (Warks) 6-0 6-2
Women's Final
N Egorova bt Samantha Smith (Essex) 3-6 6-1 6-1

PUMA SUNDERLAND TC   Apr 5-8
Men's Final
Laurence Matthews (Hants) bt Colin Beecher 5-7 6-3 6-1
Women's Final
Anne Simpkin bt N Egorova 6-2 6-4

WESTSIDE LTC   Apr 9-17
Men's Final
Colin Beecher bt Nick Fulwood 6-3 6-1
Women's Final
N Egorova bt S Parkhomenko 6-7 6-2 6-0

FELIXSTOWE LTC   Jul 7-10
Men's Final
Mark Schofield (Lancs) bt Colin Beecher 6-4 7-6
Women's Final
Lucie Ahl bt Mair Hughes (N Wales) 6-2 5-7 6-3

FRINTON-ON-SEA LTC   Jul 12-18
Men's Final
Danny Sapsford bt Paul C Robinson (Northants)
Women's Final
Karen Cross (Devon) bt Alison Smith (Staffs) 6-2 6-3

ILKLEY   Jul 19-24
Men's Final
Danny Sapsford bt Nick Fulwood 6-3 4-6 6-1
Women's Final
S Parkhomenko bt Alison Smith 6-7 6-1 6-2

SCOTTISH GRASS CHAMPS   Aug 1-7
(Craiglockhart)
Men's Final
Barry Cowan (Lancs) bt D Sweeney 6-3 6-4
Women's Final
Samantha Smith bt Anne Simpkin 6-1 6-3

SUSSEX OPEN TC   Aug 9-14
(West Worthing)
Men's Final
Danny Sapsford bt Michael Wyeth (Sy) 6-3 6-3
Women's Final
Samantha Smith bt D Huber 6-4 6-7 6-1

CONFEDERATION LIFE TT   Aug 16-21
(Avenue LTC, Havant)
Men's Final
Danny Sapsford bt Paul Hand 6-1 6-2
Women's Final
V Humphreys-Davies (Cambs) bt D Huber 7-5 4-6 6-2

ANZ GRINDLAYS JERSEY OPEN   Aug 14-28
(Caesarean C & LTC, Jersey)
Men's Final
Danny Sapsford bt Paul Hand 6-4 6-0
Women's Final
Lucie Ahl bt Samantha Smith 6-2 7-6

LAKENHAM, NORWICH   Aug 29-Sep 5
Men's Final
Danny Sapsford bt Paul Hand 6-2 6-1
Women's Final
E Nortje bt D Huber 6-3 retd

STOURBRIDGE, WORCS   Sept 7-11
Men's Final
Danny Sapsford bt Barry Cowan 4-6 6-2 6-4
Women's Final
Karen Cross bt Lucie Ahl 4-6 7-5 6-4

BONUS POOL POSITIONS
MEN: 1 Danny Sapsford 1240; 2 Nick Fulwood 1230 pts;
3 Paul Hand 850; 4 Barry Cowan 690; 5 Colin Beecher 520
WOMEN: 1 Anne Simpkin 880; 2 Lucie Ahl 670; 3 Karen
Cross 620; 4 Alison Smith 540; 5 Sarah Bentley 470

Tenpin Bowling

European Championships

Malmo, Sweden   July
Men
All Events
1	Raymond Jansson	SWE	5259
2	Patrik Johansson	SWE	5251
3	Tomas Leandersson	SWE	5189

Singles
1	Patrik Boman	SWE	1434
2	Paul Delany	GBR	1383
3	Achim Grabowski	GER	1379

Doubles
1	Helminen/Kuossari	FIN	2760
2	Leandersson/Jansson	SWE	2661
3	Boman/Johansson	SWE	2630

Trios
1	Sweden I	3785
2	Holland	3746
3	Sweden II	3742

Fives
1	Finland	6318
2	Sweden	6259
3	Belgium	6009
4	Great Britain	6003

(Oldfield 1247, Ellis 1114, Hood 1279, C Buck 1218, G Buck 1145)

Masters
(Round-robin between top 16 players)
1	Grabowski	GER
2	Leandersson	SWE
3	Boman	SWE

Women
All Events
1	Asa Larsson	SWE	5001
2	Pauline Smith	GBR	4997
3	Ann Nyström	SWE	4897

Singles
1	Anu Peltola	FIN	1284
2	Marianne Haukas	NOR	1275
3	Alessandra Cerbara	SAN	1259

Doubles
1	Darvill/Smith	GBR	2504
2	Nyström/Larsson	SWE	2492
3	Puhakka/Peltola	FIN	2431

Trios
1	Sweden I	3692
2	Sweden II	3572
3	France	3551

Fives
1	Great Britain	6016

(Howlett 1272, Leonard 1115, Darvill 1085, Coote 1244, Smith 1300)
2	Sweden	5948
3	South Africa	5816

Masters
1	Pauliina Aalto	FIN
2	Asa Larsson	SWE
3	Jette Lauridsen	DEN

BTBA UNITED KINGDOM CHAMPIONSHIPS

Fareham, Hants   *June*
Men
1	Chuck Carroll	3804	£2,000
2	Ron Oldfield	3671	£1,500
3	Keith Tucker	3768	£750

Women
1	Pauline Smith	3691	£2,000
2	Sue Megson	3606	£1,500
3	Kimberley Coote	3392	£750

TEAM BRITAIN RANKINGS
(After 12 events)

			Pl	Pts
Men	1	Richard Hood	10	896
	2	Ron Oldfield	10	843
	3	Geoff Buck	9	838
	4	Lol Ellis	10	836
	5	Simon Brown	10	810
	6	Cass Edwards	10	795

			Pl	Pts
Women	1	Judy Howlett	10	451
	2	Pauline Smith	10	427
	3	Gina Wardle	10	420
	4	Chris Parker	10	403
	5	Shelagh Leonard	9	394

Funeral services were held in December for Bob Bittner, the Detroit tenpin bowler who rolled his first perfect 300 game and died of a heart attack minutes later. In 31 years of bowling Bittner, 40, had come close to perfect games before, but this was the first time he actually completed one. "He really wanted that 300 game," said his wife Pam, "But then the one he shoots is the only one." After the game, Bittner felt ill, slumped in a chair and died. The American Bowling Congress sent along the ring they award for perfect games and Bittner went into the grave wearing it.

Trampolining

World Cup Series

SCANDINAVIAN OPEN
Haslen, Denmark Dec 11-12

Men's Individual		Pts
1 Anders Christiansen	DEN	37.1
3 Ben Colegate	GBR	36.0

Men's Synchronised		
1 Hennique/Schwertz	FRA	46.6

Women's Individual		
1 Andrea Holmes	GBR	36.3
2 Susan Challis	GBR	36.2
3 Hiltrud Röwe	GER	35.5

Women Synchronised		
1 Holmes/Lorraine Lyon	GBR	44.7

FIT WORLD CUP
Sens, France Apr 16-17

Men's Individual		Pts
1 Fabrice Schwertz	FRA	37.8

Men's Synchronised		
1 Kubicka/Kemmer	GER	45.5
7 Colegate/Hudson	GBR	21.4

Women's Individual		
1 Andrea Holmes	GBR	35.5

Women Synchronised		
1 Röwe/Ludwig	GER	44.5
7 Holmes/Lyon	GBR	22.9

FIT WORLD CUP
Sofia, Bulgaria June 19-21

Men's Individual		Pts
1 Fabrice Schwertz	FRA	38.3

Men's Synchronised		
1 Hennique/Schwertz	FRA	46.2

Women's Individual		
1 Hiltrud Roewe	GER	35.5

Women Synchronised		
1 Röwe/Ludwig	GER	45.90

JANNIE JANSEN MEMORIAL
Port Elizabeth, South Africa Sept 16-18

Men's Individual		Pts
1 Fabrice Hennique	FRA	37.0
2 Roustan Kachperko	BLS	36.7
3 Martin Kubicka	GER	35.8
5 Christopher Linney	SCO	34.5
6 Brian Murray	SCO	17.4

Men's Synchronised		
1 Linney/Murray	SCO	41.3

Women's Individual		
1 Susan Challis	GBR	35.7
2 Tina Ludwig	GER	35.5
3 Galina Lebedeva	BLS	32.9
6 Lorna Craig	SCO	30.6

Women Synchronised		
1 Nikitina/Lebedeva	BLS	42.1

European Youth Championship
Denze, Belgium Nov 5-7

MEN

Team
1 Germany		188.6
3 Great Britain		185.6

(Wright/Colegate/Colquhoun/McLoughlin)

Individual
1 Oleg Lupalo	LAT	102.3

Synchronised
1 Gvozdikov/Kobeza	UKR	127.4
4 Wright/Colquhoun	GBR	123.1

DMT Team
(Double Mini Trampoline)
1 Portugal		46.6

DMT Individual
1 Filip Deweer	BEL	25.4

Tumbling Team
1 Poland		192.13

Tumbling Individual
1 Adrian Sienkiewicz	POL	112.79

WOMEN

Team
1 Ukraine		183.4
4 Great Britain		175.9

(Burton/Tenn/Dixon-Jackson/Lyon)

Individual
1 Irina Karavaeva	RUS	101.1
4 Lorraine Lyon	GBR	96.1

Synchronised
1 Brushkova/Movthan	UKR	127.7
9 Lyon/Dixon-Jackson	GBR	121.3

DMT Team
1 Germany		42.8

DMT Individual
1 Nadine Intrup	GER	24.1
2 Ute Springub	GER	23.8
3 Natacha Bacque	BEL	23.5

Tumbling Team
1 Belgium		184.53

Tumbling Individual
1 Sigy Van Renterghem	BEL	106.86
2 Mireille Meermans	BEL	106.27
3 Patricia Nolf	BEL	104.62

National Championships
Bournemouth July 10-11

Men's Individual
1 Luke Porter	Littledown	37.80
2 Paul Smith	Airborne	37.7
3 Theo Kypri	Airborne	36.9

Women's Individual
1 Susan Challis	Portsmouth	37.9
2 Andrea Holmes	Dunstable	37.8
3 Nikki Stelling	Apex Harlow	33.2

Triathlon

ITU World Championships

Manchester   Aug 22

Women				Men			
1	Michellie Jones	AUS	2:07:41	1	Spencer Smith	GBR	1:51:20
2	Karen Smyers	USA	2:07:43	2	Simon Lessing	GBR	1:53:02
3	Jo-Anne Ritchie	CAN	2:08:06	3	Hamish Carter	NZL	1:53:29
4	Sonja Krolik	GER	2:09:21	4	Brad Bever	AUS	1:53:55
5	Susanne Nielsen	DEN	2:09:26	5	Ben Bright	AUS	1:54:20
6	Anette Petersen	DEN	2:09:34	6	Rainer Müller	GER	1:54:49
7	Sabine Westhoff	GER	2:10:22	7	Ralf Eggert	GER	1:54:54
8	Jenny Rose	NZL	2:10:28	8	Miles Steward	AUS	1:55:13
9	Ute Schaefer	GER	2:10:56	9	Philippe Fattori	FRA	1:55:14
10	Blanca Van Woesik	AUS	2:11:04	10	Remi Rampteau	FRA	1:55:25
	Junior Women				**Junior Men**		
1	Sarah Harrow	NZL	2:13;23	1	Olivier Hutschmid	SUI	1:56:28
2	Natalya Orchard	AUS	2:14:22	2	Ryan Bolton	USA	1:56:31
3	Marie Overbye	DEN	2:15:24	3	Alexandre Manzan	BRA	1:56:43

ITU World Cup

ROUND 1
Amakusa, Japan   *May 23*
Men
1 Miles Stewart   AUS   1:48:50
Women
1 Michellie Jones   AUS   2:00:08

ROUND 2
Orange County   *June 6*
Men
1 Michael Pigg   USA   1:46:09
Women
1 Michellie Jones   AUS   1:57:09

ROUND 3
Los Cabos, Mexico   *June 20*
Men
1 Greg Welch   AUS   1:55:20
Women
1 Carol Montgomery   CAN   2:11:51

ROUND 4
Embrun, France   *Aug 22*
Men
1 Stephen Foster   AUS   2:17:12
Women
1 Jenny Rose   NZ   2:38:21

European Championships

Luxembourg   Jul
Men
1   Simon Lessing   GBR   1:54:04
2   Thomas Hellriegel   GER   1:54:27
3   Rainer Müller   GER   1:55:00
7   Robin Brew   GBR   1:55:54
30 Jack Maitland   GBR   2:00:01
38 Tim Steward   GBR   2:01:19

Women
1   Sabine Westhoff   GER   2:08:59
2   S Mortier   GER   2:10:18
3   L Reuze   FRA   2:10:51
20 Ali Harrison   GBR   2:20:04
33 Shirley Yarde   GBR   2:24:42

BRITISH NATIONAL CHAMPIONSHIPS
Swindon   *May 23*

Men	**Women**
1 Spencer Smith	1 Helen Cawthorne
2 Tim Stewart	2 Rachel Hamilton
3 Jack Maitland	3 Ali Harrison

NATIONAL MIDDLE DISTANCE CHAMPIONSHIPS
Ironbridge, Shrops   *Jul 17*
Men
1 E Van Den Bosch   HOL   4:09:54
2 R Hobson   GBR   4:11:18
3 G Welsh   AUS   4:12:50
Women
1 B Van Woesik   AUS   4:44:46
2 W Ingraham   USA   4:49:43
3 A Hollington   GBR   5:02:06

NATIONAL SPRINT CHAMPIONSHIPS
Aylesbury   *June*

Men		**Women**	
1 Steve Burton	58:26	1 Helen Cawthorne	66:06
2 Colin Dixon	59:34	2 Ali Harrison	66:11
3 Richard Allen	59:42	3 Alison Hollington	67:29

HAWAII IRONMAN
Kailua-Kona, Hawaii   *Oct*
Men
1 M Allen   USA   8:09:09
Women
1 P Newby-Fraser   ZIM   8:55.31

Volleyball

Royal Bank of Scotland National Leagues

Men's Division 1

	P	W	L	SF	SA	Pts
1 Mizuno Lewisham	14	14	0	42	6	28
2 KLEA Leeds	14	12	2	37	12	24
3 Tooting Aquila	14	8	6	30	24	16
4 Reebok Liverpool	14	7	7	29	27	14
5 Wessex	14	6	8	22	30	12
6 Polonia Ealing	14	5	9	19	32	10
7 Newcastle (Staffs)	14	4	10	23	33	8
8 Speedwell Rucanor	14	0	14	4	42	-2 *

* Penalty points deducted

Men's Division 2

	P	W	L	SF	SA	Pts
1 Malory II Lewisham	22	18	4	57	28	36
2 Whitefield Sportset	22	18	4	55	26	36
3 Coventry	22	15	7	55	31	30
4 London Lynx Men	22	13	9	46	38	26
5 Radio Trent Rockets	22	11	11	45	45	22
6 Man Utd Salford	22	11	11	43	42	22
7 Gateshead Armitage	22	11	11	41	47	22
8 Dynamo London	22	10	12	41	44	20
9 Team Knights	22	8	14	36	53	16
10 Essex Estonians	22	6	16	38	52	12
11 Harriers	22	6	16	34	55	12
12 Wirral Thermax	22	5	17	31	61	10

Women's Division 1 (After mid-season split)

	P	W	L	SF	SA	Pts
1 Woolwich Brixton	6	6	0	18	6	12
2 Sale	6	4	2	15	14	8
3 Brit Music Hackney	6	2	4	13	14	4
4 Dynamo London	6	0	6	2	18	0
5 KLEA Leeds	6	5	1	16	8	10
6 Ashcombe Dorking I	6	5	1	16	9	10
7 Wessex	6	2	4	8	12	4
8 London Lynx I	6	0	6	7	18	0

Women's Division 2

	P	W	L	SF	SA	Pts
1 Purbook Portsmouth	20	18	2	55	20	36
2 Timeout Glos. City	20	16	4	51	27	32
3 Birmingham Ladies	20	13	7	50	31	26
4 Dynamo London II	20	12	8	45	35	24
5 Polonia Ladies	20	12	8	44	34	24
6 Team Knights	20	10	10	41	43	20
7 Liverpool City	20	9	11	40	39	18
8 Spark Jet	20	9	11	36	46	18
9 Man Utd Salford	20	6	14	31	48	12
10 Radio Trent Rockets	20	3	17	25	55	6
11 Speedwell	20	2	18	17	57	4

Royal Bank of Scotland Knock Out Cup

MEN

Final   *Mar 13*

Mizuno Malory Lewisham 3 KLEA Leeds 1
(15-7, 10-15, 15-9, 15-13)

WOMEN

Final   *Mar 13*

Woolwich Brixton 2 Sale 3
(14-16, 15-10, 9-15, 15-9, 12-15)

EVA SUPERCUP

Men

Mizuno Malory Lewisham bt KLEA Leeds

Women

Woolwich Brixton bt Sale

EVA CUP

Men

Egham bt Danes Chorleywood

Women

Chelmsford Partners bt Sheffield Wednesday

European Championships

MEN

Turku & Oulu, Finland   *Sept*

7/8th

Poland bt Czech Republic 15-10, 12-15, 16-14, 15-7

5/6th

Bulgaria bt Ukraine 8-15, 15-5, 15-3, 12-15, 15-11

Semi-finals

Italy bt Germany 15-1, 15-6, 15-11

Holland bt Russia 15-11, 15-8, 15-2

3rd/4th

Russia bt Germany 15-3, 9-15, 15-8, 15-5

Final

Italy bt Holland 15-6, 15-5, 13-15, 8-15, 15-9

WOMEN

Brno, Czech Rep   *Sept 27-Oct 2*

Semi-final Round

Croatia bt Belarus 15-12, 16-14, 15-4

Germany bt Holland 15-12, 13-15, 15-4, 15-17, 15-11

Czech Rep/Slovakia bt Ukraine 14-16, 15-5, 15-11, 6-15, 22-20

Russia bt Italy 15-9, 12-15, 16-14, 15-2

Final Round

Holland bt Belarus 15-10, 15-3, 15-12

Germany bt Croatia 51-9, 13-15, 13-15, 15-9, 15-9

Ukraine bt Italy 15-17, 15-8, 15-6, 17-15

Russia bt Czech/Slovak 17-15, 15-3, 15-6

Final Ranking

1 Russia, 2 RCS, 3 Ukraine, 4 Italy, 5 Germany, 6 Croatia, 7 Holland, 8 Belarus

Water Sports

Water Skiing
World Championships

Singapore   Sept 6-12

Teams Overall

		Slalom	Tricks	Jumping	Overall
1	Canada	2716.6	2484.2	2807.8	8008.6
2	USA	2803.7	2867.4	2335.5	8006.6
3	France	2725.2	2654.2	2449.4	7828.8
4	Italy	2732.8	2313.6	2345.5	7391.9
5	Russia	2619.9	2350.4	2282.2	7252.5
7	G Britain	2680.6	2024.2	2441.8	7146.6

MEN
Overall

1	Patrice Martin	FRA	2834.8
	(Sl: 1000, Tr: 992, J: 843)		
2	Andrea Alessi	ITA	2751.7
	(Sl: 879, Tr: 872, J: 1000)		
3	Oleg Devyatovski	BLR	2542.5
	(Sl: 901, Tr: 810, J: 832)		
4	Patrizio Buzzotta	ITA	2500.7
	(Sl: 948, Tr: 929, J: 624)		
5	Mike Morgan	USA	2387.7
	(Sl: 931, Tr: 769, J: 688)		
10	Paul Studd	GBR	2158.1
	(Sl: 785, Tr: 615, J: 758)		
12	Jodi Fisher	GBR	2098.6
	(Sl: 836, Tr: 512, J: 750)		

Slalom

1	Brett Thurley	AUS	1000.0
2	Patrice Martin	FRA	1000.0
3	Lucky Lowe	USA	982.8
4	Marco Bettosini	SUI	982.8
5	Andy Mapple	(GBR)	974.1
15	John Battleday	GBR	935.3

Tricks

1	Tory Baggiano	USA	1000.0
2	Patrice Martin	FRA	992.1
3	Andrea Alessi	ITA	872.4
4	Patrizio Buzzotta	ITA	928.8
5	Oleg Nadin	BLR	832.8
19	John Battleday	GBR	616.2
20	Paul Studd	GBR	615.2

Jump

1	Andrea Alessi	ITA	1000.0
2	John Levingston	AUS	960.7
3	Jim Clunie	CAN	946.6
4	Franz Oberleitner	AUT	918.5
5	Jaret Llewellyn	CAN	896.1
13	Paul Studd	GBR	758.4
14	Jodi Fisher	GBR	750.0

WOMEN
Overall

1	Nataly Rumiantseva	RUS	2678.0
	(Sl: 909, Tr: 963, J: 806)		
2	Kim De Macedo	CAN	2653.9
	(Sl: 891, Tr: 798, J: 965)		
3	Judy Messer	CAN	2601.8
	(Sl: 855, Tr: 871, J: 876)		
4	Olga Pavlova	BLR	2546.4
	(Sl: 864, Tr: 846, J: 837)		
5	Philippa Roberts	GBR	2501.8
	(Sl: 909, Tr: 756, J: 837)		
12	Corinna Williams	GBR	2235.4
	(Sl: 800, Tr: 653, J: 783)		
16	Nicola Huntridge	GBR	1921.6
	(Sl: 800, Tr: 300, J: 822)		

Slalom

1	Helena Kjellander	SWE	1000.0
2	Toni Neville	AUS	1000.0
3	Susi Graham	CAN	963.6
4	Kristi Overton	USA	963.6
5	Jennifer Leachman	USA	918.2
7	Philippa Roberts	GBR	909.1
8	Nicola Huntridge	GBR	800.0

Tricks

1	Britt Larsen	USA	1000.0
2	Nataly Rumiantseva	RUS	962.7
3	Frederique Savin	FRA	933.1
4	Judy Messer	CAN	871.3
5	Kristi Overton	USA	867.4
9	Philippa Roberts	GBR	755.5
10	Corinna Williams	GBR	652.5

Jump

1	Kim De Macedo	CAN	965.1
2	Britta Grebe	AUT	941.9
3	Tony Neville	AUS	938.0
4	Sherri Slone	USA	1000.0
5	Judy Messer	CAN	876.0
7	Philippa Roberts	GBR	837.2
9	Nicola Huntridge	GBR	821.7

Dragon Boat Racing
National Championships

Holme Pierre Point, Notts   Oct 11

1 Kingston Royals
2 Woodmill
3 Hartlepool

Weightlifting

European Championships

Sofia, Bulgaria   Apr 21-25

MEN

54Kg			Snatch	Cl+Jk	
1	Ivan Ivanov	BUL	115.0	157.5	272.5
2	Sevdalin Mintchev	BUL	122.5	150.0	272.5
3	Kikolay Petukhov	RUS	110.0	130.0	240.0
59Kg					
1	Nikolay Peshaloz	BUL	137.5	157.5	295.0
2	Hafiz Suleymanoglu	TUR	130.0	160.0	290.0
3	Albert Nasybullin	UKR	122.5	160.0	282.5
64Kg					
1	Attila Czanka	HUN	145.0	170.0	315.0
2	Valerios Leonidis	GRE	137.5	175.0	312.5
3	Radostin Dimitrov	BUL	142.5	167.5	310.0
70Kg					
1	Yotov Yoto	BUL	152.5	190.0	342.5
2	Waldemar Kosinski	POL	155.0	180.0	335.0
3	Razman Musaev	RUS	150.0	185.0	335.0
14	Tony Morgan	GBR	120.0	150.0	270.0
15	Stuart Cruickshank	GBR	117.5	150.0	267.5
76Kg					
1	K. Kapamaktsian	ARM	165.0	197.5	362.5
2	Oleg Kinchko	BLR	162.5	197.5	360.0
3	Andrzej Kozlowski	POL	160.0	200.0	360.0
83Kg					
1	O. Blyschyk	UKR	175.0	205.0	380.0
2	Krzysltof Siemion	POL	165.0	207.5	372.5
3	Pirros Dimas	GRE	170.0	200.0	370.0
91Kg					
1	Kakhi Kakhiashvili	GEO	180.0	222.5	402.5
2	S. Wolozaniecki	POL	170.0	220.0	390.0
3	Ivan Tchakarov	BUL	180.0	210.0	390.0
12	Peter May	GBR	150.0	180.0	330.0
99Kg					
1	Viacheslav Rubin	RUS	185.0	220.0	405.0
2	Slavomir Zavada	POL	185.0	220.0	405.0
3	Oleg Chiritso	BLR	177.5	217.5	395.0
108Kg					
1	Tymir Tainazov	UKR	195.0	232.5	427.5
2	Ronny Weller	GER	185.0	235.0	420.0
3	Aleksander Popov	RUS	182.5	235.0	417.5
+108Kg					
1	Manfred Merlingeg	GER	187.5	240.0	427.5
2	Andrei Chemerkin	RUS	185.0	240.0	425.0
3	Oleks Levandoyski	UKR	197.5	225.0	422.5

Women's European Championships

Loures, Portugal   Nov 4-8

44Kg			Snatch	Cl+Jk	
1	Csilla Földi	HUN	60.0	72.5	132.5
2	E Romao	POR	57.5	70.0	127.5
3	B Fernandez	ESP	55.0	72.5	127.5
48Kg					
1	Donka Mincheva	BUL	67.5	87.5	155.0
2	M D Sotoca	ESP	67.5	80.0	147.5
3	Sara Duarte	POR	60.0	72.5	132.5
52Kg					
1	Neli Simova	BUL	70.0	95.0	165.0
2	Siijka Stoeva	BUL	72.5	92.5	165.0
3	A Strombou	GRE	67.5	87.5	155.0
56Kg					
1	Janeta Georgieva	BUL	82.5	95.0	177.5
2	P Ljubov	CIS	70.0	82.5	150.0
3	S Adam	CIS	67.5	82.5	150.0
60Kg					
1	Gergana Kirilova	BUL	87.5	10.5	192.5
2	Maria Christoforidi	GRE	82.5	107.5	190.0
3	Erzsébet Márkus	HUN	77.5	95.0	172.5
5	A Campbell	GBR	72.5	90.0	162.5
67.5Kg					
1	M Trendailova	BUL	90.0	110.0	200.0
2	Jeanette Rose	GBR	80.0	102.5	182.5
3	Maria D Martinez	ESP	82.5	95.0	177.5
75Kg					
1	A Panagiota	GRE	85.0	122.5	207.5
2	Mária Takács	HUN	90.0	112.5	202.5
3	S Asenova	BUL	90.0	105.0	195.0
82.5Kg					
1	K Leppaloutto	FIN	90.0	112.5	202.5
2	M Riesterer	GER	90.0	110.0	200.0
3	Lyne Mary	FRA	90.0	110.0	200.0
+82.5Kg					
1	Gripurko Ljubov	CIS	97.5	120.0	217.5
2	Erika Takács	HUN	95.0	120.0	215.0
3	Sonja Vasickova	TCI I	87.5	102.5	190.0
4	Sandra Vokroi	GBR	85.0	97.5	182.5

EEC Championships

Athens   Mar

TEAM CLASSIFICATION

Men

1	Germany	249
2	Greece	236
3	France	205
6	Great Britain	136

Women

1	Greece	189
2	France	179
3	Italy	151
4	Great Britain	144

Myrtle Augee, +83kg, was Britain's only individual winner

Winter Sports

Ice Skating
World Championships

Prague   Mar 9-14

Ice Dancing
1 Maya Usova/Alexandr Zhulin   RUS
2 Oksana Gritschuk/Evgeny Platov   RUS
3 Anjelika Krylova/Vladimir Fedorov   RUS
17 Marika Humphreys/Justin Lanning   GBR

Womens Figure Skating
1 Oksana Baiul   UKR
2 Surya Bonaly   FRA
3 Lu Chen   CHN
12 Charlene von Saher   GBR

Men's Figure Skating
1 Kurt Browning   CAN
2 Elvis Stojko   CAN
3 Alexei Urmanov   RUS
18 Steven Cousins   GBR

Pairs' Figure Skating
1 Isabelle Brasseur/Lloyd Eisler   CAN
2 Mandy Wötzel/Ingo Steuer   GER
3 Evgenia Shishkova/Vadim Naumov   RUS
16 Jackie Soames/John Jenkins   GBR

European Championships

Helsinki   Jan 12-17

Ice Dancing
1 Maya Usova/Alexandr Zhulin   RUS
12 Marika Humphreys/Justin Lanning   GBR

Women's Figure Skating
1 Surya Bonaly   FRA
19 Charlene von Saher   GBR

Men's Figure Skating
1 Dmitriy Dmitrenko   UKR
9 Steven Cousins   GBR

Pairs Figure Skating
1 Marina Eltsova/Andrey Bushkov   RUS
12 Jackie Soames/John Jenkins   GBR

BRITISH CHAMPIONSHIPS
Humberside   Nov 13, 1992
Ice Dancing
1 Marika Humphreys/Justin Lanning
Women's Figure Skating
1 Charlene von Saher
Men's Figure Skating
1 Steven Cousins
Pairs Figure Skating
1 Vicky Pearce/Clive Shorten

Bobsleigh
World Championships

Innsbruck   Feb 1-14
Two-man
1 Germany 2 (Langan/Joechel)
2 Switzerland 1 (Weder/Acklin)
3 Germany 1 (Hoppe/Hannemann)
13 Great Britain 1 (Olsson/Ward)
Four-man
1 Switzerland 2 (Weder/Acklin/Meier/Semeraro)
2 Austria 1 (Schösser/Winkler/Redl/Haidacher)
3 USA 1 (Shimer/Leturgez/Kirby/Jones)
9 Great Britain 1 (Tout/Symonds/Rumbolt/Paul)

Luge
World Championships

Calgary
Women
1 Gerda Weissensteiner   ITA
2 Gabriele Kohlisch   GER
3 Doris Neuner   AUT
Men
1 Wendel Suckow   USA
2 Georg Hackel   GER
3 Wilfried Huber   ITA
Double Seater
1 Krausse/Berendt   GER
2 Raffl/N Huber   ITA
3 Brugger/W Huber   ITA
Teams
1 Germany, 2 Austria, 3 Italy

Speed Skating
World Championships

WOMEN
Berlin   Feb 6-7
500m: Ye Qiaobo (CHN) 40.41 **1500m:** Gunda Niemann
(GER) 2:06.60 **3000m:** G Niemann (GER) 4:23.15
5000m: G Niemann (GER) 7:25.83 **Overall:** G Niemann

MEN
Hamar, Norway   Feb 13-14
500m: Chen Song (CHN) 37.68 **1500m:** Johan Olav Koss
(NOR) 1:52.53 **5000m:** Falko Zandstra (HOL) 6:43.86
10,000m: Bart Veldkamp (HOL) 13:46.34
Overall: Falko Zandstra

Yachting

World Championships

FINN GOLD CUP
Ballyhome Yacht Club   *Jul 9-19*

1	Philippe Presti	FRA	28.00
2	Fredrik Loof	SWE	28.75
3	Richard Clarke	CAN	34.00
26	Richard Lott	GBR	144.00

LASER RADIAL
Tukapuna, New Zealand   *Mar*
1	Ben Ainslie	GBR

505
Travemunde, Germany
1	Ian Barker/Tim Hancock	GBR
2	Paul Brotherton	GBR

SOLING
Athens   *Sept 11-12*
1	T Boutouris	GRE
2	A Batzil	GER
3	L Doreste	ESP
4	H Johanessen	NOR
5	M Dorete	ESP

TORNADO
Long Beach, Cal   *Sept 25-26*
1	O Schwall/R Schwall		GER	13pts
2	M Booth/J Forbes	AUS	26	
3	C Clevenot/Y Quernec	FRA	30	
4	D Williams/I Rhodes	GBR	72	

Admirals Cup
Aug
Final Placings
1	Germany	279.13
2	Australia	278.88
3	France	247.50
4	Italy	242.88
5	Japan	242.00
6	Great Britain	238.38

European Championships

LASER
Cagliari YC   *Jul 31*
1	John Harrysson	SWE	72.0
2	Chris Gowers	GBR	86.0
3	Pascal Lacoste	FRA	88.0

FINN
Nautico Espartit YC   *Jun 12*
1	Stig Westergaard	DEN	19.70
2	José Van Der Ploes	ESP	34.10
3	Hans Spitzauer	AUT	56.70

LASER EUROPA CUP
Egbert Swensson ROYC   *Jul 3-6*
1	Robert Scheidt	BRA	100.00
2	Peter Luzius	SUI	96.91
3	Mark Littlejohn	GBR	95.70

European Youth Championships
Austria   July
Laser Radial
1	Ben Ainslie	GBR

RYA National Match Racing Championship
Torquay, Devon   Oct 1-4
1	Andy Beadsworth
2	Adrian Stead
3	Ian Southworth

Queen Mary SC, Ashford, Mx   Jul 30
1	Lee Sydenham
2	Mike Preston
3	Andrew Green

BRITISH STEEL CHALLENGE
(Finished May 24)

1	Nuclear Electric	151:11.49
2	Group 4	151:13.59
3	Hofbrau Lager	152:15.45
4	Cooper's and Lybrand	154:17.59
5	Pride of Teeside	155:16.06
6	Interspray	156:14.09
7	Heath Insured	157:10.29
8	Rhone Poulenc	159:04.07
9	Commercial Union	159:17.26
10	British Steel II	163:00.25

Swallow National Championships

Iltchenor   Sept 11-12
1 Echo   3.5pts
   (Body/Miller/Cheeseman)
2 Marengo   5.75
   (Ewart-Smith/Peacock/Woolfenden)
3 Bluff   12
   (Froy/Graves/Miller)

RYA UK National Youth Championships

Lake Bala, Wales   Apr 9
Laser
1 A Coates
2 A Simpson
3 I Percy
Laser Radial
1 P Mountford
2 P Wilkin
3 E Wright
405
1 A Richardson
2 A Fremantle
3 A Tobbutt
420
1 R Wilson/D Mason
2 R Lovering/S Hughes
3 D Lens/M Pullen

RYA Eurolymp UK

Hayling Island SC, Hants   Jun 10-14
Europe
1 S Robertson   GBR
Laser
1 S Cole   GBR
470
1 J Merricks/A Rice   GBR
Mistral (Men)
1 A McIntosh   NZL

RYA Seamanship Foundation

Points Series
1 Kevin Curtis   Triple Indemnity
2 Steve Gregg
3 Howard Lee   Howards Way
Thames Water Shield
1 Kevin Curtis
2 David Prentis   Jupiter II
3 Steve Clark
Peacock Cup
1 William Cowan   Go For It
2 Brian Povey   Inspire
3 Alex Hodges   Linlithgow
MacAlpine-Downie Trophy
1 Tim Marshall/Delia Dudgeon   Hydra I
2 Brian Johnson/Paul Bailey   Greenhill Bradway
3 Alf Boyling/Alan Shaw   Lion Heart

Board Sailing
World Championships
Mistral Class

Kashiwazacki, Japan   Sept
Men
1	B Kendall	NZL	5pts
2	A McIntosh	NZL	10
3	M Gebhardt	GER	21
4	N Leneyrie	FRE	26
5	N Kaklamanakis	GRE	33
6	T Renault	FRA	37
18	H Plumb	GBR	76

Women
1	Lee Lai-Shan	HKG	11
2	L Butler	USA	18
3	M Herbert	FRA	18
4	Zhang Xiaodong	CHN	25
5	E Draoulec	FRA	27
6	M Stalman	HOL	27
10	C Lapworth	GBR	53

PBA/O'Neill British World Cup

Brighton   Sept
Men's slalom
1	M Cousins	RSA	6.7pts
2	N Baker	GBR	11
3	C Tasti	FRA	11.7

Women's Slalom
1	J Müller	GER	2.1
2	C Streiter	GBR	6
3	L Ernst	HOL	9

HIGH SEAS

Wind-surfer James Andrews has had enough of dealing with crappy seas. The 26 year old contracted Hepatitis A and, reckoning it was the dodgy water off the south coast, is suing Southern Water. In Brighton, the clean-up-the-sea campaign has really taken off with 'Surfers Against Sewage' T-shirts all the rage.

Multi-Sports Events

World Student Games

Buffalo, USA   July 7-18

ATHLETICS

Men

100m	1	Daniel Effiong	NGR	10.07
	2	Sam Jefferson	USA	10.13
	3	Glenroy Gilbert	CAN	10.14
200m	1	Bryan Bridgewater	USA	20.14
	2	Chris Nelloms	USA	20.17
	3	Ivan Garcia Sanchez	CUB	20.55
400m	1	Ibrahim Hassan	GHA	45.87
	2	Evan Clarke	JAM	46.27
	3	Danny McFarlane	JAM	46.60
800m	1	Marko Koers	HOL	1:48.57
	2	Oleg Stepanov	RUS	1:49.50
	3	Nico Motchebon	GER	1:49.52
1500m	1	A-K Chekhemani	FRA	3:46.32
	2	Bill Burke	USA	3:46.33
	3	Gary Lough	GBR	3:47.77
5000m	1	Khalid Khannouchi	MAR	14:05.33
	2	Sergey Fedotov	RUS	14:06.15
	3	Toshinari Takaoka	JPN	14:06.20
10,000m	1	Antonio Serrano	ESP	28:16.16
	2	Yasuyuki Watanabe	JPN	28:17.26
	3	Vincenzo Modica	ITA	28:17.73
Marathon	1	Kennedy Manyisa	KEN	2:12:19
	2	Wan Ki Kim	KOR	2:15:35
	3	Hyoung Jae-Young	KOR	2:15:53
3000msc	1	Michael Buchleitner	AUT	8:30.82
	2	Vladimir Pronine	RUS	8:32.03
	3	Bizunch Yac Tura	ETH	8:32.07
110mh	1	Ditmar Koszewski	GER	13.48
	2	Glenn Terry	USA	13.58
	3	Stylianos Bisbas	GRE	13.72
400mh	1	Derrick Adkins	USA	49.35
	2	Yoshihiko Saito	JPN	49.61
	3	Dusan Kovacs	HUN	50.12
20km Wk	1	Robert Korzeniowski	POL	1:22:01
	2	Daniel Garcia	MEX	1:22:58
	3	Bernardo Segura	MEX	1:24:11
4x100m	1	USA		38.65
	2	Japan		38.97
	3	Cuba		39.20
4x400m	1	USA		3:02.34
	2	Japan		3:03.21
	3	Hungary		3:04.27
PV	1	Istvan Bagyula	HUN	5.70m
	2	Alberto Giacchetto	ITA	5.60m
	3	Jean Galfione	FRA	5.60m
HJ	1	Tony Barton	USA	2.30m
	2	Stevan Zoric	PIP	2.30m
	3	Arturo Ortiz	ESP	2.30m
LJ	1	K Streete-Thompson	CAY	8.22m
	2	Obinna Eregbu	NGR	8.18m
	3	Vitaly Kyryienko	UKR	8.04m
TJ	1	Tosi Fasinro	GBR	16.91m
	2	Oleg Sokirkin	KZK	16.89m
	3	Julian Golley	GBR	16.88m

Shot	1	Sashko Klymenko	UKR	19.72m
	2	Paolo Dal Saglio	ITA	19.64
	3	Chris Volgenau	USA	19.54m
Discus	1	Esteve Elizalde	CUB	62.98m
	2	Adewale Olukoju	NGR	62.96m
	3	Nick Sweeney	IRL	62.52m
HT	1	Vadim Kolesnik	UKR	77.00m
	2	Balazs Kiss	HUN	76.88m
	3	Christophe Epalle	FRA	76.80m
Javelin	1	Louis Fouche	RSA	79.64m
	2	Ed Kaminski	USA	77.52m
	3	Mike Parviainen	FIN	77.14m
Decathl'n	1	Sebastian Levicq	FRA	7874
	2	Darrin Steele	USA	7653
	3	U Ranzi	ITA	7545

Women

100m	1	Dahlia Duhaney	JAM	11.56
	2	Liliana Allen Doll	CUB	11.57
	3	Beatrice Utondu	NGR	11.59
200m	1	Flirtisha Harris	USA	22.56
	2	Dahlia Duhaney	JAM	22.79
	3	Wang Huei-Chen	TPE	22.80
400m	1	Michelle Collins	USA	52.01
	2	Youlanda Warren	USA	52.18
	3	Nancy McLeon Ferrara	CUB	52.84
800m	1	Amy Wickus	USA	2:03.72
	2	Inez Turner	JAM	2:04.14
	3	Daniela Antipov	ROM	2:04.75
1500m	1	Lynne Robinson	GBR	4:12.04
	2	Juli Speights	USA	4:12.43
	3	Sarah Howell	CAN	4:13.30
3000m	1	Clare Eichner	USA	9:04.32
	2	Iulia Ionescu	ROM	9:05.10
	3	Rosalind Taylor	USA	9:06.25
10,000m	1	Iulia Negura	ROM	32:22.99
	2	Suzana Ciric	PIP	32:26.18
	3	Camelia Tecuta	ROM	32:29.18
Marathon	1	Noriko Kawaguchi	JPN	2:37:47
	2	Franca Fiacconi	ITA	2:38:44
	3	Nao Otani	JPN	2:40:17
100mh	1	Ime Akpan	NGR	13.11
	2	Dawn Bowles	USA	13.16
	3	Marsha Guialdo	USA	13.24
400mh	1	Keike Meissner	GER	56.10
	2	Debbie Parris	JAM	56.11
	3	Trevaia Williams	USA	56.57
10km Wk	1	Yuwen Long	CHN	46:16.70
	2	Olga Leonenko	UKR	46:17.10
	3	Larissa Ramazanova	RUS	46:18.50
4x100m	1	USA		43.37
	2	Nigeria		44.25
	3	Canada		45.20
4x400m	1	USA		3:26.18
	2	Cuba		3:28.95
	3	Nigeria		3:34.97
HJ	1	Tanya Hughes	USA	1.95m
	2	Hele Ziliuskiene	LTU	1.95m
	3	Larysa Hryhorenko	UKR	1.95m
LJ	1	Mirela Dulgheru	ROM	6.69w
	2	V Monar-Enwcani	CAN	6.57w
	3	Daphne Saunders	BAH	6.53w

TJ	1 Nivrka Montalvo	CUB	14.16w
	2 Sarka Kasparkova	TCH	14.00w
	3 Monica Toth	ROM	13.96w
Shot	1 Zhou Tian Nue	CHN	19.17m
	2 Belsis Laza Muñoz	CUB	18.48m
	3 Katrin Koch	GER	16.70m
Discus	1 Renata Katewicz	POL	62.40m
	2 Jackie McKiernan	GBR	60.72m
	3 Anja Gundler	GER	60.56m
Javelin	1 Lee Young Sun	KOR	58.62m
	2 Tanja Damaske	GER	57.68m
	3 Valerie Tulloch	CAN	56.52m
Hept'lon	1 Urszula Woldarczyk	POL	6127
	2 Birgit Gautzsch	GER	5934
	3 Kelly Blair	USA	5926

BASEBALL
Men 1 Cuba
2 Korea
3 Canada

BASKETBALL
Men 1 USA   **Women** 1 China
2 Canada   2 Cuba
3 China   3 USA

FENCING
Men

Epee	1 Patric Daenert	GER
	2 Krisztla Kulcsar	HUN
	3 Arnd Schmitt	GER
	3 Jean-Marc Muratorio	FRA
Epee Team	1 Cuba	
	2 Hungary	
	3 Italy	
Foil	1 Serge Golubytsky	UKR
	2 Alexander Koch	GER
	3 Lionel Plumenall	FRA
	3 Alessandro Puccini	ITA
Foil Team	1 Cuba	
	2 Italy	
	3 China	
Sabre	1 Giovanni Sirovich	ITA
	2 Gael Touya	FRA
	3 Rafal Sznajder	POL
Sabre Team	1 Italy	
	2 France	
	3 Hungary	

Women

Epee	1 Mariann Horvath	HUN
	2 Sangita Tripathi	FRA
	3 Elisabeth Knechti	AUT
	3 Corinne Panzeri	ITA
Epee Team	1 Hungary	
	2 France	
	3 Germany	
Foil	1 Ildiko Mincza	HUN
	2 Anna Giacometti	ITA
	3 Diana Bianchetti	ITA
	3 Giovanni Trillini	ITA
Foil Team	1 Italy	
	2 Germany	
	3 France	

FOOTBALL
Men 1 Czech Rep   **Women** 1 China
2 Korea   2 USA
3 Germany   3 Russia

GYMNASTICS
Men

Team	1 Italy		165.800
	2 China		165.287
	3 USA		165.050
All Round	1 Vitaly Scherbo	BLS	56.425
	2 Jury Cheehi	ITA	56.025
	3 Igor Korobchinsky	UKR	55.712
Floor	1 Igor Korobchinsky	UKR	9.525
	2 Daisuke Nishikawa	JPN	9.375
	3 Youri Gotov	RUS	9.350
Horiz Bar	1 Chen Jian	CHN	9.600
	2 Scott Keswick	USA	9.500
	3 Vitaly Scherbo	BLS	9.475
Para Bars	1 Wang Xun	CHN	9.512
	2 Vitaly Scherbo	BLS	9.500
	3 Jair Lyneh	USA	9.450
Pm Horse	1 Eric Pou-Jade	FRA	9.612
	2 Fan Bin	CHN	9.500
	3 Chang Feng-Chih	TPE	9.487
Rings	1 Jury Cheehi	ITA	9.707
	2 Scott Keswick	USA	9.537
	3 Ruggero Rossato	ITA	9.450
Vault	1 Vitaly Scherbo	BLS	9.662
	2 Yeo Hong-Chui	KOR	9.649
	3 Chang Feng-Chih	TPE	9.568

Women

Team	1 Ukraine		114.500
	2 USA		114.025
	3 Japan		108.725
All Round	1 Tatiana Lisenko	UKR	38.462
	2 Lyudmilla Stovbchataya	UKR	9.100
	3 Han Na-Jung	KOR	9.075
Beam	1 Tatiana Lisenko	UKR	9.562
	2 Lyudmilla Stovbchataya	UKR	9.100
	3 Han Na-Jung	KOR	9.075
Floor	1 Benedicte Evrard	BEL	9.725
	2 Tammy Marshall	USA	9.612
	3 Lyudmilla Stovbchataya	UKR	9.362
Asym Bars	1 Natalia Kalinina	UKR	9.637
	2 Kyoko Seo	JPN	9.275
	3 Lyudmilla Stovbchataya	UKR	9.212
Vault	1 Natalia Kalinina	UKR	9.543
	2 Luisa Ribciro	BRA	9.518
	3 Hope Sheeley	USA	9.493

ROWING
Men

Ltwt S/Sculls	1 Vesa Keso	FIN
	2 Ulf Meyer	GER
	3 Jason Dorland	USA
Ltwt D/Sculls	1 Schottier/Weckbach	GER
	2 Mornati/Rotta	ITA
	3 Hilton/Brambell	CAN
Ltwt 4 Oars	1 France	
	2 Great Britain	
	3 Canada	

Hwt S/Sculls	1	Nicolae Tega	ROM	
	2	Derek Porter	CAN	
	3	Tom Symoens	BEL	
Hwt Qd/Sculls	1	Ukraine		
	2	Canada		
	3	Poland		
Hwt D/Oars	1	Graham/Barber	CAN	
	2	Ryan/Ryan	USA	
	3	Rotta/Mornati	ITA	
Hwt 4 Oars	1	Romania		
	2	France		
	3	USA		
Hwt Eights	1	USA		
	2	Great Britain		
	3	Canada		

Women

Ltwt S/Sculls	1	Wendy Wiebe	CAN	
	2	Phoebe White	GBR	
	3	Martina Orzan	ITA	
Ltwt D/Sculls	1	Duncan/Starr	CAN	
	2	Huang/Peng	CHN	
	3	Baur/Zillich	GER	
Ltwt D/Oars	1	Ou/Zhong	CHN	
	2	Featherstone/Brindamour	CAN	
	3	McCallum/Radcliffe-Smith	AUS	
Hwt S/Sculls	1	Veronica Cochela	ROM	
	2	Marnie McBean	CAN	
	3	Iza Wisiniewska	POL	
Hwt Qd/Sculls	1	Canada		
	2	Romania		
	3	France		
Hwt Fours	1	Romania		
	2	Canada		
	3	Australia		
Hwt Eights	1	Canada		
	2	USA		

SWIMMING

Men

50m Free	1	David Fox	USA	22.30
	2	Brian Kurza	USA	22.41
	3	Dean Kondziolka	CAN	22.93
100m Free	1	David Fox	USA	50.18
	2	Seth Pepper	USA	50.38
	3	Pavlo Khnykin	UKR	50.88
200m Free	1	Yann DeFabrique	FRA	1:51.24
	2	Rob McFarlane	CAN	1:51.69
	3	Turlough O'Hare	CAN	1:51.77
400m Free	1	Turlough O'Hare	CAN	3:55.01
	2	Yann DeFabrique	FRA	3:55.82
	3	Walter Kalaus	HUN	3:57.49
800m Free	1	Turlough O'Hare	CAN	8:04.80
	2	Lars Jorgenson	USA	8:07.84
	3	Masayuki Fujimoto	JPN	8:08.74
1500m Free	1	Rob Darzynkiewicz	USA	15:33.96
	2	Marco Formentini	ITA	15:38.43
	3	MasaYuki Fujimoto	JPN	15:40.19
100m Back	1	R Falcon-Cabrera	CUB	55.60
	2	Tripp Schwenk	USA	55.78
	3	Emanuele Merisi	ITA	56.31
200m Back	1	R Falcon-Cabrera	CUB	1:59.90
	2	Emanuele Merisi	ITA	2:00.45
	3	Tripp Schwenk	GER	2:01.05
100m Breast	1	Jud Crawford	USA	1:02.79
	2	Akira Hayashi	JPN	1:02.83
	3	Gonzalez-Montesino	CUB	1:03.51
200m Breast	1	Gonzalez Montesino	CUB	2:16.24
	2	Jean-Louis Rey	FRA	2:17.05
	3	Akira Hayasi	JPN	2:17.14
100m Fly	1	Martin Roberts	AUS	54.14
	2	Mitsuharu Takane	JPN	54.65
	3	Oliver Lampe	GER	54.66
200m Fly	1	Martin Roberts	AUS	2:00.91
	2	Oliver Lampe	GER	2:01.12
	3	Mitsuharu Takane	JPN	2:01.32
200m Medley	1	Fraser Walker	GBR	2:04.48
	2	Viatchesla Valdayev	UKR	2:04.64
	3	Jonathan Jennings	USA	2:04.71
400m Medley	1	Ian Mull	USA	4:24.08
	2	Viatchesla Valdayev	UKR	4:25.85
	3	Tatsuya Kinugasa	JPN	4:27.81
4x100m Free	1	USA		3:21.28
	2	Germany		3:23.25
	3	Poland		3:25.94
4x100m Med	1	USA		3:43.20
	2	Germany		3:45.37
	3	Japan		3:45.76
4x200m Free	1	USA		7:25.90
	2	France		7:27.70
	3	Germany		7:29.06

Women

50m Free	1	Le Jingyi	CHN	25.17
	2	Ye Beibei	CHN	25.77
	3	Richelle DePold	USA	25.86
100m Free	1	Le Jingyi	CHN	55.16GR
	2	Patricia Levesque	CAN	57.11
	3	Ayako Nakano	JPN	57.49
	3	Sarah Perroni	USA	57.49
200m Free	1	Heike Luenenschloss	GER	2:03.18
	2	Whitney Hedgepeth	USA	2:03.53
	3	Claire Huddart	GBR	2:04.05
400m Free	1	Sandra Cam	BEL	4:18.21
	2	Heike Luenenschloss	GER	4:18.39
	3	Isabelle Arnould	BEL	4:19.18
800m Free	1	Christine Stephenson	USA	8:48.82
	2	Sandra Cam	BEL	8:51.55
	3	Marie Pierre Wirth	FRA	8:52.17
1500m Free	1	Christine Stephenson	USA	16:41.75
	2	Isabelle Arnould	BEL	16:52.26
	3	Marie Wirth	FRA	16:56.29
100m Back	1	Barbara Bedford	USA	1:01.60
	2	Yoko Koikawa	JPN	1:02.93
	3	Alecia Humphrey	USA	1:03.44
200m Back	1	Whitney Hedgepeth	USA	2:11.31
	2	Alecia Humphrey	USA	2:13.78
	3	Yoko Koikawa	JPN	2:16.16
100m Breast	1	Guylaine Cloutier	CAN	1:10.90
	2	Svetlana Bondarenko	UKR	1:11.01
	3	Elene Roudkovskaia	BLS	1:11.47
100m Fly	1	Yoko Kando	JPN	1:01.59
	2	Kristie Krueger	USA	1:01.78
	3	Debbie Gaudin	CAN	1:02.07
200m Fly	1	Yoko Kando	JPN	2:14.45
	2	Paige Wilson	USA	2:14.60
	3	Kirsten Silvester	HOL	2:14.95
200m Medley	1	Marianne Limpert	CAN	2:15.46
	2	Nancy Sweetnam	CAN	2:15.90
	3	Hideko Hiranaka	JPN	4:53.80
400m Medley	1	Nancy Sweetnam	CAN	4:46.91

	2 Hana Cerna	TCH	4:50.14
	3 Hideko Hiranaka	JPN	4:53.80
4x100m Free	1 USA		3:47.83
	2 Canada		3:48.05
	3 Germany		3:53.99
4x200m Free	1 Canada		8:18.00
	2 Great Britain		8:26.67
	3 France		8:31.02
4x100m Med	1 USA		4:12.55
	2 Japan		4:14.96
	3 Canada		4:16.86

Men's Diving

1m Spring	1 Chen Sheng	CHN	380.52
	2 F Platas Alvarez	MEX	377.52
	3 Wang Yijic	CHN	376.86
3m Spring	1 Xiong Ni	CHN	433.77
	2 F Platas Alvarez	MEX	427.20
	3 Roman Volodkov	UKR	400.62
Platform	1 Xiong Ni	CHN	659.52
	2 Ying Gui	CHN	621.30
	3 Roman Volodkov	UKR	559.59
Team	1 China		2364.66
	2 Mexico		2134.98
	3 USA		2075.43

Women's Diving

1m Spring	1 Yu Xiaoling	CHN	275.28
	2 Annie Pelletier	CAN	258.57
	3 Brita Baldus	GER	257.22
3m Spring	1 Brita Baldus	GER	295.56
	2 Paige Gordon	CAN	292.68
	3 Silke Kruger	GER	269.46
Platform	1 Anne Montminy	CAN	407.79
	2 Yang Yan	CHN	403.32
	3 Ren Wen	CHN	393.42
Team	1 China		1684.20
	2 Canada		1619.70
	3 USA		1584.57

Men's Water Polo

	1 USA
	2 Hungary
	3 Italy

TENNIS

Men's Singles	1 Shi Han Cheol	KOR
	2 Jeffrey Hunter	GBR
	3 Zhang Jiu Hua	CHN
	3 Yoon Bok Kyu	KOR
Women's Singles	1 Yi Jingqian	CHN
	2 Kaoru Shibatu	JPN
	3 Olivia Gravereaux	FRA
	3 Samantha Smith	GBR
Men's Doubles	1 Kim/Kong	KOR
	2 Johl/Dvoracek	TCH
	3 Janacek/Laschinger	CAN
	3 Sell/Givone	USA
Women's Doubles	1 Yi/Chen	CHN
	2 Hiraka/Akahori	JPN
	3 Gravereaux/Boutelier	FRA
	3 Schurhoff/Gerke	GER
Mixed Doubles	1 Hirake/Harada	JPN
	2 Kuregian/Sargsian	ARM
	3 Markova/Smotlak	SVK

	3 Csurgo/Lanyi	HUN

VOLLEYBALL

Men	1 Japan	Women	1 Rumania
	2 Poland		2 USA
	3 Korea		3 Switzerland

Medal Table

Country	Gold	Silver	Bronze	Total
USA	30	25	20	75
China	17	6	5	28
Canada	12	14	14	40
Ukraine	11	6	9	26
Cuba	8	4	4	16
Rumania	7	2	3	12
Germany	6	9	13	28
Italy	5	9	12	26
France	5	8	11	24
Japan	4	13	13	30
Hungary	4	4	5	13
Korea	4	4	3	11
Great Britain	3	6	4	13
Poland	3	0	4	7
Nigeria	2	3	2	7
Belgium	2	2	3	7
Belarus	2	1	2	5
Australia	2	0	2	5
Jamaica	1	4	1	6
Czech Republic	1	3	0	4
Austria	1	0	1	2
Finland	1	0	1	2
Holland	1	0	1	2
Spain	1	0	1	2
Ghana	1	0	0	1
Kenya	1	0	0	1
Morocco	1	0	0	1
South Africa	1	0	0	1
Mexico	0	4	1	5
Russia	0	3	3	6
Indep Participants	0	2	0	2
Armenia	0	1	0	1
Brazil	0	1	0	1
Kazakhstan	0	1	0	1
Lithuania	0	1	0	1
Chinese Taipei	0	0	3	3
Bahamas	0	0	1	1
Ethiopia	0	0	1	1
Greece	0	0	1	1
Slovakia	0	0	1	1

Winter Universiade
Zakopane, Poland   Feb 6-15

ALPINE SKIING
Men
Super G
1 Dider Plaschy	SUI	1:42.21	0.00pts

Giant Slalom
1 Skip Merrick	USA	1:44.15	0.00

Slalom
1 Urs Karrer	SUI	1:38.47	0.00

Combined Men
1 Urs Karrer	SUI	18:74

Women
Super G
1 Catherine Chedal	FRA	1:03.33	0.00

Giant Slalom
1 Katrin Stotz	GER	1:44.23	0.00

Slalom
1 Shannon D Nobis	USA	1:41.66	0.00

Combined
1 Shannon D Nobis	USA	14:31

CROSS COUNTRY SKIING
Men
15 km Classic
1 Alexandr Zaikov	RUS	43:05.2

15 km Combined
1 Francesco Semenzato	ITA	1:21:52.9

30 km Freestyle
1 Kazutoshi Nagahama	JPN	1:20:56.0

4x10 km Relay
1 Russia		1:51:19.9

Women
10km Classic
1 Lubomira Balazova	SVK	33:13.4

15km Combined
1 Lubomira Balazova	SVK	1:02:13.5

15km Freestyle
1 Naomi Hoshikawa	JPN	43:00.2

3x5km Relay
1 Ukraine		0:45:56.3

NORDIC COMBINED
1 Junichi Kogawa	JPN	45:14.8

SKI JUMPING
Men

Team
1 Austria		846.2

116m
1 Yukitaka Fukita	JPN	229.6

85m
1 Naoto Ito	JPN	217.8

SHORT TRACK SPEED SKATING
Men
500m
1 Sae-Woo Park	KOR	0:45.85

1000m
1 Joon-Ho Lee	KOR	1:34.98

1500m
1 Joon-Ho Lee	KOR	2:29.30

3000m
1 Joon-Ho Lee	KOR	5:07.88

5000mTeam
1 Korea		7:27.56

Women
500m
1 Xiulan Wang	CHN	0:47.78

1000m
1 Xiulan Wang	CHN	1:45.03

1500m
1 Amy Peterson	USA	2:45.63

3000m
1 Chun Yang Zhang	CHN	5:49.80

3000m Team
1 China		4:38.27

FIGURE SKATING
Men
Single Skating
1 Yueming Liu	CHN		2.0pts

Women
Single Skating
1 Junko Yaginuma	JPN		2.0

Mixed
Ice Dancing
1 Mrazova/Simecek	TCH		2.0

Pair Skating
1 Piepenbrink/Castaneda	USA		1.5

ICE HOCKEY

1 Russia		9

BIATHLON

Men
10km Sprint
1 Franck Perrot	FRA	26:38.2

20km
1 Pavel Mouslimov	RUS	55:24.3

4x7.5km Sprint
1 Belarus		1:31:58.7

Women
7.5km
1 Jinfen Wang	CHN	25:13.1

15km
1 Elena Doumnova	RUS	52:03.4

3x7.5km
1 Russia		1:20:08.0

World Games
The Hague   Aug

ARTISTIC ROLLER SKATING
Men	Heath Maderios	USA
Women	Anna Cocco	ITA
Pairs	Ferri/Venerucci	ITA
Dance	Monahan/Waite	USA

BEACH VOLLEYBALL
Women	Brazil
Men	France

BODY BUILDING
Men
Lightweight	Eduard Derzapf	GER
Lt Heavyweight	Ian Dowe	GBR
Middleweight	Abin Abdullah	SIN
Heavyweight	Glenn Gravenbeek	HOL

Women
Lightweight	A Blanchette	GBR
Middleweight	Martha Sanchez	MEX
Heavyweight	Conny Plösser	GER

BOWLING
Men	Leandersson	SWE
Women	P Smith	GBR
Mixed	Aalto/Koiveniemi	FIN

CASTING
Men
7.5 Accuracy	B Larsen	NOR
18 gr Target	Steve Rajeff	USA
Fly dist. s-handed	Thomas Maire	GER
Dist. single 7.5 gr	Knut Meel	NOR
7.5 gr Target	Henrik Osterberg	SWE
Fly Target	Hywll Morgan	GBR
Fly dist. d-handed	Thomas Maire	GER

Women
7.5 gr Accuracy	Michaela Krizova	TCH
18 gr Target	Mona Warntorp	SWE
Fly dist. s-handed	Michaela Krizova	TCH
Dist. single 7.5 gr	Bente Skyrud	NOR
7.5 gr target	Kathrin Werner	GER
Fly Target	Tina Bagge	GER

FAUSTBALL
Team	Germany

FIELD ARCHERY
Men
Barebow	T Cleven	HOL
Compound	M Lundin	SWE
Freestyle	A Parenti	ITA

Women
Barebow	P Lovell	GBR
Compound	C Chapelin	FRA
Freestyle	M Angeli	ITA

FIN SWIMMING
Men
50m APN	Ari Palve	FIN
	David Landi	ITA
200m FS	Luca Tonelli	ITA
400m FS	Edwin Kanters	HOL
100m FS	Luca Tonelli	ITA
100m IM	Ari Palve	FIN
4x100m FS Relay	Italy	
4x200m FS Relay	Denmark	

Women
50m APN	Zuzanna Mandikova	TCH
200m FS	Kristina Nurk	EST
400m FS	Myriam Villette	FRA
100m FS	Lorena Baldi	ITA
100m IM	Myriam Villette	FRA
4x100m FS Relay	Estonia	
4x200m FS Relay	Hungary	

KARATE
Men
up to 60 kg	N Fuyita	JPN
up to 65 kg	Musat Ysal	GER
up to 70 kg	J Watenabe	JPN
up to 75 kg	W Otto	GBR
up to 80 kg	A Paul	GBR
over 80 kg	M Hamon	CAN
All categories	Rob Mol	HOL

Women
Kata	Y Mimura	JPN
Kumite		
up to 53 kg	I Senff	HOL
up to 60 kg	N Samuels	GBR
over 60 kg	Karin Ollsen	SWE

KORFBALL
	Netherlands

NETBALL
Team	Australia

PETANQUE
Men Triplette	France
Women Doublette	France

POWERLIFTING
Men
Bench Press 67.5 kg	Gerard McNamara	IRL
Bench Press 90 kg	Frank Schramm	GER
BP over 90 kg	Brian Reynolds	GBR
Dead Lift 67.5 kg	Rodney Hyppolite	GBR
Dead Lift 90 kg	Sly Anderson	USA
DL over 90 kg	Victor Naleikin	UKR
Squad 67.5 kg	Rodney Hyppolite	GBR
Squad 90 kg	Frank Schramm	GER
Squad over 90 kg	Victor Naleikin	UKR
Total Score 67.5kg	Gerard McNamara	IRL
Total Score 90 kg	Frank Schramm	GER
TS over 90 kg	Gene Bell	USA

Women
Bench Press 52 kg	Ann Leverett	USA
	Li-Min Lin	TPE
Bench Press 67.5kg	Carrie Boudreau	USA
BP over 67.5 kg	Cathy Millen	NZL
Dead Lift 52 kg	Claudine Cognacq	FRA
Dead Lift 67.5 kg	Carrie Boudreau	USA
DL over 67.5 kg	Cathy Millen	NZL
Squad 52 kg	Gemma Christobal	ESP
Squad 67.5 kg	Beate Ambahl	NOR

Squad over 67.5kg	Shelby Corson	USA
Total Score 52 kg	Claudine Cognacq	FRA
Total Score 67.5kg	Carrie Boudreau	USA
TS over 67.5 kg	Cathy Millen	NZL

RACQUETBALL

Men	M Bronfeld	USA
Women	M Gauld	USA

ROLLERHOCKEY

Team	Portugal

SPEED ROLLER SKATING
Men

300m time trial	Anthony Muse	USA
500m Sprint	Anthony Muse	USA
5000m	Arnoud Gicquel	FRA
10000m	P Derek	USA
20000m elimin.	A Campannoli	ITA

Women

300m time trial	Desley Hill	AUS
500m Sprint	Hilde Goovaerts	BEL
3000m	Anne Titze	GER
5000m	C Lagree	FRA
10000 elminin.	Anne Titze	GER

SOMBO

Up to 52 kg	N Baatarbold	MON
Up to 57 kg	K Akraliev	KZK
Up to 62 kg	S Ignatenko	RUS
Up to 68 kg	I Netov	BUL
Up to 74 kg	N Igrauchkine	RUS
Up to 82 kg	G Haibulaev	RUS
Up to 90 kg	A Dunaev	RUS
Up to 100 kg	V Raumiantsev	RUS
Over 100 kg	V Emelianov	BLS

SPORTS ACROBATICS
Men

Balance Pairs	Strijanov/Lebedov	RUS
Tempo Pairs	I Chen/B Chen	CHN
Combined Pairs	Strijanov/Lebedov	RUS
	I Chen/B Chen	CHN
Balance Four	P Nikolov/Gueorguiv/	
	S Nikolov/Vasilev	BUL
Tempo Four	S Nikolov/Gueorguiv/	
	P Nikolov/Vasilev	BUL
Combined Four	S Nikolov/Gueorguiv/	
	P Nikolov/Vasilev	BUL
Mixed Pairs Bal.	He/Ting	CHN
Mixed Pairs Temp	He/Ting	CHN
Mixed Pairs Comb	He/Ting	CHN

Women

Balance Pairs	Delcheva/Miroslava	BUL
Tempo Pairs	Redkovolosowa/	
	Antipova	UKR
	Delcheva/Miroslava	BUL
Combined Pairs	Delcheva/Miroslava	BUL
Balance Trio	Mrozowics/Pawliszyn/	
	Chmielewska	POL
Tempo Trio	Mrozowics/Pawliszyn/	
	Chmielewska	POL
	Ivanova/Pankova/	
	Petrova	BUL
Combined Trio	Mrozowics/Pawliszyn/	

	Chmielewska	POL
	Ivanova/Pankova/	
	Petrova	BUL

TAEKWONDO
Men

Up to 50 kg	A Haider	DEN
Up to 54 kg	S K Seo	KOR
Up to 58 kg	G Esparza Perez	ESP
Up to 64 kg	F Zas Couce	ESP
Up to 70 kg	O Sanchez Ortega	ESP
Up to 76 kg	J O Jang	KOR
Up to 83 kg	V M Estrada Gaibay	MEX
Over 83 kg	Hyon Il Kim	KOR

Women

Up to 47 kg	C M Lo	TPE
Up to 55 kg	C C Liu	TPE
Up to 65 kg	H M Cho	KOR
Over 65 kg	B Hipf	GER

TRAMPOLINE
Men

Single	F Schwertz	FRA
Synchronised	Hennick/Schwerts	FRA

Women

Single	S Challis	GBR
Synchronised	Beck/Röwe	GER

TUMBLING

Men	John Beck	USA
Women	Christol Robert	FRA

1/4 TRIATHLON

Men	Jan van de Marel	HOL
Teams	Netherlands	
Women	Annemie Suys	BEL
Teams	Netherlands	

TUG OF WAR

640 kg	Switzerland	
720 kg	Switzerland	

WATERSKIING
Men

Tricks	P Martin	FRA
Slalom	J Batleday	GBR
Jump	O Devyatovski	BUL

Women

Tricks	O Pavlova	BUL
Slalom	P Roberts	GBR
Jump	O Pavlova	BUL

Obituary

Bobby Moore, OBE, footballer   Bobby Moore was captain of the English football team in its finest hour, the 4-2 World Cup victory over Germany in 1966. Moore, who collected the Jules Rimet trophy from the Queen that day, did not just lead the team, but by his presence, both on and off the field, embodied the best of English football.

Moore was born Robert Frederick Chelsea Moore at Barking, Essex in 1941. He joined West Ham as a 17 year old in the summer of 1958 and came under the influence of Malcolm Allison. "Stand Big" was Allison's memorable advice to the young footballer and it was not forgotten. It was Ron Greenwood, who became the West Ham manager two years later, who converted Moore from a wing half to a central defender.

Moore was a captain by instinct: at 17 he led the England Youth team and went on to captain the under 23 team. His senior international debut was in the 1962 World Cup against the host nation Chile. Within a year and barely a month after his 22nd birthday, he was captain of England too, leading the team to a 4-2 win over Czechoslovakia. Moore went on to captain England a further 90 times, equalling Billy Wright's record. He gained 108 caps in all, which remains a British record for an outfield player. Moore made his final England appearance in November 1973 against Italy.

He stayed with West Ham for 15 years, helping them to an FA Cup victory in 1964, and a European Cup Winners' Cup triumph the following year. He was also Footballer of the Year, in 1964. After an indian summer with Fulham, including an appearance in the 1975 Cup Final against West Ham, he retired. Brief spells in management followed - with Oxford and Southend - and coaching in Hong Kong and the USA, before he moved into journalism as sports editor of *Sunday Sport*. In 1990, he joined Capital Radio as a football commentator and was working for that station a week before he died.

Moore had not been in the best of health since 1986, when heart problems were diagnosed. He had an operation for bowel cancer in 1991 and died on February 24th 1993.

"If people say England would not have won the World Cup without me as manager, I can say it would have been impossible without Bobby as captain. He was the heartbeat of the team."
Sir Alf Ramsey, England manager 1963-74.

"The man had more class than anyone else I ever met on and off the field. I have always looked up to him"   Billy Bonds, former teammate and West Ham
manager.

"He was a gentleman footballer and there are no gentleman footballers today"

George Cutterhan, 73, West Ham fan.

"Of all the defenders that I have challenged, Bobby Moore was the fairest, the best and the most honourable"   Pele.

"There is not a footballer anywhere on earth who played with or against him who does not have an affectionate memory"   Bobby Charlton.

"He was so neat, when he got out of the bath he didn't leave a puddle"

Mike Summerbee, former England teammate.

"God Must Have Had a Big Game Coming Up"

Dedication on a wreath at Upton Park.

Richard Adams, Three-day Eventer The 23 year old Adams was killed at the Royal Windsor Horse Show on the 29th May, when his horse fell on him.

John Bailey, Marathon Runner Bailey, a 47 year old engineer from Staffordshire, became the second man to die in the 12 year history of the London marathon. Bailey, an experienced marathon runner, died after six miles of the race following a heart attack.

Thomas Henry Barling, Cricketer Played for Surrey 1933-47. Died, aged 86, in January.

Charles Barnett, Cricketer A belligerent opening bat, Barnett scored over 25,000 runs, including 48 centuries and 113 fifties. As a bowler, he claimed 394 wickets with his medium pacers at 30 runs apiece. His England debut was in 1933, when he was just 23 and his first tour a futile attempt to regain the Ashes against Bradman and O'Reilly and the team of all-talents. Barnett retired in 1948 to his game and poultry business and days with the Berkeley Vale and Mendip Hunts. He died on May 28th, aged 82.

Tony Barton, Football Manager Led Aston Villa to European Cup triumph in 1982. Barton had only been manager of Villa for four months when they beat Bayern Munich 1-0 in Rotterdam to lift the trophy. He was sacked less than two years later. Attempted a manager-ial comeback with Northampton, which ended in a heart attack, then became assistant to Chris Nicholl at Southampton before moving on to Portsmouth. Died, aged 57, in August.

Tony Bland, Football Supporter A victim of the 1989 Hillsborough tragedy, Bland died on 3rd March, aged 22, following a House of Lords judgment that allowed doctors to legally end his life by removing the feeding tube which had kept him alive for almost four years.

Charles Bray, Cricketer A county cricketer with Essex in his playing days, Bray later became cricket correspondent of the *Daily Herald*, a post he held from 1935 to 1964. He died in September aged 95.

Dr Ben Brown, Footballer Played in goal for Oxford University and England. Won seven caps and played for Britain in the 1952 Helsinki Olympics. A tutor in chemistry at Oxford.

Stanley Meredith Butler, Cyclist Butler was the last surviving member of Britain's cycling team at the 1932 Olympics. He competed in the 100km road race in those Los Angeles Games but, carrying an injury, failed to make an impact on the race. He suffered when road racing was banned by the sport's governing body before the war, but as a veteran in the post-war years enjoyed some success, setting a new British record in the 24 hour time trial. Cycling passed down the family, his son Keith becoming British professional road race champion, his grandson, Gethin, the current 100 miles and 12 hour time trial champion. Butler died on March 5th, aged 83.

Diana Campbell, Yachtswoman Crippled in her youth by arthritis, Campbell realised her dream to compete on equal terms with the more physically able by becoming an avid yachtswoman. She sailed her first boat by being lashed to the deck in a typist's chair. Convinced that sailing presented a perfect medium for the physically handicapped, she inspired the Challenger project. Funded by the RYA Seamanship Foundation, it produced a yacht, the Challenger, designed for the disabled. In the mid-eighties, *Sailability* was founded to promote sailing for all and most of its disabled members since began the sport, directly or indirectly, through Challenger. Campbell died of cancer on April 8th, aged 60.

Tommy Caton, Footballer Capped 14 times as an England under-21 international, Caton was for some years groomed as a future England centre-half. However, the early promise was never fulfilled. From Manchester City, where he flourished under Malcolm Allison, he was transferred to Arsenal for £500,00 in December 1983. He joined Charlton in 1988, but in recent seasons his appearances had been curtailed by an ankle injury and he was talking of retirement. He died, aged 30, on 30th April.

Major General Eric Cole, sportsman Kent county cricketer, President of army golf society and light-heavyweight champion of the army. Died in December, aged 86.

Peter Coni, Rowing Administrator If Coni was an establishment figure, he was an unlikely one. A lawyer by profession, elevated to Queen's Counsel in 1980, and a rowing administrator in his spare time, Coni exuded a more subversive air. Yet if he behaved like a man who might rock the boat, Coni seldom did. In practice, he was an adept administrator who reshaped the structure of his sport of rowing. As chairman of the Henley Regatta from 1977, treasurer of the international federation, FISA, from 1990 and on the National Olympic Committee from the same time, he was an influential figure. Peter Richard Carstairs Coni died of a heart attack on July 14th aged 58.

Stanley Randall Couchman, Rugby Player & Administrator   President of the Rugby Football Union in 1978-79, in his playing days he was a member of the Lions team to South Africa in 1937-38. Died, aged 79, in November.

Ted Croker, Football Administrator Secretary of the Football Association from 1973-89. Played as a centre-half, for Charlton Athletic. An RAF pilot, Croker won the King's Commendation for brave conduct. He died in December, aged 68, after a long fight against cancer.

Jack Davies, Cricketer & Administrator County cricketer and rugby player with Kent until the age of 40. His most famous moment was when he bowled Bradman for a duck whilst playing for Cambridge University. A week earlier he had run out Len Hutton, who was in his first innings for Yorkshire. He was later treasurer of the MCC at the time of the Packer affair. President of the MCC in 1985-86. Died, aged 81, in November.

Colin Dixon, Rugby League Player The former Great Britain and Salford second row died in June following a stroke.

Right Rev. Gerald Ellison, Rowing Administrator Steward of Henley Regatta, umpire of the Boat Race and Bishop of London. Died, in October, aged 82.

Ian Folley, Cricketer Derbyshire and Lancashire player whose best season was in 1987, when he took 74 wickets. He was struck on the head, while playing for Whitehaven in the North Lancashire league, and admitted to hospital where he died. Folley was aged 30 and died in August.

Jack Froggat, Footballer Froggat played outside left in the Portsmouth side that won the First Division championship in 1949 and 1950. He won 13 caps for England but, of the same generation as Tom Finney, found opportunities limited. He died on 17th February, aged 71.

Bill Fryer, CB CBE, Yachtsman and Skier Fryer skippered the yacht *Ilex* in the first transatlantic yacht race in 1931 and in 1945 founded the British Kiel Yacht club. As a skier, he won the 1928 Lauberon Cup. In his day job, he was Major-General Wilfred George Fryer, the army's chief engineer, Middle East, from 1954-1957. He died on February 19th, aged 92.

Herbert Montandon Garland-Wells, Cricketer County cricketer, captained Surrey in 1939. Died, aged 85, in June.

Pat Garrow Boxing and football journalist for *The Scotsman*, the *Sunday Mirror* and *The Herald*. Died aged 79 in February.

Captain Michael Gibson, Tennis Referee   Gibson refereed at Wimbledon in the changeover days from amateurism to professionalism. He kept the position for 12 years and his theatrical approach did not always endear him to the players. "He is the worst referee in the business," said Ilie Nastase, "He thinks he is God...or a little higher". Gibson retired in 1975 and died aged 67 in September.

Lieutenant-Colonel Sir Martin Gilliatt, Racehorse Trainer   Trainer and adviser to the Queen Mother on racing matters. Died in May.

Ian Graeme, CB OBE, Administrator A Major-General in charge of recruiting, Graeme switched to sports administration when he retired from the army. He was secretary of the British Ski Federation for 12 years before, in 1976, he was invited to join the Sports Aid Foundation. In 1982, he became a governor of that body. He died on May 14th, aged 79.

Billy Griffith, CBE DFC TD, Cricket Administrator Griffith was wicketkeeper for Sussex and three times capped for England. MCC secretary, 1962-1974, during the D'Oliveira crisis when the MCC was seen to bow to the demands of the South African government to leave D'Oliveira out of the side, Griffith, in the ensuing uproar, offered his resignation, but it was refused. In 1979, he became President and the following year was responsible for recoding the Laws of the game. Stewart Cathie Griffith died on 7th April, aged 78.

Frank Hill, Footballer & Manager Played for Arsenal and Scotland and managed Crewe, Burnley, Preston, Notts County and Charlton. Died, aged 87, in August.

John Hill, Powerboat Racer Three times formula one world powerboat champion (1984, 1985 & 1990), died in a powerboat accident, in April, aged 59.

Mark Holliday, Three-day Eventer Holliday died during the Hexham horse trials when his horse fell and crushed him.

James Hunt, Racing Driver and Commentator James Simon Wallis Hunt was born on August 29th 1947. The son of a London stockbroker, he attended his father's school at Winchester and was earmarked for a career in medicine. Hunt, however, had other ideas. He began his racing career in Formula Ford in the early seventies and by the time he had graduated to Formula Three, his volatile driving technique had earned him the nickname "Hunt the Shunt". That reputation imperilled his career, but in 1974 Lord Alexander Hesketh set him on the glory trail when he signed him up as driver for his Formula One team. Hesketh, like Hunt, would probably have been happier in another age. They made a cavalier alliance; taking on the commercial empires and making their point at the Dutch Grand Prix at Zandvoort in 1975 with the team's first and last victory. Hesketh left the circuit after that summer and Hunt moved on to McLaren, with whom, a year later, he took his world title in a rain-soaked race in Japan. Niki Lauda, who had almost died earlier that summer, stood and watched refusing to take the last chance to retain his title, conscious perhaps that he had pushed Luck far enough for one year. Hunt had three more years in Grand Prix racing and was offered a tempting bait of £3 million to return in 1982. Hunt resisted. "I've made enough not to work again," he said. Yet the money did not last. Two expensive divorces and six figure losses at Lloyds left Hunt with a Mercedes in the drive he couldn't afford to run, and a battered old van or a bicycle that he could. His single income came from his job with the BBC as a racing commentator, at which his thoughtful bass proved the perfect counterpart to Murray Walker's excitable tenor. It was typical Hunt that, at the memorial service for his friend Denny Hulme last year, he arrived by bicycle and changed out of his jogging kit into a grey suit on the pavement outside the church. Hunt himself died of a heart attack on June 14th, aged 45.

Anne Ince, Hang-gliding Pilot Ince, who also acted as a reporter on gliding and dressage for the *Daily Telegraph*, died aged 64, in May.

Major Bill Ingall, Jockey Champion amateur point-to-point jockey in 1957. Died, aged 74, in August.

Reginald Ingle, Cricketer Captain of Somerset county side from 1932-37. Famed for hitting a Harold Larwood delivery out of the ground at Trent Bridge. Died, aged 89.

Cyril Kellett, Rugby League Player During a playing career with Hull Kingston Rovers and Featherstone Rovers that spanned the years 1956-1974, Kellett landed a remarkable 1,768 goals . It placed him fifth in the all-time point scoring chart. He died in March aged 56.

James Kilburn, Sportswriter Cricket and rugby correspondent of the *Yorkshire Post* from 1934-76. Died, aged 84, in September.

Seamus Lavelle, Rugby Union Player Lavelle, a back row forward, was a member of Hendon Rugby club since a teenager. He died after being knocked unconscious following a brawl in a game against Centaurs rugby club. Lavelle died on 14th March, he was 25.

Margaret Lodge, Hockey Captained England between 1946-51. Former President of the All England Hockey Association (1957-68). Died, in March, aged 83.

Sir Robin McAlpine Racehorse owner and breeder and a member of the Jockey Club. His racehorses included 1984 Oaks winner Circus Plume. Died aged 86, in February.

Archie Macaulay, Footballer Macaulay won seven Scottish caps in a career that took him to Arsenal, Fulham, West Ham and Brentford, before managership with Norwich. In 1959, he took Norwich, then a third division club, to the FA Cup semi-final with victories over Manchester United and Tottenham. Macaulay died in June, aged 77.

Brian MacCabe, Athlete A finalist in the 800m at the Berlin Olympics in 1936, MacCabe later served in an honorary capacity for the British Olympic and Commonwealth Games Associations. Died, aged 78, in November.

Myrtle Ethel Maclagan, MBE, Cricketer Maclagan was a member of the first ever touring team of Australia and New Zealand and she also scored the first ever women's Test century, 119, in the second Test at Sydney. Her career spanned 17 years and she twice captained England. She died on March 11th, aged 81.

Dan Maskell, Tennis Commentator Maskell did not miss a day's play at Wimbledon for 68 years. He was a player himself, and a coach, but it is as a commentator that he will be remembered, inextricably linked with his beloved Wimbledon. Maskell was first heard on the radio in 1949 and finally retired in 1992. As a commentator, Maskell was a great believer in allowing the pictures to tell the story and he spoke sparingly during a match. He was also a master of the understatement; his "Ooh, I say" following a fine shot, became his byword. Maskell's private life was marked with grief; his first wife Connie drowning and his son dying in a flying accident. Dan Maskell died in December, aged 84.

Lady Murless, Racehorse Breeder   Married to trainer, the late Sir Noel Murless, Lady Murless bred the 1968 1000 Guineas winner, Caergwrle. She died in January.

Edward Nicholson, Rifle Shooter   Nicholson represented England from 1938 until the 1970s. He died, aged 78, in April

Professor Francis O'Gorman England soccer schoolboy who went to become a director of Sheffield United football club. Senior honorary physician to the FA and FIFA. Died in August.

John Parrett, Racing Administrator Former point to point jockey who was clerk of Aintree racecourse from 1989-92. Killed in a hunting accident in Cheshire, aged 45.

Roy Perry, Landscape Painter Perry was an artist in the mainstream of British figurative art who became best known for his paintings of cricket grounds. Many were made into limited editions and Durham Cricket Club commissioned him to paint the scene of its debut into county cricket in 1992. His home club, Pyt House Players, often benefited when he sold smaller paintings to help boost club funds. He died, aged 59.

Keith Piggott, Jockey and Trainer The high point of Piggott's racing career was when he saddled the 66-1 shot Ayala to win the 1963 Grand National. However, history will remember him less for his own achievements than for those of his son, Lester. Keith Piggott was himself the son of a National Hunt jockey, Ernie Piggott, who rode over 1,000 winners. Keith Piggott followed his father into the sport winning his first race, on the flat, at 15. The lessons he learnt as a jockey then a trainer he passed on to his own son. At the Piggott home, they used a cinema projector to study races. Keith Piggott died on June 15th, aged 89.

Colonel Sir John Carew Pole Steward of the National Hunt Committee 1953-56 and elected to the Jockey Club in 1969. Former Lord Lieutenant of Cornwall, died in January, aged 90.

Mel Rees, Footballer A Welsh youth international, Rees earned his place in footballing lore as the youngest player to have played in all four divisions of the Football League. In turn, he joined Cardiff, West Bromwich, Watford and Sheffield United. While on loan to Norwich, in 1992, he was diagnosed as suffering from stomach cancer. He underwent treatment and was given the go-ahead to resume training last January. However, the cancer had not gone into remission and Rees died on May 30th, he was 26.

Keith Rogers, Yachtsman Died after being swept overboard off Pembrokeshire during a yacht race in December.

Sir Michael Sobell, Racehorse Owner Sobell's horses included the 1979 Derby winner, Troy, and the 1983 St Leger and Oaks winner, Sun Princess. Also a major philanthropist and funded the building of the Sobell Sports Centre in north London. Died, aged 100, on September 1st.

Arthur Stephenson, Racehorse Trainer Stephenson was the first National Hunt trainer to achieve 100 winners in a season. His biggest single success was The Thinker's victory in the Cheltenham Gold Cup.

Les Townsend, Cricketer Played for Derbyshire and won four England caps. Died, aged 89, in May.

Jeremy Tree, Racehorse Trainer Trainer of four classic winners and a Prix de l'Arc de Triomphe (Rainbow Quest), died aged 67, in March.

Lord Henry Reginall Underhill CBE Manager of the British Workers's Olympiad team in 1936 in Barcelona when the fascists marched in. Died aged 78, in March.

William Vincent, Yachtsman A self-employed carpenter from Bath, Vincent was lost overboard from the yacht Heath Insured during the British Steel Challenge round the world race. Vincent was 47.

Cyril Frederick Walters, Cricketer Worcestershire and Glamorgan county cricketer and was the first Welsh captain of England. His career average was just 30, but his Test average, in 11 Tests, was 52. Died, aged 87, in December.

Stanley Woods, Motor-cyclist Between 1921 and 1939, Woods won 10 Isle of Man TT races, a figure unbeaten until Mike Hailwood's dominance in the 1960s. Died, aged 88, in August.

Overseas

Sir Adetokunbo Ademola, IOC Member, Nigeria Died, aged 86, in February.

Harry Houston Alexander, Australia, Cricketer Nicknamed "Bull" because of his consider-able build, Alexander took part in the infamous Bodyline series of 1932-33. He was called up for the final Test, when he wanted to respond in kind to the tactics of the England captain, Douglas Jardine, but was forbidden to by his captain Bill Woodfull. Even without that con-sent, Alexander still managed enough venom to hit Jardine three times in the ribs and break Bob Wyatt's bat. However, he took only one wicket for 154 in the game and never played for his country again. He died in Melbourne in April, aged 87.

Ivan Andreadis, Czechoslovakia, Table Tennis Player From 1939, when he won his nation-al title for the first time, to 1963, Andreadis did everything but win a world individual title. On four occasions he shared in the men's doubles title, once in the mixed doubles and four times featured in the winning Czech team. Twice he was runner-up in the singles, but that crown was destined to elude him. He died, aged 68, on 28th October.

Zika Ascher, Czechoslovakia, Skier Noted textile designer, who in his early years skied for his country. Was a member of the Czech winter Olympic team in 1936. Died, aged 82, in December.

Arthur Ashe, USA, Tennis Player Arthur Robert Ashe junior was born in Richmond, Virginia. He was the first black man to win a grand slam event, winning the US Open in 1968, and followed with the Australian Open in 1970 and Wimbledon in 1975. He was top ranked in the world in 1968 and 1975 and retired, following a heart attack, in 1979. In 1983, Ashe was infected with the HIV virus following a heart by-pass operation. He developed full blown AIDS in 1988. Ashe's tennis career climaxed with his Wimbledon victory over Jimmy Connors, a victory against all expectation. However, it was the dignity of the man rather than his sporting achievements that made him so popular. A passionate campaigner against racism, he latterly set up a foundation for research into AIDS. He was, for five years from 1983, non-playing captain of the US Davis Cup team, he commentated on his sport and wrote for the *Washington Post*. At his memorial service, in New York's Morningside Heights church, over 5,000 people arrived to pay their respects. He died on 6th February, aged 49.

Davey Allison, USA, Stock Car Racer Allison, 32, died following a helicopter crash on July 13th. Allison's brother Clifford had died just 11 months earlier in a car crash.

Tofik Bakhramov, Azerbayan, Football Linesman The baggy-trousered, moustachioed man who was responsible for England's finest hour. In 1966, it was Bakhramov who sig-nalled that Geoff Hurst's shot had bounced over and not on the line and ensured that England had a 3-2 lead over Germany and were on their way to the World Cup crown. Twenty-five years later he maintained the view that it had been a goal. He died, aged 66.

Alessandro Balestrieri, Italy, Powerboat Racer Killed, in December, while practising for an offshore race in Argentina, aged 38.

Uwe Beyer, Germany, Hammer Thrower European champion in 1971, the German died of a heart attack, aged 48.

Zeno Colo, Italy, Alpine Skier A downhill specialist, Colo was one of the first skiers to use the then revolutionary tuck position. He won gold at the world championships in 1950 and followed up with Olympic gold at the winter Games of 1952 in Oslo. He died, aged 72.

Billy Conn, USA, Boxer Former world light-heavyweight champion, who was knocked out by Joe Louis in the 13th round when leading on points in a world heavyweight contest in

1941. Died, aged 76, in May.

Chuck Connors, USA, Baseball Pitcher A pitcher with Chicago Cubs, LA Angels and the Brooklyn Dodgers, Connors (real name: Kevin Joseph Connors) later became an actor. Died, in November, aged 71.

Danie Craven, South Africa, Rugby Player and Administrator President of the South African Rugby Board from 1956-1992, Craven was the dominant force in South African rugby during that turbulent period. Craven himself represented his country in four different positions, though primarily played as a scrum half. He died in January, aged 92.

René Dreyfus, France, Racing Driver The winner of the 2nd Monaco grand prix in 1930 and winner of Le Mans in 1938. Died, aged 88, in August.

Sir Edward Dunlop, Australia, Rugby Union Player Rugby international and Barbarian. Died, in July, aged 85.

Alex Ehrlich, Poland, Table Tennis Player Three times a beaten finalist in the world championship singles, Ehrlich was fated to be remembered rather for his part in contesting, with Farkas Paneth of Rumania, the longest ever rally for one point. It lasted 2 hours and 12 minutes. I shall run that past you again - 2 hours and 12 minutes. Ehrlich died on December 19th, aged 78.

Detlef Gerstenberg, Germany, Hammer Thrower The European junior champion in 1975, Gerstenberg went on to break the East German hammer record twice in 1984. His best performance in a senior competition was fifth in the 1980 Olympics. He died, of liver cancer, on January 24th, aged 35.

Antoine Gobert, Belgium, Football Administrator Gobert, vice president of the Belgian Football Association (URBSFA) died on 23rd April, aged 68.

Raul Gardini, Italy, Yachting Patron Financial supporter of Italy's Americas Cup challenge. Committed suicide rather than face charges of corruption. Died, aged 60, in July.

Lindsay Hassett, MBE, Australia, Cricketer Sir Neville Cardus wrote of Hassett that if he had batted on a snow-covered pitch, his footprints would probably resemble those of a bird. At just 5' 6", Hassett was one of the smallest of opening bats, but one of the nimblest. He first played for his country, under Bradman, in 1938 and took over from the great man as captain in 1953. He went on to lead Australia 24 times and when he finally retired had scored over 16,890 runs in first-class matches at a daunting average of 58.24. He scored 59 centuries, including ten in Tests; the highest of those was 198 not out against India at Adelaide. After playing, he became a commentator, but retired from that role in 1981, saying he had had enough of the antics of modern players. Hassett was a lifelong friend of Bill O'Reilly and after their playing days they were inseparable, "Tiger" O'Reilly towering above the diminutive Hassett. Hassett died on 16th June, aged 79 and just eight months after O'Reilly.

Denny Hulme, New Zealand, Motor Racing Driver Successful as a racing driver in New Zealand, Hulme's first job when he came to England was as a mechanic with Brabham Motors. He gained his first victory, in a Brabham Formula Junior car on Boxing Day, 1962. Three years later Hulme made his debut in Grand Prix racing. In 1967 he became world champion and, in all, won eight times from 102 starts. Driving in a high-risk era, Hulme strived to introduce higher safety standards. He retired from Grand Prix racing in 1974. Hulme died on 4th October. Ironically, it was on the track, but it was a heart attack that killed him. He was 56.

Melker Karlsson, Sweden, Orienteer One of 15 Swedish orienteers who have died in the past 14 years. Karlsson collapsed and died after a training run in November. He was 24.

Michael Klein, Romania, Footballer The international midfielder collapsed and died following a training run with his club Bayer Uerdingen. He was 33.

Oksana Kostina, Russia, Rhythmic Gymnast At the 1992 world championships, Kostina won every discipline; all-round, rope, hoop, ball and clubs. From Irkutsk, in eastern Russia, the 19 year old was engaged to the 1992 Olympic bronze medallist in the modern pentathlon, Eduard Zenovka. Kostina died following a car crash on 11th February 1992.

Reggie Lewis, USA, Basketball Player Boston Celtics guard, who died after passing out in practice in July, aged 27.

Roy Marshall, West Indies, Cricketer Represented the West Indies on four occasions, but played most of his cricket in England with 504 appearances for Hampshire, scoring over 30,000 runs. Died, aged 62, from cancer.

Bill O'Reilly OBE, Australia, Cricketer William Joseph O'Reilly played just 27 times for Australia, but in that brief time before war intervened, earned himself the reputation of the finest leg-spinner in the game's history. His name is invariably paired with Bradman. While the one tormented England with the bat, the other tortured them with the ball. They were both from New South Wales, O'Reilly from Goulburn. A big man, his hostile expression when he bowled earned him the sobriquet "Tiger". In his 27 tests, he took 144 wickets at 22 runs apiece. When he retired, he became a journalist with the *Sydney Morning Herald* and for the next 40 years wrote trenchant articles in that newspaper. He was an implacable opponent of Packer's revolution and, unsurprisingly, a long-time advocate of the virtues of spin bowling. "Just because Lillee and Thomson hit a few Poms on the head, we think we've got to play that way forever," he complained. O'Reilly, who died of kidney failure, was 86.

Cec Pepper, Australia, Cricketer A first-class cricketer for New South Wales, Pepper became a well-known umpire. He died, aged 75, in March.

Bill Peterson, USA, American Football Coach Famed for his malapropisms ("I'm the football coach round here and don't you remember it") Peterson coached the Florida State University. Died in August.

Drazen Petrovic, Croatia, Basketball Player Leading scorer for the New Jersey Nets and one of the top guards in the game, Petrovic was killed in a car accident in Germany on 7th June, returning from a European championship game in Poland. He was 28.

Emilio Pucci, Italy, Skier Italian couturier who was an Olympic skier in his youth.

Eric Rowan, South Africa, Cricketer Played 26 times for South Africa with a batting average of 43.66, his highest score was 236 against England at Headingley in 1951. Died, aged 83, in May.

Darren Smith, Australia, Cyclist Olympic cyclist, finished 16th in the individual road race in the Barcelona Games in 1992. Hit by a truck whilst training. Died in November, aged 20.

Armand Vaquerin, France, Rugby Union Player From the southern town of Beziers, Vaquerin was capped 26 times for France as a prop and played in 11 Franch championship finals for his hometown club. He died after an accident with a pistol in a Bezier bar on 10th July 1993. Vaquerin was 42.

Archie Williams, USA, Sprinter In the 1936 Olympic Games, it was another black American, Jesse Owens, who drew the headlines. If Williams' feats could not match those of Owens, they were impressive enough. Even to get in the team, he was obliged to break the world 400m record, taking it down to 46.1. In the Olympics, he edged home ahead of Britain's Godfrey Brown. When he returned from the Games, Williams recalled how people had asked him about the "dirty Nazis". He had replied: "Well, at least over there we didn't have to ride in the back of the bus." Williams died of a heart attack on June 24th, aged 72.

Zambian Football On 27th April, the Zambian football team lost virtually its entire team, 18 players and five officials, when the De Havilland Buffalo that was taking them to Senegal for a World Cup qualifying game crashed after taking off from Libreville, Gabon. The players who died were: David Chabala, Richard Mwanza, Wisdom Chansa, Samuel Chomba, Godfrey Kangwa, Robert Watiyakeni, Derby Makinka, Eston Mulenga, Kevin Mutale, John Soko, Numba Mwila, Wisdom Mumba Chansa, Timothy Mwita, Moses Masuwa, Moses Chikwalakwala, Patrick Banda, Kenen Simambe and W Changwe. The officials were: Michael Mwapo, the president of the national federation, Godfrey Chitalu, national coach, Alex Chola, assistant coach, W Sakala, federation official, W Mtonga, team doctor, and J B Salimu, press officer. The delegation leader, N M Zimba, the deputy permanent secretary at the Ministry of Sport, also died. The dead included six of the team that reached the quarter-finals in the Seoul Olympics and it was widely regarded as one of the best in Africa. Only three team members escaped the crash. Kulasha Bwalya, Johnstone Bwalya and Charles Musonda who play for European teams, and had been due to join the team in Senegal.

1994 Preview

World Cup

Don't let them fool you. They'll trot out all these fancy statistics; like 14.5 million Americans play soccer, or that it's the second most popular game among the under twelves (basketball is the big winner) and that the US just loves the game. It doesn't. America doesn't give a monkey's cuss about soccer. The crowds may even turn up, that's not beyond the bounds of possibility, but it'll be a bit like the Olympic stadium in Seoul where the only two events the Koreans understood were the opening and closing ceremonies.

The Americans are so parochial with their sport that they don't even follow their own stars if it's not one of their big five sports. So, when Carl Lewis arrived in Gateshead this summer to face Linford Christie, the world champion against the Olympic champion, America yawned. Put basketball, gridiron football, baseball, boxing or hockey (they don't bother with the word ice) in front of them and they'll lap it up for hours. But Football, no.

So why is it in America? Well, it's the final frontier for football. The sport has captured the world, bar America. Think of all that money waiting to be poured into the game. That great marketing circus that follows the sport around probably got quite giggly at the idea of that dosh. There were even plans afoot, early on, to Americanise the game. Four 25-minute quarters was proposed and the widening of the goals, and while we're on the subject how about a little padding here, and sin bins and the referees miked up..... Thankfully such proposals were soon thumped off the park.

FIFA weren't completely silly about television either. If it was a curious decision to take the biggest single-sport event in the world and take it to the only major country that doesn't play it seriously, they weren't going to risk the coverage. After all, America could sleep right through it, but as long as the rest of the world got good pictures then it could still be a major success. Uniquely, then, the host nation will not supply the host broadcaster for the World Cup. Although ABC will show the games, the host broadcaster will be the European Broadcasting Union; using European technical skills with American labour. Makes sense, can you imagine Meridian doing a baseball match?

In their favour, the Americans will do a professional job of presentation and prepare themselves thoroughly for the grand event. Maybe a bit too thoroughly if the sheriff of Orlando is anything to go by. The sheriff (we don't know his proper name) has budgeted for an armoured personnel carrier as part of his anti-hooligan measures. He may not have that much to worry about; at the time of writing, England (who could be based at Orlando) are some way from qualifying.

Should you go, or be thinking of it, take a close look at the schedule first. The distances between games is phenomenal. Boston to Dallas, which one poor team will have to handle is the equivalent of Plymouth to Newcastle and back twice over.

World Cup Timetable

June 17-July 17

In the first round, the teams are divided into six groups of four teams. They are called Group A, B, C, D, E, & F *(see below)*. Each group is headed by a seeded team. The remaining teams are drawn at random. Each team plays every other within its group and points are awarded as you might expect: two for a win, one for a draw, and none for a defeat. When the first round is completed 36 games will have been played - six in each group. The top two teams in each group will qualify automatically for the last 16. The four best third-placed teams (determined by a "system of standings and tiebreakers" say FIFA, but we are not quite sure what that means) will join them. From the last 16 onwards, the competition becomes a simple knock-out. If teams are tied after 90 minutes, 30 minutes of extra-time is played. If no winner is determined during extra-time, then good old penalty kicks will sort it all out.

FIRST STAGE

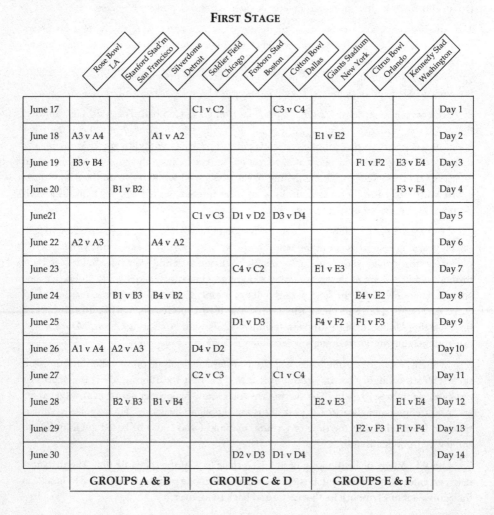

	Rose Bowl LA	Stanford Stad'm San Francisco	Silverdome Detroit	Soldier Field Chicago	Foxboro Stad Boston	Cotton Bowl Dallas	Giants Stadium New York	Citrus Bowl Orlando	Kennedy Stad Washington	
June 17				C1 v C2	C3 v C4					Day 1
June 18	A3 v A4		A1 v A2			E1 v E2				Day 2
June 19	B3 v B4						F1 v F2	E3 v E4		Day 3
June 20		B1 v B2						F3 v F4		Day 4
June 21				C1 v C3	D1 v D2	D3 v D4				Day 5
June 22	A2 v A3		A4 v A2							Day 6
June 23					C4 v C2	E1 v E3				Day 7
June 24		B1 v B3	B4 v B2				E4 v E2			Day 8
June 25				D1 v D3		F4 v F2	F1 v F3			Day 9
June 26	A1 v A4	A2 v A3		D4 v D2						Day 10
June 27				C2 v C3	C1 v C4					Day 11
June 28		B2 v B3	B1 v B4			E2 v E3		E1 v E4		Day 12
June 29							F2 v F3	F1 v F4		Day 13
June 30				D2 v D3	D1 v D4					Day 14
	GROUPS A & B			**GROUPS C & D**			**GROUPS E & F**			

Once you have surmounted the relative simplicity of who plays who in the first round, getting to grips with the second stage should be no problem at all. So here we go....

FINAL 16 STAGE
Who plays who is resolved by FIFA regulations

Game 1:	Winner of Group A v Third in Group C, D or E
Game 2:	Second in Group F v Second in Group B
Game 3:	Winner of Group E v Second in Group D
Game 4:	Winner of Group C v Third in Group A, B or F
Game 5:	Winner of Group D v Third in Group B, E or F
Game 6:	Second in Group C v Second in Group A
Game 7:	Winner of Group F v Second in Group E
Game 8:	Winner of Group B v Third in Group A, C or E

The only real problem with this round is which third team plays against which winner and again FIFA, determined not to be wooly, explain it thus...."The specific third team place is designated by a predetermined chart which is applied to the four third place qualifiers" Okay? The above matches will be played as follows (note: we did try and do a chart but it didn't help much). **Game 1** at the Rose Bowl, LA on July 3rd; **Game 2** at the Cotton Bowl, Dallas on July 3rd; **Game 3** at the Giants Stadium, New York on July 5; **Game 4** at Soldier Field, Chicago on July 2; **Game 5** at Foxboro Stadium, Boston on July 5; **Game 6** at the Robert Kennedy Memorial Stadium, Washington on July 2; **Game 7** at the Citrus Bowl, Orlando on July 4; and **Game 8** at Stanford Stadium, San Francisco on July 4.

So, on to the quarter-finals where the eight winners meet as follows:

QUARTER-FINALS

Match A:	Winner of Game 1 v Winner of Game 2
Match B:	Winner of Game 3 v Winner of Game 4
Match C:	Winner of Game 5 v Winner of Game 6
Match D:	Winner of Game 7 v Winner of Game 8

Match A will be played at Stanford Stadium on July 10; **Match B** will be played at the Giants Stadium on July 10; **Match C** will be played at Foxboro Stadium on July 9; **Match D** will be played at the Cotton Bowl also on July 9. The semi-finals (it gets easier by the minute) are played as follows:

SEMI-FINALS

Winner of Match A v Winner of Match D
Winner of Match B v Winner of Match C

Both semi-finals are played on July 13, **Match A/D** at the Rose Bowl, **Match B/C** at the Giants Stadium. The **3rd/4th play-off match** is at the Rose Bowl on July 16 and the **final** is at the same venue on July 17. So that's it. Let's just hope there's a bit of local interest.

Winter Olympics

The Winter Olympics has never had such an opportunity to shine. It has had its stars in the past; Toni Sailer, Sonja Henie and Jean-Claude Killy have all had their moments in the spotlight, but the fame is generally brief. The Games has never shaken off the all-consuming shadow of its summer cousin. What happens in the snowlands is perennially forgotten six months later when the summer Olympics takes the stage. The International Olympic Committee recognised the problem and made a fundamental change, shifting the winter Games to the mid-point of the Olympic cycle. It was probably an idea that started in the minds of the marketing men who, since they wrested control some years back, have never been happy about trying to sell two four-year products in the same financial year. However, that should not detract from the other merits in having the Games falling on the off-beat.

As well as having the stage to itself for a while, Lillehammer also has some fairly ordinary acts to follow. Calgary, in 1988, was nobody's idea of heaven and Albertville, just two years back, was close to a disaster. Lillehammer could succeed like no other snow and ice games for another reason. The return of the golden oldies. A change in the rules means that competitors that seceded to the professional ranks can now register again as Olympic competitors. It may be expecting too much for the lustre to be as sparkling as the first time around, but to have Brian Boitano, Katarina Witt and Torvill and Dean around must enhance any Games. Even ten years on, Torvill and Dean may still represent Britain's best chance of bringing a medal home. That's a sobering thought.

British interest is not likely to be overwhelming; apart from ice dance the prospects look predictably lean. Bobsleigh, freestyle skiing or speed skating are the only other disciplines where our competitors might figure prominently. There is also a very good young slalom skier, Emma Carrick-Anderson, who probably still has rather too much youth on her side. She is only 19.

Lillehammer is about 80 miles north of Oslo and the Games will be based there, with competitions at five other nearby centres. To the south and 58km from Lillehammer is Hamar, where the figure skating and the speed skating events take place; and Gvøjik (45km), where part of the ice hockey competition is based. To the north of Lillehammer, is Hunderfossen (15km), home to the Bobsleigh and Luge; Kvitjell (50km), where the downhill skiers compete; and Hafjell (15km), for the remaining alpine events. At Lillehammer itself, the Olympic Park hosts the Nordic skiing events (Cross-country skiing, Biathlon, combined and ski jumping), the freestyle skiing and the remainder of the ice hockey matches. Because Lillehammer is so far north (just over 300 miles south of the Arctic Circle), the days are short and the outdoor events are all scheduled to start between 10.00 and 13.00. Further north, in the winter months, they ski by floodlight, but that hasn't come to the Games yet.

Even the winter Games don't come cheaply. The Norwegians estimate that the stadia and additional development has cost around £450m. They are expecting 2,680 competitors from 70 countries, 8500 officials, 7000 press, and 2,500 police. You don't really need spectators with that lot around.

Winter Olympic Timetable

Opening Ceremony: Feb 12 (Olympic Park)

Closing Ceremony: Feb 27

	Bobsleigh	Luge	Alpine Skiing	Freestyle Skiing	Ski Jumping	Nordic Combined	Cross-country Skiing	Biathlon	Ice Hockey (A)	Ice Hockey (B)	Figure Skating	Speed Skating (ST)	Speed Skating	
FEB 12									16.30 21.00	18.30				day 1
FEB 13		Ms 10.00	Mdh 11.00				W15k 10.00		15.00 20.00	17.30	Prs 20.00		M5k 15.00	day 2
FEB 14		Ms 10.00	Mdhc 11.00				M30k 10.30		15.00 20.00	17.30			M500 14.00	day 3
FEB 15		Ws 10.00	Wsg 11.00	mgl 13.00			W5k 10.30		15.00 20.00	17.30	Prs 20.00			day 4
FEB 16		Ws 10.00		mgl 13.00					15.00 20.00	17.30			M1.5k 14.00	day 5
FEB 17			Msg 11.00				10.30 12.30		15.00 20.00	17.30	M 19.00		W3k 14.00	day 6
FEB 18		Mdb 10.00			K90 12.30			W15k 10.00	15.00 20.00	17.30	Dance 19.00		M1k 14.00	day 7
FEB 19	2M 10.00		Wdh 11.00			15k 10.30	M15k 12.30		15.00 20.00	17.30	M 19.00		W.5k 14.00	day 8
FEB 20	2M 10.00		Wdhc 11.00		K120 13.00			M20k 10.00	15.00 20.00	17.30	Dance 19.00		M10k 14.00	day 9
FEB 21			Wslc 9.30*	aerls 13.00			Wrly 10.30		15.00 20.00	17.30	Dance 19.00		W1.5k 14.00	day 10
FEB 22					K120 12.30		Mrly 10.30		16.30 21.00			Qual 19.00		day 11
FEB 23			Mgs 09.30*		K90 11.30			10.00 13.00	16.30 21.00	15.00 19.30	W 19.00		W1k 16.00	day 12
FEB 24			Wgs 09.30*	aerls 13.00		3x10k 10.00	W30k 12.30		16.30 21.00	15.00 19.30		Fnls 19.00		day 13
FEB 25			Mslc 09.30*		K90 12.30			Wrly 10.00	21.00	19.30	W 19.00		W5k 14.00	day 14
FEB 26	4M 10.00		Wsl 09.30*					Mrly 13.00	16.30 21.00	19.30 19.30	Exhib 15.00	Fnls 20.00		day 15
FEB 27	4M 10.00		Msl 09.30*				M50k 12.30		15.15					day 16

*Abbreviations: M-men, W-women, s-singles, db-doubles, dh-downhill, sl-slalom, sg-super giant, gs-giant slalom, ST-short track c-combined, mgl-moghuls, aerls-aerials, rly-relay. * indicates there is also a session at 13.00. NB: Norway is 1 hour ahead of GMT.*

Commonwealth Games

In competitive terms, the great days of the Commonwealth Games may be past. In Vancouver 40 years ago, Roger Bannister and Australian John Landy ran off to decide the best miler in the world. In Christchurch, New Zealand 20 years ago, Tanzania's Filbert Bayi and New Zealand's John Walker met in, perhaps, the most exhilarating 1500m race ever. Don Quarrie, a sprinter without peers, won six gold medals in three Games; Edinburgh, Christchurch and Edmonton. In Victoria, for the 1994 Games, it is unlikely that the track events will provide any competition of that ilk.

Olympic champions, world champions and world record holders will grace the games, but as Fate will have it, Britain has the sprinters, Kenya the distance runners and Australia, New Zealand and Canada have few stars at all. Colin Jackson against Mark McKoy of Canada could be the only race on the track where the Olympic champion meets the world champion and that depends on McKoy's fragile relationship with Athletics Canada, the governing body. As Jamaica's Ray Stewart illustrated in Auckland four years past, even if the stars arrive, not all of them take the competition seriously. Stewart, a reluctant starter in the 100m, virtually jogged his way to elimination.

It may therefore be an opportunity for other sports to grab some of the limelight. With the Malaysians offering stern oppostion to the England team, the badminton could be interesting. The cycling would have been, except that Chris Boardman and Graeme Obree, having forsaken the amateur world, will probably be busier elsewhere. Swimming, at least, will have some sturdy competition. Australia is not the force it was, but in Kieran Perkins it has the best long-distance swimmer in the world.

In truth, the timetable could be more exciting; wrestling and shooting do not compensate for the absence of sports like judo and rowing. The choice of sports was Canada's; only two are obligatory, athletics and swimming, and the remaining ten are chosen from a list of 15. Canada presumably has a strong team of marksmen and women, but no sport is less designed for the spectator.

Yet the compensation comes with the atmosphere; no event is more athlete friendly, no Games is more embracing. In an age when marketing, promotions, publicity and attendant kudos has all but taken over, the Commonwealth Games is the antidote. Auckland, four years past, was the perfect example. It's biggest sporting star, Sebastian Coe, did not even run in the final of the 800m. It didn't matter; Sammy Tirop of Kenya won gold and everybody applauded. They also noted another Kenyan who made his breakthrough there; William Tanui, the Barcelona Olympic champion.

There are no bribes to get the Commonwealth Games to your country, no post-mortems when you fail. No hysteria when you win gold, no bitter recriminations should you fail. Only 33,000 will be at the opening ceremony (this is no Olympic stadium) and a mere 300 million (a relative drop in the ocean) will watch it on television. Prince Edward will be at the opening and Mrs Queen herself at the closing and I'd rather be in Victoria than Atlanta.

Commonwealth Games Timetable

Opening Ceremony: Aug 18 (Centennial Stadium)

Closing Ceremony: Aug 28

Event	Venue	Day 1 Aug 18	Day 2 Aug 19	Day 3 Aug 20	Day 4 Aug 21	Day 5 Aug 22	Day 6 Aug 23	Day 7 Aug 24	Day 8 Aug 25	Day 9 Aug 26	Day 10 Aug 27	Day 11 Aug 28
ATHLETICS	1					M	M	M	M*	M	M	M
BADMINTON	3		M/A/E	M/A/E	M/A		M/A	M/A	A	A	A	
BOXING	5		A/E	A/E	A/E	A/E	A/E	A	A		A	
CYCLING	4		M/A**		M/A***			M/A	M/A	M/A	M/A	
GYMNASTICS	6		M/A(R)	M/A(R)	A(R)			M/A	M/A	M/A	M/A	
LAWN BOWLS	4		M/A/E	M/A/E	M/A/E	M/A/E	M/A/E	M/A/E	M/A/E	M/A/E	M/A/E	
SHOOTING	7		M/A	M/A	M/A	M/A	M/A	M/A	M/A	M/A	M/A	
SWIMMING	2		M/E	M/E	M/E	M/E	M/E	M/E				
DIVING	2		A		A	A		A	A	E		
SYNCHRO	2			A			A		M/E	A		
WEIGHTLIFTING	8						A/E	A/E	A/E	A/E	M/A	
WRESTLING	4		A/E	A/E	A/E							

THE VENUES

1 University of Victoria, Centennial Stadium
2 Saanich Commonwealth Place
3 University of Victoria McKinnon Gymnasium
4 Juan de Fuca Recreation Centre
5 Esquimalt's Archie Browning Sports Centre
6 Memorial Arena
7 Heal's Range
8 Royal Theatre

ABBREVIATIONS

M   Morning Session
A   Afternoon Session
E   Evening Session
(R)   Rythmic Gymnastics
*   Walks only
**   Team Time Trial
***   Road Race

TIMINGS

Victoria is minus eight hours from British summer time.

Goodwill Games

The raison d'être of the Goodwill Games is now history; it was conceived by television magnate Ted Turner as a boycott-proof games in an age when the Olympics was in its tit-for-tat era. The first was held in Moscow in 1986 and the second edition at Seattle in 1990, not too long after the Berlin Wall came down. The subsequent political thaw might easily have rendered the Games redundant. That it didn't is partly due to the persistence of its founder, partly due to the economic curtain that still exists.

The third edition will be in St Petersburg in August and is a succinct reminder that those economic barriers are still formidable. Since the rebuilding of the former Soviet states, sport has taken very much a back seat. Where finance was once available to support the propaganda of sport, now it no longer exists. Events like the grand prix athletics meetings have been downgraded and nobody entertains the idea of a major competition in the new republics (Tashkent's gesture of an Olympic bid was mere Uzbekistan flag-waving) - except for the Goodwill Games.

The Goodwill therefore has a new viability, and sponsors as formidable as Anheuser-Busch, Reebok, Pepsi and SmithKline Beecham, but it does not yet have the stature of a major Games; few people can remember who did what in the first two editions and that is a sure indication. Still, it has already mustered a formidable cast for St Petersburg. The mainstay of the programme will be the Americans and Carl Lewis, Mike Powell, Mike Conley, Gail Devers, Jackie Joyner-Kersee, Gwen Torrance, Quincy Watts and Kevin Young have all agreed to take part. The Russian complement will certainly turn out in numbers and you can bet that Ukrainian Sergey Bubka will arrive if the dollars are near the table. Colin Jackson and Sally Gunnell, who now carry the cache of titles and records, have committed themselves to the event, so the track and field element looks strong. They have also amended the programme to include the mile rather than the 1500m, so that may be a signal that Noureddine Morceli, the new world record holder, will be announced at some stage.

The Gymnastics events are certain to be well-attended. Shannon Miller, the all-round champion at the 1993 world gymnastics championships, has confirmed and the fact that 75% of the world's best gymnasts come from the new republics means the competition will be of the highest class.

The swimming programme is a short one, but Alexandre Popov and Tom Jager will make the 50m lively enough. In all, they are expecting 2000 athletes from around 50 countries competing in 24 sports. The biggest problem will be for the likes of Jackson and Gunnell who will have the most cramped of schedules. The track programme in St Petersburg runs from July 24 to 29; the European athletics championship in Helsinki takes place August 9 to 14; and the Commonwealth Games starts on August 18.

Goodwill Games Timetable

Opening Ceremony: Jul 23

Closing Ceremony: Aug 7

Event	23.7	24.7	25.7	26.7	27.7	28.7	29.7	30.7	31.7	1.8	2.8	3.8	4.8	5.8	6.8	7.8
Archery									14.00							
Athletics		11.00	17.00	17.00		14.30	14.00									
Basketball	09.00	13.00	13.00		13.00	13.00					11.00	11.00	11.00		09.00	10.00
Boxing	12.00	12.00	18.00	18.00	18.00	18.00	18.00	09.00								
Canoeing												11.00	11.00			
Cycling								11.00	11.00							
Diving											19.00	19.00	19.00	19.00	19.00	13.00
Football																19.00
Gymnastics (A)							12.00	12.00	19.00	19.00	19.00	19.00			19.00	16.00
Gymnastics (R)									12.00	12.00						
Handball		19.00	19.00	19.00	17.30	19.00										
Ice Skating												19.00	19.00	19.00	13.00	12.00
Judo			19.00	19.00	19.00											
Rowing															11.00	11.00
Swimming	11.00	17.00														
Synchro Swim									15.00	15.00						
Taekwondo										17.00	16.00					
Triathlon					11.00											
Volleyball								11.00	11.00	11.00		11.00		11.00		
V'Ball Beach	09.00	09.00	09.00	10.00												
Water Polo				19.00	19.00	19.00	19.00	11.00								
Weightlifting	11.00	12.00														
Wrestling							17.30	17.00	17.00							
Yachting											10.00	10.00	10.00	10.00		

The table shows only the first time that a sport appears on each day's schedule. The timings given are local times; British summer time will be minus three hours.

1994 Calendar

Indicates that the date is provisional

AMERICAN FOOTBALL

Jan 1-2	AFC/NFC Wild Card Play-offs	USA
Jan 8-9	NFL Wild Card Play-offs	USA
Jan 15-16	AFC/NFC Div Champ Games	USA
Jan 23	AFC/NFC Champ Games	USA
Jan 30	Super Bowl XXVIII	Atlanta
Feb 6	AFC/NFC Pro Bowl	Honolulu

ANGLING

June	World Fly-fishing champs	Lillehammer Norway

ATHLETICS

Jan 15	Inter-counties X-country	Durham
Feb*	World X-country UK Trial	Durham
Mar 11-13	European indoor champs	Paris
Mar 26	World X-country champs	Budapest
Apr 17	NutraSweet London Marathon	Greenwich, The Mall
	IAAF World road-relay Champs	Greece
Apr 18 *	98th Boston Marathon	Boston
June	European Cup	Birmingham
June 11	Man v Horse v Bike Marathon	Wales
July 20-24	World Junior champs	Lisbon
July 22-31	World athletics blind champs	Berlin
July 23 - Aug 7	Goodwill Games	St Petersb'g
Aug 9-14	XVI European champs	Helsinki
Aug 18-28	Commonwealth Games	Victoria, Canada
Sept 3	Grand Prix final	Paris
Sept 8-10	World Cup	C Palace
Sept 24	World half-marathon champs	Oslo
Sept 26 - Oct 8	World Masters Games	Brisbane
Oct 2-9	World Corporate Games	Johannes-burg

BADMINTON

Feb 4-6	English national champs	TBA
Mar 16-19	All England champs	Birmingham

BASKETBALL

Jan 17	English League Cup final	Birm'ham
Mar 5	National cup finals	TBA
Mar 15	European Cup final (men)	TBA
Mar 31	European Cup final (women)	TBA
Apr 9	NBL Play-offs (1)	
Apr 16	NBL Play-offs (2)	
Apr 21	European champs for mens clubs	Tel Aviv
Apr 30-May 1	Budweiser championships	Wembley
June 17-19	Corporate Games	M Keynes
Aug 4-14	World championship	Toronto

BASEBALL

Oct 15	World Series - best of seven	

BOARDSAILING

Apr 24 - May 3*	World Cup	Omaezaki, Japan

BOBSLEIGH

	World Junior champs	St Moritz
	European champs	La Plagne, France

BOXING

Mar*	Lennox Lewis v Tom Morrison	Las Vegas

CANOEING

Apr 1-4	Devizes-Westminster Marathon	
May 15-20	Zambezi Matathon	Zimbabwe
July 6-10	1st Canoe Polo world champs	Sheffield
July 13-16	KWV Marathon	Cape Prv SA
July 23-31	Slalom & Wild Water W C jnr	Wausau, Hurley USA
Sept*	World Champ Racing,snr	Xochimilko, Mexico
Sept*	1st Canoe Polo W C	Sheffield

CRICKET

Jan 1 -31	England A Tour to South Africa	
Jan 29-31	St Kitts & Nevis v England	Basseterre
Jan-Feb*	India tour to Sri Lanka	
Jan-Mar*	Pakistan tour to New Zealand	
Feb*	ICC Trophy-World Cup qual	Kenya
Feb 3-6	Leeward Islands v England	St Johns
Feb 10-13	Barbados v England	Bridgetown
Feb 16	WI v England,1st one-day	Bridgetown
Feb 19	S Africa v Australia,1-day	Jo'burg
Feb 19-24	WI v England, 1st Test	Bridgetown
Feb 20	SA v Australia, 1 day	Pretoria
Feb 22	SA v Australia, 1-day	Port Eliz
Feb 24	SA v Australia, 1-day	Durban
Feb 26	WI v England, 2nd one day int	Kingston
Mar*	India tour to New Zealand	
Mar 2	WI v England, 3rd one-day int	Kingstown
Mar 4-8	SA v Australia, 1st Test	Jo'burg
Mar 5	WI v England, 4th one-day int	Trinidad
Mar 6	WI v England, 5th one-day int	Trinidad
Mar 10-13	WI Pres XI v England	Guyana
Mar 17-21	SA v Australia, 2nd Test	Cape Town
Mar 17-22	WI v England, 2nd Test	Georgetown
Mar 25-29	SA v Australia, 3rd Test	Durban
Mar 25-30	WI v England, 3rd Test	Trinidad
Apr 2	SA v Australia, 1-day,day/night	London
Apr 2-5	WI XI v England	Grenada
Apr 4	SA v Australia, one-day	Port Eliz
Apr 6	SA v Australia, one-day	Cape Town
Apr 8	SA v Australia, one-day	Bloemf

Apr 8-13	WI v England, 4th Test	Bridgetown
Apr 16-21	WI v England, 5th and final Test	Antigua
Apr 26	Benson & Hedges Cup 1st round	
May 10	Benson & Hedges Cup 2nd round	
May 19	England v New Zealand 1-day	Edgbaston
May 21	England v NZL 2nd 1-day int	Lord's
June 2-6	England v NZL 1st Test	Nottingham
June 7	Benson & Hedges Cup semi-finals	
June 16-20	England v NZL 2nd Test	Lord's
June 30 -		
July 5	England v NZL 3rd Test	Manchester
July 9	Benson & Hedges Cup final	Lord's
July 21-25	England v SA 1st Test	Lord's
July 26	Nat West Trophy quarter finals	
July 30 -		
Aug 1	Women's County champs	Cambridge
Aug 4-8	England v SA 2nd Test	Headingley
Aug 18-22	England v SA 3rd Test	The Oval
Aug 25	England v SA 1st 1-day Int	Edgbaston
Aug 27	England v SA 2nd 1-day Int	Old Trafford
Sept 3	NatWest Trophy final	Lord's
Sept 18	Women's League Final	

CYCLING

Mar 6-13	Paris-Nice	France
Mar 19	Milan-San Remo (WCup)	Italy
Apr 3	Tour of Flanders (WCup)	Belgium
Apr 10	Paris-Roubaix (WCup)	France
Apr 17	Liege-Bastogne (WCup)	Belgium
Apr 25-		
May 15	Tour of Spain (Vuelta)	
May 13-15	World Cup track series	Spain
May 22-		
June 12	Tour of Italy (Giro)	
May 29 -	Tour of Britain-formerly Milk Race	
June 11		
June 3-5	World Cup track series	Denmark
June 14-23	Tour of Switzerland	
July 1-3	World Cup track series	France
July 2-24	Tour de France Lille to Paris	
	inc two stages in England (July 6, Dover to	
	Brighton and July 7, Brighton to Portsmouth)	
July 15-17	World Cup track series	USA
July 22-30	National track championships	Leics
Aug 6	San Sebastian (WCup)	Spain
Aug 8-12	Kellogg's Tour of Britain	
Aug 14	Leeds Classic (WCup)	
Aug 15-22	World track championships	Italy
Aug 19	Champs of Zurich (WCup)	
Aug 22-28	World Road Race champs	Sicily
Sept 21-25	Tour of Ireland	
Oct 8	Tour of Lombardy (WCup)	Italy

CYCLO CROSS

Jan 9	National senior, jnr & women's	S'hampton
	championships	
Jan 16	Inter Area team champs	Leeds
Jan 23	Nat Trophy Series/N'allerton Int	N'allerton
Jan 29-30	World championships	Koksijde
		Belgium
Feb 12	ESCA Nat championships	Nottingham

DARTS

Jan 1-8	Embassy World Prof champ	Lakeside

DIVING

Nov 19	ESSA national championships	TBA

EQUESTRIANISM

Apr 14-18	Volvo W Cup show jumping	Holland
May 5-8	Badminton Horse Trials	
May 11-15	Royal Windsor Horse Show	Home Pk
May 19-22 *	Nations Cup show jumping	Hickstead
June 9-12	Bramham Horse Trials	
Jul 7-10	Royal International Horse Show	Hickstead
Jul 27		The Hague,
-Aug 7	World Equestrian Games	Holland
Aug 26-29	Silk Cut Derby s/j	Hickstead
Sept 1-4	Burghley Remy Martin	Stamford,
Sept 15-18	Blenheim Horse Trials	Blen Palace
Oct 4-9	Horse of the Year Show	Wembley

FOOTBALL

Jan 8	FA Cup 3rd round	
	Scottish Cup 2nd round	
Jan 10-12	Coca-Cola Cup 5th round	
	Autoglass Trophy area q-finals	
Jan 15	USA v Norway	Phoenix
Jan 22	USA v Switzerland	
Jan 29	FA Cup 4th round	
	Scottish Cup 3rd round	
Feb 2	England international	TBA
Feb 5	USA v England	
Feb 7-9	Anglo-Italian Cup semis	
	Autoglass Trophy semis	
Feb 13/16	Coca-Cola Cup semi-finals,1st legs	
Feb 19	FA Cup 5th round	
	Scottish Cup 4th round	
	USA v Sweden	Miami*
Feb 23/27	Coca-Cola Cup semi-finals, 2nd legs	
Feb 28		
-Mar 2	Autoglass Trophy area finals	
Mar 2	European Champions League	
	European CW Cup q-finals,1st legs	
	UEFA Cup q-finals, 1st legs	
Mar 9	England International	TBA
Mar 12	FA Cup 6th round (q-finals)	
	Scottish Cup 5th round (q-finals)	
Mar 16	European Champions League	
	European CW Cup q-finals, 2nd legs	
	UEFA Cup q-finals, 2nd legs	
Mar 27	Coca-Cola Cup final	Wembley
Mar 30	European Champions League	
	European CW Cup semis, 1st legs	
	UEFA Cup semis, 1st legs	
Apr 9	Scottish Cup semi-finals	
Apr 10	FA Cup semi-finals	
Apr 13	European Champions League	
	European CW Cup semis, 2nd legs	
	UEFA Cup semis, 2nd legs	

Apr 16	Anglo-Italian Cup final	Wembley
Apr 20	Germany v England	TBA
Apr 24	Autoglass Trophy final	Wembley
	FA Women's Cup final	TBA
Apr 26 or 28	UEFA Cup final, 1st leg	
Apr 27	European Champs League semis	
May 4	European CWinners' Cup final	TBA
May 7	Final day of regular season (Eng)	
	FA Vase final	Wembley
May 8	FA Sunday Cup final	TBA
May 11	UEFA Cup final, 2nd leg	
May 14	FA Cup final	Wembley
May 18	European Cup final	TBA
May 21	Scottish Cup final	TBA
	FA Vauxhall Trophy final	Wembley
May 22	England international	TBA
May 30	Endsleigh Insurance League play-off, Division 1 final	Wembley
June 17 -July 17	FIFA World Cup finals	USA
Aug 6	FA Charity Shield	Wembley
Aug 13	FA Premier League & English Football League season opens	

GOLF

Apr 7-10	US Masters	Augusta
May 5-8	Benson & Hedges International	St Mellion
May 13-15	Brabazon Trophy	LittleAshton
May 12-15	Peugeot Spanish Open	
May 18-19	Lagonda Trophy	Gog Magog
May 19-22	Italian Open	
May 25-27	English Open Seniors champs	Parkstone & Broadstone
May 27-30	Volvo PGA Champs	Wentworth
May 30 -June 4	British Amateur champs	Nairn
June 2-5	Alfred Dunhill Open	Belgium
June 16-19	US Open	Oakmont, Pa
June 23-26	Peugeot French Open	France
June 30 -July 3	Carroll's Irish Open	
July 6-9	Bell's Scottish Open	
July 14-17	123rd Open Championship	Turnberry
July 25-30	English amateur championship	Moortown
July 30-31	Curtis Cup, women	Chattanooga
Aug 3-5	British Seniors champ	Formby
Aug 4-7	BMW International	Munich
Aug 11-14	US PGA championship	Tulsa
	Weetabix British Womens Open	Woburn
Aug 18-21	Murphy's English Open	F of Arden
Sept 1-4	Canon European Masters	Crans, SUI
Sept 5-10	British Amateur champ	Nairn
Sept 8-11	European Open	
Sept 22-25	Lancome Trophy	Paris
Sept 30 -Oct 2	English County finals	Moor Park
Oct 6-9	Alfred Dunhill Cup	TBA
Oct 13-16	Toyota World matchplay	Wentworth
Oct 27-30	Volvo Masters	Spain
	US Tour Chamionship	San Fran
Nov 10-13	World Cup	TBA
Dec 15-18	Johnnie Walker World Champs	Jamaica

GREYHOUND RACING

June 25	Greyhound Derby	Wimbledon

HOCKEY

*	12th Asian Games	Hiroshima
Jan 28-30	European Inter-Nations Cup	Germany
Feb 18-20	Indoor European Club champ - ionship, men and women	Germany
Feb/Mar*	Indoor U/21 European Cup, women	
Mar 13	RB of S HA Cup semi-finals	
Mar 31 -Apr 4	U/18 & U/16 Women's Internts	Scotland
Apr 1-4	European Clubs Cup Winners Cups, men & women ; U/18 & U/16 Six Nations tournament, men	Spain
Apr 9	HA National League Play-offs	
Apr 15-24	16th Champions Trophy	Pakistan
Apr 16-17	AEWHA Senior Int; AEWHA County championship rounds	
Apr 30 -May 1	AEHA County champ final	Liverpool
May 1	Royal Bank of Scotland HA Cup final & HA Trophy final	Milton Keynes
May 7-8	Norwich Union HA County championship final	TBA
May 14	AEWHA Cup & Plate finals	M Keynes
May 20-23	European Club champs m & w	TBA
May 22	AEWHA Veterans champ finals	M Keynes
May 29-30	AEWHA Nat League Promotion/ Relegation weekend	Midlands
July 13-24	World Cup, women	Dublin
Sept/Oct*	8th World Cup, men	Australia

HORSE RACING

Mar 15-17	National Hunt Festival	Cheltenham
Mar 24	Flat season opens	Doncaster
Mar 26	William Hill Lincoln	Doncaster
Apr 4	Jameson Irish Grand National	Fairyhouse
Apr 7-9	Grand National meeting	Aintree
Apr 9	Grand National	Liverpool
Apr 12-14	Craven meeting	Newmarket
Apr 28	1,000 Guineas	Newmarket
Apr 30	2,000 Guineas	Newmarket
June 1	Derby, Diomed Stakes	Epsom
June 4	Oaks	Epsom
	National Hunt season ends	
June 14-17	Royal Ascot	
June 26	Budweiser Irish Derby	Curragh
July 5-7	July meeting	Newmarket
July 23	King George VI & Queen Eliz	Ascot
July 26-30	Goodwood meeting	
July 29	National Hunt season opens	Bangor
Aug 26-27	Ebor meeting	York
Sept 10	St Leger	Doncaster
Sept 28-30	Cambridgeshire meeting	Newmarket
Oct 2	Ciga Prix de l'Arc de Triomphe	Paris
Oct 13-15	Houghton meeting	Newmarket
Nov 5	William Hill November H'cap	Doncaster
	Final flat meeting	
Dec 26	King George VI Rank Chase	K'ton Park

ICE HOCKEY

Mar*	World champs pool C	S Africa
Apr 7-17	World champs pool B	Denmark
Apr 22-24	British champs	Wembley
Apr 25 -May 8	World champs pool A	Italy

ICE SKATING

Jan 7-8	British Ice Dance Champs	Sheffield
Jan 7-9	European speed championships, women	Norway
Jan 18-23	European Figure & Dance championships	Denmark
Jan 29-30	World sprint speed champs men and women	Canada
Feb 5-6	World speed champs women	USA
Feb 12-27	XVII Winter Olympics	Norway
Feb 19-21	World junior speed champs	Berlin
Mar 12-13	World speed champs men	Sweden
Mar 22-27	World figure and dance champs	Japan
Apr 16 -May 2	World short track team champs	Guildford
Nov 29 -Dac 4	World Jnr Figure & Dance chps	Budapest

KARATE

May*	European championships	England

LACROSSE

Mar 20	Lancashire Cup final, men	Stockport
	Stockport Cup final men	
Mar 27	Stockport Easter Festival Eights, men	Stockport
Apr 3	ELU LN Senior Flags final	Didsbury
Apr 10	David Beesley Trophy final	
	Nigel Wayne Trophy	
	Norman Barber Cup final	
July 20-30	World Cup, men	Manchester

LIFE SAVING

Sept 1-11	Rescue '94 - World Life Saving champs, Pool (Indoor) champs, Sept 1-6 (Cardiff), Ocean (Beach) champs (Fistral Beach, Newquay

MODERN PENTATHLON

Aug 20-23	World championships	Windsor

MOTOR CYCLING

May 30 -June 10	TT Races	Isle of Man
Aug 7	British Grand Prix road races	Donington

MOTOR RACING

Mar 13	S African Grand Prix	Kyalami*
Mar 20	PPG Indy Car series	Australia
Mar 27	Brazilian Grand Prix	Interlagos*
Apr 10	Grand Prix of Europe or, Apr 17;PPG IndyCar series	Donington* Phoenix
Apr 17	Grand Prix of Europe or,Apr 10;PPG IndyCar series	Donington* California
May 1	San Marino Grand Prix	Italy*
May 15	Monaco Grand Prix	Monte Carlo
	FIA Formula 3000 Int champ round Nurburgring	Germany
May 20-21	RAC Leaders & RAC Nationals Hillclimb champ rounds	Isle of Man
May 23	FIA Formula 3000 Int championship round Pau	France*
May 29	Indianapolis 500/PPG IndyCar series	USA
June 5	PPG IndyCar series	Milwaukee
June 12	Canadian Grand Prix	Montreal*
	PPG IndyCar series	Detroit
June 18-19	Le Mans 24-Hour Race	France
June 26	PPG IndyCar series	Portland
July 3	French Grand Prix	Mgy Cours
July 10	British Grand Prix	Silverstone
	PPG IndyCar series	Cleveland
July 17	FIA Formula 3000 Int championship round	Pergusa*
	PPG IndyCar series	Toronto
July 31	German Grand Prix	Hockenheim
	PPG IndyCar series	Michigan
Aug 6	NASCAR Winston Cup series	Indianapolis
Aug 14	Hungarian Grand Prix	Budapest*
	PPG IndyCar series	Ohio
Aug 21	FIA Formula 3000 Int championship round	Nurburgring
	PPG IndyCar series USA	New Hamp
Aug 28	Belgian Grand Prix	Spa Franc*
Sept 4	PPG IndyCar series	Vancouver
Sept 11	Italian Grand Prix	Monza*
	PPG IndyCar series	USA
Sept 18	PPG IndyCar series	USA
Sept 25	Portuguese Grand Prix	Estoril*
Oct 2	PPG IndyCar series	USA
Oct 9	FIA Formula 3000 Int championship round	Nogaro FRA
Oct 16	FIA Formula 3000 Int championship round	Mgy Cours
Oct 23	Japanese Grand Prix	Suzuka*
Nov 6	Australian Grand Prix	Adelaide*
Dec 3-4	British Rallycross Grand Prix	BrandsHatch

MULTI-SPORTS

Feb 12-27	XVII Winter Olympics	Lillehammer
July 23 -Aug 7	Goodwill Games	St P'burg
Aug 18-28	Commonwealth Games	VictoriaCAN
Sept 26 -Oct 8	World Masters Games	Brisbane
Oct 2-9	World Corporate Games	Jo'burg

NETBALL

Feb 5	Scotland v England	TBA
Feb 19	England v N Ireland	TBA
Mar 19	Rep of Ireland v England	Dublin
Mar 26	England v Wales	TBA
Apr 29	England international date	Birm'ham
Nov 5	England international date	Wembley
Nov 9	England international date	TBA

OCTOPUSH

Apr*	OCTOPUSH: World champs	Rennes

RALLYING

Jan 1-17	Paris-Dakar Rally	
Mar 31 -Apr 4	Safari Rally	
Apr 7-10	Costa Smerelda Rally	Italy
Apr 8-9	Rallye Hautes Fagnes	France
Apr 22-24	Olympic Rally	Greece
May 5-8	Targa Florio	Italy
May 7-8	Rally of the Lakes	Ireland
May 14-15	Rallye Zlatni	Bulgaria
May 19-21	Saturnus Rally	Slovenia
May 20-22	Rota do Sol	Portugal
May 27-29	Isola d'Elba	Italy
June*	W Cup Rally (start Monte Carlo, finish Los Angeles	
June 2-5	Hessen Rally	Germany
June 3-5	Perth Scottish Rally	
June 10-12	Polish Rally	
June 16-19	SIV Abruzzo Rally	Italy
June 17-19	Barum Rally	Czech
Jun 23-26	24 Heures d'Ypres	Belgium
Jun 30 -July 3	Rallye dos Acores	Portugal
July 7-10	Bohemia Rally	Czech Rep
July 9	Jim Clark Memorial Rally	Scotland
July 15-17	Rallye Rouergue	Fracne
July 21-24	Rallye della Lana	Italy
July 29-30	Ulster Rally	
Aug 4-7	Madeira Rally	
Sept 1-4	Paincavallo Rally	Italy
Sept 9-10	Rally Tatry	Czech Rep
Sept 9-12	Asturias Rally	Spain
Sept 14-17	Manx Rally	IOM
Sept 19-21	Rallye Terre de Corse	France
Sept 22-25	Rothmans Cyprus Rally	
Sept 27-30	Rallye du Valais	Switzerland
Oct 14-16	Rally Hermes	Greece
Oct 22-28	Hong Kong-Beijing Rally	
Oct 27-30	San Marino Rally	
Oct 29-31	Algarve Rally	Portugal
Nov 4-6	Criterium des Cevennes	France
Nov 10-12	Semperit Rally	Austria
Nov 19-23	Greece Off-Road Raid, X-country W Cup series	Greece

ROWING

Mar 26	Oxford v Cambridge, University Boat Race (Putney to Mortlake)*	
June 29 -July 3	Henley Royal Regatta, inc World Cup	Henley-on-Thames

RUGBY LEAGUE

Jan 22	Regal Trophy final	TBA
Feb*	World Sevens	Australia
Feb 18	Wales v France	TBA
Mar 12	Silk Cut Challenge Cup, semi-final (1)	
Mar 26	Silk Cut Challenge Cup, semi-final (2)	
Apr 10	France v GBR	TBA
Apr 30	Silk Cut Challenge Cup final	Wembley
May 8	Stones Bitter Premiership, 1st rd	
May 15	Stones Bitter Premiership, semis	
May 22	Stones Bitter Premiership finals	Old Trafford
June*	W Cup Challenge - Stones Bitter champions v Aus Premiership winners	Sydney or Brisbane

RUGBY UNION

Jan 4	Scotland A v Spain	Murrayfield
Jan 14	Wales U/21 v Scotland, U/21 (Cardiff)	
Jan 15	Five Nations champ	
	France v Ireland	Paris
	Wales v Scotland	Cardiff
Feb 5	Five Nations champ	
	Ireland v Wales	Dublin
	Scotland v England	Murrayfield
Feb 19	Five Nations champ	
	Wales v France	Cardiff
	England v Ireland	Twickenham
Feb 20	France A v Scotland	*
Mar 4	Ireland U/21 v Scotland U/21	Dublin
Mar 5	Five Nations champ	
	Ireland v Scotland	Dublin
	France v England	Paris
Mar 18	Scotland U/21 v France U/21	Inverleith
Mar 19	Five nations champ	
	Scotland v France	Murrayfield
	England v Wales	Twickenham
Apr 16	County Champ final	Twickenham
May -June*	Ireland tour Australia	
May -June*	England tour South Africa	
May -June*	Wales tour Argentina	
May -June*	Scotland tour to Argentina	
May 7	Pilkington Cup final	Twickenham
May 14	SWALEC (Welsh) Cup final	Cardiff
	Save & Prosper M'sex Sevens	Twickenham
May 18	Portugal v Wales, W Cup qual	Lisbon
May 21*	Spain v Wales, W Cup qual	Barcelona
June -July*	South Africa tour to N Zealand	
Oct *	S Africa tour Scotland & Wales	
Oct*	Canada tour Wales & France	
Nov*	Scotland v South Africa	Murrayfield

SHOOTING

Mar*	European airgun champs	Strasbourg
July*	World champs	Milan
Aug*	European junior champs	Wroclaw

SKIING

dh-downhill, sl-slalom, gs-giant slalom, sg-super G

Jan 5-6	Alpine WCup, w sl w gs	Morzine
Jan 6	Alpine WCup, men's dh	Saalbach
Jan 8-9	Alpine World Cup	Kranjjska
	Men's slalom, giant slalom	Gora, SLO
	Women's slalom, super-G	Altenmarkt
Jan 11	Alpine WCup,men's gs	Hinter-storder AUT
Jan 14-16	Alpine WCup, w dh, gs, sg	Cortina
Jan 15-16	Alpine WCup, m dh,s, comb	KitzbuhelA
Jan 18	Alpine WCup, m gs	AdelbodenS
Jan 22-23	Alpine WCup, m dh,sg w slalom, gs	WengenSU MariborSLO
Jan 29-30	Alpine WCup, m dh, sg, comb w dh, w sg	ChamonixF Garmisch-P'kirchenG
Feb 4-6	Alpine WCup, w dh, sl, sg	Sierra Nev S
Feb 5-6	Alpine WCup, m dh	Garmisch-P
Feb 12-27	XVII Winter Olympics	Lillehammer
Mar 5-6	Alpine WCup, m dh, gs W dh	Aspen USA WhistlerCA
Mar 12-13	Alpine WCup m dh, sg w sl, sg	Whistler SteamboatU
Mar 17-20	Alpine WCup finals, m & w dh, gs sg	Vail USA

SNOOKER

Jan 30 -Feb 5	Regal Welsh Open	Newport
Feb 6-13	Benson & Hedges	Wembley
Feb 14-18	International Open	B'mouth
Mar 5-13	Nescafe Asian Open	Bangkok
Mar 22-27	Irish B & H Masters	Goffs
Mar 31 -Apr 7	British Open	Plymouth
Apr 16 -May 2	Embassy World Prof champ	Sheffield

SPORT FOR THE DISABLED

Mar 10-20	Winter Paralympics	Lillehammer
Mar 30 -Apr 3	ISMWSF (Wheelchair) World Fencing champs	Hong Kong
Apr 4-12	World W'chair Snooker champs	Gits BEL
May 4-12	EDSO (Deaf) Euro Volleyball	FlorenceIT
May 27-28	EDSO (Deaf) Euro X-c champs	St P'burgR
June*	BWSF National champs	Stoke Mand
June 20-25	EDSO (Deaf) Euro Bowling ch	Brussels
July*	IPC World table tennis champs	San Diego
July - Aug*	CPS World champs	Assen HOL
July 22-31	World athletics (Blind & Locomotor)	Berlin
Aug*	IPC World Powerlifting champs	Sweden
Aug*	IPC World Shooting champs	Linz AUT
Sept*	Nat Wheelchair Games	Stoke Mand
Sept 17-21	EDSO Euro Swimming champs	Budapest
Sept 21-24	EDSO (Deaf) European Water Polo champs	Budapest
Oct 1-8	EDSO (Deaf) European Wrestling champs	Voronege CE
Oct 23-29	EDSO (Deaf) European Badminton champs	Copenhagen

SQUASH

Jan 12-23	Asian Senior champs	Kuala L
Mar 11-13	Burton International Open	Cheadle
Mar 15	Woolwich Nat Schools finals	Lilleshall
Mar 18-20	Wimbledon Cup	Wimbledon
Mar 19-20	SRA Men's Over-35 Inter County - stage II finals SRA Women's Inter County League finals, Premier Div	
Mar 30 -Apr 4	4th Euro Jnr Individual champs	BolanzoIT
Apr 1-11	Hi-Tec British Open	Lambs SC & Wembley
Apr 4-7	10th Euro Jnr team champs	BolanzoIT
Apr 28 -May 1	21st Euro men's team champs & 16th Euro w's team champs	Amsterdam
Apr 29 -May 1	Hamburg women tournament	Germany
May 13-15	1st Euro Jnr Champion of Champions	Brussels
May 21-22	National Club champ finals	*
May 27-29	Bournemouth Open	B'mouth
Aug 1-13	8th Jnr m's WC's	Christchurch NZL
Oct 1-15	10th Women's World Ind & Team champs	England
Oct/Nov*	Men's World Open	Barcelona

SURFING

Aug - Sept*	European junior champs	Portrush, N Ireland

SWIMMING

Jan 21-23	Speedo British Grand Prix	Gloucester
Jan 25-27	Speedo British Grand Prix	Leeds
Mar 19	Speedo Schools International	Glenrothes
Mar 30 -Apr 1	Speedo British Grand Prix	Edinburgh
Apr 23	ESSA synchronised champs	Leicester
Apr 30 -May 2	Speedo British Grand Prix finals	Cardiff
July 4-10	5th World Masters champs	Montreal
Aug 1-6	ASA Nat age group champs	Coventry
Sept 1-11	World championships	Rome
Oct 1	ESSA team championships	Oldham
Oct 29	ESSA national champs	Guildford
Nov 19	National Diving champs	TBA
Dec 8-11	National winter champs	Sheffield

TABLE TENNIS

Jan 5	England v Japan	M Keynes
Mar 5-6	English National snr champs	TBA
Mar 19	ESTTA National team finals	TBA
Mar 25 -Apr 4	19th European champs	Birmingham
May 7	ESTTA Nat Ind champs	TBA
May 28-30	English Jnr Open	TBA

TENNIS

Jan 17-30	Ford Australian Open champs	Melbourne
May 23 -June 5	French championships	Paris
May 30 -June 5	Direct Line Insurance champs	Beckenham
June 6-12	Stella Artois Grass Court chps Men	Queen's Cb London
	Birmingham Classic, women's	Edgbaston
June 13-18	Direct Line Ins M'chester Open	Didsbury
	Volkswagen w's int tournament	Eastbourne
June 20 - July 3	All England Champs	Wimbledon
Aug 29 - Sept 11	US Open champs	Flushing MeadowNY
Nov 14-20	IBM/ATP Tour World champs	Frankfurt
	Virginia Slims Champs	New York
Nov 21-28	Standard Bank/ATP Tour World Doubles champs Men	Jo'burgSA
Dec 2-4	Davis Cup, World Group final	
Dec 6-11	Compaq Grand Slam Cup	Munich

TEN-PIN BOWLING

| Apr 24-25 | General Tyre Tournament of Champions | Fairlawn, Akron,USA |

TRAMPOLINING

| Oct* | FIT 18th World champs | Lisbon |
| Nov* | FIT Euro youth champs | Sofia BUL |

TRIATHLON

Jan 9	Angus Biathlon series III, event 3, run/bike/run	Carnoustie
Feb 6	Angus Biathlon series III, event 4, run/bike/run	Carnoustie
Nov 27	World champs 1500m, 40km cycle,10km run	Wellington

VOLLEYBALL

| Nov* | World Beach League champs | Penang |

WATER POLO

| May 7 | ESSA championships | Luton |

YACHTING

Jan 5-10	Flying Fifteen world champ	N Zealand
Jan 9	Whitbread Round The World Race 3rd leg start	Fremantle, Australia
Jan 24-28	OK Dinghy World champs	Napier Nzl
Feb 20	Whitbread RTW - 4th leg	Aukland
Mar 5-12	Fireball World champ	Durban SA
Apr 2	Whitbread RTW - 5th leg	Punta Del Este
Apr 24 -June 1	Pan-Pacific (LA-Osaka)	
May 8 -June 1	Pan-Pacific (Brisbane to Osaka)	
May 21	Whitbread RTW - 6th leg	Florida
May 22 -June 1	Pan-Pacific (Vladivostok to Osaka)	
May 29 -June 1	Pan-Pacific Race (Pusan to Osaka)	
May 30 -June 1	Pan-Pacific Race (Shanghai to Osaka)	
June* -June July*	Finn European championship 470 World & European champ	Turkey Robel GER
June 18	Round The Island Race	Cowes
June 18-26	Kiel Week	Germany
July*	Flying Dutchman Euro champs	Dublin
July*	Soling world champ	Nylandska
July*	Finn Gold Cup	Tallinn,
July 2-15	Europe Class world champ	La Rochelle
July 15-23	Yngling world champ	Oslo
July 30 -Aug 6	Cowes Week	Isle of Wight
July 31 -Aug 13	Kenwood Cup	Hawaii
July 30 -Aug 14	420 Women's world champ	Britain
July*	GP14 world championship	Lee-on-Slt
Aug*	Etchells world championship	Newport US
Aug 1-6	420 world championship	Britain
Aug 1-7	Tempest Week	Ullswater
Aug 6-12	Topper national champ	Torbay
Aug 15-19	Torbay Royal Regatta	Torbay
Aug 20-26	Cork Regatta	Kingst'n Can
Aug 21-26	Tempest world champ	Ravenna
Aug*	505 European champ	Holland
Aug*	5.5m world champ	Croquesty
Sept 17	4th BOC Challenge starts	S Carolina
Sept*	Mazda World champ Match	La Rochelle

The Governing Bodies

AMERICAN FOOTBALL
British American Football Association
92 Palace Gardens Terrace, London W8 4RS
Tel:071 727 7760

ANGLING
National Federation of Anglers
Halliday House, 2 Wilson Street, Derby DE1 1PG
Tel:0332 294704

ARCHERY
Grand National Archery Society
National Agricultural Centre
Seventh Street, Stoneleigh Park
Kenilworth, Warwickshire CV8 2LG
Tel:0203 696631

ASSOCIATION FOOTBALL
The Football Association
16 Lancaster Gate, London W2 3LW
Tel:071 262 4542
Fax:071 402 0486

The Football League Ltd
319 Clifton Drive South
Lytham St Annes, Lancs FY8 1 JG
Tel:0253 729421
Fax:0253 724786

Football Association of Wales
3 Westgate Street, Cardiff CF1 1DD
Tel:0222 372325
Fax: 0222 343961

Scottish Football Association
6 Park Gardens, Glasgow G3 7YF
Tel:041 332 6372
Fax:041 332 7559

Womens Football Association
448-450 Hanging Ditch
The Corn Exchange
Manchester M4 3ES
Tel:061 832 5911
Fax:061 839 0331

ATHLETICS
British Athletic Federation
Edgbaston House
3 Duchess Place, Hagley Road
Edgbaston, Birmingham B16 8NM
Tel:021 440 5000
Fax:021 440 0555

BADMINTON
Badminton Association of England
National Badminton Centre
Bradwell Road, Loughton Lodge
Milton Keynes MK8 9LA
Tel:0908 568822

BALLOONING
British Ballon and Airship Club
Alder House, Whiteleaf, Aylesbury
Bucks HP17 OLQ
Tel:0844 274475

BASEBALL
British Baseball Federation
19 Troutsdale Grove, Southcoates Lane
Hull HU9 3SD
Tel:0482 792337

BASKETBALL
English Basketball Association
48 Bradford Road Stanningley
Pudsey, W.Yorkshire LS28 6DF
Tel:0532 361166
Fax:0532 361022

BILLIARDS AND SNOOKER
World Ladies Billiards and Snooker Association
3 Felsted Avenue Wisbech
Cambs PE13 3SL
Tel:0945 589589

World Professional Billiards and Snooker Association
27 Oakfield Road
Clifton, Bristol BS8 2AT
Tel:0272 744491
Fax:0272 744931

BOBSLEIGH
British Bobsleigh Association
Springfield House, Woodstock Road
Coulsdon, Surrey CR5 3HS
Tel:0737 555152

BOWLS
English Bowling Association
Lyndhurst Road
Worthing, W.Sussex BN11 2AZ
Tel:0903 820222
Fax:0903 820444

BOXING
Amateur Boxing Association
Francis House Francis Street
London SW1P 1DE
Tel:071 828 8568

British Boxing Board of Control
Jack Petersen House
52A Borough High Street, London SE1 1XW
Tel:071 403 5879

CANOEING
British Canoe Union
John Dudderidge House
Adbolton Lane, West Bridgford
Nottingham NG2 5AS
Tel:0602 821100

CRICKET
Test and County Cricket Board
Lord's Cricket Ground
London NW8 8QN
Tel:071 286 4405

Womens Cricket Association
41 St Michaels Lane
Headingley, Leeds LS6 3BR
Tel:0532 742398

CROQUET
The Croquet Association
Hurlingham Club
Ranelagh Gardens
London SW6 3PR
Tel:071 736 3148

CURLING
English Curling Association
66 Preston Old Road
Freckleston, Preston PR4 1PD
Tel:0772 634154

CYCLING
British Cycling Federation
36 Rockingham Road
Kettering, Northants NN16 8HG
Tel:0536 412211
Fax:0536 412142

DARTS
British Darts Organisation
2 Pages Lane
Muswell Hill, London N10 1PS
Tel:081 883 5544
Fax:081 883 0109

EQUESTRIAN
British Equestrian Federation
British Equestrian Centre
Stoneleigh Park, Kennilworth
Warwickshire CV8 2LR
Terl:0203 696697
Fax:0203 696484

FENCING
Amateur Fencing Association
1 Barons Gate, 33-35 Rothschild Road
London W4 5HT
Tel:081 742 3032
Fax:081 742 3033

GLIDING
British Gliding Association
Kimberley House
47 Vaughan Way, Leicester LE1 4SE
Tel:0533 531051

GOLF
Professional Golfers Association
Apollo House
The Belfry, Wishaw
Sutton Coldfield, W Midlands B76 9PT
Tel:0675 470333

Womens Professional Golfers European Tour
The Tytherington Club
Dorchester Way, Tytherington
Macclesfield, Cheshire SK10 2JP
Tel:0625 611444

GREYHOUND RACING
National Greyhound Racing Club Ltd
24-28 Oval Road
London NW1 7DA
Tel:071 267 9256
Fax:071 482 1023

GYMNASTICS
British Amateur Gymnastics Association
Registered Office, Ford Hall
Lilleshall National Sports Centre
Newport, Salop TF10 9NB
Tel:0952 820330
Fax:0952 820326

HANDBALL
British Handball Association
60 Church Street
Radcliffe, Manchester M26 8SQ
Tel:061 7249656
Fax:061 7249656

HANG GLIDING
British Hang Gliding and Paragliding Association
The Old School Room
Loughborough Road
Leicester LE4 5PJ
Tel:0533 611322
Fax:0533 611323

HOCKEY
All England Womens Hockey Association
51 High Street
Shrewsbury SY1 1ST
Tel:0743 233572
Fax:0704 233583

The Hockey Association
Norfolk House
102 Saxon Gate West
Milton Keynes MK9 2EP
Tel:0908 241100
Fax:0908 241106

HORSE RACING
British Horseracing Board
42 Portman Square
London W1H 0EN
Tel:071 396 0011
Fax:071 935 3626

ICE HOCKEY
British Ice Hockey Association
Second Floor Suite
517 Christchurch Road
Boscombe
Bournemouth BH1 4AG
Tel:0202 303946
Fax:0202 398005

JUDO
British Judo Association
7A Rutland Street
Leicester LE1 1RB
Tel:0533 559669s

LACROSSE
All England Womens Lacrosse Association
4 Western Court
Bromley Street, Digbeth
Birmingham B9 4AN
Tel:021 773 4422

English Lacrosse Union
Winton House, Winton Road
Bowdon, Altrincham
Cheshire WA14 2PB
Tel:061 928 9600

LAWN TENNIS
All England Lawn Tennis & Croquet Club
Church Road
Wimbledon, London SW19 5AE
Tel:081 944 1066
Fax:081 947 8752

Lawn Tennis Association
The Queens Club
Barons Court West Kensington
London W14 9EG
Tel:071 3852366
Fax:071 3815965

MARTIAL ARTS
British Kendo Association
36 Finn House
Bevendon Street, London N1 6BL
Home Tel:071 608 3502

British Taekwondo Council
Eastney
58 Wiltshire Lane, Pinner
Middx HA5 2LU
Tel:081 429 0878
Fax:081 866 4151

English Karate Governing Body
12 Princes Avenue
Woodford Green, Essex IG8 0LN
Tel:081 504 6162

MODERN PENTATHLON
Modern Pentathlon Association of Great Britain
Wessex House, Silchester Road
Tadley, Basingstoke
Hants RG26 6PX
Tel:0734 810111
Fax:0734 819817

MOTOR CYCLING
Auto-Cycle Union, ACU House
Wood Street, Rugby
Warwickshire CV21 2 YX
Tel:0788 540519
Fax:0788 573585

MOTOR SPORTS
British Automobile Racing Club
Thruxton Racing Circuit
Thruxton, Andover
Hants SP11 8PN
Tel:0264 772607
Fax:0264 773794

RAC Motor Sports Association Ltd
Motor Sports House
Riverside Park, Colnbrook
Slough SL3 0HG
Tel:0753 681736
Fax:0753 682938

NETBALL
All England Netball Association
Netball House
9 Paynes Park, Hitchin
Herts SG5 1EH
Tel:0462 442344
Fax:0462 442343

ORIENTEERING
British Orienteering Federation
Riversdale, Dale Road North
Darley Dale, Matlock
Derbyshire DE4 2HX
Tel:0629 734042
Fax:0629 733769

POLO
Hurlingham Polo Association
Winterlake, Kirtlington
Oxford OX5 3HG
Tel:0869 50044
Fax:0869 50625

POOL
English Pool Association
44 Jones House
Penkridge Street, Walsall WS2 8JX
Tel:0922 35587

RACKETS
Tennis and Rackets Association
c/o The Queens Club
Palliser Road, West Kensington
London W14 9EQ
Tel:071 381 4746

ROWING
Amateur Rowing Association
The Priory, 6 Lower Mall
Hammersmith, London W6 9DJ
Tel:081 741 5314
Fax:081 741 4658

RUGBY LEAGUE
The Rugby Football League
180 Chapeltown Road, Leeds LS7 4HT
Tel:0532 624637
Fax:0532 623386

RUGBY UNION
The Rugby Football Union
Rugby Road
Twickenham, Middx TW1 1DZ
Tel:081 892 8161
Fax:081 892 9816

Irish Rugby Football Union
62 Lansdowne Road
Ballsbridge, Dublin
Tel:010 3531 684601

Scottish Rugby Union
7/9 Roseburn Street
Edinburgh EH12 5PJ
Tel:031 3372346

Welsh Rugby Union
PO Box 22, Cardiff CF1 1JL
Tel:0222 390111

Womens Rugby Football Union
Meadow House, Springfield Farm
Shipston-on-Stour
Warwickshire CV36 4HQ
Tel:0703 453371 Ext. 4348

SHOOTING
National Rifle Association
Bisley Camp, Brookwood
Woking, Surrey GU24 0PB
Tel:0483 797777

SKATING
National Ice Skating Association of UK Ltd
15-27 Gee Street, London EC1V 3RE
Tel:071 2533824
Fax:071 4902589

SKIING
British Ski Federation
258 Main Street
East Calder Livingston
West Lothian EH53 0EE
Tel:0506 884343
Fax:0506 882952

SPEEDWAY
Speedway Control Board Ltd
57 Villa Crescent, Bulkington
Nuneaton, Warwickshire CV12 9NF
Tel:0203 643336

SQUASH
Squash Rackets Association
Westpoint, 33-34 Warple Way
Acton, London W3 0RQ
Tel:081 7460580

SWIMMING
Amateur Swimming Association
Harold Fern House, Derby Square
Loughborough, Leics LE11 0AL
Tel:0509 230431
Fax:0509 610720

TABLE TENNIS
English Table Tennis Association
Queensbury House, Havelock Road
Hastings, E.Sussex TN34 1HF
Tel:0424 722525
Fax:0424 422103

TENPIN BOWLING
British Tenpin Bowling Association
114 Balfour Road
Ilford, Essex IG1 4JD
Tel:081 478 1745
Fax:081 514 3665

TRAMPOLINING
British Trampoline Federation Ltd
146 College Road
Harrow, Middx HA1 1BH
Tel:081 863 7278
Fax:081 861 2591

TRIATHLON
British Triathlon Association
Dover Leisure Centre, Townhall Street
Dover, Kent CT16 1LN
Tel:0304 202565

TUG-OF-WAR
Tug-of-War Association
57 Lynton Road
Chesham, Bucks HP5 2BT
Tel:0494 783057

VOLLEYBALL
British Volleyball Federation
27 South Road, West Bridgford
Nottingham NG2 7AG
Tel:0602 816324
Fax:0602 455429

WATER SKIING
British Water Ski Federation
390 City Road, London, EC1V 2QA
Tel:071 833 2855
Fax:071 837 5879

WEIGHTLIFTING
British Amateur Weight Lifters Association
3 Iffley Turn
Oxford OX4 4DU
Tel:0865 778319
Fax:0865 249281

WRESTLING
British Amateur Wrestling Association
41 Great Clowes Street, Salford
Greater Manchester M7 9RQ
Tel:061 832 9209

YACHTING
Royal Yachting Association
RYA House, Romsey Road
Eastleigh, Hants SO5 4YA
Tel:0703 629962
Fax:0703 629924

The Guinness Sports Yearbook 1995

All the results from the 1994 World Cup, the Commonwealth Games, Winter Olympics, European Athletics Championships and much, much more. . . .

You can reserve your copy of **The Guinness Sports Yearbook 1995** simply by completing the form at the foot of this page.

AND be the first to hear about the many more sports books published by Guinness every year.

You'll be amazed at the range of sports covered by the Guinness library. And whether it's the **Guinness Record of the FA Cup**, the **Formula 1 Fact Book**, **Cricket Facts and Feats** or perhaps our superb new **International Who's Who of Sport** that takes your fancy, you'll find Guinness is always the best place to come for quality sports reference.

Just complete the card below and return it to us at the address printed overleaf.

Please send me the latest details on:

☐ The Guinness Sports Yearbook 1995 (available November 1994)

☐ All Guinness publications
(tick as appropriate)

Name ....

Address ....

....

.... Postcode ....

It would also help us if you would answer the following questions (tick box as appropriate):

Age: ☐ Under 20 ☐ 20-25 ☐ 26-30

☐ 31-35 ☐ 36-40 ☐ Over 40

Sex: ☐ Male ☐ Female

Your favourite sports: 1 .... 2 .... 3 ....

The Sports Editor

Guinness Publishing

33 London Road

Enfield EN2 6DJ